POLAR ESKIMO

WEST GREENLAND ESKIMO

EAST GREENLAND ESKIMO

IGLULIK ESKIMO

BAFFINLAND ESKIMO

NETSILIK ESKIMO

AIVILIK ESKIMO

CARIBOU ESKIMO

LABRADOR ESKIMO

WYAN

MONTAGNAIS

BEOTHUK

R E E

MICMAC

MALECITE

OJIBWA

ALGONKIAN

ABNAKI

MENOMINI

OTTAWA

HURON

IROQUOIS

This Land Was Theirs

This Land Was Theirs

A Study of the North American Indian

Wendell H. Oswalt

University of California, Los Angeles

John Wiley & Sons, Inc.   New York · London · Sydney

10 9 8 7 6 5 4

Library of Congress Catalog Card Number: 66-21037
Printed in the United States of America

To Edward H. Spicer

. . . so long as the waters shall flow and the sun shall shine . . .

Preface

The writer of every book reasons, or feels, that he is able to offer something that exists nowhere in published form. No matter what the topic may be, it is likely that an author somewhere aspires to present old information in a new form or a new interpretive point of view. It may seem that far too much already has been written about North American Indians, and even a casual survey of the literature is staggering. There are, for example, the accounts of explorers, missionary records, biographies and autobiographies, fiction, poetry, histories, vehement crusades, and anthropological studies. Also, books published in recent years have attempted to bring some order to these voluminous writings. Still, in spite of all that has been written, I feel or know, depending on my frame of mind at the moment, that yet another book on the American Indian is both desirable and needed. This book is designed to present descriptive accounts of various tribes free, it is hoped, of highly technical terminology, and to trace their diverse ways of life from historic contact to their extinction or to modern times. Additionally, because I am concerned with the concept of the Indian in modern society, I have in a final chapter summarized the position of Indians in modern Canadian and American life.

In the presentation of the ten chapters devoted to geographically representative tribes I have attempted to deal with the same range of topics as far as this has been possible. In general, the topics are presented in the same subject sequence. I sometimes have departed from this general plan because sections organized in an identical manner are boring to write as well as to read. By varying the topical order I had an opportunity to elaborate on diverse subjects in different contexts. Although the subjects are, in general, the same, the emphasis varies considerably from chapter to chapter. This variation is in part due to the nature of the archaeological, ethnographic, and historical literature. When a relatively complete study of a tribe's history exists, the historical dimension is stressed. In other instances stress has been

placed on continuities or discontinuities with the past or on a particular dimension, social or cultural. In making the tribal selections a
number of factors were considered. Since the culture area approach, as
described in the introduction, has been the organizational point of
departure, it was deemed essential to obtain a broad geographical
sampling of North American tribes; as far as possible, a diversified
representation in terms of culture, society, and language was also
sought.

The attentive or casual reader will find that the chapters are free
from any particular theoretical orientation. This approach was decided on only after pondering the problem of presentation at length.
Rather than include an analysis of sociocultural change, an obvious
theoretical approach, I considered it more appropriate to offer straightforward descriptions of representative Indian tribes.

Comments on the use of some words might be appropriate since
I have attempted to follow a patterning. When generalizations are
made about American Indians, they should be considered to encompass Eskimos as well. This approach is justified on the grounds that
the cultural and linguistic differences separating Indians and Eskimos
are no greater than those separating many Indian tribes. Additional
justification is found in the fact that the United States government,
although not the Canadian government, has for many years considered Alaskan Eskimos and Indians as one for administrative purposes.
It will be noted that maize has been used most often rather than
corn, except for cornmeal and green corn, whereas bison is employed
instead of buffalo; these usages offer a modicum of exactness. The
reader with an eye for terminology will note that I have sometimes
applied the proper noun "Sioux." The word is imprecise because there
was no such Indian tribe. There were, however, diverse tribes which
spoke Siouan languages. The only justification I have for using Sioux
is that often historical records refer to the Sioux as an ethnic group
and do not specify the particular tribe of Siouan speaker involved.
Throughout the book the terminology that has come to be accepted
in anthropological usage has been kept to a minimum. When a technical word has been employed, it is defined in context, which should
present the reader with little difficulty. It will be noted that the term
clan does not occur, for this is a word with many meanings; I have
preferred to use in its place the partial substitute *sib*. One final comment on words is my usage of tribe or ethnic group. These are not
exact terms but refer to a population which considers itself, or is considered by others, to be different from other similarly conceived units.

Whenever possible, in writing about a people, I have attempted to limit my descriptions to a particular segment of a tribe. This was desirable in order to present as nearly as possible an actual culture-carrying unit. For example, in writing of the aboriginal Chipewyan, I found it necessary to draw together information about diverse segments of the population, and even then the descriptions are far from complete. When dealing with modern Chipewyan life, however, the descriptions have been limited to one community. While the chapters were being assembled, I made an effort to consult works both lengthy and authoritative. I did not attempt to survey all of the literature on most tribes. At the end of each chapter is appended a list of the references consulted; the key items are marked with a single asterisk and annotated. A brief bibliography of references employed in many if not all chapters appears at the end of the book.

Wendell H. Oswalt

Los Angeles, California
March 1966

Acknowledgments

Dr. James W. VanStone read and commented on the manuscript chapter about the Chipewyan, and Mr. Lowell J. Bean did the same with the Cahuilla chapter; I am indebted to them for their meaningful help.

Permission has been granted by the publishers for the use of excerpts from the following copyrighted material: Joan Ablon, "Relocated American Indians in the San Francisco Bay Area," *Human Organization,* vol. 23, no. 4, 1964, published by The Society for Applied Anthropology; John W. Caughey, ed., *The Indians of Southern California in 1852,* Huntington Library Publications, 1952; John Dunbar, *Collections of the Kansas State Historical Society,* Kansas State Historical Society, 1918; Peter Fidler, *Journal of a Journey with the Chepawyans or Northern Indians, to the Slave Lake & to the East and West of the Slave River, in 1791 & 2,* Champlain Society, v. 21, 1934; Fred Gearing et al., *Documentary History of the Fox Project 1948-1959,* Department of Anthropology, University of Chicago, 1960; George Grinnell, *Pawnee Hero Stories and Folk-Tales,* University of Nebraska Press, 1961; George Hyde, *Pawnee Indians,* University of Denver Press, 1951; James Howley, *The Beothucks or Red Indians,* Cambridge University Press, 1915; Nathaniel Knowles, "The Torture of Captives by the Indians of Eastern North America," in *Proceedings of the American Philosophical Society,* American Philosophical Society, v. 82, 1940; Aurel Krause, *The Tlingit Indians,* University of Washington Press, 1956; Ralph Linton, ed., *Acculturation of Seven American Indian Tribes,* D. Appleton-Century Company, Inc., copyright 1940 (reprint by permission of Appleton-Century-Crofts); Wendell Oswalt, *Mission of Change,* Huntington Library Publications, 1963; Wendell Oswalt, *Napaskiak,* University of Arizona Press, 1963; Dalip Saund, *Congressman from India,* E. P. Dutton & Co., Inc., 1960; Leo Simmons, *Sun Chief,* Yale University Press, 1942; Laura Thompson, *The Hopi Way,* University of Chicago Press, 1945; Laura Thompson, *Culture in Crisis,* Harper & Row, 1950; Mischa Titiev, *Old Oraibi,* Peabody Museum of American Archaeology and Ethnology, Museum Papers, v. 22, no. 1, 1944; Samuel H. Young, *Hall Young of Alaska,* Fleming H. Revell Co., 1927.

W. H. O.

Contents

This Land Was Theirs

Introduction

CULTURE AREAS

WESTERN ARCTIC

YUKON SUBARCTIC

MACKENZIE SUBARCTIC

CENTRAL AND EASTERN ARCTIC

NORTHWEST COAST

Pacific Ocean

Hudson Bay

EASTERN SUBARCTIC

PLATEAU

PLAINS

PRAIRIES

GREAT BASIN

CALIFORNIA

EAST

Atlantic Ocean

OASIS

BAJA CALIFORNIA

NORTHEAST MEXICO

Gulf of Mexico

0   400   800 mi.

Map by J. Donovan *(after Driver, 1961)*

The purpose of this introduction is to provide a general view of major variations in the lifeways of aboriginal Americans at the time of historic contact. Whereas in the body of the text specific tribes from widely separated areas are discussed in detail, the introduction places these peoples in a broad comparative context and in terms of culture areas. The concept of culture areas is a widely accepted means for generalizing about regional variations; in fact, broad comparative studies of American Indians at the time of historic contact have almost always been approached from the culture area point of view. A culture area is a continuous geographical region in which the inhabitants share more important facets of culture and society with each other than with the peoples in adjacent regions. Such an area may include tribes with similar or very different languages. The culture area concept makes it possible to deal with hundreds of separate tribes on a comparative basis by organizing them into a small number of groups. One disadvantage of the concept is that often it is difficult to draw firm lines between culture areas, since tribes at the borders often share characteristics of peoples in adjacent areas. This disadvantage, however, is not important enough to negate the usefulness of the concept.

Considering the close relationship of primitive peoples to their environments, it is not surprising that their culture areas tend to coincide with major geographical regions and biotic provinces. In fact, it is customary to refer to culture areas in terms that are geographical; these areas may be divided into subareas, with recognition given to more localized variations. In the descriptions to follow, certain major characteristics of the culture areas are summarized and subarea variations cited when appropriate. The information leading to the definition of each culture area has been drawn largely from the classic study by Harold E. Driver and William C. Massey (1957); the system for designating biotic provinces was established by Lee R. Dice (1943).

The reasons for selecting the particular tribes in this book are offered in the respective chapters. In terms of representation by culture area, it will be noted that one tribe, the Kuskowagamiut, represents the Arctic; two tribes, the Chipewyan and Beothuk, the Subarctic; the Tlingit, the Northwest Coast; the Plateau is unrepresented, as is the Plains. However, of the two Prairie tribes, the Fox and Pawnee, the latter borders the Plains and shares many aspects of Plains Indian life. The Eastern culture area is represented by the Iroquois and the Natchez; the Great Basin, by the peripheral Cahuilla; and the Oasis, by the Hopi. California is unrepresented, except that the Cahuilla of the Great Basin is a borderline population which shares some California characteristics.

Arctic. The treeless region with tundra vegetation which extends from Greenland across northern Canada to southwestern Alaska constitutes the Eskimoan biotic province. In southwestern Alaska the coniferous forest area is a part of the Sitkan biotic province, whereas the Aleutian, another separate biotic province, is found mainly on the Aleutian Islands. Thus there is a great deal more environmental homogeneity in the northern part of the Arctic culture area than there is in the southwestern sector. The Arctic culture area is divided into two subareas: the Western, which includes mainly coastal Alaska, and the Central and Eastern, which is everywhere east of the northern extreme of the Alaska-Canada boundary. Arctic tribes virtually all spoke languages belonging within the Eskimoan phylum, with a linguistic homogeneity of Eskimos extending from a short distance south of Bering Strait to Greenland. The people of the Aleutian Islands spoke Aleut, a stock within the Eskimoan phylum. In southwestern Alaska Eskimo was spoken, but the dialects could not be understood by the northern Eskimos or Aleuts.

A consideration of distinctive characteristics of clothing, dwellings, settlement patterns, and subsistence pursuits provides a further perspective. In the Arctic the people wore parkas tailormade from animal pelts; these were often duplicated with similar but lighterweight inner garments. The hands were protected by fur mittens. Long fur stockings or trousers of double thickness were worn, and footwear consisted of moccasins with separate hard soles. The dwellings in the Central and Eastern subarea were typically dome-shaped, snow block houses in winter and skin tents in summer, each occupied by a single nuclear family, that is, a man, his wife, and their children. In the Western subarea, semisubterranean houses of logs covered with sod were the winter dwellings, and skin tents were used in summer. Usually more than one nuclear family occupied the winter residence. In the Central and Eastern subarea sea mammals were the dominant source of food, whereas in the Western subarea, which included most of littoral Alaska, fish, particularly salmon, supplemented or replaced sea mammals in importance. In the Western Arctic the people lived in settlements that were permanent for at least a few generations, whereas the other Arctic peoples were less sedentary.

Sea mammals were taken by means of toggle harpoons and harpoon darts; they might also be netted, particularly in the Western subarea. Land mammals were taken with the aid of enclosures, disguises, or dogs. Otherwise, land mammals most frequently were taken with deadfalls and snares. In fishing, gill nets, hooks, weirs, and associated traps were employed, as were harpoon darts and leisters. Other notable examples of the technology in the Arctic culture area may be listed as follows: chest yokes in part of the Western subarea for help in carrying loads; snowshoes, of complex forms in the Western subarea and simpler forms elsewhere; hide or baleen toboggans in much of the Central and Eastern subarea; dogs as draft animals for pulling sleds almost everywhere; dogs as pack animals, scattered throughout the Arctic; elongated hide boats, with sail usage confined to the western and eastern sectors; basketry containers made by twining and coiling in most of the Western subarea, and coiling in parts of the eastern region; pottery in most of the Western subarea; copper was cold-hammered in the Western subarea and a portion of the central region; in northwestern Greenland meteoric iron was cold-hammered.

In the characteristic social pattern marriages were monogamous, but under 20 percent of the men practiced polygyny. After marriage the couple might live with or near either the husband's or the wife's family, and descent was traced bilaterally. Among the most important ceremonial involvements was the ritual associated with killing a bear; this was found over the Arctic except in the extreme eastern sector. Everywhere there was ritual recognition of the first animals killed by youths. Only in a portion of the Western Arctic were there rites for the first mammals killed during the year.

Subarctic. The coniferous forest of the Hudsonian biotic province is the dominant form of vegetation in this vast ecological band which spans northern North America. The Subarctic culture area is usually divided into three subareas: the Yukon River drainage, just short of where it empties into the Bering Sea, constitutes the Yukon subarea; the Mackenzie, named after this river drainage; and the Eastern Subarctic, largely adjacent to the southern sector of Hudson Bay. In the Yukon and Mackenzie Subarctic we find that languages of the Na-Dene phylum were spoken, whereas in the Eastern subarea the languages were usually of the Algonkian-Mosan phylum.

The Subarctic Indians wore a sleeved shirt, usually made from de-haired skins and fitted to the body. Among most groups a breechclout was worn, and leggings were separate and reached the thigh. The soft-soled moccasins, along with other items of apparel, were often decorated with porcupine quills. In some sectors leggings or trousers had soft-soled moccasins attached. Mittens were worn to protect the hands, and in much of the Eastern Subarctic separate sleeves were added to the basic shirt. Over most of the area the single-family, conical-shaped, skin-covered tent was the most important form of dwelling, but in the western sector the semisubterranean log house and the double lean-to are reported also, the latter forms being occupied by two or more nuclear families. The double lean-to consisted of a pole frame against which were leaned bark, hides, and brush. In the Eastern and Mackenzie subareas game was usually the most important food, whereas in the Yukon subarea it was replaced in part by fish, especially salmon and whitefish. In exploiting the environment these Indians moved about frequently, although they often returned to an established winter settlement.

Among the subsistence methods were the sporadic use of nets and pitfalls for taking game; the widespread practice of driving animals, especially caribou, into water and spearing them there from canoes; the use of enclosures or fences along which game was driven; the employment of dogs in the chase; the extreme importance of snares and deadfalls; and in the two eastern subareas, calling game with the aid of bark trumpets. Fishing was extremely important throughout this culture area, and the major fishing technology included gill nets, a combination of weirs and traps, leisters and spears, harpoon darts, and hooks. Other technological devices included snowshoes which, over the entire area, were of complex design although simple forms were also found in the Eastern subarea, and toboggans of hide, boards, or bark, which were widespread. Sleds—pulled by humans—were confined mainly to the Yukon subarea, and dogs were used for pack animals in much of the Yukon and Mackenzie subareas. Boats everywhere were made of bark. Containers in the Yukon were twined or coiled when important; pottery occurred at the western margin of the Yukon Subarctic and the southeastern margins of the Eastern subarea, and copper was cold-hammered everywhere except in the northeastern portion of the Eastern subarea.

In their social life we find that more than 20 percent of the marriages were polygynous only in the central Subarctic; more typically, marriages were monogamous. After marriage the couple was most likely to reside with or near the husband's family. Descent usually was traced along both sides of a family, except that over much of the Yukon subarea it was reckoned through the female line. In the sphere of supernatural ideas we find that bear ceremonialism occurred everywhere, and over most of the Subarctic special recognition was given to youths when they killed their first of any animal species. There also was ritual involvement with the first mammals killed annually in the Eastern Subarctic, and less important but similar rituals involving fish were important in the Yukon subarea. Both first animal and fish rituals were found in one section of the Mackenzie subarea.

Northwest Coast. Extending from Cook Inlet, Alaska, to the

northern coast of California, this culture area includes most of the
Sitkan and Oregonian biotic provinces. The culture area is a rather
narrow band of coastline, where the vegetation is dense, and is characterized by great conifer forests. The peoples were most likely to be
speakers of Na-Dene languages. Their clothing was made from skins or
woven plant fibers. Men wore robes on ceremonial occasions and on
cold days, but in the summer they might go about naked. In rainy
weather a poncho-like garment of woven plant fiber was worn along
with a cone-shaped woven hat. Normally neither sex wore moccasins.
Women usually wore skirts made from woven fibers, with the addition
of a robe when it was cold. The multifamily dwellings were substantial
rectangular plank structures, and a group of these dwellings might at
times be surrounded with palisades. The primary source of food for the
people was salmon. Any particular community was likely to be stable
for many generations; movement to another settlement was due more
often to feuds than to the necessity of changing locale in order to make
a living.

Whales were hunted, in some sections, with harpoons, but in
general sea mammal hunting was not extremely important in the food-
getting activities. Deadfalls and snares were employed for obtaining
land mammals, and dogs were used to aid in hunting. Fish were taken
in nets, weir and trap combinations, or with leisters, toggle-headed
harpoons, or hooks. Included in the definitive cultural traits and trait
complexes were the following: complex or simple snowshoes in all but
the most southerly sector; dogs used as pack animals in the north;
dugout boats, plus elongated hide boats in the north; twined basketry
containers and, in the central area, plaited containers; and cold-
hammered copper over all but the southern sector.

Socially, it is found that polygyny was common, occurring in more
than 20 percent of the marriages. In the north residence was with or
near a maternal uncle, but in the southern two thirds the couple lived
with or near the man's family. Descent was traced in the north through
the female line and through both sides of the family elsewhere. Ceremonial involvement on killing a bear was widespread, and either
important or minor rituals were involved when the first fish were
taken during the year. Involvement in first fruit rituals was sporadic
but widespread.

Plateau. The Montanian and Palusian biotic provinces are the
primary ecological associations in this culture area. The Montanian
consists of rugged mountains with varied biotic associations at different
elevations. The Palusian is mountainous but also contains high hills,

rolling country, and some flat areas of sagebrush and bunchgrass. In linguistic terms the most important languages were of the Algonkian-Mosan phylum.

Clothing was made from dehaired skins, fur, or wild-plant fibers. Men wore breechclouts, shirts, and leggings; women wore plant-fiber skirts, leggings, and basketry hats. During cold weather fur robes were worn, and mittens protected the hands. Moccasins were of both hard- and soft-soled forms, and in one section hide sandals were another form of footwear. The most widely occurring house form was made of planks and was semisubterranean, but in the eastern sector the Plains type of tepee was built. In both house forms the occupants usually were members of two or more nuclear families. The inhabitants depended mainly on fish or large game animals for food. To make a living the people were frequently on the move, although in the western half of the region they were more sedentary than in the eastern part.

In certain sectors of the Plateau, game was driven with the aid of fire, and land animals were netted. Surrounding game with or without an end enclosure was more widespread, as was driving game into water or over cliffs. Pitfalls, deadfalls, and snares were the major trapping methods. Calling game and using disguises or dogs in hunting were rather common. Fish were taken with the weir and trap combination, hooks, gill nets and seines, leisters, and some form of harpoon. Other items of material culture included carrying baskets, which were found occasionally in the western section, and the more common easterly parfleche; snowshoes, which might be simple or complex in the same area; toboggans of brush or hide were employed in some localities, and dogs were used as pack animals in much of the north; boats were of the dugout form in the south and of the bark variety in the north; over most of the area baskets might be twined or coiled, but twining in one locale was unimportant; finally, over the western sector copper was cold-hammered into implements.

Marriages were most often polygynous, and the couple usually lived with or near the husband's relatives. Descent was traced through males. In this area we find that bear ceremonialism might be present or absent, depending on the region. Furthermore, first kill rites for boys might or might not occur. Rites for the first animals killed during a year and major fish rites might occur within the same tribe, among different tribes, or not at all. In about half the culture area there was ritual acknowledgment of the first fruits of each year.

Plains. The North American steppe country extends from the southern sections of the Canadian prairie provinces almost to the Gulf of Mexico. It is in general a flat or rolling grassland setting. The major biotic provinces represented are the Saskatchewan, Kansan, Coloradan, and Comanchian. The Algonkian-Mosan, Hokan-Siouan, and Macro-Penutian were the most often represented linguistic phyla.

A Plains Indian man's garments were made from dehaired skins and included a breechclout, long leggings, a loosely fitted shirt, and moccasins with either hard or soft soles. Women wore calf-length dresses of dehaired skins, leggings which reached the knees, and moccasins similar to those of the men. Both sexes, but the men in particular, wore bison skin robes on important occasions and for protection from the cold. The skin-covered tepee was the dominant dwelling form throughout the area, and the residents of such houses usually belonged to a single family. In this vast area one animal alone, the bison, was the most important food source. The people followed or intercepted the bison herds and could gather in large numbers only when the herds were locally great.

Game was driven with fire, occasionally trapped in pitfalls and deadfalls, or commonly driven into surrounds with or without enclosures at the end. Likewise animals, meaning mainly bison, were driven over cliffs; other game was taken in snares. Disguises were used in hunting, as was the trick of calling animals so that they approached the hunter or could be approached by him. Fishing was everywhere unimportant, but when practiced hooks were the primary device. Sporadically, wild seeds were utilized, and seed beaters plus digging sticks were employed in collecting wild-plant products. Material traits among the Plains, paralleling those presented for the other culture areas, are the following: parfleches, or folded skin containers, as the most widespread carrying devices; snowshoes of simple or complex forms were found over much of the northern Plains; hide toboggans are reported but only from the northern reaches of the culture area; the dog-drawn travois was common everywhere, and often dogs were employed as pack animals; boats were rounded to oblong with hide covers over a wooden frame, a form commonly termed a bull boat; and pottery vessels were made in much of the northern half of the area.

In marriage arrangements more than 20 percent were polygynous. The couple resided with or near the man's family in the northern and southern sectors, but with or near the woman's family in the central sector. Over most of the Plains bear ceremonialism was practiced, and there were special observances when a youth killed his first game.

Prairie. The prairies in the heart of North America include virtually all of the Illinoian and Texan biotic provinces, along with a large area of the Canadian. This is a somewhat varied culture area in terms of ecology. The Illinoian was dominated both by prairie country and by deciduous forests; the Texan reflected a similar combination, but the grasses were often subtropical forms; in the Canadian biotic province hardwood forests were the vegetation climax. The representative tribes were most likely to be speakers of languages in the linguistic phyla of Hokan-Siouan or Algonkian-Mosan.

The clothing of the Prairie peoples was in general like that of the Plains Indians, although only soft-soled moccasins were worn by some tribes. The tepee and sod-covered earth lodge occupied by more than one family were the housing forms in the western sector; elsewhere, the multifamily residences were dome-shaped, with bark or other materials for covering. These Indians were usually hunters of diverse species of game, but they also relied heavily on the crops they raised, particularly maize. The Prairie tribes, with their farming orientation, would gather in villages near their crops during at least the planting and harvesting seasons, and sometimes for longer periods.

The most important economic division in food-getting activities was between the gathering and farming aspects. Game was driven with fire in some sectors, and surrounds were widely used; deadfalls and pitfalls were most common in the northern part of the Prairie culture area. Again in the north the weir-trap combination, along with fish spears and hooks, was employed in fishing. The digging stick, to dislodge plant products, was about the only artifact widely used in collecting activities. The people raised maize, preparing the land first by burning it over, then planting with the aid of a sharpened stick and chopping out the weeds with a hoe. Among the other technological devices were the following: the parfleche in the west; complex, simple, or unknown forms of snowshoes in the north; the dog travois in the northwest; three types of boats, the dugout in the east, bark canoe in the north, and bull boat in the southwest; and twined and coiled baskets, found throughout, sometimes together but in scattered localities, with plaiting common in the eastern sector. Finally, pottery and cold-hammered copper were widespread.

Following marriage the couple was most likely to reside with or near the husband's family. Polygyny exceeded 20 percent. Descent was traced along the male line except in the northwest, where it was calculated along both sides of the family. Bear ceremonialism and rituals for the first animals killed by a youth occurred sporadically, but they were found together only in the northeastern sector. Only in the extreme northwest were there reported rituals for the first animals killed during a year and first fruit ceremonies. A green corn ceremony was held in the more westerly localities to the north and south.

East. From southern New England to the Gulf of Mexico is a major culture area which includes three biotic provinces: the Canadian, dominated by hardwood forests; the Carolinian, where deciduous forests are the norm; and the Austroriparian, where there are forests of pines and hardwoods. The tribal languages were of the Hokan-Siouan or Algonkian-Mosan phylum.

Clothing for men included breechclouts, long leggings, soft-soled moccasins, and, in some areas, skin robes. Women wore either long dresses made from two deerskins or wrap-around, knee-length skirts, with nothing above the waist. Leggings, when worn by women, usually were short. In the southern sector the Indians lived in rectangular houses covered with gabled, thatched roofs. In the central and northern portions the houses were rectangular but had rounded roofs with an overall bark covering. Although there were local variations in house forms, the residence units throughout this culture area usually included more than one family. Most of the aboriginal occupants depended on maize cultivation as their most important source of food; because intensive farming was practiced, the settlements tended to be permanent, at least until the local soils were depleted.

In this culture area gathering pursuits played a significant role in economic life. Land mammals were taken by driving them into water to be dispatched by a hunter in a boat; fire drives and surrounds were also used. Pitfalls and snares had a scattered distribution, but deadfalls were confined to the north. Calling game was practiced sporadically, and in the southern sector disguises were employed to enable the hunter to attract or draw near to his prey. In fishing the people often used small hand nets, weirs and traps together, and fish spears; hooks were more scattered in occurrence. For plants a straight-handled digging stick was employed. Maize was the most important domestic crop and was cultivated with a straight stick with a point at the end. The area was burned over before cultivation, and later the plots were weeded with hoes. Among the technological devices reported were the following: carrying nets and also litters for the nobility in sections of the south; snowshoes of varying or unknown form in the northeast; bark or board toboggans in the extreme north; packing with dogs in one area of the central Atlantic seaboard; dugout vessels for water travel; and the use of sails sporadically in the eastern and northern sectors. Plaited containers or mats were common throughout, as was pottery; copper was cold-hammered everywhere.

In the southern part of the Eastern culture area polygyny was uncommon; the north central region was exclusively monogamous, and in the extreme northeast there was the rare occurrence of polygyny. Most often married couples lived with or near the wife's family, although in the central and extreme southwest they lived with or near the husband's. Virtually everywhere descent was traced along the male line. Bear ceremonialism and rites for boys who had killed their first game were scattered throughout much of the area and occasionally were found together. Ceremonial involvement with the first mammals killed during a year was rare; however, green corn and first fruit rites were more common.

Great Basin. This culture area is primarily within the Artemisian biotic province, but it includes a portion of the Navahonian province. The latter is characterized by pinyon and juniper trees, and mesas and canyons are outstanding physiographic features. The Artemisian is mainly a plains environment which is covered with sagebrush. Its Indian occupants spoke languages of the Macro-Penutian phylum.

The general Plains type of clothing was found in the eastern sector of the Great Basin; in the west it might be abbreviated. The women, however, unlike those of the Plains, often wore basketry hats. The dwellings were crude, cone-shaped tepees covered with skins or thatch and housed a single nuclear family. In the Great Basin the Indians subsisted on a diet of animal meat and plant products. They usually made excursions from their camps or villages to exploit the surrounding environment. They tended to move about a great deal, and camps might be highly impermanent.

Land animals were captured with the aid of disguises worn by hunters, fire drives, and nets. Enclosures for capturing game were widespread, and in the eastern section game was driven into natural traps. Pitfalls and snares were used sporadically over the area, but deadfalls had a wider distribution. Fish were taken in weirs and traps arranged in conjunction with each other or in other forms of similar obstructive devices. The fish spear, harpoons, and hooks were present but not widespread. Plant collecting was important, and among the implements employed were woven basketry seed beaters, straight-handled digging sticks, and gathering poles. Among the other manufactures were the following items: carrying baskets present in most of the culture area and carrying nets in the west; the parfleche in the east; widespread simple snowshoe forms; dogs utilized in packing and pulling travois in the northeast; balsa boats in the northwest and rafts of poles or logs among east central tribes; finally, coiled and twined baskets, as well as pottery, which were important almost everywhere.

In social life we find that marriages were monogamous, with a frequency of less than 20 percent polygyny except in a few areas. In the western sector residence after marriage was most likely to be with or near either family, but in the east it was with or near the wife's. Descent was virtually always traced through both males and females. Rituals for the first game kills of youths were prevalent, and in the east they were accompanied by bear ceremonialism.

Oasis. The Oasis culture area consisted mainly of land in the Navahonian biotic province and small northern sectors of three other provinces intruding from northern Mexico. The core of the area was dominated by mesa and canyon country in which there were pinyon and juniper stands at higher elevations, grasslands, and a desert environment at lower altitudes. Macro-Penutian, Na-Dene, and Hokan-Siouan were the linguistic phyla of the represented tribes.

The clothing styles of men usually included a breechclout of cotton cloth or skin and above it a kilt of similar material. A cotton or skin shirt and hard-soled moccasins were worn, plus a robe of woven rabbit fur in cold weather. Women wore leggings joined to moccasins, and dresses which were rectangular pieces of cloth passed under one arm and fastened over the other. Over most of the area the single-family house was either a dome- or tepee-shaped structure covered with hides, matting, bark, or thatch. The sedentary farmers had rectangular dwellings with stone walls and a flat-beamed roof, and the occupants were drawn from more than one nuclear family. The people of the Oasis culture area subsisted primarily on maize or on maize freely supplemented with hunted animals and collected wild plants. The farmers of the Oasis were permanently sedentary, whereas the people who depended more on gathering frequently moved about the countryside.

Plant cultivation, especially of maize and beans, supported most of the people of the area. The crops were planted or tended with an end-pointed digging stick and often a bladed stick; hoes were restricted to a portion of the area. It was in the Oasis, too, that garden plots were irrigated either by natural flooding or by diverting water into ditches. Fishing was unimportant, but plant collecting was a significant pursuit. The people used seed beaters of diverse forms, the straight-handled digging stick, gathering poles, and tongs for obtaining cactus. Hunting was a supplementary means of obtaining food, and game was driven by fire or surrounded by enclosures. Likewise, animals were taken with the aid of disguises and in some sections were called with auditory decoys. Pitfalls, deadfalls, and snares were employed in some areas. Other material culture usages included carrying baskets used everywhere; the parfleche in the southeast; dogs as pack animals only in the extreme east; boats, when they were present at all, built of logs or poles; twined and coiled baskets which were common almost everywhere, with plaited objects more scattered in distribution; pottery, made throughout the area; and copper, which was pounded into forms while cold.

Polygyny occurred with low or high frequency, depending on the area, and monogamy was the other marriage form. Residence after marriage was most often with or near the wife's family, but most other forms of marriage residence have been found to exist. Descent was traced through both sides of the family, except in the north central area, where it was established through the female line. Bear ceremonialism and rites for the first kills of youths were most likely to occur together, but there were tribes in which one was found without the other or neither was reported. Throughout much of the Oasis first fruit ceremonies are known to have been observed.

California. The smallest of the culture areas, California is also essentially a biotic province. The biotic province consists of the state of California with the exception of the northeastern and southeastern limits. California in general varies greatly in environment from low-lying deserts to high, conifer-covered mountainous regions, with oak forests and grasslands in between. Most California tribes belonged to the Macro-Penutian phylum, although the Hokan-Siouan and Na-Dene phyla also were represented.

Often the men went without clothing, but they might have worn breechclouts. Fur blankets protected them in cool weather. Some wore sandals, but most went barefooted. Women wore short skirts made from skins or plant fibers and sometimes fur blankets. The multi-family dwellings were most often tepee- or dome-shaped, with diverse types of covering, depending on the locally available materials. The acorn was the most important food source, and the diverse tribes tended to range from central bases to exploit local products over a restricted area.

In the California culture area plant products were the most important source of food; hunting was supplementary. In the plant-collecting activities poles and seed beaters, which usually were woven, were employed, but straight-handled digging sticks were the most important tool. For taking game, hunters disguised themselves and used calls; they made snares, deadfalls, and enclosures, but less frequently pitfalls. In those localities in which fishing was possible associated techniques were the use of poisons, hooks, harpoons, weirs and traps or other obstructions, gill nets and seines, and rarely spears. Additional artifacts of the forms cited for the other culture areas included carrying nets and carrying baskets; simple snowshoes in the northeast; boats of balsa in the north and south, but plank vessels

BIOTIC PROVINCES

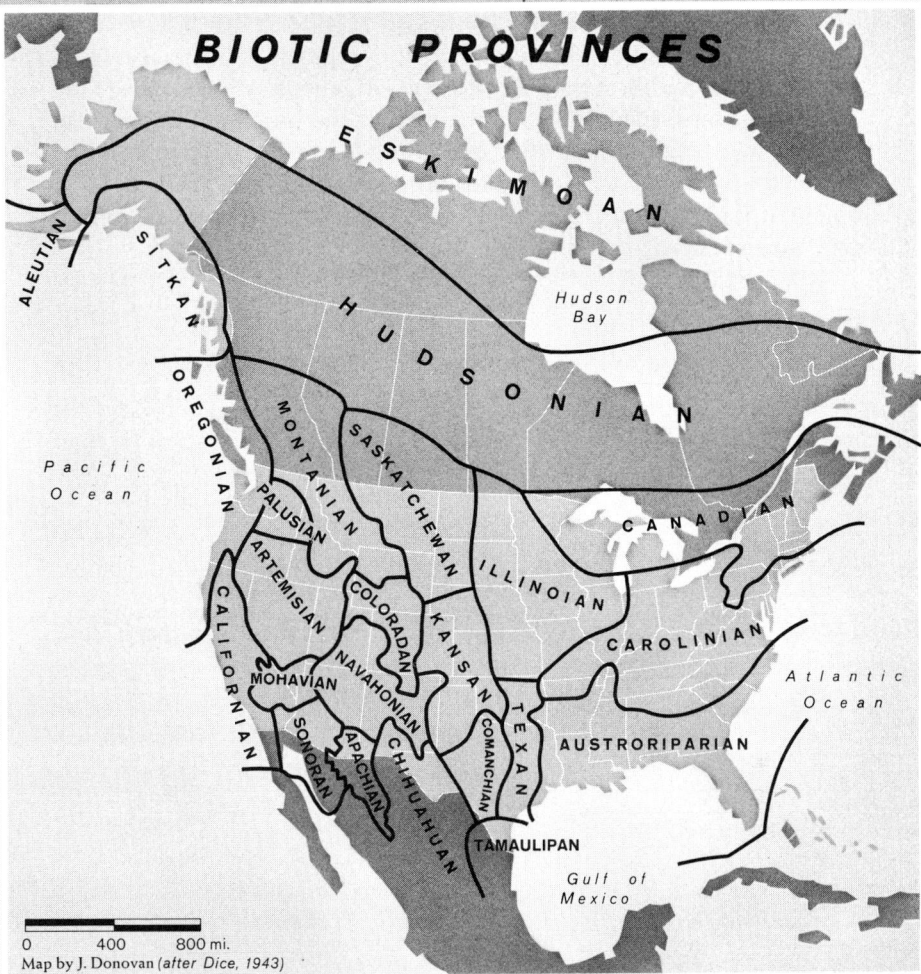

ALEUTIAN

SITKAN

E S K I M O A N

*Pacific
Ocean*

OREGONIAN

*Hudson
Bay*

H U D S O N I A N

MONTANIAN

SASKATCHEWAN

PALUSIAN

C A N A D I A N

ARTEMISIAN

COLORADAN

ILLINOIAN

CALIFORNIAN

NAVAHONIAN

KANSAN

CAROLINIAN

MOHAVIAN

SONORAN

APACHIAN

CHIHUAHUAN

COMANCHIAN

TEXAN

*Atlantic
Ocean*

AUSTRORIPARIAN

TAMAULIPAN

*Gulf of
Mexico*

0   400   800 mi.

Map by J. Donovan *(after Dice, 1943)*

along a section of the southern coast; twined and coiled baskets common everywhere except in the north, where twining alone was found; and pottery, made only in the southeast.

Throughout most of California the majority of marriages were monogamous, with less than 20 percent polygynous. After marriage the couple was most likely to live with or near the husband's family, and descent was usually traced through the male line. Bear ceremonialism and first-kill ceremonies for youths occurred widely either alone or in combination, but first fruit rituals were confined mainly to the central and northwestern sectors.

1

The Chipewyan:

Hunters and Fishermen of the Subarctic

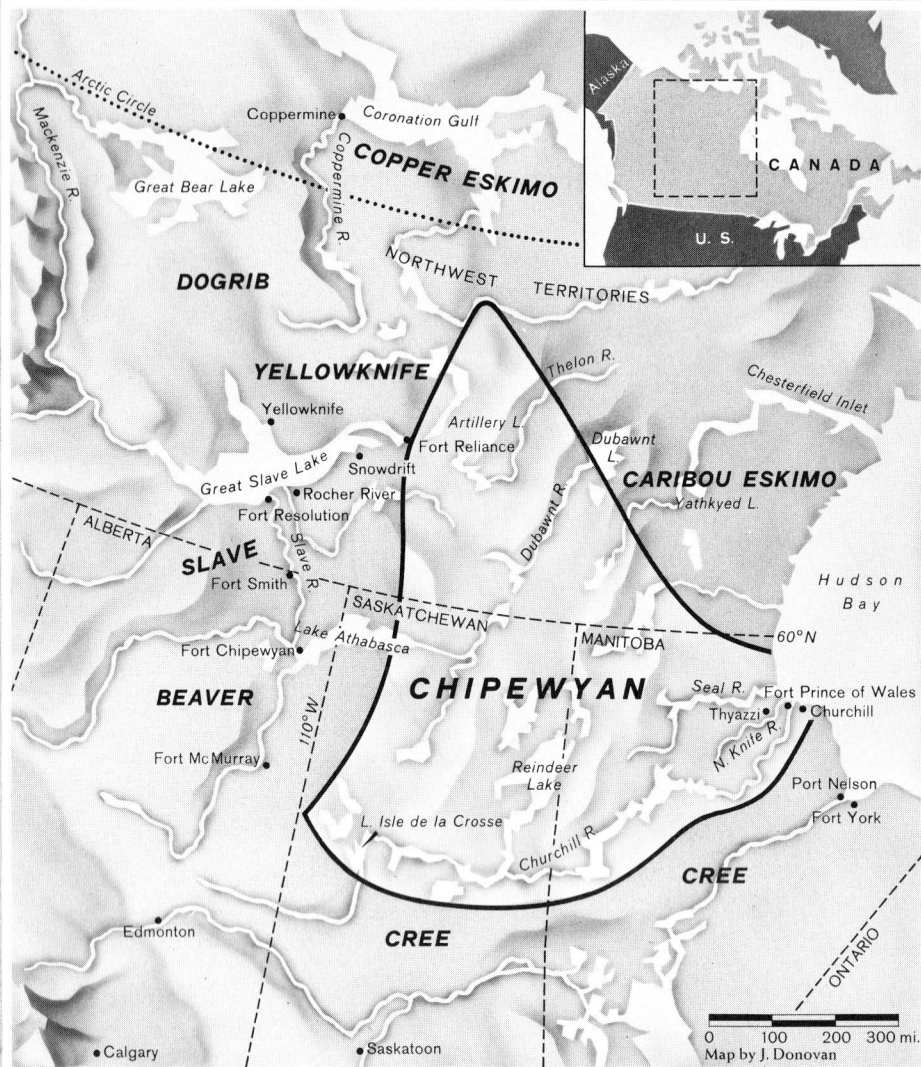

Map by J. Donovan

The territory of the Chipewyan covered a great expanse of subarctic tundra and forest, extending some five hundred miles from east to west and as many as six hundred miles from north to south. The entire area is a part of the vast Canadian shield and lies within the Hudsonian biotic province. The climate is continental; its winters are long and cold and its summers short but relatively warm. Everywhere there are interlaced networks of waterways, including foaming as well as hesitant streams and rivers, a concentration of great lakes, and countless scattered smaller lakes. The barren rocks show obvious signs of glacial wear on their smoothed or striated surfaces. The glaciated nature of the country is particularly evident in the north, where rolling masses of bedrock give way to boulder-strewn valleys. The highland areas support thin layers of lichens or nothing at all, whereas the valleys present a vegetation dominated by mosses and lichens. This area is known to the Chipewyan as the Barren Grounds, a fitting appellation which has been incorporated into the geographical literature. As one moves southward in the Barrens, gnarled individual spruce appear as outriders of their species, and farther south the spruce form small stands in sheltered draws. This is a taiga environment, where the tundra meets the northern forest, and the area in which the Chipewyan were most at home. Still farther south the spruce become dense, and juniper, aspen, and birch stands are fringed by marshy bogs and upland tundras. The land was forbidding to an outsider. It was a country that offered little to primitive man, yet was and still is in part the land of the Chipewyan.

The Chipewyan have been referred to by three different terms in the published literature. At first they were called the Northern Indians, reflective of their geographical relationship with the Hudson's Bay Company traders, who introduced the term. The easternmost bands have been called Caribou Eaters, indicating their primary dietary staple. The name Chipewyan is the accepted contemporary designation for the entire group, and in casual conversation in modern Canada they are often called "Chips." The word Chipewyan is taken from Cree and means "pointed skins," a graphic reference to the dangling point on the front and back of the caribou-skin, poncho-like garments of the men. These people term themselves "Dene," which means "humans." They were never numerous, and at the time of contact with Europeans their population is estimated at 3500. If one considers the vast extent of the country occupied by them, their population density was one of the lowest for a North American Indian tribe.

Appropriately enough, it may be asked why these Indians are described as representative of the subarctic. The reasons are linguistic, ecological, historical, and sociocultural. The Chipewyan represent one of the aboriginal variants of Northern Athapaskan Indians in language and culture. Since it was the Athapaskans who occupied most of interior Alaska and western Canada, it is desirable that one people or tribe of this aggregate be included in any description of the major variants of North American Indian culture. Among subarctic peoples there were two major subsistence sources, fish and caribou, and most tribes utilized both; the Chipewyan were such a people. They are a better group to present than most other Northern Athapaskans largely because of historical chance. They were reasonably well described by Europeans soon after initial historic contact, and added references were made to them as late as 1960, when a thorough study of one modern community was begun. For no other Northern Athapaskan tribe have we so much documentation through time. The information available, however, is not so plentiful nor so detailed as that for many other American Indians. The sociocultural reasons for describing the Chipewyan are equally significant, for in complexity of lifeway they were among the simplest of Indians. They illustrate a family-based social type in which there was a minimum of extrafamilial contact or feeling of community cohesion. They represent, too, a people among whom women were oppressed. Together the simplicity of social organization and the subordination of women form a rather unusual set of enduring circumstances in any human society.

The Chipewyan speak a language that belongs to the Na-Dene linguistic phylum, and the origin of their language has been considered by some linguists to be from the same root as the Sino-Tibetan phylum of the Old World. The importance of this remote and tenuous tie is that it suggests an ultimate Old World origin for Na-Dene speakers, which is what anthropologists currently would expect. A notable fact about Na-Dene is that it was the most widespread linguistic phylum in aboriginal North America. Its speakers ranged from near Bering Strait and the western shore of Hudson's Bay to the Mexican border. The Chipewyan are distant but recognized linguistic relatives of the Haida, Eyak, and Tlingit, who live along the northwest coast of North America, but their closer ties of language are with the other peoples of the Dene stock. Dene includes the Athapaskan family and subfamilies of Northern Athapaskan, Pacific Athapaskan, and Apachean. The Northern Athapaskan subfamily, in turn, embraces at least twenty-eight different peoples who lived in western Canada and Alaska. The Pacific Athapaskans were a small enclave of thirteen tribes concentrated in the Pacific Northwest of the United States, whereas the best-known tribes of Apachean are the Apache and the Navajo. The Na-Dene were essentially an inland people and relatively recent migrants into the New World. Their major dispersal took place during the Christian era. It appears at present, on the basis of current applications of lexicostatistics, that the Dene stock, including, of course, the Chipewyan, consisted of one closely related group of Indians around A.D. 700. These people then dispersed, and the Pacific Athapaskan subfamily virtually completed its diversification by A.D. 1000. The Apachean subfamily also began moving south about A.D. 1000, but internal Apachean splits were not completed until about 1800. Diversifications in the Northern Athapaskans took place beween 900 and 1400, with the Chipewyan completing its divergence at the later date.

The span of human occupancy in historic Chipewyan country may not be stated with even superficial exactness. It is possible only to interpolate from scattered archaeological finds to arrive at a tentative statement in this regard. One site, near the extreme eastern sector of the early historic Chipewyan range, is adjacent to North Knife River and is called Thyazzi. It is an inland site, of unknown age, at which the artifacts are blowing out of sand hills. The recovered lithic products fall within the range of a tool tradition most commonly associated with Eskimos and called the Denbigh Flint Complex, after the type site on Cape Denbigh in western Alaska occupied around 1000 B.C. At Thyazzi were found burins, end blades, side blades, and an assortment of scrapers, but not the microblade that is so typical of the Alaskan finds. These tools give no clear clues to their makers, but in type they are unlike Athapaskan artifacts. Furthermore, aboriginal Athapaskan stoneworking does not appear to have been derived from this base. At another series of sites, along the Thelon River in an area of seasonal penetration by the Chipewyan in historic times, are archaeological remains assigned to an era shortly after 3000 B.C. These sites reflect an Indian type of hunting economy adapted to an inland setting. The characteristic projectile point has a tapered stem and lanceolate outline; it is suggestively an Agate Basin point prototype. Other forms include various scrapers and knives which are less distinctive. There is evidence of some continuity of this general tool complex through time and eventual identification with the Caribou Eaters. The inference to be drawn from the North Knife and Thelon River artifacts is that there were at least two different prehistoric hunting peoples in Chipewyan country. One tool complex is associated with Indians and the other, the Denbigh Flint Complex, with Eskimos. If we accept the general premise that the Chipewyan are relatively recent migrants into the country they occupied, the early archaeological finds represent non-Athapaskan peoples who logically must be associated with Archaic Indian and Paleo-Eskimo developments. Summarily, the Chipewyan were not the first caribou hunters to adapt to the Barren Grounds.

The Chipewyan receive their earliest historical notice in connection with the Hudson's Bay Company efforts to expand the trade in furs to the lands west of Hudson Bay. The company administrators at the trading center of York Fort, founded in 1684 and located along southern Hudson Bay, were anxious to bring the Northern Indians into their post. The difficulty in accomplishing this purpose stemmed from Cree Indian success in pushing the Chipewyan to the west from their Churchill River territory. In 1715 William Stewart set out with a Chipewyan woman to induce her people to settle their differences with the Cree and to trade at York Fort. Accompanied by a small party of Cree, they sought out the various Chipewyan bands. In a year's time their purpose had been accomplished. Peace was made, and ten young Chipewyans went to York Fort to learn to speak Cree and become interpreters. Through the efforts of Stewart the country to the south of Great Slave Lake was opened for trading. The next move for the Hudson's Bay Company officials was to establish a trading center at the margin of Chipewyan country along the western shore of the bay. The selected site was the former whaling station at Churchill, where earlier still the Danish exploring party under Jens Munch had wintered in 1619-1620. Before the establishment of the Hudson's Bay Company post at Churchill, Eskimos occupied the area. In fact, the point of land on which Fort Prince of Wales was constructed was called "Eskimo Point." However, when the Indians, presumably Chipewyan, received guns from the traders, the Eskimos were forced north. It was not only the desire for pelts that led to this northward movement but the additional hope of exploiting reported copper deposits about which we will learn more. The post was constructed in 1717, while the great stone fort named Fort Prince of Wales was built between the years 1732 and 1771 and destroyed by La Perouse in 1782.

Still the heart of the Chipewyan area had not been brought under any realistic control. It appears that in 1720 James Knight traded with Yellowknife Indians, and in 1766 three Dogrib Indians traded at Churchill. Thus there was some knowledge of the great area to the north and west. Moses Norton, governor at Fort Prince of Wales, was anxious to open trade relations in this area and at the same time settle the exact whereabouts of the copper deposit. The problem of a proposed overland expedition to the "Far Indian" country was that the Chipewyan, who were making tremendous profits as middlemen in the trade with more distant tribes, were reluctant to guide the Hudson's Bay Company explorers. Official Company support for a land expedition was forthcoming, and at this point the name Samuel Hearne becomes intimately associated with the Chipewyan, copper, and the exploration of northwestern Canada.

Samuel Hearne was born in London in 1745. His response to formal education was indifferent, and he went to sea as a captain's servant before he was in his teens. He served on two different frigates during the Seven Years' War. When the war ended in 1763, Hearne's service with the Royal Navy was terminated. In 1766 he became a seaman on a small Hudson's Bay Company vessel engaged in trading and whaling along the western shore of Hudson Bay. He remained in this capacity until 1768, when his fortunes came under the influence of Moses Norton, the governor of Fort Prince of Wales. In 1768 Norton consulted with Company officials in England and convinced them that a search for the copper deposits known to exist somewhere to the north and west of Fort Prince of Wales would be an important enterprise. By this date, however, Norton must have known that the search would not be rewarding. Nevertheless, once official sanction was forthcoming, Norton organized the trip. The small party of whites and Indians under Hearne's direction was to be guided by a Chipewyan named Chawchinahaw. This was the unsuccessful trip of 1769, for the Indian guide was a fraud who hindered rather than aided the endeavor. When they were some two hundred miles from the fort, they were forced to return, largely because of the refusal of the Chipewyan hunters to supply the whites with game. The trip, although a total failure in terms of their purpose, did teach Hearne that the average Chipewyan was not reliable in his dealings with Europeans and could not be led if he did not choose. Again Hearne set off for the copper deposits in early 1770, this time under the guidance of Connee-queese, but this Indian leader was as bad as the first, if not worse, he had no authority among his people and to compound the confusion did not know where the copper was located. He led the party north to the Dubawnt and Yathkyed Lake area. At this point Hearne broke his quadrant and could no longer take the necessary observations for accurate mapping, and so he returned to the fort late in 1770. The third attempt, organized within two weeks after his second failure, was planned differently. The ultimate success of this trip hinged on the Chipewyan guide, Matonabbee, who had his own opinions about how to succeed. The key to his plan was to take women along to relieve the men of many, if not most, of the burdensome chores while traveling. To make matters even better, Matonabbee had six wives of his own at that time. The trip to the Coppermine River and Coronation Gulf was completed successfully by mid-1772, and it was one of the most noteworthy feats of individual exploration anywhere at any time. Hearne's maps were not accurate, and for this he has received periodic criticism. Perhaps what is more important to recall, however, is that such a trip has never been duplicated fully. Hearne's book describing his three trips includes our most comprehensive account of the Chipewyan and is a classic in exploration literature. The manuscript was accepted by the publisher in October of 1792, and its author died the following month. The book did not appear in print until 1795.

The map prepared by Hearne and the knowledge he gained of the country through which he passed facilitated further expansion to the northwest. The first individual to trade in the midst of the Chipewyan country was Peter Pond, who in 1778–1779 traded on a river not far from Athabasca Lake. There were North West Company and Hudson's Bay Company stations on Great Slave Lake. These trading ventures made it possible for a greater number of Chipewyan to be drawn into a fur trapping economy, for the long trip to the fort on Hudson Bay was no longer necessary for the western bands. The organization of the North West Company in 1783 introduced an era of fierce competition with the Hudson's Bay Company for the emerging northwestern fur trade. It was not until the amalgamation of the two in 1821 that trading conditions became stabilized.

To round out the history of the Chipewyan we must note the explorations of Alexander Mackenzie in 1789 which led him to the Arctic Ocean down the river that bears his name today. His account was one of disappointment, for he had hoped to reach the Pacific Ocean. The travels of Mackenzie wrote finis to speculations about a northwest water passage to the Pacific. The entire history of the Chipewyan country centered about the quest for mineral wealth, the expanding northern fur trade, and disappointing searches for a water passage to the Pacific Ocean. The search for souls by missionaries was to come later, when in 1846 Roman Catholic missionaries founded a permanent mission at Lake Isle a la Crosse and the Anglicans located at Churchill in 1912. Even today it is fur and souls that attract most outsiders into the Chipewyan country, but admittedly this pattern shows signs of change.

Most peoples in the world have at least a passing concern for their origins and seek some rationale for their existence. In the absence of systematic knowledge of the past and a scientific view of the world, most often they explain their presence in a supernatural context. The creation myth of each people provides a meaningful explanation for their very being. The Chipewyan regarded the primordial world as centering about a woman who lived in a cave and ate berries for food. Then a dog-like creature followed her into the cave and lived there with her. At night she dreamed that the animal turned into a handsome young man who had sexual intercourse with her. However, it was no dream, and the woman became pregnant. At this juncture a giant man approached; he was so tall that his head reached nearly to the clouds. With a stick he outlined the bodies of water and caused them to fill. The giant then tore the dog-like animal to shreds and threw the internal organs into the water, creating various fish. The flesh was tossed onto the land in bits and became land animals, and the skin was torn and thrown into the sky to become birds. The giant then told the woman that her offspring would have the ability to kill as many of these creatures as they required and that she need not worry about the animals' abundance, since it was his command that they multiply. The giant then returned from whence he came and was never seen again. In this way the orderliness of the world emerged, and the abundance of game was assured. This tale was a rationale for the indiscriminate killing of game and also served as a supernatural association with dogs, since the woman's offspring were human and descended from this creature related to the dog. The creation myth was not only an explanation taught to children but also formed a guide to thoughts about men and the environment they occupied.

The clothing that the people wore was made from caribou skins taken from animals killed in the early fall, from late August until mid-October, when the skins were strong and light and the fur dense but not extremely long. In general, eight to ten skins were necessary to outfit one individual for the winter. The upper garment of a man consisted of a loose-fitting, sleeved poncho with the fur side out. It did not have an attached hood or an opening cut into the front, and it extended down to the thigh with the skins cut to a point in front and also in the back. At least two skins were required for such a garment, and the seams along the sides were sewn with an awl, not an eyed needle. A fur boa was sometimes worn when the temperature was low, and the ears might be covered by a fur band, a fur cap, or a cap made from the skinned-out head of a caribou. Leggings reaching from the thighs to the ankles were of dehaired caribou skin, and moccasins at the bottom completed the normal garment. In severe weather a caribou skin cape was draped over the shoulders. The garb of a woman included a sleeved dress, again made from two skins and sewn at the sides. This garment reached to the woman's knees or even to her ankles. In order to hold the dress up from the ground a belt girdled the waist. Vanity was not unknown, even to Chipewyan women. On an extremely cold February day described by Hearne one woman held her dress high with her belt so she could "shew a clean heel and good leg," and managed at the same time to freeze her buttocks and thighs so badly that huge blisters developed as she thawed. It was a joke to all except her. The leggings of the women reached from below the knee to the ankle and may not have had attached moccasins. The moccasins of men and women were decorated over the instep with split porcupine quills which were dyed and arranged in patterns. The women also wore capes, and both sexes used mittens, not gloves, of double thickness. The inner mitten was made from dehaired skin; the outer mitten had the hair side facing the hand. They were attached to a leather harness that hung about the neck and made it convenient to slip the hands out of the mittens without the chance of losing them.

These fur-clad people were described in less than glowing terms by those Europeans with whom they first had contact. It is evident that the ideal of an honorable man was not the same for the Chipewyan and the English. First there was the haughty attitude that the Indians assumed with Europeans. The Chipewyan firmly believed that they were more intelligent than the whites. This, of course, could not have endeared them to the English. The men are described further as being patient and persevering but morose and covetous. Still they were peaceful insofar as this meant not shedding the blood of another Chipewyan male. When they were angry with one another, they wrestled, pulled their opponent's hair or ears, or twisted his neck. In a scale of honesty for the eastern tribes of the Northern Athapaskans, the Chipewyan were ranked as superior to all others; they abhorred thievery and the thief. It would appear, however, that this standard prevailed primarily within the tribe, judging from the experience of most Europeans. It is likely that the Indians thought of the whites as not quite human, since they obviously were not Chipewyan.

No description of these people could be complete without some comment on the status of women. Females were subordinated to men in every way, and the men were oppressive. Women were treated cruelly and held in gross contempt by the men. Female infants were on occasion permitted to die, a practice viewed by adult women as kindly. In fact, they are said to have wished their mothers had done it for them. Furthermore, women were beaten not infrequently, and, although it was an odious crime to kill another Chipewyan man, if a wife died from a beating by her husband, it was no crime.

The settlements in which these Indians lived ranged from an individual family dwelling in total isolation from others to clusters of as many as seventy separate households. The size of any community was a function of the time of the year and the availability of food resources. In general, it is clear that aggregates which included more than a few families were rare or of brief duration. The dwelling in which the people lived was a subarctic variation of the tepee, which is best known from the plains of western America. The Chipewyan tent consisted of a framework of poles set in a circle and bound together at the top. The cone was covered with sewn caribou skins and measured a few feet to more than twenty feet across, depending on the number of occupants, the mobility of the household, and the hunting success of the attached males. A large tent required as many as seventy caribou skins for the cover. At the apex of the poles was an opening which allowed the smoke from the central fireplace to filter out. Spruce boughs, when available, would be laid around the fire, which was lighted with sparks struck from iron pyrites. Over these boughs were caribou skins on which family members reclined and slept.

One would expect to see most of the household manufactures of these people in and around their tents. Among the possessions of the women would be cooking and storage containers of birchbark or skin. A basket of folded bark was commonly used for cooking by filling it with preheated stones, water, and raw meat. The women probably had skin bags in which they kept sewing awls and thread of caribou sinew. The men's tool kits included wedges of antler or wood for splitting planks from logs; a crooked knife with a copper blade and antler handle, the most important form of knife; a curved, wooden-handled knife with a beaver incisor for a blade, another highly useful tool for cutting small sections of wood; and a hand drill with a copper bit and an antler handle, the only drill form known. There were also awls of copper, and a copper-bladed ax hafted on a wooden or antler handle. All of these uses of copper, in addition to its further utilization in ice-pick points, arrowpoints, spearheads, and spoons, reflect a reliance on this metal over stone. The copper tools were made by pounding a raw lump of the metal into shape. These people never treated copper as a metal by heating or smelting it, but processed it in the same manner as they would stone. The Chipewyan were metal users, but only in a broad technical sense.

The preparation of food in a Chipewyan household was a major reason for the household's very existence. The favorite items were primarily caribou products: the head and fat from the back, a fetus either raw or cooked, and grubs from under the caribou's skin. These Indians did not consider steaks and chops as luxuries. Food, which most often meant caribou meat in the east and bison in the west, or fish at times when these animals were not to be found, could be eaten raw or cooked. In addition to being boiled in a birchbark container, flesh could be roasted over an open fire. One might cook by using the stomach of a caribou as a container and the contents as food. To the fermenting lichens in a stomach were added shredded fat, blood, tender meat, and cut up heart and lungs. The caribou stomach was hung over a low fire for roasting and then served. The diet of the Chipewyan only rarely included plant products, although a moss soup is reported and moss also could be added to soup as seasoning. At a winter camp a compact lump of snow was skewered on a stick and tilted toward the fire over a birchbark container to catch the dripping water. The meals at camp were prepared by women, but it was the men who ate first. The women received only what the men had not consumed, which might at times amount to nothing. One other food was pemmican, which usually is thought of as characteristic of the Indians of the Plains. Pemmican, from a Cree word meaning "manufactured grease," was made from lean meat that had been cut into strips and sun-dried or dried by a fire. It was then pounded into a powder, mixed with fat, and stuffed into caribou intestines. It was a highly concentrated and portable food and a particular favorite of travelers.

Scattered around the camp would be other items of the material culture inventory. A well-supplied camp would have tripods of poles from which caribou skin bags filled with dried meat were hung. On the ground would be a canoe, but not the well-known form made famous by the Algonkian Indians and carried over into modern canvas or metal-covered canoes. The Chipewyan variety was about thirteen feet in length and some twenty inches at its greatest width, which was toward the stern. The cover of birchbark was supported by ribs of spruce, and it was decked over the forward third. The seams were caulked with pitch for summer, and fat was added to the pitch as the weather turned cold. Such a canoe, propelled with a single-bladed paddle, was used for hunting caribou as they swam across streams or lakes and to pursue molting birds in the water. A canoe was carried by summer travelers so that they could hunt from it and also ferry across rivers or lakes. Another item of transportation likely to be seen was the toboggan. A conveyance of this kind ranged in length from eight to fourteen feet and was some fourteen inches wide. It was made from quarter-inch thick juniper planks which were steamed at the front and bent upward. The planks were bound together at two-foot intervals with crosspieces probably fixed in place by means of thongs passed through holes made with a hand drill. Chipewyan women, not dogs, pulled the toboggans. If wooden toboggans could not be constructed because of a scarcity of wood, caribou leg skins sewn together provided a temporary substitute. The cariole, which is a more complex toboggan with sides and a back, was an introduction of Europeans.

If the summer camp was in a region in which caribou or bison were unavailable, it would be located near a lake or stream known to contain fish. A principal fishing technique was to take the fish in a gill net, made of strips of unprocessed caribou skin. Nets of this form had wooden floats attached along the top and two heavy stone sinkers at each lower corner. They were set across narrow streams or at favored spots on lakes. Various species of fish would be taken, depending on the time and place, but those most commonly caught were whitefish and pike. There was a supernatural involvement in netting fish. The Chipewyan felt that each net had its own personality. For example, one net was not joined to another for fear that they would be jealous of one another, with the result that no fish would be caught. Other precautions were necessary in gillnetting. Charms were attached to the four corners of the net, and without them it was believed that no fish would be taken. These magical associations point to a supernatural concern for fish, in contrast to any similar involvement with caribou. The wooden, bone, or antler fishhooks often had charms attached. The first fish caught with a new net or hook was boiled and the articulated bones removed intact and burned in a fire. Other fishing implements included dip nets used in association with weirs, which were brush fences across shallow stretches of water. Barbed arrows were shot from bows, and fish spears were hurled from canoes. It is probable that the hooks and fish arrows were most important for travelers, for the take with these devices would be limited.

The women while in camp prepared the meals and cared for the children, as would their counterparts throughout most of the world. To these obligations may be added the task of processing raw skins, particularly those of caribou. This was one of their most important activities. After a caribou had been killed by a man and retrieved by his wife, it was skinned with a copper- or stone-bladed knife. During the skinning, bits of flesh and fat clung to the cutaneous layer. This adhering matter was scraped away by drawing a one-handed scraper toward the user. The scraper was artificed from a caribou leg bone. The distal end of the bone had been removed so that there was an oblong cutting edge which sometimes was serrated; a leather thong fitted around the user's forearm to complete the tool. If the hair on the skin was to be removed, a two-handed scraper was employed. To dehair a skin, the woman first set a wooden beam obliquely into the ground and then draped the skin over the beam with the hair side up. She scraped toward herself against the grain of the hair, using a scraper made from a caribou leg bone cut longitudinally along a medial surface. A dehaired skin was then most often smoke-cured by hanging it over a pole framework under which a small fire burned decayed wood. A skin to be used with the hair intact was scraped with a one-handed scraper, softened in water, wrung out and dried, and rubbed on the inner surface with a paste of partly decayed caribou brains. Afterward it was permitted to dry once again and finally scraped with a copper-bladed end scraper with an antler handle. The skin probably was rubbed by hand to make it pliable and relatively soft. This process of skin preparation is detailed because it was an important area of technological knowledge among a people who relied on skins not only for clothing but for bedding, dwelling covers, containers, and ropes. It should be added that American Indians did not tan skins in the technical sense of the word.

In the early spring the easternmost bands ranged into or along the Barren Grounds to hunt caribou. A hunting party first gathered at the northern edge of the forest in a birch grove. Here they cut poles to be carried with them to the north or west, and canoes were made for crossing deep or swift water. Two hundred persons gathered at one such spot in the time of Hearne. Women were taken along on these trips so that they could carry most of the camping equipment. Hearne records that a strong woman could carry one hundred and forty pounds, which is an impressive burden, considering the nature of the terrain. While traveling, the men hunted on both sides of the trail taken by the women and young girls as they pulled the heavily loaded toboggans along the most direct route. Dogs, laden with parcels of tent skins, containers, and poles, accompanied the women. In the early spring snow was still abundant, and snowshoes were essential for travelers. The snowshoes were made of birchwood frames laced with babiche (thin, dehaired caribou skin strips) through holes in the frames. Five wooden crosspieces supported each frame. These snowshoes had slightly turned-up tips and were asymmetrical in outline; the outer edge flared, but the inner edge was relatively straight. The men prepared the frames, and the women laced the babiche into place with eyed needles. When traveling on snowshoes, the men jogged along at a pace that was faster than a walk, and they traveled in this manner by the hour.

If a party needed food, they selected a camping place near a lake thought to contain fish. After locating a dry spot for their tents, they unloaded the frame poles, which were carried along when they went beyond the range of timber. The snow was cleared away to ground level by using a snowshoe as a shovel. The pole frameworks were erected and the skins lashed into place. Afterward caribou skins were placed on the ground, and snow was shoveled over the structures and packed into place. As the hunting party ranged beyond the tree line, where the snow had melted, they discarded their snowshoes and toboggans. They were then forced to backpack the camping equipment and place small parcels on the backs of their dogs. Hunting as they moved, the men paused only when food was in abundance or when they anticipated abundance. Ducks, geese, and swans were killed on their flight northward; musk-oxen were hunted in open country; caribou were lanced from canoes as they crossed a river or lake; and fish were taken with set nets or spears.

Once they had arrived at a well-known caribou crossing, they were joined by a large number of other hunting parties, so that there might be as many as six hundred persons in the same locality at one time and an average of nine individuals per tent. Families or groups of families who were seeing each other for the first time in months or years followed an established procedure at their reunion. They sat some thirty yards apart saying nothing at first. Then an old person of one party would recount all the disasters that had transpired in their lives since their last meeting, and the women of the other group would wail on hearing of their misfortune. The second party's fate was then unfolded in the same manner until all had been told. The men would then greet the men, and the women joined the women to exchange presents and good news.

When the Barren Ground caribou arrived, their number was truly fantastic. Sometimes so many were killed that only the skins, long bones, fat, and tongues were taken, and the remainder of the carcasses were left to rot. As the caribou drifted along the northern forest border, the Indians followed, drying as much meat as they could carry conveniently. The caribou were killed at this time with arrows shot from bows or by spearing them from canoes. The bow employed in hunting was the self-bow, a rounded section of birch tapering toward both ends and strung with babiche. Arrow shafts were feathered with three split feathers attached by means of sinew. Different types of arrowpoints were prepared for various species of animals. The caribou arrowpoint was unbarbed and of bone or stone, whereas bird arrows were tipped with blunted points simply to stun the bird or hare. Arrows used for fishing were barbed but did not detach from the shaft.

During the caribou rutting season in October a man sometimes attached lengths of caribou antler to his belt so that they clashed together as he walked. A bull caribou in the vicinity was deceived by the sound into sensing that two other bulls were fighting over a female. The bull would lose his habitual caution at the prospect of leading off the female and could be killed more readily than by the usual method of stalking against the wind.

It might appear that summer treks into the Barrens served little purpose save to provide a temporary food supply, which was essentially the case. However, when the caribou abandoned the northern forest border in the early spring, the most important source of food was lost unless the animals were followed, which is precisely what the Chipewyan did. The westernmost bands were able to exploit the bison that ranged along the southern shore of Great Slave Lake, and the northern forest dwellers could take the woodland caribou. Both the bison and woodland caribou were slain by essentially the same hunting methods used among the Barren Ground caribou.

In the eastern sector winter and early spring camps were established on promontories along the edge of the forest, in a locality habitually frequented by caribou, and probably at the same time near lakes known to contain fish. If a camp were situated ideally, the people would be obliged to move only once or twice during a winter. Such camps were accessible to lakes or wide rivers along which the caribou normally passed. There surrounds were constructed. Converging lines of brushy poles were erected, with poles at about twenty-yard intervals. When the caribou approached the wider end of the funnel, they were unaware of the poles, which sometimes extended over a three-mile span. As the animals walked farther toward the surround, the women, boys, and some men appeared from behind to herd them. The caribou were driven into the trap, which was a large round enclosure of branches made at the end of the funnel; here snares were set at narrow exits. The entrance was then blocked with trees, and the confused caribou were killed inside this surround by hunters who shot arrows at the loose animals and speared the ones caught in snares.

When the snow was deep and soft, the caribou were sometimes tracked on snowshoes, but this technique necessitated following a single animal until it was exhausted from floundering in the deep snow. It was easier to track and kill a moose in this manner, but moose were not common in Chipewyan country. In the winter, too, the men might set gill nets beneath the ice of lakes or jig for fish through a hole in the ice with a lured hook. In the western areas of Chipewyan country fishing was more important than among the more eastern bands.

Other significant, but secondary, methods for taking game included the erection of deadfalls for bear, wolverine, marten, and squirrels. Nets were used for taking beaver in summer, but in winter their lodges were broken into and demolished. The animals were then taken from retreats beneath the ice along the banks of a stream or lake. Babiche snares were made to entangle hares or ptarmigan. Finally, even though these Indians reached the sea at Churchill, they did not hunt sea mammals, which were locally abundant at certain seasons.

Additional facts of Chipewyan hunting and fishing activities could be detailed, but enough has been said to make it obvious that caribou and fish were the primary staples of life. Relying as they did on very few species, there were often periods when food was scarce and people starved. Famine was probably more common among the Northern Athapaskans than among any other block of American Indians. At these times the people would collect berries, mosses, or rose hips, and after the more edible plant products were consumed they turned to the most appetizing items of clothing (see Note 1) and finally, under extreme conditions, to cannibalism.

Social life exhibits a general organizational simplicity which has come to be associated with many primitive peoples at a subsistence-based level of economy. In this environment each household was durably self-sufficient and could exist in total isolation from all other such units until it came time for one of the members to find a wife. Hence it is not surprising that individualism was well developed. Each man assumed complete responsibility for himself and his family, and each woman was responsible totally to her husband. Feelings of group identity hardly existed, and the concept of community cohesion or *esprit de corps* was unknown. Neither were family units restricted in their utilization of the environment to particular geographical localities; thus the concept of family hunting territories did not exist. What we do recognize in the structure of their social lives beyond the family level are reactions to threats from outside the tribe and more rarely from within the tribe, plus the emergence, at times, of an outstanding individual within the group.

External threats came from the neighboring Algonkian-speaking Cree or the Inuit-speaking Eskimos. The Cree, called simply "enemy," and the Eskimos, called "enemies from the flat land," posed the greatest threats. The hostility stemmed primarily from the belief that the shamans of these people could and did send evil by supernatural means to cause illness among the Chipewyan. Although one of their own shamans could and sometimes did harm one of his own people with the aid of spirits, this was not common. The Chipewyan believed that no death or illness occurred from natural causes except among the aged. Thus, in theory, each physical disorder resulted from the hostile activities of a shaman. The shamans of the Chipewyan attempted to negate the effects of such evil. Shamans controlled personal spirits, and they performed feats of magic. When someone fell sick, the shaman sang and danced to summon his supernatural aids or "shadows," who were animal, bird, or imaginative supernatural familiars. He then sucked and blew the intrusive disease substance from the patient, but he was able to cure the individual only when his guardian spirits were more powerful than those of the rival shaman who had caused the sickness. If the case became extremely serious, the people erected a small square tent which had no opening at the top. The shaman here treated the patient in the usual fashion and then followed it with a sword-swallowing performance. During this entire procedure the shaman was naked. Death and lingering disease were causes of constant hostility between these people and their non-Athapaskan neighbors. This knowledge united all the Chipewyan and sent their men on sporadic forays into the lands of their tormentors. A raid on the Eskimos by a party of Athapaskans was described by Hearne, who was with the Athapaskans. The participating individuals carried wooden shields on which they had painted different designs, such as sun, moon, animals, or supernatural beings. These figures, which represented individual guardian spirits, protected their makers. After the encounter the Indians were obligated to observe numerous taboos in order to placate the spirits of those they had killed. A raid of this nature stemmed from long-standing feelings of hostility. It bound together the participants against a common enemy, but at the same time it did not require elaborate organization. Raids were bizarre melees for individual prestige, plunder, potential glory, and tribal security.

Diverse families could be united by the prowess of a charismatic leader. An individual of this nature seems first to have been an outstanding provider, a man with inordinate ability to take game and fish. Thus the leader Matonabbee supported his six wives, himself, his seven biological children, and two adopted children. Such a person probably would be thought to have the supernatural on his side. Once a reputation of this sort was established, men with marriageable daughters would be anxious to have such a man as a son-in-law. A potential father-in-law did not think of his daughter's welfare so much as the personal advantage of having the younger man attached to his household, for the pattern of marriage residence was seemingly matrilocal. A second or third wife could be the sister or sisters of the first, but in general it seems that the selection of second and subsequent wives in plural marriages was determined by the man's ability to take advantage of immediate opportunities. Such a man was physically strong, for he had to validate his claim to any particular wife, especially a young one, by successfully wrestling to keep her. A leader attracted to his camp less successful hunters, relatives, and nonrelatives, who cast their lot with him in an effort to find greater security. An important characteristic of this form of leadership was that it was highly transient. A man could hold his wives and other followers only so long as his powers of persuasion, hunting skills, and physical strength endured. After he began to fail physically, he sometimes could retain his position of authority through craft and intrigue, but this would be only a temporary respite before he slipped into obscurity.

These people calculated their ancestry through both their male and female relatives; thus they maintained a system of bilateral descent, the same general type found in the United States today. There is evidence that when a man married he attached himself to the household of his father-in-law. His ideal mate was his father's sister's daughter, that is, a patrilineal cross-cousin. In *recent* times at least some Chipewyan termed a fathers' sister's daughters (and mother's brother's daughters) the same as they would a "sweetheart," a practice that gives strength to the possibility of cross-cousin marriage. As the anthropologist Fred Eggan has pointed out, a man would rely on his son-in-law for support, and the son-in-law in turn would be aided by his wife's brother's son. It appears that in the aboriginal system of kinship terminology the cousin terms were of the Iroquois type.

Father's brother's children and mother's sister's children were termed the same as siblings, but different terms were employed for a father's sister's children and mother's brother's children. This terminology would not be incompatible with the existence of cross-cousin marriage. For the generation above Ego the kinship terms for father and father's brother are alike and mother's brother is distinct. Mother, mother's sister, and father's sister are all termed differently. Thus the terminology on the first ascending generational level was bifurcate collateral for females and bifurcate merging for males. What this terminology meant in light of actual behavior may only be inferred, since the details are not recorded in the literature. It is likely that siblings and parallel cousins of the same sex (who were terminological siblings), particularly if they were males, extended mutual aid to one another and regarded their cross-cousins as possible mates. With the further presence of wife exchange, we would find established an integrated network of blood relatives on Ego's generational level. On the parent's generation the same social distance separated aunts and uncles from one another as from parents. The inference is that these individuals were not so important socially or economically as those near relatives of one's own generation.

The number of games and amusements was small, and dancing was unknown except for one step borrowed from the Dogrib Indians. The popular and widespread hand game was known. This was a guessing game in which two opponents sat opposite each other with ten to twenty counters beside them. One man hid an object in one hand and, behind a skin, shifted it. His opponent then guessed the hand that contained the gaming piece. A correct guess gave the winner one counter, and the game was won when one man had all of the counters. A drum, of the tambourine form, was played, a rattle of skin with pebbles inside it was shaken during the guessing, and songs, too, were sung.

A composite sketch of an individual's life cycle, from birth to death, provides at least some understanding of the people operating in a sociocultural system. The information available on an aboriginal Chipewyan's life is neither balanced nor reasonably complete. It does, however, permit a sketch in broad outline of key events and behaviors. It is a virtual certainty that these Indians, as all others in North America, realized that conception resulted from sexual intercourse. As the time for delivery approached, a small tent or brush-covered structure was erected for the pregnant woman away from the main camp. Here she bore her offspring and remained apart from normal camp routine for about a month. Her isolation was enforced whether the group was traveling or at a relatively permanent camp (see Note 2). The mother was cared for by other women, but she had no contact with men. The father did not see his infant until the period of isolation was completed. Physical isolation of this nature was also the norm for a menstruating woman and for an adolescent girl at her menarche. It was the blood associated with those persons that was considered potentially harmful if it came into contact with male hunters because game and fish were thought to dislike any contamination of this nature. Apparently the women were successful in keeping the true nature of the menstrual cycle a secret from the men. When a woman wanted to avoid her husband, which might be several times in one month, she simply crawled out of the tent beneath a side and went to the menstrual hut.

During the first year of its life the naked infant was carried on the mother's back next to her skin and beneath her skin garment. The infant was held in place by a belt which passed from the middle of the woman's back over her shoulders and breasts, and it wore only a diaper padded with moss in this secondary "womb." The conventions surrounding the naming of an infant were such that a female was named after a form or characteristic of a marten. Examples are White Marten, Summer Marten, and Marten's Heart. The names for males were taken from the seasons, a place, or an animal. Unfortunately, virtually nothing is known concerning the social environment of these children. It has been reported that in at least some households considerable affection was shown them. Males occupied a favored position in comparison with their sisters, but children in general were treated by adults as adults. Conversations in the presence of children were as free and frank as though they were not there.

Childhood betrothal was practiced, and parents were careful to prevent a girl from participating in sexual intercourse before she married. The matches were made by the parents or relatives, and the girl had no choice. The usual marriage was between a pubescent girl of about twelve and a man who was about twice her age or older. An ideal partner was a father's sister's daughter. Since there was no marriage ceremony, the man simply attached himself to the household of his wife. The marriage assumed at least some degree of stability only after an infant was born to the couple. Children seldom were born during the early years of marriage, and from this it may be assumed that the young brides were passing through adolescent sterility, which would delay conception. The nuclear family, a man, his wife, and children, were neither a stable nor a long-lasting social unit. The possibilities of death by accident, disease, or starvation always existed, and life expectancy was probably less than thirty years for the average individual. These factors, plus a growing dislike for a spouse, could rupture a household. Furthermore, wrestling to retain one's wife whenever challenged did not lead to familial stability. Skill in wrestling was developed during youth, and the standard rule was that the man first thrown to the ground was the loser. An opponent could be downed most readily by grabbing his hair—thus it was cut short—or by seizing his ears—so they were greased. The woman being fought over had no voice in these matters but was expected to follow the winner dutifully. Sometimes, however, a newly won wife had to be taken by physical force. In one instance a group of Chipewyan chanced upon an enterprising Dogrib woman who had lived alone for seven months after having escaped from her captors and was attempting to find her way back home. The Indians who found her considered her as a fair and desirable prize; she was won and lost in some six wrestling matches during a single evening. It is noted also that the Chipewyan were not averse to the group rape of women belonging to their own tribe but not known to them previously.

A wrestling match for a wife did not always end well. One case is recorded in which the husband killed a potential rival. He and his wife were forced to live in isolation, and whenever other Chipewyan happened on the couple they would take everything they owned except their clothing. Women did desert their husbands, but because of the physical isolation of most camps this was a dangerous undertaking. The woman might be caught and beaten by her husband or seized by another man before she found refuge with a man she desired. Men guarded their wives jealously, not allowing them out of their sight if the opportunity for adultery existed. Wives generally were faithful to their husbands, even though a particular wife sometimes shared her husband with as many as seven other co-wives. The exchange of wives for a night perhaps helped temper any urge to seize a woman for sexual purposes alone. These exchange arrangements were made between two men and had implications that were more economic than sexual. The bonds between the men were those of continuing friendship and mutual aid. Then, too, if one man died, his partner in a wife exchange would assume, at least temporarily, the responsibility of caring for the surviving wife and her children.

As an individual aged and became less capable of supporting himself, he, or she, was regarded as an unwanted burden. The aged had the poorest of tattered clothing, and their meals consisted of the least desirable foods. Their abandonment usually took place when the camp was moved. A shelter was constructed for them, and the survivors would say, "They were dead; they appeared alive, but they were dead," and move on. A sick or senile individual who could not keep up with the travelers was left to starve alone. A person dying in isolation was not buried subsequently, and even the corpse of one who died in camp was simply placed on the ground. In any case, the bodies were consumed by animals. The personal property of the deceased was destroyed, and the immediate relatives also destroyed their own property. A mourning widow cut her hair short as an overt sign of her bereavement, and some of her shorn hair might be placed beside the deceased. For a dead husband a woman wailed about camp, stripped of her clothing and other possessions, to be aided and soothed by relatives and friends but not to remarry for a year.

The supernatural world of the Chipewyan included animistic spirits which hovered about constantly. Some of them were more potent than others, but any change from the normal and habitual was caused by these forces. The spirits of wolves and wolverine were dangerous, and these animals were not usually hunted or killed. The bear, too, was dangerous; its skin was burned and the large bones scattered in the four recognized directions. A woman could not touch or step over a bearskin; thus one placed before a door was a means of keeping women out of a tent. The spirits of a shaman were powerful, and the spirit of a deceased human was sometimes feared. There was only a vague notion of a future life, which was like that on earth but free from cares, according to one observer. Not all accounts agree, however. One states that the soul of the deceased crosses a river in a stone canoe, and if the individual has been good on earth he reaches an island on which life is free from worry. The soul of an evil individual struggles up to its neck in the river forever.

The foregoing descriptions are of life among the Chipewyan as it was observed by explorers or reconstructed by anthropologists. The manner of living for these people changed as a result of the fur trade and through the efforts of missionaries. The era of change from about 1770 to 1960 is little known, but it is possible to see that life moved in new directions. The resulting reorientation is not spelled out in the published literature and in all probability will remain vague.

The exact geographical range of these Indians at the time of historic contact is somewhat uncertain, but they did control the Barren Grounds by early historic times. Likewise, they occupied the northern forest border from the upper Churchill River to Hudson Bay. Probably by 1820 they controlled Lake Athabasca once again, after temporarily giving it up to the Cree, who subsequently became decimated by disease. In the 1890's some Chipewyan bands ranged along the western edge of the Barrens. In the winter they trapped principally marten, which they traded at Lake Athabasca, Reindeer Lake, or Churchill. In summer they lived off fish and in the fall no doubt took caribou. By 1913 the Chipewyan were concentrated near Churchill on Hudson Bay, along the western sector of their aboriginal territory, and westward around the settlements of Fort McMurray, Fort Chipewyan, and Fort Resolution. By this time the Barrens were virtually abandoned. This movement westward by the Chipewyan was probably brought about by Caribou Eskimo reoccupancy of the Barren Grounds and took place when the Eskimos received enough guns to defend the area. The process was facilitated by a decrease in the Chipewyan population. The general population movement to the western edge of the aboriginal territory no doubt also coincided with their commitment to the fur trade. The principal fur animals, the beaver, otter, and marten, are animals of a boreal setting.

It is probable that during the era of very early historic contact the Chipewyan lost much of their vitality as an ethnic group by exposure to diseases that had been previously unknown. The most destructive epidemic was that of smallpox in 1781–1782. It was Hearne's estimate that only 10 percent of the population survived, but this reference is not clearly to the total Chipewyan population, as it is assumed when it is quoted in the literature. In 1819 there was another epidemic of smallpox (Simpson, 1938, 81) which "carried away whole bands." Thus the Chipewyan were a remnant people near the beginning of their history. It is likely that because they were weakened by disease they were less able to support themselves, and there were associated famines. Another momentous change took place as a direct result of the fur trade. Once the people spent more energy trapping and less time hunting caribou or fishing, they lived within a more tenuous economic system. They wanted trade goods and trapped to obtain them, but at the same time they deprived themselves of the opportunity to acquire their basic foods. Thus, if they did not take large numbers of fish and caribou at certain seasons, they faced starvation, and this occurred more often than in aboriginal times. Famines made devastating inroads into the vitality of the society, but famines were not new. It is reported (Back, 1836, 209) that at Fort Resolution in 1833 some "forty of the choicest hunters" died in a famine, and between 1879 and 1881 "many died in hunger and misery."

In aboriginal times the charismatic leader was respected because of his unique abilities, and a number of such individuals, among whom Matonabbee was an outstanding example, are reported. It is possible that this same type of individual supervised, in a vague manner, such activities as raids. However, any real leadership embodying the qualities of power and authority was not present. With the advent of the fur trade and intermittent contact with traders, a new and different form of leadership developed. The traders desired to deal with a group representative and not with individual Indians; from this stimulus arose the role of the trading chief. The traders furthered the trading chief's standing by deferring to him and presenting him with clothing, medals, and a formal reception on his arrival at a post. By the late 1800's it is noted that the "chief" distributed the meat of caribou and moose to whomever he chose, irrespective of the wishes of the man who killed the game, although the hunter personally kept the skins and the pelts of animals. If this was indeed the norm, we are forced to the conclusion that the position of chief carried not only the quality of influence but of authority and some form of power. By 1908 the chief represented the group in their dealings with officials of the Federal Indian Affairs Branch, but, as we would expect, he was not an effective representative.

It is insightful to consider the changing status of dogs over the years. It will be recalled that a dog-like creature was thought to have fathered these people, and the dog, along with wolves and wolverine, had strong supernatural associations. In one variation of the basic creation myth the dog is identified, and a "Great Spirit" tore the dog apart, the pieces becoming the men and women from whom all people are descended. Thus dogs and men are linked closely in mythology. In the 1820's the people were convinced by a powerful man that they should not use such closely related animals to do their work, and consequently they destroyed all of their dogs. It was for this reason that during the early period of contact the people had very few dogs or none at all, and clearly they did not use them in hunting, although dogs did at times carry packs. It would appear that dogs were not widely used as beasts of burden for carrying packs, nor were they required to pull toboggans until some time in the mid-1800's. Still

Hearne mentioned that in his time dogs hauled birch poles as hunters moved into the Barrens. As recently as the early 1930's there were taboos surrounding dogs. For example, dogs were not shot, and to feed a dog a moose head or bear intestines brought ill fortune.

The vague and unformalized supernatural system of the aboriginal population came to assimilate Cree concepts, which were unreported at an earlier period. By the early 1800's they had borrowed the concept of manitou from the Cree. An evil manitou was blamed for sickness, disease, or bad luck; in the past it was often a Cree shaman who was held responsible for misfortune. The Chipewyan, by 1908, had learned many of the Cree folktales, including the trickster-hero complex.

Through time subsistence activities have depended on fish and caribou, but interestingly enough the prohibitions surrounding the treatment of these creatures were far from balanced. It has been noted that there were precautions needed for dealing with the wolf, wolverine, and bear, as well as in setting fishnets or using fishhooks. Yet references to taboos surrounding caribou hunting are rare. The logical implication is that this animal could be taken adequately by existing means so that any supernatural appeals were unnecessary. This was not the case, however, for caribou migrations were erratic and to miss one meant famine or at least severe privation. The only reasonable conclusion is that caribou, although important in subsistence, were unimportant in the aboriginal religion. In the early 1940's taboos surrounding caribou were recorded for the Chipewyan living along the eastern sector of the Great Slave Lake. For example, if a woman's skirt were to pass over a hunting knife, there was fear that the caribou would not migrate in that direction during that year. Again a woman must pierce the caribou's eyeball before she butchered the carcass to prevent the spirit of the deceased animal from reporting its fate to others. The implication might be that the caribou-hunting emphasis among the Chipewyan took place quite recently, perhaps even in early historic times, and the network of taboos did not have time enough to develop until very recently.

One interesting aside about the religion of these people is that about 1812, at Fort Chipewyan, a shaman predicted a change in the configuration of the world that would bring prosperity to the Chipewyan (see Note 3). The network of anticipated events shares many specific features of the Cargo Movements so well known in modern ethnographic accounts from Melanesia.

By the early 1900's the caribou skin tent was rare; it had been replaced by a similar but cotton-covered form. The cotton was said to be superior because the dogs would not eat it as they did the skins. At the same time the apex of a cotton tent was still made from caribou skin, for it was less likely to burn than a cotton-cloth top. This blending of the old with the new to arrive at something better is what we often have found in aboriginal adjustments to Western technology.

One of the points of disagreement about peoples in the subarctic of Canada has been whether they possessed family hunting territories that were the exclusive domain of a particular household or group of related households. Family trapping territories are reported among the Chipewyan by Penard for the period around 1900, and they are likewise recorded by Seaton for the same time. When the owner of a trapline died, his most capable son inherited the trapline; he was not necessarily the eldest son. The weight of evidence reported from the modern community of Snowdrift, however, is that family hunting territories did not exist among the Chipewyan.

In the year 1908 the anthropologist Robert H. Lowie visited the Chipewyan in an effort to record their way of life as it existed at that time and as it could be reconstructed for an earlier period. It is significant to note that Lowie was unable to gather anything more than superficial information about these people. As he stated (1959, 40), "Scientifically, it was the least fruitful trip I ever made." Athapaskans have no reputation among anthropologists of being ideal subjects for study, and Lowie's failure among them becomes somewhat understandable. Lowie did record fragments pertaining to these people. He noted that the Indians were receiving $5 a year per person from the Federal government for ammunition and twine for nets. The Chipewyan were, of course, drawn deeply into fur-trade economy, for the Hudson's Bay Company gave them trade goods in exchange for pelts. By this time the entire population around Fort Chipewyan wore trade clothing. Although their social life had undergone change as a result of contacts with Roman Catholic and Anglican missionaries, they still retained a few old customs, such as naming girls after marten.

In 1923 the Danish ethnographer Kaj Birket-Smith visited Churchill to study the Chipewyan of that region. At this time he recorded an annual subsistence cycle which was undoubtedly stabilized. The people shifted from the forest in winter to the tundra in summer. Late in summer they ascended the Seal River to known caribou crossings, where they met other Chipewyan from the east. After

tundra caribou hunting was concluded in the fall, they moved southward to the edge of timber, where they fished and hunted on snowshoes. They began trapping in November, and in late December, as
well as again in February, they returned to Churchill to trade pelts,
caribou meat, and skins. In the summer they reassembled at Churchill,
where they fished and collected their treaty money, of which more is
said later.

All knowledge of contemporary Chipewyan life is a result of the
anthropological studies of James VanStone at the community of
Snowdrift on the southeastern shore of Great Slave Lake. From the
data of these researches it is possible to observe continuity with the
old and influences of the new elements which have given a different
cast to Chipewyan culture and society. The modern information is
presented organizationally in much the same sequence as the aboriginal descriptions; whenever possible, interpretive comments are incorporated in the descriptions.

Snowdrift is located along one of the many indentations of the
southeastern shore of Great Slave Lake. It occupies a subarctic forest
setting; tree line is about one hundred miles east of the village. In terms
of aboriginal Chipewyan territory, Snowdrift is slightly beyond the
western margin. Most people of this general area traded at Fort
Resolution, which was founded in 1786. The Hudson's Bay Company
post at Snowdrift was built in 1925 in response to pressures from free
traders who were intercepting the Indians as they carried their furs
to a Bay establishment. After the store was built, families from the
eastern sector of Great Slave Lake, Lake Athabasca, and along the
Slave River traded at Snowdrift in order to avoid trips to more distant stores. It was not, however, until 1954 that the majority of the
current residents made their home at Snowdrift. They created the permanent village in response to urging by the Federal Indian Affairs
Branch agent at Yellowknife. In 1960 the settlement consisted of
twenty-six houses, most of which were constructed of logs; the Hudson's Bay Company and Northern Affairs and National Resources
physical plants centering about the store and school, respectively; an
Indian Affairs Branch freezing and cold-storage building; cabins of
sport fishing and mining entrepreneurs who are white and do not live
permanently in the community; a Roman Catholic church and residence for the transient priest; and small cabins for visiting administrators of the Department of Forestry, the Department of Fisheries,
and the Royal Canadian Mounted Police.

The commitment to settled village life was a momentous and radical change with far-reaching implications. Before their arrival here the people had lived in scattered temporary campsites and ranged out from them to hunt, fish, and trap. Previous settlements had been established according to the availability of local resources. Their settlement in Snowdrift, in contrast, was a response to governmental pressure and the presence of the store. The move radically changed the nature of social contacts, and subsistence activities were maligned. Now many people are clustered together, exploiting the same resources. Thus it is increasingly difficult to maintain their previous standard of living. Furthermore, the Indians now come under regulatory controls by Federal agents, whereas these ties earlier were tenuous or absent. In studying this process of change, it is essential to recognize the importance of Federal intervention, which led to the new circumstances.

The clothing of a modern Chipewyan bears no resemblance to the aboriginal forms. It is true that a few men still wear hooded and sleeved ponchos of caribou skin in preference to manufactured parkas bought in the store, but most persons depend almost entirely on the Hudson's Bay Company inventory for their apparel needs. Men wear long underwear, cotton or wool shirts, denim trousers, sweaters, and skin moccasins. The women wear petticoats, briefs, skirts and sweaters or cotton print dresses, and heavy cotton stockings with short socks over them, plus footwear of skin slippers in summer or shoes in winter. Young girls may wear clothing like that of the women, or they may prefer slacks, colorful lightweight jackets, and commercial shoes. Young girls often curl their hair, and young women as well as girls wear lipstick. The girls use commercial perfumes and favor brooches, earrings, and finger rings to set off their appearance. The young men are particularly fond of wide leather belts with large buckles and short, ornamented, black leather jackets. Sweatshirts with "Snowdrift, N.W.T." printed across the front likewise are popular among younger males. All men wear billed caps, often with decorative buttons, and the women and girls usually wear colorful cotton kerchiefs on their heads. The implication of the contemporary clothing styles is at once obvious. Most of the items may be obtained only from the store, and something that has value to the outside world must be offered for their purchase.

The houses of the villagers have an air of permanence unknown in the tents of the past. It was probably in 1912 that the first ridged commercial canvas tent was bought locally; these soon replaced the conical tents of old. After 1950 most families began constructing more substantial dwellings. The Indian agent obtained Federal support for the construction or renovation of cabins at Snowdrift. The Indians have been reluctant to participate in the program, for they are still hesitant to commit themselves permanently to the village. Most of the existing dwellings are one-room log cabins with board floors. The furnishings include homemade beds, chairs, a table, and shelves. Light is furnished by kerosene lamps, and heat is supplied by a wood-burning sheet-iron stove. A household inventory likewise would include trunks or bags for extra clothing or bedding, a battery-powered radio, a hand-operated sewing machine, and cóoking and eating utensils. Additional items are to be found in nearby storage sheds, which are also made from logs. Here are found frozen or dried fish, dog harnesses, outboard motor parts, traps, snowshoes, rifles, fishnets, and other equipment necessary in supporting a family. The accumulation of all these items makes the previous family mobility unlikely to recur in the future.

Each established family now owns a large, square-ended, commercially manufactured canoe, an outboard motor, and a small canvas-covered canoe of modified aboriginal design. Although a form of toboggan still exists, it is purchased from the Hudson's Bay Company store and is constructed of hardwood, and screws replace the babiche bindings. The toboggan is more correctly a cariole, for it has a rear panel and canvas sides. Dogs, not women, pull the cariole. The animals, usually about five, are chained near the houses of their owners. Unquestionably, the use of dog teams and outboard motors as sources of power has increased the mobility of the people.

The foods consumed include those used in aboriginal times plus additions from modern Euro-Canadian inventories. The Indians still prefer meat or fish with every meal, but since these items are often not available, bannock has become an important staple. Bannock is the standard fare of poor Eskimos and Indians throughout Alaska and Canada. It is made of white flour and baking powder mixed with water into a paste and spread in a greased skillet to be fried. Often this is the only food a family will have; bannock and tea are the bread and water of depressed subarctic living. The dominant method of cooking flesh is by boiling; after the dish is well cooked, it is cooled and then eaten. When families are able, they purchase prepared foods from the store. The most sought after imported items are flour, sugar, tea, coffee, crackers, peanut butter, canned meats and fruits, evaporated milk, and various seasonings. There is now more potential variety, but at the same time more factors stand between a man and what has come to be considered the necessities for his family.

Traditionally the economic lives of the people revolved around caribou and fish; this still is true, but with added emphasis on trapping. There are Snowdrift men who will not go out to their traps if caribou are not in the vicinity to be hunted, and most men do not hesitate to abandon their traps if caribou appear. The lure of the hunt is still very strong, and as recently as about 1930 hunting was more important among these Chipewyan than trapping. A man who traps today still must hunt for food while on the trapline, even though he may take only spruce hens, ptarmigan, or hares. Likewise, he fishes through the ice with a gill net for dog food. A trapline is reached in one to three days of travel by dog team. The traps a man sets are checked ideally each third or fourth day and three or four times before being removed, but in practice most traps are visited once and then removed. Sets are made by using commercial steel traps or wire snares for mink, marten, white fox, lynx, and wolverine. Red, silver, or cross fox are not purposefully trapped, for their market value is low. Trapping is a difficult pursuit surrounded by frustrating uncertainty. There are the problems of obtaining food for the dogs and trapper; a wolverine may steal animals caught in the sets or spring a line of traps and remove the bait; and a Canada jay, ermine, or other creature may spring a trap. In addition, conditions on the trapline are far from comfortable. The canvas trapping tent is small and impossible to heat adequately, and the men find it difficult to work alone for weeks at a time. The increasing tendency is for trappers to range out from the village for only short periods during November and December when most fur animals are in their prime rather than intensively throughout most of the winter.

The economic life of the trapper is linked with the Hudson's Bay Company, for it is only here at the Company store that a man can exchange his furs for trade items. The descriptions by Hearne of the Indian's relationship with the Hudson's Bay Company traders are in many ways similar to those of VanStone for the modern Chipewyan. The Indians attempt to outwit the trader and devise all sorts of subterfuge to gain credit from the store (see Note 4). In Indian eyes the only good traders are those who are concerned with the Indian's welfare. In spite of this conflict, the Indians and the Hudson's Bay Company are integrated within one economic system based on fur. The present prices of pelts are not extremely high; for example, in 1959-1960 white fox pelts brought up to $40; mink, $20.50; beaver, $25; marten, $12.50; wolverine, $18; and muskrat, 90 cents. The thirty-five village trappers live in twenty-three separate households, with one to three trappers per household. One dwelling unit with two trappers derived a trapping income for 1959-1960 of $1390, yet another household with one trapper took only $41.02 in pelts. These represent the extremes; the average take per trapper is about $320. Since white fox prices are high at present, they are trapped conscientiously during the winter, but the most important fur animal taken in the spring is beaver. There are Federal restrictions on the beaver take. In theory no man may trap more than five animals, and each pelt must be tagged before it is exchanged at the store. Energetic trappers, however, buy unused tags issued to someone else and illegally increase their catches in this manner. In all trapping activities the individual trapper normally works alone and frequently shifts from one area to another. Few trap in one locality for more than five consecutive years. The concept of family trapping areas as an outgrowth of family hunting areas is not a reality for the Chipewyan at Snowdrift, for restricted areas of familial exploitation have not existed. When the Indian agent recently proposed the registration of traplines, the people were staunchly opposed to the suggestion, saying that it would limit their mobility.

In recent years the subsistence cycle has exhibited a declining emphasis on trapping. It is a universal pursuit, but not one in which most men have faith for the future. There was a time in the recent past when men took their families along while trapping, but this is no longer possible if there are school-aged children who must attend classes. Furthermore, the income from trapping is not sufficient to meet subsistence needs. Understandably, VanStone finds that the area trapped and the intensity of trapping are steadily declining.

Other economic pursuits are highly significant, and of prime importance is the late summer hunting of caribou. A household head feels that he requires about one hundred caribou per year, of which twenty to twenty-five should be obtained in the fall. This has not been possible over the last few years, however. To hunt caribou the people go by large canoes to the Fort Reliance area. If there are no caribou at the eastern end of Great Slave Lake, the hunters portage eastward to the vicinity of Artillery Lake. Burdened by their families, large amounts of equipment, and big canoes, they are unable to reach the best hunting grounds. As a result they are unlikely to take many animals. The meat of those killed is smoked and brought back to the village to be stored in the Indian Affairs Branch cold-storage unit. In 1960 nearly half the households were unrepresented in the fall caribou hunt, although some families shared in the catch of those who did go by providing equipment in exchange for meat.

In mid-September the men set a series of nylon or cotton gill nets in the lake or along nearby rivers. The nets are anchored with large stones at each end, as in aboriginal times, and fitted with stone sinkers at intervals along the net bottom and with wooden floats along the top. Most frequently caught are lake trout and whitefish. The fish are skewered and hung to dry partially before they freeze and are stored as winter food for both dogs and people.

The Indians have come to consider trapping, fishing for themselves, and caribou hunting as less desirable pursuits than wage labor, but the possibilities for such work are limited and temporary at best. Jobs such as helping with the construction of the Federal school are few and of brief duration; work on commercial fishing vessels is unpredictable and physically demanding; fire fighting is seasonal and sporadic; serving as guides for tourist fishermen is just beginning. Clearing brush and trees from the right-of-way for a road is a steady form of employment, but it is seasonal. All of this means that the uncertainty of making a living by wage labor equals or exceeds that which existed as a part of the old subsistence pattern.

The only reliable monetary benefits are provided by the Federal government. The Snowdrift Chipewyan were encompassed by Treaty Number 11, which was signed between the Indians and the government of Canada in 1921. The Indians gave up their aboriginal rights to the land but at the same time were protected in their exploitation of local resources. In exchange the Indians received certain tangible advantages such as formal education, health services, and material goods. Every year each band member receives a cash payment of $5; the band chief receives $25, and counselors, $15 each. In recent years the Indian Affairs Branch has provided the equipment necessary to subsistence activities: fishnets, ammunition, and items such as roofing and doors for house construction. Furthermore, families in need, as defined by the Indian agent, receive a "ration" allotment from the Indian Affairs Branch through the Hudson's Bay Company store. Eligible for aid are persons with physical disabilities, families supporting foster children, the families of men in the hospital, or households in which the family head is permanently absent. A national program of old-age assistance provides for the welfare of persons sixty-five or older. Even more important is the "baby bonus," which applies throughout Canada. The Family Allowance, as it is called, is paid to each family every month; $6 is received for a child under ten and $8 for ages ten through sixteen. The program was designed to improve child care, and probably it has done so at

Snowdrift. At the same time it has made the people more reliant on Federal assistance.

With so much change in subsistence activities and material culture from an aboriginal base line, we may expect equally significant differences in other aspects of living. This seems clearly to be the case. There is no remnant of the old attitudes toward women and the treatment of women. Although VanStone is not explicit on the subject, he gives the distinct impression that domestic harmony exists. Certain activities, such as food preparation and child rearing, still clearly female obligations, may be undertaken willingly by men when the need arises. Violence, when it occurs, is exhibited against other men rather than against women. A further indication of the improved status of women is the fact that they now profit from the efforts of their own labors. A woman who processes a moose or caribou hide or sews moccasins or a jacket of skin for someone outside her family is paid directly and retains the profits for herself. The present treatment of women at Snowdrift may result from the fact that women are in the minority, and as a scarce item they are handled with care.

In terms of their formal social structure, these Indians trace their descent bilaterally, as did their ancestors. The cousin terminology, however, is now the Eskimo type, which is organizationally similar to that found in the United States today. When it is realized at the same time that preferential cousin marriage no longer exists and is not known even by informants as an aboriginal pattern, the consolidating of all cousins under one term is an understandable development. It may be, too, that over the one hundred years of contact with Roman Catholic missionaries the Church denial of cousin marriage has been influential in the change. At the same time, premarital fornication between cousins exists today.

The kinship terms on the first ascending generation (e.g., Ego's father, mother, uncles, and aunts) exhibit an inconsistent mixing of types. Separate terms for father and mother exist as before, but now mother's sister and father's sister are termed alike, a designation not known in the reported old system. By contrast and in keeping with the old, father's brother and mother's brother are termed differently. From these terms alone one would expect to find differential treatment accorded to such individuals, but meaningful interpretive data are not available.

When a person marries, he is most likely to select a mate within the community, and immediately after the marriage the couple resides with the in-laws who are best able to receive them. As soon as possible the couple will build a separate dwelling and live alone. The pattern is thus of initial and temporary bilocal residence followed by permanent neolocal residence. Among the twenty-six households in 1961, twenty-one were nuclear or nuclear core families, the latter being composed of a nuclear family to which is added a near relative or two of the husband or wife. Two unmarried men, one old and the other young, lived separately and alone. In one household were two nuclear families whose male heads are cousins. Finally, two other households included married individuals in the dwellings of relatives, but the intrusive couples planned to build their own houses shortly. It is obvious that the residence units are the same as in aboriginal times with two exceptions. First, plural marriages no longer exist, and second, capable providers have not attracted followers who live with them.

With the encouragement of marriage within the community, that is, village endogamy, plus the facts that everyone is closely or distantly related and that descent is traced through both males and females, we have what has come to be called a "deme." Insofar as kinship influences daily life, it is striking that individuals are referred to most often by their Christian names or by Chipewyan nicknames. The set of Chipewyan kin terms is not known to many adults in spite of the fact that the aboriginal language is still spoken by all adults. The overall impression is that the nuclear family is still the most important social unit, but at the same time a wider network of social relations is emerging.

Social ties that exist beyond those based on kinship alone are new or intensified. Living together in one settlement has led to feelings of village unity, and inhabitants now think of themselves as physically, economically, and morally superior to the people of adjacent settlements. Other evidence of village cohesion is the widespread sharing of game. By the time a hunter who has killed a moose has beached his boat he has given away most of the meat. The same applies to fish, which leads VanStone to term the sharing as "indiscriminate." The sharing of food existed in aboriginal times, but it was probably neither so pervasive nor so egalitarian as at the present time. Furthermore, there exists an intensive pattern of reciprocal borrowing which includes major as well as minor items of material culture. These attitudes and their behavioral manifestations clearly are means of integrating the community on a social as well as physical basis.

One result of living in a stable community has been an intensification of contact with the Indian agent stationed at Yellowknife. The agent visits Snowdrift at least every two months and sometimes more often if the occasion arises. When there is business to be presented to the villagers, the agent calls a meeting. Attendance is usually poor, however, and it is difficult for him to keep the participants talking about the subject at hand. The Indians are prone to bring up matters of individual and personal interest. This usually takes the form of specific requests for aid to themselves, and the process of democratic group action fails. Unity, when it is manifest, usually takes the form of a negative stand against a proposal rather than of building on it constructively. The Indians much prefer to deal with the agent on an individual basis and privately, almost secretly, seek him out for specific requests. The Chipewyan attitude toward the agent is that he is in the position to grant favors, and for him not to do so is regarded as stubbornness alone.

In 1960 the bands were reorganized to make allowances for the physical movements of people from one band to another. Shortly before the reorganization the chief for the Snowdrift people lived at Rocher River, and the counselors were at Snowdrift. Under the reorganized system the Snowdrift Indians have their own chief as well as two counselors. The Indians clearly have formulated what they expect from a chief. Ideally, he would not interfere in the affairs of individual villagers but would adopt a stern attitude toward Euro-Canadians in general and toward the Indian agent in particular. The whites, in contrast, expect the chief to be cooperative; if he does not cooperate, they will bypass the formal village organization and act through the trader or teacher. This pattern of the whites for accomplishing their purposes, as reflected in dealing with the counselors of the past, undermines Indian authority and contradicts the purpose in having a chief, counselors, and recognized Indian authorities in the first place.

Visits to the village by the Royal Canadian Mounted Police are more a show of power than the result of actual need. Crimes embraced by the Canadian legal system are rare, and the most important cause for police action is the making of home brew. Since everyone is secretive in manufacturing home brew and carefully avoids appearing intoxicated on the village paths when the Mounted Police are present, few arrests are made for this, the most prevalent offense. The Indians feel also that it is wrong to appeal to Canadian legal authorities for the settlement of personal disputes, and they rarely do so, although they may make the threat.

Political life for the Snowdrift Chipewyan is now organized formally along the lines of Canadian ideals, but the present product is not what the Euro-Canadians hoped it would be. The same situation exists in the sphere of religion. Today everyone is a participating but nominal Roman Catholic. The priest serving the village is stationed at Fort Resolution and is of the Oblate order. He visits the settlement frequently throughout the year and may stay for as long as two months at a time; he is always present during the Christmas and Easter seasons. The beliefs of the Church are understood poorly by the people, but participation in the formal ceremonies is high. In general, the Church is regarded as something beyond the context of daily living. The Indian attitude is that the Church is wealthy and the people should be paid for any physical labor performed on its behalf. The priest is regarded as another potential source of income; thus the feeling of belonging to a church and strengthening its purposes is not understood by the members. Interestingly enough, it is in the sphere of supernaturalism only that the people admit openly that there are differences between Indians and whites. The concept of a "bush man" prevails here as it does among most Athapaskans. This creature is a man who wears manufactured shoes and appears at a distance during the summer. He is a bogeyman since he searches for children to steal, but apparently he does not harm adults so long as they stay beyond his reach. The Indians believe that supernatural beings may harm them but will not affect white men. There are also beliefs that have to do with trapping; these are of unknown dimension but are an intimate part of trapping lore. The curing of physical illness now has passed out of the hands of the shaman, who no longer exists, into the domain of the Indian and Northern Health Services and a lay dispenser, usually the Hudson's Bay Company manager. It is the trader who cares for the supply of scientific medicines furnished by the Indian and Northern Health Services. He dispenses medicines without any formal training. If a case is serious, the nurse at Yellowknife is telegraphed, and she decides what course of action is to be followed. Likewise, the Indian and Northern Health Services nurse, sometimes accompanied by a medical doctor, visits the village. Both come every three months or oftener. Immunization shots, vaccinations, and X-rays are given routinely, and seriously ill persons are sent to the Yellowknife hospital or another one for treatment. The Indians are concerned about their health problems but do not use patent medicines or turn freely to the Euro-Canadians for help. They seem to enjoy talking about their aches and pains, but they seek treatment only if they are quite sick.

The physical stability of families and the political and religious structure of today have given rise to some associated rituals and ceremonies. Perhaps the most important surrounds the annual payment of treaty money. The payment is presented ceremonially to each individual by the Indian superintendent, who is accompanied by the Indian agent and a R.C.M.P. constable. In the evening of the same day a "tea dance" is held to the accompaniment of large tambourine-like drums, made from dehaired caribou skins stretched over circular wooden frames. The dance is a shuffling, clockwise step performed to both drumming and chanting. Roast moose meat and other foods are served at a feast the following day. Christmas Eve is another time that stimulates general interest and participation. Church service is attended, the store stays open late for last minute purchases of gifts, and home brew is made beforehand and consumed. Some houses are decorated with crepe paper and balloons, and many people play cards for money. All of this activity on Christmas Eve makes the next day one of recuperation and rest.

A popular form of entertainment is square dancing. The Indians probably learned to perform the steps from commercial fishermen who dock periodically at Snowdrift for a few days of relaxation during the summer fishing season. Most families own a guitar or violin, which is played by young or old men. They learn dance music by listening to records on one of the four village phonographs or to the Yellowknife radio station music. The square dances are called expertly by village men, and participation at the dances is good. Less formal entertainment includes nightly card games, which are extremely popular, particularly blackjack and gin rummy. Men and women often play together, and stakes may range from small change and ammunition to $3 hands in the gin rummy games among men who are temporarily affluent. While the adults play cards, the children may gamble by pitching coins to a line. The hand game of old is known, but it is played with considerably less frequency. Card games are considered to be more interesting and exciting.

The consumption of alcohol is as much a ritual as it is a form of entertainment, and prescribed patterns of drinking rarely are bypassed. Virtually the only alcoholic beverage consumed is home brew, produced from yeast, raisins, sugar, and water. It is made in secret by two or three men and allowed to age about twenty-four hours. Ideally, it should age longer, but anticipation negates the possibility. The brew is drunk in the home of one of the makers or in the brush near the village if it is summer. The object of drinking is to become intoxicated, and into the three-gallon pail a cup is dipped, the beverage drunk, and the cup passed to the next participant. Normally, some brew is stored in bottles and cached, to be consumed after the brew pail is drained. After the participants become reasonably intoxicated, they visit from one house to the next, regardless of the time, and drink as they chat with their reluctant hosts. Sometimes they offer their hosts a drink, but this is not consistent. The conversations of intoxicated men are about village life, and the Indians become more gregarious and outgoing during such sprees than at any other time of their adult lives. Younger men talk in general about sexual activity but do not mention individual experiences. Eventually, if their bottles do not become dry first, the drinkers become boisterous, and fist fights, usually having to do with women, result. Women like to drink home brew, but they must rely on the men for their supply. Drinking is reasonably common, and nearly all the men become intoxicated about once a month. There is no "dry" faction in the community, but neither are there any alcoholics.

Time and historical circumstances have added new dimensions to the life cycle of the individual. To term the present process as a blend of Chipewyan and Euro-Canadian customs would be a simplistic point of view. There are attitudes from both Indian and white sociocultural systems as well as things that are new. Conception is understood, and scientific techniques of birth control are known but not employed. If female infanticide is still practiced, it is accomplished covertly. Informants say that infants of either sex are desired. Yet there is a disproportionate number of adult males, and male infants are preferred, for they are looked on as a means of economic support in old age. For the pregnant women there are no food taboos or prohibitions, and it is increasingly common for women to deliver at the Yellowknife hospital. If the birth takes place in the community, several midwives are present, although only one or two aid in the birth. If the delivery is normal, the mother resumes her normal routine within a few days. There is no isolation as there was in aboriginal times, but as before there is no out-of-the-ordinary concern over the event.

The neonate is greeted with affection, and as an infant it is played with and enjoyed by both parents. Diapers from cotton cloth are changed frequently, and babies are breast-fed whenever they are discontent. The infants sleeps and rests in a hammock or crib, and at least some are swaddled in a blanket. Infants are dressed in baby clothes purchased from the store, and when carried they are held in the arms. They are not, incidentally, the frequent charges of their older siblings. Between the ages of one and two children are expected and encouraged to walk. Babies are noticeably fat, perhaps because milk is considered the only normal food and exercise is not a part of the infant's routine. Weaning begins at about two years, although it may be earlier if the mother becomes pregnant again or takes the nurse's advice and weans the baby after a year. The infant is weaned to a bottle, and Pablum or meat and other staples in the adult diet may supplement the milk.

As in many, if not most, contemporary Indian communities in North America, there are more children than any other category of individuals. In the total population of some one hundred and fifty, half are under fifteen years of age. Until a child is about six, he is treated with warmth and affection by both parents. Men will take small children with them on walks and are demonstratively affectionate, kissing and hugging their offspring. Like an infant, a child is permitted to play with almost anything that draws his attention, save those objects that are obviously dangerous. At the same time, a small child may be permitted to cry and scream with vigor if the parents are busy at other pursuits. After the age of ten the child is treated differently. He is regarded essentially as an adult, and independence is encouraged, especially among males. A father may proudly refer to a small boy as "my son who is almost a man," when the child displays skill or intelligence.

In the recent past an infant was not named at birth, but as soon as he developed some distinctive personality trait he was called by this trait. Later, as he exhibited other characteristics, he would be nicknamed accordingly. The Roman Catholic missionaries, who were of French background, assigned Christian names of French origin. At the time of the treaty in 1921 and as contacts with governmental agents increased, a distinct need arose to refer to specific Indians accurately. The result was that families took surnames which were French or English translations of Chipewyan or Euro-Canadian names or were derived from a geographical location. Today an infant receives a Christian name at baptism and various nicknames later in life. It was observed, too, that Chipewyan kinship terms are seldom employed either as terms of reference or address.

The young child in Snowdrift has few restrictions on his wanderings so long as he is home for meals and by the time it is dark. Children have chores to perform, but parents are not demanding if the task is forgotten or avoided. Until they are about ten years old, boys and girls play together freely, but after this age there is an increasing division of the play groups along sexual lines. By the time a boy is thirteen he has a regular routine of duties which must be performed. He feeds the dogs, hauls the water, and disposes of the garbage. By the time he is eighteen, he has more demands on his time than any other household member. He releases his father from many subsistence activities, such as checking fishnets, running the outboard motor on trips, and maintaining household equipment. The responsibilities of a teen-aged girl have been increasing in intensity since she was about eight years old. She has many household duties, and the care of younger siblings becomes important. Thus enculturation at home is a cumulative process, in which few actual demands are made but in which the number of responsibilities is increased as the child grows older. There is more obvious continuity in the rearing of a daughter than of a son. The boy, when in his late teens, is suddenly expected to assume tasks that are adult in nature.

A new and different enculturative force originates in the obligatory participation of children in the Canadian school system. There was no village school until the fall of 1960. Before that time the children were sent to government boarding school at Fort Smith or Fort Resolution, but the new Northern Affairs and National Resources school has eliminated this practice. The Snowdrift school provides instruction through the first eight grades, and attendance is compulsory between the ages of six and sixteen. Because the children speak only Chipewyan at home, they have no proficiency in English, which seriously delays their formal education. The curriculum is not adapted to Indian needs but includes the normal round of arithmetic, languages, social studies, art, and music. One of the anticipated results of better educational facilities is that there will be an increasing number of village children who will continue their education beyond the elementary level. The majority of these individuals are not likely to return and make Snowdrift their home. If they do so, it is not improbable that their formal education will hinder, not help, them. At high school they will not have learned the subsistence skills as their stay-at-home cousins have, and they will be less psychologically prepared to settle down to village life.

Sexual activities, which are a commonly observed facet of life from a tender age, do not become a subject of conversation among young people. Fornication occurs among teen-agers, with males of sixteen and females of thirteen having had at least some experience. The one difficulty in arranging such affairs is to find an isolated spot to carry them out. The rather pervasive fornication of young men may result from the fact that most of them are not married and cannot find a wife in the village. There are fifteen unmarried men between the ages of eighteen and thirty-one, and only three married males in this age group. In contrast, there are no unmarried females over twenty and only three who have reached sixteen. This poses a dilemma for males, and they see no solution to the problem.

Today, if possible, females marry at about nineteen, and males marry when about twenty-eight. A few influential old women make the formal arrangements between the families of the potential couple. The couple may or may not have a voice in the decision. The wedding ceremony takes place in the Roman Catholic church. Afterward there is an evening feast, and later still a dance may be held. Divorces do not exist, and adultery seems reasonably common, especially with certain married women when their husbands are absent from the village.

It is assumed that after marriage the couple will soon adjust to fully adult responsibilities, especially after they set up their own independent household and begin to raise children. The couple is then expected to participate in normal community life as it has been described in this chapter. A family picnics together, visits friends and neighbors frequently, and the parents play cards with other couples. The men and women consult with one another on family matters and share common interests in daily life. This generalized ideal does not always manifest itself in fact, but it does apply to most couples.

As the Indian grows old, he faces the traditional Chipewyan rejection of the aged, which is still apparent. Old people are unwanted, scorned, and ridiculed. Tempering these feelings, however, is the fact that old people receive aid from the Federal government, and thus they are a potential source of economic gain. Exploitation by their children has led some old people to establish independent households. Old age and impending death are accepted with the philosophical calm that has come to be expected of the Indian stereotype. After death the body is wrapped in a blanket, then sewn into a shroud by old women, and placed in a plywood coffin. The funeral service is Roman Catholic, and afterward the body is transported by toboggan or boat to the cemetery a few miles away. If the burial takes place in summer, the mourners have a picnic before returning to the village. Inheritance seems to pose no particular problem, for generally the children of the deceased simply divide the material goods.

In a study of folktales Ronald Cohen and James W. VanStone explored the nature of self-sufficiency and dependency among the Chipewyan. They analyzed the published early twentieth-century folktales and compared them with original stories by contemporary Chipewyan children as well as with a sample of Grimm's fairy tales for control material. They recognize that, "taken broadly, self-sufficiency and dependency refer to a basic and universal quality of all human social experience, namely, action by ego which affects his environment, i.e., self-assertiveness or self-sufficiency, and action directed towards ego over which he has no control, i.e., dependency." Every social system may be expected to exhibit both qualities but in varying proportions. As expected, the analysis of Grimm's fairy tales, reflecting the Protestant ethic, exhibited a high degree of self-sufficiency. The folktales of the Chipewyan exhibit about equal proportions of self-sufficiency and dependency, suggesting that a balance had been established by these people in their relationship with the environment. An increase in dependency, reflected in the children's stories, suggests to the authors that Federal welfare programs have made the Chipewyan less capable and less desirous of caring for themselves or that the contact situation has caused them to feel that now their actions to affect the environment are more likely to fail than to succeed.

VanStone sees the Snowdrift Chipewyan as moving into the stagnation of deculturation. The people have lost most of their old design for living and have not replaced it with comparable design along Euro-Canadian models. It is particularly in the economic sphere that this trend is evident, since trapping has only partly replaced the subsistence-based economy; the resulting mixture does not provide a satisfactory standard of living. This leads VanStone to use such characterizations as "poor white" and "lower class" for the contemporary scene. The depressed standard of living at Snowdrift indicates that these Chipewyan are at the fringes of modern cultural developments in the Canadian north. They not only lack skills and formal education, but they have not made the changes in values necessary to improve their standard of living. Therefore the more rewarding positions in the north go to white Canadians from the south. Developments at present require skilled individuals such as pilots, commercial fishermen, teachers, administrators or mechanics, but the Snowdrift people can do none of these things. As such opportunities increase, it is most likely that the Chipewyan, with their current rate of change, will fall even farther behind. They may, as Jacob Fried has recently commented in an article on settlements in northern Canada, become, like the Metis to the south, an increasingly socially and economically depressed class of mixed-bloods. The future is not bright, but neither is this course of events a certainty. The Federal government is largely responsible for the present set of circumstances, and it is within the government's domain to change what at present seems a steadily deteriorating situation.

Note 1.   Starvation at Fort Resolution in the early 1800's as described by Richard King (1836, Vol. 1, 165–166).

Men, women, and children, notwithstanding, slowly moved towards their place of destination, expecting death at every step; yet, strange to say, some reached their elysium: many, however, met their fate in a sepulchre of snow. The feeble gait of the torpid and downcast father—the piercing and sepulchral cry of the mother—the infant clinging by a parched mouth to a withered breast, faintly moaning through its nostrils—the passive child, calmly awaiting its doom—the faithful dog, destroyed and consumed—the caribou robe dwindling almost to nothing—can give but a very inadequate idea of their sufferings.

Note 2.   The birth of a child while on the trail, as described by Peter Fidler (1934, 548) in 1792.

March 13.   Moved NNE 2 miles & was necessitated to put up short of where we intended to go on account of the deceased mans wife being delivered in the Track when hawling a very heavy Sledge. The other womin wished to erect the small Tent for that purpose but she was too quick for them. She had a boy.

March 14.   Moved NNE 6 miles to the edge of the Stony Ground about 8 miles from the Thay thule dezza bearing North. The woman that was delivered yesterday took her heavy sledge to drag as usual the same as if nothing had happened to her. She sleeps in a small brush hut not having permission to come into the Tent along with the men & other women.

Note 3.   A Chipewyan "Cargo Movement" is described by John Franklin (1823, 152–153). It took place at Fort Chipewyan around 1812. The following prediction was made by a shaman.

. . . that fertility and plenty would succeed to the present sterility; and that the present race of white inhabitants, unless they became subservient to the Indians, would be removed, and their place be filled by other traders, who would supply their wants in every possible manner. The poor deluded wretches, imagining they would hasten this happy change by destroying their present traders, of whose submission there was no prospect, threatened to extirpate them.

Note 4.   A Snowdrift Chipewyan and his relationship with the Hudson's Bay Company trader is described by James VanStone (1963, 14).

Often the relationship between the Indians and the Company manager might almost be characterized as involving a battle of wits, since the goal of the Indians at all times is to obtain credit, often by fair means or foul. The following is an example of the kind of difficulty that can arise under these circumstances. An informant was working on a commercial fishing boat late in the summer of 1960 and on one of his periodic visits to the village, he asked the manager for credit, saying that he was going to make over $300 before he finished work. He even brought the captain of his boat into the store to verify his statement. On this basis, the manager advanced him $100 in credit. However, when the informant's cheque arrived, it was for less than $100 since he had already spent much of the money that was coming to him at the fishing company commissary. Then, when he was trapping the following winter, he gave his furs to someone else to sell in order to postpone the time when he would eventually have to pay his debt to the Company.

References

Back, George. *Narrative of the Arctic Land Expedition.* London. 1836.

*Birket-Smith, Kaj. *Contributions to Chipewyan Ethnology.* Report of the Fifth Thule Expedition, v. 6, no. 3. 1930. The bulk of the information in this volume applies only to the Churchill area Chipewyan as they were in 1923 and as the past was reconstructed with the aid of informants. The primary descriptive emphasis is on material culture; other aspects of culture and society are incompletely described. In spite of its shortcoming this study is second only to Hearne's work in importance.

Blanchet, Guy H. "Emporium of the North," *Beaver,* Outfit 276, 32–35. 1946.

Bryce, George. *The Remarkable History of the Hudson's Bay Company.* Toronto. 1904.

Campbell, Marjorie W. *The North West Company.* Toronto. 1957.

Cohen, Ronald, and James W. VanStone. "Dependency and Self-Sufficiency in Chipewyan Stories," *National Museum of Canada, Bulletin 194,* 29–55. 1963.

Curtis, E. S. *The North American Indian.* v. 18. Norwood. 1928.

Eggan, Fred, ed. *Social Anthropology of North American Tribes.* Chicago. 1937.

Fidler, Peter. "Journal of a Journey with the Chepawyans or Northern Indians, to the Slave Lake, & to the East & West of the Slave River, in 1791 & 2," *Publications of the Champlain Society,* v. 21, 493–555. 1934.

Franklin, John. *Narrative of a Journey to the Shores of the Polar Sea.* London. 1823.

Fried, Jacob. "Settlement Types and Community Organization in Northern Canada," *Arctic,* v. 16, 93–100. 1963.

Giddings, James L., Jr. "A Flint Site in Northernmost Manitoba," *American Antiquity,* v. 21, 255–268. 1956.

Harp, Elmer, Jr. *The Archaeology of the Lower and Middle Thelon, Northwest Territories.* Arctic Institute of North America Technical Paper no. 8. 1961.

*Hearne, Samuel. *A Journey from Prince of Wale's Fort in Hudson's Bay to the Northern Ocean.* London. 1795. (Two more recent, noteworthy editions of this work have appeared. The earlier was edited by Joseph B.

Tyrrell and published by The Champlain Society in 1911, and the second was edited by Richard Glover and published by the Macmillan Company of Canada in 1958.) Hearne's book is the standard source on the Chipewyan as they lived soon after historic contact. It is indispensable reading for any serious attempt to understand the culture of these Indians.

Hoijer, Harry. "The Chronology of the Athapaskan Languages," *International Journal of American Linguistics*, v. 22, 219–232. 1956.

*Jenness, Diamond. *The Indians of Canada*. National Museum of Canada, Bulletin 65. 1963. A reading of the chapter on the peoples of the Mackenzie and Yukon river basins provides a view of the Chipewyan in their relationship to other Canadian Athapaskans.

*———, ed. "The Chipewyan Indians: An Account by an Early Explorer," *Anthropologica*, v. 3, 15–33. 1956. This article contains abstracts of the Chipewyan information from a previously unpublished manuscript probably written by John Macdonell in the early 1800's. The descriptions are very good and provide a supplement to Hearne.

King, Richard. *Narrative of a Journey to the Shores of the Arctic Ocean*. 2 v. London. 1836.

Lowie, Robert H. "The Chipewyans of Canada," *Southern Workman*, v. 38, 278–283. 1909.

———. "An Ethnological Trip to Lake Athabasca," *American Museum Journal*, v. 9, 10–15. 1909.

———. *Robert H. Lowie, Ethnologist, A Personal Record*. Berkeley and Los Angeles. 1959.

*MacNeish, June H. "Leadership Among the Northeastern Athabascans," *Anthropologica*, v. 2, 131–163. 1956. Historical sources are evaluated and the Chipewyan discussed along with other Canadian Athapaskans. The major contribution of this paper is a classification of leadership patterns in aboriginal and historic times.

———. "Kin Terms of Arctic Drainage Dene: Hare, Slavey, Chipewyan," *American Anthropologist*, v. 62, 279–295. 1960.

Mason, John A. "Notes on the Indians of the Great Slave Lake Area," *Yale University Publications in Anthropology*, no. 34. 1946.

Munsterhjelm, Erik. *The Wind and the Caribou*. London. 1953.

Penard, J. M. "Land Ownership and Chieftaincy among the Chippewayan and Caribou-Eaters," *Primitive Man*, v. 2, 20–24. 1929.

Petitot, Emile. "On the Athabasca District of the Northwest," *Canadian Record of Science*, v. 1, 27–53. 1884.

Rich, Edwin E. *Hudson's Bay Company, 1670-1870*. 3 v. Toronto. 1960.

Richardson, Richard. *Arctic Searching Expedition*. New York. 1854.

Robinson, J. "Among the Caribou-Eaters," *Beaver*, Outfit 275, 38–41. 1944.

Robson, Joseph. *An Account of Six Years Residence in Hudson's Bay*. London. 1752.

Ross, Bernard. "Notes on the Tinneh or Chepewyan Indians of British and Russian America: The Eastern Tinneh," *Smithsonian Institution Annual Report, 1866*. 304–311. 1867.

Russell, Frank. *Explorations in the Far North*. University of Iowa. 1898.

Seton, Ernest T. *The Arctic Prairies*. New York. 1911.

Simpson, George. "Journal of Occurrences in the Athabasca Department, 1820 and 1821," *Publications of the Champlain Society. Hudson's Bay Company Series*, 1. 1938.

Tache, Alexander A. *Sketch of the North-West of America*. Montreal. 1870.

Tyrrell, Joseph B., ed. "David Thompson's Narrative," *Publications of the Champlain Society*, v. 12. 1916.

VanStone, James W. *The Economy of a Frontier Community*. Northern Coordination and Research Centre, Department of Northern Affairs and National Resources. 1961.

*———. *The Snowdrift Chipewyan*. Northern Co-ordination and Research Centre, Department of Northern Affairs and National Resources. 1963. This report and the preceding one contain virtually all of the reliable information on the modern Chipewyan. Although the data are limited in scope to the community of Snowdrift, the generalizations most probably have wider applicability for other Chipewyan populations.

———. "Changing Patterns of Indian Trapping in the Canadian Subarctic," *Arctic*, v. 16, 159–174. 1963.

2

The Beothuk:

Hunters of the Subarctic Forests

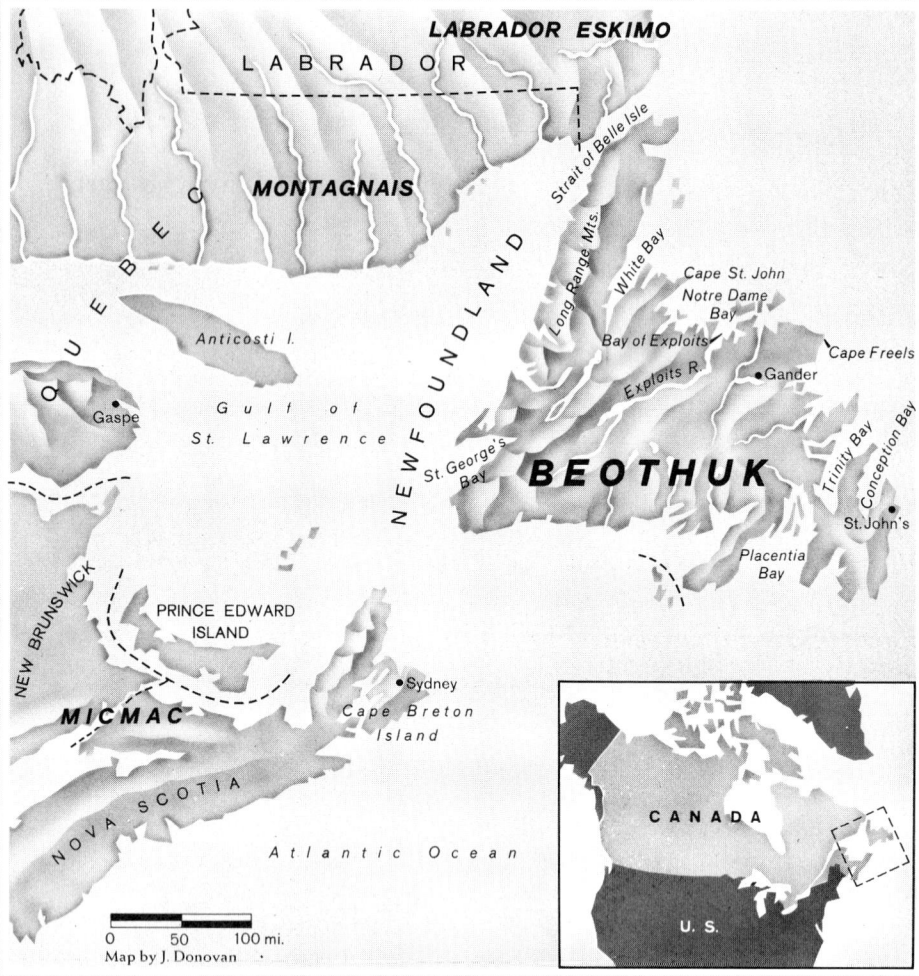

LABRADOR ESKIMO

LABRADOR

MONTAGNAIS

QUEBEC

Strait of Belle Isle

Long Range Mts.

White Bay

Cape St. John
Notre Dame
Bay

Bay of Exploits

Exploits R.

•Gander

Cape Freels

Anticosti I.

NEWFOUNDLAND

Gulf of
St. Lawrence

Gaspe

St. George's
Bay

BEOTHUK

Trinity Bay

Conception Bay

St. John's

Placentia
Bay

NEW BRUNSWICK

PRINCE EDWARD
ISLAND

•Sydney

Cape Breton
Island

MICMAC

NOVA SCOTIA

Atlantic Ocean

0   50   100 mi.
Map by J. Donovan

CANADA

U. S.

In many respects the Beothuk are a poor tribe to single out for description, for comparatively little has been written about them. Unfortunately, it is unlikely that we ever will know more about these people than already has been published, except for information that may be derived from archaeological studies. The Beothuk, who were aboriginal residents of Newfoundland, became extinct in 1829. The ethnographic information about them is derived from scattered and incomplete historical records and from reasonably systematic interviews with one Indian. These people lived a relatively simple life on their isolated island home and were never an important North American Indian tribe. It is their unknown qualities and general lack of historical significance that make them an intriguing people for discussion.

The name Beothuk is the word that the people used for themselves, and possibly it means "man" or "human being." Europeans and other Indians, however, usually termed the Beothuk the Red Indians, a reference to their habit of covering their bodies and material goods with a red, ocher-based pigment. These islanders were most familiar with the Micmac of Cape Breton Island and Nova Scotia, and they were friendly with the Montagnais and Eskimos of Labrador. They traded and visited with the Montagnais and Micmac and hosted them on Newfoundland. On the other hand, there was hostility in their contacts with some Eskimos, even though the Eskimos frequented northern Newfoundland by crossing the Strait of Belle Isle. The Beothuk were thus on friendly terms with all nearby peoples except a segment of the Eskimo population. In their language classification George L. Trager and Felicia E. Harben place the Beothuk, Micmac, and Montagnais in the Algonkian-Mosan phylum and the Algonkian-Ritwan stock. Furthermore, they classify Beothuk as a single language at the family level, whereas the Micmac and Montagnais are of the Algonkian family. The linguists Carl F. and E. W. Voegelin join earlier linguists and do not regard Beothuk as an Algonkian language. The identity between Algonkian and Beothuk words may be viewed as Beothuk borrowings, as an indication of an early relationship between Beothuk and proto-Algonkian, or as evidence that Beothuk preceded Algonkian in the region and was the donor rather than the recipient. The existing Beothuk vocabularies indicate that there were dialectic differences between segments of the Beothuk population, but the extent of these differences has not been defined.

The Beothuk population in 1776 was estimated at less than five hundred individuals. By the year 1768 the Beothuk had become concentrated in the central sector of Newfoundland, both south and north of the Exploits River between Cape Freels and Cape St. John. In this area of many islands and small bays the Indians could fish and seal with comparatively little fear of being surprised by parties of hostile whites. The Beothuk had by this time abandoned the area fronting the Gulf of the St. Lawrence, since it was on this northwestern sector of the island that the early French and English fishermen most commonly landed and killed the inhabitants. Newfoundland is within the Hudsonian biotic province, and the dominant vegetation over the island consists of dense coniferous forests, interlaced with bogs in the lowlands and stands of deciduous trees.

It might be hoped that archaeological studies at Newfoundland sites would contribute to our knowledge of Beothuk origins. Ultimately this may be true, but at present the information is only suggestive. Elmer Harp, Jr., who conducted an archaeological survey in northern Newfoundland, states that no sites of unquestioned Beothuk associations occur for the prehistoric period and that the artifact forms recovered from historic sites, when procured elsewhere, have not been attributed to the Beothuk. The forms are most similar to those in mainland sites associated with Algonkian speakers. It is clear also, from the archaeological recoveries, that Eskimos of the Dorset culture were once established on the island. Dorset Eskimos probably came to influence Beothuk technology in comparatively recent times, perhaps just before historic contact. Diamond Jenness has postulated that the Beothuk, some time before historic contact, lived in Labrador, where they knew the Dorset Eskimos, but under pressures from Eskimos or other Indians in Labrador migrated to Newfoundland.

The extinction of the Beothuk before they had been described systematically led the pioneer linguists Albert S. Gatschet and J. W. Powell to consider Beothuk as a separate and independent linguistic stock. Frank G. Speck, in his attempt to salvage ethnographic facts about these Indians nearly a hundred years after their disappearance, made a number of significant observations about their cultural position. He noted that although there are certain characteristics of Beothuk culture which make them stand apart from the Algonkians in northeastern North America they share some Algonkian cultural items and may perhaps be viewed as retaining an archaic Algonkian way of life.

The earliest contacts of Beothuk with Europeans are shrouded in the confusion of the early voyages to northeastern North America. In 1497 the English expedition under John Cabot possibly, if not probably, sailed along the coast of Newfoundland but saw no people, although artifacts were found on shore. On the voyage of John and Sebastian Cabot in 1499 three Indians from Newfoundland were brought back to England and presented to Henry VII. When the Portuguese learned of the English success, they considered the English as infringing on their New World claims and in 1500 sent two ships from Lisbon under the command of Gaspar de Cortereal. The seven individuals brought back to Portugal by Cortereal may have been Eskimos, not Indians, and were regarded as potentially good slaves. In any event, Cortereal did visit either Newfoundland or Labrador, more likely Labrador. In 1501 Cortereal again sailed for the New World but was never seen after he set out on this voyage. A subsequent searching expedition likewise was lost. The earliest unquestionable observations of the Beothuk were made by Jacques Cartier in the year 1534. Along northern Newfoundland he traded with these Indians, and he described them briefly (see Note 1).

In the early seventeenth century, when English interest in eastern North America was being nurtured, a company was founded to settle and exploit Newfoundland. This organization, the Council and Company of the New-found-land Plantation, received a royal charter. John Guy of the Company sailed to Newfoundland and passed the winter of 1610–1611 establishing a colony along Conception Bay on the southeastern part of the island. Guy returned to England briefly, but in 1612 he was back in Newfoundland exploring the country to the north of his settlement. On this trip contacts were made with the Beothuk, and a brief description of them has been preserved.

Through the seventeenth century the Beothuk seem to have followed their aboriginal pattern of living, modified only by trading and raiding contacts with French and English fishermen. The picture was to change in the first half of the eighteenth century, when the fishermen began actively searching out the Beothuk and destroying them because of their thievery and sporadic killing of whites. It was during this century, too, that the Micmac Indians from Cape Breton Island and Nova Scotia often crossed from the mainland and other islands to hunt on Newfoundland. The Micmac were armed with guns obtained from the French of Acadia. Reportedly, the French offered the Micmac a bounty for every Beothuk head brought to them, and these Indians raided Newfoundland for the purpose of obtaining such heads. The forays of the Micmac into Beothuk country became a source of constant hostility between the two tribes. The Micmac and the European fishermen soon succeeded in driving the Beothuk into the interior regions of Newfoundland which were not readily accessible. In 1768 the governor attempted to end the hostilities with the Beothuk by sending a naval party up the Exploits River, the only large river leading into the interior. This particular group of individuals led by John Cartwright attempted to make peaceful contact with the Beothuk, but they were unable to locate them. They did not see any Indians on the entire journey, but they did find numerous abandoned settlements. By this period in history the Beothuk had become very wary of whites, for white trappers and fishermen had slaughtered many of them. In 1769 a distinct effort was made by the Newfoundland governor to end the depredations against the Indians by threatening to punish offenders. Indians sometimes were being killed solely for amusement (see Note 2). Indian-white relations by this era were so bad that it seemed that the Beothuk were doomed. The whites were fishing more and more salmon streams, English trappers were pursuing beaver and other fur animals into the interior at the expense of the Indians, and the offshore islands on which birds and bird eggs were abundant were being exploited by outsiders as well. During this period Indians might be seen at a distance, and English officials might arrive at an Indian camp where a fire was still burning, but no Indians were met close at hand.

The only Beothuk captured by the English were children, except for one man who lived with the whites of Newfoundland and made intermittent contacts with his relatives until he was accidentally drowned. In 1803 a young woman who was captured for a reward was taken to the settlement of St. John's, where she was kindly treated in the hope that she could help the English to establish contact with other members of her tribe. About a year later she was returned to the spot where she had been captured, but further meetings did not develop from this attempt. Another effort to find the Beothuk entailed a rather elaborate but unsuccessful plan. A painting was commissioned in which an English naval officer was depicted shaking hands with an Indian chief as sailors piled bales of goods near him. Other Indians included in the painting were giving pelts to naval officers; a white and an Indian child embraced as their mothers watched, and finally a sailor was shown courting an Indian girl. The painting, along with trade goods, was taken to the Bay of Exploits area in 1809, but no contacts were made. Later the painting was returned to St. John's, but it was subsequently lost.

In January of 1810 a party under William Cull, the captor of the one woman who was taken, led a party up the Exploits River to locate the Beothuk. They discovered a large rectangular-framed structure, covered with birchbark and deerskins. The building contained a sizable cache of caribou meat and some pelts. The Cull party took three small beaver skins and left manufactured goods in place of them; no Indians were seen, although they were assumed to be living nearby.

The offer of rewards notwithstanding, the various parties who in 1810 sought the Beothuk were not successful. Then in the winter of 1810–1811 a group under the command of Lieutenant David Buchan ascended the Exploits River to continue the search. By following a sled trail early in the morning to a settlement of two cone-shaped bark houses part of the group of Europeans were able to surprise the Beothuk as they slept. Friendly relations soon were established, during which the Indians built a fire and presented the whites with meat and fat; the whites also gave the Indians presents. In the settlement were approximately thirty-five adults, two thirds of whom were women, and it was assumed that some of the men were away. In addition, there were about thirty children, most of whom were under six years of age. Four of the Indian men agreed to help the party of whites bring up the remainder of their supplies. Two of the whites remained with the Indians in order to repair their snowshoes. Leaving them behind was a gesture of good faith by the Europeans. Only one of the Indians continued all the way to the spot where the remaining whites were waiting with the bulk of the supplies. When the group returned to the Indian camp, they found that the other Indians and the two whites had disappeared. The party, which included the one Indian, spent the night on the alert for fear the other Indians might attack. The next day the Indian discovered the bodies of the two whites his group had murdered, and he immediately fled. The Indian could have been shot (Howley, 1915, 80), "but as his destruction could answer no end" and they could not capture him he was permitted to escape. This is certainly a touching example of magnanimity for the whites, who had every reason to be vindictive. Arrows stuck out of the backs of the dead whites, and they had been stripped of their clothing and decapitated. Buchan feared that the Indians would attack the balance of his party, which was moving forward, and so he returned to the men that he had left behind. The whites abandoned most of their outfit and descended the river, for ice conditions were making it increasingly difficult to travel. Of the two subsequent attempts by Buchan to contact the Beothuk, the first was unsuccessful, and it is assumed that the second was likewise.

In 1819 the next contacts were made with the Newfoundland Indians. During 1818 a man named John Peyton was fishing with a crew in the Bay of Exploits. His house and stores had frequently been raided at night by Indians, who took diverse and innumerable useful items. On this occasion, as the fishermen were preparing early one morning to sail southward, their loaded boat was stolen. The vessel was found a short distance away, but it had been stripped of everything useful and portable. The Indians made a successful escape, and the next winter Peyton, with government sanction, returned to the area in an attempt to recover his property. In March of 1819, when the snow was packed and traveling was at its best, Peyton ascended the Exploits River with a small party. They surprised the Indians at a camp near the spot where they had been found by Buchan. A young woman of about twenty-three was captured by Peyton and later was taken to St. John's. During her capture a man who tried to help her was killed. The captive, named Mary March after the month of March, was treated kindly by the English, who hoped to return her to the Indians and thereby to establish contact. The plan failed when the woman died on the return trip in 1820. The search for the Indians continued in that same year, however, with Peyton and Buchan joining forces. This particular endeavor, like most of the others, ended in failure.

In the spring of 1823 three women, a mother and her two daughters, gave themselves up to the whites. They were taken by William Cull to St. John's, where they were cared for by John Peyton. One daughter was very ill with tuberculosis, and the other two women were in poor health. Fearing that the women would die in the white settlement, they were returned quickly, laden with gifts in the hope of establishing firm contact with the Beothuk. The women searched for the other Indians, but were unsuccessful in locating them and found their way to an English settlement on the coast. Here the mother and one daughter died within a short while, and the surviving daughter, named Shanawdithit, but later called Nancy or Nance, was cared for by John Peyton (see Note 3). She revealed that when she left the Beothuk there were only fifteen people remaining, two of whom were shot by trappers, one drowned, and the three women, including the informant, surrendered themselves to the whites. The remaining nine apparently died in the winter of 1824–1825. Nancy perhaps by this time was the only living Beothuk, although in 1824 and again in 1826 Indians, probably Micmac, reported having seen Red Indians or recent signs of them.

In 1827, under the guidance of William E. Cormack, the Beothick Institution was founded in Newfoundland, with the purpose of finding the Indians who were thought to be at large. The further purpose of the Institution was for "opening a communication with, and promoting the civilization of the Red Indians of Newfoundland"

(Howley, 1915, 184). In the fall of 1828 Cormack, accompanied by a Micmac, an Abnaki, and a Montagnais Indian, began to search for wild Beothuk. Signs were found, interpreted as being left by these Indians the year before, but subsequent searchers failed to locate any additional Beothuk. In 1828 Nancy was returned to St. John's, where she was cared for by Cormack until early in1829 when Cormack left for England. Subsequently, she was cared for by the Attorney General of Newfoundland, but she died in June. Virtually all that we know about the Beothuk was told by Nancy and recorded by Cormack. Unfortunately, Cormack was not a good ethnographer, but Nancy seems to have been a willing informant.

The most striking characteristic of the Beothuk or Red Indians was their habit of painting themselves with red ocher. Their faces, clothing, and bodies—all were ocher-covered. The hair of the men was cut short in front and tapered to a longer length in back, with the addition of a long scalp lock decorated with feathers. In summer they usually wore nothing on their heads and feet. During the winter months leggings, moccasins, and mittens were worn, all with the hair side turned in, and, of course, covered with a mixture of ocher and oil. Typical of the men was a caribou-skin garment made of two pelts, with the hair side inward, gathered at the shoulders and extending below the knees. This poncho-like shirt was sleeved to the elbow or sometimes sleeveless. Separate armlets then covered the arms. A neckpiece of skins, which was attached to or separate from the poncho, was also worn. The skins apparently were sewn together, not with an eyed needle but by making holes in the skin with an awl and then lacing them with sinew. The only difference between the clothing of men and women seems to have been that the women's ponchos were hooded.

As seen in 1612, the Beothuk summer houses were constructed of poles driven into the ground to form a circle ten feet across at the base. The poles met at their upper ends and were covered with caribou skins. In the center of the circle was a fireplace. A more elaborate description of this type of shelter dates from 1768; it was noted then it was cone-shaped and varied in size, depending on the number of persons in the family. Oblong depressions dug in the ground and covered with small branches served as beds. The pole frame was covered with overlapping sheets of birchbark which were held in place with exterior poles. The sheeting did not reach the top of the structure, and there the smoke drifted out from the fire. There appear to have been two varieties of cone-shaped house. The form used in winter was surrounded by an octagonal frame of sticks dug into the ground and extending two feet above it. Inside this frame was the birchbark-covered dwelling, with earth piled between it and the outer framework. The summer house lacked both the outer frame and earth filling. Inside the pole frame, possibly six feet above ground, a wooden hoop was bound, from which clothing could be suspended for drying. Another form of dwelling noted in 1612 was square and roofed, although later descriptions indicate that it was not nearly so common. It has been described as rectangular, with walls built of vertical planks on three sides and horizontal squared logs on the fourth. This structure was chinked with moss, and the low, dome-shaped roof was covered with three layers of birchbark except at the opening through which the smoke from the fireplace escaped. Along the inside walls the Indians placed their implements, and in the rafters meat was stored. Their form of cache had a gabled roof, with a ridgepole at the top. This structure was probably plank-framed or covered with crossed poles, topped with a layer of birchbark. The bathhouses were probably made with bent poles tied together at the top and then covered with skins. Stones were heated in a fire outside the bathhouse and were carried in while still extremely hot. Water was brought in birchbark containers and ladled with a birchbark dipper onto the stones to make steam. Sweat baths appear to have been taken only for the treatment of disease.

A Beothuk canoe was some twenty feet in length and four and a half feet wide at the beam. Its greatest height was amidships, and the frame curved from amidships to the bow and stern. The ribs were made from conifer wood, and the frame was covered with birchbark sewn together with split roots. The most unusual feature of the canoe was that it was constructed with a V-shaped cross section so that the bottom and sides formed a continuous line, with lath running lengthwise to give the vessel rigidity. The seams were caulked with ocher combined with oil or pitch. A typical canoe was said to have carried four people. These vessels were used not only on coastal and inland waters but on ocean trips as well. The Indians frequented Funk Island, which was some forty miles from the mainland and so low that it could not have been seen from the mainland. To venture there for seabirds and their eggs required not only some navigational skill but also considerable daring.

The oblong snowshoes of the Beothuk were some four and a half feet long and slightly more than thirty inches wide at their broadest spot. They were built in such a manner that the outer edge was bowed and the inner edge formed a relatively straight line. Each snowshoe apparently was slightly bow-shaped in profile, and probably the greatest upsweep was at the tip.

The Beothuk possessed a form of toboggan, consisting of sealskins over an interior framework, which they used for hauling loads over ice and snow. Sacks were made from half a sealskin and apparently were used for backpacking goods.

A common weapon of these Indians was a self-bow some five and a half feet long and made from diverse species of wood. The arrows of three-foot pine splints were feathered with goose wing quills, and the arrowpoint, some six inches in length, had a double-edged blade. Arrowpoints for land mammals and large birds were made from stone or bone. A blunted wooden point which was a continuation of the arrow shaft could kill small birds. The spears, used mainly against caribou, were some twelve feet long and had bone spearpoints. For taking seals a toggle-headed harpoon was employed. The wooden shaft was perhaps twelve feet long; the harpoon head was attached to a foreshaft which in turn was attached to a socket piece. A caribou-skin line was tied to the toggle head, and the unattached opposite end was held by the hunter. A harpooned animal could be played with the line until it was exhausted. The Indians appear not only to have harpooned seals but also occasionally to have killed dolphins.

That comparatively little is known about the technology of the Beothuk is not surprising, considering the very fleeting contacts the whites had with them. We do know that the people used iron pyrites in order to make fire. We know, too, that birchbark containers were made in a wide variety of shapes, from small rectangular forms with straight or flaring sides to large water buckets which were rectangular. There were wide-bottomed styles with sides sharply constricting to a narrow neck as well as forms with a narrow base and widely flaring sides which ended at a broad rim. Small birchbark containers, usually rectangular in profile, were used as drinking cups.

Thanks to one particular drawing by Nancy, with labels by Cormack, we know something about their ways of preserving food. Salmon were split and dried, and lobster tails were dried and strung together for storage. The bladders of caribou and seals were filled with oil, and roughly triangular sections of sealskin with the blubber attached were cut for future use. Small sections of fat were cut from this large piece as they were required. Bird eggs were boiled in birch-bark containers and then dried in the sun.

James P. Howley, in his definitive Beothuk study, illustrates and describes diverse artifacts from Newfoundland, all of which were assumed to be of Beothuk origin. It is impossible to establish any chronology from the forms, but the sample does offer insight into a technology that may have been Beothuk. The productions in stone included items that were flaked and others that were ground. However, grinding was more common than flaking among the illustrated artifacts. Furthermore, some of the chipped forms were basely ground. Among the more common finds of stone were ground adz blades and ground gouges, along with both chipped and ground skin scrapers in a variety of shapes. Shouldered and tanged end blades of ground slate were formed in elongated triangles and were probably used as spearpoints. Triangular arrowpoints of ground slate had concave bases, but the chipped arrowpoints had side notches and were tanged. Small pieces of slate and flinty material with sharp edges are described as possible gravers. A variety of small and large grinding or whetstones also were found. Manufactures of soapstone included oblong grooved pieces, which may have been line or net sinkers; cooking pots, and lamps. About the only other stone manufactures included a rare platform pipe.

Items described as made from bone included barbed dart heads, probably for taking fish, toggle harpoon heads, socket pieces, probably foreshafts, and combs, as well as an assortment of toggles. One class of richly ornamented artifacts was made from sections of bone. Usually they were formed into an essentially rectangular shape, with a suspension hole at one end and a squared base or a base with two or three prongs. These specimens were always recovered from burials, and in one instance they were found attached as a border for a poncho. Usually the strips were etched with long parallel lines, and short parallel lines might be engraved at right angles to them. Other motifs included circles, triangles, squares, and other simple geometric forms. Work in shell apparently was confined to the manufacture of disk beads, but bone beads also have been recovered.

The caribou of Newfoundland, like those of most other sectors of arctic America, migrated northward in summer and returned south in winter. At river crossings and where the riverbank was steep, Indians felled trees for a distance of half a mile to a mile and a half. The cut trees formed a fence, ranging up to ten feet in height. When there were no trees, they drove sticks into the ground at an angle and suspended a cord from the top of each stick. Tied to the end of the cord was a piece of birchbark, and with every slight breeze the birchbark moved in the wind. The caribou were frightened by these markers and would never approach them. The surround was completed when the people erected semicircular mounds of dirt nearby, from which they appear to have shot at the confused caribou. Along one sector of the Exploits River the caribou fences extended at least thirty miles. Another method of killing caribou was to hunt them from canoes as they swam the lakes and rivers.

We know extremely little about the social life of the Beothuk, and with reference to religion there are only a few fragments learned from Nancy. For instance, Nancy illustrated a group of wooden shafts, at the top of which were different figures. One figure was of a European fishing vessel and another of a whale's tail. The other forms were geometric, and all have been interpreted as totemic in their association. We know, too, that these people performed a dance around a pole, on top of which was placed the head of any white man they had just killed. About Beothuk marriage we know only that the ceremony was validated in part with a feast which lasted a full day and night.

A few recorded examples of the treatment of disease included washing sore eyes with mother's milk, consuming a liquid that contained dogwood bark, taking vapor baths for stomach disorders and for rheumatism, and finally, for soreness about the body, rubbing a mixture of sulphuret of iron added to oil on the locus of the pain.

Interment was varied and included at least six different methods. Most commonly, a body was encased in birchbark and placed either in an excavation to be covered with dirt or on the ground surface to be covered with stones. A body also might be flexed, placed on its right side, covered with birchbark, and buried in a small birchbark-lined coffin made of horizontal poles joined by notching at the corners. Scaffold burials, again with the body encased in birchbark, were raised on four posts with a floor some seven feet above the ground, on which grave goods were also placed. The tomb of Mary March and her husband was approximately ten feet long, eight feet wide, and some four feet in height. It was floored with squared poles and covered with birchbark, and it included grave goods. Burials in caves are reported for a few areas. In one example an excavation was made in the floor of a cave, and into it were lowered the extended body and the grave goods. A birchbark covering was placed over the grave, and soil and rocks were heaped on it. Another form of cave burial had the body in a sitting position with a grass rope tied around it; the body was then covered with caribou skins and a layer of birchbark. Finally, the cave was filled in with stones.

It is perhaps a fitting epilogue to record the efforts of Frank G. Speck, the great ethnographer of Indians in eastern North America, to locate remnants of the Beothuk. He once traced a woman whose father was reportedly a Red Indian. This woman, named Santu, was supposed to have been the offspring of a Beothuk father and a Micmac mother. Santu was born in Newfoundland but was taken to Nova Scotia when she was about ten years of age. She spent the rest of her life in the Maritime Provinces and New England. She was old and partly senile when interviewed by Speck and could recall only fragments of ethnographic information of dubious merit. The Beothuk ethnographer James P. Howley did not consider Santu of Beothuk ancestry, but somehow I like to think that she was. Santu died in 1919.

Note 1.   Jacques Cartier describes his initial contact with the Beothuk of northern Newfoundland in 1534 (Burrage, 1906, 10).

To be short, I beleeve that this was the land that God allotted to Caine. There are men of an indifferent good stature and bignesse, but wilde and unruly: they weare their haire tied on the top like a wreath of hay, and put a wooden pinne within it, or any other such thing instead of a naile, and with them they binde certaine birdes feathers. They are clothed with beastes skinnes as well the men as women, but that the women go somewhat straiter a ld closer in their garments than the men do, with their wastes girded; they paint themselves with certaine Roan colours: their boates are made of the barke of birch trees, with the which they fish and take great store of Seales, and as farre as we could understand since our comming thither, that is not their habitation, but they come from the maine land out of hotter countreys, to catch the saide Seales and other necessaries for their living.

Note 2.   A British Parliament committee was established to investigate the Newfoundland trade, and in 1793 the committee interviewed George Cartwright about the treatment of the Indians. Extracts of his testimony follow (Howley, 1915, 50).

George Cartwright, Esq., being examined, informed your Committee, that he was an Officer of Foot in His Majesty's service. And being asked whether he has been in Newfoundland? he said, "Yes; several times." And being asked in what capacity? he said, "Twice on pleasure, five times on business, on his way backwards and forwards to Labrador; the last time he was there was in 1786; he has been much in that part of Newfoundland inhabited by the native Indians; he has reason to believe that their numbers are considerable, but he cannot state what the numbers are, as they have been so much chased and driven away by the Fishermen and Furriers [trappers]." And being asked, How near to any of our settlements do the Indians come? he said, "They frequently come in the night into the harbours to pilfer what they can get, to supply their necessities."—And being asked, What were the articles which they mostly steal? he said, "Sails, hatchets, boats, kettles and such other things as they

think will be of use; they use the sails as coverings for their wigwams or tents."
And being asked, Could he state any particulars respecting the condition of
the Indians in Newfoundland? he said, "He thinks their condition is very
wretched and forlorn indeed; our fishermen and furriers shooting at the
Indians for their amusement." He said, "He has heard many say they had
rather have a shot at an Indian than at a deer: A few years ago there two
men, one of whom he knew personally, went up the Great River Exploits
in the winter, on purpose to murder and plunder such Indians as they could
meet with; when they got to the head of the river where it comes out of a
great lake, they met with an Indian town, containing above one hundred
inhabitants; they immediately fired upon them with long guns loaded with
buckshot; they killed and wounded several, the rest made their escape into
the woods, some naked, others only half clothed; none of them provided with
implements to procure either food or fuel; they then plundered their houses
or wigwams of what they thought worth bringing away, and burnt the rest,
by which they must necessarily have destroyed the remainder, as they could
not exist in the snow." And being asked, If he meant to state that the conduct
of the Fishermen and Furriers towards the Indians was in general of that
cruel nature, or that these were only particular instances? he said, "He has
reason to believe from the conversations he has had with the fishermen of
these parts, that there are very few who would not have done the same
thing."

Note 3.   A description of the Beothuk woman Shanawdithit, or Nancy
as she was called by her captors. The interview with Mrs. Jure was conducted
by James P. Howley (1915, 175).

An old woman, Mrs. Jure, of Exploits Island, whom I met in 1886, and
who resided with the Peyton family at the same time as Nancy, gave me the
following particulars concerning her. Nance, as she was familiarly called, was
swarthy in complexion but with very pleasing features, rather inclined to be
stout but of good figure. She was bright and intelligent, quick to acquire the
English language, and of a retentive memory. She was very pert at times, and
when her mistress had occasion to scold her, she would answer very sharply,
"what de matter now Missa Peyton, what you grumble bout." At times she got
into sulky fits, or became too lazy to do anything. When such moods were
upon her she would go off and hide in the woods for days together, only
returning when the sulks had worn off, or when driven back by hunger. She
would allow no familiarity on the part of the fishermen who frequented
Peyton's house, but on one occasion, when amongst others, an individual
possessing an extremely red beard and hair was amongst the number, she
showed the greatest partiality to this man, even going to the length of sitting
on his knee and caressing him; to the no small confusion of the big shy
fisherman, and to the great amusement of his companions. She was very in-
genious at carving and could make combs out of deers' horns and carve them
beautifully. She would take a piece of birch bark, double it up and bite with
her teeth into a variety of figures of animals or other designs, i.e., to say when
the bark was again unfolded, the impressions thereon would be such.

References

Burrage, Henery. *Early English and French Voyages.* New York. 1906.

Gatschet, Albert S. "The Beothuk Indians," *American Philosophical Society, Proceedings,* v. 22, 408–424, 1885; v. 23, 411–432, 1886; v. 28, 1–16, 1890.

Harp, Elmer, Jr. "An Archaeological Survey in the Strait of Belle Isle Area," *American Antiquity,* v. 16, 203–220. 1951.

*Howley, James P. *The Beothucks or Red Indians.* Cambridge. 1915. Howley in this volume has compiled virtually all of the historical references to the Beothuk and has presented the ethnographic descriptions along with all of the known variations in recording.

Jenness, Diamond. "Notes on the Beothuk Indians of Newfoundland," *National Museum of Canada, Annual Report for 1927.* Bulletin 56, 36–39. 1929.

Speck, Frank G. *Beothuk and Micmac.* Heye Foundation. 1922.

Voegelin, Carl F., and E. W. Voegelin. "Linguistic Considerations of Northeastern North America," in *Man in Northeastern North America,* Frederick Johnson, ed., Papers of the Robert S. Peabody Foundation for Archaeology, v. 3. 1946.

3

The Kuskowagamiut:

Riverine Fishermen

Map by J. Donovan

0   50   100   150 mi.

The word Eskimo, applied initially to people in eastern Canada, is an Algonkian term meaning "eaters of raw flesh." In both old and new descriptive accounts Eskimos most frequently are described as a happy, fur-clad people who live in snowhouses, munch on raw meat, and lack the refinements of taste and manners noted among many of the world's peoples. Stereotypes such as these arise easily and for good reasons. The first ethnographies about Eskimos were for those in Greenland and Canada. The people described possessed most if not all of the characteristics mentioned, but at the same time there were significant sociocultural variations among the widely separated population segments. Later, when Alaskan and Siberian Eskimos were described, it was acknowledged readily that these Eskimos differed significantly from those to the east. The basic linguistic homogeneity was not questioned, but local cultural variations became particularly obvious with more intensive study. Today "typical" Eskimos in the literature are the Polar Eskimos of Greenland and the Canadian Netsilik or Copper groups. These peoples represent extreme adaptations to arctic conditions, and all speak the Inuit form of Eskimo. At the time of historic contact the Inuit speakers, who lived in the extreme northern portions of North America, numbered about 30,000 individuals. For the same time period there were at least 20,000 Yuit speakers in southwestern Alaska. Because the stress in the descriptive literature is on northern Eskimos, and yet the Yuit are a sizable population, a tribe of Yuit speakers has been singled out to represent Eskimos; these are the Kuskowagamiut.

Among the three linguistic subfamilies of Yuit—Yuk, Cux, and Sux—the largest population segment is that of the Yuk speakers. Some 2000 Yuk speakers live along the Kuskokwim River which flows into the Bering Sea from southwestern Alaska. This particular riverine Eskimo population is presented because there is a greater continuity of information about it than about any other Yuit. The authoritative but brief ethnographic account compiled by the Russian explorer Lavrentij A. Zagoskin in 1843–1844 provides a general description of aboriginal life. This information is supplemented by the findings in the excavation of the historic Kuskowagamiut site of Crow Village by James W. VanStone and Wendell H. Oswalt. There is, furthermore, an ethnographic reconstruction from Moravian missionary records for the period around 1900, and similar information was obtained from informants by Oswalt. The data from a 1955–1956 community study of the village of Napaskiak by Oswalt provide a glimpse into the very recent past. The amount of information available for the Kuskokwim Eskimos is not nearly so full and illuminating as might be suggested by this outline, but it does offer an intermittent record of one hundred and thirty years of Western Eskimo culture and society. In a description of the Kuskowagamiut a neglected form of Eskimo culture is revealed. These people subsisted primarily on salmon, they lived in relatively stable communities, and most villages contained a ceremonial structure which was an important center for social and religious life.

The Yuit may be termed Southwestern Alaskan Eskimos, for this is the primary sector of North America in which they are concentrated. The easternmost Yuit live along Prince William Sound, but between them and their close linguistic relatives to the west on the Alaska Peninsula intrude the Athapaskan Indians of the Tanaina tribe. Kodiak Island is Yuit territory, as is the Bering Sea coast of Alaska south of Norton Sound and the Bering Sea islands of Nunivak and St. Lawrence. The only other Yuit speakers live along a coastal strip of eastern Siberia. The Eskimoan linguistic phylum is composed of two stocks, Aleut and Eskimo. Within the Eskimo stock are two families, Yuit and Inuit. There is comparatively little dialectic difference within Aleut, considerably more within Inuit, and a great deal of diversity within Yuit. From linguistic evidence alone it is inferred that there is greater local time depth for Eskimo culture among the Southwestern Alaskan Eskimos than for any other area.

The Yuit lived in the most bountiful of all Eskimo environments, and over time they divided to form three distinctive linguistic groups with accompanying sociocultural differences. Their major ecological adaptations were to coastal promontories, inland lakes, and the larger rivers. The coastal people were seal hunters above all else, but some were in a position to hunt walrus as well. However, because of the shallow seas, the hunting of great whales was practiced rarely by the Yuit. Groups that lived away from the coast but not on a major river were mainly lake fishermen who were most concerned with taking whitefish. The riverine peoples usually focused their economy on salmon fishing. All groups hunted caribou during at least part of each year if these animals were present in their areas. This tripartite division of ecological adaptations is more schematic than real, for there existed a great many variations which depended on local conditions.

The segment of the Yuit population with which we are concerned lived along the banks of the central and lower Kuskokwim River system. These people term themselves the Kuskowagamiut, meaning "people of the cough river." They also have the generic term Yupik, which translates "real people," and they apply this designation to all other Eskimos with whom they can converse easily. Each settlement, whether a village or an isolated house, has a specific designation, and the residents take their name from the location. The aboriginal Kuskowagamiut occupied the Kuskokwim River from the river mouth upstream to the combined Ingalik Indian and Yuit settlement of Kwigiumpainukamiut, which is about two hundred miles upriver. Edward W. Nelson, in preparing the widely accepted designations of ethnic boundaries in southwestern Alaska, has considered the Kuskokwim estuary people also to be Kuskowagamiut, but this lumping fails to consider the very different ecological conditions of the estuary peoples from their riverine neighbors and the cultural dissimilarities that exist. The estuary Eskimos, termed Sinukmiut or "coastal people" by the lower river Yuit, should probably be regarded as a separate population. In the present conception of ethnic boundaries the Kuskowagamiut exclusively occupied both banks of the river from the mouth to Crow Village; the aboriginal population of this region is estimated at 2800 individuals.

The Kuskokwim River is broad and gently flowing as far inland as the Eskimos ranged during aboriginal times. For convenience and for ecological reasons the lower river is considered as the area between the contemporary villages of Eek and Kalskag. The central river is designated as the area from Kalskag to Sleetmiut, but only the section from Kalskag to Kwigiumpainukamiut was occupied by Eskimos in aboriginal times. Along the lower river the current flows at a rate of about four miles an hour over a mile-wide riverbed. Tides from the Bering Sea carry a flow of river water back into the river and again draw it out; the difference in water level averages about four feet. Near the estuary the land is low-lying and spotted with diverging waterways, lakes, and ponds. In unprotected areas a tundra vegetation flourishes, but in depressions sheltered from the wind there are dense willow thickets, rare stands of birch trees, and numerous growths of cottonwood trees. Then, too, a few dwarfed spruce trees form tongues of dark green vegetation extending into the tundra. This is a transitional zone between the coastal Eskimoan biotic province and the Hudsonian biotic province of the interior. On such land the animal species of economic importance were caribou, muskrat, mink, hare, and an occasional land otter. Most of the riverine settlements have stands of trees nearby, but away from the banks of the lower river there is tundra. Farther upstream the tundra is less common, and spruce growths become denser, although at higher elevations tundra vegetation reappears. As the central sector is reached, higher hills are encountered, and soon hills and low mountains front the river.

Animals along the central river include black bear in addition to the animal species known from the lower river. Migratory birds pass through the country in the spring and again in the fall, but they do not remain to nest in any numbers. Spruce hens and ptarmigan, however, live in the vicinity throughout the year. The fish in the river and adjacent waters include the annual runs of diverse species of salmon, among which the king, red, dog (chum), and silver are the most important. In the main river, lakes, and sloughs, depending on the time of year, whitefish, cod, pike, and blackfish abound. The only other fish of importance is the smelt, which ascends the lower river to spawn early each spring. It is the salmon in the main river and the whitefish in the lakes and river that contribute most to the stability of the Kuskokwim Eskimo economy.

Archaeologists have yet to focus attention on the prehistory of the Kuskokwim River area occupied by Eskimos. No sites have been excavated fully, and only Eekchuk, below Napaskiak, has been sampled reasonably well. It is possible to obtain some idea of what awaits the archaeologist by dealing with the excavated materials from the adjacent Bering Sea coast and ethnographic information from the Kuskokwim. The oldest systematically sampled site along the southern part of the coast is near Platinum and shows a relationship to the Ipiutak remains discovered at Point Hope. The Platinum Ipiutak finds were left by sea-mammal hunters who knew the use of pottery and stone lamps. They ground slate and chipped flint. This complex seems to be a later manifestation of classic Ipiutak forms and was adapted to open water sea-mammal hunting throughout the year. Near the village of Kipnuk the ethnographer Edward W. Nelson purchased an Old Bering Sea Culture artifact, which may mean that this form of Eskimo culture will some day be found to the south of the Bering Strait region where it is best known. The excavations of coastal sites by Mark Kowta at Togiak, VanStone on Nunivak Island, and Oswalt at Hooper Bay Village show that essentially there has been a stable form of Eskimo culture along the central and southern coasts for the last three or four hundred years and perhaps longer. In each sample the people were oriented primarily toward the sea and sea-mammal hunting. These adaptations to coastal living included the occupation of favorable sites for long periods, and large accumulations of midden are evidence of continuing occupancy. Along the Kuskokwim River no evidence of similar continuity in Eskimo adaptations to a riverine setting has been found. However, no one has searched extensively for prehistoric sites in this area. Unquestionably, numerous sites exist, but they are probably in the form of dwelling remains without deep accumulations of midden. It is quite possible that local riverine Eskimo culture lacks great antiquity. As pointed out in a later section, an evaluation of early historic riverine Yuit culture suggests that the people are relatively recent intruders into this very un-Eskimo setting.

The earliest known historical reference to the Kuskokwim and its people is in the 1796 diary of the Russian Orthodox-Greek Catholic missionary Hieromonk Juvenal. While he was in the Lake Iliamna area attempting to convert the local people, he recorded that three men arrived from the Kuskokwim. One of these visitors made the sign of the cross to the missionary, and although he did not know its meaning, it demonstrated that he had prior knowledge of the Russians. Where this contact may have been made is not known. It should be added, however, that the Juvenal diary may be a fabrication. It was not until 1818 that the first meaningful step toward exploring the Kuskokwim was made; it occurred with the founding of a trading station, Alexandrov Redoubt (modern Nushagak), at the mouth of the Nushagak River. From Alexandrov, probably in 1828, the Russian explorer Vasil'ev went up a branch of the Nushagak River system in an unsuccessful attempt to reach the Kuskokwim drainage. During the following summer the divide to the Kuskokwim was located, and Vasil'ev descended a river, probably the Holitna, to the Kuskokwim. The small party then made their way downriver to the mouth and returned to Alexandrov Redoubt. The travel journal of Vasil'ev never has been published, although ethnographers and historians have consulted it. In 1832 a one-man trading post was established at the junction of the Holitna and Kuskokwim rivers. It soon became apparent, however, that the post was accessible to only a few of the residents along the main river, and it was moved downstream to Kwigiumpainukamiut, the community occupied jointly by Eskimos and Indians. The move was made apparently in 1833, and during the winter of the same year the explorer Andrei Glazunov attempted to establish an overland route from the Bering Sea redoubt of St. Michael to Nicholaevskij Redoubt (modern Kenai) along Cook Inlet on the North Pacific Ocean. With a small party he left St. Michael, sledded to the Yukon River and across to the Kuskokwim drainage. Here he visited the newly constructed trading post and pushed on upstream to the Stony River junction. Ascending the Stony River, the last major barrier to his destination, he was forced to turn back when supplies of food became exhausted. The Glazunov journal has never been published in its entirety, but from the excerpts which have appeared it would seem that it contains relatively little ethnographic information. In 1841 the second post was abandoned, and a redoubt was constructed across the river. It was named Kolmakov and became the most important trading center for the balance of the Russian period. By far the most important explorer along the Kuskokwim was L. A. Zagoskin; his 1843–1844 descriptions of the Yuit, supplemented by Vasil'ev's observations, constitute the base line ethnographic data and virtually all of the published information for the Russian era. After Zagoskin's time we have the diary of the Orthodox missionary Hieromonk Illarion who worked among the Indians and Eskimos of the Yukon and Kuskokwim rivers from 1861 to 1866. In anticipation of the purchase of Alaska by the United States, the redoubt of Kolmakov and the secondary Kuskokwim trading stations of Mumtrekhlagamiut Station (modern Bethel), Ogavik, and Vinasale were abandoned by the Russians in 1866.

Time and tradition have joined to unite the Kuskowagamiut. A strong sense of local identification exists, which finds its clearest reflection in the attachment of persons to the settlement of their birth. To be born beyond the bounds of a community in which one later lives is always to be something of an outsider. To have moved frequently during one's lifetime means individual maladjustment. No traditions that record the early movements into the Kuskokwim River system are known to exist. The myths that seek to explain the origins of these people speak of the Raven as the creator in a primeval time. The Raven, too, was the culture hero and trickster as well, but today it is regarded as just another bird, one with sometimes strange behavior and no usefulness. Versions of the creation myth vary with the locality, but the essence of them all stressed a supernatural relationship between man and the ravens of old.

In physical characteristics the people are racially Eskimo, as would be expected; they are relatively short in stature and tend to be long-trunked and short-legged. The men are lean and muscular, and the women may be plump, although neither men nor women are fat in the manner often regarded as typical of Eskimos. The long keel-shaped head of classic Eskimo description is not typical; instead, the people tend to be roundheaded and lack the distinctive keel. Eskimos, as the most mongoloid of New World aboriginal populations, have extremely high cheekbones, distinct epicanthic folds, and shovel-shaped incisor teeth, all reflections of a clear racial affinity with Asian populations. The people are darkskinned only on their faces and hands where they are exposed to the elements and color deeply from weathering. Many of the men have rather heavy beards and in aboriginal times plucked all facial hair. They wore their hair in two styles, either long over the shoulders or tonsured, but with bangs falling over the eyes. The women permitted their hair to grow long, and when they concerned themselves about their appearance they gathered it back into a lock or braid. The hair of adults and children was often, if not normally, infected with lice, and one description from the early American period mentions that their hair sometimes looked as though it had been powdered because of the large numbers of lice eggs in it. Facial adornment for women included the insertion of a sinew thread through the nasal septum. Beneath the hole was suspended a string of small blue glass beads which were obtained in trade from Siberia before direct contact had been made with the Russians. The women usually had pierced ears, in which earrings were worn or strings of beads suspended. Likewise, their faces from lower lip to chin were tattooed, and they are reported to have worn two lateral labrets at the outer corners of the lower lip. Men wore either paired lateral labrets or a single large medial labret, again just beneath the lower lip, but they were not tattooed.

The most typical winter garment for both sexes was a loose-fitting, sleeved garment reaching to the calves or ankles. This type of parka most often was made from the skins of ground squirrels, with the claws and tails still attached. Some parkas were manufactured from marmot, muskrat, or caribou skin, depending on local fashions and the skins available. On the basic parka form there were modifications. Those of the women were hooded and had splits up the sides, but a man's parka was hoodless, and the sides were not split. When an individual of either sex found the length of the parka to be an impediment, he attached a belt about the hips and gathered the excess length above the belt. The parkas were trimmed elaborately, particularly those of the women. White caribou hair was added to the cuffs and lower border, and strips of animal fur dangled at the breast and from the middle of the back. The parkas of men had similar but less elaborate border trim, and a man protected his neck from the cold with a bearskin collar sewn about the opening in the parka. Males wore head coverings of skin or fur, although some men wore headpieces made from a complete goose skin split open at the breast. Men apparently wore short caribou-skin undertrousers, over which were added trousers fitted to just below the knees. Their boots were knee-length and made from caribou leg skins, with attached soles of sealskin. Inside the boots socks of caribou skin or woven grass were worn, and grass insoles cushioned the feet. Women preferred to wear long sealskin boots which reached to the hips, although it is likely that other skins were substituted, particularly along the central river. The only other major clothing item for winter was mittens. These were of caribou skin and were worn by persons of both sexes. Items intended for summer use included rain parkas made from sewn strips of intestine or from fish skins. These garments were hooded and probably reached just below the knees. During rainy summer weather people also wore fish-skin boots of varying lengths and fish-skin socks.

The Kuskowagamiut population was scattered along the river in settlements located on both banks. The number of persons occupying any particular settlement varied from ten living in an isolated house to villages of about three hundred. The isolated household-community was not uncommon, but people usually occupied larger settlements. It seems likely, judging from the settlement pattern about 1900, that few if any families lived away from the riverbanks throughout the entire year. The most detailed information available about the village dwellings is obtained by referring to the excavation of houses at the early historic site of Crow Village and by viewing these remains in the context of diverse ethnographic descriptions. A square to rectangular anteroom usually was constructed in a shallow excavated pit. The roof style is uncertain, but the sidewalls probably were supported by vertical poles set into the ground. Entrance was gained through an oval opening in a vertical wall plank. Inside the room was a fireplace where meals were cooked, and smoke from the fire drifted outside through a hole in the roof. In summer food could be cooked outside the house. Stored in the anteroom were various wooden dishes, ladles, baskets, and pottery containers, all of which were associated with domestic activities. Some houses, with or without anterooms, had short, ground-level passages which led into the living room. Others had long subterranean tunnels leading indoors. In either form the passage served to prevent cold air from penetrating the living area. Usually during cold weather and even at other times of the year the family's dogs slept in the tunnel and were a minor hazard to anyone entering. The living room, which tended to be square, with walls measuring about fifteen feet in length, was separated from the tunnel with a woven grass mat or skin curtain. Inside the house, which was built in an excavation about three feet deep, were horizontal base logs near the outer edge of the excavation. Behind the base logs were either vertical or horizontal planks or logs which formed the sidewalls. Two stout posts were set into the front wall and two into the rear wall; each post was about three feet from a corner. These were the main roof supports. However, an alternative position set them in the room away from the walls. When the posts were in the front and rear walls, they supported horizontal beams which paralleled the sidewalls. When the four-post-center arrangement was used, the beams spanned each quadrant. Against these beams rested split logs which extended from the edge of the wall excavations to the beams. The front and back walls apparently were vertical or horizontal posts and were sometimes split. The center of the roof was covered with short, split logs, but allowance was made for an opening over which was placed a framework covered with sewn fish skins or animal intestines to serve as a window. The entire structure except the window was covered with sheets of birchbark (in houses along the central river) or bundles of grass (along the lower river). Above this protective layer earth or sod was added to complete the construction. The house floor consisted of packed earth, which often if not always was moist and soggy. Near the center of the floor in houses along the central river was a fireplace, but some houses along the lower river appear to have lacked this feature. Benches usually paralleled the sidewalls, and in some houses they also paralleled the rear wall. It was on these benches that people lounged during the day and slept at night. On top of the benches were planks, slabs or birchbark, or layers of grass. Animal skins were used for mattresses and blankets.

To a non-Eskimo the odor inside a house would have been its most striking feature. The smells of stale urine, skin clothing which had never been cleaned, women who had never bathed, and dried salmon, in addition to decayed salmon heads at a certain time of the year, must have been an impressive combination. The houses were relatively dark inside because of the accumulation of soot on the walls, but some light penetrated the translucent window. This covering could be set aside during warm days for still more light from outside. Artificial light came from the fireplace or from bowl-shaped clay lamps. The lamps were placed on stands in front of the rear bench or at the edge of a sidewall bench. Oil, preferably seal oil, burned on a wick of moss. The central floor space was filled with wooden food trays, deep water buckets with sides of bent spruce root fitted into a flat bottom, and cups made in a similar manner but on a smaller scale. The pottery cooking vessels standing about were flat-bottomed with nearly straight sides or sides that flared to the shoulder, then constricted at the neck, and flared again at the rim. If there was a form of surface treatment, it consisted usually of horizontal bands of dots and lines which had been incised into the moist clay just below the rim. In the central river houses round stones were kept near the fireplace. These were heated and then dropped into birch-bark vessels for cooking food. A household such as this would include also a woman's sewing equipment in a neat, folded leather container, her semilunar slate-bladed knife, or *uluak,* wooden cutting boards, chipped and ground stone scrapers for processing skins, and awls, to mention some of the more important items. Such a dwelling was occupied by a woman, her daughters, and her young sons.

The residence of the men and older boys, the bathhouse, the workshop, and ceremonial room were combined in one structure which was called the men's house, *kashgee* or *kashim.* It was by far the largest and most complex building in any community. A typical *kashgee* was square and measured about thirty feet along each side. The walls were made of vertical planks or split logs and the roof was cribbed. A tunnel, either at ground level or beneath the ground, was the means of access, but some *kashgees* apparently had a wide entry which served also as a tunnel. At the entrance to the main room hung a brown bearskin if the tunnel or entry was at ground level. When there was an underground passage, a person entered the *kashgee* through a hole in the floor. The *kashgee* floor was covered with planks except for an area some four feet square at the center of the room. This opening was the fire pit, and it had planks over it when not in use. Above the fire pit was a window like those found in the women's houses. *Kashgee* furnishings included two or, less often, three tiers of benches around the sidewalls. A *kashgee* contained at least two large bowl-shaped clay lamps which sat on the floor or on stands before the sidewall benches.

Inside the *kashgee* would be found all of the typical tools and equipment used by men. Conspicuously absent were cooking vessels and eating containers, for they were brought in by the women at mealtime and removed after the men and boys had eaten. The wood-working tools included wooden and antler wedges, mauls of wood or hammerstones for driving the wedges, slate-bladed adzes, whetstones of various grades of fineness, paint mortars, engraving tools, and the ubiquitous crooked knife, to cite a few of the most important tools. Other belongings of a personal nature would include snuffboxes, tobacco pouches, pipes, and quid boxes. Near each man's assigned position on a bench might be seen his sinew-backed bow and arrows, spears, and other weapons. Hanging from the ceiling were the bladders of animals and the skins of birds and small animals which would play an important part in certain ceremonies.

Scattered about the settlements were excavated pits which served as storage containers. Along the lower river these pits might be lined with grass. They usually contained silver salmon, taken so late in the season that they could not be sun dried, or fish heads being made into headcheese. On the banks of the central river the pits often were lined with birchbark and not only functioned as did those on the lower river but were used also for storing dried salmon. Most processed fish, however, were placed in caches built on four raised poles, with an overhanging wooden platform on top. Above the platform was the cache itself, a rectangular wooden structure with a gabled bark- or plank-covered roof and an oval entrance at the front. Inside a cache were stored not only dried but frozen fish, herbs, and equipment such as snowshoes and nets which were not in current use. Sleds often were stored on the cache platform, where they would be out of reach of the dogs.

Pulled up above the riverbank was a variety of boats. Along the lower river each man owned a kayak, which was a driftwood frame covered with dehaired sealskins. This particular form had a large manhole amidships, a rectangular projecting stern piece, and a bow with a large hole in the wooden stem. This hole was grasped to lift the vessel out of the water or to moor it securely. It was probably an extended family as a unit which owned the open type of skin boat, or *umiak,* as it is known among many Inuit. Along the Kuskokwim it was called a *bidarra* and the kayak a *bidarka*. These skin boats were used along the central river, as was a small type of birchbark-covered canoe, built around ribs of birchwood and decked a short distance fore and aft. The only other vessel was an improvised form wider and shorter than a *bidarra*. It had a rough wooden frame covered with the skins of freshly killed large animals. This type of vessel was used to carry meat to the village from a distant hunting camp.

The ordinary winter conveyances were sleds of spruce or birchwood with built-up beds suspended on stanchions mortised and bound with babiche through lashing holes. Sleds with low flat beds were used to carry *bidarras* over the snow to camps where they would be used after the spring thaw. Smaller but similar sleds were placed over the aft section of a *bidarka,* or canoe, to be used in portaging the vessel from one lake or slough to another. Finally, snowshoes were another essential item for traveling overland at certain times of the year. Along the lower river snowshoes were needed only when traveling in timbered country where the snow was loose, for the snow on the lakes and tundra soon crusted from the action of the wind. The only time snowshoes were needed on the tundra was in the spring when the

crust could not always bear the weight of a man. Then short birch-
or spruce-framed snowshoes were worn. Along the central river, where
powdery snow was more often the norm, snowshoes were used frequently. The central river form is not known for certain, but most
likely it was longer than that of the lower river villages and had more
babiche webbing.

All of the Kuskokwim Yuit were dependent on fish as their primary source of food, and to them the salmon catch was most important. In the spring, after the winter's ice had broken up on the
main river and the high water accompanying the breakup had subsided, all the people moved from scattered camps to riverbank residences. Here they prepared their fishing equipment for the summer
to come. Along the lower river a fisherman who was in his village
just after breakup first made certain that his long-handled, small-
meshed dip net was in good repair for use during the coming run of
smelt. These small fish were dipped from the river's edge at certain
localities where they swam near the bank. Probably, too, they were
dipped into an anchored *bidarra*. In either case the smelt were taken
by the thousands, but only over a period of a few days, for the run
was of brief duration. The smelt were strung through the gills on
willow branches and hung to dry on racks placed in the sun. After
they were thoroughly dry, they were cached for winter, at which time
they would be dipped in seal oil and eaten whole. Following the smelt
run, the gill nets were readied for use. These nets were made of the
knotted inner bark of willows or of rawhide thongs and probably
were about thirty feet long and six feet deep. First large-meshed nets
were set in river eddies and tended daily from a canoe or *bidarka*.
The nets had oblong, cottonwood bark or spruce floats strung at intervals along the top, and sinkers for the bottom were made of bone,
antler, or, less often, notched stones. During the manufacture of a
net a wooden net shuttle was employed to manipulate the netting
material easily as it was being knotted; a wooden net gauge was used
to ensure a uniform mesh size. The eddy in which a man set his net
was the one he had used the year before; the right to an eddy was
lost, however, if it was not claimed each year. Since the river channel
shifted frequently, there was no real permanence for any eddy. The
first fish likely to be caught was the sheefish, a species of large whitefish. Few of these were taken, and as a result they were likely to be
boiled and eaten immediately rather than preserved for winter consumption. A fisherman was most anxious to take the first king salmon,
and after a number had been caught in set nets he took up the set
and joined together all the king salmon netting he might have. He

then placed the net in a wooden bucket or birchbark basket in his
bidarka and paddled to a straight stretch of river where the current
flowed evenly and where there were no obstructions beneath the
water. Here he threw out a large wooden float which, along the central river, was duck-shaped and attached to a line leading to the gill
net paid into the water. After the net was set, the end nearest the
bidarka was tied to the vessel, and the fisherman paddled upstream
so that the net floated at right angles to the current. When he saw a
floater on the net bob violently, he knew a fish had struck the net,
and he detached the net rope from the vessel, tied a large wooden
float to the rope, and threw it overboard. After paddling to the spot
where the fish had thrashed, he gently lifted the net from the water
and either clubbed the salmon to death or stuck a bone bodkin into
the base of its head. The fish was killed as efficiently as possible, for
if it thrashed violently a section of the net was likely to be destroyed.
The fish was put in the *bidarka* and the net straightened into an
even drifting pattern with the current. After a drift of about two
miles the net was taken in and the process repeated if the take
had been small. This technique is called drift netting and probably was the most important means of taking salmon among all
the riverine Eskimos. Not only were king salmon caught in this
manner, but with small-meshed gill nets red, dog, and silver salmon
were entangled.

When a man returned to his fish camp or village, depending on
which he preferred to fish from, he put the fish in a low wooden bin
and covered them with a mat of grass. Then his wife or daughter
processed the fish. The salmon to be eaten during the summer were
cut into chunks and boiled in water or partly dried and later boiled.
Most of the fish taken were dried for winter. The heads were cut off
first with an *uluak*; these were cooked for human or dog food, dried
and split, or buried in the ground to make headcheese. The body
cavity was split and the contents, except for the roe, kept for dog food.
The roe was mashed and eaten mixed with oil or dried and later
mixed into soups or *agutuk*, better known as Eskimo ice cream, which
consists mainly of rendered fat of any type mixed with berries, greens,
fish, or roe. When the mixture is chilled, the fat turns white. The
body of the fish being prepared for drying was split through to the
backbone and the flesh around the backbone detached as far as the
tail. With a small stick inserted into the skin to help the air circulate
around the flesh the fish was hung by the tail over a drying rack
made from poles. It was hung in the sun and covered during rainy
and damp weather with grass matting. Beneath the fish a small fire

of alder wood was sometimes built to prevent flies from laying their eggs on the fish and to smoke-cure the salmon. After the fish had dried, they were bundled together and stored in caches. Any fish caught late in the season or which for one reason or another could not be prepared for drying were placed whole in the ground. Here they decayed slowly and became "stink fish," as later whites termed them. It would seem from late nineteenth-century ethnographic reports that families did not fish intensively throughout the salmon season. They fished only until they felt that they had enough to last them through the winter. If a man took a large number of king salmon, he was desultory about fishing for other smaller species. The salmon always ascended the river to spawn in the small adjacent streams, but high water made it difficult to net them during certain years. However, starvation from a failure of the salmon run apparently did not exist.

Along the lower river, particularly when the smelt appeared, small white whales (beluga) ascended the river from the sea. Seals, too, swam into the lower river in the spring after the ice had broken up. These sea mammals were hunted from skin boats with toggle-headed harpoons or the harpoon dart. A harpoon head had an attached line and a skin bladder or sealskin float tied to the end of the line. As one of these mammals was struck repeatedly with harpoon heads, it was forced to surface frequently for air, until finally it could be dispatched with a slate-bladed lance. The meat and skin of a whale were divided according to an established system, with the man who thrust the first harpoon that became embedded in the whale receiving the greatest share. Lesser portions went to the other men whose harpoons or lances had struck, but every family in the settlement received at least a small portion of the kill. The division of a seal is not known to have been recorded, but probably the arrangement was similar to that for a whale, except that the first man to harpoon the animal received the sealskin.

Some, or perhaps even most, families did not remain at the winter village to fish for salmon. Instead they scattered to small fishing camps along the banks of the Kuskokwim or sloughs leading into the main river channel. On the central river some families remained in the winter villages but moved into temporary structures. These were round in outline, about ten feet across, and had a pole framework covered with slabs of spruce or birchbark or even bundles of grass. Inside was a fireplace, and out of a hole in the roof drifted the smoke. Along the lower river the summer fish camp dwelling was a small, winter-type house without a tunnel or anteroom. Some central river Eskimos located their fish camps away from the villages along a stretch of the river where shallow water ran over a gravel bottom adjacent to the main channel. Here weirs were built across the current, and funnel-shaped fish traps of spruce splints were set at intervals along openings in the weir, with the mouths of the traps facing downstream. In these traps were taken not only salmon but whitefish and pike. More ambitious individuals along the river set and maintained similar traps in the narrow streams leading from lakes into sloughs and rivers. With the end of the salmon fishing season the families who were away from their winter settlement moved back, taking with them their winter supply of dried fish.

The lower river families either went to their fall camps by *bidarra* before the lakes and the flowing waters froze or waited until after freeze-up and traveled by dog sled. Some time during the winter the men of the families who went to camp by dog team returned to the village for their *bidarras,* which they brought back on low-bedded sleds in order to have them there ready for the next spring. Once they were settled at camp and had collected a supply of firewood, the men prepared their fish traps and set them in small streams leading from the lakes. Their primary purpose was to take the small blackfish which left the lakes via small streams during the fall. These fish were caught in great quantities and stored frozen in woven grass bags. Later in the winter they served as food for both people and dogs. To the dogs they were served raw and frozen, but they were boiled for human consumption. The women and girls collected the last of the season's berries to supplement the supply they had gathered during berry-picking excursions in the early fall. Another fall activity of the men was to trap various species of animals. Trapping probably was relatively unimportant, but it was essential to obtain skins for clothing and bedding. Squirrels, hares, and marmot were taken with snares along their runways; mink and an occasional land otter were caught in fish traps or in smaller traps of the same type but made with heavier splints so that they could not break away. Ptarmigan snares were set in clusters around willow thickets. In areas in which beaver lived these animals were taken with nets set beneath the ice. If caribou were about, they were hunted with bows and arrows in the late fall when their skins were prime, the animals fat, and their meat at its best.

In the early fall the central river men, without their families, made extended trips up the Kuskokwim or adjacent rivers by birch-bark canoe. Their prime purpose was to take caribou and bear. They also trapped and hunted fur animals; just before the river froze they built large skin boats, using the hides of the animals they had killed for the covering. They then returned to their villages with the fall catch. The pervasiveness of this pattern is not known, and perhaps the extended fall hunting and trapping trip was a response to the fur trade and was not aboriginal.

With the onset of winter, the people were in their riverbank settlements with their food caches well stocked and hopefully prepared for the forthcoming winter. As the season wore on and grew colder, there was less and less subsistence activity. Fish traps were set through river ice in association with weirs, and set hooks baited with live blackfish were set for cod. As the ice thickened, these forms of fishing ceased. It was now the ceremonial season; one settlement hosted another for major ceremonies and held lesser ceremonies among themselves. When supplies of fish were plentiful, there were few cares to disturb the tranquillity of winter.

With the approach of spring, the villagers became restless and were eager to return once again to their camps on the tundra. Traveling by dog team before the trails became free of snow and before the sloughs and rivers were covered with melt water, families went to their traditional camps. Here, as the last snows were melting, ptarmigan were hunted and early migratory birds were snared or shot with bows and arrows. The women gathered berries, particularly highbush cranberries, which still clung to the dried bushes from the year before; the men refurbished fish traps to take blackfish, as they once again ascended the small streams to their summer habitat in the lakes. Gill nets were set in larger sloughs and streams for pike and whitefish. The surplus fish were cleaned and dried for later use. Men traveled widely by *bidarka* once there was open water; they hunted and snared muskrat, mink, and land otter or squirrels and marmot in the higher country. When they judged that their take was sufficient or when they simply wearied of the tundra camps, they returned by *bidarra* to their riverbank communities. They would do so, however, only when reasonably certain that the river ice had broken up and the flood waters had subsided.

Along the lower sector of the river, men lived with their families only at their tundra camps or at fish camps. Among the central river people summer may have been the only time of the year that nuclear families lived together in the same house. When in the village, the men and older boys lived in the *kashgee,* while the women occupied other dwellings. By piecing together various reports it would seem that most houses were occupied by a line of females. A woman raised her daughters in the house and would see her young sons move into the *kashgee.* Ideally, daughters would remain with their mothers after they had married and would raise the next generation of children in the same house. Only when the number of females overcrowded a dwelling (this by Yuit standards was rare) or when a house became uninhabitable did they move. Because the practice of female infanticide was common, the number of girls to grow up in any family was limited artificially. The surviving females lived in a lifelong intimacy with closely related women and female children, whereas males were most closely associated with others of their own sex. Under social conditions of this nature we would not expect, nor do we find, a close-knit domestic unit in Kuskowagamiut society.

In an early but brief description of the Kuskokwim Eskimos by Wrangell, which was, at least in part, drawn from observations by Vasil'ev, the activities in the village are recounted. *Kashgee* residents included all of the men except the shamans, old men, and sick persons, who are said to have occupied the houses of the women. Early in the morning, before dawn, a designated boy lit the bowl-shaped lamps in each house, and the women rose to prepare the morning meal. In the meantime, the *kashgee* residents dressed, and the shaman with his assistants went to the *kashgee* and performed a ritual which included the use of the tambourine drum. Women then took food to the males in their families. Following the meal, the women and children collected the day's supply of wood for the *kashgee* and houses. The men then went out on their subsistence activities by dog team or *bidarka,* depending on the season. After being away for the day, the men returned to the settlement, left their sleds or boats, and went directly to the men's house. It was the duty of a close female relative to unload the catch and put away the equipment of each man. Afterward the women prepared the evening meal and dried the men's clothing. It is quite apparent that village life gravitated around what happened in the *kashgee,* especially since it was here that decisions of village-wide concern were made by the men and here, too, that the ceremonial life found its focus. Furthermore, the *kashgee* was the village bathhouse, but only for males. The procedure of bathing was to build a great fire in the fire pit; after the wood was reduced to an ash bed, the men stripped off their clothing, covered the skylight with the gut window, and absorbed the intense heat, after which they washed in urine. When the bath was over, some men sat in the snow or had water from a hole in the river ice ladled over their heads.

The normal workload imposed on women included the preparation and processing of food, caring for the children, manufacturing and repairing clothing, picking berries and a few other plant products, and collecting firewood. The men were obligated to provide fish and land mammals for food and clothing, but their obligations did not extend beyond bringing the subsistence items to the settlement. This arrangement probably was not so rigid as suggested; more likely the men sometimes processed food for storage or cooked a meal and women fished or hunted. Still it would have been difficult for an unmarried adult to lead a normal life. The same applied to an orphan who was without close relatives; such an individual was dependent entirely on the kindness of other persons. In terms of specialization, the only part-time specialists were the shamans and dance leaders. A shaman lived in part on his earnings as a specialist in supernatural matters and did not hunt or fish with the same intensity as other men, but the dance leader received no material rewards for his efforts.

We deduce that among the social forms the ideal marriage pattern favored matrilocal residence and village endogamy. Considering the size of most communities, it is doubtful that this ideal was frequently realized. It seems more likely that on marrying some men left the settlements of their birth and moved into the *kashgees* of the villages of their wives. Polygyny when it did occur was likely to have been sororal, and the sororate seems to have existed. Most men maintained one wife, but successful shamans frequently had more than one. People traced their descent through both the male and female lines and were thus nonunilineal or bilateral in their kin calculations. Tracing one's descent through both father and mother to a given degree of collaterality meant that each person, except for siblings, was a member of a different bilateral kin group, or personal kindred. The system for designating cousins was of the Iroquois type, with the brother and sister terms being extended to include parallel cousins. Cross-cousins, however, were assigned a separate or "cousin" term. There was a term for mother and a separate one for mother's sister, although the latter was the same as father's sister. The first ascending generation categories were the same on the father's side as on the mother's, which resulted in a lineal system of avuncular terminology.

With villagers clustered together in a settlement for at least half of each year, we might expect diverse forms of political action, but group decisions that affected the entire community must have been relatively rare. This condition is a reflection of a subsistence orientation which was largely on an individual, not a community, level. Most likely a man supervised the hunting and fishing activities of his sons, and an older brother, in the absence of a father, was in a superordinate position in the economic life of a younger brother. It is likely, too, that it was the older men who resolved informally the routine problems of community life, such as disputes over property or hunting and fishing rights. Possibly a wider range of opinion was sought concerning differences with persons in other settlements or the formalities of arranging ceremonies. If any one individual had a prominent voice in the decision making, it probably was the shaman because of his supernatural affiliations. The nonconformity of any individual would lead first to gossip and then to mild ridicule, which was usually sufficient to bring deviant behavior into line with the community norms. If a father was annoyed with the behavior of a son, he would relate the cause of his dissatisfaction to his best friend during a sweat bath, and this person would make known the father's feelings to the son. Ridicule songs appear to have been sung as a more forceful and face-to-face means of pointing up the failings of an individual. Witchcraft was the most serious form of misbehavior of which one could be accused. If the witch lived in a distant village, it was a threat to security, but its malevolence could be counteracted by a powerful local shaman. If the witch lived in one's own settlement, this was more dangerous. Examples of witches using their powers within their own community are rare, but one recorded instance exists. In this case an old woman reportedly killed several of her own children, and the accuser was her husband. The man clubbed the woman to death, and then severed all of her joints. Afterwards her remains were burned with oil to make final her demise.

The type of occurrence most likely to rupture social harmony was the murder of an individual by an outsider. When this happened, an influential relative of the deceased assembled the men from his and adjacent communities. He entertained them, gave each man a gift, and then recounted the offense, requesting that they take blood revenge. The situation became balanced if someone in the family of the murderer were killed and there were no additional murders. Sometimes revenge flared out of hand, and a family feud erupted. This would cease only with the displacement or murder of one faction. Formalized warfare did not exist. In one feud two boys were throwing darts at targets in a *kashgee*. Each boy had a target set before him, and by accident one boy's dart struck the other boy in the eye. The father of the injured boy in a fit of rage gouged out the eyes of the boy who had thrown the dart. The males living in the *kashgee* were separated along moiety, or perhaps pseudo-moiety, lines, with each moiety occupying an opposite side of the *kashgee*. The boys had been of different moieties, and a blood bath resulted from the enraged father's revenge. The men fought their *kashgee* mates with fury until the moiety of the boy who was struck in the eye killed all their opponents. They then attacked the villages containing relatives of the men they had murdered. The rampage did not cease until the raiders were trapped and all but one, an old man, were killed. This sole survivor was mutilated and sent back to his village to carry the message of defeat. Another account of Kuskowagamiut hostilities notes that old people and children were never killed in raids; they apparently were taken captive, but male prisoners were killed.

A shaman probably was more powerful among the Yuit than elsewhere among Eskimos; in general, shamans tended to occur in particular family lines. Although a woman might become one, female shamans were not normally so powerful as the males. A young male with a predilection toward shamanism would be apprenticed to a successful shaman, and later in adult life he would practice independently. Among other things, his training necessitated acquiring supernatural aids and learning tricks, songs, and drumming. Shamanistic performances were given to diagnose, to predict, to cure by supernatural means, and to demonstrate the power of the shaman. Shamans likewise knew of cures that did not require the aid of spirit helpers, which also made them secular curers. Finally, it was the shaman who saw to it that people observed the sociocultural prohibitions. A settlement sometimes had more than one shaman, but a single individual would be considered more capable than the others. It was he to whom the villagers turned in the most critical circumstances.

When a person was taken ill and there was no obvious cause for the disability, a shaman's help was enlisted by the afflicted and his family. A shaman was paid for his services, but if a patient did not improve or died the shaman stood the chance of being accused of witchcraft, which could lead to his murder. A curing session involved the use of assistants who drummed and sang the shaman's songs while the shaman summoned his spiritual helpers, who often took the forms of animals. Once his body was host to these forces he behaved strangely, reflecting the motions and sounds of the helping spirit involved. The disease substance was then driven from the person's body by sucking or brushing it away. It happened, too, that while a shaman was possessed by a spirit he sometimes learned that a villager had broken a taboo, which had caused the illness. When the offender confessed harmony was restored to the universe. When a shaman performed during a traditional ceremony in the established round of rituals, he did so as an actor and trickster showing off his skills before an audience. His legerdemain and vanishing acts are legendary. As long as no one knew the key to his trickery the people were impressed, but it is most likely that they knew it for what it was. Shamans also interpreted present but unusual events that could give insight into the future. An eclipse of the moon was expected to usher in illness and death; it was an ominous sign when the earth quaked, and comets foretold starvation, to list a few examples of the folk beliefs. Not only the shaman but other persons, especially the old, knew of particular cures for nonsupernatural ailments. The pharmacopoeia of the people was limited in scope and significance. The castor of beaver was a pervasive cure. It is recorded, too, that the leaves of certain plants were considered effective cures for a wide range of internal complaints, that broken bones were set and splinted, and that bloodletting was practiced.

It is unlikely that a clear record of the *kashgee* ceremonial round ever will be assembled. All we have is incomplete and fragmentary information about particular ritual activities and certain generalizing statements. Common features of the *kashgee* rituals included ceremonies that spanned a four-day period, during which time the people of one or more adjacent settlements attended. The host villagers prepared for the celebration by storing large quantities of food, composing new songs, and manufacturing new dance masks, along with practicing their parts, whether in dance, song, or drumming, until they were perfected. The general supervision, at least along the lower river, was in the hands of a dance leader whose duty it was to act as host and make certain that the activities were carried out in the traditional manner. This office tended to be passed down a particular male line from father to son. The dance leader appears to have had little if any power but was respected as an authority on the rituals. The most important ceremonial event was the Great Ceremony for the Dead, which was performed every four to ten years, depending on the number of deaths and the time required to assemble the necessary assets for holding the event. On alternate years reciprocating villages held a Sending a Messenger Ceremony, which was the climax to yearly ceremonials. Others held each year were the To Call, Woman's Dance, Boy's Dance, and Bladder Festival, plus minor exchange feasts within a community. Along the central river the annual Doll Ceremony was important, but whether it was held along the lower river is not certain, although it is likely.

Observations of what is assumed to be a Boy's Dance were recorded by the Moravian missionary Weinland (see Note 1); this is one of the rare examples of a firsthand description of Kuskokwim Eskimo rituals. The representations of birds mentioned are reported in another account of a different ceremony by Wrangell, suggesting that birds may have been an important focus of supernaturalism. A small exchange ceremony of unknown name was also described by Weinland, and it probably reflects the casual tenor of many such celebrations. This was a diminutive potlatch. The term potlatch, as it is used with reference to the Indians along the north Pacific coast of North America, means a highly competitive redistribution celebration, but among Eskimos of Alaska this extreme form of rivalry did not exist, although the term has in recent years been applied to any ritualized gift giving. The Sending a Messenger Ceremony was described by another Moravian missionary for the late 1800's, and except for the trade items exchanged it probably retained the aboriginal form and meaning. The Sending a Messenger Ceremony as described in this instance was in honor of the recently deceased and included the institutionalized giving of gifts. The person or persons hosting the celebration were relatives of the deceased and had accumulated food and property in large quantities. Messengers were sent to the guest community with a mnemonic stick on which symbols were carved or appended. The announcement was made formally, and the signs on the stick were supposed to help the messengers not to confuse the details of the invitation. When the guests arrived, they were greeted ceremonially, and during the evenings of the festivities dances and songs were performed to commemorate the dead and his merits. If the deceased was not a noble individual about whom any good could be recounted, the praises of his ancestors were sung. The climax of the ceremony came a few days later when gifts were distributed to the guests in honor of the deceased, but there was no obligation to make a return gift. The Great Ceremony for the Dead was designed to free the souls of the dead so that they could rest forever in a world in the sky. It differed from the Sending a Messenger Ceremony in that anyone was welcome to attend and gifts were distributed to everyone.

Another ceremony, the Bladder Festival, was extremely important among the Bering Sea coast Eskimos. It was known to have existed along the lower Kuskokwim, and its purpose everywhere was to ensure a continuing supply of game. It was not important, however, on the lower Kuskokwim. This is not surprising in light of the dependence of the people on fish rather than game. What is surprising is that no major ceremonial involvements had developed around the taking of fish. Nonetheless, there was some sort of magical association drawn about the head of the first king salmon taken, for it could never be sold; also, dogs were never allowed to touch fresh salmon. On the central river there was a ritual for foretelling the species of salmon that would arrive during the spring fishing season. Since salmon were the major source of food, it is genuinely surprising that they did not become a major ceremonial focus of attention.

Along the central river the Doll Ceremony involved retrieving from their hiding places three small human figures of wood dressed in skin clothing. When they were unwrapped from their container, the clothing was inspected for a piece of animal hair, fur, or fish scales which would indicate the species that would be taken in abundance during the forthcoming year. In this area, too, there apparently existed more complex staging effects than on the lower river. These included curtains before a stage, dramatic entrances of the performers, and the extensive use of stuffed birds, fish, or animals which moved across the stage in the context of certain songs. Evidently, Yuit ceremonial life was quite complex along the Kuskokwim, and, although the details of the complexity have not been recorded, there is the suggestion that the rather rich environment afforded opportunities for more elaborate group ceremonies than were possible among most Eskimos.

From the writings of Wrangell we learn that a year was divided into eleven months which took their names from the conditions of animals, fish, or birds at particular times of the year or from climatic conditions. The months corresponded to the current Western calendar except that December and January apparently were combined. Furthermore, the equinox could be predicted, and certain constellations and planets were known and named.

The prospects of survival were not equal for all infants born into a Kuskokwim Eskimo household. The pregnant woman gave birth at home and was aided by her mother or another female relative. Delivery was made from a squatting position, and downward pressure was applied to a woman's abdomen if the process was delayed. The birth of a female offspring was not a particularly joyous occasion, except for the woman who desired a daughter. If there were daughters already in the family, or if it was a lean time of the year, female infanticide was likely to be practiced. Infanticide was not restricted to the newborn but might take place at any time during the next two or three years. The attitude was that since one portion of the soul of any deceased individual returned to the body of the next one born, there was no real destruction of life, only of individuals. The name of a baby became that of the person who had died most recently in the local area, and the relatives of the deceased behaved toward the namesake as they had toward the deceased. For obvious reasons, names were not associated with a particular sex, and they were changed if their bearer was plagued with misfortune. Infants and small children growing up in a household dominated by older females must have received almost constant attention, judging from more recent observations on the treatment of offspring. They were pampered and catered to; this treatment was based on supernatural beliefs as much as, or more than, natural affection. The reason for this behavior was that since an infant had the soul of a recently deceased individual he mirrored the feelings of the deceased and was appeased in order not to offend the watching spirits. This association decreased in importance as the individual grew older and acquired a distinctive personality of his own.

As a girl grew up, she was integrated rapidly into the household routine of the older females. Her toys were small facsimiles of the artifacts used by her mother, and by the time she was eight or ten years old she was a reasonably capable housekeeper. One set of household roles of fascinating dimensions was the relationship inferred to have existed between a grandmother and her granddaughter. The granddaughter's activities and world view seem to have been molded largely by this older woman who occupied the rear bench in a large household. The reason for considering the grandmother so important stems from a study of stories told by contemporary Eskimo girls. These stories, or storyknife tales as they are known, were illustrated with stylized figures of people, houses, and other physical forms. The illustrations were made on a moist mud or snow surface with an oblong-bladed implement known as a storyknife. It has been deduced that grandmothers originally made up the stories and illustrated them for their granddaughters. There is no evidence whatever of either men or boys telling or listening to storyknife stories. The tales of a grandmother served to entertain and to instruct. The main characters most frequently were a grandmother and her granddaughter; the males in the plots played a secondary role. Some of the significant ideas repeatedly occurring in the stories are that one should offer food to people when they come to visit, that nonrational behavior is to be expected from males, and that if a granddaughter disobeys her grandmother it is not unlikely that the grandmother will suffer for the girl's transgressions.

By the time boys were ten years old they had left their natal home and moved into the *kashgee*. Here they came under the supervision of the older males in their families and under the indirect control of all the older men who were *kashgee* residents. The boys were no longer regarded as children; more and more was expected of them, even though their activities were supervised casually. The steps toward adulthood were achieved by an adolescent as he increased his hunting skills. The birds and small animals killed by each boy were skinned and then stuffed by his mother and hung from strings in the *kashgee*. In the fall or early winter ceremonial recognition was given to the boys' accomplishments. The boys were feasted, and they danced in places of honor. At the completion of the rituals the skins were secreted away to a location in which they would not be stepped on. After a male had killed one of each species of animal, he was considered to be marriageable. For a girl, ceremonial recognition was given when she picked the first of each species of berries, but a more important event was the ceremonial acknowledgment of her menarche. At this time she probably was restricted to one corner of the dwelling, she wore old clothing, and she observed food as well as other taboos. Possibly it was after this time that an adolescent girl had sexual intercourse with a shaman. This was necessary for a maiden before she could be admitted to *kashgee* ceremonies.

A female was nubile at around fourteen years old, but the male was likely to be at least four years older and perhaps as much as twenty years her senior. The marriage itself was without ceremony and was arranged by the families of the couple involved or by an older man and the girl's family. Thereafter the man slept with the girl openly, and she was responsible for the preparation of his meals as well as caring for his clothing and processing the subsistence items he obtained. In the event either of the couple became dissatisfied with the other they ceased cooperating and cohabiting. A marriage might also be terminated with a wrestling match. Any man was free to challenge any other man to wrestle, and the man thrown to the ground was obligated to give up his wife. Usually it was only young women without children for whom they wrestled. No stigma was attached to divorce, and most individuals had at least two partners during their lifetimes. It is true that marriages tended to stabilize after the woman bore a child, particularly if it were a male.

As adults, the routine of daily living came to focus on the complementary activities of a man and his wife. The labors of a wife and husband formed a subsistence unit, and, although marriages may have been brittle, an adult did not willfully remain unmarried for long. In the early years of marriage the partners probably remained distant and cool toward one another and normally would not converse as Americans conceive of conversation. As time went on they were more likely to become outgoing when together, but still some husbands and wives found very little about which to talk. The personality of an adult Eskimo manifested a phlegmatic realism, in which the even-tempered person who was jovial was the ideal. Verbal aggression or physical dominance was abhorred, and to be taciturn or caustic was symptomatic of the sick or diseased. As people aged, they were not killed but often came to be respected for their knowledge. Some old men were great storytellers and passed the traditions of their fathers on to the men and boys of the next generation. Old women held forth from the back benches of their dwellings with advice and criticism, both of which were offered freely.

A dead or even an expiring person's body was flexed with the knees bound up to the chest. The women wailed, and the men killed the dogs of the deceased. His clothing and other property save those items that were kept as mementos or were deposited on the grave were probably destroyed. The body was removed through a hole made in the wall of the *kashgee* or dwelling so that the spirit of the deceased could not find its way back into the structure after the opening was closed. The body was placed in a small plank coffin with mortised corners, and it was raised above the ground on four short poles. The cemetery was usually located on an adjacent hill or a rise near the settlement. Over the coffin were placed sheets of birchbark, and above this covering were deposited those possessions that had not been destroyed. At the head of the coffin might be placed a board set between two poles, and on it were pegged wooden carvings of human faces. Sometimes, too, the coffins of men were painted with animal representations of the species taken by the man during his lifetime. Were a person to die and be buried away from the settlement, poles decorated with feathers would be erected and animal figures of wood attached. At Crow Village there existed a unique form of memorial pole. At the top of it was the carving of a bird, and beneath was the figure of a young girl in partial relief. This memorial was erected by the leading man in the community in memory of a favored daughter.

Between the time of the first direct historical contact with the Russians in 1829 or 1830 and Russian withdrawal in 1866, two institutions came to have a major influence on the lives of the Kuskokwim Eskimos. These were the Russian-American Company and the Russian Orthodox Greek Catholic Church. By far the most immediately important was the trading concern, but the Orthodox Church influence was the more lasting. The primary impetus for Russian explorations and settlement was commercial. The Russians were searching for new areas to draw into the fur trade, and with southward expansion limited by the 1820's they turned to the region north of the Alaska Peninsula. Of the earliest traders we know comparatively little. The two outstanding traders were Kolmakov and Ivan Lukin, both of whom came from mixed racial backgrounds. Kolmakov was of aboriginal Alaskan and Russian ancestry; Lukin was mixed Spanish and Russian, born at Fort Ross, California. Both men traveled widely, exploring the Kuskokwim drainage and adjacent areas. From the beginning the pelts the Russians most desired were beaver, and thus the lower Kuskokwim held little attraction. In 1853, however, white fox pelts were traded into Kolmakov Redoubt, which suggests that it was about this time that the Russians opened their lower Kuskokwim River trading post at Mumtrekhlagamiut Station. The Russians stimulated the existing trapping pattern, and it is possible that the long trapping excursions of the central river men began because of the Russians. One serious drawback to trading was the general inaccessibility of the Kuskokwim. From 1832 to 1844 its supplies came from Alexandrov via the Nushagak and Holitna rivers, after a long sled or boat trip. Later, supply lines were developed to the north which cut across to the Yukon River and on to St. Michael, but this again meant portages and small loads. As a result, the trade items available were usually small, portable, and not readily destructible. Thus items such as beads, knives, strike-a-lights, metal pots, needles, copper ornaments, and similar goods were traded. The most important nondurable goods were items of European clothing and tea.

The primary trading center, Kolmakov Redoubt, may be imaginatively regarded as a bastion in the north, but it was not. It consisted of a single blockhouse, a cabin in which persons coming to trade could stay, the store and residence for the administrator, a cabin for the employees, a bathhouse, and outbuildings. At one time, too, there was apparently a stockade surrounding the settlement. From a few scattered sources it seems that after the redoubt began to function in 1841 the physical plant deteriorated slowly so that by the early 1860's it was in a sad state of disrepair. The largest known population for the redoubt at any one time was in 1855 when eighty-eight persons resided there. The administrator usually seems to have been a person of mixed Russian and native American ancestry who identified with the people and married an Eskimo woman. The administrators appointed "chiefs" for the various villages to formalize trading relations, and the earliest traders, Kolmakov and Lukin, were granted the authority to baptize heathens. The overall impression is that the Russians adapted to Eskimo ways and made very few radical changes in the traditional patterns. Even the trading complex was not a radical innovation, for the

Eskimos had obtained Russian goods before the arrival of the Russians on the Kuskokwim. Trade items from the Russians were bartered just as there had been barter with other Eskimos and Indians.

The first Orthodox missionary to consider the spiritual welfare of the aboriginal peoples north of the Alaska Peninsula was the illustrious Father Veniaminov, who was later to become the leader of the Russian Orthodox Church. In 1829 he baptized individuals at Nushagak, and in 1832 he returned there and held church services for seventy persons. It was Veniaminov who gave Kolmakov the authority to baptize the heathen. The first Orthodox priest to visit the Kuskokwim was A. Petelin who traveled there from the Nushagak station in the 1840's, but we have no knowledge of an Orthodox missionary stationed along the river until the arrival of Hieromonk Illarion in 1861. He visited Kolmakov Redoubt intermittently until his departure from the area in 1866. It would seem that by the end of the Russian era many if not most of the Kuskokwim Eskimos along the central river considered themselves to be Christians. They were baptized and were given Russian names, but the core of Christian dogma was certainly poorly understood. What is important about the effects of the early Orthodox missionaries is that they did convey to the Eskimos the essential elements of Christianity, and the church as an institution became an established part of their lives.

Yet another complex of Russian origin must be mentioned briefly, and this is the Russian steam bath. A bathhouse was constructed by Lukin at the Kwigiumpainukamiut post, and another was built later at Kolmakov Redoubt. The Eskimos trading into these posts were familiar already with bathing in intense heat, but the Russian bath was somewhat different from the aboriginal type. It was taken in a small structure and included the use of stones which were heated above a stove or in an open fire. Water was poured over the stones to create hot vapor, while the bathers sat back and enjoyed the heat. Initial Eskimo reaction probably was unfavorable, but as time passed the Russian type of bath was to assume more importance.

From the excavation of the five houses and the kitchen midden debris at Crow Village, a central river settlement visited by Zagoskin in 1843 and 1844, we would expect tangible evidence of Russian influence. In spite of the fact that this community was occupied throughout all or at least most of the Russian era and that nearly 1600 artifacts were recovered, there were no remains which were identified positively as of Russian origin. A few artifacts such as a copper bracelet and certain bead types are most likely of Russian derivation, but this is all that may be said regarding a span of more than twenty years of direct contact. It is possible that if we had more exact information about the inventories of trade goods it might be possible to identify a few more items as of Russian origin. The logical conclusion is that Russian material culture did not make a significant impact on the Crow Village Eskimos, despite the fact that the settlement was only thirty-five miles downstream from Kolmakov Redoubt.

Crow Village continued to be occupied during the American period and was most likely abandoned between 1906 and 1912. Material items left at the site which date from the outfits of American traders include a woman's high-laced shoe, a man's square-toed shoe, a man's wide-brimmed felt hat, a kerchief, metal pendant, an assortment of metal containers, metal axes, a strike-a-light, cartridge cases and musket balls, and American-made pottery. Another important category of artifacts includes items that reflect traditional craft skills applied to new mediums. For example, mending holes were drilled in a broken sherd of imported pottery so that sinew could be laced through the holes to bind the break; the same technique had been employed in aboriginal times when a vessel of local manufacture cracked. These Eskimos also attempted to make *uluak* blades by recutting tin-can metal into blade form. However, the softness of the metal must have produced a blade of very limited utility, and slate *uluak* blades continued to be manufactured and used. The people folded sheets of tin-can metal to make small metal containers, just as they folded birchbark to make vessels. One salmon harpoon dart head had been cut from metal, although the traditional outline of the antler type was retained. These and other items reflect a flexibility in dealing with new material media. At the same time, few of the traditional Eskimo artifact forms were remade into secondarily derived forms, a situation quite contrary to the pattern found on the adjacent Bering Sea coast.

For nearly twenty years following the purchase of Alaska by the United States the only interest in the Kuskokwim was of a commercial nature. Hutchinson, Kohl & Company of San Francisco bought all the assets of the Russian-American Company, which had held a monopoly on the Alaskan trade since 1799. The Hutchinson, Kohl & Company was in turn bought by the Alaska Commercial Company in 1868 and began to function independently two years later. Kolmakov Redoubt continued as a trading center, but the main post was located at Mumtrekhlagamiut Station near the mouth of the river. Supplies were brought to this station and others farther up the river from a transfer point along the south shore of the estuary. The station at Ogavik appears to have been abandoned, but the one at Vinasale continued. For a brief period, beginning in 1877, the Western Fur and

Trading Company of San Francisco competed for the Kuskokwim trade, but its station at Kwigiumpainukamiut was abandoned in 1883. The most important observation to be made about Russian and early American trading activities along the Kuskokwim is that neither was a major commercial enterprise. The stores were not a great source of profit, and consequently their inventories were quite limited. From the Russian to the American period there was no abrupt change in policy; in fact, two of the three traders during the early American period were Russian or of Russian-Eskimo extraction.

Then, in 1883, a series of events occurred in Bethlehem, Pennsylvania, which were to have a major influence on the Kuskowagamiut. During this year the Presbyterian missionary and Federal agent for education in Alaska, Sheldon Jackson, spoke to an audience of Moravians at the Moravian College and Theological Seminary in Bethlehem. He convinced the officials of the church that they should take an active interest in the Eskimos of Alaska. Inasmuch as the Moravians had long maintained missions to Eskimos in Greenland and Labrador, it is not surprising that they responded favorably to this request. In 1884 an experienced Moravian missionary from Canada, Henry Hartmann, accompanied by a seminary student, William H. Weinland, set off for Alaska to find a site where a mission could be located. They traveled on an Alaska Commercial Company vessel as far as Nushagak and found this area to be clearly the territory of the Russian Orthodox Church. The Moravians went on to the Kuskokwim, for the Orthodox priest at Nushagak had led them to believe that the Kuskokwim Eskimos were heathens. They traveled by *bidarka* up the Kuskokwim slightly beyond Kolmakov, looking for an ideal location. They concluded that the small, lower river community of Mumtrekhlagamiut Station (modern Bethel) was best suited to their purpose. The following year Weinland graduated from the seminary, and he, along with another graduate, John H. Kilbuck, and their brides, set off for the Kuskokwim. They were accompanied by a lay minister, Hans Torgersen, who was also a skilled carpenter.

The establishment of the mission center, which came to be known as Bethel, was delayed because of the drowning of Torgersen before the mission buildings could be constructed. With the aid of the Eskimos, the missionaries were able to construct a small dwelling, and when winter arrived they were reasonably well prepared. Weinland stayed at the station for two years with his family and then left for the United States, where he was to spend most of the remainder of his life as a missionary among the Indians of southern California. Kilbuck remained at Bethel until he left the service of the Church in 1898. In

1921 he again became a missionary and went to Akiak, where he died the next year. There has been an unbroken line of missionaries at Bethel since the founding of the mission, and although some stayed for very brief periods others devoted the greater part of their lives to working with the Eskimos. The Moravians established a substation at the old Russian trading post of Ogavik in 1892, but it probably was closed in 1907 because of the virtual depopulation of the village. They successfully founded an orphanage on lower Kwethluk River in 1925, and it, along with the Bethel mission, has endured down to the present time.

The feverish search for gold in northwestern North America around the turn of the twentieth century profoundly changed the history of many areas of Alaska, but this was not the case along the Kuskokwim. Men searched for Kuskokwim gold during the Russian period, and a small number of Americans prospected in the 1880's. It was not, however, until 1907 that a significant deposit was discovered along the upper Tuluksak River. This operation has been productive through the years, but it has not been a major influence on the local economy. Likewise, the Russians seem to have been aware of the cinnabar deposits near Kolmakov but never exploited them successfully. Farther up the river, near the community of Sleetmiut, mercury has been mined intermittently since 1910. The major effect of American mining was to introduce the Eskimos to whites who were neither missionaries nor traders. The Alaskan aborigines came to have a better perspective into the variety of behaviors of Westerners. One significant material innovation introduced by the miners was the fish wheel. This device is a log raft with a large opening at the center over which is mounted a horizontal axle hung with large baskets and paddles. The river current propels the paddles and baskets which move in the direction of the current. Fish swimming upstream within reach of the baskets are lifted from the water by them. They then slide down a chute into a box at the side of the raft. The fish wheel is an extremely clever method of taking fish, for it does not require constant tending. However, it can be used successfully only under certain circumstances. The water must be opaque and must flow rather fast, and the fish must swim relatively close to the shore. This means that only in regions above tidewater would this device be practical. The fish wheel was brought to Alaska around the turn of the century after it had been employed in the northwestern United States. It was known earlier, however, in the eastern United States.

Through Moravian efforts a small number of reindeer were brought to the lower Kuskokwim in 1901. The introduction of reindeer herding among Alaskan Eskimos in 1892 had been another of Sheldon Jackson's accomplishments. The Kuskokwim herds increased until in the 1930's there were about 40,000 head being grazed along the river system. Then in the early 1940's the herds decreased rapidly so that by the end of the decade they were no longer in existence. Thus the early hope of creating a new basis for the economy was a failure. As time passed, the herds owned by the Moravian mission became an economic liability, and it was the rare Eskimo who owned a profitable herd. The deer came to be concentrated in the hands of whites and Lapps who had been brought to Alaska originally to teach herding to the Eskimos. Finally, it was vacillating Federal policies that wrote finis to the reindeer industry.

As time passed, Bethel emerged as the most important urban area on the Kuskokwim. One of the most significant factors in its early growth was the discovery in 1908 that a deep channel reached from the estuary to Bethel. Before this time all imported goods had been transferred from large ships to small riverboats. The channel was adequately charted in 1914, and an oceangoing vessel anchored at Bethel in the following year. Shortly after the turn of the century, too, there was an increase in fur prices which encouraged independent traders to open posts. The Moravian Church also opened trading establishments, using the missionaries as traders in order to offset the mounting cost of its Alaskan missions.

In terms of education and health it is again Bethel that led the field. The first formal school opened at Kolmakov Redoubt during 1861–1862 under Hieromonk Illarion, but it functioned only briefly. It was not until 1886, when the Moravians opened a mission school at Bethel, that the Eskimo children first became formally exposed to American education. This school received Federal aid until 1913, when the U.S. Bureau of Education opened another. In 1923 a territorial school was built for white children. The first doctor, a medical missionary for the Moravian Church, practiced at Bethel from 1896 to 1905. Then, in 1918, a small hospital was built at Akiak, but in 1937 another was constructed at Bethel and the earlier one was abandoned. Since that time the hospital at Bethel has served the entire Kuskokwim River and adjacent areas.

Before turning to more recent happenings among the Kuskowaga-miut, two major changes with long-range effects should be discussed briefly. The first was brought about by a severe epidemic which took place in 1900–1901. Before that time there had been epidemics along the river, for example, when smallpox struck the area in 1838–1839, but this epidemic and others seem to have claimed relatively few lives. The next major outbreak of disease was in 1900, when influenza accompanied by whooping cough, measles, and pneumonia devastated the riverine population. One estimate, made by a doctor who was there at the time, is that half the population, including all of the babies, perished. Some villages were deserted completely, and there is every reason to believe that the people were demoralized. The major impact was that continuity with the past was interrupted or perhaps even broken in most settlements. The cultural and social effects must have been great, particularly since this was the period in which Anglo-Americans were penetrating the area during the gold rushes. The Eskimos seem to have reacted by giving up many of their old ways and rapidly adopting American customs.

The second change, which probably was accelerated by the 1900–1901 epidemic, was for the Eskimo population to push farther and farther up the Kuskokwim. The country they came to occupy formerly belonged to the Ingalik Indians, but their number seems to have been relatively small and the epidemic was likely to have hit them harder than the Eskimos. By Zagoskin's time, in 1843–1844, the Eskimos were already as far inland as Kolmakov Redoubt, for it was across the river from here that they shared a village with the Ingalik. The traditional hostility between most Indians and Eskimos cannot be said to have existed along the central river. By 1960 the Eskimos had come to occupy the banks of the main river as far inland as just above the Stony River junction, nearly two hundred and fifty miles from the sea and nearly eighty miles above Kolmakov Redoubt. A number of genealogies among the people in this area indicate that the surviving Ingalik married Eskimos and became acculturated to Eskimo ways. Thus we see the riverine adaptation of the Eskimo continuing to be highly successful and the people aggressive in their movement into new country.

Shifting the descriptive emphasis to one particular village makes it possible to see the direction in which Kuskokwim Eskimo culture is currently moving on the community level. For a few days short of a year in 1955–1956 and for two weeks in 1960 the author lived at Napaskiak and gathered anthropological information. The resulting community study offers a broad view of life in one modern settlement but fails to provide depth in many topical areas. Also, Napaskiak can be considered as representative of modern Kuskowagamiut culture only tentatively, for we know very little of the way of life in the other riverine communities.

The oldest people recount that the village has been occupied for many generations. At the same time, there are traditions among residents who were born in the community that their ancestors once lived at a settlement about a mile upstream and then moved about two miles downstream before establishing the present village. The upstream site has washed into a slough, but the lower site, Eekchuk, still remains. An archaeological sampling unearthed no trade goods, and the remains are tentatively assumed to date from the early 1800's or possibly before that time. It is only with these three settlements that the Napaskiak people associate themselves. They have no traditions of their movement into the area at an earlier time. The modern village stretches along the southeastern bank of the river at the lower end of a slough. The twenty-seven frame and seven log houses at Napaskiak are occupied by one hundred forty-one persons. The most imposing structures are the Bureau of Indian Affairs school with attached teacher's residence and the Russian Orthodox Church; these buildings are better maintained than any others. Across the river at Oscarville live forty-two persons in twelve log, frame, or sod houses. Here also the store and trader's residence are located. The settlements of Oscarville and Napaskiak are dealt with together as a community, for they use the same school, store, and church and maintain close social ties. Scattered around the community is an assortment of drying racks and smokehouses for fish, caches, steam baths, and privies.

Historically we know that Vasil'ev must have passed the community on his downriver return to the Nushagak station, but the earliest reference to Napaskiak discovered so far is on a map dating from 1867. Again, Napaskiak is recorded in the Federal Census of 1880 and in the writings of the Moravian missionaries Weinland and Kilbuck who visited there repeatedly in the 1880's. Napaskiak has always represented a failure in the Moravian mission program, for the settlement is only about seven miles downstream from Bethel, yet few of its residents ever became Moravian converts. As early as 1886 an effort was made to found a mission school, and Eskimo lay preachers for the Moravian Church wintered there in 1897–1898, but made little progress with the people. Today virtually all residents are members of the Russian Orthodox faith. The small settlement of Oscarville began about 1912 as the home of Oscar Samuelson, who maintained a trading post until his death in 1953. Over the years a few families have elected to live near the store, which has continued to function under the management of the founder's daughter and her husband. For a very brief span in the mid-1950's, a store served the inhabitants at Napaskiak, but it soon failed. The people at Oscarville attend the Napaskiak church, which was constructed in 1931, and all the children go to school in Napaskiak. The school was opened in 1939 and has held classes continuously except for a brief period during World War II.

The most intensive contacts, integrating the community with the rest of the lower Kuskokwim region, exist with the urban settlement of Bethel. The five large stores, the U. S. Public Health Service hospital, two pool halls, four restaurants, and two theaters are among the greatest attractions in Bethel for the villagers. It is here, too, that they meet friends and relatives from other settlements, and it is in Bethel at the Alaska Communications System telegraph office that intoxicants may be ordered to be brought in by air from Anchorage. Thus Bethel is the center of diverse forms of socializing. Less intensive forms of contact with adjacent villages are largely social or religious in nature. A family travels to visit relatives, attend a funeral, or arrange church business. A man hunting or fishing in the vicinity may stop to visit a friend or relative. Still, the number of such visits tends to be few, even for gregarious persons with many friends, and this leads to the conclusion that the people most often socialize at home in Napaskiak and Oscarville. The only other trips are taken by men down the Kuskokwim in the spring to hunt seals and upriver in the fall to hunt moose. A few men have worked at distant urban centers in Alaska, but this practice is not common. Many of the men, however, are members of the local U. S. National Guard unit and attend an encampment near Anchorage each spring. The only other contact with the outside world is through hospitalization at Anchorage, Seward, or in the state of Washington.

Not all exotic contacts necessitate leaving the community, for one may listen to the radios which are found in most houses and learn what is happening beyond the local area. One program broadcast from Fairbanks and called "Tundra Topics" is particularly popular, for it deals mainly with news of isolated settlements. Then, too, there are the people who come to the village from urban areas in connection with some form of governmental work. There is first of all the teacher employed by the Bureau of Indian Affairs, the only outsider to reside in the community. The Bureau's supervisors and maintenance men visit occasionally, as do the U. S. Public Health Service field nurses and those working with the special program for the control of tuberculosis. Scientists are other rather frequent callers; their work usually has to do with some aspect of public health. An occasional U. S. National Guard officer or enlisted man from the Bethel head-quarters visits on official business, and the same applies to the U. S. Deputy Marshal from Bethel; sometimes there is even a stray tourist seen in the village.

All of the clothing worn today by the men is purchased ready-made from a store or mail-order house. An exceptional man, particularly one who is old, may wear sealskin *mukluks,* but these boots are passing out of style rapidly. Some men wear long cotton underwear in summer and winter; others wear T-shirts and jockey shorts in summer. Trousers are woolen or cotton, depending on the season, but wool or cotton flannel shirts are worn throughout the year. Footwear includes light cotton or wool socks, shoepacs or rubber boots, and leather shoes for use around the village in summer. The most popular form of outer winter garment is a surplus U. S. Army parka, but in fashion among some of the younger men are rather tight-fitting, lightweight cloth jackets. Conservative women, young and old, wear knee-length cotton bloomers and cotton petticoats, both of which are usually handmade. More cosmopolitan older girls and women wear nylon panties and brassieres beneath ready-made slips. Women usually prefer cotton dresses of the housedress style, but some may wear knit sweaters and slacks. Older women wear *mukluks,* but most of the younger ones wear shoes or short rubber boots. Many women, especially the middle-aged and older, still have squirrel-skin parkas which often are adorned elaborately with calfskin trimmings, but parkas are passing out of fashion and are being replaced by ready-made jackets. In summer, particularly when cleaning fish, a woman wears a hooded cloth parka over her dress. A male child has the same general type of clothing as his father but is more likely to wear *mukluks,* and a girl's garments are similar to those of the more conservative women.

In this community of one hundred eighty-two individuals there are forty separate physical households, and there is a tendency for closely related families to live in adjacent structures. In twenty-two of these homes live members of nuclear families, and in seven others one person lives alone. In the remaining houses the residents are related to one another by an extension of nuclear family ties. The larger families usually have houses with two or three rooms, but the smaller households consist of a single room. If there is more than one room, the second room is used primarily for sleeping and storage. It is the main room that contains the stove and in which people eat, and this room is the most lived in. All of the houses have some sort of anteroom or storage shed appended to them. The anteroom may often seem to contain a jumble of assorted items. A gasoline washing machine is often found along with a gasoline cookstove, food brought from a cache but not yet consumed, winter parkas, a chamber pot, and an assortment of axes and other woodworking tools. All of these items rest on the floor or are arranged on wooden shelves. An outside door leads into the unheated storage room, and usually at right angles to it is another door into the house. Irrespective of the external covering of the dwelling, whether it is log, plank, or sod, the inside is usually rectangular and has at least one curtained window on each side. The floor is of planks, and the walls and ceiling are usually covered with painted wallboard. The furnishings include a cast-iron woodburning stove with a drying rack above it. A teakettle rests on top of the stove, and perhaps a pair of sadirons are off to one side. A homemade wooden cupboard contains the dishes, pots, and pans, and on top of an adjacent washstand is an enameled basin partially filled with soapy water. Above the stand is a small mirror, and off to one side on the floor a five-gallon gasoline can with its top cut out contains waste water. A wooden table, frequently with an oilcloth cover, is placed along one wall, and around the table are either locally made or imported wooden chairs or boxes for seats. On the table are knives, forks, and spoons in one or more drinking glasses, along with salt and pepper shakers and a bowl of sugar. Overhead hangs a gasoline lantern which supplies the only light in most households; two families have their own gasoline-powered generator to supply their houses and those of near relatives with electricity. The largest items in a room are the metal-framed beds with mattresses, blankets, and preferably chenille bedspreads. Beneath a bed are cardboard boxes filled with clothing, cloth, and sections of pelts. Each house also contains trunks or suitcases piled somewhere in the room and filled with clothing not currently in use. Next to the bed of the husband and wife is usually a small, shelved nightstand. On the shelves are magazines, mail-order catalogs, letters, and an assortment of smaller possessions. On top of the stand is a battery-powered radio which is played frequently. On the walls there may be framed pictures of family members, and there is always an Orthodox Church calendar for the current year surrounded by prints of icons. A container of holy water is hung by a cord from a nail. It is clear from this description that an inventory of household items includes nothing aboriginal.

In most dwellings the only material item of aboriginal derivation is likely to be an *uluak* with a blade cut from an old wood saw blade and mounted on an ivory or antler handle.

A diligent search would uncover few material culture traits anywhere in the village that would link these people with the past. The most obvious exceptions are the continuities in the *bidarka* and canoe forms, but both now have canvas covers. The large plank boat made of spruce and powered with an outboard motor has replaced the *bidarra*. The cache structures retain their form of old, as do the dip and gill nets, but nets are now made of cotton, linen, or nylon twine. The weapons include rifles and shotguns. Only a few boys use bows and arrows, and even they prefer slingshots or air rifles. Most of the equipment necessary to subsistence welfare is purchased ready-made from the stores. The few items of local manufacture, such as plank boats, sleds, or fish traps, are usually constructed of imported materials.

The food habits of the people reflect greater continuity with the past than does the material inventory. This is largely because salmon continues to be the most important everyday food in virtually all of the households. The aboriginal methods for processing salmon continue; that is, drying, smoking, or burying them. There is the possible addition of the smokehouse, which may not be aboriginal along the lower river. The principal method of cooking salmon is still by boiling, and dried salmon continues to be stripped from the skin in pieces and dipped in seal oil before eating. The people have come to consider, however, that a meal of salmon alone is one of poverty. They now eat unleavened bread for breakfast with coffee or tea; coffee is preferred, but tea is substituted if the family's resources are low. The Russians introduced the people to the use of tea, which was most likely traded to them in brick form. Bread, too, was probably a Russian innovation. From an analysis of the tin-can types from Crow Village it appears that the most popular imported foods at the turn of the century were fruit, meat, and fish, as well as syrup, salt, lard, and baking powder, with flour inferred. Today every family regards sugar, flour, salt, canned milk, tea, coffee, tobacco, and cooking oils as necessities. They also buy canned meats and fish, crackers, candy, and canned fruits, depending on their resources.

For any family to thrive, the head of the unit must have varying skills. This diversity must compensate for factors over which the individual has little or no control. Each man must be a fisherman for salmon, and, to vary the diet, fish traps, nets, or hooks must be set for other species. A man must be a good trapper to obtain pelts which can be traded at a store for imported foods and manufactured goods. A man should work for wages whenever possible, again to buy items from the stores. Then, too, he should be a carpenter and hunter. If he has this adaptability, it is possible to compensate for a poor trapping, fishing, or laboring season by giving increased emphasis to some other activity. Versatility is thus essential if his dependents are to prosper. He must retain this flexibility, for it is almost impossible to fall back on the gains of a previous year. As a result any deficiency in a man's efforts resulting from bad luck, sickness, or injury leads to a rapid decline in the family's living standard.

When the Kuskokwim freezes over in late October or the beginning of November, the surrounding environment cannot be exploited successfully for nearly two weeks. The thin river ice makes it impossible to travel over water, and since water virtually surrounds the village, everyone must stay near home. When the ice will bear a man's weight, it is usually the boys who first skate to the opposite side of the river or on up to Bethel. As the ice thickens, and will carry the weight of a loaded dog sled and team, trips are made to Bethel for medical care at the hospital, to make purchases at the stores, or perhaps to pick up intoxicants at an airline office.

Before the sloughs and lakes freeze, some men travel by plank boat and outboard motor to their tundra camps. Here from one to three nuclear family heads live in a single camp and range from it in different directions to trap later in the year. The principal activities before the freeze-up are to haul firewood and shoot migratory birds as the last of them begin to fly southward. After the small streams leading from lakes freeze over, the men at camp set traps for blackfish. They take these fish by the thousands and freeze them in burlap sacks for dog food later in the winter. When it is safe to travel by dog team, they return to the village with meat and fish for their families. The men who do not go to their fall trapping camp before the freeze-up, and this includes the majority, will set blackfish traps within about half a day's journey from the village by dog sled. It is important to note that fall trapping camps are no longer frequented by the entire family, but only by older boys and the men. The people are torn in two directions. A man must trap to obtain furs with which to purchase manufactured goods, but he despairs at remaining at the tundra camp without his family. The women and children stay behind when there are children who must attend school, and furthermore the women have come to consider the conditions at fall camp as primitive and are reluctant to live there even temporarily.

With the approach of winter men fish for cod through the ice in front of the village, using set hooks baited with live blackfish. Each man is likely to have nine hooks on three different lines. He catches about three fish a day; these are boiled and eaten soon after being caught. Gill nets may also be set beneath the ice, and the catch from them is usually good, although it requires so much labor to tend these nets that most men are unwilling to make the effort. Late fall is the time when men and boys bring in large loads of green alders for firewood; these small trees are cut from an adjacent island stand and are carried by dog sled to the village, where the wood is chopped and stacked. Men who are concerned about keeping their homes warm for their families when they are away trapping have large woodpiles; others lay in no wood supply at all.

With the beginning of the mink trapping season in November, the men travel by dog team to their tundra camps if they are not already established there. Most of the camps are about four hours' traveling time from the village, and a particular trapping area may have been in one patrilineal line for a number of generations. However, there is no reason to regard family trapping areas as an aboriginal development. As fur animals become scarce in one area, a man will move his camp to an unoccupied expanse of tundra or trap out of the camp of a relative. One to two dozen steel traps are set out for mink, and these are checked every few days. While checking a line of traps, a .22 caliber rifle is carried on the sled for shooting ptarmigan, which are likely to be the only edible creatures about at this season of the year. A good correlation exists between the distance a man travels to his camp and the number of mink he is likely to take. When he goes a long distance, he probably will not return frequently to the village and is more likely to spend his time setting and checking his traps. In 1956 most mink pelts brought $20 to $25 from the local traders, and a mean catch totaled $250 to $375 for the season, which extends into January. Each man, before he begins trapping in the late fall, obtains credit for supplies against his potential catch. The amount of credit depends on the trader's evaluation of him as a trapper and a credit risk, but about $100 worth of goods would be a maximum. Then, too, the man's family will most likely charge items against his account when he is away trapping, and this debt should be covered by his mink pelts. Most of the men stop trapping about a week before Christmas, when it is often quite cold, but the real reason for gathering up their traps is to be at the village during the Christmas festivities.

During the extended celebrations of Russian Christmas and American Christmas, the men do not replenish their food supplies but rely on their surpluses. Furthermore, there is very little that anyone can do in the way of subsistence activities until early March. It is then that ptarmigan become plentiful in the willows along the sloughs and the hare become more active and thus are more easily snared in their trails. Again the blackfish begin to ascend the small streams and are trapped through the ice. In the middle of winter the local unit of the U. S. National Guard begins its drill sessions, and the seventeen members must attend forty-eight such drills each year. Most drills are held in January through March when there is little activity in the village. The National Guard earnings are a small but welcome addition to a family's income.

When the snow begins to melt, the cod hooks again are set beneath the river ice, and women in particular jig for pike through holes in the ice. Then, as the days lengthen and the snow leaves the southern exposures, preparations are made to move to the tundra camps, virtually always those at which the men trapped mink in the fall. If the family head did not visit the camp by boat before freeze-up the previous fall, it will be necessary for him to haul a plank boat overland by dog sled in order to have a means of returning to the village after the breakup, the traditional time of return. By late April most families will have settled in tents or small wooden houses at their tundra camps, and the school will be virtually devoid of children, although classes are still held. A spring camp bustles with diverse subsistence activities. The first concern of the men is to kill as many ducks and geese as possible to satisfy their hunger for quantities of fresh meat. The girls and women gather last year's berries, and the men set small-meshed gill nets in the sloughs for pike and whitefish. When the men have completed this work, they and the boys begin their hunt for muskrat, which is the real purpose for going to spring camp. They travel by canvas-covered canoes from one lake to the next, hunting along the way. In 1956 a muskrat pelt was worth 40 to 85 cents, and the value of the take per man ranged between $20 and $200. This was considered a relatively poor muskrat year. As the number of muskrat shot begins to diminish and the ice clears from the lakes, the people return by boat to the village, arriving just after the Kuskokwim breaks up.

Not all families went to spring camp in the spring of 1956; in fact, it seems that the same trend as that observed for fall camp may be emerging. A dozen families remained in the village; some of the men were sick, another did not have the equipment necessary for making the trip, one worked for the Bureau of Indian Affairs school, and a few men were just not inclined to make the trip. Those who did stay and a few who returned from spring camp before the breakup were on hand when the ice swept from the river. The principal activity at this time is to snake logs out of the high water which carries vast quantities of driftwood downriver. These logs are used for construction purposes or more often as winter firewood. When the river waters drop into their normal channel, smelt are dipnetted from anchored boats or from the banks of the main channel. They are strung and dried just as in aboriginal times and are stored in raised caches for winter consumption. About this time, too, some men hunt seals in the estuary; with four or five men making the trip, about half a dozen seals are killed. At present it is only rarely that a seal or beluga whale ascends the Kuskokwim as far as the village. By the beginning of June large-meshed gill nets are set in the river eddies, and a few sheefish are taken. Before long the first king salmon of the year are entangled. After three or four king salmon have been taken in a net during one night, the owner takes up the net and begins to drift for them. The drift-netting method today differs from aboriginal times only in that the nets now are commercially made and longer, drifting is done from a plank boat, and clubs are used to kill the fish. The catch from a drift is placed in wooden bins; there the fish remain until the women of the fisherman's household cut them up for drying, using the same techniques as of old. The cleaned and split fish are hung in the sun on pole racks for about two weeks and then removed to a smokehouse. This is a pole-framed structure about eighteen feet square and as much as fifteen feet in height. It is usually covered with planks or oil drums which have been cut apart and flattened; the metal sheets are nailed to the frame. The intensity with which other species of salmon are sought later in the season is, as of old, dependent on how many king salmon have been taken. The last salmon of the season, the silvers, are still buried whole in the ground, but now they are packed in old oil drums and serve as winter dog food. At present the men do not fish on Saturday afternoon or night, so that the women will have no fish to process on Sunday, and neither do they fish on Sunday. Thus nearly two days of fishing are lost in each week. A few persons may at times fish or clean fish on Sunday, but this would be exceptional.

Summer salmon fishing is village-based, for only two families went to nearby fish camps. The shift from scattered family camps to the current pattern most likely is a function of the mobility afforded the fishermen by plank boats and outboard motors. Efficient boats and motors also make it possible for men to travel to the mouth of Johnson River, some nine miles downstream, to gillnet whitefish when they concentrate there in the fall or to travel about a hundred miles up the Kuskokwim and its tributaries to hunt moose.

The dominance of salmon fishing is decreasing, for men have come to consider wage labor during the summer as essential. As many as twenty men earn about $100 each in the spring and fall for helping to unload the supply vessels which dock across the river from Bethel. As many as twenty men also are flown to the Bristol Bay salmon canneries for the period from late June through early August and earn $300 to $600 each for the season. A few others have summer jobs working for visiting scientists, for the U. S. Public Health Service hospital at Bethel, or with the Oscarville trader. Only one man in the village, the general assistant at the Bureau of Indian Affairs school, has a permanent job, and he earns around $3000 a year. As the summer begins to pass, family excursions are made to gather berries, particularly salmonberries, which are placed in small barrels and stored for winter use in *agutuk*.

A form of income unassociated with the immediate environment are the funds received from Territorial (in 1956) and subsequently Federal agencies. Thirteen persons receive monthly checks from the Alaska Department of Welfare because they are more than sixty-five years of age and completely or partly without means of support. Two men receive assistance from Aid to the Blind, and eight families are helped by Aid to Dependent Children funds. Social Security earnings are received by two men over sixty-five and by three heirs of men who qualified. The total community income from these sources is about $18,000 a year.

The economic lives of the villagers are dominated by their relations with the traders and with other commercial enterprises beyond Alaska. The first local trader, Oscar Samuelson, whose store at Oscarville opened about 1912 and who managed it until his death in 1953, maintained a paternalistic relationship with the villagers. He exchanged food and other trade goods for furs and provided many additional services. Usually when a villager had occasion to deal with a white or to correspond with some government agency, it was Samuelson who served as the intermediary. Samuelson's daughter inherited the store and, with her husband, has managed it since 1953. The relationship between a trader and his customers is shifting in emphasis. As late as just before World War II trade was primarily in pelts which were exchanged across the counter for staples, hardware, and clothing. The amount of credit extended to a man was always small, and the inventory was likewise small. Today the trader stocks a wide variety of goods, and he prefers to deal in cash or government checks rather than pelts. Therefore the trader is a strong advocate of extensive welfare programs. The village Eskimos of today are much more sophisticated in their purchasing habits, and some are careful comparison shoppers or buy through mail-order houses. One man even places his year's order for food through a wholesale outlet and has it shipped in on a supply vessel from Seattle.

In this community, in which only the persistence and good fortune of the male family head make it possible for a household to prosper, we find the relationship between father and son or sons to be of key importance. A man and his son are joined by the closest ties of kinship. They share a common residence until at least a few years after the son marries, and a son learns his skills largely through informal instruction from his father. When in the company of his father, a son is withdrawn; although he might covertly disagree with his father, the younger man would never overtly express his dissatisfaction in a face-to-face situation. The pelts from animals he traps and the wages he earns are at the disposal of his father even after he has married and brought his bride home to live. It is the father, too, who has the first call on the use of the dog team or plank boat and outboard motor. Ideally, as the father ages, he is cared for by his son, but in all likelihood the elder man will receive old age assistance and have fewer financial obligations than ever before. In this case, because of his cash income, a father may continue to dominate the economic activities of the household. The relationship between father and daughter is much cooler and more distant. Girls are expected to marry and move into their husband's household, thus offering a father little comfort or reward. In times of stress a father may vigorously defend his daughter, but causes for such defense are rare.

The bonds between mother and daughter are close and overtly warm. After bearing a son, every mother hopes for a daughter to help her with household activities, and a certain degree of affection binds the pair. A conscientious mother will work hard to marry the girl to someone in the community so that she can keep her daughter near, and she vigorously defends her against real or imagined abuse from her husband or his family. With a son, too, the mother is the most outspoken defender, or critic at times, but there is not the warmth expressed toward a son that there is toward a daughter.

The relationship between siblings, which extends to parallel cousins, is one of friendship and mutual aid. Siblings of the same sex, particularly males, may live in the same household, draw food from a common cache, and share boats, motors, and dogs. The older male is the one to dominate the subsistence affairs of the household in the absence of his father. Siblings of the opposite sex are not physically close during their adult lives, but they may be depended on in times of crisis. The husband or wife of a sibling may visit and borrow more freely from one's household than almost any other person. The ties with a cross-cousin are looser, and the degree of closeness is largely dependent on the personalities of the related persons. It is these individuals who joke and, if called on, would not hesitate to help one another.

In this society in which the nuclear family is the most important unit it is the social relationship within the family that dominates their lives. Cooperation beyond the nuclear family is desirable and present, but it is not essential for subsistence welfare. The abilities of the man are critical, for he must provide for his family's material needs. He may help his wife with the cooking and caring for the children, but it would be a rare event for a man to process fish. A woman has as her duties the processing of foods, the care of children, and other domestic tasks. She is no longer charged with bringing in the wood supply, but she may chop wood if her husband or an older boy is not available to perform the chore. It is clear that the division of labor is rather sharply drawn between the sexes, and, because it is complementary, to be without a spouse is a serious condition and, it is to be hoped, a temporary one, especially if there are growing children in the family.

The system of kinship terminology has separate terms for father and mother, as well as uncle and aunt terms for the brothers and sisters of one's parents. Thus the first ascending generational usage is lineal. For cousins, however, cross-cousins are "cousins," whereas parallel cousins are grouped with siblings. This is the Iroquois type. Furthermore, terms exist for older and younger biological siblings which are not normally extended to include parallel cousins. The most important set of relationships seems to be between males who are classificatory or biological siblings, as previously mentioned.

A reconstruction of the emergence of modern political life, which is in part speculative, reveals a chain of changes over the last sixty years. From as long ago as anyone can remember until 1950 there was a *kashgee* in the community which served the same functions as those in other Kuskowagamiut settlements. Within the *kashgee* older men were respected because of their wisdom, and two or three of them constituted an informal council of elders. Their judgment in any situation would not likely be challenged nor would the opinion of an important shaman be disregarded. In rare instances of irreconcilable differences the weaker family and its allies would leave the settlement. Such differences arose from the murder of or injury to a member of an important family. Then, in 1906, a Russian Orthodox priest came to the community and appointed a representative who was sympathetic to Orthodoxy. The appointee, who became the first "chief," appears to have been the head of a large extended family. He was soon replaced by his son, for he was an old man at the time of the appointment. There have been four chiefs before the current one. The original duty of the chief was to arrange matters pertaining to church affairs, and this obligation continues to be one of his major functions down to the present time. Today, however, the chief is an elected official; in 1947 the first elected chief took office. The office of chief has come to include secular as well as sacred obligations, and at present his duties are confused in the minds of most villagers. Some say he is the head of the village, but others regard the Orthodox Brotherhood as the head. Still others think that the village leadership is in the hands of the council as a collectivity. The authority of any particular chief is dependent on his personality rather than on the pervasiveness of his kinship ties. Part of the confusion of his role is a result of the efforts of the Bureau of Indian Affairs officials to introduce an elected village council organization into the village. In 1939, when the first teacher arrived, the Indian Reorganization Act, as extended to Alaska in 1936, was being promoted by the local Indian Affairs personnel. The teacher at Napaskiak attempted to induce the villagers to organize under the terms of the act but never was successful. The villagers did nonetheless organize an elected council in 1945, without requesting Federal recognition. The governing laws were drafted by the villagers with apparently little direct aid from the teachers (see Note 2). The laws are unrealistic in terms of fines and punishments but typify Kuskowagamiut ideas of law and order. These laws, incidentally, apply only to Napaskiak residents, and the Oscar- ville people have no comparable rules or organization. The ineffec- tiveness of the council down to the present time stems in part from the reluctance of the people to take any overt action against anyone else. The major problem dealt with by the council has been intoxica- tion of a villager. The usual course of action is to warn the guilty party, but on rare occasions the U. S. Deputy Marshal from Bethel has been summoned. Meetings have been called for additional rea- sons, such as to collect funds for village medical needs, to establish a curfew for school children, or to request that the airline offices in Bethel refuse to accept orders for intoxicants from villagers. How- ever, there is really very little reason for council action or meetings, since little community cohesion exists along secular lines.

Perhaps one important reason for the ineffective nature of the council is that the Orthodox Church Brotherhood has long fulfilled the crisis needs of the community and holds regular monthly meetings to deal with ongoing problems. The general purpose of this organization is to coordinate Church matters and provide welfare aid for members. Because all of the families participate in at least some Orthodox Church activities and only one family and one single man claim membership in another church, the welfare provision embraces everyone. The Brotherhood membership includes all but two adult males and has elected officers with established duties. The specific activities of the Brotherhood are to prepare coffins when needed and to bury the dead; to make arrangements for the annual trip of the bishop to the area; to aid the aged by providing services, such as taking an old man a load of wood; to maintain the church structure; and to perform certain ceremonial obligations. From the time of its organization in 1931 until just after World War II the Brotherhood provided food and funds to families without means of support, but this function has since been assumed by the Alaska Department of Welfare and the Bureau of Indian Affairs and is no longer a part of the Brotherhood program.

Warfare is not a part of the life of the villagers except when it is imposed on them, for they are under the political control of the United States. Early in World War II the Alaska Territorial Guard was organized as a scouting unit for the U. S. Army at a time when an invasion of the mainland of Alaska seemed likely. In the village unit older men were appointed as officers, and the younger ones became enlisted men. There was little military discipline, but there was the wholesale issuance of military equipment which the men were permitted to use daily. Thus real material advantages were to be gained from Alaska Territorial Guard membership. After the war ended this organization was replaced by the U. S. National Guard, and the tenor of policy changed drastically. The older men were not encouraged to re-enlist, especially if they spoke no English. Promising younger men were sent out for special leadership training, and regular drill sessions became a routine part of membership. Today the organization of the village unit more closely reflects military norms and has become a seriously disruptive institution in village life, particularly since it bestows rigid overt authority on young aggressive men, an unprecedented innovation in village social life. The younger men regard the National Guard as romantic, and the yearly two-week encampment in Anchorage is a great adventure. The older men who have remained in the unit have done so because of the income derived.

As explained earlier, Christianity was introduced to the Kus-kokwim in its Russian Orthodox form, but there is no evidence that any of the priests lingered among the people of the lower river in Russian times. The attempts of the Moravian missionaries to win converts have failed, although they did at one time number among their members a few village families. An Orthodox priest baptized some persons during a visit in 1905, and in the following year a priest and a songleader held services in the *kashgee* and appointed a village chief. The reason the people give for accepting Orthodoxy and reject-ing the Moravians is that their relatives at Kwethluk are Orthodox and they want to be like them. At the same time, it is likely that the Orthodox Church was identified with the old ways, and the vil-lagers chose to align themselves with conservatism. The local church was built in 1931, and a dwelling for visiting church officials was con-structed in 1948. The villagers do not support a resident priest; the priest from Kwethluk or the one from the tundra area to the west of Bethel serves the community. However, the most important person in village religious life has been Matthew Berezkin. He is of Aleut and Russian ancestry and was the songleader who came to the river in 1906. He was ordained a priest in 1908 but left the priesthood in the 1920's and moved to Oscarville in the early 1940's when he became blind. Berezkin has been a powerful influence in furthering Ortho-doxy in the community over a period of fifty years. The village lead-ers in the Church are four deacons appointed by the bishop in 1954. Their prime duty is to preach sermons, which are in Eskimo, and to interpret the Scriptures. The people use the American Bible Society translation of the Bible into Yuk, made by Moravian missionaries, and a standard Orthodox service book to guide the conduct of the rituals. The service book is understood by two men who are quite active in the church and who read English rather well. Thus the services follow the pattern of the Russian Orthodox congregations elsewhere in the world.

Everyone in the community considers himself to be a Christian, including an old man who is a practicing shaman. Still, the dogma of Orthodoxy is not understood except in a superficial manner (see Note 3). Among the villagers there is considerable variation in what is regarded as proper Christian behavior, but most would agree that helping other people when they are in need is an important Christian ideal. After an individual dies, his soul automatically goes to hell if he had not been baptized or if the death resulted from suicide. Other-wise God evaluates a person's deeds during his life, and the spirit is admitted to heaven or hell. At times the ghost of a dead person re-turns to the community, and to decrease the likelihood of its return the windows are opened after death and closed after burial. An icon is hung on the door to prevent the spirit from returning through the doorway. Although a ghost may return if it disapproves of the behavior of someone in its former house, this is not usual, and ghosts are not a great concern to the people.

The cycle of ceremonials duplicates the Orthodox calendar elsewhere in the world. Along with regular church services, special observances are held at the Russian Christmas and New Year, the Epiphany, the Easter season, and during the annual Church conference. Of far greater importance than any other ceremonial event is the celebration held at Russian Christmas. This time of the year brings forced inactivity because of the cold weather and is an ideal period for prolonged ceremonies. The preparations are elaborate, by village standards. The choir practices Russian Christmas songs in both Russian and Eskimo; the men haul and chop enough wood to heat their houses during the holiday season, wine is ordered through an airline, the ceremonial equipment is made ready, and special foods are prepared. Finally, visitors arrive at Napaskiak from surrounding communities, especially from Oscarville. The central theme of the three days of processions is to announce the birth of Christ in each household by singing Christmas songs and carrying a guiding star made of metal. The performers and the crowd of observers are fed at each house so that most of the three nights are taken up with eating vast quantities of food. The Russian New Year is celebrated by lighting kerosene lanterns on the graves of the dead, as was done also at Russian Christmas. Later, about midnight, the Christmas trees, which had decorated the houses for the season, are burned in front of the village, as fireworks and guns are shot off. The climax of the event is a short service in church; this is mainly a sermon about the ideals of behavior for the coming year. Again at the Epiphany a special church service is held and water from the river, collected in containers, is blessed by a priest. In theory, the Easter season should be the highlight of the ceremonial year, but when it falls late in the season, as in 1956, most families are at their spring camps. Again there are numerous services and some ceremonial feasting. Finally, each year, when the bishop arrives from Sitka, there are three days of special services and sermons, in which a particular religious theme is developed.

It is expected that a woman will conceive soon after she marries, and children usually are born when the mother is between the ages of eighteen and forty. It is not uncommon for a wife to conceive eight to eleven times, but families average three children because of high infant mortality. Every couple hopes that the firstborn will be a son; ideally, a woman would have two sons who live and then a daughter or two. Because no effective means of birth control is known, family size is not regulated except by giving males up for adoption if the parents feel they have enough boys; no one would consider accepting a girl for adoption. The rules that a woman should follow during pregnancy are regarded as necessary for a safe delivery and a normal offspring. For example, chewing either commercial chewing gum or spruce gum is thought to result in a difficult birth, and the same problem would develop if a pregnant woman stood in a doorway. Likewise, the offspring probably would be sickly if the mother ate food left over from a meal. Not only should a woman observe these and other rules, but it has come to be accepted that she should seek prenatal care at the Bethel hospital. The delivery may take place at home or at the hospital, with hospital births becoming more common. About two weeks after birth the newborn is baptized and given an Eskimo and an English name, both of which usually are those of a dead relative but not necessarily the same one. An infant is nursed whenever it cries, and weaning begins at about six months by more acculturated mothers. Among conservative women it may not take place until the child is three. The first solid foods usually are chewed first by the mother, but commercial baby foods are becoming more popular. Toilet training may be the concern of some mothers after the first few months, but not until a child is about two years old are elimination habits relatively controlled. A child is not expected to talk until it is about two, and by this time it has been walking for about a year. Village children unquestionably are spoiled by modern American standards. They may be mildly scolded at times, but it is more common to hold, feed, divert, or simply give in to an unhappy small child.

Young children most frequently play with individuals of the same sex and age category, and favored games are imitations of adult pursuits. There are few toys, but little girls have dolls and jacks or boys have toy guns and trucks. A favorite and almost obsessive pastime of small girls is to tell and illustrate stories. Today it is more common to see a metal tableknife used for illustrating the stories than the old form of storyknife. Likewise, the stories with plots involving a grandmother and her granddaughter are being replaced by reworked European children's stories which the girls have learned in school. Some effort is made by adults to instill the values of the community into the minds of the children, but the attempts are not systematic. An old person often tells stories to an informal gathering of children, and occasionally a church official will call all of the children together and lecture them on proper behavior. One recurring theme is that children should obey parental authority. The compulsory school law makes it necessary for all children between the ages of six and sixteen to attend school, but progress through the grades is slow because most beginners do not understand English. Commonly, by the time a sixteen-year-old child leaves school he or she is in the third or fourth grade. The classroom instruction is much the same as that found in the elementary grades in the United States, but no attempt has been made to adapt to specific Eskimo needs. As a part of school activities special celebrations are held at school at Halloween, Thanksgiving, and American Christmas. On the last occasion one pupil dresses as Santa Claus and distributes presents, most of which the students have made, to the assembled villagers.

Adolescents are expected to contribute directly to family welfare by assuming some of the responsibilities of their parents. If an adolescent works hard at chopping wood or caring for a younger child, he will be praised, whereas to avoid responsibilities brings silent disapproval from parents. By the time girls are thirteen they are usually courted by boys who are at least four years older, but since marriages are still arranged by old women and parents, courtship does not lead to any permanent marital ties. A girl is usually regarded as ready for marriage when she is thirteen or fourteen, but territorial and now state law prohibits marriage before sixteen. Because of school birth records, it is now impossible to falsify a girl's age. A girl is expected to acquiesce to her parents' decision about whom she is to marry, but a young man may state some preference or at least reject someone for whom he has a real dislike. If at all possible, the parents attempt to find a mate for their child in the village, but when this is impossible it is the girl who moves to another village, or very rarely to Bethel. A marriage license is obtained from the U. S. Commissioner at Bethel, and the ceremony is performed in the Russian Orthodox Church, following the established ritual pattern. For the initial period after marriage the couple is most likely to live with the husband's parents, and the girl becomes subordinated to her mother-in-law. The older woman is never very patient with the bride and often makes life difficult for the girl. There is no discontinuity in the man's life, and he is likely to lounge in a steam bath for many hours with friends and make frequent trips to Bethel, as he did before his marriage. Within a year or two he is expected to be more diligent in providing for the welfare of the household. Sexual freedom before marriage makes settling down with one person difficult for both members of the union, and adultery is a norm during early married life. After a number of children have been born to a couple, they will establish a more normal adult routine, and the man will probably then construct a separate residence near the home of his parents.

For an adult male the seasonal round of subsistence activities keeps him away from the village for as long as six weeks at a time, and, partly as a result, his wife must frequently be concerned with the day-to-day management of the household. If the husband makes arrangements for his absences by providing adequate supplies of wood and fish at home and credit at the store, the family will not be deprived of what are considered necessities. Some men do not make these provisions, and their families may be in need. In cases of real deprivation the relatives of the couple will aid the woman. The relative freedom of a man is expressed in other ways as well, for virtually all men spend many hours taking steam baths four or more times a week. The small Russian-style bathhouse has an outer dressing room and an inner steam room which will accommodate up to a dozen persons. There are nine such bathhouses in the community, and certain combinations of men bathe together frequently in one or the other of the bathhouses. These structures have in one sense replaced the *kashgee* as the place in which men may relax in the company of other men. Unlike the *kashgee* of old, women bathe in the bathhouses, usually in a group. Sometimes a woman bathes with her husband; only in rare instances would she bathe with any other man. It would seem that the old sexual dichotomy still exists, in which the woman is still primarily responsible for the home and the man is something of an outsider. Thus there is a subdued but pervasive individualism which dominates social life. It is likewise reflected in the behavior of old people, both men and women, who frequently live alone in houses of their own, a condition made possible by old age assistance funds.

The village problem considered most critical by the people and the government officials alike concerns individual health. Tuberculosis is the biggest threat. Among the one hundred eighty permanent residents in 1956, forty-five had active cases of the disease, and at that time there unquestionably were additional cases. Villagers have only vague notions of the germ theory of disease and recognize that no one cure is invariably successful. Therefore, in an effort to increase their chances for recovery, they attempt diverse cures for this or any other ailment they consider serious. They probably turn first to patent medicines and the traditional pharmacopoeia, then perhaps to taking steam baths, to consulting a shaman, to drinking holy water or praying in church, and finally to scientific medicine dispensed by the teacher and the Bethel hospital. Recent major progress toward decreasing the number of tuberculosis cases has been accomplished largely through the chemotherapy program at the village level by the U. S. Public Health Service.

The most common forms of diversion are steam bathing for males and visiting for females, but a more formal entertainment with village-wide appeal consists of motion pictures shown twice a week at the Napaskiak school during the winter and at the Oscarville Trading Post three or four nights a week during the summer. The favorite plot types are Tarzan and cowboy pictures, with war as a third choice. Another form of socializing is the drinking of intoxicants. All village men have at one time or another participated, but today some persons are outspoken in favor of abstinence. The nondrinkers are usually outstanding leaders in the church, but this is not consistently the case, for a few church elders consume and enjoy intoxicants. The favored alcoholic beverages are port or muscatel wine, vodka, and gin. Beer is liked by some men, but it is expensive to ship in by air and therefore seldom ordered. Men usually drink with a few friends. About a dozen men will become intoxicated one to four times a year, and some eight others are more likely to succumb every month or two. However, the heaviest drinker spent only $60 for intoxicants while in the community in the winter of 1955–1956. It is the men who drink the most, for boys and women must rely on the men to bring intoxicants home. Although consumption of alcohol is of concern to some villagers, it does not seem to be a major disruptive force in community life.

With the approach of old age, villagers become more independent and are fond of talking of the past and how the younger generation lacks the vigor of their parents and grandparents. They are willing to concede, however, without being challenged, that life today, in spite of all its shortcomings, is much easier and more secure than when they were young. Old people realize that they may die at any time and are content as long as they die at home where they know they will receive a good burial and will always be near their village.

Note 1. The Moravian Church missionary to Bethel, William H. Weinland, recorded in his diary for February 23 and 25, 1886, an account of a ceremony which took place at the village of Napaskiak (Oswalt, 1963b, 59–61).

We also learned that a small Ekorushka was to take place at Nepaskiagamute [Napaskiak] today, & John [Kilbuck] and I at once felt like going. . . . John & I started from the house at 11.30 A.M., walked fast, & reached

Nepaskiagamute at 1.5 P.M. On entering the kashima, we saw the men hard at work making masks, & finished masks standing around everywhere. We were greeted very cordially, different ones inviting us to their seats on the benches. The heat was not excessive, & the smell bearable. Feeding time came around, & the fish which we had given a few days ago to Aguliagani in pay for wood, was passed around. Before long four drums were brought in, & a practice of the real ekorushka was held. A young man, masked, & holding a [wood?] chip in each hand, took his seat on the floor of the kashima. A young man knelt opposite him, & back of this one, stood a woman & young girl. At a given time one of the drummers opened the performance by beating time on his drum, while the masked young man began some peculiar jirations, which were imitated by the young man opposite to him, & by the females standing further back. In a few minutes the other drums joined in, an old man dictated a song, & the entire company joined in singing. Following this came an interlude, during which the singing ceased, while the drumming & the corresponding jirations continued. Thus six parts were gone through with, the entire performance lasting about fifteen minutes. This performance was repeated several times. Hiagulvea put on the mask several times & seemed to be the best performer, for he seemed to cause the most merriment. The entire performance was not regarded as anything serious, for the more ridiculous it could be made, the better it was liked. We remained in the kashima until 2.40 P.M. when we looked for a suitable situation for the school house. . . .

A slight fall of snow occurred last night, and this morning the weather was still somewhat unpleasant. After breakfast John & I considered the question of going to Nepaskiagamute, & finally concluded to go. Starting at ten oclock, we reached the village at twelve, having walked at a comfortable pace. We were met by Nepaskiagani, who told us that the natives from Lomavigarmute [Loamavik] & Nepachiachagamute [Napakiak] were expected, & that until they came, the performance proper would not take place. He told us to go to the kashima meanwhile, where we found some of the natives practicing their parts. A large number of masks were hung around the kashima, & my first thought when I entered the place was, "This looks like a fair." Four male performers, wearing large masks of most wonderful designs, and one female performer, occupied the stage, & were going through peculiar jirations, keeping time with the beating of eight drums, four on each side of the stage. Soon after our arrival an intermission was taken, during which the women & children filed out. This gave me an opportunity to count them, & I found that one hundred & twenty people had been in the kashima. Some changes were now made about the stage, the masks covered with grass matting etc, during wh. time John & I took our dinner. . . .

Near the roof of the kashima hung two representations of birds, the one of an eagle, the other of a sea-gull. On the eagle stood a stuffed representation of a male native & on the sea-gull that of a female. Upon inquiry I learned that these represented the spirits of deceased natives being borne upward after death. The kashima was cold & draughty, and, as I had wet feet, I began to feel very uncomfortable.

Note 2. In 1945 the men of Napaskiak organized their village council and formulated the following set of local laws (Oswalt, 1963a, 68).

1. These are the words already made. Men will not drink; the drunk man will not fight others in the stores, pool hall, or in the show house. If a man disobeys he will be punished by six months in jail and he will pay $300.00.

2. And these are the words, a man will not give or sell another man intoxicants, beer or wine. Punishment will be $500.00.

3. The drunk man will not have a gun. If he disobeys he will pay $100.00.

4. A man will not make intoxicants without a license; if he does, he will pay $500.00 or he will be sent to jail for one year.

5. If someone brings a bottle of intoxicant into the village, the council will tell him not to do this, and after that if he continues to disobey, the council will take him to the marshal. After that if he does not change his mind, they [the council] will kick him out of the village. If somebody from another village comes here drunk, the council will let him go right away.

6. If somebody steals something from the village or a camp, if the council finds out about it they will tell him not to do so one time, and after that if he does not obey they will tell the marshal.

7. If the village has a big sickness [an epidemic] and is closed, people will not come here from other villages and people from this village will not go elsewhere except where there are no people.

8. If the council sees somebody playing cards for money, they will tell him once not to do so; after that, if they see him again, they will tell the marshal.

9. If a pulling dog is loose all the time, they [the council] will tell the man [who owns the dog] to tie the dog, and if he does not listen, they will shoot the dog.

This paper was made by the Napaskiak council and everyone should know it.

Note 3. A summary of the Russian Orthodox Church belief system at Napaskiak, as Oswalt (1963a, 144) attempted to view it through Eskimo eyes.

In essence, the Orthodox dogma is as follows: God lives in heaven and He created the earth, and man, and everything in the world. After the creation He rested, and thus men today should go to church on Sunday to honor God and rest on Sunday as He did. God had a son, a *gussuk*, named Jesus who was born "outside." Jesus was sent to earth by God to teach all people to lead a good life, but there were evil men who killed Jesus and in so doing sinned. Communion is taken in memory of Jesus, who loved people, even those who harmed him, and we should likewise love even those people who do not like us. We should also hold the memory of Jesus as sacred since he died for everyone, *gussuks* and Eskimos alike. Jesus also said that the people should help one another and lead a good life. Since Jesus was baptized, each person today should be baptized as soon after birth as possible so that he may be purified.

References

Anderson, Eva G. *Dog-Team Doctor*. Caldwell. 1940.

Hammerich, Louis L. "The Western Eskimo Dialects," *Proceedings of the Thirty-second International Congress of Americanists,* 632–639. Copenhagen. 1958.

Hoffman, Bernard G. "A Daily Journal kept by the Rev. Father Juvenal, One of the Earliest Missionaries to Alaska," *Kroeber Anthropological Society Papers,* no. 6, 26–59. 1952.

Hrdlicka, Ales. *Alaska Diary, 1926-1931.* Lancaster. 1943.

Nelson, Edward W. *The Eskimo about Bering Strait.* Bureau of American Ethnology, 18th Annual Report, pt. 1. 1899.

Oswalt, Wendell H. "A Western Eskimo Ethnobotany," *Anthropological Papers of the University of Alaska,* v. 6, no. 1, 16–36. 1957.

———, "Historical Populations in Western Alaska and Migration Theory," *Anthropological Papers of the University of Alaska,* v. 11, no. 1, 1–14. 1962.

*———. *Napaskiak: An Alaskan Eskimo Community*. Tucson. 1963a. This 1955–1956 study of one Kuskokwim Eskimo community supplies virtually all that we know of contemporary riverine Eskimo life in southwestern Alaska.

*———. *Mission of Change in Alaska*. San Marino. 1963b. A historical reconstruction, supplemented by the author's field notes, of Kuskokwim Eskimo life, with concentration on the period from 1884 to 1925. Additional summary information is provided on the Russian era and events subsequent to 1925.

———. "Traditional Storyknife Tales of Yuk Girls," *Proceedings of the American Philosophical Society,* v. 108, no. 4, 310–336. 1964.

———, ed. "Eskimos and Indians of Western Alaska, 1861–1868: Extracts from the Diary of Father Illarion," *Anthropological Papers of the University of Alaska,* v. 8, no. 2, 101–118. 1960.

*———, and James W. VanStone. *The Ethno-Archeology of Crow Village, Alaska* (in press). The excavation of the Crow Village site, which was occupied by Eskimos from ca. 1830 to 1912, provides insight into the material changes which took place during the Russian and early Anglo-American periods.

Petroff, Ivan. *Report on the Population, Industries, and Resources of Alaska.* United States Department of the Interior, Census Office. 1884.

Schwalbe, Anna B. *Dayspring on the Kuskokwim.* Bethlehem. 1951.

VanStone, James W. "Russian Exploration in Interior Alaska," *Pacific Northwest Quarterly,* v. 50, 37–47. 1959.

Weinland Collection. The William Henry Weinland collection of manuscripts, letters, and diaries. Henry E. Huntington Library, San Marino, California.

Wrangell, F. P. *Statistical and Ethnographic Data Concerning the Russian Possessions on the Northwest Coast of America.* St. Petersburg. 1839 (in German).

*Zagoskin, Lavrentij A. *Account of Pedestrian Journeys in the Russian Possessions in America in the Years 1842, 1843, and 1844.* St. Petersburg. 1847 (unpublished Hotovitsky translation from Russian). The Zagoskin travel account is the best, and virtually the only, source on Kuskokwim Eskimo ethnography for the period shortly after historic contact. It is an essential reference.

4

The Cahuilla:

Gatherers in the Desert

Map by J. Donovan

In the beginning, there was no earth or sky or anything or anybody; only a dense darkness in space. This darkness seemed alive. Something like lightnings seemed to pass through it and meet each other once in a while. Two substances which looked like the white of an egg came from these lightnings. They lay side by side in the stomach of the darkness, which resembled a spider web. These substances disappeared. They were then produced again, and again they disappeared. This was called the miscarriage of the darkness. The third time they appeared, they remained, hanging there in this web in the darkness. The substances began to grow and soon were two very large eggs. When they began to hatch, they broke at the top first. Two heads came out, then shoulders, hips, knees, ankles, toes; then the shell was all gone. Two boys had emerged: Mukat and Tamaioit. They were grown men from the first, and could talk right away. As they lay there, both at the same time heard a noise like a bee buzzing. It was the song of their mother Darkness (Hooper, 1920, 317).

With this great event the world of nature and of man began to emerge as an orderly system; at least it was said to be so by the Iviatim, the descendants of Mukat and Tamaioit, who have come to be known in the ethnographic literature as the Cahuilla (Coahuillas, Kawia).

Once the twin creators were in existence, Mukat reached into his mouth and into his heart, removing a cricket, another insect, a lizard, and a person. These creatures were charged to drive away the darkness, but they did not succeed. From their hearts the creators removed tobacco and then pipes and a coal to light one pipe. Mukat and Tamaioit maintained a rivalry over which one was born first and which was the more intelligent. Mukat became associated with making things black, and Tamaioit made items that were white. Together they created the earth, ocean, sun, moon, people, and some plants and animals. Finally Mukat and Tamaioit disagreed so violently that Tamaioit disappeared beneath the ground, taking with him many of his creations. It was then that the mountains emerged, the earth quaked, and water from the ocean overflowed, making streams and rivers. After this Mukat lived in a big house with people and with animals who had human qualities. The moon was there as a lovely female who instructed women about marriage, menstrual and pregnancy taboos, and raising children. Mukat, who had created her, desired to make the moon his wife. She knew this but said nothing. Since she could not marry him because he was her father, she traveled to her present home in the sky. When she was asked to return, she said nothing; she only smiled. Then one day, while in a humorous mood, Mukat caused the people to speak different languages. As the sun grew hot, some of these people sought shelter and were transformed into different plants and animals. Those who had stayed with Mukat remained human. The creator instructed the people how to make bows and arrows and told them to shoot at each other, which led to the first deaths. It was about this time, too, that the sun turned people different colors. Those people who were nearest to the sun's rays became Negroes, those that were far away became whites, and the Indians became brown because they were in between.

The people were angry with Mukat, for he had caused a rattlesnake to bite a friendly little man, he had caused the moon woman to leave, and he had shown people how to kill one another. Thus they decided to kill Mukat but did not know how to accomplish the deed. Mukat lived in the middle of the big house and only went outside to defecate when everyone was asleep; this a white lizard discovered. One night a frog caught the feces of Mukat in his mouth, and Mukat grew ill. The shamans pretended to try to cure him, but Mukat became sicker. As he was dying, he sang songs, and before his death he told the people how to conduct a mourning ceremony in memory of the dead each year. Mukat died and was cremated, the big house was burned, and the essence of the world was established.

The Cahuilla lived, and continue to live, in an interior region of southern California. Possibly they numbered about twenty-five hundred at the time of the earliest historic contact. By 1885 their number had dropped to around eight hundred, and it remained at this level for some sixty years. In the early 1960's some five hundred thirty retained their identity as Cahuilla and were in three separate groups: the Desert Cahuilla of the Torres-Martinez Reservation, about two hundred twenty-five and Palm Springs Reservation, one hundred; the Pass Cahuilla of the Morongo Reservation, one hundred twenty; and the Mountain Cahuilla of the Cahuilla and Santa Rosa reservations, eighty-five. Not all of these people lived on their respective reservations in the early 1960's, but they were listed on the tribal roles and claimed Cahuilla affinities. A sense of tribal identity did not exist in the aboriginal period but emerged in historic times under Mexican-American and Anglo-American influence. There did exist among the Cahuilla in the early period of contact a sense of local identity which is reflected in the subtribal and ecological groupings of Pass, Mountain, and Desert. The region is within the general biotic province of Sonoran, but there is considerable environmental variability among the three sectors. According to the traditions of the people, their original homeland was in the desert, but they were forced into the San Jacinto and Santa Rosa mountains by a great flood. This is a region of steep granite ridges and barren tablelands at the medium elevations, but at higher elevations are streams, open meadows, and forests of oak and pine. The Desert Cahuilla moved into the Coachella basin after the flood, according to tradition. The flood was probably the formation of the sea, which covered much of the present desert lowland and subsided some five hundred years ago. The desert area supports an arid type of vegetation, which includes various forms of cacti, mesquite, agave, and screw beans as economically important plants. This is an area of very little precipitation so that settlements were located around excavated wells, water holes, or streams at the base of the San Jacinto Mountains. The desert in the summertime is extremely hot, with temperatures as high as 120°F. Although it seldoms rains, precipitation, when it comes, is often torrential and causes widespread erosion. Furthermore, severe duststorms may whip across the valley. Some sectors, particularly in the eastern part of the Desert Cahuilla range, are completely devoid of vegetation. One unique environmental feature is the indigenous palm tree found in the well-watered canyons along the western slopes of the San Jacinto Mountains. The Pass Cahuilla occupied the country surrounding San Gorgonio Pass, where they found more open grassland and some oak groves, as well as desert areas.

The Desert subtribe is a striking example of an adaptation to an extremely arid sector of America. For these people we have the fine ethnobotany compiled by David P. Barrows and additional ethnographic information collected around the turn of the present century by Alfred L. Kroeber, later by Lucile Hooper, and then William D. Strong. Only sporadic anthropological interest in the people was manifest from 1925 until 1959 when Lowell J. Bean began his ethnographic reconstructions. At the present time Bean is the ranking authority on the Cahuilla. However, not only anthropologists have a vested interest in these people; they have become a significant focus for journalists, lawyers, farmers, land speculators, Bureau of Indian Affairs employees, congressmen, and municipal officials, particularly those in and around the resort center of Palm Springs. The concern is for the most part clearly neither philanthropic nor humanistic but monetary, for certain reservation lands are of fantastic value. The situation is quite ironic because so few Indians are involved. Thus a study of the Desert Cahuilla affords an excellent opportunity to consider in detail the relations of a now prosperous Indian group with the greater Anglo-American society which surrounds them. It is customary to think that the old and well-established policy of grabbing

Indian lands is a chapter in American history that is not only past but best forgotten; however, the Cahuilla example is a clear demonstration that Anglo-Americans have not changed their course of action, simply their methods. All of this is particularly interesting when it is realized that among the Palm Springs Cahuilla it is the women who have dealt most efficiently with the land problems. These people have, or had until very recently, the only Indian tribal council composed exclusively of women. The Cahuilla manifest many other characteristics that make them appropriate for consideration, not the least of which is their thoroughgoing romantic appeal. The once fabulously popular novel *Ramona* was about the life of a Cahuilla woman, and its writer, Helen H. Jackson, was to play a significant role in the lives of southern California Indians just before the turn of the century.

In the following discussion of the Cahuilla the major stress is on the aboriginal lifeway of the Desert and Palm Springs (Agua Caliente) Cahuilla. In considering the recent past, events that occurred with reference to the Palm Springs people have been emphasized. The knowing reader may object mildly or strongly to the inclusion of the Palm Springs with the Desert Cahuilla rather than with the Pass Cahuilla. Kroeber in his monograph on the Cahuilla in general includes Palm Springs with the Pass area. Strong, in his much more thorough study of Cahuilla territoriality, arbitrarily grouped the Palm Springs people with the Pass Cahuilla as did Kroeber but would have preferred, according to his text, to make the Palm Springs and Indian Wells Cahuilla a completely separate entity. According to George H. Shinn, who was interested in the San Gorgonio Pass area Indians and lived among them between 1885 and 1889, the San Gorgonio Cahuilla were not an indigenous population but entered the region shortly after 1842. According to Bean, however, the Pass Cahuilla of this region belonged to an old and well-established segment of the Cahuilla tribe. My primary reasons for dealing with the Palm Springs and Desert Cahuilla together are to present a reasonably complete account of the people, which can be accomplished only by combining the ethnographic data, and to point out the localized variations in the culture and society within one general environmental setting. The key difference between the two groups is that the Palm Springs people had reliable sources of water and the Desert people did not. The general approach has been to present both groups as one entity and to spell out the similarities and differences between these or between other Cahuilla groups whenever possible. In drawing from the ethnographic sources it was not always possible to establish the specific group of Cahuilla discussed. Thus, like the vast majority of ethnographic reconstructions, the descriptions to follow probably do not apply in every detail to any single community but rather represent the people of the general area.

Within the linguistic phylum of Macro-Penutian is found the Azteco-Tanoan stock; under the Uto-Aztecan family the South California subfamily includes the language Cahuilla. The emergence of the Cahuilla as a separate people is revealed through linguistic rather than archaeological researches. Unfortunately, no archaeological sites have been excavated and published on to provide clues to their past. Linguists, however, do offer some insight into the past affinities of these people. Kenneth Hale, after analyzing the vocabularies of certain Azteco-Tanoan languages, deduced, on lexicostatistical grounds, that at about 1000 B.C. Cahuilla became separated from the subfamily of which it was a member.

In physical appearance the Cahuilla are tall; they tend to be corpulent, and their skin is a deep brown from weathering. In aboriginal times their footwear consisted of sandals made from pads of mescal fibers. The sandals were attached to the foot with a twisted fiber thong fastened behind the heel, fitted around the ankle, forked at the front to receive the second toe, and attached to the front of the mescal fiber pad. The women sometimes wore ill-fitting, flat-topped caps made of coiled basketry. Women were tattooed on the chin, and certain men, most likely the leaders, had their nasal septums pierced and inserted a deer bone in the opening. Both males and females wore strings of beads in their pierced earlobes. The beads worn were thin curved and circular pieces of shell received in trade from the coastal regions of southern California. Clothing seems to have been nonexistent, although it is possible that the women wore short skirts of plant fiber and the men breechclouts.

The settlements of the Desert Cahuilla were clustered around handdug wells and water holes, whereas the Palm Springs people lived near the permanently flowing streams in Andreas, Palm, and Murray canyons at the base of the San Jacinto Mountains. The communities were permanent in nature as long as the local water supply was lasting. Their houses were rectangular in outline; at each corner was a forked post of mesquite on which rested roof beams. Along the sides, except at the entrance, and on top of the beams were laid lengths of brush which were held in place with horizontal poles. On some houses the brush was smeared with a covering of mud, and a layer of dirt was added to the roof. Attached to the front of a house was a ramada which was constructed like the house, with open sides in all but the windward direction. Another form of structure found in a community was the sweathouse, which has been described in detail for the Pass Cahuilla. In the central sector of an eight by twelve foot area, excavated a foot in depth, two vertical forked posts were set about four feet apart, and a log beam was placed in the crotch of the forks. On this basic framework poles were laid from the beam to the ground level, with a space left for an entry on one of the longer sides. Over the structure probably was piled brush and then earth. The fireplace was placed between the entrance and the posts, and because there was no hole for the smoke to escape it eased out the doorway and through gaps in the walls or the roof. Another type of structure that would have been seen in all Cahuilla settlements was the cache, usually raised, for the storage of plant products. A cache was made of poles and beams topped by small branches intertwined in successively smaller circles. The finished product looked very much like a bird's nest some two to four feet in height. The only other structures were a brush enclosure used for certain ceremonies and a large enclosure, walled on three sides and attached to the house of a sib leader. Among the Palm Springs Cahuilla the *net*, or social and ceremonial leader, occupied his sib's dance house, which in 1925 was about forty feet in diameter with walls of fitted boards and a palm-thatched roof. At the back was a room in which the sacred sib bundle was kept; in front of the structure was a fenced enclosure.

Artifacts made from plant fibers formed the largest category of manufactured items. Basketry was constructed by using a species of grass for the warp and either reedgrass or sumac for the weft. If a design was to be woven into a basket, the most common color employed was black. The dye was made by soaking the berry stems of elders in water for about a week with the grass warp. One particular form of reedgrass differed in color from its base to the upper portions. The split and scraped sections produced colors varying from deep red through shades of brown to a yellow. A basket usually was coiled, using a multiple foundation of reedgrass or sumac. Baskets made by the Cahuilla for their own use were not extremely well-constructed, for the wrapping of the weft was neither close nor tight. The variety of coiled basketry forms included the already mentioned basket hats for women, a flat, circular tray about a foot in diameter, a flat-bottomed basket for food or seeds which had eight-inch sides flaring slightly from the bottom, and a larger variety of the preceding type which was used in association with a carrying net. Small globular baskets serving as receptacles for utensils and miscellaneous items were flat-bottomed with flaring sides which usually constricted at the neck. The designs woven into all the basket types except the globular form included encircling bands or zigzags, a series of short stripes, rectangles, triangles, or stepped elements. If the design was in two colors, black usually was combined with red or dull yellow. The small globular baskets, which always seem to have been decorated, did not have horizontal design patterns like the other forms but were decorated with vertically patterned designs. Furthermore, the small globular baskets were coiled counterclockwise, whereas all other forms were coiled clockwise. In addition to coiled baskets the Cahuilla made twined baskets, but these vessels were of little importance. In the twined forms the warp elements casually varied from one to two, which produced an irregular-appearing finished product. One such form was a shallow, rounded basket with an unspecified use. A jug-shaped twined basket, covered with asphaltum, may have been made, but it is not certain that this was an item of Cahuilla manufacture. A net for carrying burdens in baskets was formed like a small hammock and made from the fiber of mescal leaves. At each end was a loop, and from one loop was attached a cinching cord. The cord passed over the forehead of the woman carrying it and rested against her basket hat.

The next major category of artifacts was that of stone, but in comparison with basketry, stonework decidedly was secondary. Gathering peoples the world over who collect plant seeds usually possess stones upon which to spread the seeds for grinding. Such a stone is often slightly hollowed and irregularly shaped, a form often termed a metate when found among the Indians of western America. The Cahuilla utilized metates as well as another, smaller stone which served to grind the seeds set on the metate base. The smaller stones are termed manos. A second way of grinding seeds was with a mortar made by pecking an inverted cone into a stone. The seeds were spilled into the depression and smashed with an oblong, natural stone pestle. At least some of the women had one or more mortars of bedrock at the site of the oak trees where they collected and processed acorns. Another object of stone was a block of soapstone (steatite) with a groove along one surface. Apparently the stone was heated and a cane arrow shaft fitted into the groove in order to bend it and make it true. One additional artifact type of stone belonging to at least certain Desert Cahuilla sibs was the extremely sacred pipe, details of which are unrecorded.

Indians of California were not normally pottery makers, but the Cahuilla are among the exceptional peoples in the southern part of the state who made pottery. It was not extremely important, for basketry served most of the functions of pottery found elsewhere. The vessels were constructed by building up the sides from rope-shaped bands of moist clay. The inside of a damp but completed vessel was smoothed with a stone, and the outside of the coils was flattened with a wooden paddle. The vessels were fired in an oxidizing atmosphere, and the finished product was a thin, rather brittle, red ware. Only red paint, probably hematite, was used for decorating. Surface designs on pottery were very rare and similar to styles known among the Mohave. The vessel forms included round-bottomed pots with narrow necks for water, a widemouthed, round-bottomed type for cooking, and dishes with flat bottoms.

Entering an aboriginal house, an observer would have been impressed with its relative coolness even in the hottest weather. The inside was dark from the soot on the smoke-blackened walls, and natural light filtered in only through the doorway. On one side of the entrance stood the woman's metate and mano, covered with a mat when not in use. On the other side of the doorway was a pottery water container which was filled each morning. Toward the center of the room fire-blackened cooking pots stood around the fireplace; beyond, at the back of the house, animal skins which served as mattresses and blankets were kept. Attached to the roof beams or in the thatch were bundles of plants or dried meat stored for future use.

Somewhere near every house a section of log was set vertically into the ground, the upper portion of which was cut off square and hollowed out a foot or more in depth. A slender stick some two feet in length served as the pestle for this mortar. The combination was adapted to pulverizing mesquite beans, which were an important item in the diet. Other manufactures of wood included a self- or unbacked bow made from a shaft of mesquite or willow wood some four feet in length with a nearly square cross section. The bowstring was made from mescal fiber or sinew. The arrows were about three feet in length and vaned, with two split feathers which were attached to the notched end with sinew and given a quarter twist on opposite sides of the shaft. One form of arrow shaft, made from wormwood, was simply sharpened to a point and probably used only for small game. The second form had a cane shaft in addition to a wooden foreshaft bound to the cane with sinew; the foreshaft tapered to a point but was not tipped. Apparently the latter type of arrow was used against larger game as well as against enemies. Stone arrowpoints were not manufactured by the Cahuilla in late historic times, but on the surface of recent prehistoric Cahuilla sites such arrowpoints are relatively numerous. Another weapon of wood was the boomerang, commonly called the throwing stick when found among Indians of western North America. It was a flat piece of wood shaped in a curve and was thrown at small game such as birds or rabbits. It did not sail back to the thrower if he missed his prey.

The subsistence economy was based much more on plant collecting than on any other form of gathering activity. Hunting did exist, however, and was surrounded by numerous restrictions. Among the Desert Cahuilla the mountain lion and grizzly bear were considered as shamans. If at all possible the people avoided killing these animals. In one recorded instance in which a mountain lion was killed, the claws were made into a dog collar and the skin kept to decorate images used in the Mourning Ceremony. If a young man killed a wildcat or coyote, he would leave the body and notify an old man or woman where the animal could be found. The old person was free to retrieve it and make use of the animal. It was said that only young men hunted, and before they went out, they observed certain food taboos and restricted their water consumption. Specific restrictions were observed in handling a slain deer. When a man killed his first deer, he presented it to the sib of his mother. The usual custom was to take it to the dwelling of the *net*, where the people gathered to sing all night and then to eat the deer in the morning. In general, a man or boy did not consume any of the animals he had killed. Rabbits and other small game taken by a young boy in a communal hunt usually were given to his mother's family. Early in his marriage his wife would eat most of the game he killed and his parents the balance. Later, however, a man's kills were given alternately to his own family and to his wife's family.

The only domestic animal, the dog, does not appear to have been important as an aid in hunting, but served as a pet and a watchdog. The dog was not an ordinary pet, for it possessed certain supernatural powers. Dogs could understand human conversation but could not speak, and they had souls just as people did. At the time of Mukat's death, the people had only one dog, and among some twentieth-century Desert Cahuilla, dogs still were named after the first dog. Other dog names referred to their appearance or to some characteristic behavior.

These gathering people of the desert lived by collecting plants. They recognized at least three major seasons: the budding of trees, hot days, and cold days. Some divided the year into eight more specific seasons; each of these was named in association with the development and maturation of the mesquite bean. Another calendar was lunar and based on thirteen months, but this one probably was not of equal importance with the eight stages of the mesquite. In order to predict when a season was to begin, old men gathered in a dance house and discussed when a particular star would appear to usher in a season. When the star did appear, they rejoiced and prepared for the collecting activities to follow. These observations were particularly important in the spring when stores of food were low and when plants which could be eaten were ripening in the mountains.

The most important plant in the collecting activities of the Desert Cahuilla was the mesquite tree which grew plentifully in groves found anywhere between the desert floor and heights of up to 3500 feet in better-watered areas. Stands were particularly numerous near springs, streams, and in washes. In the early summer the blossoms were picked, roasted in a pit of heated stones, formed into balls, and stored in pottery containers, to be eventually boiled in water and eaten. During June, July, and August, depending on the locality, the mesquite beans ripened. At this time, or earlier if the unripe pods were to be artificially ripened in the sun, they were picked by entire families. The children were helpful in climbing the trees to dislodge pods from smaller branches. The pods were not gathered indiscriminately, for the beans from some trees were regarded as more palatable than others. The pods could be stored from one year to the next, which may have been necessary upon occasion, since the trees of a particular grove were not necessarily as productive each year. The ripened pods were crushed in an upright wooden mortar with a stone or wooden pestle, and the juice was made into a beverage. The pods might be ripened artificially, picked ripe, or gathered after they had fallen from the trees. The dried pods, either complete or broken into small sections, were stored in raised brush framework caches. Further processing included grinding up the pods in a mortar or on a metate. The meal then could be placed in shallow round pottery or in basketry containers and moistened; when it had dried, the caked meal was removed and stored in the rafters of a house. Sections of the cakes were broken off and eaten as a snack or carried by travelers as food. The meal could also be made into a gruel or soaked in water to make the mesquite juice beverage. Loose ground meal was stored in pottery or basketry containers to be made into gruel later.

The mesquite bean was the most important staple, but the people of the desert areas likewise collected screw beans as a subsistence item. The screw bean or tornillo grew under the same general conditions as the mesquite and was processed for consumption like the mesquite pods. In ethnographic studies of California Indians acorns are generally considered to be an important staple. This clearly was the case over much of the state, but the acorn was not so important among the

Cahuilla as it was among other aboriginal groups. The favored acorn of the four varieties available was from the Kellogs oak, preferred for its taste and consistency. As was true with the mesquite beans, when the first acorns were collected, they were eaten ceremonially in the home of the *net*. If an individual were to collect acorns prior to this ceremony, it was anticipated that he would be taken ill or die. In the sib-controlled groves, each family owned particular trees, and from October to November when the acorns were ripe, families visited their trees and men climbed the trees to knock the acorns to the ground. The women removed the nut by cracking the shell between two stones, spreading the kernels out to dry for several weeks and then grinding them in mortars of stone and leaching them. To remove the bitter tannic acid from the meal it was spread out on a loosely woven basket or in a depression in the sand. In either case grass or leaves were placed in the leaching basin to prevent the meal from washing away. Then water, either cold or warm, was poured over the meal several times; during this process the mixture was stirred. The capabilities of a woman were measured by her skill in leaching and grinding acorn meal. Very finely ground meal was made into cakes and baked in hot coals, while coarse meal was made into a gruel. Acorns which were not ground at the time they were gathered were stored in raised platform caches like mesquite beans.

David P. Barrows recorded the use of over sixty plants for subsistence, with the mesquite and screw bean serving as the most important staples. In well-watered localities grew a species of *Chenopodium* which locally was called careless weed. The seeds from this plant were collected, ground, and baked into cakes. One of the most important seed-producing grasses was chia, which is a member of the sage family. The seeds were dislodged from the whorls with a seed beater onto a flat basket. They were parched and ground to be baked into cakes or mixed with water to make a nourishing drink. When the century plants or agave of the canyons produced stalks, the stalks and "cabbages" were roasted in sand pits heated with stones. The yucca of the hillsides and sandy canyons were visited when the stalks produced fruit, which was picked while green and roasted among coals. Fruit which had ripened on the stalk was consumed raw. The ocotillo, which grows near the base of the San Jacinto Mountains, is a desert shrub with thorny branches. The flowers produced are in bright red clusters, and after the flowers had bloomed, oblong capsules remained filled with seeds. The blossoms as well as the seed pods were eaten. The wild plums growing along the canyons were utilized; they produced fruit with little pulp but a large pit. The plums were dried in

the sun, and then the pits were broken open. The kernels were removed, crushed, leached, and cooked as gruel. The berries of elders
were collected and dried. Before being consumed the berries were
cooked into a thick sauce. To this listing could be added many other
plants, but the enumerated species and their utilization provide a
gauge to the wide range of plants collected for food.

The social life of the Desert Cahuilla literally was built around
water—the wells and water holes. The settlements were organized into
sibs, which were the most important units for social action. These
people traced their descent through the male line, that is, patrilineal
descent, and after a couple married, they resided with or near the husband's family, that is, patrilocal residence. Considering the principle
of descent further, we note that there were partrilineages in which by
definition all the members traced their descent to a known common
ancestor. There were additionally groups of patrilineages where the
common ancestor was assumed but was not traceable in an actual
genealogy; these were patrisibs. In 1924–1925 the anthropologist William D. Strong attempted with the aid of an old Desert Cahuilla
informant to reconstruct the disposition of the sibs for the period
around 1870. This era, although not aboriginal, probably reflected
rather well the patterning of settlements before the creation of reservations.

The sibs were lumped into two groups or moieties. In primeval
times when Mukat and Tamaioit were created, each stressed an affiliation with an animal, Tamaioit with the coyote and Mukat with the
wildcat. It is from these animals that the moieties derived their names
and continuity with the mythological past. The Wildcat moiety contained eight or perhaps nine named sibs, and two of these contained
two and three separate named patrilineages. The sibs of the Coyote
moiety numbered ten, and two contained separate named patrilineages. Theoretically, in aboriginal times one sib occupied a particular
settlement, but with the passage of time and an increase in numbers
a sib could become separated into named lineages. These in turn
might eventually acquire the position of separate sibs. The fully separate status of a sib was achieved only when it acquired its own *net*.
The Desert Cahuilla community of Touched by the River, for example,
existed before 1880. An artificial well and a nearby mesquite grove
made the location desirable until the well went dry with a lowering
of the water table. The village took its name from the name of the
first sib to settle there. These people were of the Coyote moiety and
traced their earlier residence to the Santa Rosa Mountains. The next
sib to settle by the well belonged to the Dogs of the Wildcat moiety

who also came from the Santa Rosa Mountains. With the latter sib came the Wantcinakiktum people, who derived their sib name from a Santa Rosa mountain. The Wantcinakiktum, however, were subordinate to the Dogs, for they had no *net* of their own. The former was once an independent sib, but apparently the members decreased in number or moved apart. The patrilineage of the *net* died out, leaving at least this patrilineage without a leader. These people, however, identified themselves with the Dogs in a relationship which could be regarded in the nature of a suprapatrisib or phratry.

In the Touched by the River village the members of the original sib occupied seven small nuclear family households. When the former leader of the sib died, presumably his elder son did not possess the necessary qualities to serve as the next leader. By a decision of the sib members, a younger son succeeded the father as the *net*. The house of the *net*, unlike all the others of his sib, had a dance house attached to it. The living arrangements of the Dogs were different, for they occupied two large houses containing extended families. The eldest son succeeded his father as *net* in the one known instance; this was the ideal form of succession. Like the Touched by the River sib the Dog *net* had a dance house appended to his residence. The Wantcinakiktum lived in four nuclear family households and were very poor, seemingly quite dependent on the Dogs for much of their food. Since they had no *net* of their own, they were responsible to the *net* of the Dogs. Each sib ranged out of the relatively permanent community to collect on its traditional lands; for example, the Touched by the River sib owned a nearby foothill area where there were groves of mesquite and cacti in the canyons. The Dogs collected on their ancestral lands in the Santa Rosa Mountains over an area shared with another sib. Each spring when they moved with the other sib to the mountains, they did so under the leadership of the oldest *net* of the two sibs. The Dogs additionally collected from scattered groves of mesquite which were near a village they had occupied on the desert. The Wancinakiktum collected in the desert area used by the Dogs and also in a canyon area in the Santa Rosa Mountains. The people of any sib were free to hunt mountain sheep, deer, rabbits, or other game on the collecting territory of any other sib.

The major social division among the Desert Cahuilla was along moiety lines. The Coyotes and Wildcats were prohibited from marrying each other; thus, these were the exogamous units in the society. It is interesting to note additionally that all animals were regarded as belonging to the moiety of their creator in the same manner as human beings. When the songs of a sib were sung, birds were mentioned which belonged to the moiety of that sib, and this established the singers' affiliations. The evidence of whether or not members of the opposite moiety aided in certain ceremonies for the dead is contradictory, but this problem will be discussed later. The members of the moieties did, however, joke with one another, but this relationship was friendly, not malicious.

Hereditary leadership among the Desert Cahuilla did not extend beyond the sib level, but in cases where some necessary decision was important to a number of sibs, the respective *nets* would sit in council collectively. The routine decisions which were not personal in nature were under the control of one's sib *net*, a man who ideally possessed inordinate abilities. Among the specific qualifications required of a *net* were a knowledge of the boundaries of all the sib lands and of the ceremonies and traditions; he also was expected to be a good orator and a fair-minded individual. He did not possess more material property than anyone else, but the families gave him the first fruit of any plant harvest, which in part compensated for the time he devoted to sib activities. The theory of passing the office from eldest son to eldest son had obvious advantages, for it is rather clear that a potential *net* was required to learn and retain a great many specifics about his sib. It was stated that a woman never held the title of *net*.

A woman retained the name of the sib of her birth and the name of her patrilineage as well if the sib were divided into a number of such lineages. She did, however, come to associate herself ceremonially with the sib of her husband. Any ceremonial ties she might retain with her personal sib depended on how far away she was from the community of her sib. From the more esoteric activities of her husband's sib a wife appears to have been excluded, but older women participated in at least some ceremonial activities.

As mentioned in reference to the dwellings of the Touched by the River and Dog *nets*, each had an attached dance house. In aboriginal times it probably was of the same materials as an ordinary dwelling but was rounded in outline. At the rear of the *net's* house was a small room, and here in a rolled mat of tules were kept sacred objects and ceremonial paraphernalia of the sib. Included in at least some of the sibs' sacred bundles were stone pipes, and in the bundles of all were eagle feathers. In one particular bundle were the feathers, part of an eagle skin, and an eagle feather kilt. Clearly the *net*, as guardian of the most sacred sib objects, which collectively were termed the "heart" of the sib, was the most important ceremonial specialist. It was this possession which led to his importance as a social leader as well.

The *net* was the outstanding socioreligious leader among the

Desert Cahuilla, but there were other leaders of stature who were more specialized. Included was the *paha*, whose role existed only for the northernmost Desert Cahuilla. Even here his functions are obscure and of uncertain dimensions. Among some sibs the *paha* did not exist, but when the office was known, the individual who filled it was powerful and feared. His prime duty was to make the preparations for ceremonies and to maintain order on such occasions. It seems that he may have performed his duties for a sib of the opposite moiety. Upon his death he was replaced by his son or another near male relative.

The only other leader of importance was the shaman. This was not a hereditary office among the Desert people, nor was there any restriction on the number of shamans in any one sib. A potential shaman usually was ill frequently as a child and was treated by a shaman, who would become aware of the boy's potential as a curer, magician, and seer. When he was about eighteen years old, he would dream a song, which was the tangible source of his inordinate powers. It was Mukat, one of the twin creators and culture heroes, who conveyed the dreams and the association with a guardian spirit. The next step was for the youth to dance before the people of his sib in the dance house for three nights, after which he would be known as a shaman. In time he acquired other songs, dances, feats of magic, curing and bewitching methods, all through his dreams. In his dreams, too, the shaman learned of specific herbal cures for particular ailments, while at other times he learned specific "spells" which were harmful or curative. When not drawing from his pharmacopoeia, he attempted to cure a patient by sucking directly on the afflicted part of the patient's body. He reputedly removed the disease object without breaking the skin. When plant products were employed, they usually were applied externally, such as an application of golderino weed to a snake bite or an unspecified plant product to the bite of a poisonous spider. Few plants were recorded as having been used in curing, which is in contrast with the diverse knowledge of plants and their uses as foods. Certain animals, birds, and insects, such as the coyote, fox, owl, hummingbird, and fly, were messengers for the shamans; they brought warnings of someone's impending illness. As a shaman succeeded in his calling, his reputation increased. While a youth, he did not accept material rewards for his cures, but as he grew older he charged for his services. If a shaman became malevolent in the use of his spirit powers, he became a threat to the security of the community, and in some instances such individuals were killed by common agreement.

In the Palm Springs area were four sibs, each of which was localized at one settlement. The From the Rock sib occupied one or more canyons near Palm Springs, and the *net* maintained the ceremonial house. According to the mythology of this group, they wandered from the mountains into the canyons on the eastern flank of the San Jacinto Mountains. It was said that this was the oldest of the local sibs. A second sib was Daylight, which occupied Andreas Canyon. Both of these were of the Wildcat moiety, and as with the desert inhabitants, moiety exogamy prevailed. Two other sibs, both of which were extinct in 1925, were of the Coyote moiety and lived to the east at Indian Wells; their names were Good and *Nonhaiam*. Another nonfunctioning Coyote sib, the Deep Water Hole people, formerly lived near Palm Springs. All of these sibs except the last one mentioned formed a ceremonial group which exchanged shell money at their Mourning Ceremony.

The *net* in the Palm Springs area functioned in the same manner as that of the Desert Cahuilla except that the former had greater authority. People feared disobeying a decision of the *net*, for by possessing the sacred sib bundle he could make someone ill or even kill him by supernatural means. The *paha*, as an important official, was known from the beginning of the world according to the Palm Springs area people. He served as an assistant to the *net* in all of his activities. He kept order at sib functions, saw to it that each family provided food enough for ceremonies, and was the messenger of the *net*. Only among the From the Rock people was there a ceremonial official called *takwa*. His primary function was to oversee the preparation and division of food during sib ceremonies, and during the Mourning Ceremony he made the presentations of gifts to the guests.

Probably the major religious activity which did not have to do with the life cycle of an individual was the Eagle Killing Ceremony. The ceremony was virtually the same at Palm Springs and among the other Desert groups. The mountainous lands of some sibs contained eagle nests which were watched carefully when the eagles nested. A guard observed the nest from a high vantage point, and when eggs were laid the sib was notified and a feast was held. When the eaglets were well-feathered, the sib *net*, regarded as their owner, sent men to retrieve one or more of the eaglets. The captured bird was kept caged in the *net's* home and fed by his family. When the bird reached its full plumage, the neighboring sib or sibs were notified and the ceremony arranged. All night long a guest sib sang the special songs pertaining to the death of eagles. They were joined in singing and the accompanying dances by all of the attending people. The eagle was rolled into the sib's ceremonial mat and held by the *net's* nuclear family members as they danced in a circle. With the dawn of morning the eagle screeched and died, probably from being squeezed gradually. The body of the bird was placed by the fire, and the people wailed to lament its death. After the sun had risen completely, the eagle was skinned. The *net* kept the feathered skin; the body most likely was burned. The skin was rubbed soft and kept in the sacred bundle. Some feathers might be made into a ceremonial skirt and others set aside for adorning images in the Mourning Ceremony.

When sibs were assembled, particularly when a girl was tattooed or when a boy's nasal septum was pierced, songs known as "enemy songs" might be sung. The complex was best recalled by Desert Cahuilla informants. Between certain sibs, usually those who were geographically distant from one another, there was a rivalry of unknown origins. Members of the competing sibs originated songs into which they incorporated the names of persons in the rival sibs. The names sung were the personal appellations bestowed by one's sib *net* ceremonially and secretly. The fact that the personal name of someone in a sib had been learned was shameful, and these names were used in the derisive songs (see Note 1). The performance was by first one sib and then the other, and the dubious victory went either to the side mentioning the most names of rivals and heaping the greatest abuse or else to the sib whose members were physically able to sing longer than the other side.

The enemy songs were an obvious means for giving vent to aggressive behavior in a socially approved manner. The joking relationship between moiety members served the same function in a milder and friendlier atmosphere. From the literature it is evident that serious, overt ingroup hostility was rare, but petty quarrels were rather common. It would seem that the *net* of a sib had rather firm control over those persons responsible to him, and quarrels between members of different sibs were handled by the *nets* of the sibs involved. There did arise occasionally persons who became a threat to group harmony; these were usually malevolent shamans. One recorded example well illustrates the course of events and action in such a situation. In the latter part of the nineteenth century an old man, a powerful shaman of the Touched by the River sib, was considered to be the world's most powerful shaman. This was proved by the fact that when the shamans gave an exhibition of their abilities, he always performed last and challenged the others to kill him. None was able to do so because he was protected by spirits on all sides. Finally the old shaman was told by a man of a different sib to stop killing people. The man who gave the warning was soon struck by a "pain" which none of the shamans consulted could remove, and he died. Everyone knew that the old Touched by the River shaman was responsible. A man from the shaman's sib and men from other sibs met and decided that the old shaman must be killed. It was decided that the *net* of the Dog sib should be the executioner since he was both strong and brave. This man, along with a shaman from another sib, visited the old shaman and was invited to spend the night. They did so, and when everyone was asleep, the *net* thoroughly crushed the old man's skull with a stone pestle. At the head of the victim's bed were found many small feathers of different birds and the skin of a gopher snake. It was these items that the old man had made into pains. As they were trampled into the ground, a thunder-like sound was heard. In the morning people came to view the body, and later the same morning the body and the house were burned separately. It was then agreed by the sibs involved that if the Touched by the River sib sought revenge, all of its members would be killed. No action was necessary, however. There were threats of vengeance by some young men of the sib of the deceased man's wife, but since they did not have the support of their *net*, no action materialized. This case is one of the rare recorded instances in which collective sib action was taken for the good of all the people.

Formalized warfare or even feuds with neighboring ethnic groups were rare. The peoples to the west were either Mountain or Pass Cahuilla who were closely related by language and tradition, and conflict with them was minimal. To the east was an area of desert with no permanent occupants until the Colorado River was reached, where the Yuma lived. The latter were aggressive and warlike. The Cahuilla feared the Yuma, but the intervening desert was an effective barrier to intensive contact. The Chemehuevi who lived to the east along the Colorado River and into the deserts of California were quite friendly with the Desert Cahuilla. The southern neighbors of the Desert Cahuilla were the Yuman-speaking Kamia, but the dimension of intercourse with these people has not been reported upon and is assumed to have been relatively unimportant.

In the kinship terminology a male Ego distinguished among his older and younger male and female siblings, and in the first ascending generation he made similar distinctions between his father's brothers and mother's sisters. He employed other terms for his father's sisters and mother's brothers; these did not take their relative age into consideration. In his own generation a male Ego referred to his parallel female cousins with the same terms as for his sisters. For these cousins the older and younger distinctions depended on the age of the mother's sister or father's brother in relation to Ego's father and mother. For example, a man's older sister was termed *kis*; his mother's older sister's daughter was also termed *kis*. Likewise, both a younger sister and one's father's younger brother's daughter were called *nawal*. Cross female cousins, however, were termed similarly to each other but different from sisters or parallel female cousins. What we have is a bifurcate collateral terminology in the first ascending generation above Ego and an Iroquois cousin terminology. The Iroquois cousin terms make particular sense since there existed moiety exogamy. Thus certain near relatives, such as father's brother's children and mother's sister's children, were of one's own moiety and called brother and sister. Parallel cousins on the other hand were of a different moiety and termed differently, but in spite of the terminological difference one could not marry such a person.

Of all the forms of diversion probably the most important was the game of *peon*. It was played avidly at the Mourning Ceremony, at other ceremonial events, and at secular gatherings. George H. Shinn, who knew the Cahuilla rather well in the late 1880's, described the game as he saw it played among the Desert people. A team from one village played against one from another settlement; perhaps it was one sib against another. Shamans aided their respective sides, while women sat behind the men of their team and sang at certain times during the game. One person was assigned the role of mediator, and it was his duty to keep a fire burning by which the game was played, hold the stakes, settle disputes, and take charge of the tally sticks. The game was played by eight men, four to a side, who knelt or sat cross-legged with a blanket between them. Lots were drawn to determine which side would first have the *peons* in hand. A *peon* was a small bone tied to a string about two feet long; at the opposite end of the string was a small piece of wood. Each man on the starting team held a stick in one hand and a *peon* in the other and crossed his arms with his fists beneath his armpits. These men then took the blanket, probably a skin in aboriginal times, in their teeth to hide the manipulation of their hands from the view of the guessers. The holders of the *peons* swayed from side to side in time with the singing of the women on their side, switched the *peons* back and forth, and then suddenly dropped the blanket from their teeth, revealing their arms still crossed and fists beneath their armpits. They continued swaying from side to side, and their opposites attempted to guess which hand held the *peon*. For every correct guess the second team took the *peon*, but with each incorrect guess the first team received one of the fifteen tallies. A particular game ended when one side had lost all four *peons* or had won all of the tallies. Then a new game was started and new stakes put up. *Peon* was played frequently throughout the night, and as one player tired he was replaced by another.

Other games mentioned include a race between two pairs of men. Each pair kicked a wooden ball for several miles and then back again to the starting point. The men on each team took turns kicking the ball, and the team which returned first was the winner. Another race took place on the night of a new moon. The first boy to see the moon would call the others, and they would race to some water in which they could swim. After swimming they then raced home, and by so doing they would bring good luck to the coming month. Cat's cradles were made by the people of both sexes. This skill had supernatural implications since a person's spirit, before it could pass into the world of other spirits, was first required to demonstrate its ability to make string figures.

The course of an individual's life from womb to tomb was sur-rounded at critical times with numerous prohibitions. One of these periods was pregnancy. The potential mother refrained from eating any more than necessary; she drank only warm water, ate very little meat, and consumed no salt. If the woman ate fruit pecked by a bird, her infant would have sores; if she ate meat from the legs of game, a breech presentation would result; and if the woman were industrious when pregnant, her offspring would be an energetic person. These are but three of a number of specific rules of behavior to insure a safe delivery and a normal offspring. When a woman gave birth, she was in a sitting position. As soon as she had dispelled the placenta, she lay in a specially prepared trough dug into the floor of the house. This trough was lined with sand which had been heated with stones, and after the woman stretched out, additional hot sand was piled over her body. Here she remained for about ten days, leaving the trough only to urinate and defecate, to have the sand reheated, and to be bathed with hot water each morning. During the month following par-turition the mother still was subject to food taboos, and the father could eat no foods containing salt. A nursing mother did not have sexual intercourse with her husband, for to do so was thought to spoil the mother's milk, and a woman who weaned her infant early became the subject of mild teasing.

An offspring was not named formally until several children had been born into the sib and each child's parents had accumulated an abundance of food and wealth for a feast and for distribution. This meant that the child was between the ages of four and twelve before it received its name. In the event that a child had not been formally named by the time he was thirteen, he would have nothing but nicknames throughout his life. The special naming ceremony was held in the sib dance house, and to the event were invited the members of the father's and the mother's sibs. The participating children received traditional sib names of deceased ancestors selected by the sib *net*. The names for males tended to be those of animals, birds, or insects, and those for females were most often from plants or household artifacts. The climax of the ceremonial dancing and singing occurred when the *net* held each child up and shouted its name three times, after which the name was repeated by the audience. It sometimes happened that a *net* would not state the real name for fear an "enemy" sib would learn of it and incorporate it into their songs. In this case the correct name was revealed in secret. The father also might acquire a new name at this ceremony and in the process gain additional standing. Following the naming ritual, presents such as food, baskets, a deerskin, or even ceremonial equipment were distributed to the guests. This gift giving ended the ceremony.

As a Desert girl approached adolescence, she was tattooed. The sib of the mother was invited to the event, and it was the mother's sister who tattooed the girl. Using a cactus thorn, she pricked straight lines or angled lines from the lower lip to the chin of the girl. Into the openings was rubbed a black paint obtained in trade from the Yuma Indians. At this time the earlobes of the girl were pierced. At the time of each girl's menarche the *net* summoned the sib of the girl's mother to a ceremony which began that evening. A fire was built in front of the net's house to heat the ground. After it was hot a trough was dug, and the girl was placed in it, her body then being covered with hot sand. Throughout the night the members of the girl's sib danced and sang around the pit. In the morning the girl was removed, bathed in warm water, and her head was covered with a white paint or a powdered mineral. For the next three weeks she was subject to food taboos very much like those surrounding pregnancy. The girl stayed in or near the house, and she scratched her head with a special implement, not with her fingernails, in order to prevent her hair from dropping out. Subsequent menstrual periods were surrounded by the same taboos, and a married menstruating woman must never touch her husband; the good health of the couple depended on how well the woman obeyed these rules.

William D. Strong records that his informants denied the existence of an initiation ceremony for Desert Cahuilla males, but Lucile Hooper described male initiation for the Palm Springs group. Boys between the ages of ten and eighteen were selected by the elders for initiation and taken to a brush enclosure outside the dance house. The boys remained secluded here for five days and saw only those persons who brought them food, which could not have grease or salt in it. During the last three nights that the boys were in the ceremonial enclosure, the old people danced throughout the night. The climax came on the fourth night when the initiates were brought out and given a drink of cooked jimsonweed, or toloache as it is known in Spanish. After taking it, the boys danced briefly but then became dizzy and were placed in a corner while the older people continued to dance. The following evening the effects of the jimsonweed had worn off, and for the next five nights the boys were taught how to dance, sing particular songs, and otherwise instructed concerning correct adult behavior. The function of this ceremony seems to have been to dramatize the ritual death of the initiates as children and their rebirth as adults knowledgeable about the norms of the group. The only forms of body mutilation among males were piercing the ears and piercing the nasal septum. The latter operation was not common and was said to have been performed only on young boys with promise as leaders. Into the opening at the base of the nose were inserted pieces of deer bone.

Desert Cahuilla marriage patterns included moiety exogamy and a prohibition of seeking a spouse from any known relatives on either side of the family. Genealogies were not remembered over many generations so that it was possible to marry a fourth or fifth cousin, so long as that person was in the opposite moiety. Instances of infant betrothals were known, in which the prospective in-laws exchanged gifts of food and baskets frequently to bind the agreement. A person was most likely to marry someone from a nearby community. Most commonly a girl was about thirteen years old and the male about eighteen at the time of marriage. The match was arranged by the parents, and the proper procedure was for the mother of the boy to ask the girl's parents if the girl would help her collect mesquite beans. The girl's family delayed responding until they considered the match; if they judged it desirable, the girl's father notified the boy's father. Presents were taken to the bride's home by a relative, who returned with the girl alone. She was led into the house by the boy's mother and seated facing a corner, with her back to the assembled relatives of the groom. The groom then sat next to the girl, and the couple was given food as the boy's relatives ate. After the feasting was over, the couple was considered married, and that night the newlyweds were given a single blanket with the theory that if affection did not bring them together the cold desert night would. A girl who was unhappy in the home of her in-laws might return to her mother's home, but if she did this repeatedly, the presents which had been given were returned and the marriage considered dissolved. The groom and his parents had the right to expect the bride to bear an infant within two or three years. Failure to do so might annul the marriage and again mean a return of the marriage presents. A man could, if the woman's parents agreed, receive a younger sister of his wife if the latter died, that is, the sororate. It was less common for a woman to marry her deceased husband's brother, that is, the levirate. Among these people monogamy was the prevailing form of marriage, and familial relationships appear to have been quite stable. Among the Palm Springs people the details of marriage arrangements varied slightly from those for the Desert, but the essence of the ceremonial arrangements was the same. The Palm Springs residents married either into the Desert or Pass groups, with somewhat greater frequency among the latter.

In the routine of adult life a woman was the outsider in the nuclear or extended family household of her husband. The husband and wife were expected to be reserved with one another in the presence of others, and the wife generally retiring when with her in-laws or around men. Ideally, younger persons were thoughtful and unselfish in their dealings with older persons, values instilled in children when they were still quite young. Young boys who hunted or collected the first plant products of the season were expected to take them to the aged. The most virtuous adults were those men who hunted the best and the women who could work more efficiently than the others.

Death brought destruction to a Cahuilla household. It was recalled that in the distant past on the morning following the death of a person, the house in which the death had occurred was burned, and at a specific site the body of the deceased was likewise burned. More recently, however, this archaic pattern was modified. When an individual died, the members of his and other sibs assembled, bringing presents. The body was washed, dressed, and taken to the sib dance house of the deceased. Here the assembled mourners sang over the body throughout the night. If a man had died, the creation narrative was sung; for a woman, a song about the moon was sung, since it was the moon who had originally instructed women. The body of the deceased was burned on the morning following death, and within a week his house and possessions were likewise burned. Within a month of the cremation the Pass Cahuilla held a ceremony to prevent the spirit of the deceased from returning. The members of the dead person's sib took food to the dance house and sent for the members of neighboring sibs. Bolts of calico—probably reed mats in aboriginal times—were dragged about the dance floor to destroy the tracks of the dead, and then songs were sung to propitiate the deceased. Relatives of the deceased threw out gifts which were gathered up by the guests, and any possessions of the dead person which had not been burned previously were now destroyed in a fire.

During the fall or winter of every year, a Mourning Ceremony extending over seven days was held for those sib members who had died since the last such ceremony was held. This was the most complex of all Cahuilla ceremonials, and its essential core was the retelling of the creation myth. The ceremony had been held for the first time after the death of Mukat, and it was he, before he died, who taught the ancestors of the people how to conduct the rituals. The sib *net,* with the aid of the *paha* and others, was the director and organizer. Arrangements were made months in advance. Guests were people from sibs related by marriage to the deceased as well as those persons who had brought gifts after the death. Each sib was invited to arrive on a specific night so that the assembled group would not be too large. The first three nights the shamans of the host sibs or other sibs performed tricks and danced. They attempted to communicate with the spirits of the dead in the process. One shaman's performance at such a Mourning Ceremony has been described thus: he tied a band about his head and inserted three clusters of owl feathers in it, and then another cluster of owl feathers was attached to a stick about eight inches in length which the shaman held in his hand. He sang and shuffled around a fire and began to tremble violently. He then pushed the stick down his throat three different times, and the third time he brought up a small black object said to have been a lizard. After the "lizard" was removed from his heart, he stopped shaking. A favored performance upon such occasions was for the shaman to place live coals in his mouth and to swallow these (see Note 2). Throughout the three nights to follow, different sibs led by their respective singers sang all night long. Those individuals singing the last night aided the relatives of the deceased in making images of each person who had died and for whom the ceremony was being held. The images were nearly life-sized and were constructed from reed matting and clothed with deerskins. The male images had bows and arrows and eagle-feather headdresses; the female images had baskets decorated with eagle feathers. They were further adorned with ornaments, or decorative skins such as that of the wildcat, and eagle feathers. At sunrise on the final day of the Mourning Ceremony the assembled guests were given presents of food or artifacts. Then the host *net* led a procession around the inside and outside of the dance house. He was followed by women, each carrying the image of a near relative. Then came the throng of participants and attendants. The people gathered in a circle in front of the dance house, and the images were placed in the center of the circle as the people danced, sang, and wailed. Objects of wealth were then thrown over the images to show respect for the dead. These items could be retrieved but not by members of the sib hosting the ceremony. Next, the images were carried to a designated place and burned. The sib members who had been invited to the ceremony were presented by the *net* with strings of beads made of small round shell disks, and then the people left for their homes. The souls of the dead were now released, further mourning was unnecessary, and their names were no longer mentioned.

After the cremation and the burning of images, the soul or spirit of an individual continued its existence. The presence of a soul in a living person was considered a reality, for when people fainted or dreamed their souls seemed to wander. Spirits also left the bodies of persons months before they died. A spirit might wander unknown to the possessor, or else the individual might become ill and a shaman be summoned to retrieve it. When the soul of a person was beyond recall, it went to a place created in the east by Mukat. Here stood two mountains which clapped together and then separated. The souls found their way to these mountains, and once there a deathless guardian spirit questioned and tested them. After passing the tests, which included making cat's cradles and answering questions, the soul attempted to go between the clapping mountains, but only those who had lived according to the rules of Mukat while on earth were able to pass untouched. Otherwise they were crushed by the mountains and became butterflies, bats, trees, or rocks nearby.

The Cahuilla often have been grouped under the general category of Mission Indians, but this designation is not accurate. They were not subject to the same mission environment associated with the Indians of the coastal region of southern California, nor did most

Cahuilla have more than indirect contact with the Roman Catholic priests of the missions. The first European to skirt the fringes of Cahuilla country probably was Pedro Fages. In 1772 he followed deserting soldiers from San Diego into the Colorado desert, went northward to the Borrego Valley and then on to the vicinity of the San Gabriel mission. About this time too the Spanish were intent on establishing a land access route to Alta California from Mexico. Supplying the new Spanish colony by sea was precarious, and it was hoped that an overland link with northern Mexico could be developed. Juan Bautista de Anza was selected to pioneer the trail. He set out with a small party from Tubac in early 1774, wending his way from one water hole to the next without any expectation of difficulties until he reached the Yuma Indians along the Colorado River. The aggressive and bellicose Yuma were in a position to contest his crossing of the Colorado River. De Anza, however, gained the support of their chief, Palma, who made the crossing incidental. The desert beyond was more of a challenge, and the first attempt to cross it was a failure due to the lack of forage and water for the horses and mules. This forced them back to the Colorado River. A smaller party was organized to attempt a crossing, and the second push into the unknown was successful. They passed through a portion of Cahuilla country, crossed the San Jacinto Mountains, and finally arrived at the San Gabriel mission, which had been founded in 1771. De Anza traveled on to Monterey, returned across the desert to the Colorado River and on to Tubac. In September of the same year he again set out for Alta California, but this time with settlers and large herds of livestock. The route taken was a more northerly one than before. Although the Colorado River crossing was difficult, it was negotiated, and the party reached the San Gabriel mission. In 1780 a Spanish settlement was authorized among the Yuma Indians as a belated attempt to secure the Colorado River crossing and to give the Indians the mission they had requested, but the Yuma in 1781 destroyed the outpost and killed the settlers, missionaries, and soldiers. This negated effectively the usefulness of de Anza's efforts and his hopes for an overland trail. When the War for Independence in Mexico ceased, attention again was turned inland, especially as the Mohave Indians, linguistic and cultural neighbors of the Yuma, were raiding ranchos and settlements from the east. In 1819 the Indians in the San Bernardino area requested a mission, and seemingly as a result an outpost or rancho was established among them. In 1823 Jose Romero left Tucson with a small party to reestablish the overland route, and he traveled westward without serious difficulties. On the unsuccessful return trip it was noted in the diary of Jose Maria Estudillo that the most eastern rancho passed was at San Gorgonio. It was shortly after this that the party met some "Cohahahuilla" Indians traveling to San Gabriel.

From the 1823–1824 diary of Jose Estudillo and its annotations by Lowell J. Bean and William M. Mason it is apparent that the Desert Cahuilla, at least those as far south and west as Palm Springs, were in rather close contact with the San Bernardino mission rancho. Surprisingly, some of the people of the Coachella Valley were horti-culturists by this time, raising the aboriginal American domestic plants maize and pumpkins that they had unquestionably acquired from some Colorado River Indians who were farmers. The Cahuilla of the Desert also were growing watermelon, which is an Old World domestic plant introduced into the Americas by Europeans. It might be expected that the Old World domestic barley and wheat would likewise have been cultivated, but these were not mentioned. At the same time it is known that both crops were being grown by the Yuma prior to the travels of de Anza among them. What we are led to conclude is that wheat and barley cultivation probably was known to the Cahuilla but not practiced by them.

Before 1834 the California missions were under the control of Roman Catholic clerics, and the mission setting maintained by these Franciscans had been the primary acculturative influence upon the Indians. After this date some missions, including the one at San Gabriel, passed through the administrative process of secularization, and the missionaries lost their control. In the year 1834, the San Bernardino rancho was sacked and burned by Indians. With seculari-zation the rancho passed into private hands, but there were serious difficulties in keeping the herds of livestock out of the hands of marauding Indians. The Mountain Cahuilla leader, "General" or "Captain" Juan Antonio, and his small band were retained to stop the raids, which they did with great success. In 1846 the United States acquired California, and a few years later, in 1852, the San Bernardino rancho was purchased by Mormon settlers. Juan Antonio's followers then moved to the western end of San Gorgonio Pass. All during the late Mexican and early American periods the raids by Indians for livestock, particularly horses, contributed to the hostile feelings of the whites toward most Indians in southern California. It was the combative Mohave, Yuma and Paiute who were the greatest villains; it seems unlikely that the Cahuilla took a significant part in these raids. The sequence of early American period events did not lead to serious militant resistance by the Cahuilla, for they were not by nature combative and were beyond the interests of any major segment of the white population. Thus they were left very much to their own devices.

As early as 1847 the military governor of California, General Stephen W. Kearny, appointed Indian agents, including one for the southern part of California. Apparently they did nothing of importance, however. Then in 1850 the U. S. Congress sent three commissioners to California to negotiate treaties with the Indians and assign lands to them. O. M. Wozencraft was the commissioner who arranged the Cahuilla treaty of 1852. This treaty set aside lands from San Gorgonio to Warner's ranch, an area about forty miles in length and thirty miles in width. The U. S. Senate, however, refused to ratify any of the eighteen treaties with California Indians. Congressional resistance stemmed from a number of facts; the commissioners had committed the government to the expenditure of a great deal of money, the white citizens of California were vigorously opposed to the treaties, and possibly it was thought that some of these lands might contain gold. In the fall of 1852 a Superintendent of Indian Affairs in California, Edward F. Beale, was appointed. He was the colorful and extremely capable administrator who selected Benjamin D. Wilson as the subagent for the southern part of the state. Wilson was a former mayor of Los Angeles, a landowner who had married a Spanish-American, and a leading merchant. In a report, possibly if not probably written by Wilson's friend Benjamin Hayes, we have some comments on the Cahuilla as they were in 1852 and a good account of conditions among the Indians of southern California in general. The Wilson Report was twice rescued from oblivion, once by its publication in the Los Angeles *Star* in 1868, and again in 1952 with the annotated republication by John W. Caughey.

By 1852 old ethnic groupings had been disrupted, for the Wilson Report noted that among the Desert Cahuilla there were Luisenos, Dieguenos, and a leader who was a Yuma. Although the elders still spoke Spanish, as did many others, and there still was the claim of being Christian, the last Christian ties with the San Bernardino rancho had been severed with its destruction in 1834. In general the Indians worked as laborers and domestics on the ranchos of whites. They were paid at a much lower rate than white laborers and frequently were intoxicated. One of the major problems concerned the rights of Indians to mission and other lands under the new government. Wilson, or Hayes, pointed out that under Spanish law the Indians had rights to their settlements and pasture lands, and in theory the state of California recognized Indian landrights. A number of recommendations were made in the report concerning the future, including the suggestion that a subagent and others with skills such as farming and carpentry be located at principal settlements. At the beginning at least, missionaries would be recruited to teach the Indians about American ways. It was pointed out that the present state laws were "*All* punishment. *No* reform!" (See Note 3.) It was proposed further that lands be set aside for the Indians and that administrative centers be established in different areas, including one among the Cahuilla. The people would be encouraged to concentrate in these towns and be regulated largely by a legal code derived from the Spanish administration of Indians. These and other proposals sound very much like a re-creation of a mission type of environment.

The Wilson Report stands as a perceptive document on southern California Indians during the early American period, but it made no recognized impact on policy. Probably the principal reason for inaction was the rejection by the U. S. Senate of the treaties. Beale reorganized the Indian Affairs agencies in 1853 and retained Wilson for a short time as an assistant agent. In late 1852 Beale had recommended that lands be reserved for Indians. These lands would be military reservations as well as areas in which the Indians could be instructed in farming and other skills. Soldiers were to be in their midst to maintain order, and the military would be supported from the surplus Indian crops. He successfully convinced his superiors of the advantages of this plan, and the first such reserve began operating at Tejon in 1853. This was the beginning of the modern reservation system in the United States. Initially, the Tejon Reservation was strikingly successful; however, in 1854 the political enemies of Beale brought against him the charge that he was making a personal profit from the reservation. He was fully vindicated, but the system lost impetus and did not become a vital force in the lives of most California Indians. Wilson passed into politics and Beale out of Indian affairs in California; the scope and importance of the reservation were never fully developed in the area where it was conceived.

In the mid-1850's the Cahuilla numbered about thirty-five hundred males, of whom fifteen hundred were of fighting age. These figures unquestionably include many non-Cahuilla, but in any event they far outnumbered the local white settlers. The Indians were discontented after the government's failure to live up to the treaty negotiated by Wozencraft, and the Cahuilla leader Juan Antonio attempted to form an alliance with the Yuma and Mohave to force their demands. Formal agreement among the Indians could not be reached, and it became obvious to Antonio that the whites would resist in force. The Indian complaints included not receiving farming implements as promised in the treaty and the trespassing and squatting of whites on traditional Indian lands, from which they took water and wood. Then in 1862 an epidemic of smallpox spread inland from Los Angeles, and among those who died was Juan Antonio. How many others perished is not recorded, but the epidemic was probably another significant factor in eroding away the people and their way of life.

Throughout the latter part of the nineteenth century some Cahuilla worked on the ranches of whites, the men as laborers and the women as domestics. The men worked also in orchards and vineyards; they cut mesquite wood and labored at salt works. Still they continued to gather products of the desert as they had for a long time in the past. In some of the better-watered areas, they cultivated gardens and fields as they had learned to do from the Spanish-Americans. Likewise they worked as laborers when the Southern Pacific railroad was being built through the area in the early 1870's. The effects of increasingly intensive contacts with whites never were recorded by anthropologists, for by the time ethnographers conducted field studies among the Cahuilla, they were interested primarily in reconstructing the aboriginal way of life. We do have a few fragments of information reflecting the changing scene. For example, by around the turn of the century pottery was fired with dung, which is a non-aboriginal method, and some of the metates used were the three-legged variety made from lava and obtained from Mexicans. There is also the fact that wire was used for bowstrings instead of sinew or fiber. Then too the women made baskets for sale to whites. The designs included figures of lizards, snakes, men, animals, and birds, none of which are demonstrably of aboriginal provenience. From 1918 through 1925 there are additional remarks published by anthropologists regarding more specific changes in Cahuilla culture and society. Again the observers were most interested in the past, and their information about changes is usually parenthetical. The economic changes by this time included the possession of farming lands by sibs, but this probably had been the case for about a hundred years previously. The amount of land actually arable was negligible because of the scarcity of water. Time had brought changes in dwelling forms, and there were changes in the settlement patterns. A frame house was not burned after one member of a household died but rather after three deaths occurred there. Among the Desert Cahuilla a sib dance house still was occupied by a *net* and his family, but it had assumed a new form. Although the outline remained rectangular as of old and although it still was covered with cane and palm fronds, the roof was now pitched like a shed. By the late 1950's very few of the aboriginal traits remained. Acorns were still processed for food but were used only for special social and ceremonial occasions.

The sociopolitical life moved in new directions, for the rule of moiety exogamy was no longer being observed with great care. The Desert people, perhaps because of their greater numbers, were able to maintain moiety exogamy longer than the Palm Springs people, who increasingly were prone to marry someone within their own moiety. At the marriage in aboriginal times presents were given to the bride's family; during the early American period money was substituted. The girl's family received $30 around the turn of the century, but by 1925 a female infant was termed scornfully "a paper," meaning a marriage license which no longer brought a gift. The pattern of leadership had long been in the process of change due to various outside influences. It is obvious that in aboriginal times suprasib leaders did not exist, but in the mid-1800's one outstanding charismatic leader, Juan Antonio, did emerge. The whites dealing with the Cahuilla, in order to exercise control efficiently and to implement desired changes, appointed "chiefs" or "captains" through whom they dealt with the Indians. It was said by informants that one such person, a man at Cabazon, was appointed as the leader of the Desert Cahuilla, but his effectiveness must be doubted. He was given "papers" and a horse by the Mexicans as symbols of his authority, and when he died the office passed to his son. Even as late as the 1920's the leader at Palm Springs, although elected by the people, was not an effective spokesman in dealing with the Federal government.

The ceremonial life reflected disintegration and reintegration during the early part of the present century. The major shift was toward combining unrelated ceremonies with the Mourning Ceremony into a "fiesta" week. For example, among the Pass Cahuilla in the late 1880's, the Mourning Ceremony included performing the Eagle Killing Ceremony on a Friday; the feathers then were used to decorate the images which were burned two days later. In aboriginal times the people had cremated their dead; under Spanish, Mexican and Anglo-American stimulus, they began burying the dead. Coffin burial sometimes included placing food, clothing, and bedding with the body in the hope that these things would be useful to the spirit if it did not soon find a permanent resting place. The additions to the Mourning Ceremony came to include dressing the images in manufactured clothing, even including such items as hats and veils. Coins and buttons came to replace shells for the eyes of the images, while the nose and ears were appliqued pieces of cloth. Coins were thrown on the exhibited images near the end of the ceremony, and Indian-owned lunch counters sold food and coffee to the participants and observers. In 1931 it was recorded that at Palm Springs the Mourning Ceremony was biennial, held by alternating sibs for the dead of the previous two years. Among the Desert Cahuilla one of the last *nets* died in 1958. Prior to his death he had directed local ceremonial life, but when he died, the ceremonial structure, his house, and all of the ceremonial equipment were burned; this was the end of the end.

Returning to the course of Desert and Palm Springs Cahuilla history from the late 1860's, we see that the dominant theme running through the record concerns land and Indian rights to it. In 1869 the Superintendent of Indian Affairs for California hoped to be able to set aside lands for Indians before whites encroached further, but he did not succeed until the following year when some small reservations were established in San Diego County. Then in 1875 President Ulysses S. Grant authorized the establishment of the Agua Caliente and Cahuilla reservations. A Mission Indian agency began to function out of San Bernardino in 1879. Now for the first time slight but realistic efforts were being made to recognize the needs of southern California Indians. In 1881 Helen H. Jackson published a book called *A Century of Dishonor*, which was a scathing indictment of the manner in which American Indians had been treated. As a result of her crusading interest in Indians, she was retained to make a report to the Commissioner of Indian Affairs on the Indians of southern California. A field study of conditions was conducted with Abbott Kinney and a report submitted in 1883. It is partly a chronicle of wrongs against the Indians, particularly by Anglo-Americans, and partly a series of recommendations. One of the suggestions was that honest boundary surveys of Indian lands should be made and monuments erected to indicate the limits, that white settlers on such lands be removed, and that in some instances additional lands be purchased for the Indians. Then, too, Indian communities on lands which had been granted to whites should have the Federal government support their claim for prior occupancy and ownership, particularly because the Indians were in no position to press their own claims. Furthermore, Indian lands should be held under a trust patent by the Federal government for twenty-five years, and then the patent should be turned over to the Indians. The desirability of establishing additional schools, both day schools in the villages and a boarding school for children from isolated settlements, was stressed. Then there was the need to have a government agent visit the Indians at least twice a year in order to keep various types of disputes from getting out of hand. A law firm or lawyer should be retained to protect the legal interests of the Indians from the numerous diverse forms of injustices now suffered at the hands of whites. Direct economic needs were acknowledged in the suggestion that farming implements be distributed wisely and some provision be made for the needs of old and infirm individuals. The report of Jackson and Kinney did not make the impact that they had hoped. This led Jackson to write a novel about the plight of these Indians, thinking that this would lead to the desired reforms. The novel, *Ramona,* was highly successful, but its crusading purpose was ignored by most of its readers.

The problems of the Palm Springs Indians over the legal rights to their land have followed a confused and meandering course. The original reservation was set aside in 1875, but subsequent Executive orders changed the original grant. The reservation of today was formed in 1896 under the authority of the 1891 Mission Indian Relief Act. The reservation consists of approximately 32,000 acres of land in essentially a checkerboard pattern around the town of Palm Springs in Riverside County. The general policy attitude which guided the formulation of the Mission Indian Relief Act grew out of the General Allotment Act or Dawes Act of 1887. The keystone of this legislation was to allot reservation lands to individual Indians who were family heads. After a period of twenty-five years the Indian allottee could, with the sanction of the Secretary of the Interior, receive a fee patent title whereby he would be the legal owner and could do with the land whatever he might choose. As the result of a Federal act of 1917 the Secretary of the Interior was directed to make such allotments on the Palm Springs and other Mission Indian reservations. The allotted land per family was to be limited to a total of one hundred and sixty acres. In 1923 a Federal agent went to Palm Springs and made allotment selections for the band members irrespective of any particular Indian's attitude toward the program. Then in 1927 an allotting agent made allotments only to the Indians who requested them; nearly half of the members made requests. These allotments consisted not of one hundred and sixty acres but of five acres of irrigable land, forty acres of dry land, and two-acre lots in the town of Palm Springs. None of the 1927 selections were approved by the Federal government, and legal action was taken by the Indians in the late 1930's to force approval. At this point it should be noted that with the passage of the Indian Reorganization Act of 1934 there was a basic change in Indian policy. First and foremost in the context of the Palm Springs land dispute, further allotments were prohibited if a recognized Indian group did not vote against coming under the provisions of the act. The Palm Springs band voted against it, and thus allotments were still possible. The atmosphere among the Bureau of Indian Affairs officials was very much against the allotment program, and they obstructed the granting of allotted lands at Palm Springs as elsewhere. The courts held that the Secretary of the Interior could not be forced to make allotments, which brought the litigation down to 1940. New action was taken the following year to have the allotments approved. The action was carried to the U. S. Supreme Court, which required a review of the litigation; the result was the 1946 verdict that the allotments were valid. Some but not all allotments were approved in 1949. The ones which were unapproved involved cases of conflicting claims, but finally selections were approved for the entire band.

Additional complexity was added when one of the suits involving allotment selections resulted in a 1950 court decision that the allotted lands should be of approximately equal value for each individual since this was the original intent of the allotment law. The problem then came to center about the disparity among the values of the allotments. Based on 1949 estimates, the allotment values ranged from approximately $17,000 to $165,000, with a total value of lands allotted and pending allotment being about $7.4 million. In order to equalize the allotments it was estimated that additional allotments of land worth nine million dollars would be necessary; the total value of unallotted tribal lands was around twelve million dollars. The major difficulty in allotting the remaining land was that the value of the land would be reduced by what necessarily would be a complex parceling. By breaking the land up in small allotments it would be less desirable for developers and its value would be decreased. Then too, equalization would in some instances require that allotments be greater than one hundred and sixty acres, which was impossible under the law as it stood. Since the Indian lands around Palm Springs were tied up in litigation, real estate developers were beginning to bypass Palm Springs; this was adversely affecting the value of the lands. The solution proposed by the Secretary of the Interior was to organize a tribal corporation and convey to it all of the tribal assets. This organization would be empowered to issue equalization stock to individuals with unequalized allotments and to redeem the stock from the sale of or income from the lands managed by the tribal corporation. Persons who held equalized allotments would receive only membership stock until the equalization process was complete. Then all members would receive dividends equally.

The U. S. Senate Bill 2396 of the Eighty-fifth Congress, first session, 1957, was to provide equalization of allotments along the general lines noted above. The Indians, however, objected to the proposed bill, and tribal representatives went to Washington, D.C., to attempt to have their suggested modifications accepted. The Bureau of Indian Affairs representatives refused to make any changes and stated that if this legislation were not passed, the tribal reserves would be used to equalize the allotments. These reserves, the cemeteries, hot springs, and particularly the canyons, were the prime centers of tribal identity. To allot them would be to destroy the tribe as a social and political unit. The Bureau of Indian Affairs forwarded the bill to the Committee on Interior and Insular Affairs of the House of Representatives, and since the bill involved persons from his district, Dalip S. Saund was given the privilege of introducing it. Saund studied the bill and stated later, "I came to the conclusion that under no circumstances would I be a party in introducing the bill." He was then instrumental in having the bill set aside until a hearing could be held in Palm Springs. The hearing was held in October of 1957. It became evident during the session, as was originally obvious to Saund and the tribal council, that the bill was not in the best interest of the Indians nor could it be conceived of as just. Probably the most dangerous provision was that a tribal corporation was to be established and given the title to all unallotted lands. It would issue equalization stock to bring each individual's allotment to the value of the most valuable allotment and redeem these shares from income or from disposal of the land. For the first two years the Agua Caliente members were to appoint three individuals to a board of directors consisting of seven persons. The four other members were to be appointed by the Secretary of the Interior. This proposed organization was a liquidation corporation, and it is highly questionable that either legal or moral justification could be offered in its defense by the Bureau of Indian Affairs (see Note 4).

At the hearing, diverse issues were aired, including the previously discussed problems of the control of the proposed tribal corporation and the status of the reserve lands. The city attorney for Palm Springs favored the bill with certain changes so that the city would be able to tax Indian lands to aid in the support of the city government. The subcommittee was outspoken in its condemnation of this stand. Another problem involving taxation was whether or not the State of California might tax the tribal corporation if the bill were passed. Federal immunity against taxation was to be provided, but such assurances were not forthcoming from the state officials. Further evidence was given concerning the inadequacy of the present leasing laws. Under these laws leases are granted for two periods of twenty-five years each. Much of the testimony was devoted to conflicting interpretations of the various court decisions by different lawyers for the Indians.

In 1959 as a result of the 1957 hearing Congressman Saund submitted two new bills before the Eighty-sixth Congress, and these became law. The major provisions of the equalization bill, Public Law 86-339, are as follows. Allotments will be made to all band members who have not received them, but no future born members will receive allotments. Equalizations will be made on the basis of 1957–1958 appraised land values, but the cemeteries, Roman Catholic church, hot springs, and certain canyons are to be tribal reserves and not subject to allotment. The remaining lands are to be allotted regardless of prior acreage limitations and in proportion to the highest monetary value of the prior allotments. The second bill, Public Law 86-326, provided that reservation lands could be leased for a period not exceeding ninety-nine years except for grazing land which could be leased for not more than ten years. The 1957–1958 allotment appraisals ranged from approximately $75,000 to $630,000, in contrast with the 1949 appraisal range of $17,000 to $165,000 cited previously. Obviously the land was rapidly becoming fantastically valuable. Even with the passage of the first bill mentioned above, it was impossible to equalize the allotments fully. Some 80 percent of the band have obtained allotments valued at not less than $335,000; the remaining 20 percent of the allotments are valued in excess of $335,000. It is true that most of the land was still in trust status by 1962, and the Indian "owners" were not free to do with it as they might choose. Most of the land was thus not producing income. However, with the changes in the leasing laws, it is likely that within the next ten years individuals will derive considerable profit from leases. By delegating most leasing authority to the Sacramento office, the Bureau of Indian Affairs has taken a further step to make it administratively less difficult to lease Indian lands. The major leasing enterprise thus far has been in connection with the Palm Springs Spa at the hot springs. The Spa was completed in 1960 at a cost of $1.8 million, and an adjacent hotel, also on Indian land, was completed in 1963. In 1961 the city of Palm Springs purchased sections of lands allotted to eight adults and twenty-two children for $2,979,000 which was shared by the allottees. The future looks very bright, but without the honesty and integrity of the

"Congressman from India," Dalip S. Saund, there is every reason to believe that the future not only would have been clouded but dismal.

The most remarkable aspect of all the Palm Springs band land problems is that in 1957, when the issues were coming to a climax, they involved only thirty-two adults and sixty-four minors. At that time there were ten adult males and twenty-two females; of the males two were in the U. S. Navy, two were over seventy years of age, and two were incapable of handling their own affairs. At this point one of two courses of action was possible; either the band could trust the Bureau of Indian Affairs and its lawyer to handle their business affairs completely, or the women could assume the roles of leaders. The latter alternative was pursued. In aboriginal sociopolitical life there was no precedent for female leadership. The *net* was always a man, and all other offices were held by men. There is at the same time the probability that a woman did occasionally hold an office in trust for a son and that old women were sometimes very active in sib ceremonial life. In the early historical period the whites concerned with directing Indian life appointed "chiefs," "captains," or "generals," to act as intermediaries. With the creation of the various reservation units, leaders for the reservations were selected by the Indian agents. These leaders seem to have been sib leaders as were the earlier appointed leaders. From 1900 to 1945 Palm Springs band affairs were managed by a three-man business committee which was elected. During this same period the aboriginal pattern of leadership and ceremonial life was eroding away, and band identity came to center on common problems surrounding the protection of their rights to the land. In the acculturation process which was taking place, there is evidence suggesting differential acculturation for males and females. The men continued to follow a "gathering" pattern in their wage labor. They worked, but only sporadically, as grape pickers, ranch hands, woodcutters, or railroad laborers. In their employment setting their most frequent contacts were with other Indians. The women, on the other hand, who worked outside of their homes, were employed primarily as domestic servants, and they came to understand the world of whites on much more intimate terms than did their husbands. For this reason women became the stable core around which the society functioned. From 1935 to 1939 a woman was the secretary for the band business committee, and in 1939 two members of the committee were women. Then in 1945 the business committee was accused of graft, and for about the next ten years band business was handled in town meetings. In 1954 an all-woman tribal council was elected, with Mrs. Vyola Olinger as its chairman. Mrs. Olinger, who was an active member of the band, was an apt choice, for she was not only intelligent and articulate but willing to work constructively with the Bureau of Indian Affairs officials. The men had by this time come to distrust virtually all proposals by the Bureau. It was under the tribal council of women that the major land disputes were solved. In 1961 a young male was elected to the council, and this brought an end to the era of all-female political dominance, but it was the women who had won the most important battles.

Note 1.   Lucile Hooper (1920, 345) recorded a number of "enemy songs" among the Desert Cahuilla. Three of these are as follows:

> His food gave out, his water gave out,
> Leave him now, go away from him:
> Isilwelnet. (enemy name)
> (Repeated as many times as desired.)

> Bury him now, plant him now:
> And then they buried him, and then they planted him:
> Pehuetematewilwish.

> There stands the whirlwind, there stands the whirlwind
> Where they burned him, where they burned him:
> Puchueulchalmalmia.

Note 2.   Lucile Hooper (1920, 331) described a shaman eating fire at a Mourning Ceremony held among the Desert Cahuilla at Torres.

After Casimiro took the dark object from his heart [a previous trick], he reached into the fire with his foot and kicked out a few coals. One of these he picked up: it was about the size of a dollar. He immediately put it into his mouth. I was only a few feet away and one of the sparks from his mouth, as he blew, fell on my hand, so I can testify that they were hot. The glow from the coal could be seen on the roof of his mouth. He swallowed it in about a minute. He swallowed three coals in this way. I saw two other men do the same thing.

Note 3.   In the Wilson Report, (Wilson, 1952, 51–52) "The Indians of Southern California in 1852," are recorded the state's attitudes toward handling Indians.

We may fairly presume that the State law now in force was not intended to be permanent. In addition to the provision above quoted touching lands, it extends the civil and criminal laws of the State over all Indians within its limits; prohibits their punishment, except by justices of the peace, with a jury (if required); subjects them to fine or whipping, not to exceed 25 lashes for stealing; gives the Indians power to require the chiefs and influential men of any village to apprehend, and bring before the justices any Indian charged or suspected of an offence; and "if any tribe or village refuse or neglect to obey the laws, the justice of the peace may punish the guilty chiefs or principle men by reprimand or fine, or otherwise reasonably chastise them." If convicted, Indians may be hired out to pay the fine and costs for a time fixed by the justice. A white man is finable for "abducting an Indian from his home, or compelling him to work against his will," and for selling or giving him intoxicating liquors (except in sickness)—and, for the last offence may be imprisoned not less than five days. Contracts for hiring must be in writing made before a justice of the peace. In like manner a minor Indian child may be bound out by parents or friends till the age of 18, if a male, and a female till 15, these being their ages of majority. For vagrancy—"loitering and strolling about, or frequenting public places where liquors are sold, begging, or leading an immoral or profligate course of life," he is hired out at public auction, a term not longer than four months, to be subject to the law regulating guardians and minors, unless he can give bail for good behavior for twelve months; the proceeds of his hire, after deducting certain expenses, to be paid to his family, if he have one, if not, like fines to be paid into the county treasury. The only additional remedial provision is one making it "the duty of justices of the peace, in their respective townships, as well as all other peace officers in this State, to instruct the Indians in their neighborhood in the laws which relate to them, giving them such advice as they may deem necessary!"

All punishment. *No* reform!

Note 4. Congressman D. S. Saund (1960, 139–140) in his autobiography commented on the Agua Caliente equalization bill which he was asked to introduce and support.

I had heard about the controversy of the Agua Caliente tribal lands in Palm Springs during my campaign, and so I studied this bill very carefully. It turned out to be a fantastic piece of legislation. Its most shocking provision involved the creation of a new commission to take care of the tribal properties of the Agua Caliente tribe. This commission would consist of four members appointed by the Secretary of the Interior and three members of the tribal council. Not only that, the bill authorized the Secretary of the Interior to turn the title of the Agua Caliente lands over to the commission and grant it authority to sell, lease, or dispose of this property in any way its members thought to be in the best interests of the members of the tribe.

In other words, this was a proposal to turn not the *management,* but the *title* of the Indians' property over to a commission in which the majority of the membership would be appointed by the Secretary of the Interior. Now, according to the Department of the Interior's estimate, the property involved has a value of $12,000,000!

There were other provisions in the bill that would have violated the normal regulation which stipulated that Indian lands be free from local taxation: such as one that permitted the city of Palm Springs to tax the land immediately. Furthermore, the bill did not in any way limit the amount of money the commission could spend, but left that to the discretion of the commissioners.

The bill seemed to me completely obnoxious.

References

Ames, Walter. "Palm Springs Indians Still Protest Land Split," *Los Angeles Times,* November 12, 1961.

Bancroft, Hubert H. *History of California.* 7 v. San Francisco. 1890.

*Barrows, David P. *The Ethno-Botany of the Coahuilla Indians of Southern California.* Chicago. 1900. A general history of the Cahuilla is followed by a description of the local geography. These sections are followed by a discussion of houses, baskets, and the utilization of plants. The botanical information in particular is quite comprehensive and serves as a standard source.

Bean, Lowell J. Verbal statements.

*Bean, Lowell J. and William M. Mason. *Diaries & Accounts of the Romero Expeditions in Arizona and California.* Los Angeles. 1962. The publication of these records offers a previously unknown historical dimension to the Cahuilla. Their primary value is in conveying certain details of Cahuilla acculturation by Spanish-Americans.

Bean, Lowell J. and Katherine S. Saubel. "Cahuilla Ethnobotanical Notes: The Aboriginal Uses of the Oak," *Archaeological Survey, Annual Report 1960-1961,* Department of Anthropology & Sociology, University of California, Los Angeles, 237–249. 1961.

———. "Cahuilla Ethnobotanical Notes: The Aboriginal Uses of the Mesquite and Screwbean," *Archaeological Survey, Annual Report 1962-1963,* Department of Anthropology & Sociology, University of California, Los Angeles, 55–76. 1963.

Beattie, George W. and Helen P. Beattie. *Heritage of the Valley.* Oakland. 1951.

Bolton, Herbert E. "In the South San Joaquin Ahead of Garces," *Quarterly of the California Historical Society,* v. 10, 211–219. 1931.

Bourne, A. R. Some Major Aspects of the Historical Development of Palm Springs between 1880 and 1938. (Occidental College, Master of Arts thesis.)

Caughey, John W. *California.* New York. 1940. (See also Wilson, Benjamin D.)

Ellison, William H. "The Federal Indian Policy in California, 1846-1860," *Mississippi Valley Historical Review,* v. 9, 37–67. 1922–1923.

Gifford, Edward W. *California Kinship Terminologies.* University of California Publications in American Archaeology and Ethnology, v. 18. 1922.

Hale, Kenneth. "Internal Diversity in Uto-Aztecan: 1," *International Journal of American Linguistics,* v. 24, 101–107. 1958.

*Hooper, Lucile. *The Cahuilla Indians.* University of California Publications in American Archaeology and Ethnology, v. 16, no. 6. 1920. Most of what is known about the aboriginal Cahuilla will be found in this ethnographic reconstruction, a similar reconstruction by Alfred L. Kroeber, or the analysis of social life and settlement patterns by William D. Strong.

Jackson, Helen H. *A Century of Dishonor.* New York. 1881 (an 1890 edition contains the Report on the Conditions and Needs of the Mission Indians of California).

James, Harry C. *The Cahuilla Indians.* Los Angeles. 1960.

*Kroeber, Alfred L. *Ethnography of the Cahuilla Indians.* University of California Publications in American Archaeology and Ethnology, v. 8, no. 2. 1908. A brief but valuable ethnography which concentrates on material culture. It supplements the reconstructions by Lucile Hooper and William D. Strong.

Land Allotments on Agua Caliente Reservation, Calif. Hearing before a Special Subcommittee of the Committee on Interior and Insular Affairs, House of Representatives, 85th Congress, 1st session. Serial No. 17. 1958.

Ringwald, George. "Agua Caliente Story," *Riverside Press-Enterprise and Riverside Daily Press,* October 20–26, 1957.

Rush, Emmy M. "The Indians of the Coachella Valley Celebrate," *El Palacio,* v. 32, 1–19. 1932.

Saund, Dalip S. *Congressman from India.* New York. 1960.

Shinn, George H. *Shoshonean Days.* Glendale. 1941.

*Strong, William D. *Aboriginal Society in Southern California.* University of California Publications in American Archaeology and Ethnology, v. 26. 1929. The best information about aboriginal social structure, the movements of people, and settlement patterns.

Transmitting Report by Subcommittee on Indian Affairs. State of California, Senate Committee on Rules Resolution No. 8. Sacramento. 1961.

Wilson, Benjamin D. *The Indians of Southern California in 1852.* John W. Caughey, ed. San Marino. 1952.

1962 Progress Report, Agua Caliente Band of Mission Indians. Long Beach. No date.

5

The Fox:
Fighters and Farmers of the Woodland Fringe

MINNESOTA

CANADA

OJIBWA

L. Superior

YANKTON

MENOMINI

WISCONSIN

SAUK

MICHIGAN

L. Huron

SANTEE

KICKAPOO

Wisconsin R.

Green Bay

WINNEBAGO

Fox R.

POTAWATOMI

IOWA

L. Winnebago

Wisconsin Dells

L. Michigan

Prairie du Chien

FOX

ILLINOIS

Detroit

L. Erie

IOWA

Tama

Chicago

INDIANA

OHIO

Saukenuk

Rock R.

Rock Island

Des Moines R.

Iowa R.

ILLINOIS

OTO

MISSOURI

Tippecanoe R.

KANSAS

Illinois R.

Mississippi R.

Greenville

Missouri R.

Miami R.

St. Louis

Wabash R.

Ohio R.

Osage R.

OSAGE

KENTUCKY

Cumberland Plateau

OKLAHOMA

ARKANSAS

TENNESSEE

SHAWNEE

0 50 100 150 mi.

MISS.

ALA.

CHEROKEE

Map by J. Donovan

Today, at a time when most of the Algonkian tribes of the east-central United States have long since disappeared, the Fox still survive as a small but separate ethnic group. Yet it was these people the French set out to destroy completely; although they were nearly successful, the Fox struggled on. The Fox obstructed American settlement of their lands and harassed settlers until the turmoil climaxed in an Indian war. Following the war, the Indians were displaced, and their numbers were further depleted. Fox resistance against either the French or Americans was not a matter of chance but one of choice. By possessing haughty independence, brave warriors, and capable leaders, they, apart from the other tribes in the central states, reflected a nobility and purpose which made them stand out as exceptional. The most striking example of their independence and originality occurred in 1854. After having been defeated and displaced a generation earlier by the Americans, they began to leave their Kansas reservation and to settle on land they had once owned but now purchased from whites in Iowa. The intriguing and instructive question to be asked is why and how the Fox managed to survive at all in the face of the long-lasting hostility of most people with whom they have had contact.

The Fox know themselves as the Mesquakie, which is translated "red-earth people." This proper name stems from their creation myth which records that they were made from red earth. According to one account they received the name Fox when some members of the Fox sib met a party of French. When the Indians were asked who they were, they responded Fox, meaning of the Fox sib and Mesquakie tribe. It is estimated that together the Fox and Sauk (Sac) numbered about sixty-five hundred individuals at the time of historic contact, of whom possibly two thousand were Fox. An estimate for 1728 gives two hundred warriors, and an estimate for 1805 is for three hundred warriors in a total population of twelve hundred persons. In the 1950's nearly one thousand Fox lived in Oklahoma, five hundred in Iowa, and one hundred twenty-five in Nebraska.

In terms of one linguistic classification the Fox, together with their cultural and linguistic neighbors the Sauk, belong to the Algonkian-Mosan phylum; they are members of the Algonkian-Ritwan stock and the Algonkian family. It was the Algonkians who occupied a vast sector of eastern Canada and a smaller area in the eastern United States. Remarkably, the other groups with whom they are clearly affiliated linguistically include two small northern Californian tribes, the Yurok and Wiyot, representing the Ritwan family.

Two major difficulties in assembling materials on the Fox make presentation of the balanced account impossible. The first is that the information on Fox ethnography does not date from an early period of historic contact. Thus it is not possible to establish with authority an aboriginal base line; the Fox way of life was modified by the fur trade before being described by ethnographers. However, the Fox have been described by virtually all observers as being highly conservative, and, except for superficial changes such as the introduction of trade goods, we might expect that recent ethnographic accounts about them reflect the past more accurately than would be the case for most American Indian groups. A second difficulty in dealing with the Fox is their intimate association with the Sauk throughout much of their history. It is difficult if not impossible in some instances to separate the Fox historically from the Sauk. Whereas the descriptions will be confined to the Fox insofar as it is possible, frequent reference will be made to the Sauk. The Fox have been singled out for analysis for many specific reasons. First of all, they are people who lived in an eastern woodland environment but maintained a way of life that had affinities with the Indians of the prairies. The Sauk occupied a similar position, but the ethnographic information about them is not nearly so comprehensive. Additionally, the Fox historical and ethnographic data have a great deal of continuity when compared with those of the Sauk or other adjacent people. There are ethnographic accounts by an anthropologist, William Jones, who was part Fox, and by the anthropologist Truman Michelson, as well as William T. Hagan's history of the Fox and Sauk. For purposes of continuity the Fox Project of the University of Chicago, Department of Anthropology, under the direction of Sol Tax, is an invaluable source of information for the period from 1948 to 1959. In addition, the ethnographic information about the past collected and published by Natalie F. Joffe and Tax supplements the earlier accounts of Jones and Michelson. Studies have been made also of recent acculturation, biculturation, and their political structure.

The earliest historical records locate the Fox along the Fox River of eastern Wisconsin. In the general area which they occupied were three different types of environmental niches: deciduous forest, mixed forest, and prairie country. The general area is characterized by Dice as being in the Canadian biotic province. Here the forest climax is in terms of hardwoods, but coniferous forests may be important localized climaxes.

In the Great Lakes region the earliest human occupants were unsettled hunters whose general way of life is reflected in scattered assemblages of stone tools. These people are described as Paleo-Indians.

The lithic traditions often include fluted projectile points of the Clovis type as a recurring and distinctive form. It is clear that these mobile mastodon hunters came to occupy the Great Lakes region by 10,000 B.C. and continued hunting these huge beasts until about 7000 B.C. when the climatic picture changed and mastodons became less common. Indians characterized as of the Aqua-Plano group dominated the area from about 7000 to 4500 B.C. The people involved in this chipped stone industry must have hunted deer, caribou, and elk as important species of large game animals. By the end of the era there emerged two other patterns of culture, termed Boreal Archaic and Old Copper. Each was adapted to a forest environment and possessed woodworking tools, such as the ax, adz, and gouge, which were not present in the earlier periods. The methods of working stone shifted from flaking to grinding; some of the copper tools were annealed. The bearers of these traditions were hunters, fishermen and collectors, with hunting possibly of the greatest importance. Their principal weapon was not the bow and arrow but the spear used with the spear-thrower or atlatl. The technologies of these Indians developed increasing efficiency until about 500 B.C. when two radical innovations appeared, artificial burial mounds and pottery, both of which probably spread into the area from Asia. Still the basic economy appears to have remained much the same until the era of the Hopewell culture of the Early Woodland tradition. These people were centered in the Ohio River valley and built great earthworks upon which they must have expended an inordinate amount of time and energy; they had elaborate manufactures in stone and organic materials; they used a great deal of care in producing grave goods for the important dead; and their economy, although still dependent on hunting, had a firm foundation in the domestic crops they raised, maize, beans, and squash. The Hopewell Indians pushed into the Great Lakes region and reached a climax in complexity around A.D. 400. During the Late Woodland period, from about A.D. 800 until historic contact, there was an essential continuity with the past but a wide variety of local variations in the cultures indicative of no overall unity. In the Lake Winnebago area the Indians of this period planted maize, beans, squash, and tobacco. They hunted small and large game and collected nuts, berries, and mussels. Their material culture is of the type which we associate with early historic Indians of the area. The bow and arrow was the principal weapon; fish were taken with hooks, leisters, and nets, and their stone manufactures were of both the chipped and ground varieties. What is most apparent is the basic continuity with the earlier Woodland traditions, which stand in contrast with the

Paleo-Indian and Archaic developments of the earliest period of human occupancy.

The earliest known reference to the Fox Indians occurs on a Jesuit map which was made up in the year 1640. At this time they lived near Green Bay, Wisconsin, and neighboring tribes included the Sauk, the Kickapoo, the Menominee, and the Winnebago. According to tradition the Fox arrived in this area after being driven to the west by other Algonkian tribes. Historically, the first Fox contacts with persons of European descent were made in 1665 when French traders and explorers pushed into the western part of the Great Lakes region. In the year 1670 a mission was founded among the Fox, and the famous Father Allouez attempted to convert the Fox to Christianity. Despite all his labors he was not able to win converts except among people who were dying or were ill. The Fox received the French with hostility during the period of initial contact, but they liked being able to obtain trade goods. When some Fox went to Montreal in 1671, they were ill-treated by the French and later sought revenge. When the French pushed on to the west of Fox country and offered trade goods to the Ojibwa and to some Siouan-speaking tribes, the Fox resisted since the French were arming Fox enemies. The Fox began systematically to plunder the French trade canoes; this brought them into direct and lasting hostilities with the French. With the establishment of Detroit in 1699 contact between the French and the Indians in the Great Lakes region intensified. In 1700 the French made a treaty with the Iroquois, and in this treaty the Iroquois promised not to disrupt the trade to the west. In 1701 many of the tribes of the western Great Lakes area met at Montreal to make peace with the French. The Fox were among those tribes establishing peace, and they along with the Iroquois and the Siouan speakers to the west were not to interfere with the French trade. However, the French continued to supply weapons to Indians who were at war with the Fox. Meanwhile, the British were anxious to establish themselves in the fur trade in the northwest. They incited the Fox against the French and offered higher prices for pelts besides. By 1712 the French and Fox conflict could not be resolved peacefully, and the Siege of Detroit led to heavy Fox losses. The Fox became bent on wiping out the French, and the French were equally determined to destroy the Fox as a people. In order to make an efficient resistance against the French, the Fox invited the Abnaki to settle among them. The Fox received assurances from the Iroquois that they could live among them if defeated by the French; they also made peace with the neighboring tribes. They even pushed southward among the Omaha and the Chickasaw in order to ally them with the cause of French removal, but the Fox could not convince the latter tribes to support their efforts. The French and Fox hostility came to a climax in 1728 when nearly five hundred whites and twelve hundred Indians moved against the Fox. The party destroyed Fox villages but failed to destroy the people. However, with French support the Indian enemies of the Fox succeeded in virtually destroying the tribe by 1730. Over a period of about two years nearly twelve hundred Fox were killed, and the tribe was no longer an independent entity. However, the Fox consolidated again when the prisoners held by other surrounding peoples were released. In 1731 some two hundred remaining Fox took refuge among the Sauk villages. Two years later the French attempted to obtain the Fox from among the Sauk and planned to ship them to the West Indies as slaves, but the Sauk refused. The French attempted to take the Fox by force, and a fight developed in which some French were killed. The Sauk fled southward to avoid French reprisals and were joined by the Fox. It was not until the year 1737 that peace was made between the Fox and the French, but by this time the Fox were no longer an independent ethnic group.

Toward the end of French political control of the Great Lakes region the Fox once again moved to Wisconsin, but it was not until the British replaced the French at the Green Bay post in 1761 that the Fox felt reasonably secure. Fox and British relationships were always very good. However, they were forced, not by the British but by the Ojibwa, to abandon their Wisconsin lands permanently around the year 1780. The Fox were not to remain undisturbed long in their new home in Illinois. Around 1800 increasing contact was made with the Americans in the Northwest Territory. The Indians lived in scattered communities along both banks of the Mississippi River north of the mouth of the Des Moines River. By this time the Fox had become dependent upon the fur trade in order to receive goods that they considered necessary to maintain their way of life. They were most often in debt to traders for the goods that they obtained against their next year's take. Still the relationship between the Fox and the Sauk and the traders, especially British, seems to have been very good. The Fox expected certain privileges, such as being entertained when they were at the trading post, receiving gifts from the traders, and being taken care of in times of stress. At the same time they relied on trusted traders to help guide tribal and village affairs. The traders were important in molding the attitude of the Indians toward both the British and the American governments. The Fox and Sauk were brought into contact and conflict with the Americans through the actions of William Henry Harrison, governor of the Northwest Territory. The Americans had no reason to consider the Fox and Sauk sympathetic to them, since the British had been aided by these Indians during the American Revolution. With the influx of settlers into the Northwest Territory there was increasing pressure on all Indian groups of the Midwest to sign treaties with the American government and to move westward. In the year 1804 a small party of Fox and Sauk went to St. Louis, and here they became intoxicated and signed a treaty with the United States for the release of their lands along the Mississippi River. Some $2000 worth of goods were distributed to the Indians plus an annuity of $1000 with 600 assigned to the Sauk and 400 to the Fox. The treaty authorized further settlement of Illinois lands by settlers from the United States. Not only were the Indians at St. Louis unauthorized to contract the treaty, but the tribes as a whole did not know of it until after the chiefs had arrived back from St. Louis. The Treaty of 1804 always was to be a great cause for Fox anger against the Americans. They felt that the Americans had deceived them and that these lands had been taken from them illegally. This treaty was to be the one document to which the Americans referred constantly in asserting their claims to Fox and Sauk lands. The treaty was made, the damage was done, but the bitterness was to linger always in the minds of the Indians involved. The area ceded to the United States included western Illinois, north and west of the Illinois River, a small section of southern Wisconsin, and another small section of eastern Missouri. One provision of the treaty stipulated that the Indians could continue to occupy the land so "long as the lands which are now ceded to the United States remain their property."

The Americans found that one of the major difficulties in dealing with the Indians was the tribal wars. These not only disrupted trade routes but made settlement of the country difficult. In an effort to bring the warring tribes to peace with one another a council was held at St. Louis in 1805 to which were invited all the major tribes in the upper Mississippi drainage. The tribal chiefs met with Governor Harrison and the Indian agent for the area, and they signed a treaty of peace with one another. In order to impress upon the Indians the power and strength of the United States it was arranged for selected Indians to visit Washington, D. C. About one third of the group to meet in Washington were Fox or Sauk Indians. The journey east was an impressive sight for all involved. However, at the same time that some chiefs were in Washington others were on the warpath against the Osage and the Chickasaw. Thus this effort to bring about a peaceful settlement of Indians affairs was unsuccessful. During the winter of 1805–1806 Fox and Sauk war parties roved along the Missouri River to search out the Osage camps and right wrongs they felt were done to them by the Osage. Because Americans were also killed by these warriors, there was increasing pressure on the government of the Northwest Territory to bring about an effective settlement of Indian differences. To add to the governor's administrative difficulties additional settlers entered the Northwest Territory between the years 1806 and 1812. They were particularly active in clearing the land and establishing farms in the region between the Ohio and the Mississippi rivers, precisely the region where there was the greatest Indian unrest. At this point the Fox and Sauk came under the influence of the Shawnee. With historic contact the Shawnee, who were Algonkian speakers and linguistically related to the Fox and Sauk, centered in the Cumberland region of Tennessee. Later many of the tribe moved to Ohio during the Revolutionary War and assisted the British against the colonists. At the treaty of Greenville in 1795 they were forced to give up their lands along the Miami River in Ohio. In 1798 some joined the Delaware who were by now in Indiana, but the ones who were most hostile to the Americans moved to Missouri. In 1806 the half brother of the great Shawnee leader, Tecumseh, rose to prominence. His name was Tenskwatawa, but he is better known as the "Shawnee Prophet." He reportedly died and was reborn; while dead he visited the land of the spirits and was given a view of the future. This messiah saw contentment only for those who gave up white ways and returned to the old Indian way of life. With Greenville, Ohio, as the center of his activities he received tribal representatives from the surrounding region. The movement coalesced into an effort to rid the country of the "Long Knives" or Americans.

With the Treaty of 1804 as the rallying point for their grievances against the Americans, the Fox and Sauk were ready and willing to follow the confederation organized by the Shawnee and actively fostered by the British. In the Battle of Tippecanoe Creek of 1811 the Shawnee Prophet's prestige was destroyed by William H. Harrison's stand against the Indians, but the battle was not decisive. Afterwards, however, it was unlikely that an Indian confederation could emerge. In early 1812 an Indian delegation which included Fox and Sauk went to Washington, D. C., and this time they were well received because the War of 1812 had erupted into open conflict. The most the Americans could hope to do was to keep the Indians from participating in the conflict on the side of the British. In order to make Fox and Sauk aid impossible the Americans decided to move the Indians to Missouri, where they would be beyond effective contact with the British. They were partially successful, for approximately fifteen hundred members of the combined tribes were eventually moved to these new quarters.

Black Hawk was the only major leader who was an active supporter of the British. He was born in 1767 as a member of the Thunder sib of the Sauk tribe. When he was fifteen years of age, he distinguished himself as a warrior, and at seventeen he led a raid on an Osage camp, bringing back the scalp of a warrior. By the time he was nineteen he had led a party of two hundred warriors against an equal number of Osage. Nearly half of the Osage were killed, with Black Hawk killing five men and one woman. By 1812 his reputation as a leader and warrior made him the most honored and respected man of the combined tribes. At the opening of hostilities in the War of 1812 Black Hawk journeyed to Green Bay, Wisconsin, with two hundred warriors and was heartily received by the British. They convinced him that the first task was to secure the Great Lakes region. Black Hawk and his warriors traveled to Detroit to participate in the British siege. Although they arrived after the victory, they remained to fight for the British during the war. At the same time many members of the combined tribe, but particularly the Fox, were moving to Missouri under pressure from the Americans to neutralize potential Indian participation.

While Black Hawk was away, there was the threat that American troops would destroy the principal village of Saukenuk near the mouth of the Rock River in the present state of Illinois. The people were ready to flee after deciding to do so in council, but at this juncture Keokuk asked to speak. This man's mother was said to have been half French, but he was an unimportant member of the Sauk tribe. His sib affiliations were not those of a leading political group, but he was the host charged with entertaining visitors to the tribe. By exploiting this position he was able to foster his own ambitions. He spoke up at the council meeting and said that the people should resist the American invasion. He was a fine orator, and the persuasiveness of his speech convinced the people that they should not abandon their village. When the American force failed to arrive to oust them, he became a hero. By his oration and his convincing stand against the Americans, Keokuk established himself as a political leader among the two tribes, a leader who was to rival and eventually outdistance the great Black Hawk.

Keokuk became friendly with the Americans, and Black Hawk continued actively to aid the British. When an American military party attempted to ascend the Mississippi River in force in mid-1814, a party of Sauk, Fox, and Kickapoo, under the leadership of Black Hawk, successfully prevented the American vessels from reaching their goal. The victory was an indecisive one, but the British were pleased with the Indian effort, particularly with their concerted attempt to prevent the Americans from taking the Rock River country. As time went on, however, particularly by the end of 1814, there was a marked division among the members of these two tribes. The Missouri faction attempted consistently to be neutral although a few of its members, from time to time, fought for Black Hawk and the British. By the fall of 1814 the course of the War of 1812 in the Northwest Territory had changed. It was obvious that the Indian war was not being successfully managed by the British, and the Americans were consolidating their forces. The Treaty of Ghent brought an end to the War of 1812, but there was no mention in the treaty of Indian participation. The Fox and those Sauk who had remained on the Missouri signed a treaty, but it was not until 1816 that the peace treaty between the United States and the Sauk who had supported the British finally was signed. The Indians were obliged to reaffirm the Treaty of 1804, giving up their lands along the Mississippi River. The breach between the Sauk and Fox, brought on by their division during the war, continued over the years.

In order to impress on the Indians the strength of their arms, the Americans founded Fort Armstrong at the lower end of Rock Island, at the mouth of the Rock River. The fort was established primarily to demonstrate that the Americans were fully prepared to defend the frontier against complete reoccupancy by the Indians. In spite of the fact that the Americans were victorious in the War of 1812, many of the Indians of the Northwest Territory still looked to the British for aid in their struggle against the American penetration. The unsettled conditions among the Fox and Sauk from 1815 to 1817 led to sporadic raids against frontier settlements and the beginning of clashes with the Sioux, upon whose lands they encroached as they were pushed west. In an effort to end the conflicts among the Indians, in 1820 a meeting was held of the Fox, Sauk, the Winnebago, and the Sioux who lived along the Mississippi. An agreement was reached, although some Sioux groups were not represented. The primary American interest was to settle the frontier conflicts among the Indians in order that the Indian trade would not be interrupted and so that settlers would not be harassed. It was during these unsettled years that Keokuk became a powerful instrument of white appeasement in the central prairies. Keokuk was quite willing to abide by American decisions so long as they furthered his own ambitions; meanwhile the effective influence of Black Hawk declined radically.

In 1824 a tribal delegation again visited Washington, D. C. The meeting was arranged in order to show the chiefs the power of the United States. Unfortunately, Black Hawk was not among the individuals who made the visit nor had he visited Washington previously. The primary purposes of the Washington trip were to reach an agreement about differences over land sold to the United States and to bring peace among the Fox, Sauk, and Sioux. Finally, in 1825, the Treaty of Prairie du Chien was signed by the Fox, the Sauk, and the Sioux. It was agreed that the tribal boundaries set up by this treaty were binding for all the members involved. It further was agreed that the Indians were not to seek any additional aid from, nor to be in contact with, the British in Canada. It was apparent at this time that the encroachment of white settlers on the lands ceded by the Fox and Sauk, but still occupied by them, would cause additional hostilities. In the winter of 1828–1829 there were some twenty white families settled on tribal lands in the vicinity of Rock Island. Black Hawk heard about the invasion of this land and journeyed there to observe the scene himself. He would not believe the Americans were as numerous and powerful as the delegates who had gone to Washington had reported. He was appalled by the willingness of Keokuk and other chiefs to bow to the Americans. He was angry to find fences of white settlers enclosing Indian cornfields and that many of the houses of the Indians had been destroyed. In council he advocated further resistance against the Americans, but Keokuk always spoke of peaceful settlements and resettlement. As the Americans occupied Fox and Sauk country, so these tribes in turn invaded the lands of the Sioux, which caused additional hostilities among the Indians. In an apparently unending quest for land by the Americans, once again in 1830 the Fox and the Sauk along with other adjacent tribes gave up their claim to all the lands between the Missouri and the Mississippi rivers. The amount of money received in this settlement could not begin to compensate the Indians for their loss. It was also made clear to the Indians that they could no longer return to Saukenuk; that they were to leave and never come back was an injunction issued by the government in 1830. Black Hawk, however, intended to reoccupy the village in 1831. It was difficult for the Indians to live in the traditional Illinois lands because settlers were constantly selling the Indians intoxicants; finally, the Indians did not have enough food to take them through the winter of 1830–1831. They had sold virtually all of their equipment in order to obtain intoxicants. To complicate conditions further, in the winter of 1830–1831 there were heavy snows in the Illinois region which made it impossible for the Indians to hunt efficiently. By this time Black Hawk was desperate. He appealed to other Indian tribes in order to organize a confederation to resist the whites. He turned to the very unstable Winnebago Prophet, sent parties to visit the Creek, Cherokee, and even his old enemies, the Osage. However, the emissaries were not successful in enlisting systematic Indian aid. In the spring of 1831 Black Hawk and his "British Band" returned to Saukenuk, and the women began to plant maize. The three hundred warriors in the party were not openly hostile to the encroaching whites, but the settlers and Black Hawk's band were antagonistic with one another. In an effort to bring about a peaceful settlement in the removal of the Indians, troops were dispatched to the Rock River country. If they had been regular troops, the difficulties which were to arise might not have been nearly as complicated. However, the anxious officials dispatched militiamen in order to put down what was termed an Indian uprising. On the 26th of June in 1831, Saukenuk was bombarded even though the Indians had left, and the village was destroyed. It was clear that the Americans planned to take firm action against the Indians under the leadership of Black Hawk, and Black Hawk was finally forced to sign an agreement in which he promised not to return to Saukenuk and to submit to Keokuk as the leader of the combined tribes. This did not mean the end of the Indian raids in the Illinois country, for numerous small parties of warriors went out on the warpath against the will or with the passive approval of their chiefs. There was little that the chiefs, including Black Hawk, could do to stop these depredations. At this point it would seem that resistance against the Americans was no longer feasible, but Black Hawk was told that the Winnebago, Potawatomi, Chippewa (Ojibwa), and British would support an attempt to retake Saukenuk. The Indians supposedly had promised to send braves to fight the Americans, and the British had promised to supply the army with guns and ammunition as well as provisions. However, this report, unknown to Black Hawk, was false and had been misrepresented by one of his own subordinates.

In the spring of 1832 the British Band, including two thousand persons with something more than five hundred warriors, crossed the Mississippi River and moved toward Rock Island. By this time the frontier was in turmoil, volunteer militiamen were called out, troops were reassigned and moved into the area in an effort to prevent Black Hawk from reoccupying his traditional country. The American military effort was hopelessly confused, and at the same time Black Hawk was unaware that he had been deceived by his lieutenant. The British would not be coming to their support, and neither could they count on any major aid from other tribes. After arriving on the eastern bank of the Mississippi River, Black Hawk began to ascend the Rock River. A short distance behind him was the volunteer army of the Americans, which was ahead of the regular troops and completely out of effective control of the general in charge of the operation. These volunteers burned the lodges in the Winnebago Prophet's village and then moved on in their pursuit. As Black Hawk traveled up the Rock River, he came in contact with the Potawatomi. They told him that they could not possibly give to his people the corn they needed, and they also warned that no British were going to aid the Indians. Under these circumstances, Black Hawk felt that he must surrender before being overtaken by the whites. He sent a party of warriors back to the camp of the whites beneath a flag of truce in order to secure terms for peace. The volunteers, however, who were not under any realistic military command, misunderstood the purpose of the warriors and soon poured across the prairie after the Indians. One of the three Indians carrying the flag was killed. The other two and the Indian scouts who had followed them raced back to their encampment. Black Hawk now was forced to fight. He rallied around himself forty warriors to hold off the whites. The Indians ambushed the rush of oncoming whites, and soon the militiamen were fleeing in panic. The rest of the troops were routed, and all were swept along in the retreat. These disorganized volunteers fled to relate exaggerated stories of the Indian numbers and of the defeat they had suffered. After the skirmish Black Hawk and his followers returned to the American camp, looting and mutilating the bodies of the slain whites. Afterward they withdrew to the headwaters of the Rock River, knowing that an overwhelmingly large American force would be pursuing them. When the regular military contingent reached the battleground, they found the bodies of only eleven individuals who had been killed by the Indians. As the Indians retreated, they massacred a group of whites on a farm, causing settlers and the government to demand decisive action, and sent scalping parties into the settlements along their path. The American forces were reinforced, and by the end of June the United States military operation included four hundred regular soldiers, three thousand militia, and two or three hundred Indian auxiliaries. By this time the campaign had cost the Americans approximately $300,000, and the Indians still were not defeated.

On June 15 Major General Winfield Scott took charge of a large contingent at Chicago with the purpose of trapping the Indians between his forces and the Mississippi River forces of the Americans to the west. As conditions grew more desperate for the Indians, not only from losses of individuals in battle but also deaths from exposure and starvation, their few allies began to desert at every opportunity. Thus it was not long before the position of the British Band was desperate. Black Hawk decided to try a breakthrough. If it was successful, the Indians could move west and rejoin Keokuk or escape on the prairies. The Americans caught up with them, however, and by mid-July were making an increased number of contacts with the British Band. The banks of the Wisconsin were reached before the Americans were close enough to attack the entire Band. Here the Americans occupied a small plain, with Black Hawk and his followers in the surrounding hills. It was only after considerable effort that the Indians were driven from the hillside down into the river bottom. In this engagement nearly seventy of Black Hawk's warriors were killed, but the Americans lost only one man. In spite of this loss and the desperate position in which he found himself, Black Hawk successfully crossed the river bottom and maintained his followers as a cohesive group. At this point the Americans paused to reconsolidate their forces, but at the end of July they once again made contact with the retreating Indians. On the trail of the Indians abandoned equipment was found, together with individuals who had died from starvation, and others who had died from wounds. It was very obvious that the party was no longer able to fight effectively. On the first of August, approximately five hundred members of the original British Band arrived along the eastern bank of the Mississippi River. Black Hawk advocated retreating farther to the north, but the majority felt that their best chance for survival was to cross the Mississippi River. However, an American vessel in the Mississippi River effectively prevented the Indians from any large-scale crossing. It fired on the Indians, killing twenty-three and preventing many others from crossing. After the attacks of troops on land and on the steamboat, only one hundred and fifty Indians were alive. Fifty had moved northward with Black Hawk, and a hundred had escaped across the Mississippi River. Unfortunately for those who had crossed the Mississippi, the Americans asked the Sioux to search them out. The Sioux killed approximately seventy individuals when they found them in a starving and defenseless state. Black Hawk eluded capture until he had reached the vicinity of the Wisconsin Dells. Here he was finally taken by a party of Winnebago who were to receive a reward for the capture. Black Hawk surrendered to the Winnebago and was delivered to the military forces.

The price the Indians were to pay for their defeat was to forfeit some 6,000,000 acres of land, except for a small reservation, along the western bank of the Mississippi River in the present state of Iowa. Among the stipulations were that they were to remove themselves from this land and never again return there to "reside, plant, fish, or hunt." In return for the lands that they were to give up, the Indians were to receive a blacksmith, a gunsmith shop and an annual allotment of tobacco and salt. They also were given winter provisions and $40,000 to pay their debts to the traders. Over the next thirty years they were to receive $660,000 for their cession. Another stipulation in the treaty was that Black Hawk and other leading chiefs should be taken to Fort Monroe on Chesapeake Bay as prisoners. It was thought necessary to remove the Indian leaders in order to prevent any further violence along the frontier. Black Hawk arrived in Washington, D. C., in late April but was a prisoner at Fort Monroe for only a brief period of time. He was released to the custody of Keokuk in May and was given a tour of the major cities in the eastern United States in order to impress upon him the power of the Americans. He was duly impressed when he saw the seventy-four gun *Delaware*. He was amazed by the mobs of people that surrounded him and awed by the arsenals that the Americans maintained. According to the historian William T. Hagan, if only Black Hawk had accompanied one of the earlier Indian parties to Washington, D. C., and had come to realize at that time the power of the Americans, the Black Hawk War in all probability never would have been fought.

In their defeat the Fox and Sauk settled in Iowa where they had a small, inadequate reservation which could not possibly accommodate their needs if they were to follow their old way of life. They attempted still to hunt and plant their crops; however, the lands were soon depleted of game, and they turned to the west to hunt bison. As time passed, this, too, was unprofitable, and they came to spend more and more time wintering among whites. Here they had contact with unscrupulous traders, with dishonest agents, and with whites who were hostile toward them. The Indians were plagued with disease, and the consumption of intoxicants became almost a way of life for the Fox and the Sauk. As if these troubles were not enough, there was additional dissension in the combined tribes. There were those individuals who favored Keokuk and supported his policies, and there was a faction that was against Keokuk. Then, too, there were the tribal differences between the Fox and the Sauk and various minor disagreements. Additionally, as if to compound their already tremendous problems, the Fox and Sauk were thrown into closer contact with their traditional enemies, the Sioux. There were raids by parties on both sides, and their embittered attitude toward one another continued to be manifest. To climax all their problems, there was an increase in the number of settlers into the accessible lands from the Mississippi Valley. Once again, the Fox and Sauk were forced to move. Americans, with the interests of the Indians at heart, attempted to introduce scientific farming to them, but the Indians would have no part of the program. Neither would they permit schools to be established, and likewise they rejected the efforts of missionaries to convert them to Christianity. What we see is a crystallized hostility against white culture emerging from the nature of their two hundred years of direct contact with persons of European descent. Again, in 1837, the Indians were forced to cede a portion of their land to the United States, and there was the usual monetary compensation. In 1842 the Fox and Sauk were forced to sell all of their land in Iowa, embracing approximately 10,000,000 acres. They moved to western Iowa temporarily and in the fall of 1845 traveled on to their new home at the headwaters of the Osage River in Kansas.

In Kansas the Fox obtained nearly 400,000 acres of land. This was mostly prairie country ill-adapted to their horticultural hunting economy. In order to sustain themselves the people were forced to turn more and more to annuities from the government, but they still continued to hunt bison on the prairie and to seek other game in more sheltered country. Yet they were never successful in maintaining themselves in this manner. Hunting on the prairies brought them into conflict with additional groups who had not previously been their enemies. The Comanche, the Kiowa, and Arapaho all resented the intrusion of the Fox and Sauk. The intruders, however, were fully capable of defending themselves against the prairie tribes. The number of warriors that the Fox and Sauk could assemble always was small, but they were brave warriors and defeated many parties of greater numbers and strength. One reason that they were able to maintain themselves against these tribes was that the Fox and Sauk had weapons that were superior to those of the other Indians in the area. However, by the 1860's, with their numbers depleted by disease and by losses in warfare, they could no longer effectively cope with the more numerous hostile groups. Thus, it is not surprising that during the Civil War the Fox and the Sauk did not actively participate, although a few individuals volunteered to serve with the Union Army.

The Fox never were reconciled to their Kansas reservation; they bitterly were opposed to the Treaty of 1842 and rallied around the chief, Poweshiek. Poweshiek, because of his disgust with the Sauk for ceding the Rock River country, had moved to Iowa with many of the

Fox. He later was joined by Keokuk and the other Sauk who were unwilling to aid the British Band in the Black Hawk War. Soon after the Fox removal to Kansas, Poweshiek died under mysterious circumstances. After his death many Fox became discontented, and during the winter of 1851–1852 nearly a hundred, most of them Mesquakie, returned to Iowa. The Indians purchased eighty acres of land in Tama County and settled again in Iowa. Legal recognition of the Fox in Iowa was given by the state government in 1856, and the land was held in trust by the governor of the state. Then in 1858 other Fox from Kansas defied the Federal government and moved to Iowa. By doing so, they forfeited their annuity payments until the U. S. Congress granted them once again in 1867. Amazing as it may seem, the Indians were welcomed by the white settlers. Altruism was not their motive, but the ease with which the Indians could be separated from their annuity payments was what brought the friendly reception by the whites. In 1862 an additional group of Fox moved back to Iowa after there was a disagreement about annuity payments on the Kansas reservation. Finally, when the Fox and the Sauk were forced to give up their Kansas reservation and move to Oklahoma in 1869, still more Fox returned to Iowa. By about 1870 there were some three hundred Fox Indians in Iowa, and they began to settle down to a new way of life in an old environment.

The history of the Fox and Sauk Indians, with their many moves from lands that were traditionally theirs to new lands they occupied briefly, is complex. However, it may be summarized briefly. Originally the Fox occupied the Green Bay, Wisconsin, area, and from there they moved into western Illinois. In 1804 they unknowingly ceded their lands in Illinois and a small sector of Missouri and Wisconsin to the United States. Then they were given lands in Iowa. In 1832 they ceded their lands along the Mississippi River, and then in 1837 another small parcel of Iowa land was taken away from them. Finally, in 1842, they were obliged to give up their remaining Iowa lands and move to a reservation in eastern Kansas. Except for those who moved to land they purchased in Iowa, they remained on the reservation in eastern Kansas until they were resettled on another reservation in northern Oklahoma. The reservation in Oklahoma was procured for the Indians in 1867, and they moved there in 1869. In Oklahoma the Fox and the Sauk have retained their identity as an integrated group; however, they always remained aware of their separateness. When the move to Kansas was made in 1842, many of the Fox were unwilling to remain in Kansas and returned to Iowa. At the time of the move from Kansas to Oklahoma, additional Fox returned to Iowa; thus the Iowa segment of the combined tribes has retained its separate identity much more clearly than those who remained in Oklahoma.

The information which follows about the Fox is very different from that which has been compiled for the other tribes in the study. None of the Fox ethnographic material dates from a very early period of historic contact. Most of the data were collected around the turn of the present century, or shortly thereafter. Fortunately, however, a great deal of this information was compiled by a Fox who also had Welsh and English ancestry and who became a professional anthropologist. This individual, William Jones, was born in 1871 on the Sauk and Fox reservation in Oklahoma. When Jones was nearly a year old his mother died, and he was taken care of by his Indian grandmother. However, she died when Jones was nine years of age, and his father sent him away to school. After three years of schooling he returned home and became a cowboy, but in 1889 he went to the Hampton Institute, then to Andover, and finally to Harvard. Jones had planned to study medicine; however, financial difficulties and persuasion by the anthropologist Frederic W. Putnam convinced him that he should become an anthropologist. He graduated from Harvard in 1900 with an A.B. degree and completed his professional training at Columbia where he received a Ph.D. in 1904. Jones worked among Algonkian tribes, but he could not obtain a permanent position in Algonkian research and finally began working at the Field Museum in 1906. He made a field trip to the Philippine Islands in 1907, and in the spring of 1909 when he was ready to leave he was murdered by the Ilongots. During the course of his life Jones had compiled a considerable amount of information about the Fox; his notes were subsequently edited and published by Franz Boas, Margaret W. Fisher, and Truman Michelson. It is primarily from these sources that we are able to reconstruct in a reasonably systematic manner the way of life of the Mesquakie.

At a place which is not on earth and of such great distance that no one is able to travel there, a place where it is always winter, lives Wisaka. In the remote past he lived on earth with his younger brother, but the manitous met in council and plotted to kill the brothers. They killed the younger brother, but the older brother, Wisaka, survived their attempts. First they tried to kill him with fire. Then they created a great flood, but Wisaka climbed a tall tree on a mountain top, a canoe appeared at the top of the tree, and he paddled about on the water. Then a turtledove brought him twigs, and a muskrat brought some mud. Wisaka made a ball from the mud and stuck twigs into the ball. He threw the ball into the water, and from it grew the earth as we know it today.

It was Wisaka, too, who created all the things on earth and man as well. The Fox, according to their own traditions, are people with such antiquity that they do not know when they first arrived on earth. They were the first people to dwell on the land made by Wisaka, and they lived by the sea. Out of the sea came a great fish with the head of a man. As this great fish walked on the land, he became fully human, and he was followed by other fish who made the same transformation. These individuals established a community near the Fox, and every aspect of Fox life was copied by the fish-turned-to-men. The Fox were created by Wisaka, and when he formed them they were red, the same color as blood. This was the way that the Fox lived when they were on earth among the manitous. The first Fox were manitous and lived among manitous, but eventually they assumed the form that they have today. As time went on, people grew more distant from the manitous, and the lands and world in which they lived changed. In recent years animals and birds are beginning to disappear, and the manitous which control the universe are unhappy about this new state of affairs. Sometime in the future the manitous will destroy the earth, the Fox will revert to their original red condition, and then the world will begin again.

Fox tradition records when they lived along the northern sea they were surrounded by enemies who harassed them constantly. Finally there was such overwhelming strength against them that they were forced to flee from their traditional home. They were warned by their friends who were among the enemies, the Kickapoo and Sauk, that the hostile tribes planned to kill all of the tribe. The Fox were able to escape after a young man prayed to the manitous that it would snow heavily. As the snow began to fall, the enemies secured their camps and retired to their lodges. When they slept the Fox escaped from the trap and tricked the Indians who they knew would pursue them. One group of individuals followed the trail of a man one direction, and a group of warriors made a wide trail in another direction. Their enemies, thinking that a large party had moved along the wide trail, followed this path, only to be ambushed by the party of Fox. Somewhat later the Fox built a fort, and their enemies found the fort but were unable to take it. The Fox later felt that it was safe to leave their stronghold, and they traveled to a place where the seas were joined by narrow waters. It was here that they met their enemies, the Ojibwa, the one tribe that had been most active in making war against them. A fight took place, and the Ojibwa were defeated. The Fox then continued to move westward, and finally they came to the country around Green Bay and the Wisconsin River. It was this country that they chose for their own, and here they settled.

Fox men were particularly striking in their appearance, largely because of the manner in which they wore their hair. Their hair style is called *moconi*, which is a form of roached headdress. A man shaved all the hair from his head except for a palm-sized tuft left at the crown and cut approximately two inches in length. To the center of this tuft grew a long scalp lock that was never cut and was usually braided. From his crest of hair hung an eagle quill, and along the middle of the crest were attached long lengths of deer hair which very frequently were painted red. The typical clothing of a male included a breechclout made from processed deerskin, leggings of deerskin, and long moccasins which reached just below the knee. When the weather was cold, a man wore a cape of skins. The women dressed their hair by parting it in the middle and drawing it to the back of the neck where it was joined in a twisted roll which was sometimes two inches in diameter. Most probably the women wore long buckskin dresses, along with short buckskin moccasins. The children, at least the very young children, usually wore only a long, loose shirt. As he grew older, a boy wore the same type of clothing as a man; girls followed the clothing styles of their mothers. By the end of the last century most of the Fox had given up their old hairdressing and clothing style. A few men still wore the *moconi* hairdress, but most men allowed their hair to grow down the back of the neck. Behind the neck the hair was gathered and braided into a small pigtail from which were hung ornaments of silver and beadwork. By this time store-bought shirts became everyday apparel for men; at home, however, they wore only the breechclout and blanket. Moccasins changed in the material from which they were made. The shift was from buckskin to cloth, and the skin cape was replaced by a blanket or shawl. The Fox males in particular were given to wearing a wide variety of jewelry, including earrings, rings, wristlets, and armlets, all preferably made of German silver. The shirts and skirts of women were made from calico, and a woman would wear at least two shirts which were loose at the waist, buttoned at the front, and were without a collar. The skirts, of which they wore two or more, hung loosely from the hips to just below the ankles for younger women and girls and reached just above the ankles for older women. The women also were attracted to jewelry made from German silver; ornaments included beads around their necks, earrings, and finger rings as well as wristlets. Women wore short leggings which were made from woolen material and reached as far as the knees. They preferred beaded shawls, but those who could not afford shawls wore blankets. By the turn of the century small children who were unable to walk were dressed in long loose shirt-like garments; older children wore clothing similar to that of adults.

The summer settlements of the Fox were along rivers and streams in the valley lowlands where the women could find adequate ground to clear and plant. The village dwellings were oblong bark-covered structures with pole frameworks and were as much as forty feet in length and twenty in width. Inside and along each sidewall was a platform of poles resting on posts and raised about four feet above the ground. These platforms served as seats and beds. Bark was placed on top of the poles and then skins over the bark. In the open space at the center of the house were fires for cooking and for heating. Clusters of lodges were occupied during the summer from April through mid-September. After this time small family groups dispersed and lived a nomadic life during the winter. The winter dwellings were oval structures made by placing the ends of poles in the ground, bending the poles together at the top and tying them. Over the structure were placed reeds or mats, and at the doorway hung a bearskin.

An inventory of Fox material culture is incomplete, and most descriptions date from the period around 1900. The material goods were for the most part portable since much of every year was spent in scattered hunting camps. The principal hunting weapon was the bow and arrow; the bow was sinew-backed, and arrows were placed in a quiver of buckskin. Other material goods listed in their inventory included wooden mortars for pounding maize and other grains. The people also had digging sticks to prepare the ground, and they made various forms of bark and skin containers, in which they placed not only household goods but products from the hunt and from their horticultural pursuits.

By the turn of the century the Fox were reconciled to the clothing and everyday household equipment which they purchased from whites. During any important religious or social event, however, they wore clothing and adornments which they had come to regard as traditional finery. Anything made from silver was regarded as "good medicine," particularly when made into jewelry on which were executed certain designs. The silver once came in long processed strips from Mexico, but by about 1900 it was obtained from Colorado. The standard silver-working tools seem to have been only a knife, a hammer, and an awl. A silver hair comb for a woman was a particularly potent charm, for it was inserted near an individual's soul, located just beneath the scalp lock, the teeth of the comb being arranged so that they touched the soul. To wear numerous silver bracelets was also desirable, even if they stretched in an almost continuous band from the wrist to the shoulder, for the bracelets with designs on them represented prayers. On ceremonial occasions girls and women wore a wide variety of decorated beaded ornaments. Most important among these was the strip of beaded leather which was wrapped around the roll of hair at the back of a woman's head. Furthermore, attached to the hairwrapper were long woven strings which dangled nearly to the ground. These hairstrings were regarded as particularly sacred, and the owner's welfare could be controlled by possession of her hairstring even temporarily. Strings of beads were worn by girls and women, and it was felt that four pounds was the most one should wear. Beaded bands with geometric designs on leather were fitted tightly about the necks of young girls, whereas similar necklaces for married women fitted loosely about the neck. A necklace in which black beads were woven indicated that the ornament had been blessed by a shaman, and turquoise beads were added to increase the fertility of the wearer. The ceremonial dance skirts of women or girls included embroidery which was geometric in its pattern if it was to have religious significance. The ornate floral patterns were regarded strictly as ornamental in their conception and execution. A man's most important ornament was that which protected the scalp lock, which was just above the seat of the soul. Habitually, each chief wore an eagle feather set in a small bone mounting, and at the end of the feather was a red dye which indicated that the man had killed a warrior. The feather also was decorated with golden-winged woodpecker feathers since this was a bird that was important in the supernatural system. Eagle feathers adorned in this manner could be worn only by an individual who possessed a hereditary rank of importance. Like the women, the men wore silver ornaments—earrings, bracelets, and finger rings. The men wore strings of beads around their necks and necklaces with beads sewn to strips of leather as well as beaded headbands.

The eating habits while in permanent camps included partaking of three meals a day, a light breakfast and lunch and a large meal in the early evening. Habitually each person had a spoon, but one wooden food container might be used by more than one person. They sat either on the platform or on the ground to eat. Men habitually sat cross-legged, while women sat with their legs together or under them. In a large encampment where men were numerous they ate first, but normally the entire family ate together. The meals were prepared at the central fireplaces in the bark houses or at the single fireplace in the center of the winter wigwam. The food was prepared most frequently by boiling, and in aboriginal times the cooking containers were made from clay. By the time the records about Fox food preparation are reasonably complete, however, we find that an iron kettle hung from a hook above the fire was the usual cooking utensil. When they lived in Wisconsin, they harvested wild rice as an important food, but the only wild rice that they were able to obtain in later years was supplied by the Winnebago and Menominee. The most important food staple for the Fox was maize. The varieties raised were white, red, yellow, and blue. The Fox designations for the varieties were based on a word stem which meant maize and then on its color designation. As might be expected a wide variety of maize dishes were prepared and consumed. Corn was boiled or made into hominy by leaching the shells away with wood ash and washing away the lye. Corn also was parched in a fire, but most frequently it was ground into a meal and made into gruel which was consumed after boiling. A wide variety of beans were grown; these had been domesticated in Mexico and reached the Fox from the Southwest. Pole beans were from the Southwest, and a few beans had been introduced by whites during historic times. Another domestic plant was squash, which was prepared for consumption by cutting the fruit in rings which were placed on a pole and half dried in the sun. Then the rings were plaited and placed between two mats which were pressed by walking over them. The strips again were dried in the sun and finally stored for winter. Among the wild plants gathered were broad-leafed arrowhead corms, either collected from the plant rootlets or robbed from muskrat caches. These "potatoes" were boiled, sliced and strung on strings which were hung from the rafters of a bark house. A potato-like growth was the groundnut which grew along the plant roots and was as much as three inches in diameter; it was peeled, boiled, sliced, and then dried to be cooked with meat in the winter. A third plant, rootstock from the yellow lotus, was dried for winter; when needed, it was soaked and cooked with meat, corn, or beans. Additionally, the Fox collected sugar-maple syrup, which was an important seasoning in cooking, and a few plants were collected specifically for seasoning. Hickory and butternuts as well as walnuts were appreciated, and diverse forms of wild fruit were consumed either at the time of collecting or later in the winter after they had been dried.

The subsistence activities of the Fox around 1820, and most likely before, were divided into two distinct phases. In the spring and summer they occupied traditional villages and tilled the lands adjacent to their bark-covered lodges. The women planted and maintained the gardens while the men hunted. The most important game animal was the deer, not only for its meat but for its skin and fat. Small game and birds were hunted, as was the bear which the Fox considered a choice form of meat. The basic staples, however, were maize, beans and squash cultivated by the women and the wild plant foods which they collected. All of these foods were dried and stored in cache pits, in bark baskets, or in the rafters of a bark house. In mid-September when individual families left their summer settlement they took a small quantity of corn and other possessions to their winter hunting area. The scattered families lived in their dome-shaped, mat-covered structures which easily could be abandoned and rebuilt by carrying the mats from one camp to the next. Some families ranged into the headwaters of the Iowa and Des Moines rivers. Others who owned horses ranged westward and hunted into the Missouri River drainage. When winter hunting became less rewarding, they assembled in large encampments and were not again active until time to trap beaver in the spring. Then they traveled back to their villages and planned the trip so they would arrive together. This was to minimize exposure to hostile peoples and to prevent someone from illegally taking the provisions of another's cache.

According to the able analysis of early contact Fox culture by Natalie F. Joffe, the functioning social and economic unit was built around the small extended family. This unit conceivably could include about forty individuals since a man had two to five wives, and their children brought their spouses into the household somewhat less often than they set up a new household or joined the wife's family. In addition, there might be household members from other tribes who had been adopted or were captured in raids. Female captives might marry Fox men, and their offspring were regarded as Fox. Furthermore, it was likely that a family group would include individuals adopted to take the place of deceased persons. The adopted person did not take up residence in the household but was regarded as a member of it.

The Fox were divided into patrisibs, which were the most important social and religious groups within the society. There were apparently fourteen exogamous sibs, named primarily after animals and birds, during the early historic period. Among the leading sibs we find the Bear, Fox, Wolf, Thunder, Swan, Eagle, Sturgeon, and Bear Potato. The largest patrisibs were the first four mentioned, and it is possible that these were among the oldest sibs. From one Bear sib lineage was derived the line of paramount chiefs. The Fox sib was known also as the War Chiefs and had split into named sub-sibs which in at least one instance formed a lineage. The Fox, Thunder, and Bear sibs contributed most of the chiefs, the leaders of war parties, and council members; the other sibs normally provided the tribe only with councilmen. The sibs appear to have been divided into moieties which provided reciprocal services in ceremonial activities; the Bear and Wolf reciprocated with the Eagle, Fox, and Thunder sibs. It must be added, however, that the exact nature of these mutual obligations is not known.

A second type of moiety division has been recorded. In this arrangement each person was assigned to one of two groups, the To'kana or Kicko, depending on birth order and the father's affiliation. A first-born was usually assigned to the division to which his father did not belong, and the second to the group of his father's affiliation. The third belonged to the moiety of the first and so on. Assignment was irrespective of the sex of the person and had nothing to do with marital arrangements. Between the members of the moieties there was a friendly rivalry. They played games against one another, and the division was important in certain festivities, hunting arrangements and the assignment of camp police.

In the Fox kinship terminology collected by Sol Tax in the 1930's we find that on a male Ego's generational level there were specific terms for older brother and older sister, whereas younger brothers and sisters were considered as younger siblings. These terms were extended to father's brother's children and to mother's sister's children. There were additionally distinct and separate terms for father's sister's son and daughter as well as for mother's brother's son and daughter. Furthermore, the terms for father's sister's son and daughter were the same as for sister's son and daughter. This form of cousin terminology is termed Omaha. On the generational level above Ego we find that the word for father was extended to father's brother, but there was a different term for mother's brother which was extended to all males in the direct line from mother's brother, for example, mother's brother's son, mother's brother's son's son. The terminology for males on the first ascending generation above Ego is bifurcate merging. For females, however, we find the term for mother was different from mother's sister, and both were different from the word for father's sister. This is a bifurcate collateral terminology for the female line. Furthermore, the mother's sister term was extended to the mother's brother's daughter and mother's brother's son's daughter. The most important observation to be made about the terminology is that there was the inclination to group individuals of both sides of one's family into a small number of categories and to ignore separations by generation. In kinship behavior between sets of individuals there tended to be egalitarian relationships. For example, even recognizing the age and status differences between a father and his son, we still find the behavior between them tended to be as between two brothers in the ideals of modern American society. Among the Fox, the mother-son relationship was more like that between sister and brother; restraint was necessary without avoidance. Again between a father and his daughter there was the brother and sister attitude, while the mother and daughter relationship paralleled that of a father and son.

Political life was organized around the tribe and the village. The paramount chief was from a particular lineage in the Bear sib, although the Fox, Thunder, and Bear sibs contributed lesser chiefs who, like the tribal chief, must be from a particular patrilineage. In the event that the elder son of a chief could not or would not succeed his father the title and position were passed to a younger son, a brother, or a nephew of the chief. At the village level it is apparent that the chief was an important individual, for it was the village that organized subsistence activities and raiding or war parties. An individual village chief was in office for an extended period of time, and although his influence was great he was not powerful. Expected to be nonaggressive in his behavior and mild mannered in disposition, he served as an arbitrator when there was dissension in the council. That organization made important decisions which affected the community as a whole; its membership was drawn from the different patrilines and would include any other men with outstanding qualities. The village chief listened to discussions and attempted to reconcile conflicting views until a decision could be reached. It may, from the above descriptions, appear that the chief and council were quite powerful, as they in fact were, although it is true that they were most often guided by tradition. The Fox, as Walter B. Miller stresses, were rugged individualists who knew what was expected of them, and in normal activities they strongly resented anyone's attempt to direct their behavior. As the Jesuit missionary Father Allouez (Miller, 1955, 286) wrote long ago, "These people are self-willed beyond anything that can be imagined!"

In order to obtain some idea of the functioning of the political system, it is highly instructive to recount briefly what took place when an individual was murdered by another member of the tribe. In this one recorded instance a man had murdered his wife and was instructed by the sib of his wife to appear in their main lodge. He did as he was directed and squatted on the floor. The men of the woman's sib came in and seated themselves on the platforms. A man at the end of the line held an ax which would be used the smash the back of the murderer's skull if he were judged to die. Once the men were assembled a man at one end of the line silently nudged the man next to him; this was a vote to kill the murderer. This man nudged the one sitting on his far side and so on until one man failed to nudge his partner. This indicated that he did not approve of the death penalty, and since decisions of guilt by tradition must be unanimous, the murderer was not doomed to die. Instead, his relatives were permitted to present gifts as compensation. This example demonstrates that the serious crime of murder was not handled at the tribal or village level but was considered as an offense against the murdered individual's kin group. It illustrates too the alternatives of action, death or compensation.

One activity in which the Fox excelled and which consumed much of their time and energy was warfare. Aggression against another Indian group or against whites was either at the tribal or individual raiding party level. A national war such as was fought against the French, the Americans, the Sioux or Osage met with overall tribal approval but very rarely included large numbers of warriors and large-scale battles. More common were the raids led for a specific purpose by an individual against an enemy. The circumstances leading to warfare were to secure one's hunting area, to acquire new lands upon which to hunt, to avenge the death of a Fox, or to gain prestige and honor. A war leader at any level was able to organize a raid because of success and because he had been granted power by a manitou. A war leader supervised the party strategy, but he had limited power, for no participating warrior ever was obligated to follow the war leader against his will, and he could at any time defect and return home without loss of honor. Even though a warrior might submit to the authority of a war leader and follow instructions, the participants were obliged to bend to the war chief's modicum of authority only during the period of the raid. The important point is that the Fox war leader had more authority and power than any other individual at any other time, and yet his prerogatives were very few indeed. As if to emphasize the temporary nature of his position he was obligated after returning from a raid not to enter his settlement until he had been ceremonially purified. Within Fox society a great deal of prestige and honor was heaped upon the successful warrior. To be a great warrior was a value instilled in boys from early childhood. A child was given portions of the eyebrow or heart of a brave but slain enemy in order that he might eat them and acquire the qualities of the deceased. A boy attempted to join a war party as soon as possible in order that he might boast of his exploits according to the custom for all warriors. Anyone could attempt to lead a war party. If he dreamed and if his dreams were judged propitious by other warriors, they would pledge themselves to join the raid. Before departure, war songs were sung, and men abstained from the company of women. Although a woman might join her husband on a war party, she would not have sexual intercourse with him during the trip. A party against an enemy advanced slowly, hunting along the route and caching the dry meat for the return trip. If the party numbered twenty or more individuals, a sacred bundle was taken along for supernatural protection; a smaller party had to rely on the party leader's medicine bundle to secure supernatural aid. Scouts were sent out in advance, and one man was designated to cook for the attackers. An attack was always planned to surprise the enemy, and if the party were successful the return was led by the man who made the first kill. In defeat, each warrior returned home as best he could. If scalps were taken and captives secured, the elderly ones were often killed on the way home. A successful raid ended with a scalp dance and feasting at the village of the warriors. A woman could gain important status and rights among men if a male relative permitted her to club the head of an enemy he had killed. For a Fox man to steal horses was honorable; however, such theft did not have the important social value which we find among the more typical Indians of the Plains and prairies. The warrior could and usually did take a new name repeatedly if he excelled in warfare. The warfare complex among the Fox is not nearly so elaborate as among many Indians of the Plains, but it does nonetheless manifest most of the important features found in this area among the aboriginal Indians.

Individual experience in supernatural matters centered in the concept of manitou. Manitou was sacred and mysterious, a fickle but necessary power with which an individual must communicate if he were to be successful. As a supernatural, manitou was a pervasive quality in nature. It was approached with humility and apprehension, and yet one was aware of the moment when a manitou had manifested itself simply by the thrill felt and by a sense of feeling different. The normal way in which one sought out a manitou was through prolonged fasting, and yet at a critical or even unanticipated time the force might be heard or seen. The manifestation of a manitou might be conveyed in a song, an object, or a ritual to be performed. Walter B. Miller in discussing supernatural experience among the Fox, stresses the important point that religious systems are essentially projections from one's social experience and an extension of the manner in which men deal with other men. The central religious concept of manitou was a pervasive supernatural force; it was abstract and impersonal. Yet, it was received by an individual, and it was a personalized manitou that was drawn into the experiences of an individual. The blessing and cooperation of a manitou had no built-in permanence; it could at any time be lost inadvertently or through carelessness. The varieties of manitou were endless and pervasive. The force could be animal, human, organic, inorganic, material, nonmaterial, natural or supernatural, and an individual receiving such power always sought to reinforce it.

Each individual sought his own personal experience with the supernaturals, for personal welfare and success depended on the individual's relationship with his own manitou. Each boy when he reached adolescence fasted, but not without eating something, for four days and four nights or even longer. He darkened his face with ashes and stayed alone in the forest. At the end of his isolation he dreamed of a manitou or received a vision which included instructions. The receipt of a manitou's power was contingent on following certain rules set down by the manitou. These usually included, among other things, the avoidance of menstruating women and a periodic offering of tobacco to the manitou. In addition, other instructions might be given such as wearing a certain item of clothing, singing a particular song, or possessing a particular object which became the basis of his medicine bundle. All of these things could be a part of the instructions from a manitou. If the boy conducted himself correctly in his relationship with the manitou, the association would endure, but if the boy failed the manitou would withdraw his support. Then the boy again would fast and isolate himself in order to obtain the affiliation of another manitou. A faithful manitou would not only remain with the man during his lifetime but continue to be with him even after death.

The supernatural forces in the religious system were conceived around the idea of the manitou, the most important of which, called Gitche Manitou, was the great manitou. There was also the creator and culture hero Wisaka who was addressed as "my nephew," which among the Fox implied a rank of equality. Additional mythological creatures, usually animals, could bestow power on men. Medicine power could be granted by bears and snakes, and the deer made one swift of foot. An individual's contact with these creatures served as a sacred basis for bundle rituals, which were the essence of Fox ceremonialism. Around each bundle ritual a cult developed, and it was the cult's founder who had learned from one of the supernaturals the essential rituals. Affiliation with sacred bundles and their ceremonies was passed along sib lines, or it could be achieved by learning the ritual and by being invited to participate. Other ceremonial groups did not pass along sib lines, and membership was granted through initiation. Although there were differences in the details of sib ceremonies, the rituals of different sibs had much in common. The spring and summer rituals included dancing in a bark house of the sib. In the winter, when the ceremonies were held in the wigwams, there were rituals but no dancing. In the summer rituals the singers and the drummer consistently sat on the south side of the bark structure. Hoof or gourd rattles were used by certain sibs, and rasps were used by others. The dance directors blew flutes. The participants consistently performed four dances and ate three times, with the main feast following the third dance. Ceremonial attendants often were drawn from particular sibs who reciprocated with one another. An emphasis also was placed on dogs as ceremonial food, seating position according to moiety, the sacrifice of tobacco, and numerous other specific traits and trait complexes which demonstrate the essential homogeneity of the ceremonies, which were conceived of by the Fox as quite diverse in origins and details. A leader of the Fox ceremonies committed to memory the ritual speeches which were punctuated by other episodes. Such a leader followed established tradition in his performances, and the authority he had was limited to the activities involved in the ceremony.

Apart from the manitous, there were other supernatural beings. Probably the most important single category was that of witches who were envisaged in human form and as either male or female. It was reported that witches, who often were members of the Bear sib, learned their skills from other witches. They ventured about during the night, flashes of light which illuminated the landscape came from their mouths, and furthermore, they made a hissing sound in passing. The evil created by witches took diverse forms; for example, for a part of an individual's body to swell was caused by the touch of a witch. Then, too, when someone died for no apparent reason, a witch was thought to be behind the death. If an individual became bewitched, there were techniques which could turn the malevolent power against the witch. When a witch entered a house, it turned into a feather if discovered.

In the Fox concept of the world an effort was made to relate most natural phenomena to the sphere of the supernatural. Thus, the sun was a man, the grandfather of the Fox, and also a manitou; he was not always considerate of the people. The moon, their grandmother, had a gentle quality and could be looked upon at any time. The months were named and associated with the arrival of each new moon. The Milky Way was a river of stars, and other stars in the sky either were persons who had died and had gone to live in the sky, or else they were great manitous. The four stars forming the body of the Big Dipper were thought of as a bear followed by three stars who were hunters. The hunters followed the bear each year until the fall when they killed it and its blood fell to earth where it turned the leaves of some trees red and faded the color of others. Then the bear came back to life, and the hunters pursued it for another year. The color red came to symbolize the fall of the year; it also signified hostility and was used for decoration. Black was the color for winter, for fasting, and for mourning. Green was for spring and peace; it was the special color of the chief's sib. Yellow symbolized only summer.

Curers among the Mesquakie used plant products and to a far lesser extent animal substances to heal patients. As a plant was collected, it was necessary for the gatherer to follow a set of rules. Songs were sung before removing roots, and an offering was placed in the ground where a root had been. This procedure was necessary to appease the grandmother earth, for plants were the hairs from her head. The earth was the grandmother of Wisaka and the Fox as well; her name was Mother-of-all-Things-Everywhere. Her hairs, the plants, were alive and the grandparents of the Fox. Plants knew about the behavior of people, and they were able to talk with one another. Their conversation was heard as the sound produced when the wind blew through the trees. Plants could be happy or sad, they mated in the spring, and they bore fruit in the fall. Appeasement was necessary for Wisaka so that the plants would be potent cures. Not only was there a proper manner but a proper season in which to collect medicinal plants, and only stipulated amounts were to be taken.

In attempting to effect cures it was possible to mix herbs and roots of diverse plants according to the diagnosis of the disease. Sometimes as many as nine plants were combined in a single medicine. The ethnobotany published by Huron H. Smith for the Fox was compiled largely from a collection made by William Jones about 1900. It contained nearly two hundred plant substances used in curing, most of which were taken internally although some were applied externally and a few burned, using the smoke as a cure. More items in the pharmacopoeia were used to cure or ease intestinal disorders than for any other treatment. They composed nearly a seventh of the known medicines. The next large category consisted of diverse types of poultices, followed by plant products used to treat urinary or bladder ailments and those surrounding some aspect of menstruation or childbearing. At least five different plant medicines were used against colds, snake bites, to stop or impede the flow of blood from artificial wounds, to strengthen one or as love magic. Only rarely were plants used in a diagnosis, or for some less tangible ailment such as being afraid. Rarely, too, were botanical cures borrowed from whites. The use of animal products as cures is limited to a few items, and likewise inorganic substances only rarely were employed.

In order for a woman to conceive the Fox believed that it was essential for her to copulate repeatedly with one man. During the course of her pregnancy many restrictions surrounded her behavior. For example, to ensure a normal birth the woman abstained from eating nuts in order to prevent the embryo from breaking through the membrane; nor could she touch a corpse for fear her baby would die, and to stare at a corpse would make the baby cross-eyed. Parturition took place in a small hut away from the family dwelling where the mother was cared for by some old woman. Here she remained for ten days after the birth. In childbearing a woman knelt and leaned forward supported by a rawhide strap. She could not cry out no matter how severe the pain. If the delivery were long and difficult, a shaman or woman sang around the outside of the hut but usually offered no other assistance. For the next twenty days the woman slept in the main house but apart from the other members and ate in the birth lodge. Finally, after thirty days, she assumed her normal role in the household. During her isolation she was avoided by men, and at the end her garments were discarded.

The baby was placed on a cradleboard and carried by its mother for nearly a year. As children grew older, the parents did not favor one child over the other until a boy became outstanding in hunting skills. The ideals of childhood behavior were recorded by Truman Michelson from a Fox text. From it we learn that children were told not to visit other families often, for if they did people would think that they always were searching for something good to eat. Children were expected to be retiring and honest and, when someone died, to fast and not be noisy. The fasting prepared the boys for additional fasts which were an important part of growing up and becoming an adult. Fasting was emphasized for girls also, particularly around the time of the menarche, in order that they have a good and a long life. These ideals of childhood behavior may not have been followed closely, but they did nonetheless constitute the normal expectations for children. One activity undertaken by young males of high social standing was to become a "slave" for two years in the service of a chief to do any menial task. After this period the volunteer was freed from the drudgery of performing menial tasks such as cooking and camp chores throughout the remainder of his life.

By the time a boy was about seven years old he began to be trained as a hunter, with his father as his principal instructor. A feast was given to celebrate his first animal kill, and a meal from the animal was prepared for someone who was not a member of his household. As mentioned earlier, the relationship between a father and his son was somewhat comparable to the relationship between two brothers in our society. The boy was given a gun when he was about twelve years of age and was expected to hunt small game. He was instructed by his father in hunting magic and in the objective skills for taking game. A son who disobeyed was not punished physically but was instructed by his father to fast. To fast and seek solitude was not new to the child, but it did become intensified. Then, when the boy was still young, he was expected to seek out a manitou. When he went alone into the forest on his quest, his parents mourned the loss of their son, for after establishing this supernatural relationship he would no longer be a child. To fast and paint one's face with ashes made a manitou approachable and encouraged it to grant the young man success in the hunt and in war, and give him longevity as well.

At about the same age that a boy began to receive instruction for later life, a girl was taught the domestic skills by her mother. She learned to sew, to cook, and to care for the garden. About the age of twelve, she began to acquire the more complex skills necessary in making moccasins and house mats. At the onset of her first menstruation she was isolated from the settlement in a small hut where she lived for ten days with a blanket over her head. Her companion during this isolation was an old woman who instructed the girl about adult behavior. At the end of this initial isolation the girl bathed in a stream, and her skin was pierced, especially about the back and sides, until she bled freely. The bleeding was to ensure that the girl would not menstruate excessively. She then moved within sight of the settlement, living here for twenty days. After this time she took a second bath and finally was permitted in the family dwelling once again. During all subsequent menstrual periods, a woman was isolated in a hut.

She was not only potentially dangerous to herself but to the men and the supernatural. If she were to touch her hair, it might fall out; if she ate sweet or sour food, she might lose all her teeth. She could kill a tree with her touch or cause a crop to fail if she ran through a garden. Most important, the manitou abhorred menstruating women, and such women were avoided by men so that they would not lose their special powers (see Note 1).

A girl was prepared for marriage only after she had acquired the skills of making fine beadwork and ribbon applique. Her behavior was supervised carefully by her mother and her mother's brother, who was a joking relative. He not only joked with her but saw that she behaved properly since he would be shamed if she did not. She was instructed not to be promiscuous nor to giggle, for giggly girls were open to sexual overtures. As a boy became a young man, he was expected to be respectful toward girls and to have sexual intercourse only with the girl he planned to marry. A young man sometimes courted a girl by playing a flute near her home, which was an attempt to lure the girl outside. The melody of the flute conveyed his desire. For a girl to accept the lure was to accept the man's advances. Parents of a courting couple, however, preferred to have the man visit their home openly to win their daughter in marriage.

The principal means for obtaining a wife was by bride service or elopement, with the former being more common. The suitor first became friendly with the girl's brother and mentioned the subject of marriage to him, although he could approach the girl directly. The girl was of necessity a member of a different patrisib than the man. If the match were acceptable, the girl's family usually required the services of the groom until the first offspring was born. An alternative was for a man's family to present the girl's family with gifts so that the period of service would be unnecessary. This was attempted especially if the parents of the boy did not want to lose their son as a hunter. When gifts were accepted in lieu of bride service or when the service was completed, the couple was free to establish an independent household or to join either set of in-laws. An elopement and marriage occurred when a man convinced a girl to go with him on a summer hunt. Upon their return he presented the parents of the girl with gifts. Another less common means for obtaining a wife was for a warrior to have a bride offered him by the girl's father. This happened when a man had greatly aided the family of the girl. For example, if a warrior prevented the scalping of a man's dead son, gave the son a warrior's interment, or rescued the son from an enemy, he might be offered the deceased man's sister as a wife.

At least a few Fox appear not to have married but to have lived as transvestites. A dance held annually centered about and emphasized the position of such a person. The *berdache,* as he was termed by the French traders and trappers, was danced around by men who had had a sexual relationship with him. The transvestite wore the clothing of a woman, and because of his highly unusual role he was regarded as sacred.

The dissolution of a marriage usually resulted from sterility or from an inability of a couple to tolerate one another. Some personality characteristics such as extreme jealousy or having an ill-tempered mate led to divorce. When a marriage was dissolved, any presents which had been exchanged during the marital arrangements were returned, and the woman was free to retain her personal property. Sometimes a marriage was dissolved after a few days, with the husband leaving his wife. Instances such as these were said to have occurred when the bride was not a maiden. Examples of a wife committing adultery are recorded, and in extreme instances the husband might kill the couple; another alternative was to cut off his wife's ears or bite off her nose.

One conspicuous characteristic of adult life was that each individual knew what was expected of him and was resentful of being instructed in any manner. A person's behavior was dictated by tradition; he did as his father had done before him, or as he had done the year before. He communicated with the supernaturals as an individual with no other person standing between him and the manitou. He functioned in the institutions of the society without supervision, and in his personal life, again, he was his own authority. Thus, it is not surprising that individualism was the social norm, and strong resentment was exhibited by any Fox who was told to do anything.

When an adult died, there were three possible forms of interment reported as aboriginal. In one form the body was placed on a scaffold or in a tree. A deceased warrior was interred in honor by placing him in a sitting position above the body of a slain enemy. The bodies were not covered. Most common perhaps was to excavate a shallow pit and arrange the seated body so that the head was above the ground and rocks or a small shed covered the head. Food and water were included with the body, and the feet were faced to the west. Weapons were not placed with the dead for fear that the spirits would use them against the living. A stake was erected at the foot of the grave, and the bark was peeled from it. Among the final acts were for those present to sprinkle tobacco on the body and then to kill a pup or a grown dog on the site of the burial. The spirit of the dog was not only to protect but to guide the dead to the next world. The interment arrangements were conducted by an appointed person who was assisted by others. Just before the body of a warrior was abandoned, an old warrior recounted the number of individuals the deceased had killed, which meant that the souls of these persons would serve as his slaves in the land of the spirits. The funeral director distributed to his helpers the property of the deceased, along with items contributed by relatives of the deceased.

Each individual had two different souls which served different purposes. A small soul came from a particular manitou and was equated with the individual's life; it left the body at the time of death and through subsequent adoption ceremonies was reborn three more times. The larger soul, from Wisaka, entered the neonate's body at birth but was never to be reborn. In the world of spirits a division was made. In one section lived persons who had been good on earth, and in the other, persons who were evil. Some of these ideas may very well have been inspired by Christian missionaries.

After disposing of the body, the sib to which the deceased belonged held a mourning ceremony. A dog was killed for the event and its hair singed by four firebrands taken from the hearth of the deceased. The dog was cooked, and the sib's mourning songs were sung until about midnight when the mourners ate the dog. The ceremony then continued through the night. Persons mourning for the deceased dressed in tattered clothing and blackened their faces. They remained in this state up to four years, which was the maximum time limit before performing an adoption ceremony which brought an end to mourning. The adoption ceremony was performed by the relatives of the deceased and served to release permanently the soul of the dead. The soul had left the earth after four days but returned at intervals until the adoption rituals were completed. If this did not happen within four years, the soul became an owl. The actual adoption process was to select an unrelated friend of the deceased of the same sex and approximate age. This individual did not live with his adopting family; he assumed the kinship position of the deceased and also retained his own prior kinship ties. In instances where the deceased was a warrior killed by an enemy, the adopted warrior was obligated to kill an enemy in order to release the widow from mourning.

Following the course of Fox history once again and tracing what happened to the Fox in Iowa brings events down to 1867 when Congress restored their annuity payments. During their initial reentry into Iowa beginning in 1851, the Indians who struggled back were miserably poor. Their economy was based on hunting and trapping, gardening, begging and selling curios. When they obtained their annuities once again, they used some of the money to purchase additional lands, as they continued to do whenever money was available. New problems developed concerning their annuities and their claim to the land, but these in each instance were resolved. The Indians still were extremely distrustful of outsiders, and in 1876 when a school was built, it was not attended since the families continued to scatter into hunting and trapping areas in the winter time. In the late 1880's the Fox still refused to allow their children to attend school, and the men would not learn the skills necessary to be farmers. In 1894, after the sale of land allotments in Oklahoma which had been held for them, they were able to expand their holdings in Iowa to twenty-eight hundred acres. It apparently was about this time that they began to rent farmlands to whites, lands that did not belong to the core of their holdings, and to use the rent money for the payment of taxes. In 1895 the Secretary of the Interior became the trustee for Fox lands in Iowa, replacing the governor of the state in this capacity, but this change was not actually completed until 1908.

A visitor to the Fox lands in Iowa in 1897 and 1898 reported that the population was about four hundred, and the winter dwellings were described as oblong, pole-framed structures with mat covering, just as in aboriginal times. The ground inside such a structure was covered with old blankets, and a fire in a central fireplace provided warmth, light, and heat for cooking; the only items seen in one such dwelling were containers and food. The standard fare seems to have been flour, lard and maize. The flour was fried in lard to make a bannock which was eaten with dried sweet corn. Dogs remained an important meat for a festive occasion. A few families, particularly those of younger men, lived in frame dwellings with adjacent outbuildings. One of these residence units measured twelve by twenty feet, and a sleeping platform was built along one side and at the end of the house. This particular residence was provided with a coal heater, and other furnishings included a table and chairs. In the summer the people lived along the bottomland near the Iowa River in dwellings sixteen feet wide and twenty feet long, covered with boards and bark over which mats were placed. Inside, a platform extended along the length of the room on both sides. The structures were supplemented with a hut nearby for menstruating women.

Violence seems to have been rare, but about this time an Indian agent appointed three Indian policemen to stop the liquor traffic. The only murders known to occur since they returned to Iowa were of a Pawnee, a score settled against an old enemy, and the murder of a loose woman killed by an offended wife.

By 1911 when another brief summary of the Iowa Fox is available, we learn that many families hunted and trapped, earning as much as $20,000 for pelts in a good trapping season. Only about a quarter of the men were then farmers, and the crop value was about $10,000, a substantial recent increase. At the same time only about $3000 was earned from wage labor. The most noteworthy change in the physical settlement was that around this time a third of the houses were rebuilt or remodeled. There existed at the same time a marked shift to frame dwellings with half of the population living in this type of structure. Thus, it would seem that more people were becoming increasingly sedentary, although the economic system continued to be based more on trapping than on farming or wage labor.

By 1937 the ordinary daily attire of both men and women followed the style of the dominant white society. The only aboriginal survival was in the moccasin footwear of some persons, and the women still wore shawls. At this time women wore their hair in a variety of styles; it was plaited, hung freely over the back and was held in place with a comb or barette, put up in a knot at the back of the neck, bobbed, or permanent-waved. The hair styles of the men, however, were exclusively those of whites, and instead of plucking their beards, they shaved.

The landholdings near Tama, Iowa, in 1937 consisted of one large parcel of twenty-eight hundred acres on which the people lived, and another five hundred twenty acres which were tilled by white farmers on leases. The population of four hundred fifty supported themselves either by farming or by wage labor on small family plots which could not be alienated by individual occupants but could be leased to another Fox. A family dwelling consisted of a frame house with usually one or two rooms and adjacent outbuildings such as a barn, corncrib, chicken coop, roofless privy, and a canvas menstrual hut. During their monthly period or if they had a baby at home, the women ate in the menstrual huts, but they slept in the houses. Another important structure was made of canvas or mats covering a frame of poles. It was rectangular, resembling the summer house of old, and was often attached to an arbor. On the arbor platform the men sat and the children played, and much of the cooking was done by the women over a nearby out-of-door fire.

The average family income in 1937 was about $500 per year, which includes funds from all sources. The total landholdings were worth about $225,000, and tribal assets held by the Federal government yielded a return of $6500 a year. Individuals could draw the funds held by the Federal government for specific projects if they had tribal and Bureau of Indian Affairs approval. About half of the ninety-one families farmed; the other half was supported by wage labor. In 1936, a year of a drought, seventy-six families received some form of relief. In the farming activities women cultivated the garden plots after the land had been prepared by the men, and the men raised the field crops which were important sources of cash income for those who had land. Men who did not till the soil worked in nearby towns.

The food habits retained a certain degree of continuity with the past, for maize was shelled and dried or made into hominy as of old, and sections of squash were dried, grated, and stored for future use. The people still collected local plant products and took small game. New items produced in their gardens and fields included oats, alfalfa, potatoes, beets, and onions. They obtained wheat flour and most meat and dairy products from store purchases, and their maize was ground at a commercial feed mill. It might be expected that families would raise dairy cattle or cattle and hogs for sale, but few families were inclined to do so since they apparently disliked the chores associated with stock raising. They did raise chickens which they purchased from mail-order houses, but their success in this enterprise was not striking. Innumerable dogs were kept, and puppies remained an important ceremonial food. About half of the families owned horses for hauling buggies and wagons or for plowing and for riding, but it was primarily younger persons who rode horses. The material culture in the late 1930's seemingly was typical of rural Iowa. About half of the families owned automobiles, and most shopping was done in Tama, where some effort was made by the storekeepers to stock goods with an appeal to Indians, including shawls, silk neckerchiefs, and beads. Special items for use on festive or ceremonial occasions, such as seed beads, were purchased from mail-order houses. Deerskins were obtained from other Indians in Oklahoma or Wisconsin.

The residence units consisted of a man, his wife and their biological children, unmarried relatives and perhaps children by a former marriage. These nuclear-core households were the economic units as well, although all residents might not contribute equally to the family's support, and the near relatives of the couple often were quite transient. In general, the household was established near the home of relatives, and there was a tendency to be more closely linked to a wife's family residence than to a man's family residence. The kindred groups offered the average individual a widespread network of relatives numbering between fifty and a hundred persons and distributed among about a dozen other households. It is important that although the Fox were patrilineal, the important social ties in their daily lives were with both sides of the family. Family ties were extended through adoption, which was of the same nature as in aboriginal times, that is, to replace a deceased relative with an adopted individual of the same approximate age and sex.

The political life of the Iowa Fox has undergone extensive changes, but it does exhibit certain continuities. The most marked continuity is in the continuing presence of two groups, the To'kana and Kicko. As formerly, the firstborn was of the moiety opposite his father, the second was of the same moiety as the father and so on. In the 1930's these groupings functioned mainly in games and ceremony. More meaningful is the political factionalism which has a very real place in the daily lives of all the people. Its immediate origins seem to stem from a controversy over the giving of individual names for the compilation of a tribal roll in 1876. One faction, the conservatives, refused to tell their names to the Indian agent; that the progressive faction consented led to eventual inequities in the annuity payments. In addition, a chief was appointed in 1881 who was not of the Bear sib. No controversy was raised at the time, but when the chief later led the progressives, the conservatives questioned his hereditary right to the chiefship. This division continued to be important in the 1930's. Families, but not sibs, tended to act as units in the factional disputes, but these disputes did not affect ceremonial activity in which sibs are important. Marriages tended to stay within one faction, but when they did cut across it was most often the woman who joined the side of her husband.

In 1916 the last chief appointed a council which functioned until an election in 1929 when a council was elected. The elected members of the contending factions, however, could not agree, and they never met. Although elections continued to be held, the council remained inactive, owing to internal differences. Then in 1937 the tribe organized under the Indian Reorganization Act, and the elected members of the council, seven in all, began to work together. However, the details of council operations were not recorded. In their political relationships with the state and Federal governments their lands continued to be held in trust by the Federal government. Still the land is subject to taxation, eminent domain, and other judicial procedures which would apply to any other individually owned land in the state. Differences among themselves were settled usually by arguments, although women sometimes fought and one man might strike another on the head. The most common offenses to be prosecuted were drunkenness and differences over property rights. These suits were often brought by the Indians, although they would not seek settlement from whites for problems such as theft.

The concept of manitou persisted; meanwhile, formal religious activities gravitated around sacred bundles of the patrisibs or voluntary religious associations. Christianity, the use of peyote, and the nonaboriginal Drum Society offered additional outlets for religious energies, but participation in one did not exclude one from partaking of another. Membership in the peyote cult was small in 1937, although ceremonial use of the cactus had been known since around the turn of the present century. The attraction of peyote is for its reported curative properties, and a person who tries everything else and then turns to peyote continues to use it after he recovers from an illness. The Drum Society is a religious organization of comparatively recent origin in 1932 and was probably derived from the Potawatomi. The members were progressive individuals even though the power of the ceremony was derived from the manitou. The ritual involved the use of four drums, and the ceremonies were held four times a year. The drums were associated with particular leaders, and they had specific functions.

In the early 1930's the religion still focused on the sacred bundles which were either hereditary along a patrisib line or else crosscut sib affiliations. Forty sacred bundle groups in eleven major categories existed, and within each of these categories were major and minor bundle groups. Membership in a group was patrilineal, but additionally a person might become a member of another group because his personal name was different from his father's affiliation. Thus a Bear sib member with a name from Thunder participated in the sacred bundle ceremonies of both the Bear and Thunder sibs. It was possible to acquire sacred bundle group membership through invitation, which most often happened when an individual was a good singer and knew the songs associated with the particular bundle group. Certain reciprocal functions linked the groups into various activities. The bundle affiliations did not regulate marriage although this was apparently an old ideal. The ceremonies were held in summer longhouses and extended from morning until sunset of a single day. Food was prepared by the hosts, and the most important dish was stewed puppies, ceremonially killed with clubs, served by members of another sacred bundle. The dances were in sets of four, and the sacred bundle was opened and its various items used in the ceremony. The dancers, either male or female, were introduced with flute music played in the four directions or to items in the bundle. Both men and women participated in the summer rituals, but only men were active in the winter festivities. The dog feast was eaten between the third and fourth dances, and after the meal the bones were carefully collected and burned.

Witchcraft and sorcery were still very much a part of Fox life in the 1930's, and malevolent power was obtained in a vision quest. It was in a sorcerer's power at any time to take the form of a bear or a snake. If a potential victim could shoot a gun at the spot where a witch was thought to be, the sorcerer would die within four days. One important use of sorcery was for love magic, and, if properly employed, it led to an uncontrollable attractiveness for the user. The medicine at the same time would drive a nonresponding victim to insanity and eventual suicide.

The ability to cure came from a vision, and a variety of means was displayed. A shaman visited the patient, and if he was compensated enough he accepted the case. The curing procedure entailed singing, administering herbs, and sucking out the disease. Because it was a bear or snake that gave supernatural aid to the medicine man, a claw or bone formed the core of his medicine bundle and might be used to suck out the substance causing the illness. A foreign substance taken from the body of the patient was placed in a saucer of alcohol which had been kept ready for this particular moment.

A brief but revealing composite reconstruction of an individual's life cycle in the 1930's may be obtained from the descriptions of Sol Tax and Natalie F. Joffe. As in the aboriginal era, pregnant women were obliged to refrain from certain activities which were considered harmful to the embryo which they carried. One taboo was that a pregnant woman could not eat bologna for fear the embryo would be harmed since it too was covered with skin. The father as well as the mother had restrictions placed on his behavior for the safety of the infant. Parturition took place in a separate structure built for this purpose, and the woman was aided by her female relatives. After childbirth the mother was separated from her husband for only ten days.

When a child was six years old, it began to attend school, and it was only just after the turn of the present century that schools became intermittently important in the life of a child. Regular day schools have functioned since 1912, and in 1937 the children started to a consolidated grade school for Indians. Two were attending the boarding high school maintained by the Bureau of Indian Affairs at Haskell, Kansas. Two other individuals had attended college, but neither of them completed his college work. At her menarche a girl lived apart in a hut and was visited only by old female relatives. She lived alone for ten days and then for another ten days she cooked for herself. No similar ritual existed for boys, nor was there any longer much of an opportunity to teach him to fast.

Adult life centered about supporting and raising a family, but there existed the wide variety of entertainment forms outside of the family unit. Tama provided pool halls frequented by men and boys; a men's baseball team and a girls' softball team were active; and during the winter gambling was an extremely important form of diversion for men and women. The varied ceremonial life also continued to be important, and the Indian Pow-Wow, organized in 1913, provided entertainment for both Indian participants and white observers.

The Fox of Iowa came to develop stabilized relationships with whites and other Indians. Their ties with the Sauk remained warm and friendly. They visited with these Indians in Oklahoma and received from them products that were locally unavailable. A similar attitude was maintained toward the Potawatomi of Kansas and Wisconsin. Old Indian enemies such as the Ojibwa and Sioux were now friends. Not all Indian tribes, however, were well regarded, and the Winnebago were considered with hostility. Toward whites their general feelings were split between Bureau of Indian Affairs employees and others. The former were regarded as persons supported by Fox funds, to whom requests for government help were made freely and from whom compliance was expected. Toward other whites, whose functions were largely commercial, there existed a warm and friendly relationship (see Note 2).

When a person died, messengers were sent to spread the word, and the same evening a ceremony was held. It was supervised by the patrisib to which the individual belonged. The following day the grave was dug; the body was washed, dressed, and carried to one of the three cemeteries on a truck. A sib symbol later was erected at the grave. About a year after the death there was the traditional adoption ceremony with the accompanying ritual and a replacement of the dead by the living.

The changes between the 1930's and 1948–1959 are at times striking, but the general feeling is that continuity has been much more important than change. In 1948, when Sol Tax returned to the reservation, he was impressed with how little change had taken place.

There were in 1949 eighty-two Fox households and a total population of 489. Most of the households were two-room dwellings in which an average of seven persons lived. At this time it was estimated that of all the reservation land, about fifteen hundred acres was farmland. A third of this was tilled by white tenant farmers, and the rent money used to pay taxes. The Mesquakie families residing on the reservation have continued to find personal identity in the old kinship structure which retains its vitality. The changes that seem most striking are in the political structure of the tribe.

Once again, warfare and the status of being a warrior became an important part of Fox life in World War II. Of the forty-seven veterans, twenty-two became members of a local American Legion post which was organized in 1949. The Fox post was founded through the efforts of a white legionnaire from a nearby community. Initially, the Fox veterans joined the Tama post, but when they were refused intoxicants they resigned. The Federal restriction on selling intoxicants to Indians was still in force, but it had been suspended when the Indians were in the armed services. Thus the distinction at the Tama American Legion post between Indians and non-Indians once again made them aware that they were different from the other residents of Iowa. The Fox Legion post, which they organized, served primarily as a means for members to find greater recognition in white society through the common ground of being a veteran and a legionnaire. The large public meetings involving Fox and whites were attended well by both members and nonmember veterans. The Fox community as a whole turned to the veterans for leadership, but this was not provided because the veterans as a group were no better able to cope with community problems than any other segment of the population. As the post began to function, the leader preserved the Fox idea of unanimity in making decisions. He did this by taking on any authority and any initiative reluctantly. Although the next leader exerted more authority, the organizations would have foundered except that a white veteran assumed the organizational responsibilities. When he left, the right to use a government building for meetings was denied the Indians, for it was learned by Federal officials that they stored beer in the meeting place. After this episode the organization passed out of its functioning existence. Another attempt by a local white to organize the Legion in 1959 did not meet with any realistic Indian participation.

One of the most pleasurable and lasting of all new Fox institutions has been the previously-mentioned Pow-Wow held in late August of each year. Before 1913 and probably from the time the Fox arrived in Iowa, whites had been invited to attend certain rituals. In later years nonreligious attractions were offered, although the religious core of the celebration was retained. In 1913, in response to white enthusiasm, the Pow-Wow was formally organized as a four-day affair, primarily intended as entertainment for whites. The committee controlling the Pow-Wow was structured along tribal council lines, with fifteen members being chosen by the chief and representing the major family lines. In 1922 the group reorganized along American organizational lines, with a constitution, officers, and committee members. By 1951 the committee membership had been expanded, and although the positions were elective, there was a great deal of continuity in the elected representatives. In spite of the popular election, the idea of representation by all the major family groups was preserved. By the early 1950's the rather elaborate arrangements for the Pow-Wow were guided largely by the committee secretary, a person familiar with whites; since such matters as publicity and the various forms of local arrangements had to be managed through whites, he served as a link between the Indian and white communities. Still, however, there is no real authority to guide the event. The participants follow traditionally established norms for the event which resembles a county fair with a strong Indian emphasis, expressed specifically in dancing and singing. By 1951 there were twenty-four separate family souvenir concessions, food concessions, the performance of the old dances and songs, and a guitar group singing cowboy songs. In good weather it is not unusual for seven thousand persons to attend the four-day celebration. Virtually every Fox participates in the event, and most families camp at the Pow-Wow grounds during the celebration. All normal routine ceases when the time approaches, and this is the one time of the year that all the people work together as Fox.

In the 1950's the supernatural system still was organized around the traditional ceremonials. Apart from the yearly Pow-Wow, it was still the sib-affiliated religious activities which most often brought the people together. The sib organization is weak and somewhat vaguely defined, serving primarily as the structure around which the traditional religious ceremonies are organized. This tentative judgment was made by Charles Callender of the Fox Project, and he is inclined to believe that the patrisib in past times only served the same general function. The greatest support for the old religious system comes from the elder members of the community, and they are aided by some persons who are middle-aged. Younger Fox tend to be nonreligious or seemingly are ready to adopt Christianity, were it not for the pressures from the older people. Four sib-affiliated ceremonial groups continue to function. These are the Bear, Fox, Wolf, and Thunder sib ceremonial organizations. The Drum Society members still tend to be progressive, and participants number between thirty and forty individuals. In the late 1940's participants in the peyote rituals included about a dozen persons. Membership in the two Christian denominations is limited to about thirty persons. The missions represented are the United Presbyterian and Open Bible Gospel, both of which are maintained and encouraged by whites, although some meaningful Fox leadership is beginning to emerge.

In the mid-1950's the Fox supported themselves as skilled and unskilled laborers and as artisans in the communities which surrounded the reservation. Most often they commuted to their homes each day, but in some instances they returned to the reservation only on weekends. The Fox of Iowa have all the obligations of other United States citizens; they pay all the diverse forms of taxes, and they have the same rights to vote or to receive relief if they are without economic means. At this time about eight families receive relief, paid for by the state and Federal governments. At the same time the Federal government provides the Indians with services that are not available to non-Indians. They have a grade school maintained by the government, and a medical doctor holds a clinic in the school for Indians. The services provided cost the Federal government approximately $60,000 a year. In spite of the comparatively little aid that the Indians receive and which seemingly they deserve in light of what historically has happened to the Fox, the local whites have a stereotyped view of the benefits the Indians derive from the Federal government.

The local white and Fox attitudes toward each other are an important matter of concern, since these views form the background for social interaction. The whites regard the Fox as lazy, which they are by white standards, and as living off Federal dole, which is untrue since it is only Federal medical care and schooling that the Indians receive. The whites consider that these Indians are sexually promiscuous and physically dirty. These attitudes are probably reasonable in light of observed Fox behavior; nevertheless, they are clearly not so lawless as the whites think. Furthermore, the whites regard the Fox as temporary and expect them to be assimilated into the American melting pot; however, this assimilation has not as yet taken place. By contrast the Fox think that the whites are greedy and aggressive, which they are by Indian standards, that they are temporary, and that their behavior is artificial. The Indians also believe that they are discriminated against. Both groups agree that the Fox have been maltreated in the past; this brings feelings of guilt to the whites and of hostility to the Fox.

Some anthropologists in their studies of people conceive their role as that of a scientific observer whose duty it is only to record the diverse ways of different people. This certainly is a valid intellectual stance and is perhaps the one which prevails today. There are other anthropologists, however, who feel that recording the facts of social and cultural behavior is not enough. They feel that it is a duty, if not a moral obligation, to lend their skills to make life somewhat easier and adjustments smoother between primitives and moderns. Anthropologists with this point of view are not rare, but for them effectively to make changes is unusual. The one satisfying exception is Dr. Sol Tax of the University of Chicago who organized and directed the Fox Project. The work by Tax and his associates is a fine testimonial to what can be accomplished under dynamic and effective leadership. It is therefore fitting to follow the course of this Indian anthropological project (see Note 3) which began in 1948. Tax had previously studied the Fox in 1932 and 1934, and Joffe had made her study in 1937. With this anthropological background and the course of Fox history available for study a group of anthropology students from the University of Chicago embarked on the Fox Project.

As Fred Gearing has stressed, the stereotyped views held by the Fox and whites are being constantly reinforced. As long as this continues, any hope for change is unrealistic. The Fox Project members after careful preliminary studies initiated a campaign to change these attitudes by reaching the whites through newspaper articles, radio and television presentations, and by speaking before various white organizations as well as to individual whites. The Fox on the other hand were reached largely through conversations with individuals and in group meetings. Some of the attitudes of white toward Indian which were considered most amenable to change are as follows: the Fox are temporary residents of the state; the Fox live in poverty; the Fox are not good farmers; the Fox are improvident. These are among the values under attack by the Fox Project propaganda in order to help the whites understand the Indians. At the same time an effort has been made to destroy Fox misconceptions about the whites.

The most dynamic and successful of the Fox Project innovations has been the college scholarship program they initiated for Indians who had completed high school. Initial discussion of the idea took place between Tax and the tribal council in 1954. When the idea moved into the planning stage, the Fox overwhelmingly approved. By 1955 the problems of sponsorship were solved, and Fox youth began to attend local colleges under the program. At that time there were three students, and the next year five more participated. It was expected initially that over ten years some twelve to fifteen individuals would be drawn into the program, but it is likely that participation will perhaps double this original expectation.

Finally, under Fox Project encouragement a community industry organized as Tamacraft was founded. It was originated as a cooperative to produce tile kits, decorative tiles, greeting cards, and jewelry in quantity, along with craft items produced individually. The Fox reaction to the proposal was enthusiastic, and by 1957 the Indians were actively engaged in the industry. Much of the stimulus has come from the local artist Charles Pushetonequa, who is very much an Indian and interested in his own artistic production as well as in devising means for bringing others into the program as participants. Tamacraft has been successful, and the products well received by whites.

The Fox Project personnel of the University of Chicago made studies basic to an understanding of Fox society and culture before they launched the program of change. The programs they had originated or fostered had succeeded or were clearly likely to succeed when the project was terminated in 1960. It appears that through this interest by anthropologists a dynamic program has begun for effecting change in the lives of one American Indian group. The tribe now is a little more viable. In the future it perhaps will not only survive but may begin to thrive. One of the basic assumptions made by Fox Project personnel was that Mesquakie culture need not be assimilated into American culture; rather, it had something to offer the modern world. Therefore, the projects initiated were designed to lend stability and durability to the sociocultural lives of the Indians.

The question is whether or not the social survival of the Fox will continue. An answer is in part provided in a study by Steven Polgar of the Fox Project in connection with boys' gangs in 1952 and 1953. It was found that one group of boys who interacted habitually with one another was a gang, as this term is used in American society, but that other groups of boys were not gangs in the same context. The members of the first group had a high rate of absenteeism in school, and they were suspected of theft and property damage. The clothing they wore was "Indian" in its type; they preferred bright colored clothing and Navajo jewelry. Most of them were from non-nuclear families, and their relatives were not active in local politics. The members were cold to both white and Indian worlds; likewise, they were delinquent in both worlds. The second group of boys was oriented toward white society as well as their own in a positive manner. This was especially true of its leader. These boys did not wear flashy clothing, and they were participants in the traditional sib ceremony. Members of the first gang were participants in these ceremonies and the Pow-Wow, but the second gang did not habitually participate in the Pow-Wow or other less traditionally oriented activities. It is from the second gang that Polgar expects the traditionally oriented leaders of the next generation to emerge. The third gang is much more oriented toward the attitudes held by the dominant white society. All the members had spent at least a few years away from the reservation, and they are able to compete successfully for jobs in white society. In addition, there is the fact that three of the eight members later entered college. Six of the eight still dance in the Pow-Wow, however, and most attend the sib ceremonies. These boys have begun to find acceptance in white society and are able to move away from Fox traditions although they do not wish to sever their ties with Fox culture.

From this analysis of Mesquakie boys' gangs, it is apparent that one gang is composed of boys whose behavior is antisocial in the eyes of both the whites and the Fox. The members of the third gang are moving rapidly and successfully toward assimilation in the dominant white society. It is the members of the second gang who seem to have the greatest potential for the continuity of Fox life. They appear to be adapting to both societies successfully and exhibit a pattern of biculturation, which means straddling the sociocultural fences. If the Fox are to continue their separate ethnic identity, it is these individuals who provide the greatest hope for the future.

Note 1.   A Fox woman in her autobiography describes the approach of her menarche and her mother's warnings (Michelson, 1925, 303).

And then I was thirteen years old. Now is the time when you must watch yourself; at last you are nearly a young woman. Do not forget this which I tell you. You might ruin your brothers if you are not careful. The state of being a young woman is evil. The manitous hate it. If any one is blessed by a manitou, if he eats with a young woman he is then hated by the one who blessed him and the (manitou) ceases to think of him. That is why it is told us, 'be careful' and why we are told about it beforehand. At the time when you are a young woman, whenever you become a young woman, you are to hide yourself. Do not come into your wickiup. That is what you are to do. She frightened me when she told me.

Note 2.   Natalie F. Joffe (1940, 323) in 1937 wrote about the existing relationship between the Fox of Iowa and non-Indian Service whites in general.

The Fox does not want the affection of the Whites if it has to be bought at the price of his integrity. Persons who have developed servile attitudes to accommodation are looked down upon. Fox life is so full for the average Indian that he does not need to go outside of his own group to achieve satisfaction and prestige. The working adjustment that Fox culture has reached by acculturation is vigorous and living, so strong that the great in-group feeling has been buttressed. There is remarkably little sexual traffic with Whites. It is striking that any Fox-White affairs of serious proportions within recent years have been between Fox men and White women, and not the converse picture which is usual in such cases. Indian and White half-breeds suffer practically the same handicaps as Indian-Negro crosses. There was considerable infiltration of White blood about three generations ago, but it has practically ceased now, and the descendants of such unions regard themselves as Indians. It would be literally impossible for any White woman to come and live as the wife of a Fox man.

Note 3. Early in August of 1948 when the fieldwork of the Fox Project had just begun, one of the anthropology students from the University of Chicago, Davida Wolffson, wrote something of her changing views of the Fox (Gearing et al., 1960, 30–31).

Late this afternoon we went over to Jim Bear's for the harvest ceremony of the Drum Society. It has been very cool in the evenings lately, and today was almost like an early autumn day: gray, and with a slight chilly breeze. When we arrived, the ceremony had almost begun; a fire was burning at the far end of the summerhouse, and from time to time a whiff of woodsmoke would come our way—the perfect finishing background touch. _____ uttered what appeared to be the opening prayers, after which we ate. There was a sort of effortless hush throughout even the meal, a hush that corresponded with the solemnity of the prayers and the intentness of the drummer-singers. I could see only patches of green through the open windows, and it seemed as though we were set off from the rest of the world, bound together by mutual appreciation and attentiveness to the words and music. It was really an enchanting time for me. I understood, finally, why the hard wooden shelves seem not to bother the Indians; even my comfort-loving soul detached itself from restless thoughts of hard wood.

This was the first time—with the exception of a few moments during the Wolf clan dance—that I really appreciated the emotional pull of native religions. . . .

As I can see clearly now, when I first came out here I was unconsciously biased in favor of having the Indians become just like white rural Americans. _____'s powerful appeal, and _____'s undemonstrative progressiveness (toward white ways of living) exerted a strong influence on me. Now for the first time I am becoming aware of the validity of the non-white ways of living, of the meaningful quality of something "pagan" like the Drum dance. I am beginning to see why there is a value in preventing the total assimilation of the Fox—not so much because Indians' ways are any better (in an absolute sense) but simply because they are the chosen and accepted, and therefore the "natural" ways for a good many people here.

References

Bicknell, A. D. "The Tama County Indians," *Annals of Iowa,* (3rd series) v. 4, 196–208. 1899–1901.

Caldwell, Joseph R. *Trend and Tradition in the Prehistory of the Eastern United States.* American Anthropological Association, memoir no. 88. 1958.

Catlin, George. *North American Indians.* v. 2, 207–217. London. 1844.

English, Emory H. "A Mesquakie Chief's Burial," *Annals of Iowa,* (3rd series) v. 30, 545–550. 1951.

*Gearing, Fred, et al. *Documentary History of the Fox Project 1948–1959.* Chicago. 1960. The Fox Project of the University of Chicago, Department of Anthropology, was designed to compile information about these Indians and to apply anthropological knowledge in the solution of Fox problems. The volume includes documents relative to the project as well as selections of various published and manuscript studies. The information provided is basic to any realistic understanding of the development of modern conditions among the Fox of Iowa.

Green, Orville J. "The Mesquaki Indians, or Sac and Fox in Iowa," *Red Man,* v. 5, 47–52, 104–109. 1912.

*Hagan, William T. *The Sac and Fox Indians.* Norman. 1958. Hagan's definitive history of the Sauk and Fox begins with the early historic period and is carried through in detail to the reservation period in Kansas. There is very little information for the time after 1860.

Jenks, Albert E. "The Wild Rice Gatherers of the Upper Lakes," *Bureau of American Ethnology, 19th Annual Report,* pt. 2, 1013–1137. 1900.

*Joffe, Natalie F. "The Fox of Iowa," in *Acculturation in Seven American Indian Tribes,* Ralph Linton, ed., 259–331. New York. 1940. The 1937 field study of the Fox near Tama, Iowa, by Joffe, when consulted in conjunction with the 1932 and 1934 field data for the same people of Sol Tax, provides an excellent view of the historical background and emerging modern conditions for the group.

Jones, William. "The Algonkin Manitou," *Journal of American Folk-Lore,* v. 18, 183–190. 1905.

———. "Notes on the Fox Indians," *Journal of American Folk-Lore,* v. 24, 209–237. 1911.

———. *Ethnography of the Fox Indians.* Bureau of American Ethnology, Bulletin 125, Margaret Welpley Fisher, ed. 1939. Jones, who was of mixed Fox and white descent and an anthropologist, was killed in the Philippine Islands in 1909. Some of his field data on the Fox were edited and published by Truman Michelson and Franz Boas a few years after his death. About twenty years later his notes were presented to the Smithsonian Institution and were edited for publication by Margaret W. Fisher. This volume is ably annotated and is an essential source on the Fox. In it is provided a rounded view of Fox life for the period just before 1900.

Michelson, Truman. Review of: *Folk-Lore of the Musquakie Indians of North*

America by Mary A. Owen, in *Current Anthropological Literature,* v. 2, 233–237. 1913.

———. "How Meskwakie Children Should Be Brought Up," in *American Indian Life,* Elsie C. Parsons, ed., 81–86. New York. 1922.

*———. "The Autobiography of a Fox Indian Woman," *Bureau of American Ethnology, 40th Annual Report,* 291–349. 1925. The Fox woman recounting the story of her life supplies a wide range of ethnographic details concerning her people for what must have been late in the nineteenth century. It is only to be regretted that the autobiography is not longer and more detailed.

———. "Notes on Fox Mortuary Customs and Beliefs," *Bureau of American Ethnology, 40th Annual Report,* 351–496. 1925.

———. "Notes on Fox Gens Festivals," *Proceedings of the Twenty-Third International Congress of Americanists,* 545–546. New York. 1930.

———. "Miss Owen's 'Folk-Lore of the Musquakie Indians,'" *American Anthropologist,* v. 38, 143–145. 1936.

Miller, Walter B. "Two Concepts of Authority," *American Anthropologist,* v. 57, 271–289. 1955.

Owen, Mary Alicia. *Folk-Lore of the Musquakie Indians of North America.* London. 1904. It is difficult to know how much of this volume is reliable in view of the criticisms by Truman Michelson (1913, 1936). In compiling the material on the Fox, only Owen's information on material culture was utilized. This section of the book does not come under fire from Michelson and, in fact, is almost praised.

*Polgar, Steven. "Biculturation of Mesquakie Teenage Boys," *American Anthropologist,* v. 62, 217–235. 1960. During the summers of 1952 and 1953 the field study of teen-age boys was made, and it was established that although some of the boys seemed on their way toward assimilation in white culture, others were delinquent in both Fox and white cultures, and still others were able to participate successfully in both white and Indian cultures. This is a very insightful paper and probably reflects an acculturation patterning for many Indians other than the Fox.

Quimby, George Irving. *Indian Life in the Upper Great Lakes.* Chicago. 1960.

Rideout, Henry M. *William Jones.* New York. 1912.

Smith, Huron H. *Ethnobotany of the Meskwaki Indians.* Bulletin of the Public Museum of the City of Milwaukee, v. 4, 175–326. 1928.

*Tax, Sol. "The Social Organization of the Fox Indians," in *Social Anthropology of North American Tribes,* Fred Eggan, ed., 243–282. Chicago. 1937. The core of this article is devoted to the Fox kinship terms and the social units, but there is additional information provided about conditions among the Tama area Fox as they lived when Tax visited them in 1932 and 1934. The emphasis of the chapter, however, is on a reconstruction of the social system of the past.

White, Leslie, ed. *Lewis Henry Morgan, The Indian Journals, 1859–62.* Ann Arbor. 1959.

6

The Pawnee:

Horsemen and Farmers of the Western Prairies

WYOMING
SOUTH DAKOTA
★ Pierre
MINNESOTA
CANADA
U.S.
YANKTON
SANTEE
ARIKARA
Missouri R.
IOWA
NEBRASKA
PONCA
MEXICO
TETON
PAWNEE
OMAHA
★ Des Moines
N. Platte R.
Loup R.
● Omaha
ILLINOIS
COLORADO
S. Platte R.
Platte R.
● Fort
Childs
★
Lincoln
MISSOURI
★ Denver
Republican R.
OTO
★ Springfield
KANSAS
CHEYENNE
Topeka
Saline R.
●
Kansas R.
★
Kansas City
Missouri R.
★ St. Louis
KANSA
Jefferson City
★
KIOWA
OSAGE
Mississippi R.
NEW
MEXICO
OKLAHOMA
Cimarron R.
Arkansas R.
TEXAS
WICHITA
ARKANSAS
COMANCHE
Canadian R.
★ Oklahoma
City
Memphis
●
Red R.
★
Little Rock
0   50   100   150 mi.
Map by J. Donovan

The border between the prairies and the plains of mid-America is thought to have been occupied in aboriginal and early historic times by small bands of mobile hunters and collectors. These Indians readily adapted to the horse as a domestic animal, which increased their mobility but did not change their basic relationship to the environment. On the prairies there were other Indians who were not wanderers, who adopted the horse but lived in semipermanent communities; among these were the Pawnee. They were farmers, living in scattered earth lodge communities, and thus they represent a very different way of life from that found among the Sioux, Cheyenne, Comanche, or Kiowa, who occupied the plains to the west. The Pawnee in particular represent Indians who accepted the horse as a domestic animal but failed to deal realistically with the rapidly changing sociopolitical environment in historic times. The Pawnee took the horse, but suffered dreadfully from diseases and at the hands of their enemies; this then is a tribe that did not succeed. Another reason for describing Pawnee life is its majestic quality; another, the aesthetic appeal of Pawnee ceremonies and poetry. Unquestionably there may be found among other Indians a similar aesthetic orientation, but the literature on the Pawnee seems to represent this facet of Indian life better than that for most tribes. Thus the Pawnee, to the author at least, seem more romantic than all the rest. Their religion was a beautifully integrated system which defined with precision man's relationship with the gods.

The name Pawnee was not employed by the Indians of this group until very recent times, after it was in common usage among whites. The origin of the name is unknown. The people knew themselves as Skidi, Chaui, Kitkehahki, or Pitahauerat, depending on the subgroup of the Pawnee to which they belonged. Pawnee as a name for these people was not used until the 1600's, and then it was a term applied to them by the Indians to the north and to the east. Furthermore, according to the historian George Hyde, who has studied these Indians most exhaustively, there was no name to designate the entire tribe in early historic times, and the derivation of the name Pawnee, from the word *pariki,* meaning horn, seems to be a false etymology.

It is probable that the Pawnee entered their historic range in Kansas and Nebraska by ascending the Arkansas River and pushing on northward to the Kansas River drainage. At this point they divided and settled in two different environmental niches. One segment settled in the plains of southwestern Nebraska, and the other established itself in eastern Nebraska and along the eastern bank of the Missouri River in western Iowa. Both populations lived in small settlements; they raised domestic plants and hunted. The eastern segment of the Pawnee placed some emphasis on fishing, while the western branch stressed bison hunting. Another group remained in eastern Oklahoma and southern Kansas. In 1825, about three hundred years after initial historic contact, the tribe numbered about ten thousand. In 1840, with the first actual count, their number was 6244, but in 1862 the population had declined to 3414. In 1881 there were only 1250; again in 1940 the population was 1017. In 1962 the Pawnee associated with their reservation in Oklahoma numbered 687. In linguistic terms the Pawnee are of the Hokan-Siouan phylum, the Iroquois-Caddoan stock, the Caddoan family, and the Pawnee language, with dialects.

In east-central Nebraska, the historic area of the Pawnee, the prairie environment included open country with a grassland vegetation, but in the alluvial valleys of the easternmost section were well-watered streams, with fertile soil and groves of trees. According to Waldo R. Wedel, who has had an abiding interest in the archaeology of the Plains and prairies, the first occupancy of the central plains began around 8000 B.C., and the earliest people were hunters of big game. The great Plains and adjacent areas were populated initially by hunters who made large, multifluted spearpoints of flintlike material, of the type designated as Clovis. When the elephant population became extinct, the people hunted smaller but more plentiful species, of which the bison was most important. The remains of these bison hunters, who preyed on now extinct forms of the animal, are more widespread and numerous than those of the earlier hunters; kill sites and campsites are not unusual. Among the most important types of spearpoints associated with these people are the famous Folsom points, which were fluted like the Clovis points but were smaller and had only one flute on each face. These technologies were replaced by other lithic industries, and new peoples entered the area around 5000 B.C. As man killed off the herds of large bison, and as new influences from the Great Plains came to bear on the local cultures, different economic patterns emerged. Around 1500 B.C. there developed small populations who favored butte areas for occupancy. Hearths have been found, some of which were lined with stones, and associated small pits probably were used for storage. The bison hunted were contemporary forms, and vegetable foods also were collected by these people. The inventory of stone tools was more diverse and complex than previously had been found.

In central Plains prehistory there exists a period of nearly two thousand years just prior to the Christian era about which we have very little information. By about A.D. 200 Indians from the east with Hopewellian traditions had introduced maize and beans as domestic crops along the Missouri River near Kansas City. These people were hunters as well as farmers, and they possessed a technology which included the manufacture of ground as well as chipped stone tools. Furthermore, they manufactured pottery in a rather wide variety of forms. The Hopewellian influences, which orginally came from the Ohio River valley, brought the first domestic plants and ushered in the potential of a new subsistence base; however, the people themselves never became established on the Plains. What did emerge as important was Plains Woodland culture. The general configuration included pottery, but no direct and substantial evidence of horticulture has been found to date. Poles covered with reeds were probably the form of dwelling, and there may have been interior fireplaces. These hunters possessed a technology adapted to the collection and processing of vegetable products, and they manufactured a wide variety of ornaments.

Shortly after A.D. 1000 life on the Plains assumed new directions, and although there were regional variations, the most significant changes were as follows: maize, beans, squash, and sunflower cultivation for which there is unquestioned evidence; an inventory of material items far more extensive than found in the earlier periods; earth-covered houses with tunnel entrances, central fireplaces, and four posts for supporting the roof; and clusters of houses in small communities. There is good evidence from the nature of certain artifact forms that the people maintained contact with the central Mississippi valley but had less intercourse with the peoples to the south and to the north. The relationship of these Indians with the historic Pawnee is still unknown, although the general similarities with early historic Pawnee culture seem apparent.

Pawnee culture and society were deeply influenced by the introduction of the horse obtained in raids against the tribes to the south and west, but little else was obtained from these directions. At about the same time in the early historic period the old material culture was replaced largely by trade goods from whites. The early historic dwellings of the Pawnee were of the circular earth lodge type, and they were clustered in villages. Skin tepees or dome-shaped, brush-covered dwellings were the types of structures used on hunting trips in the Plains. In the nineteenth century some villages were surrounded by a sod wall some three to four feet in height, with a moat in front of it. These earthworks and moats served to make the villages more defendable. In the period just before white traders arrived, pottery was made and utilized, but work in stone, while known, was not elaborate. The work in bone and horn was, as might be expected, more complex, since these people relied heavily on the bison. The observation most impressive to Wedel was the similarity of Pawnee material culture to the technologies of the Indians to the east and to the southeast, particularly the Caddoans of the lower Mississippi River, and with the Eastern Woodlands, as represented by the Iroquoians. By contrast there were very few borrowings from peoples in the Southwest.

Pawnee history is not a continuous record of events dating from the earliest historic contacts with whites. After initial contacts a virtual blank exists for the next three hundred years before these people again emerge in a historical perspective. A tradition among the Pawnee records that the Skidi Pawnee once were a separate people conquered by the other Pawnee, and vague tales record a movement into the north from a southerly direction.

When the Spanish explorers under the command of Hernando de Soto crossed the Mississippi River and moved westward in 1541, they encountered sedentary Indians, but farther west in the prairie country they came on the Caddoans, who, unlike the Indians along the Mississippi proper, were unsettled and put up fierce resistance against the Spanish. Since the Caddoans were able warriors and the area offered no potential for looting, the Spaniards turned back to the Mississippi River. In 1541 when Francisco Coronado and his party moved to the north and east from New Mexico, they were guided by an Indian whom the Spanish named the Turk because of his appearance. He was to take them to Quivira, which the Spaniards were led to believe offered untold riches. The exact location of Quivira is not known for certain, but probably it was somewhere in southern Kansas. Quivira offered no riches, and the Turk was murdered by the Spanish who regarded him as a charlatan. In all probability Quivira was then the homeland of at least some Pawnee. By the late 1600's mounted and armed Apache effectively were raiding the Caddoan villages for slaves and plunder. Unquestionably the Pawnee were drawn into these hostilities. Those Pawnee on the Republican River, the Skidi branch, probably moved to this area during the seventeenth century. Pressure was being exerted on them from the east by Siouan speakers, particularly the Oto who were pushed west of the Mississippi River by the Iroquois. Soon the Pawnee acquired horses and metal weapons and consolidated their settlements. By 1715 the Skidi were grouped into eight villages. It was not long before the Pawnee came into contact with French traders who were present along the eastern drainages of the Mississippi River from the period immediately following the Sieur de La Salle expedition of 1679–1682. The traders came to offer more and more goods, including guns, to the tribes in the West. When word of the French intrusion reached the Spanish of the Southwest, the Spaniards became alarmed over potential French penetration of their northern and eastern frontier. In 1720 a Spanish party accompanied by Pueblo and Apache Indians left Santa Fe to investigate the extent of French domination. The guide took the party north of their destination, and in Nebraska, possibly where the Platte River forks, the party was attacked. Most of the Spaniards were killed, along with some of the Pueblo Indians, but the Apaches escaped when the attack began. It was possibly the Pawnee and adjacent tribes who destroyed the invaders. It was asserted by the survivors that the Indians were aided by French troops, but there is no reason to think that the French were directly involved. The French in turn exaggerated the Spanish loss and in 1724 sent a party from New Orleans to establish peace among the warring tribes in order that French influence could be more firmly entrenched. Surprisingly enough, an enterprising French representative, Etienne V. de Bourgmont, succeeded in establishing peace among the Apache, the Oto, the Skidi Pawnee, and the Iowa, which were the most important contesting tribes. Two years later French traders pushed into eastern Colorado, but this link was soon broken by Comanche raids. The result was that the Skidi Pawnee came temporarily to dominate the Nebraska country.

A smallpox epidemic plus hostile Indians on almost every quarter reduced the eight large Skidi Pawnee villages of 1725 to a single village during the early 1800's. Through the mid-1700's the Skidi were the only Pawnee to occupy Nebraska in any number; the Black or Southern Pawnee had not yet moved northward from the lower Arkansas River. Just after 1770 the Black Pawnee were located on the tributaries of the Missouri River and were to become known as three tribes: the Chaui, or Grand Pawnee; the Kitkehahki, or Republican Pawnee, who were an offshoot of the Chaui; and the most southerly branch, the Pitahauerat or Tapages, who sometimes are designated as the Smoky Hill Pawnee. The arrival of the new peoples brought conflict with the Skidi. The disagreements were largely over hunting territory, and the Skidi were defeated in their attempt to remain the exclusive occupants of some key areas. The terms for peace included the stipulation that the Skidi would leave their villages. They did so temporarily, and they were forced to recognize the Grand Pawnee as the leaders of the combined tribe. This conflict probably took place around 1770, but the Skidi never became subordinated as their conquerors had hoped.

The Omaha, under the leadership of Blackbird, a singularly able chief, came to dominate, or at least to intimidate the Skidi Pawnee in the late 1700's. In one instance, also, a group of Omaha warriors were grossly insulted by the Kitkehahki, and Blackbird assaulted the offenders, destroying most of their houses, plundering the dwellings and killing around a hundred persons. All of this was done with the Grand Pawnee standing aside and not aiding their neighbors. Likewise the Grand Pawnee did not aid the Skidi when the latter were attacked by the Ponca. Omaha power, however, waned around the turn of the nineteenth century when smallpox spread to them from some Pawnee who had brought it from New Mexico.

The Spanish of New Mexico continued to be anxious to develop regular contacts with Pawnee country and prevent the spread of French as well as American influence. None of the expeditions sent from Santa Fe were particularly successful in realizing this desire. Countermoves were organized by the Americans, and in 1806 Zebulon M. Pike was sent to visit the Pawnee and then the Comanche to win the support of these tribes and pave the way for the westward advance of the Americans. Pike's efforts to establish friendly contacts with the Comanche through the Pawnee were not successful because the two tribes were at war. At the same time there was a struggle by rival Pawnee factions for internal political control, which erupted as intratribal warfare. When the Pawnee did consolidate against the Kansa, they were defeated by them in 1812. They were more successful, however, in stealing horses from the Comanche at about this time. In all of these machinations the Skidi Pawnee seem to have remained somewhat apart, and their activities are obscured by scarcity of reference to them. They were apparently interacting most frequently with the Sioux, either peacefully or in raids.

In the year 1818 four Pawnee chiefs, one representing each branch of the tribe, went to St. Louis at the request of General William Clark, who was the Indian superintendent at St. Louis. Here the Pawnee signed a treaty of peace and friendship with the United States and began to be drawn into a new and different type of relationship with foreigners. Unlike the French and the Spanish with whom the Pawnee had earlier contact, the Americans were more aggressive in their interest in the Pawnee, and this interest extended beyond trading relationships. The Indians who went to St. Louis were impressed greatly by the Americans, but those remaining at home who only occasionally saw an American were not convinced of the power of the Long Knives. The harassment of Americans who were either traders or soldiers led to the withholding of trade goods to the Pawnee area, which induced the Pawnee to return looted items and even to promise a whipping of the Pawnee warriors who had attacked the Americans. The promise was not kept, however, and as soon as the Americans were out of sight, the Pawnee tended to do once again as they thought best. In 1825 the Pawnee signed another treaty of friendship with the United States, agreeing not to interfere with Americans traveling to New Mexico. Pawnee battles at this period were not with whites but with other Indians. One group was defeated badly by the Osage, and the Skidi defeated a party of Cheyenne, who had enlisted the aid of the Sioux and Arapaho to move against the Pawnee. The Cheyenne withdrew when a lance with sacred arrows attached was captured early in the battle by the Pawnee. The Skidi were badly defeated by the Comanche, but no battle took so many persons as did the smallpox epidemic of 1832, which is said to have killed more than three thousand individuals, including nearly everyone over thirty years of age. Then in 1837–1838 another smallpox epidemic struck, killing about two thousand persons. In the 1830's the Pawnee were not only fighting without success against the Cheyenne, the Sioux, and the Arapaho, but also against Indians who had been moved west of the Mississippi River. To prevent the annihilation of the Pawnee by the diverse tribes bent on their destruction, the agents of the United States intervened by signing a treaty in 1833 granting hunting rights in western Kansas for most immigrant tribes. In this treaty the Pawnee gave up their exclusive rights to a great area south of the Platte River. They thought this involved merely sharing hunting rights, but it was actually a government attempt to make them settle down as intensive farmers. Then in 1834 two now famous Presbyterian missionaries, John Dunbar and Samuel Allis, wintered with the Pawnee to learn the language and to begin their mission activities.

By 1838 the situation among the Pawnee was desperate. The dreadful epidemics had destroyed the core of the population, raids of enemy tribes were more and more devastating, and the Pawnee had no reliable allies. Frequently when they returned from bison hunts in the plains they found their settlements and cached supplies looted and destroyed. At the time they received their annuity payments in 1839, they requested the Indian agent to establish a mission and to teach them American agricultural techniques. When the time came to settle down in one community, however, the Pawnee refused to move to the location the government selected. In 1841 a Presbyterian missionary party of fifteen whites started a farm and mission settlement to induce the Pawnee to settle down around the Pawnee Mission on Loup Fork in Nance County, Nebraska. Within a few years the government built a blacksmith shop, a school, an agency center, and some of the Pawnee began to settle nearby. A terrible Sioux attack in 1843 on the Pawnee village near the mission led the people to flee south of the Platte River. When they returned, the missionaries Dunbar and Allis, who understood the people best, saw the tribe making slow but steady progress. These missionaries encouraged the Indians to settle down, but others of their group advocated what George E. Hyde has termed "muscular Christianity." They beat the women and children to try to make them conform to Christian standards. An Indian boy was shot in the back for stealing corn, and a Pawnee girl was beaten nearly to death by a missionary's son. To disgrace the scene further the Indian agent, whose background was southern and slaveholding, supported the harsh treatment of the Indians and removed those government employees who worked harmoniously with them. A worse acculturation can hardly be imagined. Finally the Sioux were too much for the government workers and the missionaries, and they were forced in 1846 to withdraw. Then came the wagon trains of settlers up the Platte River Valley on their way to Oregon and later to Utah. Depredations against migrants were attributed to the Pawnee, whether the tribal identity was known or not. Fort Childs was built in 1848 on Grand Island in the Platte River to protect the migrants. By this time the Skidi and Grand Pawnee had reconciled their differences because of the havoc brought to them both by the Sioux. It is amazing but true that during the time the Pawnee had their homes destroyed by hostile groups they themselves were raiding to the south with striking success, stealing horses which in turn were stolen from them by the Sioux.

In the early 1850's the Pawnee did more begging and stealing from wagon train immigrants than they did raiding and looting. The Skidi attempted to hunt bison in the plains in 1852, but Sioux harassment made it impossible for them to remain and only a stroke of good fortune kept the party from being completely destroyed. The next year only the organized fighting skills of their allies, the Potawatomi, saved one segment of the Pawnee population from destruction. Finally, there were intruding white settlers who built their homes south of the Platte River, making life unbearable for the Indians there. The Pawnee could not live north of the Platte because of the powerful Sioux. In 1857 the Pawnee accepted a small reservation on the Loup Fork, and Federal aid compensated them for the loss of their land. They received $40,000 per year for five years, and $30,000 a year for every year thereafter, in addition to a promise of active protection against the Sioux and an agency and agent to help them settle down as farmers. Included in the settlement was a trip to Washington, D. C., for some chiefs. In 1859 Indians took up residence in their new reservation, but during the years immediately following the Sioux raids continued. Moreover, a good Indian agent was replaced by a greedy one. The villages were exposed during the summer hunt of 1862 but were defended with valor by old and young men and even some women (see Note 1). In 1864 the Sioux raids were so devastating to the whites that troops were sent into the region, and some Pawnee aided the soldiers. However, ineffective American leadership brought no contact with the hostile Indians. In 1865 a new United States Army commander was appointed, and his military success was due largely to the Pawnee and their cooperation with the Americans. Still, the Pawnee were rovers. They refused to remain on their reservation, and the efforts of the corrupt and incompetent series of Indian agents contributed nothing to their welfare. The reservation was in 1869 put under the administration of Quaker missionaries, which was an attempt by the Indian Service to rid itself of corrupt representatives. The first Quaker missionary found that the Indians could speak no English and although the first school had been established about twenty-five years before, none of them could read or write. Horticulture by the women was still the only type of farming. The Quakers set out to destroy Pawnee customs as rapidly as possible. In 1870 some of the Pawnee chiefs were induced to cultivate fields with a horse and plow; in earlier times it was unheard-of for a man and a chief to work as a woman. Then others followed the example of the chiefs, and American farming practices were introduced for the first time. The missionaries and Indian agents were not satisfied with this progress and hoped to break up the villages and place families on separate plots of farmland. To finance the new development, the Quaker missionaries pressured the United States Congress to sell fifty thousand acres of Pawnee land to finance this resettlement program. In the summer bison hunt of 1873 some four hundred Pawnee were trapped by a force of nearly a thousand Sioux and almost one hundred Pawnee were killed. The fall of the same year grasshoppers and potato beetles destroyed their crops, while white settlers were taking timber and hay from Indian lands. With all this adversity the people were demoralized and not without good reason. A dissident two thirds of the population started south to abandon their reservation, but most returned the following spring. Still there existed a deep dispute among the Indians about whether they should move southward to Indian Territory or remain in Nebraska.

With government pressure removal became a necessity, and in 1874 part of the tribe followed the first group. The land selected for their reservation was to the west of the Arkansas River and north of the Cimarron River, the area occupied by three tribes of the southern Pawnee around 1700. By late 1875 all the Indians had arrived on their new lands. The Quaker ideal of providing one hundred sixty acres and a house for each family was fine, but the money to implement the program was not available. There could be no compromises among the Quakers, and the people were destined to live half-starved in canvas tents, with very inadequate clothing and their horses even stolen by whites. The Quakers were delighted when the warriors were forced to trade their weapons for food! The population figures make the misguided idealism of the Quakers a genocide: 1872, 2447 people; 1876, 2026; 1879, 1440; and finally, in 1890, 804. In an effort to force the Pawnee to become more intensive farmers the government in 1882 cut off the rations provided to the Indians. Some families managed to adjust, but most simply reduced their standards of living and depended on annuities and lease money provided by white cattlemen who grazed their animals on Indian lands. Finally in 1883 the government was able to establish successfully a concentration camp for children, euphemistically called a boarding school. Parents were prohibited from visiting their children, and the committed child remained in Federal custody for years on end. All of this was in an effort to force the Pawnee to give up their Indian ways.

Long ago before the present races of men occupied the earth, there lived a people who were giants. They were so big and powerful that one was able to run a bison down on foot, kill it, and readily carry the carcass away over his shoulders. Such men did not believe in Tirawa, as the Pawnee do, but felt that all power rested in their own hands. Finally Tirawa was so angry with the giants that he caused the water level to rise. All the land became soft, and the giants sank into the ground and died. Tirawa next created a man and woman in the same proportions as people today. It was from this couple that the Pawnee were derived.

In conceiving the universe, the Skidi branch of the Pawnee, and probably the other Pawnee as well, considered that in the sky there were two great forces, the male to the east and the female to the west, while all of life was derived from the zenith. The supernatural power at the zenith where the male and female forces combined was termed Tirawa and even his name was sacred, to be spoken quietly. Men sought aid from him, but he dealt with them through lesser supernatural beings, who were beneath Tirawa physically as well as in power. The first people came to earth upon the winds from the Morning Star, and from each of the seven winds one expected different qualities. The east wind swept in with the dawn, bringing life into a person's body; the west wind brought life and direction to life; the north wind was associated with the North Star; the wind of the spirits drove ghosts from north to south; another sent game, and yet another drove the animals, while the south wind came from where the star spirits dwelt.

Conflicting reports about the hairdressing style among Pawnee men exist in the literature. George B. Grinnell, who knew the Pawnee well in the 1870's, recorded that a few men still kept a roach, which was a strip of hair down the center of the head allowed to grow about an inch in length. It was made to stand upright with paint and grease. From the back of the roach a scalp lock hung down. John Dunbar considered the word Pawnee derived from the term for horn, which he thought referred to a hairstyle with an erect scalp lock possibly worn by these men formerly. The historian George Hyde doubts these interpretations. The women parted their hair in the middle and made two braids of it, one hanging down on each side of the head behind the ear. Both men and women plucked their pubic and axillary hair, which was considered unclean. Such hair could not be burned but was buried, for to burn something was to offer it to the supernaturals. Likewise, a man plucked the hair from his face. Painting the face and chest was common for a Pawnee man, and the pigments used were red, white, and yellow. These three colors were used because of their attractiveness, whereas black was kept for war.

A man's clothing included a breechclout, which was a piece of dehaired deerskin which passed between the wearer's legs and overlapped a belt in the front and back. Additionally, men wore tight-fitting buckskin leggings with long fringes at the outer edges and sometimes adorned with human hair and bead decorations. A bison-skin or wolf-skin robe was thrown over their shoulders. For adornment a man might wear a necklace of bear claws, beads, or strung sections of bone as well as body paint. The women wore leggings from the knees to the ankles, moccasins, and a wraparound skirt to below the knees. A band of skin was worn about the chest, and it was held in place with shoulder straps; women also wore bison-skin robes. Young boys went without any clothing whatsoever, and small girls wore a loose shirt.

Approaching a Pawnee earth lodge village in the early part of the nineteenth century, a visitor found well-beaten paths converging on the settlement. For miles around there were scattered gardens tended by the women, accompanied by their small children and older daughters. When enemies were about, one or more warriors went with the women as they cultivated the fields in order to prevent their being ambushed by an enemy raiding party. The cultivated spots were those where the sod was thin and could be worked readily with a digging stick or hoe. Grazing horses and mules roamed near the village and were tended by small boys or an occasional man. In a settlement were innumerable dogs and children, and many women were busy processing hides. In the community of the Grand Pawnee and Pitahauerat in 1820 were one hundred eighty earth lodges with a population of nine hundred families, totaling thirty-five hundred individuals. The lodges with their attached entryways were closely grouped with one another in an irregular pattern. These houses ranged between twenty-five and fifty feet across and were circular in form. They were log-framed structures, over which were placed layers of grass and then a covering of packed earth. About five families or twenty persons lived in a typical dwelling. Inside an earth lodge, which had its entrance to the east, along the north and south walls were platform beds. The allotted area for each family was curtained off from the next with mats, and behind the curtains were the family's possessions. The central area was open, and in the floor were caches for dried vegetable foods. There was also a central fireplace and above it a hole for the smoke to escape. The back and center of a lodge was the place of honor where the household head presided, and where there was to be found an altar on which rested a bison skull. Hanging from the west wall of every important man's lodge was a sacred bundle, wrapped in deerskin and blackened with age. The bundles were surrounded with taboos. They were opened only on special occasions and represented an important link with the past and with the supernatural. Near each home was a log corral for the horses and mules belonging to the occupants of the lodge. Before each lodge was the homeowner's tripod, on which hung his painted shield and a rawhide case of war supplies. On top of many lodges were scalps on short poles. While in the village during the summer, families slept out-of-doors under arbors, one being constructed for each family lodge.

For the summer or winter hunts into the bison country the people traveled in family groups, Indian file, with each woman and child leading a horse and the men ranging about the column on horseback or on foot. A typical day's march covered between six and eight miles, with three hours required to break or prepare a camp. It was the women who erected the bison-skin-covered tepees, built around pole frameworks, and up to about eighteen feet across at their base. They left an opening at the top and center of the covering for the smoke to pass out from the central fire pit. Reed mats were spread on the ground, and the evening meal, which was prepared over the open fire, was the only meal of the day.

Knowledge about the variety of material objects manufactured is derived both from early historic archaeological excavations by Waldo R. Wedel and from the observations of nineteenth-century travelers. The flaked chert arrowpoints of small, notched or unnotched, triangular forms, plus a few scrapers chipped from quartzite were virtually the only artifacts made from flinty material. The Pawnee apparently pounded meat and berries on boulder anvils into which cup-shaped depressions were worn from repeated use. Pounding, not grinding, seems to have been the accepted way in which to process food products. For processing hides, sandstone scrapers were ground and pecked into an elliptical shape; pecking stones were used also to shape grooved stone mauls and axes. Rectangular pieces of sandstone with a groove along one side were used to smooth arrow shafts. Tobacco pipes were made most often from catlinite and were of the elbow type with detachable wooden stems.

From bone the people made a variety of awls and needles, and a bison rib with a small symmetrical circle cut into it sometimes served to straighten arrow shafts by gently bending the shaft while it was inserted in the straightener. A most important bone tool was a bison scapula hoe, which had been cut to form a square or rounded blade at the distal end of the bone. The shoulder blade was attached to a wooden stick at right angles to the articulation of the bone. The two were lashed together with sinew; the lashing was then dipped into hot water so that the sinews shrank and made a tight binding.

Metacarpal bones of local ungulates were cut off diagonally above the lower condyle to serve as skin-scraping tools. Sections of antler served as picks, and pieces with a right-angle curve were sharpened to make adz-like skin scrapers. In order to flake flinty material a short section of antler was employed. Spoons were fashioned from bison horn by cutting the horn in two lengthwise. The people also used the lower jaw of a deer, wolf, or some similar species to remove grains of maize from the cob.

From wood the people made dishes and bowls out of which to eat, and wooden mortars were hollowed out with fire. The Pawnee bows were backed with sinew and had a sinew string. The flint-tipped arrows were distinctively Pawnee, and each arrow bore an ownership mark. Fire was made with a fire drill, the shaft of which was rotated in the hand.

Locally made pottery was manufactured into the 1800's, when it was replaced by trade vessels of copper or iron. The aboriginal clay pots were molded from lumps of clay and tempered with a fine, inorganic material such as sand or crushed rock. There apparently were no variations in the pottery among the different bands. The most common vessels in use were quite small, under ten inches in height, and globular, with constricted necks and collared rims. These collars were quite often decorated with incisions or protuberances. The incisions, made in the moist clay around the rim, were parallel lines in simple combinations. The vessels were fired and were then ready for use. The Pawnee were unimaginative potters, and their products in clay very rarely included anything but vessels for cooking.

The dependence of Plains and prairie Indians on the bison, and the diverse uses for the animal and its products are almost legendary. Still it is fitting to repeat the list for the Pawnee. The meat from a freshly killed animal could be and was at times eaten raw, and the meat from a female was in general more palatable than that from a male. Bison meat was cooked when fresh for a number of dishes, and when dried it was a primary staple for consumption during the winter months. The summer skins were scraped on both sides to make covers for tents, ropes, rawhide, and meat containers. The winter skins, with the hair remaining intact, served as blankets and robes. The sinew was used as bowstrings or as thread. The brains were smeared on the skins in order to break down the fiber and to produce a softer skin. A hoof was used as a hammer. The bison bones were made into scrapers and awls; ribs were sometimes fashioned into bows. The bladder was a water container, and dried bison dung was a standard fuel in areas where wood was unavailable. Bison skins were the major product the Plains Indians offered the traders in exchange for diverse imported items, which was still another reason for emphasizing the hunting of these animals.

The Pawnee pattern of seasonal activities in the early nineteenth century meant abandoning the earth-lodge settlements in summer and again in early winter. From their villages the people ranged to the south and west in search of bison herds. In the summer of 1835 the Grand Pawnee and their close neighbors, the Pitahauerat and Kitkehahki, traveled westward in three columns which included four thousand people, thousands of horses and mules, and about seven thousand dogs. While on the move to and from the bison country, the orderliness of the hunters contrasted with the movement of the women and the children with the tents and household equipment. The column traveled at a walking pace, with the chiefs and warriors astride fine horses and the poor men walking. The poor permitted their horses to walk along without packs so they would be fresh in case bison were to be pursued. Docile old horses were employed as pack animals or to draw the travois. A horse was controlled by tying a strip of leather around the lower jaw of the animal; the strip was then held or tied to the saddle. Behind the saddle tent poles were tied on either side; these extended from the horse's head to the ground behind the animal. Across a set of tent poles behind the horse might be tied short poles, and on this bed were laid leather containers of dried meat and bison-skin robes. On a travois or litter might ride an ill or wounded person. Tent skins, robes, and household articles were loaded on the saddle, and on top of a load a woman or two or three children might ride. A woman riding might carry a small child on her back or hang a cradleboard over the end of a tent pole near the saddle. If a child were two or three years old, it might be held by the mother as she rode along. Colts carried light packs, and young horses were ridden by young boys. Horses without loads ran freely about the column.

At this time of year trading or raiding parties traveled south in search of glory, horses, and trade goods, while other groups went to a particular deposit to obtain supplies of rock salt. The salt country was a flat area with red clay cliffs in the northern and central sectors of Oklahoma. It was a place not only to obtain salt but also to perform rituals.

Parties moving into the bison country left their camp for the night about 4 A.M. and covered about twelve miles before eating the first meal of the day. They rested, ate, and then pushed on for another eight miles before camping for the night. Once they had reached the grounds on which they were to camp, they would make camp and sometimes remain in this spot for a few days. The women unloaded the equipment and set up the residence. It was a semicircular dome, with a flat side where the entrance was located. The pole frame was covered with dressed bison skins, and inside were stored the household goods. At the back and center was reserved an area for the household head, and a bison-skin robe was spread out for him. Here the man slept, lounged, and ate, while hanging from a pole above him were his weapons and riding equipment. In front of the skin lodge of every important man was a tripod of poles, on which hung his shield; on the shield were painted figures representing the man's sib affinities.

In order to pursue and kill bison efficiently, a well-organized force of warriors guided the hunt. These were men upon whom the chiefs could rely to maintain order and plan the hunt. A column moving toward a herd of bison, after the animals had been located by roving scouts, was led by chiefs and shamans. Each man had a particular position in the riding order, and each attempted to have a special horse used only for hunting bison. When the herd was sighted, a crier relayed the decision of how the hunters were to be deployed; once they were in place, at a given signal, all the men descended on the bison together. Preferably they converged on the herd from different directions. The favorite hunting weapon was not the gun, but the bow and arrow, and each hunter rode naked, carrying only his weapons, just as he did when prepared for battle (see Note 2). After as many animals as possible had been killed, they were butchered and brought back to camp, where the women cut the meat into thin slabs and dried it on pole frames over a fire in the skin tent. They then pounded it and packed the jerked meat into rawhide satchels.

At the end of the summer bison-hunting season the people returned to their villages, where they had planted crops in the spring. This was the most pleasurable season of the year, for food was abundant, with a good harvest of corn, beans, and squash. This was the time for social as well as for religious activities.

In the fall and early winter hunting parties returned again to the bison country and made a special effort to obtain bison skins which were now prime. Some skins were exchanged with traders for imported goods, and others were scraped free of the hair, to be used as lodge coverings or folded into rawhide containers. Again in February or March they returned to their villages with the meat and skins. Although in a typical year they might be away from their villages for about eight months, nevertheless, the villages represented home for the wanderers.

Spring was the lean period when the Pawnee had to rely on dried meat, cached maize, beans, and squash. At this time the small garden plots were prepared for cultivation by the women. The most important plant was maize; it was significant both in the rituals and the mythology and was a staple food for the people. The plots were seldom larger than an acre in extent and were located at the mouths of ravines where the soil was fertile and the sod cover not extremely thick. All the cultivation was by women, who prepared the ground with hoes and planted the grains of maize in hills. Sometimes a brush fence was built around a garden patch, but more often it grew in the open, with the women protecting their plots from wandering horses during the day. After the maize was harvested, it was boiled or roasted, then cut from the cob and dried, or stored on the cob in caches. The women likewise cultivated beans and squash, and the latter were sun-dried in strips which were later woven together for convenient storage and transporting.

The most important uncultivated vegetable food was the wild potato, which was a very important item in times of food scarcity. Berries, wild plums, cherries, and mushrooms were among the more important plants collected. In general, all of these plants were supplements to maize and bison meat. According to one description, an evening meal during a bison hunt consisted of dried bison meat, followed by a combination of maize and beans, then ground parched maize, and next corn mush, and the meal was ended with an ear of roasted corn. Also hunted and eaten were elk, deer, bear, otter, and raccoon, and the domestic dog was eaten on occasion.

The only aboriginally domesticated animal of the Pawnee was the dog, and they kept huge numbers of these animals, judging from Murray's account in the 1830's. The dogs were used as pack animals as well as to drag loaded travois. The first horses possibly were introduced about 1700 or somewhat earlier, judging from the rate of spread of domestic horses out of New Mexico in the late 1600's and historical records.

It is the Skidi branch of the Pawnee that are best reported in the ethnographic literature. The Skidi, however, were culturally and socially more conservative than the other three groups, and they possessed at least some ceremonies unknown to the others. All of the Pawnee bands were divided into village units which were politically and socially distinct. Although the Pawnee were a tribe, only rarely did they act or react as a tribal unit. Each of the four bands was independent, and within each band were village aggregates. The Skidi regarded themselves as closer to the Arikara than to the other Pawnee bands. The members of any village reckoned their descent from an assumed common ancestor, and they married within the community. Descent was traced through a line of females; thus the people possessed matrisibs, practiced community endogamy, and had matrilocal residence. At the same time the Pawnee were not completely matrilineal, since the chieftaincy and priestly duties could and did pass down a line of males. Each settlement possessed a sacred bundle, which contained objects of immense religious significance for the villagers and was assumed to have been passed down a direct line from the original owner.

The village sacred bundle was a supernatural focus leading to a rationale for this social grouping, and village endogamy may have been practiced in order to keep the sacred bundle as a distinct village trust. Village political life was under the direction of a hereditary chief, his subordinates and a council. The villagers of one band were bound together through participation in joint religious ceremonies and in a joint council, where participation was rigidly controlled by tradition.

The activities of each of the thirteen known Skidi villages were supervised by a chief, who among other responsibilities allotted lands to individual users. Most important in terms of village cohesion was the fact that a village chief was the possessor of a sacred bundle which was usually passed down a male line. These bundles were either direct gifts from particular stars, or made by a distant ancestor of a chief under the supervision of a star. The chief owned the bundle; his wife was its keeper, and the associated rituals were conducted by a priest. The earth lodges of a village were either large or small, depending upon the number of occupying families. A small lodge included only a nuclear family, but larger ones accommodated two or many families. The largest lodges were the residences of the chiefs, where space was required for performing certain ceremonies.

According to the Presbyterian missionary John Dunbar, the labors of a woman were arduous, and her tasks never seemed to be completed. Besides the processing of skins, cooking and gardening, which might be expected, she was also obliged to saddle and unsaddle her husband's horse, and in the tent she occupied the coldest fringe (see Note 3). As though to compensate for their position, women talked steadily by habit and were very sharp-tongued. By contrast the men seemed devoted to warfare and hunting, with a great deal of leisure time during which they slept, lounged, talked, sang, feasted, and smoked. The duties of each sex were defined with precision, and there was little opportunity for a woman to modify her ascribed role.

A male's social position was based largely on the achievements of his immediate male ancestors; thus there was some rigidity in the social structure. At the same time, however, there existed the ideal of a poor but ambitious and honorable young man achieving great success in life. The class system which molded the lives of most persons found its sanction in supernatural origins, and the prerogatives and duties of the leaders were similarly derived. One set of divinely instituted obligations directed that a segment of the population must protect the settlement from human enemies; these were the leaders and participants in war. A second group, the priests, took charge of religious obligations, and a third, the shamans, protected the village from disease and famine. These responsibilities were those of the upper class; a lower class consisted of poor people, with little or no influence and authority.

Each Skidi village, of which there were thirteen in late historic times, contained a hereditary chief and a particular sacred bundle representing his authority, which was passed on to his eldest son if this individual were capable. The decision concerning the next chief was made by the chiefs' council, who accepted or rejected the successor. If the eldest son was not capable, a younger son or another close male relative of the chief's was chosen. From each settlement the hereditary chiefs selected warriors of highest rank to become nonhereditary chiefs, so that the number totaled thirty-one in the chiefs' council for all of the Skidi. An extremely able warrior was made a chief by being invited to join the hereditary chiefs in their lodge on four occasions. The first three invitations were refused, but the fourth accepted and gifts presented to the chiefs. The man then became a chief, but he did not pass the title on to his son.

The appearance of chiefs during their council differed from that of ordinary men. A chief wore an eagle feather in his hair, and on his bison robe were representations of stars, the sun, or battle scenes. His leggings were fringed with hair from human scalps and with eagle feathers. His face was painted red; from ear to ear across the forehead was a blue line, along with a forehead design symbolic of the Turkey's Foot constellation.

The most important duties of a hereditary chief were to promote community welfare and be the guardian of the people. The hereditary chief appears also to have been responsible for the allotment and reallotment of farmlands to persons of the village for which he was responsible. A chief was not expected to be an aggressive and constant fighter but was to provide for the general welfare of the community. A chief provided for his family's needs, although he had two retainers to perform more menial tasks. Other men, usually four in number, who were braves, served the hereditary chief. They aided the chief by helping him preserve civil order and prepare for religious ceremonies. These braves carried war clubs or tomahawks as symbols of their offices which they held for life and had acquired through an affinity with the Morning Star.

Warriors were men who through their own efforts had risen to positions of authority. Again supernatural sanctions gave rise to this class of individuals. From their group chiefs were chosen, since warriors had by their sacrifices obtained supernatural favor. They were privileged to wear into battle the sacred warrior's costume and to paint three dots on their foreheads, symbolic of an eagle's claw marks.

The decisions of a political nature were made by the hereditary chiefs and the nonhereditary chiefs, but they could be overruled seemingly by the priests. The deliberations of the chiefs in council probably centered most frequently about where and when to hunt or raid, and over issues concerning relations with other Pawnee groups, enemy tribes, and friendly tribes. In early historic times the principal chief, who apparently took precedence over all others, was from the Chaui subtribe. When the chiefs of a village met in council, they decided issues by a consensus of the group feeling even if the feeling ran against the will of the leading chief. When the chiefs met in council, they seated themselves in an arrangement followed in the Four Pole Ceremony, to be discussed later.

Half or less of the Skidi males were not hereditary chiefs, braves, or warriors, nor were they shamans or priests. Instead they were commoners without authority within the subtribe to which they belonged. These men owned few or perhaps no horses, their lodges were small, and often they received necessities from persons of wealth. It would appear, too, that some young men, and occasionally older men, attached themselves to the households of important men and performed menial tasks for these individuals in return for their support. Then, at the fringes of a settlement were the outcasts of one type or another, persons who had disregarded tribal customs.

In the kinship terminology of the Skidi Pawnee a male termed his father and his father's brothers alike, whereas his mother's brother was called by a different word. The word for mother was extended to mother's sister and father's sister. The resulting classification on the first descending generation is bifurcate merging for paternal relatives and generational for maternal relatives. In addition, the mother, mother's sister, and father's sister term was extended to include father's sister's daughter. The father and father's brother term was applied to a father's sister's son. The patrilineal cross-cousin terms were different from the matrilineal cross-cousin terms; the latter were not distinguished by sex and were the same as for Ego's son and daughter. Parallel cousins on both sides of the family were termed alike but with male-female distinctions. Furthermore, the words for brothers and sisters were extended to parallel cousins, and the latter were Ego's classificatory siblings. Ego's children, his brother's children, and his mother's brothers' children were from his mother's lineage, and Ego's paternal cross-cousins were from his father's lineage. Thus, the cousin terminology was Crow.

In behavior the closest lifelong ties were between siblings, especially brothers, and, by contrast, deep emotional ties did not exist between a husband and wife. A warm relationship probably existed between a man and his mother's brother's wife, since this woman, or these women as the case may have been, were sexual partners for the young man from the time he reached puberty until he married. The mother's brother was responsible for the marriage arrangements of both the sons and the daughters of his sister.

Routine differences which arose within a village seem to have been settled by the individuals or families along traditionally directed lines without outside interference. The most common form of dispute seems to have been between men while gambling. Contestants appear to have fought with each other but to have stopped when blood was drawn. The thefts which occurred seem most often to have been by poor people, and if they were found out, the person from whom they stole punished the offender physically by whipping or beating. In instances of adultery by a woman the offended husband was irate because he considered that what was his property had been taken away from him. The adulterous man was punished by the husband, probably beaten or whipped. Adultery apparently was not uncommon nor particularly serious, but this was not true of rape. Consent or lack of consent by the girl was not the important criterion of rape; her age was the crucial factor. To fornicate with a young girl led to a man's being beaten badly and then made an outcast. A person's unprovoked murder led his relatives to seek revenge by killing the murderer, who was not defended by his relatives if they considered him to be in the wrong. If each group of contesting relatives considered their position legitimate, a feud would erupt between them.

George B. Grinnell (1961, 303) wrote, "The Pawnees were a race of warriors. War was their pleasure and their business. By war they gained credit, respect, fame. By war they acquired wealth." The emphasis on warfare among Indians in mid-America is legendary, and the Pawnee are justly remembered as being among the best warriors. To the Indians living south of the Pawnee they were known as Wolves, possibly a derogatory designation but more likely based on their skill as scouts and horse stealers. When a group of Pawnee warriors and braves went off to raid, they actually organized a temporary voluntary association, or Wolf Society, with origins in mythological times. The supernatural patron of warfare was the wolf, and thus they patterned themselves after wolves. Items from the sacred bundle of war regalia covered with a wolf's skin were taken to provide power on a raid. A raiding party attempted to move about the landscape after the manner of wolves. One reason for assuming this guise was that because prairie wolves were common, often entering Indian camps at night, they attracted no attention. A Pawnee on a raid carried with him a wolfskin robe, and by wearing it as well as imitating the movements of a wolf he was ignored as he entered an enemy camp. To imitate a white wolf the raiders painted themselves with white clay, symbolic of the wolf. The same disguise was employed by a raiding party on the move during the day. All the raiders but one kept to a ravine or river bottom, while one man disguised as a wolf scouted along the hills where he could see great distances. Such a scout was not suspected by the enemy observer as being human.

From most accounts there is no reason to question the fighting abilities of the Pawnee, but they failed to make effective alliances with other tribes. This failure led to their ultimate defeat. The Pawnee defeated and partially absorbed the Ponca, Omaha and Oto, but these were not all-powerful peoples. They usually fought with all the adjacent Indian tribes, both those indigenous to the area and the late arrivals from the eastern United States. A partial exception might have been their relations with the Potawatomi. The established tribes who raided the Pawnee and were in turn raided included the Cheyenne, Kiowa, Kansa, Osage, Comanche, Arapaho, Ute, and Crow. They likewise warred with the Chickasaw, Choctaw, and Cherokee who were displaced from the East. The Pawnee could not even remain peaceful with the Wichita, who were their distant relatives, nor were the four Pawnee bands always friendly with each other.

The Pawnee fought under two different general sets of circumstances for two different purposes. When they left their settlements seeking an enemy, they were searching for glory, manifest in scalps and horses. The Pawnee fought defensively against enemies who came to their settlements by night to steal horses and to take scalps, or when a large enemy party came by day and by the hundreds to scalp, to kill, and to loot. Either on offensive raids or in defensive stands the Pawnee warrior was a very brave man. Still the standards of behavior in warfare differed greatly from the norms in Anglo-American society. On a raid the ideal was to slip into an unsuspecting enemy camp, kill as many persons as possible before arousing the populace, and then escape with the best horses. A raid most often was organized to steal horses, and if the opportunity presented itself an enemy was slain and scalped as well. Such raids were most like guerrilla warfare in Western society. The question of a fair fight was not considered, since the primary aim of a raid was to catch the enemy unprepared and take full advantage of his condition. There was no disgrace in not attacking a well-armed or an alert camp, nor did a man lose standing by running away if he was outnumbered.

A raiding party was organized by any man who could attract a following. He was mostly likely to be an already successful warrior, but an aspiring youth sometimes could convince others of his abilities as a leader. The leader sought supernatural help through prayers to Tirawa, offered while meditating, smoking, or eating. The men selected by a leader to take part in his raid were called together, and the plan was announced. If they wished to accompany the group, they smoked a sacred pipe. If they declined to participate in the raid, they passed the pipe on to the next man without smoking. Likewise the leader secured the aid of a priest, and certain ceremonies were performed. The priest presented the group with a sacred bundle to take with them. Every man on a raiding party provided himself with extra pairs of moccasins, since they nearly always set off on foot. Each of as many as twenty moccasins was stuffed with food for the trip. The food consisted of pounded, cooked corn and pemmican. A warrior also carried sewing awls and sinew to repair his footwear, a bow and arrows, and a robe. The leader carried the sacred pipe and tobacco. As mentioned earlier, a raiding party sent a scout ahead to watch for enemies. As they traveled into country occupied by hostile Indians, they became more cautious, and if any sign along the way was interpreted as an ill omen, they might turn back. The activities of such a party were under the direction of its organizer, who commanded the warriors. The aspiring warriors who joined the party were assigned menial tasks around the camp, and they studied the tactics of the warriors.

The primary purpose of a raid was to steal horses, but since an enemy kept his best horses near his tepee, often tied just outside the entrance, it required great daring to cut a number of horses loose and to negotiate a successful escape. The most likely time for the theft to succeed was late at night when one or more men could slip into a camp unnoticed. It was expected that the leader of a raid would be the most daring, and if he alone obtained horses, he shared them with other members of the party. He might also give a horse to the priest who had aided their success by his prayers. One privilege of a successful war party was for its members to change their names, assuming new names which reflected some great deeds.

Success in horse raids was a rapid road to prestige and riches, to which any daring man could aspire and often succeed. Great bravery was required to steal enemy horses, but it required even greater daring to attempt to make peace with an enemy tribe. To do so it was necessary to expose oneself to great danger by openly entering an enemy camp. Among the greatest chiefs were those who were chiefs of peace.

The battles in defense of a community were organized in a different way. An attacking party would number hundreds of warriors who suddenly would appear one morning on the hills about a village. Each man in the opposing force was mounted on his best horse and wore his most majestic garments, set off with an elaborate feather headdress. They did not ride pell-mell into the settlement, but waited. As soon as the party was sighted, the village men seized their weapons, their best horses, and rode out naked to meet the enemy. The women corralled the remaining horses and climbed on top of the earth lodges to watch the battle. The two long lines of opposing warriors rode slowly toward each other and stopped when about six hundred yards separated them. The men on each side chanted war songs and shouted insults to one another. A warrior from the Pawnee or enemy line would then advance before his comrades to make a speech disparaging the enemy, praising his fellows in arms, and boasting of his own achievements. When his oration was completed, he galloped toward one of the enemy's flanks, and when within bowshot he rode furiously before the mounted column but in such a manner that little of his body was exposed to the fire of the enemies. He shot arrow after arrow into the line of men. Those that he passed pursued him, and if he or his horse were not struck with arrows, he rode back to his own line and his pursuers returned to their original positions. If, however, he were disabled in any way, so that it appeared he would be overtaken, his comrades rushed to save him from the enemy. The horsemen were soon at close quarters, fighting with war clubs or anything else at hand. In this close conflict men were injured but not usually killed. If the person who made the speech were killed and scalped, his friends withdrew without attempting to recover his body. If he were not scalped, the opponents returned to their original lines and repeated the battle plan again and again until one side withdrew. The Pawnee rarely if ever were routed when taking a stand at home, for if they were, their families and the settlement would be destroyed.

If, during battle or in a raid, a captive was taken, it was decided in council what to do with him. He was most likely turned over to a woman's society which was amorphous in its organization and functioned only under this particular set of conditions. The women were young, single girls, old maids, or widows, who performed with warbonnets of corn husks, bows made from sticks, and lances of reed stalks. A captive was turned over to them to be tied and tortured for four days, during which time every indignity conceivable was heaped upon the victim before he finally was killed.

It has been the custom for anthropologists to regard Plains Indian warfare as an all-consuming game about which tribes were organized. Clearly an important value was placed on warfare, but it was more than a game, with lives, loot, and prestige at stake. According to the thoughtful analysis of William W. Newcomb, the conflicts were restricted to small numbers of participants at any one time, with results which were usually indecisive. Newcomb stresses the importance of the horse as a means of developing the specialized bison hunting subsistence pattern, and with the emergence of this pattern competition over hunting territories led to armed conflicts. There was also the displacement of eastern tribes to the West, and Anglo-American expansion brought yet another form of competition for land. The eastern tribes, furthermore, possessed guns which aided them significantly in their encroachments. The competition was particularly fierce on the edges of the Plains, where bison were not so abundant as in the heartland. The erratic seasonal movements of the bison were difficult to follow even when they were numerous. As the herds decreased and increased competition developed for the remaining animals, there was bound to be conflict over hunting territories. Additionally, there was the policy of the French, Spanish, British, and Americans of pitting one tribe against another. Thus, it would appear that the fundamental causes of Plains Indian warfare were economic in their nature, which is a more reasonable hypothesis than to accept the supposition that these Indians fought for the sake of fighting.

Pawnee religion was an integrated system, over which the supreme deity Tirawa presided. His earthly agents were priests, who supervised a yearly round of ceremonies and retained sacred bundles of supernatural origin. The religious system embraced all things in the universe in a manner which was functionally linked. To understand the system it is first necessary to explain the sacred bundles which were the concrete ties between men and the gods. For the Skidi branch the word for a sacred bundle translates "wrapped up rainstorm," a name symbolic of the origins of the supernaturals to the west, whence the bundle's powers came. Such a bundle might also be called "mother," which was a reference to the two ears of maize found in each bundle. These ears of corn were the symbolic mother of the people. In each of the thirteen Skidi villages there was one bundle. One settlement, Center Village, had associations with the Evening Star bundle, which was the greatest of the western powers, the supreme and original authority. Kept in Old Village but belonging to the Skidi in general were four outstanding sacred bundles, the Yellow Star, White Star, Red Star, and Big Black Meteoric Star bundles. It was the power of these bundles, plus that of the Human Skull and North Star bundles, that bound the Skidi together in their dealings with the gods.

Together, the thirteen organized Skidi communities (but not two others which refused the confederation) held what was called the Four Pole Ceremony. This ceremony was held outdoors in a particular enclosure made for the event. At the center of the enclosure was a fire pit, with the soil from the pit deposited in a pile on the ground beyond the enclosure entrance, which was always to the east. Around the fire pit were four equidistant poles in a square, with a cottonwood pole representing white, willow colored yellow, box elder colored red, and elm painted black. Inside the enclosure at the center of the west side a raised altar for a bison skull was erected. Circling the items mentioned above was a screen of fresh tree branches which had been placed just inside the raised earth embankment. Within the enclosure the priests and the bundles they possessed were arranged along the north or south sides, depending on whether their community was north or south of the Loup River. If we consider the center of the fire pit as representing the center of a clock, Evening Star (Venus) was located near one o'clock. According to the mythology, she was a powerful and beautiful female deity sought in marriage by all the stars. She married Morning Star (Mars) who was near three o'clock and had to overcome four powerful stars in obtaining his bride. A daughter was born to the couple and the earth created as its home. A boy placed on earth was the offspring of Sun and Moon. Then Morning Star required a sacrifice for his efforts, and Evening Star instructed a man and woman in making an Evening Star bundle, often called the Red Calf bundle. Next a man was sent out to tell the people how to perform the Four Pole Ceremony. Two villages, however, having just performed sacred bundle ceremonies, refused to participate. The details of the Four Pole Ceremony are not recorded, but it obviously was a series of rituals designed to reinforce the unity of the Skidi Pawnee with the supernaturals.

The sacred bundles were gifts from particular stars or else were made under the supervision of a star. They were symbolic of a village and united its ceremonies. The four special bundles were used in ceremonies involving the entire federation. The village bundle ceremonies led by the priest seem to have been for subtribal welfare and the general ones for the success of the entire band. The sacred bundle rituals passed from a priest to his successor, usually a relative, and had nothing to do with the hereditary chiefs. These chiefs, however, were responsible for the physical bundles, and in turn the chiefs obtained their position by virtue of this association. Another feature was that a sacred bundle was not under the care of a priest but was physically kept by a woman, who knew certain facets of the bundle's rituals but could not take part in the ceremonies.

It would appear that the four leaders of each bundle society were hereditary, and the membership was open to relatives of deceased members or other outstanding men who were invited to join. This generalization applies specifically to the lesser bundles associated with the five leading bundles. The well-established leading bundles associated with the Skidi were the Horse, Brave Raven Lance, Reds, Thunderbird, and Those Coming Behind bundle societies. Each member was initiated and underwent tests. Failure in the tests barred one from membership for life, but success led to lifelong association with a particular bundle; one man could be a member of all these societies. Among the Pawnee as a whole the bundle societies were organized for warfare, for hunting, or for both these functions. In times of crisis a war society might be selected by the chief to aid in a battle, while a priest would decide which hunting society was to take charge of a bison hunt. These societies served as sodalities or voluntary associations, in which the members found pleasure in each other's company and other rewards from the social contacts. Each society was divided into two segments, according to their seating in the lodge. Each side, the north leading the winter ceremonies and the south leading in the summer, had its own director, two drummers, singers, a lance-bearer, a messenger, and a doorkeeper.

Each society possessed specific rituals to renew the members' lances. The old lances were set aside for the graves of great warriors, and new ones were made each year. The new lances were sanctified with smoke, and a feast followed the ceremonies. The new lances were exhibited by their bearers during a dance for the members. In battle the lance-bearers planted their standards before the enemy and were the last to retreat. If it appeared that the lance would be taken by the enemy, another member of the party could carry it off, and the bearer could then withdraw. The villagers were told that the lances were made for the good of everyone and therefore must be protected. In battle the lances were stuck into the ground by their bearers and were an advance rallying point for the fighters; the lances were not taken on privately organized raids but were used only in general attacks.

The Red Society, or Red Lance Society, among the Skidi, had two lances, one associated with the South and one with the North. A pipe was kept by the head of the society, and used in the ceremonies were four rattles and four hand drums. The Red Lance Society had no duties during the bison hunt; it was a war society that existed only in one settlement. Its primary function was to act as police on formal raids or to repel attacks on hunters. The lances gave protection to the members while fighting, and they were carried in celebrating dances of victory. Each year the two lances were disassembled in the fall to be renewed the next spring.

The societies discussed above were considered permanent and official, but there was another group of societies which appear to have been most often transient in their nature. Such sodalities were organized by men who could not qualify for membership in an established society and were ambitious enough to form their own organization. After having a dream or vision to sanction the organization, the leader sought a membership and had no difficulty in finding recruits. When they helped out in a crisis, they acquired prestige, but if they failed in battle or during a hunt, or if their leader's persuasive powers failed, they were likely to disband. Among the Skidi we find six such organizations, of which the Crazy Dog Society was one. Like the other transient sodalities it had a ceremonial complex, including equipment like the established sodalities. A distinctive feature of the Crazy Dogs was that each member carried a ring-shaped rattle. When they danced, it was in the nude with a cord tied around the penis foreskin and feathers at the end of the cord. Reportedly they had a "no flight" obligation in battle, for the foreskin was tied to a cord attached to a stake in the ground; from this they could not release themselves. The Children of the Iruska was a "contrary" society. The members reversed normal expectations in their behavior. If the camp were attacked, they continued whatever they were doing before the alarm; if someone told them not to go on a raid, they went; and if a mysterious animal were near camp, which normal persons feared, they would hunt the animal. The number of contraries was small, six or seven in number. They never married and were always painted black, to be ready to fight. The members were selected by the leader because they were strange. The society apparently came to an abrupt end when most of its members were killed in a battle.

The priests derived their positions of authority from a star or a planet and were a hereditary group of wise men. The prime prerequisite for becoming a priest was to have an excellent memory, and the second was to be related to someone who was a priest. It was a priest who recited rituals associated with major religious ceremonies to ensure community success in farming, the hunt, and in warfare. A priest performed as a mediator between men and Tirawa. He was effective where an ordinary man was less so, because he knew more and was more expressive. The sacred bundles were in his charge, and he possessed the necessary esoteric knowledge for handling them. His training was that of a ritual specialist. There were four leading Skidi priests, one each for the Yellow, White, Red, and Big Black Meteoric Star bundles. Each year a different one of the four led the ceremonies and was responsible for the welfare of the subtribe from the first thunder in the spring until after the fall bison hunt. The Red Calf bundle priest was more powerful than all the others, but he was called on to perform ceremonies of his own only when the ceremonies of the other four bundles had failed. It was the priests of the five sacred bundles mentioned above who were most important; normally all were present at any particular ritual involving one of their number. The ceremonies of all the bundle groups differed in details, but they shared the characteristic that at the first thunder of each spring each bundle was opened by the priest in charge and dried bison meat was burned as an offering to the supernaturals of the west.

A priest presided over the name-changing ceremonies for individuals and was the intermediary in marital arrangements. The life of the priest was considered to be lengthened if he was most sincere in performing his duties, but his life was shortened if he took his responsibilities casually. The two retainers in each priest's lodge aided in ceremonial activities, and his criers were old and honored men who announced when ceremonies were to be held and recited certain parts of the ritual instructions.

A second major category of supernatural specialists was that of the shamans, who ultimately derived their powers from a time when the deity Tirawa created certain specific human roles. The shamans controlled the spirits of the earth to cure people but did not command as was customary of a chief. It was from Tirawa that the original shaman received a blue body paint to wear during ceremonies. He received also the wing of a black eagle and a gourd rattle. The specific powers of any particular shaman were derived from an animal, which in turn had acquired power from a particular star. An ill person could be cured only by a shaman whose animal guardian was the same as his own. An emerging shaman might receive power directly from his animal guardian, but more often he became an apprentice to an established practitioner with the same guardian.

The shamans were organized into societies of their own in which they performed specific rituals, usually twice each year, at the time of the first thunder in the spring and again in the fall, for purification as well as a renewal of power associated with their sacred objects. The rituals included the use of sacred altars, a division of the society's members into two sides, body paints, rattles and drums, and smoked tobacco as an offering.

Each of the major subgroups of the Pawnee held a Twenty Day Ceremony, or, as it was also termed, a Big Sleight of Hand Ceremony, late in the summer after the harvest and the bundle ceremonies were completed. At this time the shamans held forth for twenty to thirty days; some were aided by one or more assistants and built willow booths in one of the large and important lodges. Among the Skidi a mythological water monster was honored during this celebration by the construction of the creature's image. All shaman societies aided in its construction. The head, at the south side of the lodge entrance, was covered with a bison skin, and its teeth, made from willows, showed in the open mouth. Two long "feelers" were decorated with bright colors, and on top of the head was a plume of down. The body was constructed of willows bent into a half circle and covered with mud; the tail was forked like that of a fish and was on the north side of the entrance. The image of a turtle was made in the fire pit, and its head faced the altar to the west. A new fire pit was built on the back of the turtle and represented the sun. Small human figures cut from rawhide were symbolic of stars and hung from the ceiling. A large figure of a man, made of rawhide, was placed on a pole above the lodge; this figure represented the Morning Star. On the floor to the south side there was one additional figure, a life-sized woman, made of clay and clothed, and symbolic of the Moon. After the completion of these objects, the participants paraded around the settlement carrying the sacred animals of the shamans, which were two loons among the Skidi. Specific shamans were adorned with the representative species from which they derived their power. A secret ritual was then held in the ceremonial lodge, and afterwards the shamans gave a public display of their powers. Examples included having maize mature before the audience or a tree bear fruit miraculously. Likewise, a bear shaman took the liver from a living man, ate it, and then the man walked away unharmed. A trick performed unsuccessfully meant expulsion; its success brought permanent membership in the group. During the final days of the celebrations, the sacred bundles were visited and rituals performed in association with them. Finally, the items constructed in the lodge for this event were taken to a body of water and placed in a pile, with the mud woman on top.

The sodalities of shamans included the Bear, Bison Doctors, Deer, Blood Doctors, Iruska, and One Horn Dance. The highest ranking shamanistic society was the Bear, and in it, as in the others, the members possessed distinctive rituals, dances, equipment, and taboos. Deer Society members imitated various animals, not only the deer, and received a potion made from mescal beans upon initiation. After the initiate passed into unconsciousness from the bean's effects, the leader of the ritual ran the toothed jaw of a garfish down his spine; if the initiate moved he was refused membership. The Deer Society members had particular control of snakes and were said to be unharmed by snake bites. A unique feature of the Blood Doctors ceremony was for the members to spit up a red substance during their performance and to paint the bodies of those present with the liquid. They likewise painted their otterskins, the otter being their guardian, with the red substance. Men of the Iruska, "The Fire in Me" Society, could tolerate great heat, handle hot coals from a fire, and stand barefooted on hot stones during their performances. The member shamans treated the burns of others. The One Horn Dance Society members wore one bison horn as a part of their costume during performances. The membership was drawn from fighting men, and they performed only before an enemy attack. Magical flashes of light indicated an enemy was approaching, and then tobacco from the sacred bundles of the settlement was brought together and sacrificed to the supernaturals. The One Horn Dance Society functioned under the auspices of a deceased warrior who returned at the time of a pending attack. The details listed above occurred only once, but the society was revived when flashes of light reportedly were seen by a woman.

One of the important ceremonial events in the religious calendar centered about preparations for the summer or early fall bison hunt on the Plains. The public rituals were preceded by fasting, prayers, and sacrifices by the priests. The ceremony was under the supervision of whichever of the four sacred bundle priests was presiding for that year. He also chose the members of one of the sodalities to police the hunt. These police were different from those who supervised the villages and were appointed for the duration of the hunt only. The leader of the camp police was appointed by the chief from the honored old warriors, and he in turn selected three assistants. In a lodge at a village-wide gathering, twelve bison skulls were arranged in a semicircle at the back of the structure. Nearby stood the chiefs and shamans with bison staves, sacred bows and arrows, and other hunting equipment. Invocations were made to Tirawa for success in the hunt. Next the implements were placed on the ground within the line of skulls, and prayers continued. When the appeals to the all-powerful supernatural were over, a drum was beaten, and a dozen or more warriors formed a circle to perform the bison dance, which continued uninterrupted for three days, after which the villagers left on the hunt. During the hunt eight carefully selected men carried the bison staves at the head of the moving column. In the 1870's the staffs were spruce poles wrapped with beaded red and blue cloths to which were attached hawk and eagle feathers.

The Pawnee looked to the heavens as the source of life and as the dwelling place of the gods. As previously has been mentioned, the sky with its heavenly bodies reflected the basis of the supernatural system. It is thus to be expected that the Pawnee priests studied the stars and planets. According to Skidi lore there were two great forces in the sky, the male to the east and female to the west. At the zenith where there was "the silence of the blue sky, above and beyond all clouds" the supreme supernatural force Tirawa was present. Particular stars or planets were associated with specific events in Pawnee mythology, and an individual acquired supernatural power from a star. A Pawnee star map which was included in a sacred bundle and judged to date from precontact times includes stars of five different sizes, each drawn as a four-pointed figure. The largest three sizes were most important, and the others represented the Milky Way or served as fillers. The Milky Way was at the center of the star map, and the stars to one side represented the summer skies while those opposite reflected a view of the winter sky. The constellations recognized are those known to us; the seasonal changes were recorded as well as the presence of double stars. This map demonstrates clearly that the Pawnee had acquired a rather sophisticated knowledge of astronomy.

The Skidi Pawnee sacrifice to the Morning Star is one of the most widely known of American Indian ceremonials. In spite of its bizarre savagery there was beauty in the accompanying symbolism. The sacrifice was possible only when Mars was the Morning Star and when a man dreamed that the offering should be made. This person obtained from the keeper of the Morning Star bundle the warrior's garb which was part of the bundle. He set out with other men to find a victim from an enemy tribe. The captive, usually a young girl, became dedicated to the Morning Star as soon as the captor seized her. She was returned to the Skidi chief of the Morning Star village, and for four days rituals were performed which centered about her. The ceremonies began to climax toward the end of the fourth day when songs were sung of the quest of the Morning Star for the Evening Star, and as each song was completed, a tally stick from the sacred bundle was set aside. Evidently the captor represented the Evening

Star, and the sticks symbolized the removal of the victim from this world into the sphere of the supernatural. On the afternoon of the fourth day a rectangular scaffold was erected. The two upright poles of the scaffold represented the day and the night; the four cross-poles forming the bottom of the frame represented the four directions, and an upper cross-pole represented the sky. The girl, who, it is hoped, was unaware of her fate, was taken to the scaffold the next morning. She was stripped of her clothing, and if she climbed to the upper of the four cross-poles willingly it was regarded as a good omen. Her hands were tied to the upper bar and her feet to the uppermost of the four lower bars. As soon as the Morning Star rose, two men came from the east carrying flaming torches and touched her armpits and groin. Four other men touched her with war clubs. Her captor then shot a sacred arrow through the girl's heart, while another man hit her on the head with the war club from the Morning Star bundle. The priest for the Morning Star bundle cut open her breast with a flint knife and covered his face with the blood. The observers, men, women, and children, shot arrows into the body and then left the scene. The captor of the girl held meat beneath her body so that her blood dripped down to cover the meat. The blood-covered meat was burned as an offering to the deities. Finally the girl's body was cut down, and the arrows were removed by the priest. The corpse was left to be eaten by animals (see Note 4).

The last sacrifice by the Skidi probably took place in 1838, but the most dramatic moment known to have occurred during the ceremony was in 1817 when the son of a Pawnee chief interrupted the sacrifice. This young man, named Petalesharo, was present when a Comanche woman was to be sacrificed. He cut her free from the scaffold, rode away with her on a horse, and then gave her a horse so that she could return to her own people. Petalesharo performed his feat because his father opposed these sacrifices, and he succeeded because of his daring and high standing among the Pawnee. When in 1822 Petalesharo visited Washington, D. C., with a party of Pawnee and the chiefs of other tribes, he was presented with an engraved silver medal by the girls of Miss White's Seminary to commemorate his rescue of the Comanche girl. On one side of the medal is depicted the sacrificial scaffold and the surprised leaders of the ritual, and on the opposite side Petalesharo is shown leading the girl away. When Petalesharo died in 1841, the medal was buried with him. In 1884 the medal was taken from his grave, and eventually it was presented to the American Numismatic Society of New York City.

The Pawnee possessed an extremely rich and varied body of folk-lore and ritual texts. It is not the purpose of this study to analyze this form of ethnographic information, but one example taken from the Skidi may convey something of the richness of Pawnee oral traditions. It was recited often during the winter by the adults to the children, who were expected to memorize the text and to regard it as having been related by the Evening Star, the first mother. Like the texts of many peoples, this one is filled with symbolism meaningful only to the Pawnee, and therefore interpretive comments are offered. The text was translated by James R. Murie, a Pawnee who collected a great deal of ethnographic information about his people, and it was published by the Pawnee authority George A. Dorsey (1906, 350).

> Listen, the girl (1) in distress walks to and fro on top of the mountains.
> Listen, the girl's ears tremble, as she runs to and fro, listening.
> From the girl is truly descended a fine tribe of people.
> There are left behind grass lodges (2).
> They rub their backs upon the poles of the lodges.
> Many buffalo shall be consecrated, and shall be carried one by one at the foot of the hill.
> Yonder are high hills and low, covered with waving grass.
> Now listen, pay attention, they (3) give out their words in their own tongue.
> Yonder on the slopes of the willow-covered hills is a cave.
> Turtle (4) shall speak and say, "We will destroy you."
> Now I make holy this Comanche (5) who is brought into the lodge.
> Meat shall be taken from the back of the buffalo (6).
> The rays of the sun (7) shall enter the lodge.
> Burnt-offerings of flesh and human beings shall be made.
> The earth (8) then shall become a plain.
> When this shall happen, people shall see the streams as bows (9).
> You shall live under the heavens, and move about over the land as a tribe.
> Then the people shall come together, and all shall live as one people.
> The earth shall be fruitful.
> The owl (10); the owl.
> You shall go to the ravines (11).
> The carcass of an animal that has been eaten to the bone.
> The spotted rabbit (12) had his way, like a warrior, and he counts coup upon the enemy.
> The mouths shall look round (13).
> The noise of sticks (14) and voices shall move to and fro.
> May the fathers wave the sticks (15)!

The girl (1) was the first person on earth; she looks and listens for other people. The grass-covered dwellings (2) were reportedly the first type used by the Pawnee, and when abandoned lodges of this type were common, the bison rubbed their backs against the poles. The supernatural powers of animals, they (3), are found in different places. A turtle (4) created a flood to destroy four monsters, and this reference contains the implication that people will destroy one another and particularly that there will be the Morning Star sacrifice. The reference to the Comanche (5) is a further allusion to the sacrifice; the bison meat (6) is for an accompanying feast, and the sun's light (7) consecrates the victim. The earth (8) appears to be flat when shrouded with mist, but as the sun rises the mist disappears and shadows cast by the sun's rays reveal the hills and mountains. The reference to bows (9) is associated with killing animals, dedicating meat to the gods, and offering human sacrifices. Owls (10) are wise; the priests chant their night rituals like the owls. In the ravines (11) are the remains of animals, who like men, die. The Rabbit (12) is a star near the Milky Way who offered a way of life opposed to that of the Evening Star. When the people have an abundance of food, their mouths will be round (13) from singing and shouting. The sticks (14) are a reference to arrows shot at the Morning Star victim, while the sticks (15) next mentioned are associated with a blessing of children by waving pipe sticks.

When a woman learned that she was pregnant, she, with her husband, began to observe certain prohibitions. The most important of these was that the man could hunt and kill only deer and that only his wife could eat the meat. A wide range of additional taboos were observed by the potential father and mother. The prohibitions were necessary in order to prevent any deformity of the embryo. Each embryo acquired an animal familiar, and its nature was revealed later by the actions of the individual when ill. The shamans could identify the guardian of an individual and only attempted cures for persons with the same guardian that they possessed. When the woman began labor, her husband left the dwelling and did not return for four days. During this time he continued to follow the taboos, and he wore his hair loose, because Tirawa did so while creating. The laboring woman was aided by an old female shaman or the keeper of a sacred bundle. On the dirt floor of the dwelling fresh earth was spread and covered with soft grass to absorb the flow of blood. Birth took place from a kneeling position, with the woman leaning forward on a stick. Beforehand she took medicine to ease the process, but if the medicine did not succeed, additional women came to her aid. The navel cord was cut and tied by the midwife and was kept by the mother to be buried with her. The infant was then washed, wrapped in a blanket, and placed on a cradleboard. Finally the afterbirth was wrapped and placed in a tree where it would not be disturbed by birds or animals. The relatives of a child born at night observed the stars and the weather; if the wind did not blow and the following day was clear, they assumed the infant probably would not be ill or plagued with difficulties in his life. The near relatives of the mother cared for the neonate until the umbilical cord dropped off; then the infant was returned to the mother. Now, too, the parents' hair was braided, and the midwife was compensated. Were a woman to die in childbirth or the offspring to be stillborn, it was assumed that taboos had been broken. Infanticide was unknown and not even thought of. Male shamans were thought to be able to produce an abortion by using herbs, and an unwed woman might attempt to induce an abortion by applying pressure on her abdomen.

From the midwife an individual received a name based on his appearance or behavior just after birth. Examples of names for the Skidi included Round Eyes, Fatty, and Young Bull. The names White or Black were favorite Pawnee names for boys, and Bright Eyes was a favorite name for girls. A small child could receive another name when his father sacrificed a scalp for the occasion in a formal ritual. This name usually was retained by the individual until after marriage. A third name was bestowed by the individual's father after the marriage, and this one might be replaced to insure success in warfare or after a brave deed. Likewise a man might receive the name of an honored relative. So long as a child nursed, it was called by a word comparable to "baby," and the sex was not distinguished. This period lasted for about three years, and after this the terms for male and female children were different.

Informal adoption took place when an affluent family raised a child belonging legally to a poor family. It appears to have been somewhat less common to adopt the child formally. Formal adoption took place when a favorite boy or girl died and another resembled it. The arrangements were made if the parents approved of the adoption.

A young child was under the direct supervision of his grandmothers, who were severe instructors. Were a child to misbehave, he was reproved verbally, and if he did not obey the rules of childhood behavior, he was whipped. Among the ideals were for children to learn tribal lore from their grandmothers. They were reproved for not being quiet and withdrawn when among adults or for being inattentive during ceremonies. Also, a child could not go near the altar in the rear of a lodge. Older sisters, the mother and father, and the grandparents all served as authoritarian figures for a child. Until a boy was about twelve years of age, he helped his mother with such household tasks as hauling water. Older boys came under the supervision of their grandfathers, and to acquire skill in using the bow and arrow became an important part of a boy's life. The favorite game played with a bow and arrows was to shoot at an arrow shot by another boy. Older boys followed their fathers on bison hunts, and as soon as a kill was made, they aided in butchering the animal; the horse upon which they had ridden was used to transport the meat to camp.

A girl's training in the essential household skills was under the direction of her grandmother. When a girl menstruated for the first time, no ritual was known to be performed unless the girl's mother was the keeper of a sacred bundle. In such instances the girl was isolated, probably with her maternal grandmother; there were prohibitions on the girl's behavior and restrictions in her diet. For such a girl the same pattern was following during subsequent menstrual periods. All menstruating women were to avoid contact with sacred bundles and could not attend the accompanying ceremonies.

A boy who had reached puberty, which was not marked by ceremonial recognition, was placed in a new age group in which he remained until he married. He was identified by a word translated "grown" or "straight up." Until this time he went naked except to wear a robe in cold weather. After puberty he dressed as a man and was closely linked with his mother's brother's wife. When her husband was away, the boy served as a supplementary husband for a few years until acquiring a wife of his own. This form of mating was recorded by Dorsey and Murie in their study edited by Alexander Spoehr, whereas a different form is noted by Alexander Lesser who, although acknowledging marriage of a man to his mother's brother's wife, also stresses that a young unmarried man who had demonstrated his bravery had sexual access to his older brother's wife. Lesser would term this relationship fraternal polyandry.

Charles A. Murray, the Scot who passed a summer among the Pawnee, has left a delightful account of young men's vanity (see Note 5). When not obliged to hunt, the young braves sought to make themselves handsome and then lavished care on their favorite horses, which they groomed and adorned with paint and even a few feathers in the tail. After the rider and the steed were fully presentable, they paraded through the settlement to be admired by all. For a young man to seduce an unmarried girl was disreputable since girls were expected to be virgins when they married. Were a young couple to fornicate and be found out, the parents prevented further meetings. If, however, the girl became pregnant, a hasty wedding was arranged if the man was considered a potentially reputable husband. If not, he might be beaten badly, and no one would defend him, for it was very difficult to find another man willing to marry the girl under such circumstances.

In a normal marriage the couple were not to be more closely related than third cousins, if relatives at all, and the ideal was to find a mate from one's own community. A man did not marry until after he had participated in at least one raid, had successfully stolen horses, and had killed bison on the hunt. The woman was about twenty-two years old and fully mature. The couple lived with the wife's parents following the marriage. When a man married a woman from another settlement, they always resided in the community of the woman. The children were affiliated consistently with the village of their mother; thus there were matrilocal residence and the ideal of village endogamy.

Marriages were usually arranged by relatives of the couple, with the primary negotiations between a man's mother's brother and the possible bride's mother's brother. If the girl had no uncle, her brothers or grandfathers made the decision. Were the potential groom to object violently to the arrangements he would leave home for a year or two. A girl could try to influence the decision of her maternal uncle, but she was forced to abide by his verdict. The maternal uncle of the man, were he from a leading matrilineage, selected a chaste girl and one with a reputation for hard work. A formal wedding ceremony was performed when leading lineages were involved, but for persons of lesser standing this was not considered necessary. Marriage ceremonies were led by the priest, and formal approval was given by the girl's relatives in a ritual which included smoking and recitations of the young man's merits. Further ceremonial smoking and gifts to the male relatives of the girl followed, and finally the marriage ceremonies were completed when the couple ate and then slept together. Males were referred to by a word meaning "man" and females as "woman" after marriage. After a couple was established, their parents aided them in making a tepee in which they lived alone during the hunts into the open plains; at the same time, when the man was away on a hunt or with a raiding party, his wife or wives and children moved into the lodge of his parents. Finally, when a man was fully successful in adult activities, his family and his wife's family each built half of the earth lodge which would be the couple's new residence. The lodge was completed when the husband built the altar and he and his wife made the fireplace.

In theory, a man did not abuse his wife physically because it was through two female deities, Evening Star and Moon, that he was able to obtain bison and maize. In fact, it seems that a man rarely abused his wife so much that her relatives intervened on her behalf. Skidi Pawnee divorce seems to have been rare, and when it did occur, the grounds were most likely to be adultery or failure of the husband to be a good provider. Barrenness of the woman was not grounds for divorce. A man could leave his bride on the wedding night if she were not a maiden. Such a woman, along with others who freely fornicated before marriage, or loose widows, then lived on the fringes of a community as prostitutes. An adulterous wife was deserted, and an adulterous husband might be ordered to leave his home by his female in-laws. In cases of divorce the children remained with their mother. If a married man were to die, his younger brother acquired his widow as a wife, that is, the levirate.

Both Dunbar and Murray as well as other early nineteenth-century observers often remarked at length about the strenuous physical labor of Pawnee women. In spite of the fact that women could not be warriors, priests, shamans, or chiefs, they still were recognized in tribal, political and social life. It was the woman of a lodge who kept the sacred bundles and sacrificed maize on the lodge altar. Community welfare largely depended upon her successful fulfillment of these duties.

In instances of plural marriages the first and subsequent wives of a man were sisters; thus there was sororal polygyny. A man could obtain the younger sisters or sister of his wife if the girl's family was satisfied with his abilities as a provider. The secondary wives were acquired as they came of age, but there was no accompanying ceremony. One Skidi man had eight wives from two families, which seems to be the record number.

In the daily round of family activities while in the village, all the members bathed in a nearby stream or river in the morning. They then busied themselves around the settlement and ate their first meal around noon. Normally the women sat on the east side of the home during meals and the men opposite them, while the children ate near the women. When a number of families lived in one dwelling, the women of each unit alternated in preparing the meals. A number of food taboos were observed. Shamans and chiefs could not eat fish;

the tender meat around a bison's anus was saved for old people; and young people were not to eat the stomach of a bison cow. To break any of these taboos was to court some particular type of disaster. If the men were out hunting bison, the persons remaining in the village were cautioned to keep the lodge clean and to make offerings of maize to the bison skull on the household altar. Likewise, menstruating women were not to approach the skull for fear of angering the spirit of the bison.

Preparations of a body for burial and subsequent observances varied depending on the importance of the person during his life and the circumstances of death. For any individual the body was prepared almost immediately for the burial, which took place a few hours later. The body of an old person or a person of rank was painted with a sacred red pigment by a priest. The corpse of a man was shrouded in his bison robe, and ceremonial equipment was buried with a person who was a member of a particular voluntary association. For an old man, one who was no longer a hunter or warrior, and a woman after the menopause, both specially designated, there was no prolonged period of mourning; it lasted only the day of the burial. Also, a man who died in middle age from natural causes was not mourned, for such a death reflected the useless nature of the person.

At the death of an important chief the mourning period lasted months; it was shortened, however, to four days if the death took place just before the bundle renewal ceremonies. If a person of no consequence died, only the family mourned the loss, and then only for three days. If a man were to die at the hands of an enemy, his close friends and relatives secured an enemy scalp as soon as possible after the death. They consecrated it to a deity and tied it to a long stick above the grave. When a man died, it was his brothers and sisters who truly mourned the loss. A surviving brother mutilated himself, while a sister cut her hair. It was said of a wife, however, that she would spit on her hands to pretend tears, simultaneously peering through her fingers in search of another husband. A widow was to mourn for a year before remarrying. If she remained in the lodge of her deceased husband, it was expected that she would marry his younger brother or his sister's son at the end of the mourning period. If, however, she returned to her parents' home, these marital arrangements seem less likely to have taken place. A widower was obliged to mourn for at least two years, and it was frequently the case that he never remarried. After a man's death, his wife was considered the owner of their lodge and tepee as well as her own utensils and tools.

Personal property such as robes, horses, and riding equipment were inherited usually by the deceased's sister's sons.

The dead almost always were buried in the ground, usually on top of a hill but sometimes along the edge of a stream or a ravine, and over the body was piled a low mound of earth. The bodies were flexed, covered with matting, and accompanied by grave goods. Items never included as grave goods were objects which were regarded as having their origin in the sky. The most important category of this sort seems to have been the meteorites which were sometimes part of a war bundle. They were from the stars, which were supernatural, and they belonged to the sky. Thus they were placed on hilltops so that they could return to their home.

Information about the Pawnee dating from after the turn of the century virtually is nonexistent, but we do have the detailed study by Alexander Lesser of the Ghost Dance of 1890 as it affected the Pawnee. This was the last major effort of the tribe to reaffirm its cultural identity as Indian. To trace the development of the Ghost Dance among the Pawnee is to plot rapid change in another Indian sociocultural system. The original leader of the 1890 Ghost Dance was a Paiute Indian from Nevada named Wovoka or Jack Wilson. He reportedly died during an eclipse of the sun in January, 1889, and went to heaven, where he saw all the dead Indians living an idyllic life. God reportedly said that if Wovoka returned to earth and taught the people to perform a particular type of dance, the Ghost Dance, the dead and living would be reunited. Likewise, people must not fight with each other nor with the whites, and neither should they lie or steal. If all of these instructions were obeyed, there would be no more illness, old age, or death. By performing the Ghost Dance this happy new world soon would emerge.

Word of the Ghost Dance rapidly spread among Indians, and the doctrines were reinterpreted by different tribes. One frequent view was that Wovoka was Christ who had come to save the Indians. Rumors about the Ghost Dance had spread to the Pawnee in 1890, and in 1891 a Pawnee, Frank White, participated in a Ghost Dance in southern Oklahoma. White returned to his people and became the leader of the Ghost Dance among the Pawnee. During the dances the participants who went into trances revealed that they had seen the Messiah and the dead. The leader preached that the world was to change soon and that the whites and persons of mixed Indian and white ancestry would be blown away or destroyed by the wind. Believers, however, would see the dead return and the bison again become plentiful. The dances were held throughout 1891, and by 1892 most of the Pawnee had accepted the doctrine and were participating in numerous Ghost Dances to hasten the time when a new world would be created. Many persons were so convinced that the present world was going to end that they did not plough or plant their fields. Opposition by the Indian agent to the dance and his efforts to break up dances led to their being performed in secret. Finally, the leader of the movement, Frank White, was arrested for holding a Ghost Dance and held for about two weeks. During his hearing the judge sternly warned him against continuing his "insurrection."

At the time when the Ghost Dance movement reached its climax, the Federal government was exerting every effort to induce the Pawnee to change the nature of their landholdings. The Pawnee were living on a reservation, and with the passage by Congress of the General Allotment Act in 1887, reservation Indians were encouraged to select plots of land for which they eventually would receive clear titles. Unallotted reservation lands then were to be sold to whites. The Pawnee had resisted the program and viewed it as an attempt to destroy the tribe, which it was. In mid-1892 Federal agents told these Indians that if they accepted individual land allotments, they would pass from Federal control and could then hold their Ghost Dances as often as they wished. This argument apparently was convincing, for by late the same year the allotment process was completed. The following year the nonallotted lands were opened to white settlers. Over the next few years the Ghost Dance was continued but in a less militant form, and the Indian agents could do little to stop it.

After the death of White in 1893, or possibly somewhat earlier, the Ghost Dance changed to become a more formalized series of four-day ceremonies. The Ghost Dance focused Pawnee attention on being Indian, for one of the doctrines was to give up the goods and ways of whites. Their introspection led to a renewal of the importance of sacred bundles, the waning sodalities, and aboriginal games. By 1892 the sacred bundle rituals virtually had ceased to exist, and the elaborate shamans' performances were likewise becoming events of the past. A number of factors ran counter to a complete bundle ceremony revival. Some bundles had been buried with the last priest of a bundle group, and when a bundle did survive the priest in charge of it was not likely to know all of the esoteric lore surrounding it. Alexander Lesser (1933, 108) notes that in the late nineteenth century there was a "cultural forgetting" and that the functions of the ceremonies were fading, which made the continuity of ritual knowledge from a priest to his apprentice less likely. Then, too, many persons were dying, and with them went their store of knowledge that had not been passed on. The Ghost Dance, with its emphasis on individual vision experience, was one mechanism to revive the nonesoteric aspects of aboriginal life. An individual could acquaint himself with the past through a vision; this made unnecessary the ritual instructions of old. Such supernatural commands brought a new sanction into the performance of Pawnee dances and ceremonies.

In historic times many Indian tribes of the Plains and prairies accepted peyote and integrated its use into their supernatural system. Peyote, a small cactus plant grown in Mexico, has a small "button" appearing above the ground. These buttons were collected and dried for ritual use. The buttons contain nonhabit-forming stimulants and sedatives which produce a narcotic effect. The first knowledge of peyote was received by the Pawnee from the Quapaw about 1890 when two young men visited the latter tribe. Somewhat later more details concerning its use were learned from Arapaho visitors. When under the influence of peyote, one man learned songs and rituals which became the basis of the Pawnee peyote cult, and this individual emerged as its leader. As is common among American Indian tribes, elements of Christianity were integrated into the belief system, and in part the taking of peyote is associated in the minds of the Pawnee with the Ghost Dance.

As Lesser (1933, 117) has written, "The Ghost Dance proved not only a force for cultural revival, but with a return to the past as an inspirational source and guide, and vision sanctions as immediate drives, the doctrine was an impetus to cultural development." It appeared as though the Pawnee could once again reaffirm their Indian identity. This was not to be the case, however. With the allotment program the reservation was divided into small parcels of land, and whites who purchased unallotted lands lived next door to Indians. The Indians received an $80,000 advance for the lands they had released and a continuing $30,000 a year annuity plus interest from the balance of the sale of Nebraska and Oklahoma lands. All of these funds were either directly or indirectly available to the approximate one hundred and sixty families. Furthermore, the Pawnee leased farmlands, grazing lands, and even their houses to white cattlemen and farmers. The result was that by the turn of the century the Indians were well-to-do financially but they lived without purpose.

There was no positive side to their security, for they lived from day to day, spending their money as rapidly as they received it. There was no Protestant ethic guiding them to do otherwise. The net result was that they became deculturated, they no longer retained their Indian ways, and they adopted only the superficial aspects of white culture.

Note 1.   The historian George E. Hyde (1951, 192–194) describes a raid by the Sioux against a poorly prepared Pawnee community in 1862.

The Pawnees went on the usual summer hunt, leaving in the villages some women and children and a few men, most of the latter being sick or crippled. On August 27 six hundred Sioux, said to have been Brulés and Yanktons, appeared suddenly on the hill to the northwest of the Pawnee villages (the hill on which the Skidi burial ground was located), and came riding down toward the villages. This was in the morning, and the Sioux, who seemed to know that the villages were almost deserted, did not make a charge but advanced slowly in perfect order, the sun gleaming on their lances and guns, the fringes of their white war-shirts and the feathers of their warbonnets streaming in the breeze; as they came on at a slow steady pace, holding their excited ponies in, they were singing war songs.

In the Skidi village there was a man named Crooked Hand (*Skadiks*) who had a great reputation as a warrior although, as some informants stated, he was born with a deformed or palsied hand. According to other Pawnee informants Crooked Hand had had a leg broken in a fight with the Cheyennes in 1852, and he was lame in that leg. He was lying sick in his lodge when news was brought of the appearance of the great war party of Sioux; he instantly sprang up, threw off his buffalo robe, and seized his weapons, issuing orders for everyone to prepare to fight. Mustering sick men, old men, boys of twelve, and even a number of women, Crooked Hand got a force of about two hundred together and mounted, some of the women armed only with iron hoes and similar weapons. Some of the Pawnees wanted to stand behind the high earth wall that had been thrown up around three sides of the villages, as a protection from Sioux raiders, but Crooked Hand refused angrily to listen to their advice and led his motley force boldly out on the open plain to face the Sioux.

The Pawnees always recounted that when the Sioux caught sight of Crooked Hand's little force, including women, soft-cheeked boys and men almost too old to sit their horses, they burst into laughter and began to jeer at the Pawnees; but a fierce charge led by Crooked Hand soon ended that. The fight was the old-fashioned prairie Indian kind of affair: ride up and down and yell, shoot and charge in, kill a man or two, and then draw off for a rest before resuming the performance. As a spectacle it was prodigious: six hundred Indians careening up and down through clouds of powder smoke and dust. Sick as he was, Crooked Hand killed six Sioux during the day and had three horses shot under him. The fight started in the middle of the morning; the Sioux, who had expected to kill all the Pawnees in a few minutes and then plunder the villages and set them ablaze, were astonished to find that they could not break the Pawnee resistance. As the afternoon wore on the Sioux began to be worried about themselves and started drawing off, and as the day ended this slow withdrawal suddenly turned into a panic flight with Crooked Hand and his old men and boys (now mounted on fresh ponies brought from the villages) riding them down and killing them. The Pawnees claimed that a great many Sioux were killed in this final retreat. The Pawnees had about sixteen killed. Crooked Hand, wounded in several places, rode into the villages at dusk covered from head to heel with blood and with a Sioux arrow through his throat, the iron arrow-head sticking out at the back of his neck. Somehow the Skidi medicine-men got the arrow out and patched him up, but the throat wound bothered him for the rest of his life. It did not reduce his pugnacity in the slightest degree, and up until the time of his death in 1873 Crooked Hand continued to be a leading warrior among the Skidis.

Note 2. George B. Grinnell (1961, 296–297) describes Pawnee hunters as they approach a herd of bison.

A brief halt was made on the upper prairie, until all the riders had come up, and then, at a moderate gallop, we set off. A few yards in advance rode the twenty-four soldiers, at first curbing in their spirited little steeds, till the horses' chins almost touched their chests, and occasionally, by a simple motion of the hand, waving back some impetuous boy, who pressed too close upon them. Many of the Indians led a spare horse, still riding the one that had carried them through the day. Often two men would be seen mounted on the same animal, the one behind having the lariats of two led horses wound about his arm. Here and there a man, with his arm over the horse's neck, would run along on foot by the side of the animal which was to serve him in the charge.

As we proceeded, the pace became gradually a little more rapid. The horses went along easily and without effort. Each naked Indian seemed a part of his steed, and rose and fell with it in the rhythmic swing of its stride. The plain was peopled with Centaurs. Out over each horse's croup floated the long black hair of his rider, spread out on the wings of the breeze. Gradually the slow gallop became a fast one. The flanks of the horses showed here and there patches of wet, which glistened in the slanting rays of the westering sun. Eight, ten, a dozen miles had been left behind us, and we were approaching the top of a high bluff, when the signal was given to halt. In a moment every man was off his horse, but not a pony of them all showed any sign of distress, nor gave any evidence of the work he had done, except by his wet flanks and his slightly accelerated breathing. Two or three of the soldiers rode up nearly to the top of the hill, dismounted and then peered over, and a moment later, at another signal, all mounted and the swift gallop began again.

Note 3.   The Presbyterian missionary John Dunbar (*Collections of the Kansas State Historical Society*, v. 14, 1918, 610–611) describes the life of Pawnee women.

The Pawnee women are very laborious. I am inclined to think, they perform more hard labor, than any other women on this continent, be they white, black or red. It is rare, they are seen idle. When a Pawnee woman has nothing to do, she seems to be out of her element. They dress the skins for the tent covers, which is done with no small labor, sew them together, and fit them for the tents—make all the robes, which are many, both for their own use and the market—cut and bring all the wood on their backs—make all the fires—do all the cooking of course—dry all the meat—dig the ground—plant—hoe and gather all the corn, of which they raise an abundance, as they also do of beans and pumpkins—cut the timber, and build all their dwellings, both fixed and movable—set up and take down the portable tents—bridle and unbridle, saddle and unsaddle, pack and unpack all the horses—make all their moccasons, mats, bags, bowls, mortars, etc. etc. and if there be anything else done, beside watering, bringing up, and turning out the horses, (which the boys do) killing the bufalo, smoking and feasting, the women do it. Since the ground has thawed, they have bestowed some hundreds of days of hard labor in digging Indian potatoes. A woman does not succeed in digging more than a peck, laboring diligently from sunrise till sunset. Soon after light I have seen droves of the women and girls with their hoes or axes on their shoulders, starting off to their day's work. The men do not fail to call up their wives and daughters, as soon as it is light, and set them at work.

Their women are mere slaves. Whenever a Pawnee wishes to take a ride, he sends a boy after his horse, which, when brought up, his wife saddles. When he returns, he dismounts, and walks directly into his dwelling. His wife must without delay take off, and bring in the saddle. When he goes out to kill the bufalo, his wife must bridle and saddle his horse. When he returns, she must meet him without the village, and lead in his horse with the meat, which she throws off, and brings into the lodge, then unbridles and unsaddles his horse. If he kills the animal with a gun, and brings the meat on his back, his wife must meet him, as before, take the meat from his back on her own, and bring it to the lodge.

When together in the lodge, their wives and daughters occupy the coldest and most inconvenient part of it. If there happens to be as many men present, as can conveniently sit around the fire, the women must sit back behind them, however cold it may be. If they have more than their horses can conveniently pack, their women must carry it. They carry huge loads, as far as we travelled during the day, many of them without stopping at all to rest by the way, that I discovered. When they stop for the night, the horses are to be unpacked, and unsaddled, the furniture to be arranged, the tents set up, wood and water brought, fire made, victuals cooked, moccasons mended, etc. before taking any time to rest, thus their labor is excessive. They are naturally bright and active, but their treatment renders them what slaves always are. They are much degraded. They become, as much slaves to their sons, when they arrive at manhood, as to their husbands. They are exceedingly loquacious. Several of them often talk at the same time. They either possess the faculty of talking and hearing at the same time, or are so predisposed to garulity, that they talk without caring to be heard. They not only talk much, but often scold. Their ill treatment frequently renders them excessively illnatured.

Note 4.   John Dunbar (*Collections of the Kansas State Historical Society*, v. 14, 1918, 631) records one account of the sacrifice to the Morning Star by the Skidi or Loup Pawnee.

The Loups are far more superstitious than either of the other bands. Though they had solemnly engaged that this cruel custom should not be renewed, yet their deeprooted ferocious superstition has sacrificed another victim. Young females are the objects of this horrid infatuation devotes [devours?] and the more beautiful the subject the stronger the medicine. A man, who has thrice witnessed this revolting transaction accounted of it as follows: After having performed all the various preliminary rites and ceremonies their superstition requires, the victim is stripped nearly or quite naked, and one half of her person from head to foot is painted red, the other black, a scaffold is erected, and the feet and hands being extended, the right wrist and ankle are tied to an upright piece of timber, and the left wrist and ankle to another at a proper distance and thus the wretched creature is suspended. Various ceremonies, such as smoking the medicine pipe, etc. at different stages of the operation. The young men and boys, each having provided a handful of arrows about a foot long, made of the stems of a species of tall grass that grows on the prairies, now advance and commence shooting these arrows into the breast and other parts of the unfortunate sufferer. This tormenting sport is continued till all their arrows are expended. These arrows enter just enough to adhere and the breast is literally filled with them; but they do not destroy life. This being done an old man comes forward and shoots an iron pointed arrow through the vitals and the illfated creature is released from farther suffering. The chest is now cut open and the heart taken out and burned. The smoke that rises from this fire is considered a most potent medicine, and their implements of war, hunting and agriculture are passed through it to insure success in their use. The flesh is now wantonly slashed off with knives and thrown to be devoured by the dogs, but the skeleton remains suspended till it decays and falls.

Note 5.   The Scottish traveler among the Pawnee in the 1830's, Charles A. Murray (1839, v. 1, 317–319), describes the toilet of a young male.

About the age of twenty they are allowed to hunt, and seek other opportunities for distinction. This epoch answers to the Oxonian's first appearance in London life after taking his B.A. degree. I have seen some dandies in my life—English, Scotch, French, German, ay and American dandies too; but none of them can compare with the vanity or coxcombry of the Pawnee dandy. Lest any of the gentry claiming this distinction, and belonging to the abovementioned nations, should doubt or feel aggrieved at this assertion, I will faithfully narrate what passed constantly before my eyes in our own tent; namely, the manner in which Sâ-ní-tsă-rish's son passed the days on which there was no buffalo hunt.

He began his toilet, about eight in the morning, by greasing and smoothing his whole person with fat, which he rubbed afterwards perfectly dry, only leaving the skin sleek and glossy; he then painted his face vermilion, with a stripe of red also along the centre of the crown of the head; he then proceeded to his "coiffure," which received great attention, although the quantum of hair demanding such care was limited, inasmuch as his head was shaved close, except one tuft at the top, from which hung two plaited "tresses." He then filled his ears, which were bored in two or three places, with rings and wampum, and hung several strings of beads round his neck; then, sometimes painting stripes of vermilion and yellow upon his breast and shoulders, and placing armlets above his elbows and rings upon his fingers, he proceeded to adorn the nether man with a pair of mocassins, some scarlet cloth leggins fastened to his waist-belt, and bound round below the knee with garters of beads four inches broad. Being so far prepared, he drew out his mirror, fitted into a small wooden frame, (which he always, whether hunting or at home, carried about his person,) and commenced a course of self-examination, such as the severest disciple of Watts, Mason, or any other religious moralist, never equalled. Nay more, if I were not afraid of offending the softer sex by venturing to bring man into comparison with them in an occupation which is considered so peculiarly their own, I would assert that no female creation of the poets, from the time that Eve first saw "that smooth watery image," till the polished toilet of the lovely Belinda, ever studied her own reflected self with more perseverance or satisfaction than this Pawnee youth.

References

Buckstaff, Ralph N. "Stars and Constellations of a Pawnee Sky Map," *American Anthropologist*, v. 29, 279–285. 1927.

Catlin, George. *North American Indians*. 2 v. London. 1844.

Dorsey, George A. "Social Organization of the Skidi Pawnee," *Fifteenth International Congress of Americanists*, 71–77. Quebec. 1907.

———. "A Pawnee Ritual of Instruction," *Anthropological Papers Written in Honor of Franz Boas*, 350–353. New York. 1906.

———. "The Skidi Rite of Human Sacrifice," *Fifteenth International Congress of Americanists*, 65–70. Quebec. 1907.

*Dorsey, George A. and James R. Murie (edited by Alexander Spoehr). "Notes on Skidi Pawnee Society," *Anthropological Series, Field Museum of Natural History*, v. 27, 67–119. 1940. The definitive study of Skidi social structure with notes on the life cycle of the individual as well as information on certain aspects of political organization.

Fletcher, Alice C. "Pawnee Star Lore," *Journal of American Folk-Lore*, v. 16, 10–15. 1903.

*Grinnell, George B. *Pawnee Hero Stories and Folk-Tales.* Lincoln. 1961 (originally published in New York in 1889). Grinnell describes diverse aspects of Pawnee ethnography, but none in detail. Emphasis is on folktales and stories about warfare, but it is still an essential source for a balanced account of these Indians.

Hodge, Frederick W. "Pitalesharu and his Medal," *The Masterkey,* v. 24, 111–119. 1950.

*Hyde, George E. *Pawnee Indians.* Denver. 1951. This book is the definitive history of the Pawnee but has very little to offer about events after 1900.

Irving, John T., Jr. (edited by John F. McDermott). *Indian Sketches.* Norman. 1955.

Lesser, Alexander. "Levirate and Fraternal Polyandry among the Pawnees," *Man,* v. 30, 98–101. 1930.

*———. *The Pawnee Ghost Dance Hand Game.* New York. 1933. The focus of this study is on the Ghost Dance and the revival of a game at the time of the Ghost Dance, but the volume also contains a summary of Pawnee history down to about 1900.

"Letters Concerning the Presbyterian Mission in the Pawnee Country, near Bellevue, Neb., 1831–1849." *Collections of the Kansas State Historical Society,* v. 14, 570–784. 1918.

Linton, Ralph. *The Thunder Ceremony of the Pawnee.* Field Museum of Natural History. Leaflet 5. 1922.

———. "The Origin of the Skidi Pawnee Sacrifice to the Morning Star," *American Anthropologist,* v. 28, 457–466. 1926.

McKenney, Thomas L. and James Hall. *The Indian Tribes of North America.* 3 v. Edinburgh. 1933.

*Murie, James R. *Pawnee Indian Societies.* Anthropological Papers of the American Museum of Natural History, v. 11, pt. 7. New York. 1914. This short monograph is the most complete and readable account of sacred and secular Pawnee societies. It includes also information about other aspects of Pawnee life and is a required source of ethnographic materials.

Murray, Charles A. *Travels in North America.* 2 v. London. 1839.

Newcomb, William W., Jr. "A Re-Examination of the Causes of Plains Warfare," *American Anthropologist,* v. 52, 317–330. 1950.

Roe, Frank G. *The Indian and the Horse.* Norman. 1955.

*Wedel, Waldo R. *An Introduction to Pawnee Archeology.* Bureau of American Ethnology, Bulletin 112. 1936. Not only are the details of Pawnee archaeology presented, but historical and ethnographic data are analyzed into a fine synthesis of sociocultural data.

———. *Prehistoric Man on the Great Plains.* Norman. 1961.

Wissler, Clark and Herbert J. Spinden. "The Pawnee Human Sacrifice to the Morningstar," *American Museum Journal,* v. 16, 49–55. 1916.

7

The Tlingit:

Salmon Fishermen of the Northwest

ALASKA

Copper R.

Prince William Sound

AHTENA

EYAK

Kayak Is.

CANADA

TUTCHONE

TLINGIT

Yakutat Bay

Yakutat

Dry Bay

Lynn Canal

Klukwan

Douglas • Juneau

Stikine R.

THALTAN

TSETSAUT

Lituya Bay

Gulf of Alaska

Hoonah

Angoon •

Admiralty I.

• Hood Bay

Sitka

Baranof I.

• Wrangell

TSIMSHIAN

Prince of Wales I.

Ketchikan

Metlakatla

• Tongass

Fort Simpson

Skeena R.

HAIDA

Queen
Charlotte
Islands

CANADA

A L A S K A

0   100   200 mi.

Map by J. Donovan

One day during the summer of 1786 an Indian hunter looked seaward from above the shores of Lituya Bay on the Gulf of Alaska; he imitated the call of a wolf and then ran into the nearby village. The wolf's cry was a sign of important news, and people gathered as the hunter arrived, saying, "Raven is coming." He stated further that Raven was white and was to be seen on the horizon to the west. Everyone knew that long ago Raven was white, not black, and thus his appearance in this form was not surprising. This was a great moment, for Raven, the creator and culture hero, had said he would return to reward those persons who had obeyed his teachings and to turn the others into stone. Some persons looking seaward peered at the white object through hollow stalks of kelp so that they would not be blinded by Raven's brightness. Then Raven came into the bay and folded his wings. Individuals who expected to be turned into stone stood erect and cut their chests with stone knives; others who were unafraid began painting their faces to receive this great and honored visitor. One wise old man decided to go out to Raven and offer himself to be turned into stone so that other persons might be spared. He paddled his hunting canoe out to Raven and was lifted, canoe and all, out of the water onto Raven. Here the old man saw men with brown hair and blue or gray eyes; their faces were white and they wore strange clothing. The old man began to wonder whether he truly was in the midst of Raven. A man far better clothed than the others appeared, and he was assumed to be Raven. The old man asked for mercy, but the man in the fine clothing sent for food. One of the foods offered to the old man seemed to be a section of a human skull, and something else looked like maggots. Finally he was offered a red liquid which had the appearance of blood; he would eat none of these things. "Raven" then crossed his hands in the air twice, and the old Indian knew that this was not Raven after all since the sign he made was the one people used when they wanted to trade. The Indian traded away his hat and garments of sea otter skin for a piece of iron and a small bell. Then, without clothing, he was lowered into the water in his canoe and paddled back to the village. He carried ashore his prizes and told the people of his great experience. This is a modern account by the northern Tlingit recalling the visit to Lituya Bay by Captain Jean de La Perouse of the *Astrolabe* and Paul-Antoine de Langle on the *Boussole,* the first Europeans to explore the area.

Tlingit is the term by which these Indians call themselves and means "people," but the Russians referred to them as Kolosch, or by some variation of this word, the meaning of which is not known for certain. Their language belongs to the great Na-dene phylum, the Dene stock, and is a single language at the family level. Numerically, there were as many as ten thousand of these people around the time of historic contact, but this figure may not be reliable. A current population estimate, again of only general reliability, is that eight thousand Indians in southeastern Alaska are identified as Tlingit. The country which they occupied included nearly all of present-day southeastern Alaska from the Copper River mouth southward including the northern two thirds of Prince of Wales Island. The people were divided into named geographical subgroups, called a *kon* or *qwan* in Tlingit. Each had a principal village, and the members controlled the resources of the surrounding area. From north to south the first *kon* was Yakutat, with its most important settlement on the bay of the same name. The Yakutat Tlingit ranged northward to the Copper River mouth to dominate the Eyak Indians, who were Na-Dene. The most powerful of all the *kons* was the Chilkat, whose members lived along the shores of the upper Lynn Canal and occupied four major villages. One, Klukwan, had sixty-five houses and about six hundred residents, making it one of the largest of all Tlingit settlements. The other *kons,* each of which had at least one major village, were the Auk, Taku, Huna, Killisnoo, Sitka, Kake, Kuju, Stikine, Henya, Tongass, and Sanya. The oral traditions of the Tlingit relate that they arrived in their present area from the south, somewhere around the Skeena River, except for the Kake who came from the interior.

The Tlingit have been selected for discussion as an example of the complex way of life which emerged on the north Pacific coast of North America. They stand as one of the more complex sociocultural developments in North America which was not based on horticulture. An ethnographic study of the Tlingit was compiled in 1881–1882 by two geographers who were also brothers, Aurel and Arthur Krause. Their description of Tlingit history, culture, and society, which includes earlier observations of other whites, was published in 1885 in German and was translated and published in English in 1956. In 1904 the outstanding American ethnographer John R. Swanton studied the Tlingit, but he was more interested in mythology and language than in an overview of the lifeway. The next significant studies in the era around 1900 were by the missionaries Livingston F. Jones and Samuel H. Young. The unpublished doctoral dissertation by Kalvero Oberg, based mainly on fieldwork at Klukwan in 1931–1932, provides the most valuable factual and interpretive data on aboriginal Tlingit life. Philip Drucker's study of the Alaska Native Brotherhood is an important analysis of a major political and social force in Tlingit life. A monograph by Frederica de Laguna attempts to combine archaeological and ethnographic with historical information in order to reconstruct the culture in the area around the modern settlement of Angoon in the Killisnoo *kon*. Finally, a brief but revealing study of Hoonah, whose inhabitants are in the Huna *kon*, was conducted by Seymour Parker in 1961. Thus there are both a relatively complete series of publications about the Tlingit for the American period and satisfactory reconstructions for the aboriginal past.

Tlingit country, of the Sitkan biotic province, is composed of masses of mountains reaching to the sea, islands, deep bays, and glaciers. It is a verdant land, with tranquil and turbulent waters which proffer an environmental richness with great exploitative potential. Along the northern third of the area sheltering bays are rare; it is here that impressive mountains abruptly meet the sea. The southern two thirds of their country contains innumerable large and small islands before a fractured coastline. The channels between the land formations range from deep and wide to shallow, narrow, and rock-strewn passages. The tides may ebb and flow with a variation of twenty feet in the inlets. The coastal sector is a narrow band of land with mountains a short distance inland; thus, there are very few rivers of any size flowing into the sea, the major exception being the Stikine River.

The most impressive climatic characteristics are the warm summers and mild winters, plus heavy precipitation. In one wet year, 1856, rain fell two hundred fifty-eight days, and it snowed twenty-seven days. With the abundance of rain the vegetation is lush and varied. Stands of red cedar and mountain hemlock grow at lower elevations, but Sitka spruce, lodgepole pine, and other varieties of spruce are the most common forms of conifer. The ground cover includes a profusion of smaller plants which form a virtual wall of vegetation. The fallen trees, great ferns, diversity of berry bushes, and in some sectors the spiny devil's club, make cross-country travel impossible in the summer except along the established trails. In the winter with heavy snow cover it is possible to snowshoe through the forest. Considering the geographical configuration, it is understandable that travel by boat was far more important than walking along overland trails. It was only the trails to the interior at certain passes and along a few rivers that took people inland on trading or raiding trips.

The large variety of terrestrial fauna included both black and grizzly bears, fox, wolves, wolverine, lynx, and deer on some islands. Scattered caribou herds were on the mainland plateaus, and mountain goats as well as mountain sheep occupied the coastal ranges. Smaller species included hare, squirrel, ermine, porcupine, muskrat, and a few beaver. Among the marine mammals were numbered whales, hair and fur seals, sea lions, and sea otter. Of all the fish the most important were the salmon and candlefish or eulachon; halibut, haddock, trout, and herring also were caught. Along the edges of the sea were edible algae, crabs, sea urchins, mussels, and cockles. The avifauna included the bald eagle, raven, owl, and migratory waterfowl which summered in the area.

Tlingit prehistory is virtually unknown owing both to the difficulty in locating and excavating sites and to the fact that few archaeologists have worked in this region. De Laguna, the only field worker in the area with a major interest in archaeology, suggests a broad developmental sequence which requires verification but seems logical. From a study of north Pacific region archaeology and ethnography she suggests that contacts between Alaskan Eskimos and Northwest Coast Indians are quite old and that perhaps a thousand years ago they became more intensive, introducing elements from the Asian side which fostered the elaboration of Indian culture. Philip Drucker suggests that the coastal Indian developments emerged from an Eskimoan base and became most distinctive among the Nootka and Kwakiutl, who represent the purest forms. The Tlingit, Tsimshian, and Haida, in this reconstruction, are regarded as more recent in their emergence and as marginal to the more southerly developments; these reflect, too, a marked influence from the interior Athapaskans which interrupted the north-south continuity along the coast.

De Laguna's excavations in the Angoon area represent the only systematic work of any consequence. She has classified the remains as village sites, as fortifications, or as localities with petroglyphs or pictographs. However, from the areas of the rock carvings few cultural remains of any sort were recovered. Not only are conditions poor for the preservation of sites, but they are difficult to find because of the rapid growth of vegetation following occupancy. Of the Tlingit artifacts recovered, all probably belong to the early historic period and reveal very little new in terms of the past and their makers.

The history of the Tlingit began with explorations of the Russians who sought to determine whether the Asian and North American land masses were continuous. It was during the Second Kamchatkan Expedition under the leadership of Vitus Bering that the first contacts were made. The two expedition vessels, the *St. Peter* under Bering and the *St. Paul* under Alexei Chirikov, sailed from Kamchatka in 1741 and soon became separated in the north Pacific Ocean. Chirikov, the first Russian to reach the coast, anchored offshore near the southern limit of Tlingit country. He sent two separate small boats ashore, but neither returned to the ship. Later two canoes of natives paddled toward the *St. Paul* and then withdrew. Without another small vessel to put ashore, Chirikov was forced to return to Kamchatka. Shortly after Chirikov's landfall the Bering party anchored off Kayak Island at the northern edge of Tlingit country. This island seems to have been occupied by Eskimos, the Chugach. Bering sent a boat ashore for water with orders not to linger. It was not without difficulty that the great German naturalist, Georg W. Steller, persuaded Bering to allow him to accompany the party. No people were seen, but a camp and possessions were found, along with a still burning fire. The descriptions by Steller of the structure and artifacts he saw are the earliest such descriptions for the area. On the return voyage the *St. Peter* crew was forced to winter on Bering Island off the coast of Kamchatka. Here Bering died, but the surviving members of the crew returned to Kamchatka the next year, bringing with them the pelts of sea mammals. This led to the hasty organization of small trading and hunting expeditions to the Aleutian Islands, and before many years had passed the search for furs had reached the Alaskan mainland.

The Russians were not the first observers of the Tlingit country, however. As early as 1582 the Spanish explorer Francisco Gali saw the northwest coast in the vicinity of Sitka but apparently had no contacts with the people. The Spanish viewed the Russian explorations with alarm and in 1774 sent Juan Perez from Mexico northward. His party reached the Queen Charlotte Islands. The following year a Spanish vessel under Juan de la Bodega landed near Sitka and attempted to take possession of the land. They withdrew quickly, however, because of the hostility of the people. Next, in 1778, it was the English under the command of one of the greatest of all explorers, James Cook, who sailed to the northwest coast. Although Cook saw the Sitka area from the sea, he did not attempt to land. After Cook came the expedition to Lituya Bay by La Perouse in 1786. English expeditions and traders became particularly numerous after word reached England of the profits to be made in selling sea otter pelts in China. Americans also entered the fur trade; the earliest, in 1788, were Robert Gray, commander of the *Washington,* and John Kendrick in command of the *Columbia.* It was not until the expedition of George Vancouver in 1792–1794 that the northwest coast was mapped with enough accuracy to establish that the legendary Strait of Anian to the Atlantic Ocean was truly a fable.

Throughout the 1780's and 1790's Russian merchants moved toward an increased consolidation of the Alaskan trade until at last in 1799 the Russian-American Company was founded and granted a monopoly. The dominant local administrator was Alexander Baranov, who established a permanent base on Kodiak Island in 1791. Baranov's first contacts with the Tlingit occurred on Prince William Sound. Here he and his party were mistaken by raiding Yakutat Tlingit for Chugach Eskimos and attacked in the middle of the night. The Russians and the Aleuts who were with them fought off the Indians, but each side suffered casualties. This encounter with the Tlingit and the earlier contacts by traders and explorers of all nationalities were of an unfriendly nature. These Indians virtually always were haughty, aggressive, thieving, and bellicose, especially when they outnumbered the intruders. A fort and trading post was established at Sitka in 1799, and so long as Baranov was there the Indians did not attack, since they respected his bravery. After he left in 1801, the Indians attacked, destroyed the fort, and killed the small garrison. In 1804 Baranov returned with about nine hundred men, eight hundred Aleuts and the balance Russians. Anchored before Sitka was the *Neva* under the command of Urey Lisiansky. The *Neva* was the first Russian vessel to sail to Russian-America from European Russia. At Sitka the Russians hoped to establish a fortress on a steep hill formerly occupied by the Indians. The Tlingit withdrew to a nearby fort, and the Russians founded their hilltop settlement of New Archangel. The Indians were determined to drive the Russians away if possible, but they could not withstand the bombardment from the *Neva* and withdrew from the fort, which later was destroyed by the Russians.

With the retirement of Baranov in 1818 a succession of administrators controlled the fortunes of the Russian-American Company. Some were extremely capable, while others were weak administrators. Relationships with the Tlingit fluctuated with the capabilities of the chief administrator. Throughout the latter part of the Russian period, until the purchase in 1867, Sitka was the primary trading center for the Tlingit, but American trading vessels and traders of the Hudson's Bay Company successfully competed for Tlingit furs. The destructive Indian and Russian hunting techniques made the fur trade less and less profitable as time went on. Finally the lowering of the Russian flag at New Archangel, or Sitka, on October 18, 1867, and the raising of the American flag brought the era of Russian control to an end.

According to Tlingit mythology, the first people simply existed, and no explanation was sought for their ultimate origins. Then, according to one tale, there was once a woman who lost all her sons, killed by her brother, and who prepared to commit suicide. An old man whom she met told her to swallow a heated beach pebble. The woman did as instructed and swallowed the pebble, which made her pregnant. She bore an offspring, who was Raven in human form. He grew quickly, and as a boy he shot small birds and then larger game with a bow and arrows given him by his mother. After Raven was older, he visited his uncle in spite of warnings by his mother that his uncle, her brother, had killed his ten older brothers; his mother followed him reluctantly. The uncle attempted to kill Raven, but because of Raven's supernatural powers he was able to save himself. Finally, Raven caused a flood, and the people perished except for Raven and his mother, who donned bird skins and flew into the air. Raven stuck his beak in the sky where he hung for ten days. After the water subsided, he fell to earth and landed on a heap of seaweed. Raven then went to the house of Petrel, a man who had no beginning nor end, but who always existed. In a small locked box, on which he sat, Petrel kept water and when Raven was thirsty he was given only a little. Raven tricked Petrel into thinking that he, Petrel, had excreted in his bed. While Petrel was outside cleaning his blanket, Raven drank more than his fill of water. He flew to a tree with pitch in it. Petrel built a fire beneath the tree, and the smoke turned Raven from white to black. It was later the trickery of Raven that released the stars into the sky, the moon, and finally the sun. It was Raven who was a creator or releaser of forces in the world. He was a culture hero and above all else an inordinate trickster.

The Tlingit were medium to tall in height and lean, with skins no darker than those of persons from southern Europe. They rubbed their black hair with grease, and it hung loose over the neck. The beards of the men were not heavy and usually were plucked. When a male was young, his nasal septum was pierced, and through the opening a small ring was passed. At times several small holes were made around the outer edge of the ear, and bits of wool or small feathers were stuck in the holes. Only a man with great achievements had such ear holes. From the pierced earlobes were hung ornaments of shell, stone, or teeth. Women wore their hair loose as did the men but parted it in the middle. Body mutilation for adornment was more striking for women; in addition to earrings, each wore a large medial labret inserted through a hole beneath the lower lip (see Note 1). The initial opening was made around the time of puberty or perhaps earlier, and the hole periodically enlarged until it sometimes stretched four inches; as one observer noted, kissing was impossible for such a person. Women who were slaves did not have labrets. Tattooing, if it occurred, probably was restricted to lines beneath the chin among the northern Tlingit, who could have learned the custom from Eskimos. On certain occasions facial paintings were important for both men and women; paint was worn for special ceremonial or subsistence activities, to reflect mourning, or simply to look attractive. One's face was painted also as protection from the heat or cold, as well as against snowblindness in the spring and insects in the summer. Organic and inorganic red and black pigments were mixed with a seal oil base.

Adults of both sexes dressed in long-sleeved shirts of dehaired skin, over which they wore a sea otter skin cape with the fur side facing outward. Women were described further as having worn undergarments of processed skins which reached from the neck to the ankles. No footwear was worn except in severe weather, and then the form was the moccasin. These were traded from or copied after those of the interior Indians. Their hats for hunting and ceremonies were woven from root or grass and shaped like a truncated cone with a flat top. The Tlingit clothing hardly seems adequate to an outsider, but the people conditioned themselves to accept extremes in temperature. Bathing in cold or icy water was expected as well as sitting in a scorchingly hot house.

The permanent winter villages were located where there was good fishing nearby and where canoes could be landed safely. This meant that the Tlingit preferred sheltered bays, inlets, or the lower course of a river for their home sites. If the community was small, all of the houses were set in a line near the beach or riverbank. If the settlement was large, the houses were arranged in rows and grouped according to kinship affiliations. The essentially square, plank dwellings with gabled roofs had entrances facing the water. In the construction of a dwelling four great posts were sunk in the ground, one at each corner; these rose ten feet above the surface. In the middle of the sidewalls were support posts, and on top of these rested plates. Near the center of the front and back walls were higher posts which supported beams along the length of the house. Over secondary roof beams were overlapping horizontal planks, and these short board shingles were held in place with lengthwise poles or scattered stones. Toward the middle of the roof was an opening to let light in and smoke out. Over the skylight a plank cover was used in bad weather. To reach the roof a notched pole ladder was kept against the side of the house. Steps or a platform led to the round or oval doorway which was at the center or off to one side of the house front; entrance was gained after pushing aside a grass mat. The floor inside the smaller dwellings was on one level, but larger houses contained a central area dug down about three feet. Along the sides at ground level were compartments enclosed with matting or boards; these were for sleeping rooms, a sweat bath, or for the storage of food and possessions. This floor was planked, as was the excavated area, except near the fireplace. Around the fire pit were stones to be heated in the fire and placed in containers for cooking food. Overhead along the beams were stored various hunting and fishing devices, and fish might be hung from the roof beams to dry. Among the northern Tlingit in particular the house of the leading lineage in a sib was likely to have decorated wall partitions or panels which have been termed heraldic screens. It appears that behind these screens were the apartments of the house chief, while another report notes that behind such panels the ceremonial equipment of the household was stored. Around the entry to a house or even around the entire community were palisades which served to protect the occupants. Included among the other structures to be seen about a winter settlement were bough-covered, cone-shaped structures which were sometimes leaned against the outer wall of a house and used for women when menstruating or in childbirth. Scattered about also were pole racks for drying fish. At a short distance from each settlement, either toward the sea or forest, were the graves of the dead. It should be noted that no mention has been made of the great totem poles which usually are regarded as the most striking feature of a Northwest Coast Indian village. The reason is that totem poles were not erected during the earliest period of contact.

The land within a village was owned by the sibs and divided among the house groups. The path before the houses was used freely by anyone, but sections were owned by the adjacent householders. Trails might be cleared by community members as a group, and the beach before a settlement was common property. Each of the thirteen, or perhaps fourteen, *kons* had its geographical boundaries, and each community in turn controlled the sector it exploited. Within the domain of a village, each of the represented sibs had particular localities which they defined as their own. However, not all localities were claimed, and the unclaimed ones could be used by anyone. Each sib or portion thereof exploited sites such as fishing streams and the adjacent hunting lands of the stream's drainage, sealing islands, mountains inhabited by mountain goats, ocean banks, berry patches, and house locations, but according to de Laguna the people did not conceive of their ownership in terms of an entire geographical area but rather the specific spots used by them. Among the most important exploited localities were summer fishing grounds where a family obtained its supply of fish for winter. The structures built at these camps were of flimsy plank construction, and some were walled in on only the windward side.

The technological achievements of the Tlingit in craft skills rank high among primitive peoples anywhere in the world. Their manufactures in stone, bone, and wood are famous, and their weaving abilities merit additional comment. In a typical aboriginal household were a wide variety of wooden containers. One form was made from a thin plank of cedar which was steamed and bent into a rectangular form, then overlapped and sewn with root. A wooden bottom was fitted into place and a top sometimes added. Some of these boxes had bulging sides which were painted or carved. The largest and most elaborately decorated boxes were used for the storage of valuables, and others were for cooking or food storage. Another common form of wooden vessel was made from a single piece of wood and ranged from round, to oval, to rectangular in outline. To these basic forms were adapted various animal shapes, such as a beaver lying on its back, with the head at one end, legs on the sides, and tail opposite the head. The rim might be inlaid with the opercula of mollusks or bits of abalone shell, and the eyes of the animal might likewise be inlaid with shell. Other household items included dishes, spoons, and ladles of mountain sheep or goat horn. Oval lamps of pecked and polished stone furnished light from fish oil burning on a wick of peat moss. Stone pestles and mortars which had been pecked and ground into shape were used for mashing berries. Plant fibers were woven into a wide variety of household containers such as trays, bags, or baskets for storing or carrying various items; they also were woven into mats upon which persons lounged. All of these artifacts would have been seen in any typical household, and in each house, too, the family members gathered around the fire to rest, to eat, or to work during the day. The wood for each day's fire was brought in by the younger men and boys on the day it was to be burned. At the fireplace the meals were prepared at irregular times of the day in these large houses with as many as thirty occupants. Boiled foods were prepared in wooden or woven containers into which water was placed. Hot stones were dropped in together with meat or fish, and a lid placed on the vessel so that the contents would simmer. Fish boiled, roasted before the fire, or dried were the principal items in the diet, and they were supplemented by flesh from land and sea mammals. Included in the diet were shellfish, vegetable products and fruit, particularly a wide variety of berries, but these foods were relatively unimportant. Boiled foods were dipped from their cooking containers into large spoons which served as plates, and large quantities of water were consumed at every meal.

Carving the sib crest on any item was done by a member of the opposite moiety who held a rank equal to that of the individual requesting the carving. By preference this would be a wife's brother, but if such an individual was not a capable carver, someone else, of either moiety, could be hired and paid to make the object. The man who was first asked to do the work paid the craftsman and in turn was paid by his brother-in-law. Carvings produced in this manner fulfilled ritual obligations, and the labor involved was ceremonial.

There have been two aspects of Northwest Coast Indian life which have most attracted the attention of whites: their art and the potlatch system. About these a great deal has been written, and while the potlatch will be discussed later it is now desirable to summarize briefly Tlingit artistic and craft expressions. As Franz Boas pointed out, there were two basic artistic styles among Northwest Coast Indians. The first was dominated by men; that it was largely symbolic is manifest in the sculpture, carving, and painting. The second, or women's, style was largely formal with little or no attending meaning and was manifest primarily in basketry on which there are designs. Although the Chilkat robes were woven by women and contained symbolic designs, the women reproduced symbolic paintings made on boards by a male designer. The carving skills of men were expressed primarily in wood; red cedar was the favorite medium. The men likewise carved horn and ivory; pounded and incised copper; and further utilized shell, hair, and skin for decorative elements. The women in their artistic crafts utilized animal wool and spruce or cedar root fibers. Their basketry designs usually were geometric, and the specific motifs were named. The baskets were nearly straight-sided and were flat-bottomed. The sides were decorated, but rims usually were plain.

Among the common elements in the symbolic art was a sense of symmetry, with the figures characterized by stylization. Animals most often were the subject matter, but human figures also appeared. Sometimes these seem to have been portraits of individuals. In general, the art of the Tlingit was not so complex as that of their neighbors to the south; neither was it so monumental, possibly because of the scarcity or absence of great cedar trees in most of the Tlingit area. What the Tlingit did excel in producing was a very wide variety of highly imaginative masks which were used by performing shamans. The human form of the mask included supplementary animal figures which were the familiars of the shamans. The carvings on utilitarian objects served to enhance their beauty and bring prestige to their owners. It was not customary to create an object free from the associations of prestige and decorative art. Distortion was an important consideration in their creations since traditional forms were adapted to diverse surfaces. Carving a bear on a totem pole presented a very different problem from fitting a bear to a rectangular vessel shape, on the handle of a horn spoon, or on a flat screen painting. Thus, there was an adaptability of the motifs. Another characteristic of the artistic symbolism was making one feature of an animal a key to its identification. The beaver was characterized by its incisor teeth and tail, while the killer whale was keyed to its prominent dorsal fin. So it was also with the other totemic representations. Prominent and recurring symbols incorporated in figure representations included the skeletal motif, the use of joint markers, and the prominence of stylized eyes. The Tlingit craftsmen employing these motifs produced some of the outstanding art works of primitive men.

The most important item manufactured by men for subsistence activities was the canoe used for fishing and coastal voyages. Normally a canoe was constructed during the winter months when unhurried skill led to the production of attractive and sound vessels. The largest canoes were constructed by the southern Tlingit, since great cedar trees did not grow in the northern area. Likewise large canoes were purchased from the Haida to the south. The best wood for a canoe was from a live, straight-grained red cedar which was felled by building a fire at the base. A tree which had been blown over by the wind might be utilized, however. With an adz whose head was made from ground stone the log was hewn and scraped. In order to spread the sides of the hollowed log the cavity was filled with water, and hot stones were dropped in the water. Then pieces of wood were wedged across the gunwales, and as the log softened, the sides were spread and wider pieces of wood inserted until the desired degree of flare was achieved. The height of the sides was sometimes increased by fitting planks above the sides, and the sides of a vessel might be painted with designs and the bow carved. A small canoe carried two or three persons, whereas a large one held some sixty persons and was forty-five feet in length. The canoes were propelled with paddles, with one extra long paddle used for steering. When not in use, canoes were protected from the direct sunlight by placing mats or blankets over them and by sprinkling water over the side. A smaller variety of canoe, made from a cottonwood log, was used for fishing and traveling along rivers.

Snowshoes were essential for winter travel, especially for the Chilkat who traded with the inland peoples during the winter. The light maple or birch wood frames were heated over a fire and shaped; the netting was made from rawhide thongs. The shoes were about four feet in length and ten inches wide at their broadest point, with rounded toes which turned up at the front and pointed heels.

The subsistence cycle reached an ebb during the winter months, and even March did not yet provide reliable weather for fishing. Nonetheless, it was during March that the subsistence year began anew. The canoes were prepared, the fishing gear was readied, and the men waited anxiously. When calm weather arrived, they fished for halibut in March and April along the coast fronting the Pacific Ocean. They employed a distinctive form of V-shaped hook which had a tine along the inner side of one prong of the V; on this was baited a piece of fish. The hook was lowered on a long, stone-weighted rope, while on the surface a wooden floater bobbed when the bait was taken. Two men fishing from a canoe maintained about fifteen of these lines, and when a fish was hooked, they paddled to the bobbing floater, raised the line, and clubbed the fish to death as it was boated. Fishing for trout at this time of the year likewise was important. Several wooden, shanked hooks with bone barbs baited with clam meat or pieces of fish were attached at intervals along a main rope which was anchored at both ends with stones. A second rope was attached to the first and to an inflated seal's bladder, which floated on the surface to mark the spot where the anchored lines had been lowered. The lines were checked after about half a day, and the hooked fish were killed with a club. Following the ice breakup in March and during the following month, the women fished with gill nets from canoes; one woman usually paddled and a second handled the drifting net. The nets were made from rawhide or cedar bark rope, inflated bladders being used as floaters and stones as sinkers. Various species of trout were taken in the gill nets. Clams and mussels were collected in large quantities and were either dried and smoked for future use or else were steamed in a pit by pouring water over hot stones and leaves. The pelts of fur animals were in excellent condition in March, and wolf, fox, mink, and land and sea otter all were sought. Some of these animals were killed in deadfalls, but sea otter were hunted with darts, marmots dug from their holes, rabbits snared, and porcupines clubbed to death.

Spring came in April or May, and at this time the plants grew exuberantly. For a brief period in late February and again in late

April candlefish ascended many of the rivers. They were taken with hooks, traps, and dip nets and were dumped into a canoe which was half-buried in the sand. Stones were heated in a fire, water added to the load of fish, and the stones dropped into the mass of fish. After the stones cooled, they were reheated, and as the oil from the cooked fish came to the surface of the water, it was skimmed off and ladled into wooden containers. The primary use of the oil was with dried salmon, but it was served also with berries or drunk during feasts. In mid-April herring swarmed into the shallow bays to spawn and were so numerous that they could be impaled on sharp tines set in the side of a pole. The pole was drawn back and forth in the water, and the pierced herring were then shaken off into a canoe. They were either eaten soon after being caught or strung on ropes to dry for later consumption.

Trading ventures were a means of obtaining locally unavailable products or those that were at least scarce in the region. During the late prehistoric period iron was the most desired trade item, and it was traded into the area from across Bering Strait. In historical documents it has been recorded that in the summer Tlingit men traveled among the interior Athapaskan Indians taking fish oil as their most important item of trade. It was during the summers too that great canoes were paddled to the Haida and Tsimshian country, with Chilkat blankets being an important trade item. In early historic times the Tlingit are known to have traveled as far as the Puget Sound area of Washington state. Their travels were for diverse purposes, but in each instance the party was organized by a house group under the direction of its leader, the Keeper of the House. From the interior Athapaskan tribes they received caribou skins and sinew as well as lichens for a particular type of dye. Dentalia, haliotis, and shark teeth came from the south, copper from the Copper River to the north, and slaves occasionally from the north but more commonly from the south. The most important trade route seems to have been the one leading into the interior, and it was controlled jealously by the Chilkat.

In the late summer berries were collected and stored with candle-fish oil in airtight boxes. Salmon eggs, oil, and berries were similarly mixed and preserved. If large land mammals were killed, their flesh usually was cut into strips and sun-dried or else boiled and stored in oil. Some foods were stored for winter at this time of the year, but it was not until September that the winter food supply became a major concern. Diverse species of salmon were taken during the summer, but no great effort was made to catch and dry quantities of them until September. The species of salmon found in the Tlingit area included the coho (silver), dog, humpback, king, and sockeye, which were taken from July through December. The principal device for taking salmon was a funnel-shaped fish trap set with the mouth of the trap opening downstream. The stream was blocked with a weir, which opened only at the trap. A secondary method was to strike the salmon with a harpoon dart head which was wedged in the end of a wooden shaft. After the fish was struck, the dart head detached itself except for its leather thong fastening to the shaft. Fish were cleaned with a semilunar knife which had a slate blade. The heads, tails, and internal organs were removed; the fish were then hung on a drying rack with the flesh side up. They were covered during damp weather or smoke-cured in the house, and after being dried, they were bundled and stored. As soon as a house group had gathered enough dried salmon for the winter, the members returned from their fishing camp to their village where they settled down for the winter. Very little food was gathered throughout the winter months, for this was the season of feasting, storytelling, and leisure which did not end until April. Sometimes in the winter people fished through the ice of the rivers for flounder. A fisherman cut a hole in the ice and squatted over the hole with a blanket covering his head and a long-handled fish spear (leister) poised above the hole. As a flounder swam along, it could be seen beneath the water and was impaled on the prongs of the spear. Fishing for flounder was only to provide for immediate needs.

In the hunting of sea mammals the harpoon dart was the most important weapon. It consisted of a shaft at the end of which was fitted a barbed dart head. This head was of bone or antler, with a wedge-shaped tang and a line hole near the base. Only the northern Tlingit at Yakutat hunted great whales, and they seem to have done so under stimulus from their Eskimo neighbors to the north. Among the sea mammals taken by the Tlingit as a whole were the seal, sea lion, dolphin, and above all else the sea otter, particularly in historic times. From the ethnographic accounts it would seem that sea mammal hunting was not very important; neither does it appear that inland hunting was important for most *kons*. When they did pursue bears or mountain goats, these animals were cornered with the aid of dogs and killed with bone-pointed spears.

The people of each of the *kons* were divided into moieties, and these were represented in each of the geographical areas. The moieties were the Raven and Wolf, with the Wolf moiety termed Eagle in the north; these were in turn divided into named sibs. The Tlingit considered that there were certain personality characteristics associated with the members of the moieties. Raven people were expected to be wise and cautious, but the Wolves were quick-tempered and warlike. According to Oberg, the Raven moiety in the recent past consisted of twenty-seven matrisibs, all using the raven on their crests. The Wolves had no similar identity in their crest designations but derived their crest symbols from the diverse experiences of sib ancestors. According to Aurel Krause the Raven sibs included the Raven, Frog, Goose, Sea Lion, *Uhu,* and Salmon. In the Wolf moiety were the Wolf, Bear, Eagle, Whale, Shark, and *Alk* sibs; his list is not complete, however. A person not regarded as in any of the sibs was referred to as a stranger and was addressed as uncle or son-in-law, reflecting his in-marrying status. At Klukwan the most important sibs were the Wolf and Eagle. These sibs were divided into named subgroups which probably were lineages. Within each sib the leading lineage was the one with the greatest amount of wealth. Ideally the leadership of a lineage was passed from a man to his sister's son, but apparently this practice could be bypassed by appointing a new chief to replace an old one. Each settlement with a number of sibs would have more than one chief, but one would emerge as dominant in community affairs by virtue of his wealth and personality. The Raven and Wolf moieties were exogamous and matrilineal. Each member sib of the respective moieties recognized a particular settlement as its ultimate place of origin and was identified initially with a particular geographical area. By the time of historic contact both moieties were represented in most settlements, and a number of different sibs also were likely to be present. If one sib was large in a particular settlement, it was divided into lineages as represented in house groups. In theory, the sibs of each moiety possessed distinctive titles and associated design motifs which only members could use. These might be lent temporarily or even taken over by a more powerful sib. Again in theory, only members of the Raven moiety had the right to the raven design and those of the Wolf moiety, the wolf design. Furthermore, the animal after whom a sib usually took its name or had an association was employed in its sib designs. The clarity of design usage became confused when for example a sib of the Wolf moiety employed a modified raven design but did not take the Raven name for the design. A situation of this nature always had precedent in some mythological, historical, or quasi-historical event. Within each sib house names were derived usually from a myth of the sib, from the sib's name, or by assuming the name of another sib's house for a legendary or historical reason. The names of individuals were taken also from sib names. These were either male or female designations, but a female could acquire a male's name if there were no males to carry it on. What we see are moieties, each divided into a number of matrisibs which in turn were divided into house groups. The sibs in any one locality would be represented by their leading lineages. The house groups were composed of nuclear families, again related through females. Nuclear family unity did not exist because the parents were of different sibs and moieties. The sibs were represented in different geographical areas and would act as a unit only in rare instances of a feud which affected all the sib. The sib had no common leader or unified territory, and even crests commonly were identified with localized lineages rather than with the sib as a whole. Finally, within a sib's membership in a village were persons ranked as nobles, commoners, or slaves, depending on the social standing of their particular lineage.

In the role system of kinship we find that a single term embraced all the older people of the grandparent generation. To these persons Ego was attentive and respectful. The ties between a mother and her son were close even though the son might leave home to live with his mother's elder brother, who was for him the most powerful individual in Tlingit society and his authority figure. Fathers were considered too lenient to discipline their sons effectively, and of course the father did not belong to his son's sib or moiety. Parents especially were concerned about the welfare of a daughter, who would command a large bride-price only if she were properly mannered and a maiden; thus she was watched constantly by someone. A mother's sister was called by a diminutive mother term and was treated as one's mother. The "little mother" term was extended to all the women of her moiety in her generation. A mother's sister aided and advised her sister's children. A father's sister was termed differently from mother and mother's sister, with the father's sister word extended to all women of her moiety in her generation and the next descending generation. The father term was unique, but a diminutive word for father was employed for father's brother and again extended to the men of his moiety and generation as well as those men of his moiey in the next lower generation. A man treated his father's brother with respect, and a girl on rare occasion married her father's brother. A man ideally would marry his father's sister, and because she was a potential mate, their relationship was always warm. At one's own generational level a man distinguished between older and younger brothers, terms which were extended to men of one's generation and moiety. Older and younger male sibling distinctions were highly important because an older brother had the first rights of inheritance, greater authority, and more ceremonial responsibilities. A woman made the same distinction among sisters. There was a single term for a man's sister and one for a woman's brother, which was extended to all the members of that sex of Ego's generation and moiety. Brothers were socially and physically close since they were of the same sib and lived in the same house; with a sister a man must be distant and withdrawn, although he was concerned for her welfare. A mother's sister's children were termed as brother and sister, and the boys were raised in the same household as Ego. Father's sister's children normally were called by descriptive terms. The terminology for the first ascending generation was essentially bifurcate merging, and the cousin terminology was of the Crow type. The average Tlingit adult avoided using relationship terms in direct address in everyday conversation for fear of offending someone since there was a great deal of emphasis on an exact ranking of individuals. Thus nicknames and given names were in common usage. Relationship terms were, however, commonly employed on ceremonial occasions.

The most important social and economic unit was the Tlingit household, which had a significant place in the ceremonial life of the sib and moiety. A house group ideally was composed of Ego and his brothers, as well as his mother's sister's sons who were classificatory brothers, and the sons of the sisters of these individuals, plus the sons of the daughters of these sisters. All were members of a matrilineage, and there were additionally the in-marrying spouses in the household; if a girl married her father's sister's son, she too remained in the house of her birth. It was a household of this nature which operated as an economic unit, with the respective members working toward their common welfare. In particular it was brothers, led by the eldest, the Keeper of the House, who aided one another in feuds, potlatches, and other matters of house group concern. The importance of the Keeper of the House in directing house group life cannot be overestimated. He was an individual with very real power and authority. He directed the economic activities of household members and was deferred to by the other men in his residence unit. The house group leader was given choice foods, he allotted items obtained in trade, and was freed from any humble form of household labor. It was this man, the eldest brother, who slept behind the heraldic screen in a house and represented the household in ceremonial activities as well as in sib councils. Furthermore, when he died the rights to his position fell to the next oldest brother, either biological or classificatory. In addition to the position of Keeper of the House was the designation Rich Man. He was the wealthiest of the local household heads in his sib, and thus the ranking Keeper of the House. These men more than any others were responsible for the fortunes of their sib units.

The extensive ceremonial life centered on crucial events in the life cycle of individuals and happenings of important sib or community concern. Thus, birth and death, successful raids, the completion of a new house, or settling disputes required ceremonial acknowledgment. The duration of a ceremony depended on its importance; it might last for one night, several days, or as long as the host's food supply remained. The ceremonies as a whole included feasting, songs and dances, and the presentation of gifts to the honored guests. The most elaborate ceremonies were held in association with the death of an important individual. There was first the cremation ceremony shortly after the death; later there might be an anniversary feast which honored the dead and established the social position of his successor. The redistribution ceremonies or potlatches of the Northwest Coast Indians are famous, but detailed descriptions of them are rare. The key to Tlingit ceremonial involvement was the emphasis on reciprocity. Whenever a child's ears or lip were pierced, a person initiated into a secret society (a recent Tlingit ritual complex), or the dead buried, it was someone of the opposite moiety who was responsible for the task. Such labor was rewarded during a redistribution of property. In the associated rituals the host and his most important helping relatives were seated in a sib house along the rear wall. Lesser helpers sat along the wall where the entrance was located, while guests were seated along the sidewalls. Guests were fed and entertained with songs and dances; the guests in turn sang and danced. The hosts and guests alike were keenly alert to any affront in the words of their opponents or to notice a mistake in the dances or songs of their opposites. Offenses were grounds for property claims, or if breaches of etiquette were flagrant, fights would take place. The songs and dances conveyed meanings associated with the totemic group of the performing sib, but other potlatch songs were composed in memory of the dead. Box-shaped wooden drums and tambourine drums were used to accompany the performers, and clappers and wooden rattles were used also. The Tlingit seemed particularly prone to borrow songs, dances, and costumes from adjacent peoples.

In every important ceremonial activity the persons in a house group turned to the opposite moiety to fulfill the ritualistic obligations. In theory, it was one's brothers-in-law who performed the task, whether it was to bury the dead, erect a totem pole, build a house, or perform any other major ritual. The house group accumulated food and resources in order to compensate for the ceremonial labor performed, and it might take a year or longer before the ceremonial hosts were ready to initiate a project. The work of house building, for example, was under the direction of the Keeper of the House. He had his sons and the brothers of the wives in his house to form the major segment of the labor force. The builders were fed and entertained, and when the house was completed, the builders were publicly honored at a potlatch, each man receiving gifts according to his standing and the labor he contributed.

The institutionalized redistribution of goods played an important part in the economic lives of the Tlingit. Exchanges or gifts linked the various interdependent units of the society in diverse ways. Kalvero Oberg distinguished, as did the Tlingit, numerous forms of exchanges, beginning with barter, then gift exchange, food gifts, feasts, the ceremonial exchange of labor, and finally, ceremonial gifts or potlatches. It was through barter that one, a man or woman, acquired a needed item, with each person involved attempting to gain the advantage and tending to ignore any other factors. In the gift exchange those items manufactured by individuals were exchanged for products he or she did not produce well. Such exchanges were made by individuals even within the same house group. The protocol was to work through an intermediary, giving him a gift to carry to the craftsman and to make the request. When a major item was desired, such as a canoe, a number of gifts would be offered to the craftsman at intervals. If the gifts offered did not measure up to the product sought, the craftsman produced an inferior object. Gifts of food, particularly to members of other house groups in the same sib, were offered when a particular house group had an abundance of a product. There was no great concern to equalize such gifts rigidly, although the gifts should in time balance one another. Feasts were given on private occasions, particularly by a house group when success in hunting, fishing, or trading had been inordinate. Near relatives were invited, and the food not consumed was taken home by the guests. As mentioned elsewhere, the moiety exchange of labor was a socially integrating and economically significant force in Tlingit life. Ceremonial labor was involved in the construction of a house, the manufacture and erection of a totem pole, handling the dead and their interment as well as at other times in the life cycle of the individual. With the exchange of such labor went feasting and the exchange of gifts which were secondary to the primary obligation. These gifts, being of a ceremonial or potlatch nature, had as their purpose the giving and acquiring of property. The most important potlatch goods were slaves, who were killed or more often freed. Second, plates of native copper pounded into shield-like forms were a means of concentrating wealth, and these coppers were exchanged intact, cut into sections as mementos to guests, or thrown into the sea as an ultimate means of validating one's wealth. Finally, blankets, which were not really blankets at all but ceremonial robes, were given as gifts or torn into sections and distributed to guests to commemorate a potlatch. Items offered in a potlatch were borrowed by the house group within its sib, manufactured by the house group, and sometimes borrowed from other sibs in the same moiety. There was the constant effort to give greater potlatches than one's rivals, and as a result emphasis was placed on the production and accumulation of these goods.

The description of a potlatch held in connection with the erection of a new house was recorded by John R. Swanton, and it deserves presentation in summary form since such descriptions of Tlingit ceremonies are rare. This potlatch, which must have occurred around the turn of the present century, probably reflects the aboriginal pattern. In this instance the Raven people of Klukwan, an important Chilkat settlement, were to host the Wolves of Sitka. A Raven house builder and a secondary host at Klukwan sent the former's wife and her friends to Sitka to extend the invitation. She arrived with the others and distributed leaf tobacco, fed the people, and told of her mission. To reciprocate for the invitation, the potential guests danced for the visitors and displayed their crests to demonstrate their respect for those extending the invitation. The following day the woman and those accompanying her again feasted the people, and again the guests danced in return. The following morning the wife of the Klukwan Raven threw a piece of charcoal outside as a sign that her people should give property to her. The reason for the request was that the Wolves at Klukwan had helped build her husband's house but that the Sitka Wolves had not; therefore they were obligated to pay and the woman was sent since she was a Wolf. They gave her $1000 worth of property, but she asked for more since her husband was wealthy. She was given a total of more than $2000 worth of property. After the Wolves of Sitka had prepared all their ceremonial equipment they set off in boats for Klukwan, followed by the woman and her friends. The four dance leaders of the guest party practiced their dances when they camped. These leaders made preparations as though they were going off on a raid by abstaining from women, fasting, and making medicine. As the guests paddled along in their canoes, they rushed at each other as though they were attacking. These preparations indicated that there was to be a dance contest. In addition, while they moved north they plundered towns for provisions, for they were so powerful that no one dared stop them.

When they reached the vicinity of the host village, the hostess had them camp so that she could prepare a final meal. A nearby village chief also feasted them, distributing twenty boxes of candlefish oil; the guests then danced to show their respect. The hosts came to meet their guests before the latter arrived and made them presents of candlefish oil, berries, and firewood. They brought crest objects along with the gifts and left them overnight to demonstrate their trust of the guests. When the guests arrived at Klukwan, one of the hosts met them with bow and arrows, pretending to release an arrow. This gesture was to show how brave the host was in the face of the fact that he would be distributing a great deal of wealth. The second host, the one whose wife extended the invitation, then received the guests, and everyone crowded into one house to dance. The guests, the Sitka Wolves, danced first to the accompaniment of a Tsimshian song, after which the Klukwan Eagles danced. Somewhat later the guests were feasted, the main dish being roasted salmon, a favorite dish of the deceased chief in whose honor the potlatch was being held. Another dance was held, followed by a greater feast, and still another dance was given by the guests, competitive with that of the hosts. A Sitka song leader insulted his hosts by implying that he knew all songs and that his hosts or opposites were worthless. A Klukwan man then asked his wife for a knife; only the presence of the crests sitting in the open and the distraction of a Raven man's calling like a raven prevented a fight. After this performance food was brought, and a huge platter was set before two men who were guests. They were expected to eat it all but could not quite finish the meal, and the Klukwan people mocked them. Then all of the guests ate, using horn spoons belonging to the dead chief of the Klukwan Ravens, and after they finished the hosts had their meal.

The following morning the Sitka people discussed with those from Klukwan the reburial of the chief's remains and the erection of a grave monument. The guests reburied the bones and erected a carved monument. This was the real reason they had been summoned. The following morning the hosts instructed the women of their sib to dress in their ceremonial clothing, which indicated that the hosts were pleased. When the guests entered the house where they were being entertained, they were asked to sit at the back of the house on mats previously used by the hosts' sib relatives. The guests were served the best of foods, and the host whose wife had extended the invitation doubled the amount of property she had received and presented it to his guests. As the property was being brought out, the guests were paid to dance and sing, with the most important persons receiving as much as $200 for dancing. It required four days to give out all of the blankets. The host who had sent his wife to Sitka wore a hat which had been used by his uncles and grandmothers; by wearing it, along with distributing so much property, he established his social position as the Raven chief at Klukwan. The two hosts distributed about $11,000 worth of property in addition to those items distributed by other members of their sib. There was a final feast, and then the guests "left a dance" as a gesture of respect for their hosts. There was a song contest at the end of the potlatch to see who knew the most songs, and finally, after it was over, the overloaded canoes of the guests, the Sitka Wolves, departed for home.

The pageantry of Tlingit ritual performances brought drama into their ceremonies. The drums, either box or tambourine, served for background music along with wooden rattles on certain occasions. The ritual dramatizations were derived from the mythology and accompanied by chants as well as songs. In a house with the audience crowded along the walls the performances took place around the central fireplace. The performers were garbed in their finest apparel, and the typical dance step was to a two-four beat of the drums. The steps of the dancers were repetitive, with the greatest variations in tense movements of the shoulders, trunk, legs, and arms.

Much, if not most, Tlingit aggression was channeled through ceremonial competition, but this at times ranged out of hand when a party felt that it had been insulted. In instances of physical injuries from a member of another sib or from anyone of the opposite moiety, there was the necessity of a settlement. The cohesion between the moieties was not a binding force, and conflicts between them were common. The modern Tlingit likened the moieties to European nations in their battles with each other. The settlement of a dispute, in terms of material goods or a life, was essential for any offense. The amount of the settlement was contingent on the abilities of the guilty to pay as well as the power of the offended to collect. Any minor conflict was settled eventually at a feast which included a property settlement. When a person was grievously offended, one course open to him was to murder the offender. If this was accomplished, there was bound to be a second murder in retaliation. However, if the persons killed were of unequal rank, there was the further problem of establishing the value of each death, which led to additional complications. Sometimes when an individual felt that he had been done an injustice and had no means to right the wrong, he committed suicide. The offender was regarded by the relatives of the deceased as his murderer, and compensation still was necessary. Upon occasion disagreements between sibs were settled by a duel between representative warriors from each group. Murders were from ambush, and the same was true of campaigns against other tribes or sibs. The only crimes within a sib were incest and witchcraft, both of which were punished by death. It should be stressed again that there was no overall unity within a moiety, for some of the bloodiest and most bitter feuds took place between sibs of the same moiety.

Conditioning a warrior for combat included bathing in the sea, even at the coldest time of the year, and being whipped by an older man to demonstrate one's courage. The two most important reasons for conducting a raid were to avenge a death and to obtain slaves. The actual preparations for warfare involved abstaining from all contact with women and fasting. As the party traveled, it seized property from camps along the way irrespective of whether the residents were friendly or not. A shaman always accompanied the party and predicted events of the near future. Plans for an attack on an enemy community were kept as secret as possible, and the foray was launched at dawn. Rod or skin armor protected a man's body, his face was covered with a mask, and a wooden helmet protected his head. All the enemy men who could not flee were killed with daggers, and the women and children were taken as prisoners. Then a reprisal attack would be expected to avenge the murders. The copper-bladed dagger, a spear which was thrown, and possibly a war club, appear to have been the most important weapons. Scalps were taken at times, and the scalped person's head sometimes was impaled on a stick and exhibited. The men in a war party returning home sang of victory as they approached their village, and the paddle of each man killed among the raiders was stuck up at the spot he had occupied in the boat. Finally, in order to bind a peace settlement hostages might be exchanged and kept for a year or longer. Peacemaking required a set pattern of ceremonialism, which climaxed with the exchange of hostages, termed "deer," since deer are peaceful and the hostages should follow their behavior.

Most of the slaves held by the people were persons captured in raids or purchased from peoples to the north or south. Others were the children of indebted men who could find no way out of their dilemma except to give themselves and as many of their children as necessary to the ones to whom they were indebted. There was for these persons, in contrast with captives, the possibility that they might be redeemed. There appears to have been considerable variability in the manner in which slaves were treated. They seem in general to have been well cared for by their masters since they were a valuable form of property. Yet there are some reports which picture the lot of slaves as extremely difficult since they had to perform all the odious tasks and might at any time be killed at their owner's fancy. At times slaves were killed on purpose in order to enhance the importance of a man. They might be killed when their owner built a new house, or in order to gain prestige one man would kill a number of slaves and his rival would be obligated to kill a greater number, and so it went until one had no slaves remaining. It would appear that the owner-ship of slaves was more important in the prestige system than any economic gain from the services of a slave. The proportion of slaves to free persons is not known, but it is recorded that ten slaves in a house was a large number.

In the supernatural order Tlingit shamans were judged by Swanton to have more power than the shamans elsewhere along the coast of the north Pacific Ocean. The power of a shaman was con-tained in the spirits he controlled, and these were passed from a man to his sister's son, or to his own son on rare occasions when there was no one of his own sib to receive the position. The normal man-ner in which a sib acquired a new shaman was for the spirit of a recently deceased shaman of the sib to enter the body of an upstand-ing youth of the sib; he was then acclaimed by the people as the successor. This seems to have happened at the time of the shaman's death. Nephews who aspired to be the next shaman went into trances around the dead man's body, and the individual who remained in a trance the longest was most likely to be named the successor. After this supernatural visitation the novice, accompanied by some near relatives, went into the forest. Each of them ate little and searched for a sign, the most propitious being to see a bird or an animal drop dead. It was the spirit of this creature which henceforth would aid the tyro. After the young man had proved he had his uncle's power, he would inherit the ceremonial equipment.

Shamans controlled various spirits, and these were represented on their masks. Most spirits served specific sibs, but there were others of importance which could come under the power of any shaman. The latter category included a spirit associated with the souls of per-sons who were lost at sea or who died alone in the forest, as well as another one which was a messenger for the shamans. On a mask the primary protecting spirit was represented as the main figure, but help-ing spirits also might be on the mask. Thus a helping spirit might be posed around the eyes of the mask, and this increased the vision of the primary spirit. Distinctive characteristics of a shaman were that he neither cut nor combed his hair, and about his neck he wore a bone necklace and a small whetstone, the latter being used to scratch his head. Upon instructions from a spirit, small bones were inserted through the holes in his nasal septum. A shaman owned rattles which had spirit associations and were used in his performances. Among his charms were the split tongues of animals, especially the land otter, and claws of eagles which were sources of power. The split tongues, and probably the claws as well, were placed in bundles of cedar bark, grass, and devil's club. After a shaman bathed he rubbed himself with this bundle. Likewise, the bundle was used in all his rituals. Among the spirit helpers were spirits of the land otter, the sun and the sea, and the crest animals of the shaman's sib (see note 2). After summoning his spirit helpers, a shaman cured an afflicted individual by blowing, sucking, or passing an object over the locus of the affliction, which drew out the cause of the illness. A shaman and his family usually lived in a separate village residence, and in the forest near the house was his shrine. Shamans from time to time retreated to caves for extended periods in order to intensify their spirit relationships.

Witchcraft most often was performed by obtaining some item intimately associated with the victim and then making a representation of the victim in the specific form that the witch desired to make him. When a person was ill, the cause was attributed to witchcraft, and the offender was named by the curing shaman. Persons accused of being witches usually were either women, children, or slaves. They were tortured to extract a confession or even killed before a confession was forthcoming. An accused witch was tied up by members of his sib and refused food and water for eight days or even longer. If he refused to confess, it was expected that he would die; when a witch did confess, the bewitching substance was scattered in the sea. Other services of the shaman, apart from those mentioned already, were to locate food sources, to predict the future, or simply to demonstrate his power.

A number of charms and their uses have been recorded by Swanton, and these appear to have been employed by ordinary persons. They were made from parts of plants and used in such diverse activities as foreseeing the future, attracting a woman, making one wealthy, or improving hunting ability. A few additional items seem to have been secular cures, but these were rare and apparently unimportant. In general, it would appear that curing and supernaturalism were shamanistic matters. At the same time, it is apparent too that salmon, which were the all-important subsistence item, were not dealt with in a sacred manner. They simply were accepted as present and were caught and utilized. Even in the mythology salmon play a relatively unimportant role; again they seem to have been regarded as a constant part of the environment.

Names of the months of the year varied with the locality, and one record begins the year with the August moon. The Chilkat appear to have numbered the thirteen lunar months, but at Sitka the months were named, except for two which were numbered. When named, the designations referred to seasonal changes in the environment. Knowledge about the natural world was crystalized and integrated into a loosely ordered system. Directions were thought of as upriver, which was to the north, and downriver, meaning to the south. The world was thought of as a flat expanse with the sky as a dome above the earth. In all this space everything that existed was alive: on the sun and moon lived spirits; stars were the lights of distant towns or houses; clusters of stars sometimes were named, and Venus was identified. A rainbow was the path of dead souls to the upper world, and the northern lights were dead spirits playing. Everything on earth was possessed by a spirit quality, which had subordinates or helpers; each trait, every fire, and everything that one did had its main spirit and helpers.

Childbearing within the mother's own home was prohibited because it would have brought ill fortune to the men of the house. Thus a birth took place in a shelter built against the side of a house or nearby, to which men never went. In the birth process slaves and a midwife, always a member of the opposite moiety and preferably the woman's husband's sister, aided the woman. In the structure a pit was dug and lined with moss, and a stake was driven into the center of the hole. While giving birth, the woman squatted in the pit holding the stake. After the birth the umbilical cord of the offspring was cut and placed in a bag which hung about the neonate's neck for eight days. The mother was restricted to her shelter for a period of time recorded by different observers as five, ten or thirty days. To prevent a baby from crying repeatedly, the first cry was caught in a container and apparently buried where many people walked so that it was smothered as the baby grew. The baby was wrapped in skins, with moss for a diaper, and was tied to a board. The mother carried the cradleboard with her or hung it from a roof beam when she was in the house. Among the customs followed in child rearing was to place the umbilical cord of a boy under a tree where an eagle had nested; this was to make him brave when he became an adult. Likewise, a mother placed woodworm burrowings on her nipples so that as the baby nursed it would receive the burrowings as well as the milk and be neat in later life. A child was nursed for three or four years, and the first solids were fed to the infant after about a year. Were an infant born to a woman without a husband it normally was suffocated.

A baby was named for a maternal ancestor, the name taken from an animal associated with the sib. Later in life a child could acquire a name from its father's sib, if a potlatch was held for the event. A man who gave his son a second name soon after its birth obligated the offspring to give great potlatches. With the birth of a son the parents then referred to themselves by the son's name, as the father of or the mother of, whatever the son's name was. This is the practice of teknonymy. A family that possessed great wealth and wanted its children to have the greatest amount of prestige freed as many slaves as they had children and built a new house. Property was distributed to all those who aided in the construction, and the ceremonial climax occurred when the children had their earlobes pierced by a woman who would then receive many gifts. Such children were termed "of the nobility," and their descendants were referred to similarly. In early childhood children were encouraged to behave in a manner appropriate to adults of their sex. They were taught to restrain any emotion and to remain dignified and aloof. Physical punishment of children occurred only if they refused to bathe in cold water in the winter; they were expected to take cold baths daily from the time they learned to walk. When boys moved to the household of their mother's brother, they were switched by this man after bathing and were made to run up and down the beach until their uncle was satisfied with the amount of exercise they had had. After this physical exertion, they were instructed by the older men in the customs and history of the sib and were taught certain skills by watching men perform routine tasks. As a boy grew, he came under the direct influence of his maternal uncle and performed tasks for this older man rather than for his father. A boy tended to gravitate toward a particular uncle whom he wished to emulate in his particular skills such as carving, hunting, or those relative to the supernatural. The uncle gave honorific names to his young charges and taught them the lore of their sib, but there were no secret initiations. The most important nephew was the oldest, for he would inherit from his maternal uncle not only material property and wives but titles as well. Even while young, boys were free to use a maternal uncle's tools without permission. If a mother died, the father was obliged to place the off-spring in the custody of the mother's siblings.

When a girl menstruated for the first time, she was confined to a brush-covered shelter or a separate compartment in the house behind the heraldic screen, and her face was covered with charcoal. A high-born Tlingit girl was isolated for an entire year, and girls of lesser standing were isolated for at least three months. A girl was attended by near female relatives as well as by a slave; additionally, she was obliged to drink water through a bird bone tube. She left the compartment only at night, and she wore a broad-brimmed hat so she would not taint the stars with her gaze. During this isolation she was instructed by her mother concerning sib myths, songs, and the behavior considered proper for a woman. It was at the beginning of her isolation that her lip, nasal septum, and perhaps her earlobes were pierced by a woman of the opposite moiety. When she came out of seclusion, she was given new clothing; if her family was wealthy, the slave attending her during the period of isolation was freed. It was expected that the girl would marry soon, and she must remain chaste until then. In order to make certain that she did not have sexual intercourse, she was made to sleep on a shelf above the bed of her parents before she married. The rank of a person was reckoned through both sides of the family and depended largely on the amount of the bride-price paid by one's father for one's mother; thus it behooved the parents to provide a daughter with all the desirable advantages of careful rearing and wealth.

In marital arrangements there was strict moiety exogamy. A match was initiated by the suitor, who enlisted the aid of a go-between to broach the subject with the girl's family and with the girl. If favorably received, he sent presents to his future father-in-law. The most desirable marriage partners, in decreasing order, were a father's sister, brother's daughter, father's sister's daughter, and finally mother's brother's daughter. In the ideal form of marriage with a father's sister, the groom assumed the role of his mother's brother. However, the most common type of marriage was with a father's sister's daughter, and this was preferred by a young man. These close marriages served two important functions: keeping the wealth concentrated, and providing mates of nearly equal rank.

A wedding ceremony took place in the house of the bride, the man's relatives assembling as the future husband sat in the middle of the floor dressed in his most elaborate ceremonial garb. The bride was hidden in a corner of the house and was lured to sit beside the groom by the singing and dancing of the assembled group. The guests feasted while the couple fasted for two days. Then the bride and groom ate, after which they fasted for another two-day interval. It was only after a month, however, that they were considered married. A wealthy groom gave a potlatch for the girl's family, and marriage residence was either with his or with her family. If the couple moved into a man's household, the bride's relatives presented the man with property equal to or exceeding the value of what his relatives had presented to them. Polygyny was practiced by wealthy men, and a first wife held a rank superior to that of any subsequent spouses; five wives seem to be the most a man had. Polyandry sometimes occurred but only if the second husband was a brother or other close relative of the first husband. The levirate was customary, and if the deceased husband did not have a brother, his sister's son married the widow. If neither category of individual was available, a widow could marry any man of her former husband's sib. If his mother's brother died, a man was obligated to marry the widow even though he might already have a wife, and he inherited his uncle's wealth. In spite of the ideal that a man live in the house of his mother's brother, inherit his wealth, and marry his daughter or another person in this line, his father's sib attempted to lure him into its domain. This especially seems to have been true for a boy who had married outside his home community. When a married woman was seduced and blood revenge was not exacted by her husband, the seducer was obligated to make a property settlement. If the seduction was by a near relative of the husband, the offender was expected to become the woman's second husband.

An important pastime among adult males was gambling, and some men were so addicted that they sometimes lost prized possessions and even a wife. The most important form of gambling was a hand game in which one uniquely marked stick was put in the midst of three others. These three were selected from as many as one hundred and eighty sticks, at least some of which were named. The four sticks were separated into two bundles, each surrounded by shredded cedar bark and placed by the dealer before the guesser opposite him. A successful guess was made when the marked stick was in the bundle selected, and then the guesser manipulated the bundle. For each incorrect guess of an opponent a counter was won. After ten or eighteen counters were won, depending on the variation of the game being played, the bundle was divided into three sections. The opponent then was to find the marked stick in two out of three guesses, and if he failed, he lost the game. A variation of this game was to hold little round pieces of wood in the hands and shift them rapidly back and forth until the opponent called for a guess. Then the manipulator held out his hands, and his opposite guessed which contained the key piece. A correct guess won a counter, and one was lost with an incorrect guess. The game was played by teams, but only one man of each team handled the sticks at any one time. When the opposite team's counters were all won, and the number of counters is not specified, the stake was won. Other adult diversions included the dice games and a ball game where the purpose was to drive a ball along the tidal flats to the opponent's goal. Boys played a game which involved throwing a stick at a rolling wad of grass. They also wrestled, hunted, and swam for entertainment. A favorite diversion among little girls was to arrange beach pebbles in the form of figures.

Physicians of the Russian-American Company at Sitka in 1843–1844 described the people as follows (Romanowsky and Frankenhauser, 1962, 35): "The Kolosches are proud, egoistic, revengeful, spiteful, false, intriguing, avaricious, love above all independence and do not submit to force, except the ruling of their elders." To outsiders the Tlingit were not likable. Still adults were patient and persistent; they never seem to have hurried; and they angered only with provocation. During the fishing season they worked long hours, but during the winter there was time for leisure. At this time the women made their famous robes and baskets; in general, women appear to have had less free time than the men. The social position and respect that a woman commanded depended on her personality and standing within her sib; a woman with abilities was listened to by the men. Women had well-defined rights and relatives who were willing to come to their aid in case of any injustice from the husband's side of the family. An individual, whether male or female, was expected to behave in accord with his rank in the sib system. Persons were of higher rank if their sib was large, wealthy, and powerful. Still, not all such persons were noble in their behavior, in which case they were treated by others as though they belonged to a lesser sib. Were a person from a high-ranking sib to behave coarsely in the eyes of his fellow sib members he might be killed by them.

As soon as an individual died, the relatives began to wail, and the body was placed in a sitting position at the back of the house, in the place of honor. Along the rear wall of the house were arranged the greatest treasures of the household. For four days or longer the body remained here. Each night songs were sung, and guests of the opposite moiety were feasted and presented with gifts before the funeral was completed. The near relatives of the deceased singed their hair and blackened their faces during the ceremonies. Toward the end of these observances the body was dressed in fine clothing and then taken from the house through a hole made by removing a plank from a wall. A dog was thrown through the opening, and this gesture had the supernatural implication of driving evil from the dwelling. The body was carried to a funeral pyre at the rear of the house site and was placed in the middle of heavy logs. A eulogy was delivered and oil poured over the pyre. Slaves might be killed and placed on the pyre of a wealthy man. The fire was lit, but the mourners left before the body was burned completely. Later, women returned and took some of the bones from the ashes, wrapped them, and placed them in a small box. The mortuary box was placed on top of a post, which was sometimes adorned with carved figures or paintings. An alternative was to place the ashes in a grave house resting on the ground. After a cremation a death potlatch was held and gifts distributed to persons of the opposite moiety who had participated in the death ceremonies. All of the major duties connected with the interment were performed by members of the opposite moiety. This included preparing the body, ritual wailing, and carving a mortuary or memorial pole.

When a shaman died, his body was placed in a different corner of the house each night of the funeral ceremonies, and the survivors in the house fasted. Burial was on the fifth day, and the shaman was clothed in his best garments. Through his nose was placed a sacred bone which he had used, and another was stuck in his hair. A large basket was placed over his head, and he was buried in a coffin which was raised on four posts and placed on a point of land overlooking the sea. The grave houses of shamans differed from those of ordinary persons by being raised, but all had steep gabled roofs. If the deceased had been wealthy, the house was decorated elaborately. The body of a slave was not cremated or buried, but was thrown into the sea without ceremony. Upon the death of an ordinary person, the period of mourning was one year, and the property of the deceased went to a sister's son. If such an individual did not exist, it was passed to a younger brother; this kept the wealth in the sib of the deceased. If the person's death was not from violence or drowning, his soul traveled along a rainbow to the upper world of the stars, moon, or sun. There existence was in a state of happiness. A world above this upper world was inhabited by the souls of persons killed by violence, but one could enter this realm only if his death had been avenged. There was a world beneath the earth to which went the souls of drowned persons.

Sustained contact between the Russians and Tlingit began when the Russians reestablished themselves at Sitka in 1804. From this time until the end of the Russian era in 1867, the administrative center and trading post at Sitka was virtually the only Russian establishment in southeastern Alaska. For the Indians the most desired item of trade during the earliest period of contact was iron; it was already present in small quantities prior to the arrival of the Russians and other Europeans. Because the Tlingit were keen traders among themselves and with adjacent peoples, and since the Indians were always ready to accumulate material wealth at the expense of someone else, all the foreign traders found them cunning and dangerous hagglers (see Note 3). The fur traders who ventured to deal with the Tlingit were all eager to obtain sea otter skins. Initially, any form of trade goods was accepted, but before very long the Indians were highly selective in the items they would take. Woolen blankets were desired because they traded away their animal pelt clothing. The Tlingit desired firearms and obtained them from sources other than the Russians; standard early trade items included tobacco; vessels of tin, iron, or copper; axes; glassware; and clothing, especially gaudy uniforms. During the span of Russian contact there was never any effective political control over the Tlingit. The Indians governed themselves, and the Russians did their best to keep violence to a minimum in the vicinity of Sitka.

Russian efforts to Christianize the Tlingit never were very successful owing to the strength of the aboriginal religious system dominated by the shamans, the restricted area of Russian penetration, and the scarcity of clergy. The first priest at Sitka arrived in 1816, but not until the coming of Father Veniaminov in 1834 did an energetic program of missionizing begin. Veniaminov did not, however, rush into a campaign to make converts of the Tlingit; by 1860 only about four hundred fifty were Christians. A school was opened for children at Sitka but it was not strikingly effective during the Russian period.

For most primitive peoples the most devastating effect of contact with Europeans has been the exposure to previously unknown diseases. These have reduced populations with terrifying rapidity. In 1834 when Veniaminov went to Sitka, he attempted to persuade the Indians to be vaccinated against smallpox, but they resisted the program. Then in 1835 a smallpox epidemic struck. No Russian died, but half of the Tlingit are estimated to have perished. When the Indians found that their shamans could not cure the disease, they lost faith in these curers and turned to the Russian medical doctor for vaccinations. Europeans introduced syphilis to the area, but in 1843 it was relatively uncommon.

On the eighteenth of October in 1867 the formal transfer of Alaska from Russian to American ownership took place at Sitka. The Tlingit were not permitted in Sitka for the ceremonies, but in order to observe the transfer they watched from canoes in the harbor. With American occupancy fortune seekers of almost every variety arrived, and to the Indians this influx must have offered shocking revelations. The Russian inhabitants had the option of returning to Russia within three years or becoming American citizens; virtually all of them left within a few weeks of the transfer. For ten years civil government did not exist, and the U. S. military garrisons stationed at Sitka, Tongass, and Wrangell were a primary source of trouble rather than a means for supporting order. The Tlingit clashed repeatedly with the military over Indian deaths that were not compensated for, which led to murders and the destruction or threatened destruction of Tlingit settlements. The most important causes of the difficulties were the failure of the military to understand Indian ways, the wholesale smuggling of intoxicants, and the prevalence of stills among the Indians. After the military troops departed, only the U. S. Revenue-Cutter Service vessels and the collector of customs represented legal authority. In 1878 the customs officer at Wrangell stated that within a month he had a thousand complaints from Indians but had no way to deal with them. The difficulty became acute with the influx of miners who wintered that year at Wrangell. In 1880 gold was discovered near the present city of Juneau, which brought more miners and confusion; still it was not until 1884 that a civil government began to function in the more populous areas of Alaska.

The entry of Protestant Christianity into southeastern Alaska came in 1876 when a group of Tsimshian Indians from Fort Simpson, B. C., went to Wrangell to work. These Indians had been converted to the Methodist Church of Canada, and one whose English name was Philip McKay remained at Wrangell after the rest left in the fall and opened a school. In 1877 the Presbyterian missionary Sheldon Jackson made a survey trip to southeastern Alaska. He was accompanied by Mrs. A. R. McFarland, who formerly had been a missionary among Indians of the western United States. Mrs. McFarland remained at Wrangell and took charge of the school, and during the following year she founded a home for girls. Presbyterian missionaries arrived at Sitka in 1878, and a lasting school was opened there in 1880. In the early 1880's additional schools were established in Tlingit territory with the purpose of educating and missionizing the Indians. It is nevertheless primarily from the writings of the Presbyterians and the ethnography by Krause that we are able to piece together the major changes in Tlingit life for the forty years surrounding 1900.

The missionaries found the Tlingit women more amenable to the strictures of Christianity than the men. Since in this matrilineal society the women could be quite influential, working through the women became important. Then too the girls attended school more regularly than the boys and became interpreters more frequently than the men, which gave them a certain amount of power and prestige. Certain Biblical messages which the missionaries considered as important could be accepted readily by the Tlingit. For example, the sacrifice of Jesus Christ for the sins of mankind was fully comprehensible in terms of compensation (see Note 4). A Tlingit also considered it much better to give than to receive, which again was a desirable Christian ideal; but among the Tlingit the meaning was conceived differently. The Presbyterian missionary Samuel H. Young was a perceptive person in many ways, and he noted that one of the mistakes they made at Wrangell was to give the Indians gifts freely. The people then came to expect gifts as rewards for becoming Christians. When asked to attend church, an old Tlingit was likely to respond, "How much you pay me?" The same compensation was expected by parents when they permitted their children to attend school. The schools were the most important institution for the introduction of systematic change among the Tlingit, and it was through the schools that the missionaries were most successful in winning converts.

Among the diverse problems with which the missionaries were to concern themselves was the condition of Tlingit slaves. Except in rare instances slaves were not freed with the purchase of Alaska by the United States, because there was no effective governmental representative to handle Indian affairs. The missionaries also took a stand against cremation; the shamans; the potlatch system; polygyny; and hoochinoo. The missionaries' stand was firm on every one of these issues (see Note 5).

In the ethnography of Krause and the writings of the Presbyterians are reported certain specific changes which took place in the late 1870's and early 1880's. The innovations were largely in the nature of items added to the material culture, while some items were deleted from the old material inventory. The women had given up wearing labrets; even by 1827 they had been rapidly passing out of fashion. Some men wore moustaches and beards; this does not appear to have been an aboriginal custom. Silver jewelry, usually pounded from coins, was made locally. Women wore as many as a dozen bracelets at once, and rings for women were popular. Clothing styles shifted from garments of skins to those of cloth after European models, and woolen blankets universally were worn as capes. The women wore loose gowns of calico which were gathered at the top on a yoke. Over these were worn skirts of the same material. For festive occasions women wore jackets that matched their skirts and brightly colored kerchiefs on their heads. Small girls were clothed like their mothers, while small boys wore only a calico shirt when away from home and nothing when in their homes. The men wore calico shirts and cotton trousers.

House entrances changed from an oval opening to the use of hinged doors, but the lineage house was still the typical residence unit. Changes in food habits included raising vegetables, particularly potatoes, which was a Russian introduction; the women were the cultivators. Flour was introduced by the Russians, and it was prepared as a gruel or baked into bread. Coffee and tea were used rarely, and the same was true of eating utensils. Alcoholic drinks were unknown in aboriginal times, and during early contact with the Russians the Indians refused them because of their fear of the Russians. Soon, however, intoxicants became a favorite trade item for roving trading vessels. The Russian and American governments prohibited the sale of intoxicants, but they were smuggled in; also, a discharged American soldier taught the people how to distill their own alcohol. This drink, called hoochinoo, was extremely popular. The men became smokers, but in aboriginal times they only chewed a "tobacco-like" plant which they sometimes mixed with lime. They either carved their own elaborate pipes of wood or stone or else obtained clay pipes from the traders. Imported tobacco was chewed by both men and women. The most important changes in subsistence techniques were the use of iron points to replace those of stone or bone on fishhooks and the use of firearms in hunting; the old methods of fishing were not changed, however.

As Walter R. Goldschmidt and Theodore H. Haas have pointed out, it appears that a consolidation of settlements within a *kon* had begun prior to historic contact, and the pattern continued with intensification in historic times. Early in the twentieth century the forces leading to greater population concentrations included the following: population reduction due to wars and diseases; depletion of fish and game in some areas by whites; the availability of better boats which provided mobility from a consolidated settlement; the efforts of traders, missionaries, and Federal officials to have fewer and larger settlements for more efficient trade, Christianization, and administration; the desire of the Indians to live in larger communities; and the economic advantages in settling near white communities. During the same era, the early twentieth century, dwellings of frame construction for individual families became more popular, but at some villages, such as Hoonah, sib houses were occupied until quite recently. In 1944 Hoonah virtually was destroyed by fire, and it was only after this time that nuclear family residence units were constructed.

As mentioned earlier the house group was the most functionally integrated social unit in aboriginal Tlingit society. It was likewise the most important economic and ceremonial group within a sib. In aboriginal times, however, within a house group the trapping of fur animals was an individual pursuit with each man supplying pelts for his own nuclear family. In historic times when trapping became a primary means of livelihood, individual trappers built cabins on lands of their sib and came to claim local areas for their exclusive exploitation. The economic focus then shifted from the house group to the individual, and the cohesion of the house group began to be destroyed. This was one factor leading to the construction of nuclear family dwelling units. The essence of this particular analysis of the shift in emphasis of the economy was plotted by Kalvero Oberg.

Some families had begun to use chairs in their houses around 1900, but tables were less common. Stoves replaced the fireplace, and dishes replaced ladles out of which to eat. There were no regular mealtimes, but boiling still prevailed as the favored method of cooking. To wash clothing became a part of household routine, and sewing machines were owned and used. Although the clothing styles of whites were well accepted, the ears of persons of both sexes still were pierced for ornaments, and the nasal septum likewise was pierced to receive a ring. Jewelry made from silver, which formerly was popular, came to be replaced by gold jewelry when the value of gold was realized. Facial painting now was restricted mainly to ceremonial events, but it was used also for protection against mosquitoes and the weather.

The economy continued to be centered on fishing and the sea, but new skills associated with fishing were beginning to prevail. The halibut hooks of old were displaced by modern metal hooks. Individuals of both sexes turned to work in canneries, while other men were attracted to jobs in the gold mines. A few other individuals still continued to hunt sea otter until 1911 when the animal population clearly was headed for extinction and laws were introduced to protect their number. The skills of the men as woodcarvers and metalworkers led to the manufacture of craft items for the tourist trade, and women wove robes and baskets for the same market. Knowing the independent nature of the Tlingit, it is predictable that they would not make reliable employees. To be ordered about was to be insulted, and as domestic servants or laborers they usually did not satisfy their white employers.

The potlatch system continued to function, and it retained much of the pageantry and drama known in aboriginal times. The predilection for borrowing and imitating the songs, dances, and costumes of foreigners continued. One instance has been recorded of some shipwrecked Japanese arriving at Dry Bay in 1908; in performances by women in 1909 a memorable imitation of Japanese clothing and haircuts was presented. Other changes took place in the form of the potlatch gifts. Blankets from the traders came to be more important gifts than Chilkat robes; silver dollars were a favorite gift item, as was American store-bought food.

Of all the fascinating subjects concerning the Northwest Coast Indians none has received more attention than totem poles. The size, complexity, and romantic appeal of totem poles have long attracted description, comment, and comparison. The form usually described, however, dates only from historic times. The most detailed discussion of totem poles has been compiled by the anthropologist Edward L. Keithahn. These monuments are so large and obvious that we would expect even the most casual observer to have made note of them in the earliest historical accounts, that is, if they were present. They are not mentioned by Cook, La Perouse, or Portlock. It was not until John Meares visited the Queen Charlotte Islands in 1788 that "great wooden images" were reported (Keithahn, 1963, 38). In 1791 we have the first good description of a heraldic pole by Etienne Marchand, again for the Queen Charlotte Island people, the Haida. In 1792 there was a description of northern Tlingit mortuary poles at Yakutat by Alexandro Malaspina. When Lisiansky was on the *Neva* at Sitka in 1805, he saw many poles of the mortuary variety. The general conclusion drawn by Keithahn is that carved posts in the house interiors and mortuary posts were present among the Tlingit in prehistoric times. Again according to Keithahn, it was not until between 1840 and 1880 that the detached pole standing apart from a house was common along the northwest coast. Even during this era totem poles were not widespread among the Tlingit. Furthermore, Keithahn questions whether the great totem poles could have been carved prior to the general availability of iron-bladed tools. The erection of great totem poles became a means for house groups who became wealthy through the fur trade to record their increased prestige. Some aspiring persons did not have the right to carve the heraldic crests, and so they originated new symbols such as the bull and ship, basing their right to use these forms on the claim that they were the first to see them when they were introduced. When the Krause brothers were among the Tlingit in 1881–1882, it was noted by Aurel that only one totem pole was to be found among the Chilkat, none among the Sitka and Killisnoo groups, but many at the Stikine settlement near Wrangell.

Tlingit totem poles were erected to serve diverse purposes. The four main posts inside of houses normally were not carved, but they were faced with carved pillars or panels, some of which still stood inside modern Tlingit houses at Klukwan in the early 1960's. The pillar faces were carved with crests of the sib. Often included were abalone shell inlays, and sometimes human hair or ermine fur was attached. A second form was the mortuary pole with a box at the top for the ashes of the deceased. In historic times a crest figure was placed on top of the pole, and the ashes were in a recess at the back of the pole. The final development of the mortuary pole was to carve story figures on the pole. A third type was the memorial pole which most often was raised by a maternal nephew or a younger brother in memory of the former house group leader who had died. These poles were erected within a year of the death of the commemorated person and were not habitually raised at the site of interment. Memorial poles not only honored the dead but validated the succession of the new house group leader. Modern forms of the memorial and mortuary poles are tombstones made of granite or marble, with crests carved on them by the monument companies. The heraldic type of pole, the fourth form, was erected at the front and center of a house, and an oval opening near the base served as the house entrance. Carved and painted on a pole of this form was a tale associated with the house group. The fifth type, the potlatch pole, is historically the most recent form of totem pole to develop. These were raised to enhance the prestige of family groups which had accumulated and distributed wealth earned as the result of the fur trade or by working directly for whites. Such poles recorded an elaborate potlatch by the group that had them carved and erected. The final or sixth form was the ridicule pole, which usually was raised to force some house group to recognize and compensate for a debt. For example, a ridicule pole is said to have been carved and erected to shame a white trader for not repaying a potlatch that had been given in his honor.

One of the most interesting of all totem poles was a memorial pole carved and raised in honor of Abraham Lincoln. The details of its erection are unknown, but Keithahn offers the following reconstruction of this particular monument. He estimates that at the time of the purchase of Alaska a third of the natives were slaves, either captives, the offspring of captives, or persons who had sold themselves into bondage because of debts. A slave or bonded person could not escape, for no village would give him refuge. At one time a certain group of Raven people had given sanctuary to slaves; as a result, their neighbors became hostile and forced them to move repeatedly. Finally, they and the slaves settled on Tongass Island near an American fort which had been built to prevent smuggling from Canada. Here the Indians were not disturbed, and here they learned that Lincoln was responsible for the freeing of slaves in Alaska as well as in the United States. As a gesture of appreciation, they erected the pole, most likely using a photograph of Lincoln as a model. The fifty-five-foot pole, carved by a Tsimshian, had the figure of Lincoln at the top and a Raven crest near the bottom. The original pole was taken down in 1939 and a replica pole carved to replace the weather-worn original.

The Indian attitude toward totem poles was such that their erection was an end in itself. A pole was carved and raised for a particular purpose, and it then became unimportant as a physical object. As a pole tilted with age or threatened to fall, it was not supported in any manner. Restorations would have necessitated an outlay of wealth equal to the cost of erecting the original, for comparable ceremonies would have been held. Thus it was more feasible simply to erect another pole which would bring greater honor to the house group. Since poles deteriorate rapidly in the damp weather and few new poles were raised after the turn of the present century, they have disappeared rapidly. Then too, many poles have been removed to diverse museums and parks. Various parks and national monuments were established beginning in 1890, with the purpose of preserving totem poles. However, a concerted effort to save the totem pole was not made until 1938. By 1942, when the project was completed, nearly fifty poles had been restored, and about the same number which could not be restored were duplicated.

The totemic symbols which were exhibited on totem poles were associated with one or the other of the moieties. Other symbols represented sibs, and still others, house groups. All of the Raven moiety members employed the Raven design as their primary symbol, and they identified their primeval origins with the geographical area to the south. The Wolf moiety had the Wolf as its chief totem in the south and the Eagle in the north. Not only the actual crests but names associated with a sib were important designations, and their use had to be validated through the potlatch system. These honorific names often drawn from the sib or moiety totems tended to pass from great-grandfather to a great-grandson. The animals associated with a totem could be killed and eaten by moiety members, however, and the eating habits of all the tribe were uniform, indicating no taboo on eating one's totemic species.

One extremely satisfactory means of tracing the course of Tlingit acculturation from the turn of the present century to the 1950's is with a discussion of the Alaska Native Brotherhood (A.N.B.). This political institution, studied in detail by Philip Drucker, was founded by ten Indian men from southeastern Alaska, all of whom appear to have been Tlingit except for one Tsimshian man. These men, who met at Sitka in 1912, shared many characteristics. All were not only Presbyterians but leaders in church affairs and strongly committed to the ideal of rapid assimilation into white culture and society. They also had had prior personal experience in the social structure of Western institutions as reflected in local church organizations. One important and distinctive concept in the formation of the A.N.B. was its nonlocal nature. Chapters, or camps, as they are termed, were organized initially at Sitka, Juneau, and Douglas. In the 1920's chapters had been established in all the southeastern Alaskan Indian villages except for Metlakatla, which had a sense of local identity and a history which stood apart from other Indian communities in the area. By 1952 there were sixteen active chapters. Within a few years of its organization, a parallel group was formed for women, the Alaska Native Sisterhood, and it most often absorbed the local women's society of the church. These organizations hold a joint annual convention. The local chapters are represented by three delegates, and there are additionally the officers of the central organization and past presidents of the central organization represented. When decisions must be made throughout the year, an executive committee composed of past presidents, the Sisterhood president, and the central organization officers as ex officio members is the governing body.

The initiation fee to membership in the A.N.B. is $10, and the annual dues are twelve. Half of this money is retained by the local chapter, and half goes to the central organization. Additionally, a yearly assessment of each chapter helps to cover the costs of the annual convention. The Sisterhood usually raises most of this money. It is stated generally that all adults are members of the Brotherhood or Sisterhood, but in fact most are not active. In Ketchikan, there were eight hundred fifty-nine Indians in 1952 but only fifteen A.N.B. members and twenty-seven in the Sisterhood. At Angoon, during the same year there were twenty-two members of the Brotherhood and fifty-six in the Sisterhood out of a total of four hundred twenty-nine. In spite of the small village membership, most of the Indians support the purposes of the organization, and there is no formal opposition. Each chapter has a total of nine officers and council members; monthly meetings are held, except during the fishing season, to discuss local and general business. Virtually every chapter has a building used for A.N.B. functions. The one at Hoonah, completed for the 1952 convention, cost nearly $50,000. The better halls have a floor area large enough for a basketball court, a kitchen, restrooms, and a central heating plant. In the halls public meetings and social gatherings are held, and motion pictures may be viewed. Thus, much of the social life in a community centers in the Brotherhood structure.

The Brotherhood colors are red for salmon and yellow for gold; these are displayed on ceremonial sashes. The official song is "Onward, Christian Soldiers." The primary goal of the organization is stated clearly in the first article of the constitution. It is as follows: "The purpose of this organization shall be to assist and encourage the Native in his advancement from his native state to his place among the cultivated races of the world, to oppose, discourage, and overcome the narrow injustice of race prejudice, and to aid in the development of the Territory of Alaska, and in making it worthy of a place among the States of North America" (Drucker, 1958, 165). The aim of the Brotherhood clearly was the rapid assimilation of the Tlingit into white society in southeastern Alaska, but first the Indian's ties with the past had to be broken. This was attempted in two different ways. First, speaking English was considered to be very important; in fact, eligibility for membership was restricted in Article II to "English speaking members of the Native residents of the Territory of Alaska," and the constitution was printed in English. A second target was to destroy the potlatch system which represented the aboriginal past in the minds of both the missionaries and the Indians.

Brotherhood policy concentrated on gaining citizenship rights for Indians equal to those of whites. The matter of Tlingit citizenship was complicated by the fact that under the Russian administration no formal recognition of their legal status seems to have been given. In the Russo-American Treaty of sale it was stated that the uncivilized tribes, which included most Tlingit and other aboriginal Alaskans, were to be subject to such laws as the United States might pass. With the purchase there was no attempt to negotiate treaties nor to establish Indian reservations, and therefore the citizenship status of aboriginal Alaskans remained unclear. They were not "wards of the government" in the sense of reservation or treaty Indians. They came to consider themselves as citizens, but the whites in Alaska usually regarded them in the same light as Indians in the United States. Until they were declared citizens, the Tlingit could not file on mining claims, and this was a cause of resentment. Indians in Alaska could, under the terms of the General Allotment Act of 1887 or a Territorial Act of 1915, become citizens by demonstrating that they were following a civilized way of life, but few individuals sought to become citizens under these laws. The issue of citizenship was forced in 1922 by a Tlingit lawyer, William Paul. His was the most powerful voice in the A.N.B., and as Drucker (1958, 39) states, "he made a career of the Brotherhood movement." The case in question involved a Tlingit who had voted previously, but whose vote in the 1922 primaries was challenged. Through court action, during which Paul defended him, he was cleared of illegal voting. As a result, Indian voting rights were accepted, even before the Federal Citizenship Act of 1924 gave all Indians the rights of other citizens.

Through the years the A.N.B. has actively sought to further its ends by diverse forms of institutional action. One campaign was to have Indian children accepted in Territorial schools. Until 1931 the Federal Bureau of Education maintained schools in Indian villages, but in some communities there was both a Bureau of Education school and a Territorial school, with the Indian children attending the former and white children going to the latter. In 1929, in a case in which Paul defended the Indian father against the school board, the right of Indian children to attend Territorial schools was established by court action. The Brotherhood moved into the field of organized labor by supporting fishermen's unions. The sequence seems to have been that local unions were formed and amalgamated, and separated again until 1939 when the A.N.B. became a bargaining agent for the combined unions under the Wagner Act. Soon this union affiliated with the American Federation of Labor as the Alaska Marine Workers' Union. The Brotherhood kept its bargaining power in the A.F.L. merger and thus retained the key function of negotiating wage scales for cannery workers and fish prices for fishermen. In order to be a bargaining agent, the Brotherhood was forced to open its ranks to non-Indians and did so by creating the category of "associate member." One of the recurrent problems dealt with by the Brotherhood has been the matter of reservations. The general feeling against the creation of reservations seems to have stemmed from reservation Indian influences on Tlingit children at the Chemawa and Carlisle Indian schools. It was not until the Indian Reorganization Act of 1934, applied to Alaska in 1936, that the matter became a major issue, for it then appeared that the Tlingit would have to request reservations before they could come under the provisions of the Indian Reorganization Act. Reservations were not created, but over the years some more conservative communities have favored their formation in order to secure their landholdings and with the belief that reservations would bring more security. In 1946 the Brotherhood convention took the stand that local communities could form their own policies toward reservations and would have the support of the central organization. The issue of Indian land rights and the fact that land had been taken by whites without compensation led the Tlingit and Alaskan Haida to attempt to obtain compensation through the Court of Claims. This stemmed from the Tlingit and Haida Jurisdictional Claims Act of 1935. The Indians involved sued for $80 million, and the Court of Claims decided that they were entitled to compensation. It is estimated that they will receive $3 million to $80 million and that some eight thousand Indians will be the beneficiaries.

The Brotherhood has been active also in fighting discrimination against Indians. The matter came to a climax about 1929 when the Indians openly resented "For Natives Only" signs in the balconies of motion-picture houses. A boycott organized by the A.N.B. was effective in having theaters desegregated, but it was not until 1946 that an antidiscrimination law was passed by the Territorial Legislature. It is worthy of note that during World War II, when Indians, Aleuts, and Eskimos were organized into the Alaska Territorial Guard units, their units were composed of all natives, but this was not viewed by the people as discriminatory. Finally, in recent years the Brotherhood has attempted to expand its activities into other sectors of Alaska among Athapaskans and Eskimos. The efforts in this direction have been active since 1951, but only since about 1962 has the expansion program been implemented seriously.

In spite of the fact that one of the primary aims of the Brotherhood has been to do away with aboriginal customs, their efforts have been only partly successful. The principal target for attack, the potlatch, was regarded as heathen and most deplored; however, as Drucker points out, it actually was primarily social, not religious, in its nature. Certain potlatch customs have become incorporated into the Brotherhood structure, such as addressing persons of the opposite moiety in a ceremonial fashion; fining individuals for infractions; making gifts to the organization; and gift giving by the family of a deceased person for burial services when these are provided by the opposite moiety through the Brotherhood. In one sense the A.N.B. serves as a new institution through which the moieties reciprocate. Furthermore, although the ideal of fostering English speaking still exists, the business meeting of a local chapter is sometimes conducted in Tlingit, particularly since the older persons who are normally the most active members are not likely to speak English with ease.

From the ethnographic and historical researches of de Laguna, it is possible to develop further continuity in the Tlingit sociocultural system. Her study of Angoon on Admiralty Island, the large island just east of Baranof Island, on which Sitka is located, provides information about the recent past. References to Angoon in 1882 are numerous because of a particular chain of events which occurred there. Prior to that date, an 1875 report gives the impression that Angoon was a neat and orderly settlement and mentions that the Indians raised a fine crop of potatoes. In 1882 Angoon virtually was destroyed by a force under the command of a U. S. Navy officer. This event more than any other has become a focal point of local Tlingit resentment and hostility against whites. The incident occurred when a Tlingit employee of the Northwest Trading Company was killed accidentally when a whaling bomb exploded. The Indians demanded compensation, but the company refused. The Tlingit seized the two white men who were with them at the time of the accident, along with the boat and other company property. They threatened to kill the whites and destroy the company store because their compensation was denied. The Revenue-Cutter Service vessel *Corwin* was at Sitka at the time, and it went to Angoon to assist the American party under the direction of E. C. Merriman, a U. S. Navy Commander. He demanded that the Indians compensate the Americans for the trouble they had caused or else the town would be shelled and their canoes destroyed. When the Indians did not comply and, according to one American account, after it was learned that there were no women or children in the village, the community was bombarded and many canoes destroyed, although some houses purposely were spared. Finally, the shelled houses were burned. The white men and the Northwest Trading Company property were recovered. According to one modern Tlingit version of the attack, the Indians had stopped whaling to conduct services for the dead man. The village was shelled and burned, but the Indians did not know why. Furthermore, six children who were in the houses at the time suffocated from the smoke. An analysis of Tlingit and white versions of the event indicates that the stories of neither side are entirely logical and consistent. What is clear, however, is that the Indians did not understand the action of the whites and the whites made no attempt to adjust to the customs of the Indians in this particular instance.

In 1917 the Angoon sib leaders organized as a town with a council under a Territorial law. The town government originally seems to have had difficulty in functioning effectively due to rivalries among sib leaders. Furthermore, the younger members of the organization, who understood democratic procedures better than the older members, were in favor of more rapid change. A community hall was constructed in 1917 when the town council was founded, and in 1921 local chapters of the Brotherhood and Sisterhood were organized. In 1929 the annual convention of the Brotherhood was held at Angoon, and the building was improved for the occasion; since that time it has been termed the A.N.B. Hall. In 1939 the town organized itself under the terms of the Indian Reorganization Act as the Angoon Community Association. Then in 1948 the council, consisting of seven elected members, established the Angoon Native Village Court, which has jurisdiction over community members. The administration is maintained by a chief judge, three assistants, and a village police force of four men. The court has the authority to try civil cases involving claims up to $200 and cases involving assault, disorderly conduct, adultery, and other crimes of this nature. It is quite apparent that the Tlingit at Angoon have incorporated institutional forms from American society into their village political structure, but it is not known how effectively these have functioned within the village.

In 1918 a Presbyterian church was started at Angoon and was completed the following year. Prior to this time Presbyterian services were held in the house of one particular sib leader who was important in the local organization of this church. A Russian Orthodox Greek Catholic church was constructed in 1928–1929, and although the Presbyterians have had a local minister, the Orthodox church has not had a resident priest. At an unrecorded date the Salvation Army built a hall at Angoon, and a local Tlingit leader directs its activities. The membership of the various religious groups in 1950 was one hundred Orthodox, eighty Salvation Army, and seventy Presbyterians. Membership may be along lineage lines, but the groups seem to cooperate with one another. Some of the older villagers were educated at the Orthodox or Presbyterian schools at Sitka. A Federal school was not built at Angoon until about 1920. In 1950 some one hundred children attended, and others continued their education at the Bureau of Indian Affairs high school at Mt. Edgecumbe. In addition, two were attending college at this time.

In spite of initial opposition to the Indian Reorganization Act, owing to misunderstanding of its purpose, some provisions of the act have been most helpful to the community. The people who were purchasing fishing vessels, which in 1950 cost between $15,000 and $22,000, now could finance the boats through the community organization, which provided more liberal terms than had the fish canneries which held the mortgages previously. Of more importance is the community purchase of the salmon cannery operating at nearby Hood Bay. Purchased in 1947, the cannery was first operated by the community in 1949. The council hired a white manager who in turn hired the remainder of the workers. Now most of the men work as fishermen for this cannery, and the women process and pack fish in the production line. Union wage scales are paid all the workers, and an additional labor force of Filipinos has been hired for the operation. The community-owned cannery was in 1950 on its way to becoming a very successful venture. Commercial salmon fishing can be very lucrative; for example, in Hoonah the catch in 1961 was particularly good. Approximately twenty fishing boats operate with crews consisting of from six to nine men per boat. The captain receives five shares of the catch, two each for the boat and gear and one for himself, while each adult man receives one share and young boys less than a share. Earnings per share for the four-month fishing season ranged from $4000 to $8000. At the same time, fishing or processing seafoods is about the only way to earn cash at Hoonah.

In a brief but revealing study of Hoonah in 1961 the anthropologist Seymour Parker recorded a continuing emphasis on rank in this modern settlement. "High class people" are persons prominent as fishing boat captains or as businessmen. The former also are likely to have prominent positions in their matrisibs. Individuals in this general category are expected to finance potlatches and aid the community in funding various projects. The "common" or "average" people usually are members of fishing boat crews, and while they may accept Federal or state relief they do so with feelings of shame. The lower class is described as "living from day to day." They feel little reluctance in accepting relief funds and have the reputation for drinking intoxicants a great deal. One of the major points made by Parker is the strong sense of individualism which pervades the value system of the modern Tlingit. Familial, sib, and community ties certainly exist and are upon occasion important, but the individual thrives or wanes largely on the basis of his own abilities. This is a social characteristic identified with aboriginal times but with less stress than is found today. Previously a man was largely bound to the destiny of his matrilineage, although wealth and prestige were desired by all. Now, with a disintegration of the old sib and moiety system but a continuing emphasis on material wealth and prestige, the modern Tlingit has a very good opportunity to compete with any other person in southeastern Alaska.

Note 1.   La Perouse (Krause, 1956, 96) described the labrets worn by the Tlingit women at Lituya Bay in 1786.

All the women, without exception, have the lower lip pierced the full length of the mouth and down to the gum, and in this incision they have a kind of wooden spoon without a handle, which rests against the gum and spreads the pierced lip into a roll so that the lower part of the mouth extends out two or three inches. The young girls just have a nail in the lower lip and the married women alone have the right to the spoon. We tried to persuade them to abandon this ornament. They agreed to it reluctantly. They made the same gestures and showed the same embarrassment which a European woman would show at baring her breast. The lower lip then fell to the chin and this second picture was little better than the first.

Note 2.   John R. Swanton (1908, 451, fn. c) describes the manner in which the Tlingit conceive of the universe.

Most Indian languages, at any rate the Tlingit, do not have a true plural, but usually a distributive and occasionally a collective. This means that instead of thinking of so many different objects they think of one diffused into many. Therefore the Tlingit do not divide the universe arbitrarily into so many different quarters ruled by so many supernatural beings. On the contrary, supernatural power impresses them as a vast immensity, one in kind and impersonal, inscrutable as to its nature, but whenever manifesting itself to men taking a personal, and it might be said a human personal, form in whatever object it displays itself. Thus the sky spirit is the ocean of supernatural energy as it manifests itself in the sky, the sea spirit as it manifests itself in the sea, the bear spirit as it manifests itself in the bear, the rock spirit as it manifests itself in the rock, etc. It is not meant that the Tlingit consciously reasons this out thus, or formulates a unity in the supernatural, but such appears to be his unexpressed feeling. For this reason there is but one name for this spiritual power, *yēk,* a name which is affixed to any specific personal manifestation of it, and it is to this perception or feeling reduced to personality that the "Great Spirit" idea seems usually to have affixed itself.

Note 3. Feodor Lutke in 1827 describes the arrangements which were made for a vessel to trade with the Tlingit (Krause, 1956, 41).

The forward part of the ships was closed off by a spread of sails to a man's height. Behind this wall, the armed crew took their places, supported by several cannon loaded with grapeshot cartridges and ignited fuses. All around the ship to the height of the bower a net was spread which had an entrance only at one place for a single person. Before trading began, the commander of the ship allowed the chiefs to come aboard and be shown these preparations and given to understand that no more than a certain number of buyers would be allowed on the ship at one time. No one would be allowed more than ten steps from the rail and if anyone were killed transgressing these rules, it should not be looked upon as breaking the peace. After these directions were laid out the supercargo could begin trading without danger, but the slightest relaxation of these precautions could bring about the most serious consequences.

Note 4. The Presbyterian missionary Samuel H. Young (1927, 111-112) comments on an episode of generosity toward a Tlingit at Wrangell for the period around 1880.

Many of the natives still hold the same attitude as one of my men: I found him very ill and helpless, suffering from a form of rheumatism. I cared for him for more than a year; gave him a room in one of our houses within the fort, and my wife and I tended him and nursed him as if he were a brother. We expended upon him more than a hundred dollars in medicine, food and clothing. After he had recovered in some degree and was able to return to his home and do some work, I found him standing by his small canoe on the beach one day and I said:

"Charlie, I wish you would take me in your canoe over to Shustaak's Point," half a mile distant.

He looked at me for a moment and then said: "How much you goin' to pay me?"

"Have you no shame?" I asked. "Have you forgotten all that I have done and spent for you the past year?"

He eyed me with a look that made me want to knock him over. "That's your business," he said in Thlingit. "My canoe is *my* business."

Note 5. The famous Church of England missionary, Father Duncan of Metlakatla, gives advice to the Presbyterians on how to handle Northwest Coast Indians (Young, 1927, 159-160).

Never recede from a position once taken, even though it proves to be a mistake. The natives must learn to have implicit confidence in their missionary, and to think that he can make no mistakes and do no wrong. To them he must be omnipotent and omniscient. Even while he laments his own weakness and ignorance, he must keep up this appearance.

References

Bancroft, Hubert H. *History of Alaska, 1730-1885. The Works of Hubert Howe Bancroft,* v. 33. San Francisco. 1886.

Boas, Franz. *Primitive Art.* Dover (republication). 1955.

Drucker, Philip. *Culture Element Distributions: XXVI. Northwest Coast.* Anthropological Records, v. 9, no. 3. 1950.

*————. *The Native Brotherhoods.* Bureau of American Ethnology, Bulletin 168. Washington, D. C. 1958. The Alaska Native Brotherhood, which has been a Tlingit-dominated organization since its founding in 1912, is the subject matter for half of this study. The second half of the volume is devoted to a similar organization in British Columbia. Drucker's largely historical study is a highly significant contribution since it is devoted to one of the organized efforts by the Tlingit to promote assimilation into white Alaskan society.

————. "Sources of Northwest Coast Culture," in *New Interpretations of Aboriginal American Culture History.* Clifford Evans and Betty Meggers, eds., 59–81. Anthropological Society of Washington, D. C. 1955.

Fraser, Douglas. *Primitive Art.* Garden City. 1962.

Goldschmidt, Walter R. and Theodore H. Haas. *Possessory Rights of the Natives of Southeastern Alaska.* A Report to the Commissioner of Indian Affairs (mimeographed). 1946.

Jackson, Sheldon. *Alaska.* New York. 1880.

Jones, Livingston F. *A Study of the Thlingets of Alaska.* New York. 1914.

Kashavaroff, Andrew P. "How the White Men Came to Lituya and what Happened to Yeahlth-kan who Visited Them," *Alaska Magazine,* v. 1, 151–153. 1927.

*Keithahn, Edward L. *Monuments in Cedar.* Seattle. 1963 (revised edition). This study is particularly useful in any attempt to trace the origins, antiquity, and development of various forms of totem poles.

*Krause, Aurel. *The Tlingit Indians.* Jena, 1885; translated edition, Erna Gunther, tr., American Ethnological Society. 1956. The 1881–1882 field study by Aurel and Arthur Krause, written by the former, is the standard Tlingit source. The breadth and balance of the study make it the first to be consulted in any serious study of the Tlingit.

de Laguna, Frederica. "Some Dynamic Forces in Tlingit Society," *Southwestern Journal of Anthropology,* v. 8, 1–12. 1952.

*————. *The Story of a Tlingit Community.* Bureau of American Ethnology, Bulletin 172. Washington, D. C. 1960. Based on archaeological and ethnographic fieldwork in 1949 and 1950, this report concentrates on the Angoon area and its people. The archaeological data are supplemented by historical records and ethnographic field information.

McClellan, Catharine. "The Interrelations of Social Structure with Northern Tlingit Ceremonialism," *Southwestern Journal of Anthropology,* v. 10, 75–96. 1954.

Niblack, Albert P. "The Coast Indians of Southern Alaska and Northern

British Columbia," *Annual Report of the Smithsonian Institution, 1887-88*, 225–386. Washington, D. C. 1890.

*Oberg, Kalervo. The Social Economy of the Tlingit Indians. Ph.D. dissertation, Department of Anthropology, University of Chicago. 1937. This unpublished study based on fieldwork in 1931–1932 and conducted primarily at Klukwan stands next to the work by Krause in its merit. Oberg's discussions of the social system and economy are outstanding for their clarity and breadth; it is little short of amazing that this work has never been published.

Parker, Seymour. See Ray, Charles K., et al.

*Ray, Charles K., et al. *Alaskan Native Secondary School Dropouts*. University of Alaska. 1962. The report in this volume by Seymour Parker on the Tlingit at Hoonah is brief but very good. Parker spent only about a month at Hoonah in 1961, and his emphasis was on values, but considerable additional information is included which is the most up-to-date information in print.

Romanowsky, S., and Frankenhauser. "Five Years of Medical Observations in the Colonies of the Russian-American Company," *Medical Newspaper of Russia*, v. 6, 153–161. St. Petersburg. 1849 (translated from German and reprinted in *Alaska Medicine*, v. 4, 33–37; 62–64. 1962).

*Swanton, John R. "Social Condition, Beliefs, and Linguistic Relationship of the Tlingit Indians," *Bureau of American Ethnology, Twenty-sixth Annual Report*, 391–512. Washington, D. C. 1908. This study based on fieldwork in 1904 at Sitka and Wrangell is not a balanced ethnography, nor does it purport to be, but it does serve as a good supplement to the works of Krause and Oberg.

Wardwell, Allen, compiler. *Yakutat South*. Chicago. 1964.

Willard, (Mrs.) Eugene S. *Life in Alaska*. Philadelphia. 1884.

Young, Samuel H. *Hall Young of Alaska*. Chicago and New York. 1927.

8

The Hopi:

Farmers of the Desert

Kaiparitz

coal
(strip mining)

NEVADA

UTAH   Cedar City

COLORADO

Lake Powell

Mesa
Verde   Durango

Glen Canyon Dam

NAVAJO

Las
Vegas   Lake Mead

Grand Canyon

Black Mesa

San Juan R.

Chaco Canyon

Santa Fe

Hoover
Dam

Colorado R.

Moencopi

Oraibi   HOPI

Painted Desert

ARIZONA

Kingman

Winslow

Albuquerque

PIMA

Flagstaff

ZUNI

NEW   MEXICO

CALIFORNIA

Colorado R.

Black   Mesa

Hotevilla   Third
Mesa

Second
Mesa

Wepo
Wash

First
Mesa

Rio Grande R.

Oraibi   New Oraibi

Hano

Antelope
Mesa

Gulf of
California

Oraibi Wash

Wash

Keams
Canyon

MEXICO

Polacca

Jeddito   Wash

0   5   10   15 mi

0   100   200 mi.

Map by J. Donovan

When Americans think of Indians, their first thoughts are likely to be of Plains groups with tepees, horses, and eagle feather warbonnets. If they pause and think again, they are likely to visualize a pueblo in a desert setting, fields of maize, painted pottery vessels, and strange katcina dolls. The Hopi of northeastern Arizona represent one such pueblo people. In many respects the Hopi and other pueblo peoples better represent Indians than the warriors of the Plains or prairies. The way of life of the warriors is gone; their glory lingers only as a memory among the people involved and in the written records. The situation is quite different for the pueblo lifeway. These people continue to live in the same setting as their ancestors; they still plant maize, produce pottery, and make katcina dolls. Their cultures do not survive in all their past glory, but they still exhibit an inordinate vitality in spite of centuries of outside pressures bent on their destruction. It is striking, for example, that in the 1950's less than two percent of the Hopi were practicing Christians. The resiliency of these people against outside pressures and their tenacity in retaining the old ways seldom is found among other American Indian tribes.

The Hopi have been singled out for discussion for diverse and, it is hoped, significant reasons. First they, more than any other pueblo group, display an appealing continuity with the past. Their ancestors settled the land in northern Arizona around a thousand years ago, and the Hopi community of Oraibi is one of the oldest, if not the oldest, continuously occupied settlements north of Mexico. Nowhere else are Indians so directly and intimately tied to one locality. Nowhere else among Indians do the past and present blend into a singularly integrated whole. Another reason to write about the Hopi is the wealth of literature describing their way of life. They long have attracted the attention of ethnographers so that studies of the Hopi are diverse and detailed. In the author's opinion the greatest American Indian ethnography is a monograph about the Hopi; the study of them by Mischa Titiev titled *Old Oraibi* is monumental. Titiev collected a wealth of facts about these people between 1932 and 1940, and he presented the material in a lucid style with great analytical sophistication. The information on Hopi social and religious life in the present chapter is based primarily on Titiev's study. He offers so much that it is unnecessary to seek other sources except to amplify certain details and to add information on topics which he did not include. The amount of published information about the Hopi is almost staggering. In George P. Murdock's monograph *Ethnographic Bibliography of North America* (1960), there are three hundred eighty-one Hopi entries, representing an impressive amount of material. It compares in volume with the information available on the Navajo, Iroquois, and Ojibwa.

The word *hopi* is an aboriginal term of the people who call themselves Hopi. Hopi means good, happy, or peaceful, the ideal for all individuals in this society. The Hopi also have been called Moqui in the literature. This designation for them apparently is derived from a word applied to the Hopi by Rio Grande pueblo peoples. In the Hopi language Moqui means dead. In linguistic terms the Hopi language is of the Macro-Penutian phylum, the Azteco-Tanoan stock, the Uto-Aztecan family, and Hopian subfamily. The aboriginal Hopi population was approximately twenty-eight hundred, but dropped to two thousand in 1907, and is currently about five thousand.

The northeastern sector of Arizona occupies in part the Navahonian biotic province. The environment is one of plateaus and, at lower elevations, deserts. Along the southern extremity of two plateaus, Black Mesa and Antelope Mesa, the Hopi settlements were and are situated. This is an area of sporadic and unpredictable rainfall where horticulturalists seemingly could not survive. The only reason the Hopi and their ancestors have been able to farm this area is that the rainwater which filters into the upland sandstone seeps southward above a layer of shale to emerge at the ends of the mesas as seepages and springs. On the higher elevations of the mesas juniper and scattered pinyon grow. This flora is replaced by grassland nearer the valley floors, and in the lower sections desert vegetation including saltbrush, greasewood, and sagebrush dominate. In regions of dampness or along irregularly flowing streams cottonwoods and willows grow, and at the springs as well as bordering more dependable streams are found cattails and rushes.

In the Southwest around the time of the birth of Christ there lived an Indian population termed Basketmaker in the literature. The remains of this cultural manifestation are best known from the peoples' leavings in dry caves and rock shelters. Basketmaker sites are numerous in the area where Arizona, Colorado, New Mexico, and Utah meet. In the open rock faces, particularly in the San Juan River drainage, have been found burials and living sites. The houses located were round in outline with walls constructed of horizontally arranged poles and sticks with mud filling in the wall openings; the roofs probably were cribbed. These were substantial structures, and inside a dwelling were food storage pits and "heating pits" in the floor, as well as grinding equipment, manos and metates. Elsewhere in rock shelters were storage pits and human burials accompanied by a variety of grave goods. On the adjacent flood plains of constantly or intermittently flowing streams were grown maize and squash; these plants were cultivated with flat-bladed or pointed wooden digging sticks. The people hunted large game such as deer and mountain sheep with a spear and throwing board, called an atlatl in the Southwest. A variety of nets and snares were used to obtain rabbits and other small game. The only domestic animal was the dog, and the two types found were very different. One was most similar to a short-haired terrier, and the other resembled a collie. The manufactured goods of the people included a wide variety of baskets. They usually were made by the coiling method and were often decorated with designs in red and black. The people used deep, cone-shaped baskets which were carried with a tumpline. Pottery was just being introduced, and the dishes found were made with organic temper and dried in the sun. The idea of making pottery was introduced to the people most likely from the south. The most important clothing was a blanket of woven strips of rabbit skin with the fur left intact and sandals made from woven yucca fiber. The people appreciated ornaments, and necklaces or pendants of stone, seeds, and bone often were found. The Basketmaker burials recovered are from cave sites, usually from pits which had been employed earlier as storage basins. Multiple burials were the rule, but usually without any sign of violent death. The bodies were flexed and wrapped in rabbit-skin blankets. A large basket often was placed over the head of the deceased, and a wide variety of grave goods was included. Frequently cone-shaped pipes were found, along with ornaments, clothing, and weapons.

Around A.D. 500 the Basketmaker culture moved in a somewhat different direction. The changes were of sufficient magnitude to differentiate the new culture as an outgrowth of the earlier period. The people have been termed Modified-Basketmakers. They occupied village communities, and their earliest houses were round. Somewhat later an oval variety is found, and finally by A.D. 700, which was at the end of this era, the houses were rectangular. Houses were built in pits and sometimes had attached anterooms and entrance passages. Later, the passages became ventilating shafts, and the dwellings were entered through the roof. The roofs of these structures were cone-shaped originally and later flat; they were supported by four posts with crossbeams against which were placed vertical sidewall poles that were closely spaced with horizontal poles. On the hard clay floor of such a dwelling were a fire pit, manos and metates; there was a hole in the floor which was probably the sipapu, known in modern pueblo structures as the spot where the supernaturals come to earth from the underworld. The economy of these people was essentially the same as earlier, with new forms of maize as well as beans added to the diet. The weaponry now included the bow and arrow; new tools included grooved mauls and axes. Pottery was manufactured by the coiling process and scraped before it hardened to mask the coils. It was fired by a method which prohibited air from circulating freely about the vessels, that is, a reducing atmosphere, producing finished vessels of white or gray color. The earliest fired vessels were decorated with black designs, often modeled after those on baskets. Another category of clay objects was that of stylized human female figures with only the head and body usually represented. In spite of the increasing importance of pottery, baskets continued to be manufactured and frequently were designed with red and black motifs.

In the same general area between A.D. 700 and 1400 emerged the Indian culture called Pueblo. Three periods, Developmental, Great, and Regressive Pueblo, have been distinguished. Growing out of a Basketmaker background, with new ideas from within and from afar, the Pueblo periods represent a major climax in American Indian cultural developments. The early Pueblo peoples artificially flattened the backs of infants' skulls against cradleboards to produce the new head shape. The garb of the people began to change with the introduction of cotton as a domestic plant, and the women may have worn cotton blankets. The men possibly wore kilts as well as breechclouts, and there were new sandal styles. The living unit of the Developmental Pueblo people exhibits a direct continuity with the past. The houses evolved gradually into aboveground structures with contiguous units built of masonry. In the pit house tradition were constructed the round, subterranean ceremonial structures or kivas. The interior arrangements of the kivas included walls of coarse stone with an encircling bench, a fireplace, and a sipapu. The roofs were cribbed, with an opening left for entering. The economy remained as before, with the only new crop being cotton. The only new animal was the domestic turkey, most likely raised for its feathers rather than its meat. In the horticultural system was a new tool, a hoe of flaked stone, which was most often unhafted. The pottery was manufactured with greater skill than before. The paste was fine, and a thin slip of clay was often placed on a vessel before it was fired. The designs on pottery were made with mineral or vegetable pigments, and two-color combinations, black-on-white and red-on-orange, were most prevalent. The designs exhibited a wider range of motifs, but still they were most often conceived in geometric patterns.

Southwestern Indian culture came to a climax during the Great Pueblo period, which began around 1050. This was the era of great stonemasonry, with hundreds of residence and storage units in a single multistory pueblo. Mesa Verde was occupied at this time as well as the magnificent ruins at Chaco Canyon. The productivity of the cultivated flood plains was great, and irrigated acreage was brought under cultivation. With dependable surpluses of food individuals were freed from tilling the soil, and craft specialization developed. The potters became artists producing individualistic painted vessels, and leisure time fostered an elaboration of the religious system. Quite suddenly, by 1300, there was a virtual abandonment of the area. The reason for the exodus probably was related at least indirectly to an extended drought between 1276 and 1299. Arroyo cutting left the flood plains dry and irrigation ditches waterless. It is possible, too, that the nomadic Navajo and Apache raided these settled peoples and contributed to their downfall. The surviving population was to continue its way of life but only in a few pueblos.

The Hopi mesas were one locality in which the Regressive Pueblo period survived in the midst of what must have been drastic population displacements. Here were built rows of masonry houses constructed around plazas, and there were small rectangular kivas in which ceremonial activities focused. The striking cultural achievement was in pottery, with the bichrome and polychrome vessels numbered among the most pleasing Indian pottery made in North America. The ware was usually black-on-yellow or else red-and-black-on-yellow. Not only were fine-lined geometric designs executed, but representations from life forms also appeared. This era ended about 1700, after the first Spanish contacts but just before Spanish intrusion began to modify effectively the cultural pattern of old.

Fifteen hundred and thirty-nine was the last year of Hopi prehistory; in mid-July of the following year the first Spanish explorers arrived. A small group under Pedro de Tovar traveled from the pueblo of Zuni where Francisco Coronado, the expedition leader, rested. De Tovar arrived at one of the eastern Hopi settlements where he was met with hostility. The Hopi were attacked, the community partially destroyed, and the Indians defeated. De Tovar then peacefully visited the six other Hopi communities, and later a party of the same expedition passed through Hopi country to the Grand Canyon without any resistance. The Spanish search for gold led to the arrival of the next explorers. In the spring of 1583 Antonio de Espejo entered the country. The contacts between the Spanish and the Indians were peaceful; in fact the five Hopi settlements existing at this time openly welcomed the Spanish. More lasting contact was made by Juan de Onate in 1598 when the Hopi peacefully submitted to the authority of the Spanish king. The Spanish hoped to make Christians of these people, but Franciscan missionaries did not settle among them until 1629. Before long churches were completed at three different settlements, and two more missionaries joined the first three. The Franciscans reported they were making great progress, but the poisoning of one of the priests in 1633 suggests that all of the Hopi were not contented charges. The vigorous Franciscan efforts to destroy the old Hopi religion led to cruel punishments for backsliding Indians. In 1655 one of the missionaries caught a man performing an "act of idolatry." The man was beaten severely in public and again beaten inside the church; finally turpentine was applied to his body and ignited. The Hopi died and the missionary relieved of his post, although no punitive action was taken against the offender. In 1650 the Hopi refused to join the other pueblo peoples in a revolt against the Spanish, but they supported fully the Pueblo Revolt of 1680. Their major contribution was to kill the four missionaries stationed among them. Indirectly they aided the insurrection by permitting Indians from the Rio Grande pueblos to live among them when the Spanish struck back; two communities were constructed for these friendly allies. The Hopi did not feel secure in their remote locality, although Santa Fe and the Spanish were far away. They feared Spanish reprisals, and therefore three villages were relocated on mesa tops where they could be more easily defended than in the valley bottoms. The Spanish returned in 1692, and when the Indians willingly swore to support the Spanish king peace again was established. By 1699 the Spanish were in firm control of the Rio Grande pueblos, and this led one Hopi faction to request missionaries from the authorities at Santa Fe. A missionary visited, but after he left, the community was summarily destroyed by the anti-Spanish faction among the Hopi. The men who offered resistance were killed, while women and children were scattered among the remaining settlements. The pagan Hopi under the leadership of a man from Oraibi went to Santa Fe and told the Spanish governor that the Hopi would make peace if they were permitted to continue their old religion. This, however, was a completely unacceptable proposal to the Spanish. For the murder of the Christian Hopi the Spanish in 1701 attempted to defeat the Hopi in battle, but the small Spanish force and the adequate defensive positions of the Hopi led the Spanish to withdraw. Another attempt to control the Hopi by force occurred in 1706, but it, too, ended in failure. As at an earlier period, Hopi freedom was retained not so much by their military skill and determination as by the distance which separated them from Santa Fe and the difficulties the Spanish were having with other Indians. The next major event in Hopi-Spanish contacts was a religious jurisdictional dispute. Both the Jesuits and the Franciscans sought to have the Hopi under their control. The Jesuits won temporary control which led to a vigorous effort by the Franciscans before the conflict was resolved. The Franciscans did not succeed in their task, however, and neither did the Jesuits. Throughout the 1740's and the early 1750's the Hopi thwarted all Spanish efforts to bring them within effective control.

Beginning in 1755 the course of Hopi history was to gravitate more and more toward acceptance of the Spanish. In that year one Franciscan priest preached to them, but without success; another was well received but prohibited from discussing religion. The next year two missionaries were received, but again the Christian religion was a tabooed subject. The arid environment in which the Hopi lived was able to accomplish what the missionaries failed to do. A sequence of dry years exhausted the Indians' reserve of corn, and by 1779 many of the Hopi had gone to Zuni to survive. The next year most Hopi were so scattered that the local population was reduced from around seventy-five hundred to eight hundred. In the midst of this struggle to survive came the smallpox epidemic in 1781. In this same year, however, the rains came and the crops were bountiful, making it possible for the population to reconsolidate. It was finally pressures by the marauding Navajos that forced the Hopi to go to the Spanish in 1818 and request aid, but the Spanish, who were faced with their own problems of survival, were by then unable to help. The most striking characteristic of Hopi historical contacts with the Spanish was the ability of these Indians to withstand Spanish pressures toward acculturation, particularly in the religious sphere. It is evident that Hopi resistance toward the Spanish was not consistent, but the pro-Spanish faction seems to have been in the minority. Irrespective of the numerical importance of the factions it is suggestive that factionalism was a well-established aspect of Hopi life even before the Spanish arrived.

The next major problem faced by the Hopi was how to interpret the arrival of another group of non-Indians who began to enter their country as early as 1826. Were these the legendary Bahana who were to come from the east and aid the Hopi? It was thought that the Anglo-Americans might well be the Bahana since their men were successfully preventing the encroaching Navajo from seizing Hopi land.

In primeval times, according to a myth recorded at Oraibi, there was on earth no light or living thing but a being called Death. Three caves beneath the earth surface were likewise surrounded in darkness. In the lowest cave people existed in crowded and filthy conditions. Two brothers, The Two, lamented the plight of men and pierced the cave roof from above. They planted one plant after another so that men could climb up to the second world. A particular type of cane grew tall enough, and the many people and animals entered the second cave world. This setting was finally filled with people, and they ascended to the third cave. Some people fell from the cave back into the second world, as had also happened in the ascent from the first to the second cave. In the third cave the darkness was dispelled by fire found by the brothers. The people built houses and kivas and traveled from one place to another. Great turmoil developed when women neglected their duties as wives and mothers, preferring instead to dance in the kivas. Finally the people, along with Coyote, Locust, Spider, Swallow, and Vulture, emerged at the fourth level, which was the earth. They wandered about in the darkness with only torches to light their way. Together the men and the creatures with them attempted to create light. Spider successfully spun a blanket of white cotton which gave off some light. The people then processed a white deerskin which they painted with turquoise paint. The skin was then so bright that it lighted the entire world. The painted deerskin became the sun, and the blanket was the moon. The stars were released from a jar by Coyote. Once the earth was lighted it was realized that the land was limited in space and surrounded by water. The Vulture with its wings fanned the water, and as the waters flowed away mountains appeared. The Two made channels for the waters through the mountains, and canyons and valleys were formed.

When the people arrived on earth and lighted the darkness they saw the tracks of the God of Death, Masau'u, and attempted to follow them to the east. The people caught up with Masau'u, and a girl who was not so attractive as one whom she envied conspired with Masau'u to cause the first death. The girl causing the death was the first witch, and her descendants became the witches of the world. The dead girl was seen living in the cave world below the earth, which had become an idyllic place. Another deity helped the people by making their maize and other seeds ripen in a single day. The witch then caused conflicts with people who had emerged on earth before the Hopi, particularly the Navajo and Mexicans. Of the two brothers who led the people from the underworld, the younger brother was the ancestor of the Oraibi people. The older brother went east but promised to return when the Hopi were in need of him. After many generations the older brother's descendants, the Bahana, were to return and find the Hopi poor and in need. The ~~Bahana~~ would be rich and would bring food and clothing for the Hopi. The Hopi would reject the Bahana, but the latter would treat them kindly.

The hairstyle for men was bangs over the forehead and the remainder of the hair gathered in a knot behind the neck or else cut off evenly at the nape of the neck. A headband of fur or fiber was worn about the head to hold the hair in place. Everyday clothing for a man included a breechclout of deerskin or cotton cloth over which was worn a cotton cloth kilt, belted at the waist. A man also might wear leggings of deerskin as well as moccasins or sandals woven from yucca fiber. In cold weather a cotton shirt was worn, and perhaps a woven rabbit-skin blanket was added. A girl wore her hair long until she passed through the Girls' Adolescent Ceremony; then it was put into two disk-shaped bundles, one over each ear. After she married, her hair was parted in the middle and worn long. A woman's clothing consisted of a wraparound cotton blanket which passed under her left arm and was fastened together over the right shoulder. The garment extended a short distance below her knees; she wore leggings on her lower legs and moccasins on her feet.

At the southern end of Black Mesa, there are three tongues of land. The westernmost section is Third Mesa, and on top of it at the southeastern end Oraibi is located. The pueblo is laid out in a series of eight roughly parallel streets, with a plaza between two streets and kivas scattered about the settlement. In aboriginal times the houses were square and made from stones dressed and set in place by men. The roof beams were placed on top of the last layer of stones, and the women for whom a house was constructed prepared and applied a mud plaster to the inner wall surfaces. A woman and her friends completed the roofing by adding on top of the beams a layer each of brushwood, grass, and finally mud. The house was windowless, and no doors opened onto the street. The dwellings were owned by women, and a new house usually was constructed next to or near the residence of the woman's mother or other near female relative. The residences were often multistory, and access to a ground floor room was through an opening in the ceiling, beneath which was placed a notched log ladder. The rooms were square, extending about twelve feet along

each wall, and floored with stone. Along one side of a room were bin
metates of different degrees of coarseness for grinding maize. There
were fireplaces in such dwellings but few other furnishings. The rooms
without an outside opening were used for storage of food and material goods. A kiva or ceremonial structure was a subterranean room
with a roof entry gained by descending a ladder. A kiva was rectangular in shape and was built along a north-south axis. The southern
portion of the floor, where observers would sit, was slightly higher
than the floor on the north side. In the northern section were a fire
pit and a sipapu. Along the walls except for the south side were hollow stone compartments containing sacred objects. The usable kivas
in Oraibi numbered about fifteen. In general each was owned by the
sib which constructed it or refurbished and rededicated an abandoned
one.

The Oraibi farmlands were mainly east, southwest, and west of
the settlement. The lands were in theory owned by the Bear sib head,
who was the Village Chief. The precedent for his ownership was established at the founding of Oraibi in the mythological past. The lands
were allotted for use to particular matrisibs, and surplus land, held
by the Bear sib, could be allotted to any conscientious individual by
the Village Chief. The result was that no sib was landless although
some lands were far more desirable than others. One of the major
causes of disputes between sibs was over landholdings. In many respects it is remarkable that the Hopi were able to till the soil successfully. The winds, the cold summer nights, the early frosts, baking
sun and very sporadic rainfall all led to an unpredictable harvest.

The most elaborate manufactures were textiles, usually woven by
men, plus pottery and basketry made by women. Hopi men prepared
their domestic cotton by carding and spinning it into thread, and they
wove textiles on looms located either in their homes or in a kiva.
The fiber often was colored with vegetable dyes which turned the
cotton yellow, orange, green, black, or various shades of red. Two
loom forms were utilized for different purposes. A vertical loom was
suspended between the ceiling and the floor for making square and
rectangular cloth for blankets. The waist loom was attached to a beam
at one end and to the weaver's waist at the other, being held taut
by his body. The latter loom was employed in the manufacture of
belts. Associated with either loom form were similar component parts.
Two beams, one upper and one lower, held the warp in position;
the heddle rod held loops of yarn to draw the warp forward;
a shed rod was cast behind the warps not held by the heddle rod and
in front of those held; a batten, which was shaped like a sword, held

open the shed, and after a weft strand had been woven into place, one edge of the batten was brought down on the weft to force it firmly into place. There were two principal weaves reported; in plain weaving the weft and warp consistently intercepted at the same place and in twilled weaving the weft and the warp joined at different points. Variations on these basic forms included tapestry weaves in which the weft was pressed so tightly by the batten that it could not be seen readily, and brocade weaving was employed, which means weaving extra threads into cloth to make a design. The only weaving by women was the production of rabbit-skin blankets. These were made on vertical loom frames. The warp was probably cotton thread spirally wrapped with rabbit-skin strips, with the fur still on; the weft was probably cotton thread. The most important textiles woven by the men for women included wedding robes, belts, dresses, and shawls. For themselves men wove kilts and sashes for ceremonies, as well as kilts, shirts, and blankets for daily use.

Hopi pottery was either undecorated ware for cooking and storage or else polished and decorated for other uses. There were sources of gray or yellow clay near all the villages, and it was collected by the women. The raw dry clay was first soaked and then kneaded into a paste. For cooking and storage vessels quantities of ground sandstone were added to the paste, but little or none was mixed into the paste of other wares. The bottom of a vessel was molded from a single piece of clay, and then oblong coils of moist clay were added spirally to the base. Each coil was pinched to join with the preceding piece, and the junctures of the coils were obliterated by smoothing them with the hand. The complete containers were dried, and any cracked vessels were discarded. Utility ware then was fired without further processing. The vessels were preheated around a fire made from cedar bark. After the fire burned to a bed of ashes, the ashes were spread and wood chips placed on top along with coal. The top was covered with a layer of large sections of broken pots. Then the vessels to be fired were placed upside down on the prepared furnace; finally the vessels were covered with large sherds and additional coal, and were left to fire overnight.

Once a more elaborately processed vessel was dry, a piece of sandstone was used to smooth and thin the walls. The vessel was moistened and polished with a stone, later to be slipped and painted. The process of slipping which sometimes preceded painting involved mixing clay with water to a creamy consistency and applying it to the vessel with a rabbit tail. After the slip had dried, the vessel was polished again. The pigments used for painting were a vegetable product binder with hematite for black, yellow from a clay containing iron hydroxide which fired red or shades of orange, and white from one particular source of fine white clay. The pigments were applied with yucca fiber brushes. The Hopi pottery designs prevalent around the time of early historic contact and today are essentially the same. This is not an example of long-term stability in design styles but a revival of old designs. In 1895 Jesse W. Fewkes excavated an abandoned Hopi pueblo at First Mesa. One of his Indian workmen was a man from Hano, a settlement among the Hopi of Rio Grande Indians who arrived around 1700. The wife of the man was named Nampeyo, and her interest was attracted to the beautifully executed, painted pottery found at the site. This woman already was recognized widely as one of the best Pueblo potters. First she studied the archaeological sherds until she was familiar with the patterning. Later she developed a style derived from the original but not an exact copy of it and became renowned for her pottery. One typical vessel form, a water jug, had a rounded bottom, sides that flared up to two thirds of the height, and a rounded constriction which was nearly flat on top with a raised neck. Another form was a small bowl for serving food. On the water jugs the painted design was confined mainly to the flat upper portion which was a broad ring for the design pattern. A characteristic of the designs was that a black line which was always broken was painted just below the vessel mouth. The designs formed a continuous band, four equal sections with each design alike, or four panels with two different designs alternating. The bowl motifs in the bottom of the vessels were a single design or less frequently a series of radiating designs. Bowl designs, which were most often of birds, ranged from fairly naturalistic to highly conventional forms. Water jug designs were more formalized with the field broken by parallel lines. The designs were largely geometric as well as angular in their execution.

Rather surprisingly, basketry varied greatly in method of manufacture from one mesa to another. Second Mesa women manufactured coiled baskets, and those of Third Mesa wove wicker baskets. In the recent past, 1930's, basketry was not made at all on First Mesa. The warp elements of Third Mesa wickerwork were from wild current or another plant, while the weft elements were from sumac or rabbit brush. Different vegetable dyes included greens, yellows, blue, purple and black. The basketry shapes usually were flat or shallow trays.

Katcina "dolls" are a category of Hopi material culture which has attracted wide attention among whites. These small painted and adorned wooden images usually were made by men for children prior to katcina performances. The figures were presented to the children by the katcinas and were considered by the children as gifts from the gods. The katcina images were hung from the rafters in the home of a child in order that he might familiarize himself with the many different forms. Katcina figures frequently are called dolls, but this is a misnomer since they were not played with as dolls but served mainly to instruct uninitiated children about one aspect of the religious system. Harold S. Colton has written the most complete analysis of Hopi katcina figures, and he states that there are more than two hundred forty different forms. They are divided into six different groups which are as follows: chief katcinas, who were the leaders among katcinas; clowns; runner katcinas; katcinas appearing in a wide variety of forms at the Powamu Ceremony; those appearing during the one-day katcina performances; and katcina-manas or female katcinas. The various image forms were carved from cottonwood tree roots. After a figure was shaped, it was smoothed with a section of sandstone, after which appendages such as ears or horns were pegged into place. Over the figure was applied a thin layer of white clay, and on this base were added vivid colors, the same ones used for the body paintings of real katcinas. Various organic or inorganic substances were used to produce black. For yellow, iron hydroxide was employed, red was from hematite, and a fine white clay was used for white. A figure was painted and then adorned with small feathers representative of eagle, parrot, turkey or other large birds.

The katcina images reflect in a somewhat stylized form the disguises used by men in portraying katcinas. The head of a katcina impersonator was covered with a full face mask of leather or one made from a flat basket. The mask itself might cover only the upper part of the face, with a beard of hair or feathers hanging beneath. The most common form of mask was a cylindrical piece of leather with a circular disk sewn on top. The openings through which the performer looked were small slits or holes, which had no relationship to the eyes on the mask. Noses were highly stylized protuberances, and mouths might be tubular, beak-shaped, or painted in various ways. The top of a mask often was adorned with a wooden tablet, feathers, hair, or wool. A fox-skin boa encircled the neck where the mask met the body. A wide variety of costumes prevailed with a white cotton shirt, cotton kilt, sash, and green moccasins being common for the chief katcinas. Many of the others wore cotton kilts, sashes, a fox skin hanging behind the kilt, and red moccasins. Some might wear breechclouts in addition to skin robes over their shoulders, while a katcina portraying a bride wore a typical bridal outfit. Other female impersonators wore typical women's dresses. A katcina was made striking by the vivid color of the paints applied to the wooden image or impersonator. The colors symbolized the direction from which the katcina came. Yellow indicated a northerly direction; blue-green, westerly; red, southerly; white, easterly; while red, yellow, white and blue-green in combination indicated the zenith, and black the nadir. The mask, body, and legs were often painted with representations of heavenly phenomena, animal tracks, phallic or vegetable symbols. It seems significant that these vivid colors of the gods offered striking contrast with the drab local desert setting and the bland colors found in the village environment.

The material inventory, in addition to those already mentioned manufactured items, included a rather limited number of objects. The hunting and warring bows were of the self-bow type made from oak or shadblow; the latter is a shrub or small tree. Arrows were made either from reeds or various types of wood. The reed variety of shaft was tipped with a wooden foreshaft. The nonreturning boomerang or rabbit-killing stick was made from oak which did not grow locally and had to be imported. Cut to shape, it was then steamed over a fire so that it could be bent to the desired degree of curve. For driving or snaring small game, nets and snares probably were made from yucca fiber twine, cotton thread, or perhaps from both materials. In addition to basketry and pottery containers, vessels were made from squash and possibly gourd shells in aboriginal times. Gourds served as dippers, canteens, spoons, and other containers. Rattles made from hoofs, seeds, and shells were attached to fringed garments or worn in bands about the waist or arms. Rattles also were made by placing seeds in squash or gourd shells. A flute with five stops was manufactured and blown across the end; this instrument was employed by the flute societies. Rasps were made by notching a stick of greasewood and running a stick or animal's scapula back and forth over the notches. The bull-roarer was a sacred implement consisting of a wooden tablet attached to a cord. When the cord was whirled about, the wooden piece produced a sound which was to bring rain clouds.

The subsistence year began with the planting of crops, for it was the horticultural harvest, not what was obtained by hunting, which sustained the people. The time to plant any particular crop was established by a Sun Watcher, and his determination was made on the basis of when the sun rose at a particular spot on the horizon. It was habitual for the men of the various matrisibs to plant and harvest their crops as a group. A married man planted the sib land allotted to his wife and her immediate family. The men were considered the owners of crops until they were taken into the wife's house, after which the produce became the property of the women on whose land it had been grown. The farmlands derived their moisture from ground seepage at the foot of Black Mesa or from stream overflow; cultivation of the latter type of ground is termed floodwater farming. Maize, the most important crop by far, was planted in holes about a foot deep made with a digging stick. Some ten to twenty seeds were dropped in a single hole, and if a planting did not sprout in about ten days it might be reseeded. The only preparation of a plot for planting was to trample the weeds or cut them with a broad-bladed, spatula-shaped implement and then break the soil with a pointed stick. After the plants began to grow, in plots which were about one acre in extent, they were weeded and the soil loosened about the roots. Fields were not rotated nor was the maize hilled. Beans sometimes were planted among the maize stalks but more often were raised in separate plots. Squash and cotton too appear to have been raised on separate acreage. During planting and harvesting a Masau'u impersonator was usually present, but there were virtually no specific planting and harvest rituals. Most other Hopi subsistence activities also were group endeavors organized by individuals or societies to embrace some or all of the community. One of the cooperative communal tasks was to clear sand and debris from the village springs which were owned by the Village Chief but used by anyone. For such a work party there were sometimes katcinas who served as mock taskmasters.

Hopi knowledge about the flora of their environment probably did not exceed comparable information available to many other groups of sedentary Indian farmers. What is unusual is that an extensive ethnobotany has been compiled on the Hopi plant usages by Alfred F. Whiting. Among these people in the 1930's he found that there were about forty plants under cultivation. Of this number only five species were aboriginal (kidney and tepary beans, maize, cotton, and squash); four others may have existed prior to Spanish times but more likely represent post-contact domestics (Aztec and lima beans, gourds, and sunflowers). Five plants were introduced during the Spanish period (chili peppers, onions, peaches, watermelons, and wheat); however, all others were first introduced by Mormon farmers or other Anglo-Americans. Ten diverse species of wild plants were cared for by the Hopi, but the seeds apparently were not sown from year to year. For example, wild tobacco seeds from two different species were sown so that plants would provide leaves for ceremonial uses. This apparently was necessary since the plant did not grow in local abundance. Likewise, wild dock root was used for dye, and the seeds sometimes were planted. Some wild plants such as beeweed were not cleared from a plot in order that the young plants could be collected and cooked. Fifty-four different wild plants were eaten; ten were staples, fifteen were used as greens in the spring, and twelve others were used when there was a domestic crop failure. The balance were used as snacks or seasonings, or were made into beverages. In the manufacture or decoration of items nearly fifty plant species were utilized; sixty-five were used medicinally and forty ceremonially or for magical purposes. Although there is overlap in the above listings, the Hopi made use of a wide variety of plant species. There were about two hundred wild flowering plants in the locality, of which half were commonly utilized. At the same time it still is likely that a number of plants existed locally which were neither identified nor used.

Compared with the rituals for farming, the ceremonial preparations for a hunt were complex. The species most frequently hunted were antelope and rabbits; both jackrabbits and cottontails were considered desirable as food. Rabbits were hunted often in the late summer when it was not essential to tend the crops. A man organizing a hunt could be of any sib; he made the necessary observances to the God of the Hunt by preparing prayer offerings. The details of when the hunt was to be held were announced by a crier, and the next day further rituals were observed by the organizer. In the actual hunt men formed a surround which decreased in size until the trapped animals were confined to a small area. Rabbits were killed with boomerangs as well as with clubs, which were thrown. A rabbit killed outright belonged to the killer and a wounded one to whoever caught or killed it. The surround was formed repeatedly and additional rabbits, plus any other game, were taken until the leader called an end to the hunt. The game was taken back to the village, and each man gave his kill to his mother, sister, wife, or father's sister. The recipient "fed" the game cornmeal, and later she put some of each animal's gall on a piece of piki (cornmeal bread), added salt and rabbit fur, offered this combination to the dead animal, and then threw the offering into the fire. The ritual was performed in order to restore the game to the God of the Hunt.

For hunting antelope, deer, and mountain sheep the organizer as well as all the others in the party made prayer offerings, and there was ritual smoking. The surround method was used to capture these animals in aboriginal times. It seems to have been the pattern to run down and suffocate an antelope. A deer apparently was shot with arrows or clubbed to death but not stabbed. Once again there was a ritual propitiation of the deceased animal. Coyote hunts were conducted by kiva members collectively, and as usual the surround technique was employed. In the kiva after a hunt each coyote was given a lighted corn husk cigarette and spoken to as a child before the owner took the animal home.

The primary staple, maize, was more than a food to the Hopi; it was the symbol of life itself. To consider only the subsistence facets of maize utilization, however, it is recorded by Whiting that they grew three different varieties: flour, sweet, and flint. In early historic times the flint form was quite important, since the hull of each grain was hard and in storage could not be attacked easily by weevils. At the same time the flint variety was difficult to grind, which appears to be the reason for its decreasing importance in recent times. The most popular variety of maize in recent times has been the flour type, which was grown by every farmer; the white strain was most important, followed by one which was blue. Among the flour maize strains there were at least twenty different forms named and identified. Sweet corn was raised in small quantities, with only two different named strains.

As would be anticipated, there existed a wide variety of dishes prepared from maize. The harvested product usually was stored on the cob and shelled for use as needed. Shelled, ground maize was made into gruel, dumplings, soups, and bread. Hominy was prepared by soaking shelled maize in a juniper wood ash and water mixture, then boiling the grains and washing them to remove the hulls. Maize also was roasted on the ear, parched, or baked in pits. One dish, very much like popcorn, was prepared by soaking the kernels in salt water and parching them in hot sand. Ground cornmeal sometimes was bound in corn husk containers and boiled before eating. One very important food made of maize, piki, was used as bread. It was made from a finely ground cornmeal mixed with water, using ashes as leavening. It was baked on a special stone slab over a fire. The stone was heated and greased, and the bluish-gray liquid was poured over the stone. After baking, the piki was folded or rolled into "loaves" for later consumption. It often was eaten by dipping one end into liquid food; the moist portion was bitten off and chewed.

The Hopi knew of no term for household, and yet this was the social unit which dominated and guided the life of each individual. A child was born into this unit and retained a strong emotional identity with it throughout life. The household consisted of a core of women—grandmother, daughters, and daughters' daughters—plus unmarried sons and in-marrying husbands. All of these persons except the husbands belonged to the same matrilineage as did the males who were born into the unit but had married and moved into

the houses of their wives. When the members of a matrilocal household outgrew the residence, a new contiguous room was built to accommodate the overflow. This adjacent household retained its ties with the parent matrilineage and held farmland in common as well as maintaining a reverence to a common fetish with accompanying ceremonies. Possession of the lineage fetish or bundle would be by the oldest female lineage head, and the associated ceremonies were conducted largely by the old woman's brother or son. The ritual obligations were passed down the most direct maternal line associated with the original lineage residence. This physical structure was the meeting place at which to discuss common lineage problems, and it remained the heart of the matrilineage sometimes even after it was abandoned. Thus there was a leading matrilineage with the greatest rights and duties as well as subordinate or daughter lineages. As a daughter lineage grew in size, it might become so socially removed from the original group that the underlying ties were lost. The distant lineages would become separate entities if they created new fetish bundles and acquired distinct names. Members of a named group tracing their ties through the female line and having the same bundle, although they could not trace connecting genealogical ties, formed what would be called a matrisib.

By 1906 there were about thirty named matrisibs at Oraibi, with the number representing splits of sibs, as well as the possible settlement at Oraibi by a number of different sibs. The sib names are linked with happenings in mythological times or refer to sib ancestors and include such examples as Katcina, Bear, Bow, Butterfly, and Lizard. Sib ancestors were termed *wuya* and might or might not be tangibly represented by a sib bundle. A bundle sometimes included more than one *wuya,* and this led to sibs' having alternative names. It might be assumed, also, that a two-bundle *wuya* represented the consolidation of two declining sibs. The sibs were grouped into nine nameless phratries which contained from two to six member sibs. The union of sibs within a phratry was associated with the mythological past, and possibly sibs of the same phratry stemmed ultimately from the same lineage base. Sib members of the same phratry could not marry one another, but they shared common ceremonial and landholding interests.

Overall village control was in the hands of two individuals: the Village Chief and the War Chief. The Village Chief was from the Bear sib, and a sacred stone in his possession validated his position of authority. The stone reportedly was brought from the underworld by Matcito, the legendary village founder. Covering the stone were engraved motifs, including human figures, which on interpretation were the basis for the division of lands among the sibs. The stone was inspected as a part of each Soyal Ceremony. The Village Chief headed the Soyal Ceremony, which gave him the highest sacred standing. The most important secular duty of the chief was to settle land disputes, but he did not arbitrate other differences between villagers. He was the "father" of the community and was not to be troubled with ordinary disagreements between villagers. His sacred duties, in addition to those surrounding the Soyal Ceremony, included offering prayers for village welfare. It was the Village Chief who stayed up late each night smoking and musing about pueblo conditions after most people had gone to sleep. For any critical matter of community concern, his advice was sought although he could not compel the actions of others. The office of the Village Chief was passed to a brother or to a sister's son after this potential chief had received instructions from the existing chief during a long period of training. The Village Chief wore no badge of office, but he had a distinctive style of body painting for certain ceremonies and a sacred stick or cane of authority.

The only individual at Oraibi with permanent power as well as authority was the War Chief. He had the right to inflict either verbal or physical punishment for nonconformity, and he attained his position by being the most outstanding warrior. It was he who, carrying a stone-headed club as his only weapon, led men into battle. On some occasions, when parties of men were organized for a community project, certain katcinas assembled the workmen and directed their activities. If a man were a laggard, he might be reprimanded or even in extreme instances beaten by a katcina. The authority and power of the overt leaders never extended beyond the village. There was no means for uniting the Hopi as a tribe; in fact, the only time they clearly joined in a common cause was during the Pueblo Revolt of 1680.

From the point of view of a male Ego the terminology for designating blood relatives often is virtually coextensive with his natal household. Ego termed his mother the same as his mother's sister and would not distinguish between them in normal usage. At the same time father and father's brother were termed alike, but mother's brother was termed differently. The designations for females in the first ascending generation paralleled that for males since father's sister was distinguished from mother and mother's sister. This is a bifurcate merging terminology for aunts and uncles as well as mothers and fathers. This usage is reasonable since mother and mother's sister were of the same matrisib, and father was in the same matrisib as father's brother. In the cousin terminology parallel cousins were termed as siblings whereas mother's brother's children were termed as one's own children, and father's sister's daughter was called the same as father's sister. Finally father's sister's son was termed father. This terminology for cousins is of the Crow type. The most distinguishing characteristic of the cousin terms is the ignoring of certain generational distinctions. The kinship terminology provided the framework for lifelong responsibilities, with particular forms of behavior expected in the varying sets of relationships. One of the most bitter overt displays of anger against someone was to renounce kinship usage and its accompanying ties.

The Hopi prided themselves on being peaceful people who even dreaded shedding the blood of most animals, and yet they were organized for armed conflict. They fought to defend their pueblo, and the role of a warrior was recognized as dangerous, important, and necessary. In primeval times, when the Hopi emerged from the underworld, it was the Kokop sib which introduced a warrior society and aided the Spider sib in accomplishing the same end. Every man joined the society, but a distinction was made among members. Boys were trained for warfare with a rigorous program of cold baths, races, archery practice, and rising early. The Warrior Society held a ceremony each year during the late fall. Its membership was divided into ordinary warriors and stick-swallowers; these two categories might be regarded as divisions of one society or as two separate societies holding a joint ceremony. The sacred equipment was held by the Spider and Kokop sibs. The two days of rituals involved the usual pattern of making prayer objects, ritual smoking, offering prayers, and building altars. A war medicine was prepared and drunk, after which there were exhibitions of stick-swallowing by one branch of the membership. For the real warriors, those who acknowledged killing and scalping an enemy, there was a special initiation which involved fasting and secret rituals.

Warfare was said always to have been defensive. Men went into battle clad in ordinary clothing, with the addition of caps made from mountain lion skin to which were attached eagle feathers. A man fought using bow and arrows, a stone club, spear, and boomerang. Before embarking they prayed to the Masau'u and to long-dead warriors; they also sang songs to render them brave. The War Chief led them into conflict with his stone club. A slain enemy was scalped to the accompaniment of a scalping song, and scalps were carried into the pueblo on poles. A Navajo scalp was worthless, but one from an Apache or Ute was valued. The permanent resting place for a scalp was in the home of its taker. A scalp was washed with yucca suds and intermittently "fed" by its owner.

The Hopi ideas of man's relationship with the gods formed a well-conceived and orderly system built about continuity between life and death, with differences between these conditions ideally minimized. An integrated relationship was maintained between the living and the dead, with the spirits of the dead becoming clouds which brought rain to the living. Furthermore, the katcinas represented generalized ancestors whose activities on earth and in the underworld benefited the living. To the Hopi there was a duality in being human. Man possessed a physical body and a "breath-body," spirit or soul. When an individual died, preparations for burial were in many ways the same as for the newborn, since the corpse was sprinkled with cornmeal, bathed, and given a new name. The breath-body journeyed to the underworld, where its existence was like that of the Hopi on earth, except that when the dead consumed food they took only of its essence. Because of their weightlessness the dead could rise into the sky and become clouds to bring rain. Thus the deceased aided the living in a very meaningful manner. The katcinas were impersonations by the living of dead ancestors. The God of Death, Masau'u, logically was a god of fertility since the dead controlled the rain which led to fertility and growth. Likewise, the sun was a god of fertility, with an intimate association with the dead. The sun spent half of its time in the underworld, the land of the dead, and half of its time on earth. It was by prayers and offerings to the dead and to the sun that blessings on earth were realized.

Dual concepts integrated Hopi society still further. An individual was born to this earth, and in death he was born in the underworld, only again to "die" in the underworld and become reborn on earth. Even in death, the breath-bodies from the underworld were capable of returning to earth. As there was an earthly life cycle of the individual, there was a daily and yearly cycle for the sun. Each morning the sun left its eastern home and at sunset entered its western home; thus it furnished light equally to the earth and the underworld. On a yearly basis, winter began with the summer solstice and ended with the winter solstice, while summer began about mid-December and lasted until about mid-June. When the winter solstice occurred on earth, it was the time of a summer solstice in the underworld, and the reverse also was true. The generalized ancestors, the katcinas, were on earth from the winter solstice until the summer solstice—in the summer season—and in the underworld during the earth's winter. Finally, most major ceremonial societies held major and minor rituals;

these were separated by six months' time. While a major ceremony was being held on earth, a minor one was celebrated in the underworld by the katcinas. Thus, as would be expected, death in theory held no fears to the Hopi, for the living and the dead were one (see Note 1).

The religious system was implemented with a series of annual and biannual ceremonies held by particular religious associations or societies. Each major ceremony was controlled by a different organization, and each organization was linked to a different matrisib. An elder male of the leading lineage in each matrisib usually headed the religious association of his sib. In the possession of the matrisib was a fetish bundle called the "mother" or "heart" of the sib, which consisted of an ear of maize, feathers, and coverings as well as other sacred objects. The equipment was owned by the leading lineage, and there was an associated kiva in which services usually were held. The rituals were conducted at particular times; these were determined by phases of the moon, times when the sun rose at a particular spot on the horizon, or by the number of days since the end of another ritual set. The general pattern for all the major ceremonies of any group was similar. The rituals extended over nine days, and when kiva members were so occupied, a flag was attached to the kiva ladder to warn off nonmembers. During the rituals there was a prohibition against eating fatty foods, meat, and salt. There was the further prohibition against sexual activities before as well as during the time of these celebrations. The first day was a perfunctory beginning, and the next eight days were divided into two four-day segments, with the final day devoted usually to a ritual open to the public. The specifics of the ceremonies included the use of altars and associated wooden, stone, or clay tablets. On the tablets were painted motifs, which were symbolic or representative forms of animals, clouds, maize, and rain. There were many prayers, and there were singing and smoking. Prayer offerings to be left at the proper shrines also were constructed. Sand paintings and certain fluids with a water base likewise were important. Each secret society was associated with the curing of a particular disease, and to be taken ill with a disease controlled by a society was one means for induction. Initiation rituals usually took place around the midpoint of the major ceremony and involved among other things having one's head washed with yucca suds as well as being given a new name by a ritual sponsor who was already a member of the society.

To benefit by all the advantages of being a Hopi in this and the underworld it was essential to participate actively in the affairs of one or more secret societies. A necessary previous step was taken at about nine years of age when boys and girls were initiated into either the Katcina Society or the Powamu Society, the latter being more restricted in membership. Within the next few years a girl was expected to join one of the four women's societies; boys joined the Antelope, Blue Flute, Gray Flute, or Snake societies. Occasionally a woman joined a man's society and vice versa to fulfill a particular role, but by and large the ceremonial societies were divided along sexual lines. An adolescent boy was expected further to undergo a Tribal Initiation, and only then was he free to participate in the most sacred of all ceremonies, the Soyal.

A summary of the Hopi ceremonial year, followed by a description of the Katcina Society, provides a glimpse of the integrated complexity of religious behavior. A review of the ritual calendar may arbitrarily be considered to begin with the winter solstice or Soyal Ceremony. The Soyal was conceived around a mysterious moment each year when, in Hopi thinking, the sun rises at the same place for four days, when the days are shortest. The Soyal Ceremony was conducted by men who had completed the Tribal Initiation, which meant being admitted to membership in the Agaves, Horns, Singers, or Wuwutcim societies. At Oraibi the Wuwutcim Society conducted the most sacred of the Soyal rituals, and it was far more popular than the others. The Soyal was managed by Bear sib members with the Village Chief as the director. The principal function of the ceremony was to compel the sun to begin the trip back to its summer home so that it would bring warmth enough for the crops to be planted. The climax of the rituals came when the "Star Priest," called Sun Priest at other times, performed a dance with a sun symbol representative of the cycle of the sun. The ceremony had the complementary purposes of inducing fertility in both women and plants and participation was village-wide. There were particular men and women dancers and the performances of katcinas, as well as the usual smoking and prayers plus the manufacture of a large number of diverse prayer offerings of corn husks, feathers, and prayer sticks.

The Powamu Ceremony, which began when the new moon in February was first seen, climaxed in the forced growth of beans in the kiva of the Powamu Society, which led the activities. Fifty to one hundred bean plants were raised by each man in his own kiva. The beans were well watered, and the kiva fires burned hot day and night to force the sprouting. The beans were grown for the Eototo and Aholi katcinas, those katcina impersonators who planted maize which sprouted at the same time as the beans. If the beans and maize sprouted well and grew heartily until the harvest, it was a good omen for the forthcoming farming season. The sprouted beans were cut and bundled to be presented by katcinas to the grower's uninitiated off-spring, his ceremonial children, and favored relatives. A man made small bows and arrows or other gifts for boys and katcina images for girls or women. In each instance the gifts were presented to the recipients by the katcina impersonators. During the years when children were to be initiated into the Powamu Society, the initiates saw the sacred rituals for the first time on the fifth day. They were instructed not to reveal their new knowledge under the threat of punishment by the katcinas. By undergoing the initiation, participants became members of the Powamu Society and were permitted to impersonate katcinas, to participate in katcina rituals, and to become katcina fathers or ceremonial sponsors. Not all children were inducted into the Powamu Society; the remaining children on the sixth day of the Powamu Ceremony were inducted into the Katcina Society. Membership carried the right to function as a katcina, but these individuals could not participate in the Powamu ceremony or become katcina fathers. The initiation included revelation of sacred traditions, and the initiated again were cautioned against revealing the secrets they had learned.

In August another high point in the ceremonial round was reached with the performances of the Antelope-Snake or Blue and Gray Flute society ceremonies. The Blue and Gray Flute societies alternated with the Antelope and Snake societies in presenting August ceremonials each year. The Flute societies conducted their most sacred and secret rituals in the home of the leading lineage of the supervising sibs. The pattern of prayers, smoking, and manufactured offerings was climaxed by a ceremonial race, and later the offerings were placed at shrines. The membership assembled also at a spring where one man submerged completely in the water to the accompaniment of singing and dancing. When the man surfaced, he brought up with him gourds filled with water which symbolized water for Oraibi. Another race took place, this time for women, and a ritual similar to the one just described was held at another spring. Then there was a final race to the village by women. Even though the Flute ceremonies took place after the summer solstice they seem to have been a counterpart of the Soyal, and as with the Soyal, their performance was to bring rain and fertility. The Antelope-Snake ceremonies served the same function, alternating years with the Blue and Gray Flute society ceremonials.

The Antelope and Snake societies were separate organizations,

but they combined for their major ceremony. The two societies manufactured prayer offerings jointly, then separated to their kivas, where
they performed secret rituals. At this time the Snake Society members
collected snakes in each of the four directions on each of four different days. As with the Flute ceremony there was a race, but the
major event was a public performance in the plaza. Here the Antelope
Society men danced with vines, which they had obtained previously
from a cottonwood bower in the plaza, dangling from their mouths.
The next day the Snake Society members brought the captive snakes
from their kiva to the bower and danced with the Antelope performers. Then in pairs the Snake men went to a previously erected cottonwood booth, where one of each pair received a snake, which he held
by his lips or teeth just behind the snake's head. He danced around
the plaza several times while his partner brushed his shoulders with
a "snake whip," which was a short stick with eagle feathers attached.
Another Snake Society member danced along behind the pair. Each
snake was danced with and then released on the ground at the plaza.
The snakes were then gathered together in a circle and sprinkled with
cornmeal by females of the Snake sib. Finally, younger men of the
Snake Society picked up as many snakes as they could and took them
to shrines in each of the four cardinal directions.

The public performances of the Snake Society members have
attracted more popular interest among whites than any other American Indian ritual. The reason, of course, is that the snake dancers
carried prairie rattlers in their mouths as often as they carried harmless species such as the bull snake. The Snake Society members handled the poisonous and harmless snakes with equal ease, and yet
prairie rattler bites occasionally are fatal. Illness or death from snake-
bite among the dancers is unreported, and various explanations
have been offered concerning the Indian's ability to handle poisonous
snakes. There is no evidence to support the possibility that the members have an immunity to snake venom or that the snakes were
charmed. Neither is there reason to believe that the snakes were
drugged in any manner. Furthermore, the Hopi did not have an
effective antidote for venom; this was proven with a laboratory test-
ing of their snake medicine. Historically, there appear to have been
two different answers to Hopi success in handling rattlesnakes. In
1883 a herpetologist visited a kiva where snakes were being kept for
a dance; he inspected the fangs of one rattler and found them intact.
After the dance he sent two of the rattlesnakes which had been used
to the United States National Museum, and the venom glands were
found to contain poison. Thus it would seem almost certain that the

fangs were milked before the public ceremony. The next snake captured after a snake dance was taken in 1932; another herpetologist
recovered a rattler from a shrine following a snake dance. The snake's
fangs had been cut away rather skillfully. Similar evidence that the
fangs were cut out in recent times was obtained in 1951 when another
rattlesnake recovered after a ceremony was found to have had its
fangs removed. Thus, the weight of evidence is that the Hopi in
aboriginal times and into historic times milked the poison from the
fangs of rattlesnakes but that between 1883 and 1932 they shifted to
cutting away the fangs. The logical conclusion to be drawn is that
the Hopi came to understand white attitudes toward rattlesnakes and
eliminated the possibility of harmful bites by a surgical operation on
the dangerous snakes.

The final ceremony of major importance was the Tribal Initiation
controlled by the Agaves Society, and it was held only when this
society had at least one candidate for initation. During this ceremony
adolescent males were initiated into one of four secret societies, the
Agaves, Horns, Singers, or Wuwutcim. At Oraibi the most important
of the four was the Wuwutcim, controlled by the Chicken Hawk sib.
It should be recalled that a male could not be a fully participating
adult in Hopi society until he had passed through this initiation.
The Tribal Initiation was the most complex of the ceremonies and
a cornerstone of Hopi religion. The time for the Tribal Initiation,
which took place in November, was established by the Sun Watcher.
After the announcement that the time for the ceremony had arrived,
the four sponsoring societies began their activities by smoking, making
prayer offerings, erecting the kiva flags, and preparing altars. A new
fire was made in the Agave kiva by the kiva chief and carried to the
other participating kivas. An idol called Dawn Woman was brought
from her shrine and exhibited on top of the kivas until the fifth day
of the ceremony, when she was returned to her shrine after "deliver-
ing" her offspring. The Wuwutcim initiates of the Chicken Hawk sib
were considered little chicken hawks, and each was given a poncho-
like blanket garment, which was to represent the feathers of a chicken
hawk, by his ceremonial father. The candidates pretended they were
little hawks, calling like a nestling for food as they flapped their arms
like wings. All candidates slept in their kivas, and on the third and
fifth days dances were performed which clearly were associated with
fertility, with phallic symbols and simulated pregnancies presented.
On the eighth day, dances indicative of germination were held by
the Chicken Hawks, and on the ninth day activities climaxed with
highly sacred songs, a bonfire, and impersonations of mountain sheep

by Horn Society members. All of these events, along with others which have not been described, symbolized the ritual rebirth of male children into manhood and reaffirmed the connection between the living and the dead.

Once long ago, according to Tawaqwaptiwa, the late Village Chief of Oraibi, after the Hopi departed from the uppermost level of the underworld they wandered on earth with their gods the katcinas. The Hopi with the katcinas were attacked by "Mexicans," and all the gods were killed. The dead returned to the underworld, and the surviving Hopi divided the ceremonial paraphernalia of the dead katcinas in order to impersonate the gods. It was these impersonations of katcinas which formed a core of Hopi ritual obligations. When a man wore the sacred costume of a katcina, he became a god, and his mask was the most sacred item of his costume. As the masks wore out, became soiled, or broke, they were replaced or repaired; replacement did not detract from their sacredness. The chief katcina masks were the only ones not to be replaced or duplicated. It was possible also to vary a new katcina mask from the original without impairing its supernatural associations. During any year katcinas were present at Oraibi from the time of the winter solstice till the summer solstice, and then they were in the underworld except for Masau'u Katcina, representing the God of Death, who was about the earth the year long. A Hopi did not deceive himself to the point of believing that an impersonator was a god but rather considered his role as a friend of the gods. Small children on the other hand were taught that these were the gods.

Membership as a katcina was open to all village men under the general sanction of the Village Chief, and the direction of katcina activities was under the control of the Badger and Katcina sibs. The former presided during the early season, and the latter functioned at the end of the season. The first katcina appeared in late November as a tired, bedraggled old man in a worn costume. He performed a dance feebly at the dance plaza, and at the Chief kiva he left four prayer sticks, danced and sang, and then sprinkled cornmeal in four of the six directions. These activities indicated the kiva was now open for katcinas. Near the end of the Soyal Ceremony in December the sexually aggressive Mastop katcinas arrived. They pretended to copulate with all the women, young and old alike, who gathered to watch their arrival. Ritual sexual intercourse was performed by a katcina when he placed his hands on a woman's shoulders and jumped up and down. This was not a frivolous gesture but a very serious fertility rite. The following day, the last of the Soyal, the Qoqoqlom katcinas appeared. Some performed a dance, and others sprinkled cornmeal as though to emphasize the opening of the season. During January any of the ordinary katcinas were initiated, and nightly performances were given in different kivas with each kiva dance group performing twice in all kivas. The groups originated in different kivas, with the kiva head deciding which katcina was to be portrayed. In February in association with the Powamu Ceremony katcinas again appeared. During the time of the Powamu two katcinas in particular served to intimidate uninitiated children who were wayward. These were the So'yoko and Natacka katcinas. Any kiva might supply the katcina actors, and they were instructed by the parents of bad boys and girls concerning the specific transgressions of particular children. Another performer, Hahai'i, the Katcina Mother, announced the forthcoming event in the kivas. The children were forewarned that something out of the ordinary soon would occur. The Hahai'i left shelled maize at each house in which there were girls and small snares for boys. The girls were warned to prepare ground cornmeal and the boys to trap small mammals for the giants who were coming, or else the giants would take them away. A few days later the awesome giant katcinas arrived, wearing frightening masks and carrying weapons and a basket in which to take away children. The katcinas cited particular transgressions of the children and threatened to carry them away. The parents defended the children; the offerings of baked cornmeal by the girls were accepted, but the small animals caught by the boys to appease the katcinas were rejected. Finally, the katcinas left, but only after they had received gifts of meat from the parents. The So'yoko and other katcinas then peered into a kiva and witnessed a dance performed by members. Then the giants hauled the performers from the ceremonial chamber. The hostile katcinas, intrigued with the dance, began to imitate the performance. Finally the katcinas and the dancers went into the kiva and ate the accumulated food. The children were told that the katcinas had descended into the underworld from the kiva.

In years when initiates were to be inducted through the Powamu Society it was the katcinas who initiated them. When the beans were harvested, the katcinas distributed bean sprouts and gifts to uninitiated children. On the day that the gifts were presented Aholi and Eototo katcinas appeared. The Aholi Katcina performed in a manner which on interpretation suggested that all of Oraibi belonged to the two of them. Together they performed a ritual with water symbolizing the bringing of rain. Later the same day, to the delight of villagers, many katcinas arrived and distributed surplus gifts from the morning.

The following day unmasked katcinas arrived at the kiva in which the initiates were assembled, and the preadolescents now learned that katcinas were not real gods. An additional kiva ritual took place in years when there was a Tribal Initiation, with the He'e'e Katcina, one of the "Mothers of all Katcinas," leading the katcinas in a procession. On the third day of this performance, shrines were visited; here the He'e'e was joined by additional katcinas, and she led them to the village. Finally a tale was reenacted symbolic of the arrival of the Badger sib at Oraibi.

For the balance of the season the Katcina Society was in charge of the various katcinas who appeared. The next series of katcina dances was known as Repeat, indicative of the fact that these were a repetition of performances held just after the end of Powamu. Included in the first series of Repeat performances was the Water Serpent dance. It could be arranged by any kiva that wished to present the ceremony so long as the Village Chief approved. The He'e'e Katcina led other katcinas with her entry into the village early one morning. On the evening of the same day the serpents, a male and female with two offspring, were the center of ritual attention. The ceremonial leaders took them to the main spring at Oraibi where prayers were offered, there was ceremonial smoking, and the heads and tails of the serpents were dipped into the spring water. Then the first performance was held in the sponsoring kiva. Before an assembled audience, but in the dark, a screen was erected with forced-grown maize plants placed before it. As the kiva was gradually lighted, the serpents appeared out of unseen holes in the screen and, swaying as they emerged full length, finally broke the maize in a symbolic harvest. The ceremony then was repeated at the other kivas. The next series of performances was held out-of-doors by katcinas at irregular intervals prior to the Home Going rituals. Sponsoring kivas impersonated almost any katcina as long as they had the Village Chief's approval. There were rehearsals, with prayers and the construction of prayer sticks, and katcina dances were held in the village plaza. A particular series of dances was held during a single day, and clowns might burlesque the dancers or perform independently of the katcinas. Finally the Home Going observances took place just after summer solstice and lasted for about a month. The katcina rituals closed with offerings made at a village shrine, and when the shrine lid was closed, the katcina season ended.

Considering the katcina cult as a whole, the summary statement about it by Mischa Titiev expresses the nature of the system very well. Titiev (1944, 129) states: "The complexities of their Katcina worship are of little moment to the Hopi. They make no effort to systematize or to classify their beliefs, but are content to regard the Katcinas as a host of benevolent spirits who have the best interests of the Hopi ever at heart. To impersonate them is a pleasure, to observe them a delight. Quite apart from its more formal features, the operation of the Katcina cycle brings more warmth and color into the lives of the Hopi than any other aspect of their culture."

Participation in secret societies was not restricted to men only, since women controlled three voluntary religious associations of their own. These were the Lakon, Marau, and Oaqol. Just as the secret societies of men included a few women, so the religious associations of the women included a few males. The organization of women's societies was similar to that of males: they were controlled by a lineage in a particular matrisib, possessed fetish bundles, carried out secret rituals in a kiva, and performed certain ceremonies in public. Each held its major ceremony in the fall, and it appears that the best established of the three was the Marau, with the other two derived from it. Titiev suggested that the Marau may once have been for the initiation of girls and paralleled the Wuwutcim for men. This possibility suggests itself because of certain parallel conceptual and ritual characteristics of the two societies.

The religious dogma of the Hopi was precise, the ceremonial round was exacting, and the katcinas played a major ceremonial role. In order to maintain the balance in nature and to sustain man's relationship with the gods each individual was obligated to contribute to the best of his ability. An individual's contribution was manifest in being *hopi* or good. The anticipated behavior for an individual was spelled out in detail since being *hopi* involved more than goodness alone. A Hopi was ideally very cooperative and self-effacing. He had moral as well as physical strength and health. Such a person was not aggressive; he was a guardian of life and bowed to collective responsibilities while always thinking good thoughts. Conversely, an evil or bad person was *kahopi*, with personality traits opposite those of the ideals.

Contemplation of the Hopi religious system reveals that it was a finely tuned totality. The katcinas always fulfilled their obligations in the underworld, and if the Hopi on earth did the same, there was no privation or unhappiness within the society. It was the responsibility of each person to fulfill his social and ceremonial obligations by being *hopi*. Community-wide prosperity indicated that each individual had contributed his utmost, and the ideals of the Hopi Way thus were achieved. But what about failures? Why was it that during some years rain did not fall, winds dried the ground and blew seeds away, or the stream beds did not flow with water? Obviously, it was essential to be able to explain why it sometimes came to pass that nature did not respond to the complex ceremonies. A scapegoat or rationalization for farming failure was necessary. The burden of failure was said to rest with individuals, persons who were *kahopi*, thinking evil and doing evil; these persons were witches. The origin of witchcraft was traced to Spider Woman who caused the first human death. Hopi informants believed that in a typical community there were more witches than ordinary people and that witches were males or females of any sib. No one was considered to be incapable of witchcraft. A Village Chief or ceremonial leader might be suspect simply because he held an important office. Anyone who was self-assertive was open to the accusation of being a witch because such behavior was not *hopi*. It was possible to become a witch either by voluntarily practicing sorcery or by unknowingly being inducted into a society of witches as a child. In the latter instance, existing witches reportedly carried off a related child while it slept and inducted it into a secret society which followed the patterning of other Hopi secret societies. The initiate was taught the witches' art of assuming the shape of an animal in order to pursue their nefarious craft by night. The power of a witch was derived from association with an animal familiar, such as a coyote, owl, wolf, or small black ant, from whom the greatest forces of evil emanated; quite logically, a sorcerer possessed "two hearts," his own and that of an animal familiar. Sorcerers harmed a community by sending pestilence to the fields, by causing land erosion to increase rapidly, or by driving off rain clouds and replacing them with a conjured windstorm. A witch was not content with destroying crops but killed living people as well. Murder by witchcraft probably was the most important activity of a sorcerer since it was by killing one relative each year that the witch extended his life. A relative was killed or his illness caused by shooting stiff deer hairs, ants, a bit of bone, or another object into his body without breaking the skin.

Just as there were individuals bent on harming and killing people by a supernatural means, there were likewise shamans whose obligation it was to cure the ill. There existed in early historic times a Hopi society of curers, but it passed out of existence before it could be reported adequately. In any event, in the more recent past there were curing specialists who relied on pharmacopoeia and massaging techniques. Their knowledge appears to have been secular in nature. Some individuals set broken bones and prepared herbs for patients. They possessed a rather complex body of information which required specialized training, and a secular shaman was likely to pass his knowledge on to a sister's son. In another category were the shamans who performed supernatural cures. These individuals were "two hearted," but in theory they employed their powers only for curing illness caused by witches. It is obvious, however, that such a person would be suspect in a sorcery case and a dangerous individual in any event. Such a person might identify the source of a malady after chewing jimsonweed root or some other plant to induce a vision which aided in diagnosing the difficulty. An ordinary person could best protect himself against a witch, who was most likely a near relative, by wearing arrowpoints of stone. These artifacts were regarded as the ends of lightning flashes associated with the clouds. Another way to ward off the effects of a witch was to rub ashes from cedar wood on both individuals and objects. The Hopi attitude toward known witches, those persons seen practicing witchcraft, was that such an individual would die or encounter misfortune. Therefore, it was both unnecessary and unwise to interfere with his activities. A witch usually was identified by a brave shaman in his diagnosis of someone's illness. Occasionally when an individual was dying he revealed that a certain person was a witch. The sanctions against a witch were not in this world but in the underworld, where his spirit thirsted and hungered, as it approached the underworld by only one step a year. Once it arrived there, it was burned in an oven and became a beetle.

The composite view of an individual's life cycle which follows has been drawn primarily from the data of Ernest and Pearl Beaglehole, obtained at Second Mesa communities, and from the writings of Mischa Titiev for Oraibi.

Certain precepts, when followed, were conducive to pregnancies. A woman should pray to the sun at dawn each morning, and she was most likely to conceive if she had sexual intercourse while menstruating. If she failed to conceive, her husband might make katcina images to be presented to her each year at the Powamu and Home Going ceremonies; to these images she prayed. Conception clearly was recognized to result from sexual intercourse, and a woman recognized her pregnancy by the fact that she failed to menstruate. If, as the embryo developed, a woman suspected that she was carrying twins, a shaman's aid was sought to make the twins one. To bear twins was regarded as difficult; also if both lived a parent would die, or if one twin died the other also would die. A pregnant woman prayed to the sun and sprinkled cornmeal in the process to ease the labor of childbirth. Furthermore, she was active during her pregnancy, and she as well as her husband observed diverse taboos.

A woman bore her offspring in the house of her mother, often the same dwelling in which she had been born. In the birth process she was unaided, and she bore the offspring while squatting over a layer of sand. Most deaths in childbirth were said to result from the woman's failure to expel the afterbirth. The blood, afterbirth, and sand were covered with cornmeal and hidden in a special crevice. If a young person had contact with the blood and afterbirth, he would become ill. Immediately after the delivery, the grandmother entered the room, severed the umbilical cord, and took charge. In a short time the father's close female relatives, his mother or sister, arrived to wash the head of the neonate and to direct the activities of the next twenty days, which culminated in a naming ceremony and a feast. It was the father's close female relatives with whom one later in life developed warm social ties. The father was nowhere to be seen during the birth, and usually for forty days thereafter he withdrew to his kiva away from the bustle and confusion in the house of his wife.

An infant was nursed whenever it awoke and cried. Furthermore, it was not weaned for two to four years or even longer (see Note 2). To quiet an unhappy child a mentor might rub its sexual organ, and a small child might masturbate while either other children or adults were present. When a child was able to walk, he was encouraged to urinate and defecate outside the house; if he should defecate inside, he might be scolded or slapped on the head. Matters pertaining to sex were accepted among the Hopi with casual regard. Since a child slept in a small room with his parents, their sexual activities easily were observable. Children were not instructed concerning sexual matters but came to understand them through observation. It was habitual for males and sometimes women casually to urinate before persons of the opposite sex. Furthermore, jokes which we would consider obscene were taught to small boys to be used when they performed as ceremonial clowns. Still, shyness was a characteristic of young girls, and a licentious person was sometimes called crazy.

Small children played together or with toys provided by adults. As they grew older, they were expected to rise early and pray to the sun in order to be *hopi*. They played in water and also bathed each day in the water of a spring. A boy accompanied his father to the fields; while he was small he played, but in later years he helped his father in the farming activities. A girl became tied to her home, and the care of her younger siblings or her mother's sister's small children was an important duty.

No formal recognition was given to the arrival of puberty for either males or females. It was customary, however, for boys in their early teens to begin sleeping in a kiva rather than at home; this was a distinct break with their earlier childhood. For a girl there was a ceremony through which it was necessary to pass before she married. It was held annually for girls between the ages of sixteen and twenty. The event usually was directed by a young female who had passed through the rituals, and she was aided by two boys in supervising the girls. Most of four days the girls spent morning to night grinding maize; the grinding took place in a darkened room in the home of one of the girls' paternal aunts. They also observed food taboos and drank liquids only at midday. The boys organized a rabbit hunt on the third day, and the girls spent most of that day baking piki. Afterwards, the girls appeared for the first time with new coiffures termed "butterfly wings" or "squash blossoms." A girl continued to wear her hair in this manner until she married. She was most likely to marry someone from within the community soon after passing through the Girls' Adolescent Ceremony.

Fornication between teen-agers was a norm, and it was formalized in the *dumaiya*. After a boy began sleeping in a kiva, he was free to roam the pueblo at night. While doing so, he wrapped himself in a blanket so that his identity would not readily be discerned. As the members of his amour's household slept, he crept in carefully to the side of the girl, who in a whisper asked who it was. The boy answered "It is I," and from the sound of his voice, the girl identified her caller. If she were willing, which usually was the case since the boy went only where he thought he would be received, he passed the night with the girl, leaving just before daylight. A *dumaiya* was supposedly secret, but it could not remain so in a small community like Oraibi. The girl's parents did not interfere with a *dumaiya* so long as they regarded the boy as a potentially acceptable husband for their daughter. A girl was not likely to have only a single lover, and before long she might become pregnant. If this happened, the girl named the boy she best liked as the father, and the formalities of arranging a marriage were begun. It also was possible for a girl to propose directly to a boy during certain festive or ceremonial occasions. A couple did not court unless they stood in a proper social relationship with one another. A person could not marry another of the same sib or phratry. In the ideal system of marriage, one could not marry a person of his father's sib or phratry, but this rule was not observed with care. Neither was a person who had never been married previously supposed to marry a divorced or widowed individual, but such marriages did take place. Such individuals, who were more frequently females than males, were termed "basket carriers," indicating that they would be forced to carry heavily-loaded baskets from their place of burial to the underworld.

A formal marriage ceremony began after the relatives of a couple approved the match; the girl then went to the boy's home to grind maize for three days. This was a trial period in which the girl demonstrated her abilities as a homemaker, but there was no comparable trial for the groom. While the girl was in the boy's home, his paternal aunts attacked the boy's mother and her sisters with mud and water for permitting the girl to "steal" their "sweetheart." The forces fought with mud and water in an atmosphere of jovial hostility. On the fourth morning the couple had their hair washed in one container by their respective mothers and female relatives. A mingling of their hair symbolized the marital union. Once again the paternal aunts of the boy attempted half-heartedly to disrupt the ritual. After their hair dried, the couple went to the mesa edge to pray to the sun and then returned to the groom's home for a wedding breakfast. The couple were now man and wife but continued to live in the groom's home until his male relatives, and any other men who offered to help, completed the bride's wedding costume. The men prepared the cotton and wove two sets of wedding garments, a small robe and a white-fringed belt, in addition to preparing skins and sewing white moccasins and leggings. During the manufacture of these items the groom's family feasted the workers. After about a month or longer, the garments were completed; wearing one set and carrying the second in a reed container, the bride returned home. Her husband informally and unobtrusively took up residence in her household. The wedding garments were very important because they were required for entering the underworld after death.

All Hopi women appear to have married, but such was not the case for men. There was indirect pressure to marry applied to a girl by her brothers and her mother's brothers in order to bring another male into their farming unit. A boy was not pressured to marry, for his family then lost him as an economically productive member. Any form of plural marriage was prohibited, but many unions were not permanent. In a compilation of marriage records for somewhat more than eight hundred individuals, Titiev found that over thirty-five percent had from one to eight divorces. The most common grounds for divorce was adultery, followed by what probably would be termed in-

compatibility in modern American society. Divorce was a simple matter to effect since it was only necessary for a man to rejoin his natal
household or for a woman to order her husband from her household.
The primary pressures against a divorce came from a girl's family
since they did not relish losing an economically productive male. A
divorce was casually regarded, however, partly because the mother and
her small children continued to reside in their old abode; an older
offspring might join either parent. It is not to be assumed that Hopi
society, with its rather extreme sexual laxness and marital instability,
did not suffer from these disorganizing influences, for there was a
definitely adverse effect.

A husband and wife lived together, but often they were not socially close. The activities of a male were not shared by his wife. He
was the hunter, the farmer of the lands of his wife's sib, the weaver,
and maker of moccasins. He might remain an outsider in his wife's
home throughout his life. A wife, her sisters, and mother owned the
house and all the subsistence items deposited there or in their store-
rooms. A wife prepared the foods for consumption and cared for her
children and, at times, her sister's children. A woman was quite free
to go much her own way, and if she were unhappy with her husband
she could divorce him almost as readily as he could divorce her. It is
little wonder that a woman was socially closest to her mother and her
mother's sisters, while a man maintained his warmest ties with his
natal household.

The household in which a child was reared consisted of a line of
females. Within this setting perhaps the closest bonds were between a
mother and her daughters. Daughters were destined to spend their
lives in their mother's home or in an adjacent residence, and eventually they assumed their mother's role in the society. From her mother
a girl learned the essential domestic skills and the norms of proper
behavior. A mother guided the most important decisions in the ceremonial life of a girl and was likely to have a voice in the selection of
her mate. When the menarche arrived, the girl's mother instructed
her on how to care for herself. The girl, however, was not isolated at
this time, nor at any other menstrual period; neither was she restricted
from participating in ceremonies while menstruating. Were a mother
to die the mother's sister, who was called mother, replaced the biological mother in the girl's affection. Between a mother and her son
the social bonds were not as close as between a mother and daughter
(see Note 3). A mother indulged an offspring of either sex, but a son
in his early teens soon found his identity with a kiva group. After
marriage a man's natal home remained the residence with which he

would most likely identify. He returned there when divorced and was a frequent caller in his mother's house. Like a girl, a man also identified closely with his mother's sister, especially if the mother had died. Small girls were fond of their fathers, but as a girl grew her father was not overtly important in her upbringing. He was, however, interested in having her find a good husband, who by his farming activities could lighten the father's economic labors. A father took comparatively little active interest in a son until the latter's Tribal Initiation. Then the father selected the boy's ceremonial sponsor, which was an important decision. As a boy grew older, his father assumed a major role as his teacher. He imparted farming and ceremonial skills as well as advice about being *hopi*.

Between siblings of the opposite sex there were bonds of friendship, mutual aid, and affection. Throughout childhood this was true, and there were no restrictions leading to avoidance after the individuals had reached maturity. Girls aided their brothers in farming activities, while boys gave their sisters gifts. Each was pleased by exemplary behavior of the other, and a girl was quick to defend her brother against any slander. Between brothers the social ties were close, with the older brother helping to educate the younger one. There might be indirect competition for ceremonial offices and for girls, but this was rarely disruptive. Often a younger brother married first so that the older one might care for their natal household; in marriage, it was ideal for brothers to marry sisters. As would be anticipated, sisters were socially close throughout their lives. When the age difference was great, the older one was the instructor of the younger. Close cooperation between sisters was expected but did not always occur. They occupied the same household and raised their children together; their solidarity was a foundation stone of Hopi social life.

The maternal uncle of a young boy was the only male of his parents' generation who was of the same lineage and sib as himself. This male was of varying importance to the boy. If such an uncle were a ceremonial leader, a boy might follow him in office; this necessitated a systematic training of the youth. In any instance, a mother's brother was likely to be the most important figure of authority associated with the boy's home, and the former did not hesitate to discipline an erring boy. A mother's brother was not all sternness toward his sister's children, however. He often told them myths or tales about their sib and would give them gifts on occasion. For a girl, her mother's brother was influential in the selection of her husband, and this uncle lectured the young couple toward the end of the marriage ceremony. A father's sister offered her brother's daughter advice, particularly in ceremonial matters, and the relationship included mutual aid. However, the most important function of a father's sister was to assist the birth of her brother's children. One very warm relationship was between a father's sister and her brother's son. As a small child, such a boy soon learned that he was always a welcome guest in this woman's home. Here he received favored foods and frequent demonstrations of love and affection. As he grew older, he took game to his paternal aunt and exhibited his warm feeling toward her. Sexual relations with this aunt and her daughter were possible, and Titiev suspects a youth may have, in the not too distant past, been expected to marry a father's sister's daughter.

As a person neared death, his body was said to become swollen. Younger people as well as most adults left the house, fearing to be present at the time of death. The body of an individual was bathed, his hair washed, and the body reclothed. A man was wrapped in a deerskin and a woman in her wedding blankets. The bodies were always flexed into a sitting position. Prayer offerings were prepared by the father of the deceased or another male in his sib. A prayer feather was placed beneath each foot and in each hand, as well as over the navel; the latter was the location of a person's spirit. The face was covered with cotton, symbolic of the time the dead become clouds, while food and water were placed with the body as sustenance on the journey to the underworld. The body was carried to the cemetery by men living in the house of the deceased; here a hole had been dug just large enough to receive the bundled corpse. It was placed facing the west, and soil was spread hastily on top. Those men who attended purified themselves afterwards by washing in a boiled juniper preparation, and there was a ritual in the household of the deceased to protect the members against spirits. The next day the man who had manufactured the prayer offerings took cornmeal and five prayer sticks to the grave. The prayer sticks would help the person on his travels to the land of the dead, and the food was to feed the spirit. A prayer was offered, and the spirit was told not to return for anyone else in the community. Later, each of the household residents washed his hair and smoked himself over hot coals on which pinyon gum had been placed. The possessions of the deceased all were thrown away. A separate cemetery was provided for the stillborn, infants, and children. Bodies appear to have been placed there if death occurred before a girl passed through the Girls' Adolescent Ceremony or before a male joined a religious society. The spirit of an infant did not travel to the underworld but lingered above the house, to be reborn again as an individual of the opposite sex. The death of an adult was a dreaded event. It was surrounded with misgivings and fear in spite of the fact that most dead were to be reborn into a peaceful world which was an intimate part of the Hopi Way.

Among the earliest Hopi and Anglo-American contacts was a conflict which took place between the Indians and white trappers in 1834. The trappers raided Hopi gardens, and when the Indians resisted, some fifteen were killed. In 1850 the Hopi attempted to induce the Anglo-American authorities in Santa Fe to control Navajo depredations, but it was not until later that the Anglos finally contained the Navajo. The whites who visited the Hopi mesas favorably impressed some of the Indians. Perhaps, the Hopi reasoned, the Anglo-Americans were the Bahanas, or White Gods. Each Hopi knew the origin myth in which an elder brother of the Hopi, a Bahana, departed and promised to return when the Hopi were in need. The basic problem debated by the elders was how to identify the Bahanas when they returned. A more immediate problem was, however, the physical survival of the people, for in the late 1860's a severe drought was followed by a smallpox epidemic. After these depressing events, many of the Indians joined the Zuni temporarily. Anglo-American interest in the Hopi intensified in the 1870's. Beginning in 1869 there was a Moqui Indian agent, and a Moqui Pueblo Agency was established in 1870. From a study of the formation of the Hopi Reservation by Volney H. Jones we learn that as early as 1858 the Mormons from Utah had entered the Hopi country. One missionary worked among them, but without success, and about 1875 a small Mormon colony was founded in Hopi country. The Moqui Pueblo Reservation was created by an Executive Order in 1882, but the land set aside for Indians was not for the exclusive use of the Hopi. The rectangular area included around thirty-nine hundred square miles, most of it claimed and utilized by the Hopi. It seems not unlikely that the reservation was established as an attempt to prevent increased Mormon settlement locally. A secondary reason for forming the reservation was the increased Navajo encroachment on Hopi grazing lands. The official reservation name was changed from Moqui to the Hopi Indian Reservation in 1900. It is clear from Jones' study that the United States did not express an earlier interest in the Hopi because of the distance between their country and the administrative center at Santa Fe. Also, the Hopi did not intervene in the activities of incoming whites. On the other hand, Federal officials were occupied with the regional problem of hostile Navajo. After the Navajo confinement to a reservation in 1868, attention was turned to the Hopi. A Bureau of Indian Affairs school and an agency were established for the Hopi in 1874. The first school was administered by missionaries, but in 1887 the Bureau took over supervision of the school. The passage of the General Allotment Act by Congress in 1887 resulted in Federal pressures on the Hopi to shift from family and community landholdings to individual land allotments. The Bureau attempted to force the allotment program in 1907 but did not succeed. Conflicts with the Navajo over grazing lands intensified since there had been no boundary survey of the Hopi Reservation at the time of its formation and Navajo encroachment on Hopi lands continued. Furthermore, through a series of Executive Orders the Navajo Reservation came to surround the land of the Hopi. Around 1937 the Bureau of Indian Affairs reduced the area officially designated as Hopi to about one-fourth the original allotment, or nearly one thousand square miles. The Hopi Indian Reservation was officially recognized, and the legitimacy of Navajo occupancy in the balance of the land was likewise acknowledged by the Federal government.

After this brief survey of recent Hopi history, it is time to turn again to the community of Oraibi and to trace what has happened in this settlement during the Anglo-American era. In the second quarter of the nineteenth century the Oraibi chief belonged to the Squash sib and obtained the office because his father was of the Bear sib. Apparently, his temper was volatile, and as Titiev points out, the killing of some Hopi by American trappers hardly could have made him conciliatory toward the new group of whites. The next chief, a member of the Bear sib, was a bachelor who, on at least one occasion, was noted to be unfriendly with visiting Anglo-Americans. When he died about 1865, the succession fell between two young men of the Bear sib, Sakhongyoma and Lololoma. Since they were both young, their father, from the Water Coyote sib, functioned temporarily in their stead. The Moqui Pueblo Special Agent was well received in 1871 everywhere but at Oraibi. Furthermore, the people of Oraibi were angry with neighboring communities for their acceptance of whites. The younger of the two brothers, Lololoma, was acknowledged as Village Chief at some time prior to 1880, and he continued his father's anti-American policies. Soon after becoming established in his office, Lololoma traveled to Washington, D. C., with a party of Hopi to appeal to the Federal government to contain Navajo encroachments on their land. After the trip, Lololoma reversed his attitude toward Anglo-Americans and became the leader of the progressive, friendly, or pro-Anglo faction. The anti-Anglo faction, called conservatives or hostiles, was led by the male head of the Spider sib, called Uncle Joe by Anglos but actually named Lomahongyoma. It is important to note that he was a leader in the Soyal Society, head of the Blue Flute kiva, and from the same phratry as Lololoma; this made his challenge to the latter's leadership legitimate. Now was the time for the progressives and conservatives to group behind their able leaders, and the great drama at Oraibi began.

Because a critical issue in the dispute was the precise identity of the Anglo-Americans, each faction drew on sacred myths to validate its stand. Were the Anglos the Bahanas of the sacred myths? The hostile faction said no, for when a real Bahana returned he would be able to speak to the Hopi in their language and could produce a stone matching the one held by the Village Chief at Oraibi. Obviously, to the hostile Spiders, the Anglos were not the Bahanas. Furthermore, by accepting the whites as gods, the progressive were likely to arouse a Water Serpent, known from the mythology, which would send a flood to end the world. The progressives traced the difficulties not to Anglo-Americans but to the underworld and Spider sib witchcraft. Although the Spider and Bear sibs were of the same phratry, it was only the Bear members who were the chiefs. The Bear sib owned fewer major rituals than the Spider, but the Bear sib owned most of the land, with the Spider holdings small in proportion to their ceremonial importance. The next step in the dispute was for the members of various sibs to take sides behind the Bears and the Spiders. A number of different factors influenced the stands of particular individuals. These were their sib and phratry ties as well as the nature of their close kin ties with the outstanding personalities in the conflict.

The attitude of the conservatives was reflected by their categorical rejection of American ways. They refused to send their children to school at Keams Canyon in 1887, and when Lololoma identified the hostiles to government officials, some hostiles were arrested. The remaining hostiles then confined Lololoma to a kiva, from which he was rescued by United States Army soldiers. When in 1891 an attempt was made by Federal representatives to survey Oraibi land, the hostiles disrupted the efforts. When a small group of soldiers came to unseat the leader, they were surrounded. A ceremonial declaration of war was issued with great drama, and the soldiers prudently withdrew. A larger United States military force was sent to Oraibi shortly afterwards, and the hostile leaders were arrested without difficulty. It appears that some progressive leaders were arrested also at this time.

What happened at Oraibi affected the entire tribe, for in 1890 the village contained twelve hundred of the twenty-two hundred Hopi listed on the official census. Laura Thompson points out that behind the rupture at Oraibi was the problem of land. There were not only Navajo encroachments but also disputes between sibs within the settlement and in other Hopi villages over the lands of an abandoned pueblo. It is to be remembered also that in addition to Oraibi's large population, successful farming in the past was based on community recognition of sib holdings and sib cooperation in farming. Between 1892 and 1911, however, Federal pressures were great to have the Indians accept individual family land allotments.

By 1891 the friendly and hostile factions were at such bitter odds that there could be no reconciliation of their differences. Inasmuch as the hostiles were more numerous, their leader, Lomahongyoma, declared that he was the Village Chief. The fracture became a fissure when attention turned to ceremonial issues. Neither side would cooperate with the other in presenting the sacred ceremonies; nor would either permit the use of its ceremonial equipment by the opposite faction. The progressive leader was refused the right to hold the Soyal Ceremony in the Blue Flute kiva, and the conservative leader decided to hold his own Soyal Ceremony. In 1897 the Soyal Society members were forced to align themselves with one of the two leaders, depending on whether they supported the hostile or the friendly faction. In spite of the bitterness between the factions, each held its own Soyal Ceremony without interference from the other. Each also performed the Powamu and Niman ceremonies, but the progressives did not attempt to hold the Blue Flute-Snake rituals which belonged to the hostile faction. Between 1899 and 1906 two separate but never fully complete sets of ceremonies were conducted· annually. About 1901 there was a change in progressive leadership. Lololoma died, and a younger sister's son replaced him. The new chief of the Bear sib, Tawaqwaptiwa, was a young, aggressive man, who was selected over his older brother because of his more forceful qualities. In 1906 open conflict developed, climaxing in September when certain conservatives who had moved to Oraibi from another settlement refused to leave. After some scuffling the conservative leader drew a line on the ground, and a push-of-war was held. Before the pushing began it was decided that the losers would leave the pueblo. The hostile leader was the object to be pushed, with people pushing him from behind or in front. Finally, the hostiles or conservatives lost the struggle. The same evening about three hundred persons took their belongings and abandoned the settlement. They founded the new village of Hotevilla, about seven miles to the north of Oraibi. The nature of the split clearly illustrates that the sociopolitical structure of the community could not resolve conflicts of this nature (see Note 4).

The Bureau of Indian Affairs authorities came upon the scene soon after the rupture and sent the conservative leaders to jail. Then Tawaqwaptiwa temporarily was relieved as chief of Oraibi by the Bureau officials and was sent to the Indian school at Riverside, California, to learn to speak English and practice American ways. When he returned to Oraibi in 1910, he was extremely anti-American; Titiev (1944, 94) records accounts which describe him as "quarrelsome, stubborn, vindictive, and unusually licentious." Over the next twenty years Tawaqwaptiwa managed to antagonize most of the remaining residents of Oraibi. He forced Mennonite converts and sympathizers, in addition to those who accepted only some American customs, away from the settlement with his constant quarrels. By 1933 only one hundred nine residents were in Oraibi. Some had moved to New Oraibi, on the valley floor beneath Oraibi, and others settled some forty miles to the northwest at Moencopi on the Navajo Reservation. The disintegration of Oraibi, as Thompson has pointed out, relieved local pressures for land, but social cohesion did not develop in the offshoot communities. In Moencopi two factions emerged, one sympathetic with the Mennonite missionaries and another which retained ceremonial ties with Oraibi. The Mennonite converts' being forced out of Oraibi by Tawaqwaptiwa's hostility in turn led to the abandonment of a full ceremonial cycle at Oraibi. The most successful conservative community by the 1940's was Hotevilla. The people had a nearly complete ceremonial cycle when they left Oraibi that September night in 1906. Through the years resistance against whites became almost an end in itself; the reasons behind it were logical. After the split, most of the Hotevilla men were impounded by the Federal government, and it was very difficult for the women and children to survive until their return. Then too, children were forced by soldiers to attend school, and the people were forcefully dunked in sheep-dip during a 1912 epidemic. These people continue to scorn outside interference. They have reached the point of refusing to sign any paper for any reason; they just want to be left alone (see Note 5).

After 1906 a complete ceremonial round could no longer be held at Oraibi, but Chief Tawaqwaptiwa faced the situation calmly as he aged. He maintained that the time would soon come when everyone would abandon him and he alone would carry on the Soyal. Then there would be a great famine, and following it, all of the old ceremonies would be reinstituted at Oraibi. Again the village would thrive in all of its colorful glory. Tawaqwaptiwa waited and waited and died still waiting.

By the beginning of the present century, the subsistence cycle had undergone major changes. The primary reliance on maize, beans, and squash remained, but new crops and animals became increasingly important. Probably the most important new animal was the sheep, and virtually every man owned at least a small flock by 1900. Each animal was owned by an individual, but they were herded by men cooperatively. Most often a man herded a combined flock for a few days, and then his brother, with whom he was a herding partner, cared for the sheep. Sheep were held as a form of wealth and were butchered only for ceremonial feasts. Any unconsumed meat was dried in the sun as jerkie or dried, pounded, and mixed with fat as pemmican. Cattle were less popular because of their initial cost and the pattern of allowing them to graze freely. This led to the destruction of crops, with ensuing disputes over crop damage. The major difficulty in maintaining horses, which were broken to the saddle, was the nuisance of rounding them up each day for pasturing, usually at a considerable distance from the community. Thus, like the sheep, they often were owned and tended jointly by men.

It is possible to learn many details of recent Hopi sociocultural change by consulting the admirable works of Laura Thompson. The field studies were made during 1942–1944, and their purpose was to help solve Bureau of Indian Affairs administrative problems among the Hopi. A vast amount of diverse information was obtained; the following is especially pertinent here. In the 1940's about four thousand Hopi were located in fourteen different settlements, including Moencopi, and on land which had been set aside for Hopi occupancy adjacent to the Colorado River. The critical problems facing the people were a population increase on a smaller land base and the increasing erosion of the land. The land depletion apparently was due to a dry climatic phase as well as to overgrazing by livestock. Government efforts to remedy the situation first were aimed at a reduction in the number of livestock. The people of the Third Mesa area were required to reduce their stock nearly 45 percent, while on the other two mesas reductions were about 20 percent. Thus, the Oraibi area residents were hardest hit by the program. The Federal government had for many years encouraged herding, and sheep had become a very important item in the Hopi economy. The Third Mesa people resisted the reduction program with vigor but finally succumbed to Federal pressures. Along with stock reduction a program was instituted to encourage better stock management practices, and cooperatives were organized. The farming practices of old remained, and most of the fields were watered from stream flooding or else were dry land plots. An effort to irrigate Hopi lands has not been overly successful, and even if it were expanded it could include only a maximum of four hundred acres. The plow was replacing the digging stick in the 1940's, but the attitude toward the land remained the same. The typical farmer (and almost every man farmed) raised a wide variety of crops, but the essentially meatless diet consisted mainly of maize, white flour, beans, potatoes, sugar, and coffee. The caloric value of the diet was below normal standards for children and just barely sufficient for adults. In 1942 the Hopi economy was based on the following: wage labor, 36 percent; livestock, 34; agriculture, 22; and all other sources, 8 percent. Of the nearly six hundred families, more than half had an income of less than $300 in 1942.

All aspects of life at Oraibi have undergone tremendous readjustments owing to the 1906 rupture. When the ceremonial cycle no longer could be performed, a man's activities were affected profoundly, and the kiva-centered life of a male was destroyed. A man became more sib-directed, and there was an accompanying increase in the significance of the nuclear family unit. Tests administered by Thompson and her associates demonstrated that Oraibi children looked to their mothers as the dominant family member, while to children from First Mesa the father and mother both were important. Furthermore, boys from First Mesa were outgoing in their responses, while those of Oraibi were "definitely constricted and are troubled by a vague anxiety," according to Thompson (1950, 97). At the same time the Oraibi children were judged to reflect greater sensitivity than the others tested. In all social units males have suffered more disorganizing influences than the females; if anything, the position of women has been strengthened. The net result has been a fostering of previously unheard-of individualism. Seemingly, about the only course of action remaining for men is to seek to better their position as individuals. Since the Oraibi land base is not adaptable to the accumulation of farmlands or even male control of such lands, there has been a move toward wage labor by the ambitious males. Another avenue open to individual males is political leadership, but in this role an individual encounters the pervasive Hopi feeling against personal achievements.

One remarkable characteristic rarely reported for American Indians is that the Hopi as a group have rejected the use of alcoholic beverages; neither has the peyote cult gained a foothold among these people. On Second Mesa it was recorded in 1934 for one particular community that a single teen-aged boy drank intoxicants. He drank secretly and was said to be the only consumer of intoxicants in the settlement.

As would be expected, when the Hopi Tribal Council was organized in 1936, the residents of Oraibi refused to recognize it or participate in its activities. Since there had been no aboriginal mechanism for the various Hopi pueblos to unite, it is not surprising that cooperation among the modern settlements is lacking. The Council drew most of its active members from the more Americanized settlements, and even in 1955 the Council was not representative of all the settlements in spite of its official recognition by the Bureau of Indian Affairs. It seems impossible to obtain general Hopi agreement on any major issue. In the 1950's there were pressing decisions to be made concerning highway construction, the lease of reservation lands to oil companies, and a suit against the Federal government for lands they had lost. As Edward H. Spicer notes, the conservative Hopi considered that their traditional lands were sacred. Such land could not be alienated or modified because this would be recognition of failure in obligations to the supernaturals. Therefore, the Hopi could not sue for the loss of land; this would be to admit that the Federal government now had a claim on the land, which in turn would mean that the Hopi had transgressed against the gods. In a similar vein, to build roads or drill oil wells was to disturb the land. This could not be justified on moral grounds, nor could the Hopi stand be altered, since the gods did not compromise. This behavior seems irrational to modern whites and even to "progressive" Hopi, but when it is noted that only 2 percent of the Hopi were practicing members of Christian churches, their position is more comprehensible. The katcinas of the underworld have fulfilled their obligations for a long, long time. Their living representatives on earth, the Hopi, have kept their faith for over four hundred years against the Spanish, the Anglo-Americans, and other Indians. The Hopi Way continues, but can it endure for another four hundred years without increased tolerance from whites?

Note 1. Laura Thompson (1944, 36–37) summarizes the Hopi world view.

Implicit in the Hopi configuration of culture is an original and basically integrated theory of the universe by which the Hopi attempt to organize their world in order to cope with their life problems and obtain some degree of security in a highly hazardous environment. They conceive of the world—including man, the animals, the plants, the land base and the supernatural—as an absolute, ordered system functioning under a definite set of rules, which are known to them (and to them alone). In accordance with these rules they believe they can, through regulating their behavior, emotions and thoughts in a prescribed manner, exercise a measure of control over their environment.

Theoretically all phenomena, natural and supernatural, living and dead—including man, animals, plants, the earth, sun, moon and clouds, the ancestors and the spirits—are interrelated and mutually dependent through the underlying dynamic principle of the universe—which we shall call the law of universal reciprocity. This law implies the concept of immanent or cosmic justice. The emphasis is not, however, on the idea of rewards and punishments or on punishments alone (retribution), but on the mutual exchange of essentially equivalent but not identical values according to fixed traditional patterns, in the interests of the common weal. Man, the elements, animals, plants and the supernatural cooperate in an orderly fashion, by means of a complex set of correlative interrelationships, for the good of all.

Note 2. Don C. Talavesva, Sun Chief (Simmons, 1942, 56) records in his autobiography, his weaning process.

While I was learning the importance of food and trying to recognize the different things that were fit to eat, I kept going to my mother for milk and was still nursing at six. Whenever we boys set out to hunt kangaroo rats or other small game, I ran first to my mother, placed my bow and arrows on the floor, sat beside her, and drank from her breasts. The other fellows would say, "Come Chuka, come, or we will be late." "Wait, wait," I replied between draughts. But on account of their teasing, I finally gave up the breast in embarrassment. My mother did not wean me; I just decided to let her alone.

Note 3. Sun Chief (Simmons, 1942, 67) describes his attitudes toward his near relatives.

I had also learned to pick out the people whom I could trust. My own mother still stood at the head of the list. She was my best friend. Though always busy, she was ready to help any person who came to her. My father also was a good friend and taught me how to do many things with my hands. I liked him, except on a few occasions when he punished me. He worked hard in his fields and with his herd, and was one of the best weavers in Oraibi. He traded the garments that he wove for things for his family to eat and wear. My grandfather, who lived in the house with us, liked me best and spent most time in teaching me. I knew I could count on him. My uncle Naquima and my sister Tuvamainim were good pals to me, but my brother Namostewa was not much of a friend.

Note 4. Mischa Titiev (1944, 92–93) summarizes the chain of events leading to the factional dispute at Oraibi.

If I may be permitted to add to the statistical data the impressions gained in the field and in the frequent handling of the raw material, I should say that the division of Oraibi proceeded somewhat as follows. First, the chiefs of the Bear and Spider clans finding their phratry affiliations too weak to hold them together in the face of disputes over land and other strong differences of opinion, began a struggle for the control of the pueblo. Second, the members of their own clans quickly sided with their leaders. Third, the men of the conflicting clans brought into their respective parties their wives and children, thus emphasizing household ties and beginning to break up clan cohesion. . . . Fourth, the women of the five leading clans in the struggle generally induced their husbands and other household relatives to join their cause, thus breaking down clan ties still more. Fifth, those men who were not closely related to the leaders either through descent or marriage made their choice of sides on the basis of their most cherished ceremonial connections; for, with the establishment by the Hostiles of a full ceremonial cycle to rival that of the Friendlies, all the villagers were forced to declare themselves unequivocally on one side or the other. Sixth, when this stage was reached the original clash between Hostiles and Friendlies resolved itself into a struggle between the participants in the Spider-led ceremonies and those in the Bear-controlled rituals. Seventh, wives and unmarried children tended to follow the leads of husbands and fathers. Eighth, after the entire populace had been divided, a climax occurred when the Friendlies expelled the Hostiles from Oraibi on September 7, 1906.

Note 5. Laura Thompson (1950, 81–82) recorded from the Hotevilla leader the way these people view the world.

At first there was the same sort of confusion in the other world as exists in this world today. So the Hopi sent a messenger to Masau'u, the Being or Power of this world, asking that they be permitted to come here. The Being said that they might come if they adhered to the rules or law of this world. The Hopi agreed to abide by these laws Masau'u taught them. These are quite detailed and it would take a long time to relate them. Because the time is short I will pass on to the present. The reason why the land is denuded of covering is that some of the Hopi have given up the Hopi way and taken on the white man's way. Also those who have not done so are interfered with constantly by the white man and are disturbed in their spiritual life. They ask only that the white man let them alone so that they can continue in the Hopi way of life. There are ways to bring back the plant cover and the Hopi know how to do this. They were told that the white man would come and entice the Hopi with words and other means to leave his way and take on the foreign way, and that if they did this much trouble and difficulty would come upon them. And so that is what has happened.

References

Beaglehole, Ernest and Pearl. *Hopi of the Second Mesa*. American Anthropological Association, Memoir no. 44. 1935.

*Bunzel, Ruth L. *The Pueblo Potter*. New York. 1929. The discussion of Hopi and other pueblo Indian pottery is one of the finest studies of aboriginal ceramics. The text is particularly noteworthy when dealing with the ways in which designs were conceived and executed.

Colton, Harold S. *Hopi Kachina Dolls*. Albuquerque. 1949.

Colton, Mary-Russel F. "The Arts and Crafts of the Hopi Indians," *Museum Notes, Museum of Northern Arizona*, v. 11, 3–24. 1938.

Cushing, Frank H. "Origin Myth from Oraibi," *Journal of American Folk-Lore*, v. 36, 163–170. 1923.

Forde, Cyril D. *Habitat, Economy and Society*. London. 1934.

Hurbert, Virgil. "An Introduction to Hopi Pottery Design," *Museum Notes, Museum of Northern Arizona*, v. 10, 1–4. 1937.

Jones, Volney H. "The Establishment of the Hopi Reservation, and some later Developments Concerning Hopi Lands," *Plateau*, v. 23, 17–25. 1950.

Oliver, James A. *Snakes in Fact and Fiction*. New York. 1958.

*Simmons, Leo W., ed. *Sun Chief*. New Haven. 1942. This Hopi autobiography is an extremely valuable document, for it offers great insight into the life of one individual.

Spicer, Edward H. *Cycles of Conquest*. Tucson. 1962.

Thompson, Laura, and Alice Joseph. *The Hopi Way*. Chicago. 1944.

*Thompson, Laura. *Culture in Crisis*. New York. 1950. The ethnographic background to Hopi life is provided in summary form, with the addition of the 1942–1944 findings of Thompson, her co-workers and assistants. The volume is devoted in part to Hopi administration by the Bureau of Indian Affairs, but also provides diverse information about Hopi acculturation.

Titiev, Mischa. "Notes on Hopi Witchcraft," *Papers of the Michigan Academy of Science, Arts, and Letters*, v. 28, 549–557. 1943.

*———. *Old Oraibi*. Papers of the Peabody Museum of American Archaeology and Ethnology, v. 22, No. 1. 1944. The classic study of a Hopi community through time—a key source.

Whiting, Alfred F. *Ethnobotany of the Hopi*. Museum of Northern Arizona, Bulletin 15. 1950.

Wormington, Marie M. *Prehistoric Indians of the Southwest*. Denver Museum of Natural History. 1951.

9

The Iroquois:

Warriors and Farmers of the Eastern Woodlands

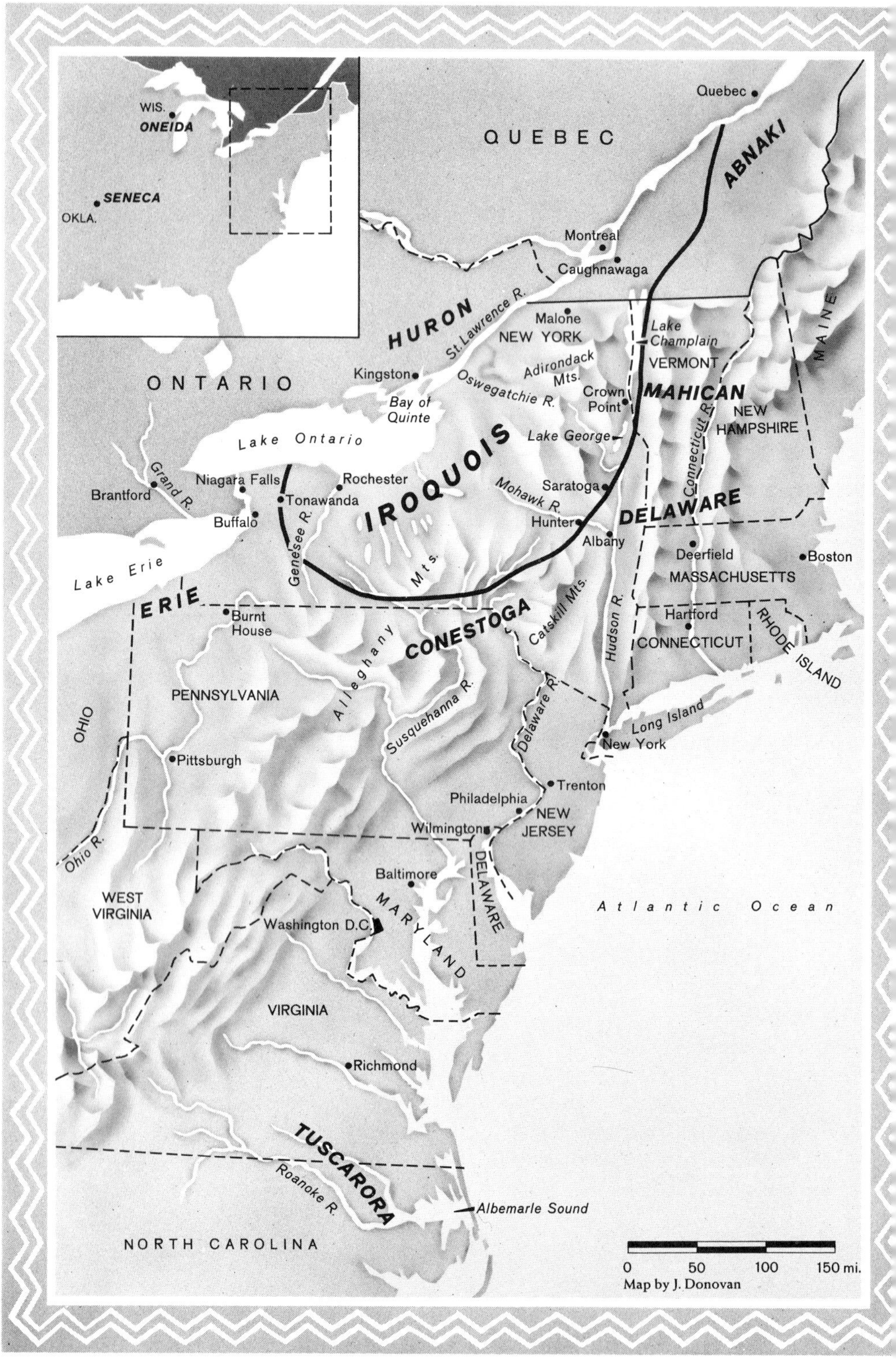

WIS.
ONEIDA
SENECA
OKLA.
QUEBEC
Quebec
ABNAKI
Montreal
Caughnawaga
HURON
St. Lawrence R.
Malone
NEW YORK
Lake Champlain
VERMONT
MAINE
ONTARIO
Kingston
Adirondack Mts.
Oswegatchie R.
Crown Point
MAHICAN
NEW HAMPSHIRE
Bay of Quinte
Lake Ontario
IROQUOIS
Lake George
Connecticut R.
Grand R.
Brantford
Niagara Falls
Rochester
Tonawanda
Buffalo
Mohawk R.
Saratoga
Hunter
Albany
DELAWARE
Genesee R.
Mts.
Deerfield
Boston
MASSACHUSETTS
Lake Erie
ERIE
Burnt House
CONESTOGA
Catskill Mts.
Hudson R.
Hartford
CONNECTICUT
RHODE ISLAND
Alleghany
PENNSYLVANIA
OHIO
Susquehanna R.
Delaware R.
Long Island
New York
Pittsburgh
Trenton
Philadelphia
NEW JERSEY
Wilmington
Ohio R.
DELAWARE
Baltimore
MARYLAND
WEST VIRGINIA
Washington D.C.
Atlantic Ocean
VIRGINIA
Richmond
TUSCARORA
Roanoke R.
Albemarle Sound
NORTH CAROLINA
0
50
100
150 mi.
Map by J. Donovan

Anthropologists long have exhibited a particular fondness for the Iroquois and not without good reasons. The first modern ethnography was written by Lewis H. Morgan about these people and published in 1851 under the title of *League of the Ho-de-no-sau-nee or Iroquois*. This work was to set the general precedent for modern ethnographic studies and is an anthropological classic. The original Iroquois League consisted of five tribes or nations, the Cayuga, Mohawk, Oneida, Onondaga, and Seneca, and was known also as the Five Nations. These Indians conceived and administered an extensive secular bureaucracy of great vitality and justness. In early historic times the League was able to extend its political power through conquest and intimidation far beyond its place of origin in present-day western New York State. It was the Iroquois, too, who played a decisive role in shaping the colonial empires of the French and British in northeastern North America. Historians acknowledge also the importance of the League during the American Revolution. From the colonial period to the present the names of outstanding Iroquois have been known to many Americans. During the colonial period there were the warrior and military leader Hendrick, the warrior and politician Joseph Brant, and Red Jacket, the great orator. Kateri Tegaquitha, born about 1656, has been beatified by the Roman Catholic Church and is well on her way to becoming the first American Indian saint. General Ely S. Parker was the secretary to General Ulysses S. Grant and drafted the terms of peace at Appomattox at the end of the Civil War. Finally, there is the contemporary Iroquois, Jay Silverheels, better known as Tonto, of Lone Ranger fame. The Iroquois have continued to retain their clear identity down to the present time with a sociocultural resilience that is rare. Today it is recognized that many Iroquois contribute significant skills within the economies of modern Canada and the United States.

One major difficulty in compiling Iroquois ethnographic sources is to separate information on the Iroquois in general from that pertaining to a single member tribe or nation. This problem has not been resolved successfully because we do not have parallel information on all the League nations. The descriptions to follow thus represent a broad and composite view of these Indians. In general, the reconstructed aboriginal scene has been drawn from the ethnography by Morgan, whose data came mainly from the Tonawanda Band of the Seneca. Furthermore, Morgan unquestionably presented an idealized form of Iroquois culture which suggests greater uniformity and nobility than actually occurred. For the later period an attempt has been made to follow the fortunes of the Mohawk in particular, and in some respects this makes a balanced reconstruction more difficult. The reason is that a major segment of the Mohawk population was Christianized early in its history and has thus attracted less attention from ethnographers than more conservative and traditionally oriented Iroquois tribes. In the more recent historical descriptions we will therefore attempt to follow the destiny of the Mohawk without ignoring the general trends in Iroquois culture and social change.

Consulting the Iroquois sources is an extremely rewarding and at the same time a frustrating experience. It is fascinating to read the studies by Lewis H. Morgan, Horatio Hale, John N. Hewitt, and Frank G. Speck, and it is equally rewarding to read the recent works of Anthony F. Wallace. Most of all, however, it has been the continuing contributions of William N. Fenton over the past thirty years which are most useful. He has examined a vast amount of historical information and at the same time has made highly original field studies. As Fenton (1951, 305) has noted, "the Iroquois and their neighbors cover a time span of three centuries and have had more written about them in the last hundred years than any other American Indian people, including the Navaho.... During three centuries their culture has undergone remarkable change which is abundantly documented; their culture has also demonstrated amazing stability." The frustration in consulting Iroquois materials stems from the failure of any specialist since Morgan to attempt a synthesis of his findings. Considering how few persons are engaged in Iroquois research and the vast number of sources available, this is understandable; nevertheless, a broad, integrative progress report would be invaluable.

The aboriginal Iroquois occupied approximately the area from Lake Champlain and Lake George on the east to the Genesee River drainage and Lake Ontario on the west. The northern boundary was the St. Lawrence River, and Iroquois domains extended southward to the upper reaches of the Susquehanna River. Each nation occupied an oblong strip of country; from east to west, the nations were the Mohawk, Oneida, Onondaga, Cayuga, and Seneca. Population estimates for the period of early historic contact vary widely. James Mooney estimated that the Five Nations in A.D. 1600 numbered about fifty-five hundred and the Tuscaroras about five thousand. William N. Fenton estimated the Five Nations population at something less than ten thousand for the period of early historic contact. By 1904 the Six Nations (adding the Tuscarora) numbered at least sixteen thousand, including some three thousand persons of mixed blood. In 1962 the Iroquois in the United States who had retained at least some identity as Indians were approximately as follows: New York, with all Six Nations represented seventy-seven hundred; Oklahoma Cayuga and Seneca, seven hundred fifty; Pennsylvania Seneca, thirty; and Wisconsin Oneida, fourteen hundred. The total modern Iroquois population, including those in Canada, is estimated at twenty thousand.

The word Iroquois is derived from the combination of an Algonkian word translated as "real adder" and a French suffix. According to the linguistic classification of George L. Trager and Felicia E. Harben the Iroquois spoke a language of the Hokan-Siouan phylum, the Iroquois-Caddoan stock, and the Iroquoian family. The dialects of the Iroquois include Cayuga, Mohawk, Oneida, Onondaga, and Seneca. Cherokee, which is of the same family as Iroquois, separated from Iroquois about 100 B.C. Separations within Iroquois among the member dialects took place about A.D. 700. All of these estimates are based on the results of glottochronology.

The lands of the Iroquois fall into two biotic provinces. The eastern area is in the Canadian province, and the western province is the Carolinian, according to the classification of Lee R. Dice. The boundary between the two is not drawn sharply since both have hardwood forests as the climax vegetation in western New York State. The sugar maple is the typical hardwood forest climax species. In Iroquois country are diverse nut-bearing trees such as chestnuts, hickories, oaks, and walnuts, while the conifers are red cedar, white pine, and hemlock. In aboriginal times the area was rich in diverse animal species. The large animals included bear, deer, elk, and moose, and there were also wild turkey, fox, and porcupine. The most important fur-bearing species were the beaver, fisher, marten, mink, and muskrat. Lake fish included bass, smelt, trout, pickerel, pike and whitefish. From this brief listing of the natural resources it is abundantly clear that the environment had a great deal of potential for an aboriginal people.

The first known inhabitants of the northeastern area of the United States presumably were big game hunters and are known only from scattered lithic finds. The people came from the south or west and manufactured spearpoints, knives, and scrapers, as well as implements from prepared or polyhedral cores. Their lithic technology was based on flaking methods, and they lived around 9000 B.C. Following this prehistoric era, which is relatively unknown in detail, the populations, usually termed Archaic, became more sedentary; this possibly represented a settling-down of the big game hunters. The earliest Archaic peoples are not much better delineated than their predecessors, but by sometime before 2000 B.C. with the Late Archaic the picture becomes somewhat clearer. The technology came to include ground stone tools. Among the latter forms were adz blades, gouges, grooved stones, and slate points. Sometime soon after 2000 B.C. pottery was manufactured, and such items as bannerstones and semilunar knives were new manufactures. This cultural complex was to be the base out of which developed the Early Woodland, around 1000 B.C., which seems to have been a localized development of the earlier peoples. Cremations became more important, as did red ocher associations with the dead and an increase in the quantity of grave goods. The climax development was the Adena culture in the Ohio River area before 200 B.C. There were burial mounds and, later in the same culture complex, earthworks, some farming, and a great diversity of artifact forms. The middle period of Woodland is associated mainly with Hopewell cultural developments which emerged about A.D. 1 from an Adena base with diverse outside influences. As James B. Griffin (1964, 241) has written, "There is a growing tendency to view Ohio Hopewell as a uniform cultural complex dominated by an elite class that marshaled its manpower for conquest and the establishment of outlying subject groups." He further doubts that Hopewell sociopolitical organization was as advanced as that of the historic Iroquois. Associated with Hopewell are complex earthworks, settled communities, farming, and a highly varied material culture. This cultural period did not dominate the New York State area; instead we find here the Point Peninsula cultural remains which were left by central-based gatherers who perhaps cultivated a few plants. Their technology included chipped as well as polished stone weapon points, knives, and ornaments. The general tradition seems to have developed from an Archaic base with a retention of a subsistence pattern based on hunting and fishing. Direct continuity exists into the Late Woodland culture reflected in the Owasco and associated developments in New York State and adjacent areas. The population was more sedentary than that previously noted for the area, the villages were fortified, and the people depended more on crops which they raised than on gathering activities. Their pipe forms and dwellings were of the Iroquois type, and these Indians have been identified as Iroquoian. Tribes related to the historic Mohawk and Onondaga were in the Montreal region in the early 1500's and moved to New York State about one hundred years later. Two conclusions reached by Griffin concerning the archaeological remains of the Iroquois are that their way of life developed in the northeastern area and that their material culture does not seem out of the ordinary in its complexity for the area in general.

No Indians played a more important role in the growth and development of the British North American colony than the League of the Iroquois. In attempting to follow the history of the League in colonial and later times particular attention will be paid to the Mohawk. The principal historical sources consulted were the pro-British study by John W. Lydekker, the more balanced study of Cadwallader Colden, and the histories of Francis Parkman.

After the French first entered the St. Lawrence River system with the explorations of Jacques Cartier in 1534, they began to establish contact with the Algonkian, Huron, and Montagnais tribes. By the time the imaginative and aggressive French explorer Samuel Champlain was ready to turn his attention from the west to the south, it was to be expected that he would ally himself with the Algonkians against their enemies, the League tribes. Little did Champlain realize what a powerful adversary he was to confront. As Francis Parkman (1901, v. 1, 9) wrote, the League was "foremost in war, foremost in eloquence, [and] foremost in their savage arts of policy . . . ." In 1609 Champlain, with a group of Algonkians, canoed to the lake which bears his name and met a party of Iroquois. In the battle which followed, the Iroquois attacked with confidence but were struck with terror at the appearance of white men clad in strange garb and employing deadly weapons. The Iroquois were routed, and the League as a whole never forgave the French and the Algonkians for the defeat. The Iroquois soon recovered from this blow to raid and terrorize successfully the French and Indian settlements along the St. Lawrence River from Montreal to present-day Quebec City.

Initial formal contacts between the Mohawks and Europeans led to their signing a treaty with the Dutch in 1644 and one with the Dutch successors, the English, in 1664. The treaty with the English was signed also by the Seneca but not by the other three nations of the League. The following year all but the Mohawk, plus some Cayuga and Seneca, made a treaty with the French; the French attacked the Mohawk because of their failure to cooperate. In response to French pressures the Mohawk requested that Roman Catholic missionaries be sent among them, but nothing developed from the proposal. The French attempted to win permanent control over the Iroquois in an attack against these Indians in 1687. The Iroquois responded to French pressure by turning to the English for help and acknowledging themselves to be the subjects of James II. With the domestic crisis in England and the abdication of James II in 1688 the French seized the opportunity to attempt the destruction of the British colony. The Mohawk took the initiative against the French by destroying the community of La Chine and attacking Montreal successfully. In a conference of the League in 1690 to decide whether to support the French or the English, the Mohawk, Onondaga, and Seneca favored the English. In 1693 the French destroyed the Mohawk settlements and persuaded the Cayuga and Seneca to remain neutral. The English in the meantime attempted to consolidate their position with the League by sending missionaries among them; meanwhile the French also intrigued with the League nations. The great debate among the Iroquois centered among the Onondaga, the seat of the League council. The French were most effective among the western nations, the Cayuga and Seneca, whereas English influence was strongest among the easternmost member nation, the Mohawk. The French, however, did not give up on the Mohawk, and Jesuit priests were able intermittently to induce Mohawk to settle near Montreal at St. Louis or Caughnawaga. By the early eighteenth century perhaps two thirds of the Mohawk had left their aboriginal home. Divorced from their traditional hunting and farmlands they developed a new means for survival. They served as the transporters of trade goods from English posts in the east to the French traders who were involved in the lucrative trade for beaver pelts from the more distant Great Lakes region tribes. The French had good trade routes but expensive and not very plentiful trade goods. The English and Dutch traders around Albany possessed desirable trade goods, but they lacked communication with the western tribes. The Caughnawaga illegally transported English goods to French traders who in turn disposed of the goods in the west.

Hostilities between the French and English erupted anew with Queen Anne's War in 1702, and the outlying New England settlements received the brunt of the attack. The Iroquois remained neutral, but the New England Indians and those in adjacent areas of Canada fought for the French. In the late winter of 1704 the Caughnawaga Mohawk and Abnaki accompanied a French-led party to Deerfield, Massachusetts, where there were about three hundred persons at the time. In a predawn attack about one hundred and ten persons were taken prisoner and about fifty others killed. During the rapid return to Canada, most of the prisoners who could not keep up with the fast-moving party were killed; only somewhat more than half of them were restored eventually to the English. It should be noted that although the Indians never hesitated to kill a man, woman, or child who fell behind they never raped women. One of the captives, Eunice Williams, who was six years old at the time, was taken with her father John, a minister at Deerfield, and brother Stephen. Their mother was taken captive too but was killed when she lagged behind the retreating war party. The son and father were redeemed finally, but Eunice was baptized a Roman Catholic and remained among the Caughna-waga to marry an Indian eventually. In 1740 she visited Deerfield with her husband but could not be induced by her relatives to remain permanently, although she did make three other visits. The French led contingents of Indians in other raids against the frontier farms and hamlets, but none was as successful as the one against Deerfield.

The first Church of England missionary to the Mohawk arrived in Albany in 1704, but his efforts ended in failure due to his inabilities. In 1710 the English took five Iroquois to England in an effort to impress the Indians. One died on the trip, but the others were grandly received in London. Among these visitors was the Mohawk named Thoyanoguen or Hendrick. As a result of their visit to Queen Anne, a renewed attempt was made at establishing a mission to the Iroquois. Queen's Fort was constructed in 1711 near an important Mohawk community at present-day Hunter, New York. The fort was stocked with one missionary, William Andrews, soldiers, and an interpreter. The adult Indians of the area previously had been baptized by Roman Catholic or Dutch missionaries, and so they were by no means unaccustomed to European men of God. During this time period the Iroquois were not deceived by the British or French, and at one conference it was stated (Parkman, 1892, v. 1, 10), "If the English sell goods cheaper than the French, we will have ministers; if the French sell them cheaper than the English, we will have priests."

When Queen Anne's War ended and the Treaty of Utrecht was signed in 1713, English control over much of eastern America was consolidated. Most importantly, members of the League nations were recognized as British subjects. The success of the missionary, Andrews, in working with the Indians at Queen's Fort was questionable. The children soon wearied of attending school, and general conditions among the adults were not what he would have desired. One of his principal complaints was the traffic in intoxicants from Dutch traders to the Indians. The Iroquois passion for intoxicants is well documented, and naturally the missionary attempted to stem its flow. His mission did comparatively little to change the lives of the Indians, and in 1719 he resigned his post in disappointment. The soldiers remained at what was now called Fort Hunter, and it became an administrative center. A mission again was opened in Albany in 1727, and the missionary stationed there periodically visited the fort. By 1742 all but two or three Mohawk had been baptized and nominally were Christians. This success was a direct result of the extremely able efforts of Henry Barclay who became an Anglican missionary in 1735. He seems to have been an ideal choice since he was born in the colonies, graduated from Yale, spoke Dutch and some Mohawk; further-more, he was eager to serve. At first he was a catechist at Fort Hunter; in 1738 he was ordained as a priest to serve Albany and Fort Hunter. The Mohawk respected him highly, as did the English, and he was able to succeed where his predecessors either had failed or could claim only limited success.

The War of the Austrian Succession, which erupted in 1740 and once again pitted the French against the English, had New as well as Old World reverberations. The French actively sought Iroquois support, and together they raided and burned outlying settlements, bringing turmoil to the Albany area. Since Barclay felt that he could accomplish little by remaining in the area, he left to serve at Trinity Church in New York City, and once again the Mohawk were left with-out a cleric. For two years the French intruded into the border area, and the English mounted little effective counteraction; they even were forced to withdraw from the border outpost at Saratoga. The English did send raiding parties into French territory under the Mohawk Hendrick in 1747, but the following year peace was concluded. When the next missionary went to Albany and Fort Hunter, he found cause for joy and anxiety. The Mohawk received him in a friendly fashion and had retained at least some of what they had been taught by Bar-clay and his predecessors. One Indian had even taken it on himself to spend most of his time preaching and instructing others. The dis-tressing aspects of the scene were that intoxicants had become popu-lar and highly disruptive in Indian domestic life and that the Roman Catholic priests at Fort Frontenac (Kingston, Ontario) had been suc-cessful in inducing more Mohawk to move to Canada. Between 1713 and 1750 the population of Mohawk appears to have dropped from five hundred eighty to four hundred eighteen, with the decrease due mainly to Indians moving into French-occupied country.

During the late 1740's and early 1750's the French actively sought to expand their control by completely dominating Lake Erie and Lake Ontario as well as by bringing about closer contacts with the Cayuga, Onondaga, and Seneca through building a mission at the junction of the Oswegatchie and St. Lawrence rivers. A major in the militia, George Washington, was sent to induce the French to abandon one post they had seized, but he was unsuccessful. A later attempt by Washington to dislodge the French by force from the upper Ohio River area ended in his defeat and greatly strengthened the position of the French with the local Indians. In the next major conflict, Major General Edward Braddock was killed and his force badly defeated near Fort Duquesne by the French and Indians, including some Caughnawaga, in 1755. About the same time William Johnson attempted to induce the League to join him and a colonial force against the French and their Indian allies. The English and French met in conflict on September 8, 1755, and after a hotly contested battle the English and their allies won the day, thanks in a large part to Hendrick, who was killed, and the Mohawk whom he led. In 1756 a formal war, the French and Indian War, was declared between England and France. The English were defeated soundly until Fort Frontenac fell to them and until the Moravian missionary Frederic Post persuaded the Indians of the upper Ohio River drainage to abandon their French allies. This forced the French to withdraw from Fort Duquesne in 1758 and led to the English founding of Fort Pitt (Pittsburgh) at the site.

In 1759 the English began a two-pronged attack against the French which led to an end of French political power in Canada. A naval force with soldiers included was sent up the St. Lawrence to take Quebec, and one overland force was to move through the Lake Champlain region to the St. Lawrence. Another land invasion, with soldiers and Indians under the command of William Johnson, was sent against the French at Niagara; the fort fell after a siege. Participating in this action were the Mohawk and other Six Nation warriors, totaling nine hundred forty. The troops under Jeffrey Amherst who were pushing into the Lake Champlain area spent the winter at Crown Point on the lake. The naval contingent under Charles Saunders and the troops under James Wolfe reached Quebec but were unable to bring effective action against the fortress of Quebec until a narrow path leading to the summit was discovered. In the famous battle on the Heights of Abraham the English line met the charging French and did not fire until the advancing army was thirty-five paces away. The French force virtually was destroyed; Wolfe died from wounds received in leading a charge. A French effort to retake Quebec ended in failure, and in the spring of 1760 the English formulated a plan to take Montreal with converging armies. The plan succeeded, and during the same year the French were forced to surrender their principal holdings in North America. Hostilities did not cease, however, for the Indians who had fought for the French cause organized under the leadership of Pontiac, an Ottawa Indian, and seized much of the Ohio country in 1763. The Iroquois in general, except for some Seneca, remained loyal to the English. The hostile Indians destroyed many frontier farms and settlements and killed many whites before a settlement was reached in 1766. Action was taken by the British government in 1763 to license traders to Indians and to prohibit the alienation of Indian lands except with the approval of the Governor-in-Council. These were two extremely important precedents in guiding future Indian policies in Canada and the United States.

Following the French and Indian hostilities, the Society for the Propagation of the Gospel of the Church of England again became concerned with the Mohawk population around Fort Hunter. The most influential member of this organization, William Johnson, sought suitable teachers and missionaries. In his eyes the need was particularly urgent because of Congregationalist efforts in the Fort Hunter locality. The major difficulty of Society leaders in the early 1770's was to enlist the services of individuals who were capable and willing to spend an extended period of time working with the Mohawk. The Mohawk were well-disposed to receiving them, but at the same time not all the Mohawk were good members of the Church of England. They continued to drink intoxicants a great deal, and their attendance at church services was not in impressive numbers. The only organized violence in this interim between more massive conflicts was "Cresap's War" of 1774, which erupted when a prospecting party exchanged murders with Ohio country Indians. Among the persons killed were relatives of John Logan, a Cayuga sachem. In retaliation Logan murdered whites but was defeated by an army of colonials. It was at his surrender that Logan made his famous speech against the whites (see Note 1).

In 1775 began the final drama in which the Iroquois were to play a significant role in American history. The Iroquois were as a whole loyal to the British, and at best the colonial rebels could hope only to neutralize them. The loyal subjects of the Crown in turn did their utmost to induce the Iroquois to support the cause of the British actively. The intrigue and counter-intrigue was led by three individuals in particular. Samuel Kirkland, a missionary to the Oneida, attempted to induce this nation and the Tuscarora to remain neutral, which they pledged to do. Shortly before the hostilities began in 1775, Guy Johnson, a nephew of the deceased William Johnson, sought Mohawk support for the British. He persuaded most of the Mohawk to accompany him to Canada, where the Governor-General induced the Mohawk to fight for the loyalists under Guy Johnson and Joseph Brant. Another loyal subject of the Crown was the son of William Johnson, John Johnson, who remained in the Mohawk valley to lead local supporters when this might prove necessary. At the second Continental Congress an Indian Department was created with Northern, Middle, and Southern divisions, and the commissioner of each was charged with rendering the Indians neutral. At a meeting of the

Northern Commissioner with the Iroquois gathered at Albany another more systematic effort was made to insure their neutrality. In early 1776 the Northern Commissioner sent a force to disarm John Johnson's troops. This was accomplished, but an attempt somewhat later to capture their leader failed. John Johnson escaped to Montreal, where he organized a loyalist force. Guy Johnson was successful in raiding rebel settlements and then with Joseph Brant visited England in 1775 to clarify the position of the loyal Iroquois. In England Brant was made a captain in His Majesty's Army and pledged Iroquois support. Upon his return he led a force of Mohawk against the American rebels. Joseph Brant, or Thayendanegea, was born in 1742 while his parents were hunting in the Ohio country. His father was a full-blooded Mohawk, and his mother was either full-blooded or half-blooded. His sister became the wife of William Johnson. Brant began his long career as a warrior in 1755 and later was sent by his brother-in-law to a school in Connecticut where he was reasonably well educated. After the organization of Brant's Mohawks, the rebels in turn attempted to create a counterforce of other Indians, but it was not a success. With the Declaration of Independence in 1776 the political break with the British was complete and the war began. The policy of unanimity among the League tribes broke down in 1777 as a result of the conflict between the British and the American colonials. The Mohawk and Onondaga were divided internally, some supporting each side. The Cayuga and Seneca supported the loyalists; the Oneida and Tuscarora were in theory neutral but in fact gave the rebels aid.

At the opening of the Revolutionary War the Church of England missionary at Fort Hunter was John Stuart; he stayed with the Mohawks who remained. Stuart was soon moved and confined by the rebels, and the remaining Mohawk joined the loyalists in Canada. As a result of the successful assault of forces under Joseph Brant and Walter Butler into the Cherry Valley to the south of the Mohawk River, the Americans organized an army against the Iroquois. In 1799 the troops of General John Sullivan succeeded well in their task of destroying Iroquois communities, crops, and grain caches. Iroquois effectiveness was broken, and many of them fled to Canada, abandoning their traditional lands forever. In Canada the Mohawk settled temporarily near Montreal where they were given lands. Here they erected a log building to serve as a church and council house. When the French entered the war on the side of the rebels, the combined army defeated General Charles Cornwallis at Yorktown, and this virtually ended the war. A treaty of peace was signed in 1783, but there was no mention of the Indians and their future status. In recognition of Mohawk aid for the British cause, these Indians were granted land along the northern shore of Lake Ontario and lands along Grand River, which flows into the northeastern sector of Lake Erie. A separate treaty was made between the Six Nations and the United States, in which the Oneida and Tuscarora, who remained neutral in the conflict, were permitted to retain most of their lands. The other League nations, who had fought for the British, were forced to relinquish claim to most of their land. Once again Joseph Brant went to England, this time to press for compensation for Mohawk losses (see Note 2).

Brant did not obtain all that he had hoped for in the way of compensation from the English government and was somewhat disillusioned by his reception on his return to Canada. Still he lobbied for a Canadian home for the loyalists of the Six Nations. The Canadian authorities willingly offered an area along the eastern shore of Lake Ontario at the Bay of Quinte, but Brant pushed for a final grant of land in the Grand River country of Lake Erie. Some of his followers preferred the Bay of Quinte site and settled there. In 1784 the Grand River area was purchased from the Indian occupants and granted to the Six Nations. Brant considered that the Iroquois who were to occupy the country were granted sovereignty over it and he was the trustee. Thus the land, in Brant's eyes, was subject only to Iroquois national control. The Iroquois began to move to the Grand River drainage in 1784, with approximately sixteen hundred people in the migration. Almost a third of the total were Mohawk, somewhat fewer Cayuga, and the balance mostly Onondaga, Seneca, and Tuscarora, with a few Oneida.

The migrants could not support themselves by hunting, and since farming by men probably was not the norm, the economy of the settlers was precarious. This was especially true because there already was a decline in the fur trade, a possible alternative means for subsistence. Brant's solution to the dilemma was to lease, sell, and grant reserved lands to whites. The Six Nations people were divided in their attitude toward this policy. The traditionalists opposed the alienation of land on the grounds that it simply was not a form of property which could be transferred, but the majority of the Indians seem to have supported Brant. Some of the younger men felt that Brant was using them to his own advantage, but they were quieted by their maternal female relatives. The Canadian officials were by and large opposed to the alienation proceedings, but vacillating policies and efforts to appease Brant did not lead to any clear course of administrative action. Officials feared that if they did not appease Brant he might swing the Six Nations people over to the American cause, which he seems to have threatened to do. Bureaucratic recognition was finally given to the leases, sales, and grants at Grand River. The original reserve of five hundred seventy thousand acres was reduced by three hundred fifty thousand acres as early as 1798.

The last time the Six Nations asserted political power in an international dispute was in the War of 1812. The Americans were quick to assure the Six Nations residents that invading forces would not disturb their interests, but the Iroquois were rightfully unimpressed; neither were they willing to commit themselves wholeheartedly to the British cause, again for good historical reasons. An initial call to arms brought forth fewer than fifty Iroquois to serve the British cause. Later victories by the Canadians induced some five hundred Six Nations warriors to fight, which they did with distinction, but before the end of the war any effective Iroquois cooperation had ceased to exist.

From an Iroquois origin myth recorded by Henry R. Schoolcraft we learn that once there were two worlds. The upper level was inhabited by creatures similar to humans, and the lower level by monsters who lived in water. A female from the upper world descended into the lower realm and onto the back of a turtle. She bore twin boys and then died. The shell of the turtle grew in size and became an island continent, and the offspring of the woman were termed words which when translated mean Great Spirit (Ruler) and Evil Spirit. Light was created by Great Spirit by transforming his mother's head into the sun and other parts of her body into the moon and stars. The light from these heavenly bodies drove the monsters deep into the water, and then Great Spirit placed on the expanded turtle shell all the geographical features, animals, and plants useful to man. He created men and women from earth and placed life in their forms. His brother made creatures of evil and geographical barriers to blight this pacific landscape. Thus the brothers were contesting forces, and this led to a fight between them. For two days they fought until finally Evil Spirit descended into the underworld.

Iroquois clothing was made principally from deerskins prepared for use by removing the hair and smearing the skin with a preparation of boiled deer brains. After a few hours the mixture was removed and the skin twisted to make it pliable. Finally it was smoked over a fire on each side and was ready for cutting and sewing. Skins were sewn with sinew, and a deer bone awl was used to puncture the skin to receive the sinew. Men wore kilts which extended to the knees and were belted at the waist. The kilts were fringed at the bottom and decorated with designs in porcupine quills. The quills were dyed blue, red, or yellow, or else left undyed. Individual quills were flattened and attached to the garment with sinew thread. The men wore shirts with fringed sleeves and bottoms, and their leggings extended from above the knees to the ankles, were fringed at the outer edge, and were decorated with porcupine quills along the outer edges and sometimes at the bottoms. The attire of a man was completed with moccasins, again with quill decorations. Women wore skirts which hung from the waist to just above the ankles, with designs in quills along the lower border. Over this garment was a dress which nearly reached the ankles and had fringed sleeves and bottom. From the knees to the moccasins were short leggings, and in cold weather a skin cape was worn about the shoulders.

Any particular community was likely to exist for about ten years, after which the adjacent farmlands were exhausted, firewood scarce, and the dwellings fell into decay. The settlement then would be relocated on another hill a short distance away. Twelve or perhaps thirteen villages, each with three to six hundred inhabitants, existed shortly before the turn of the eighteenth century. The Mohawk had three communities termed the Mohawk "castles" by whites. A series of major and minor trails connected these and other settlements of the League nations. The settlements were not dispersed widely, but clustered along an east-west line. By utilizing trained runners it was possible to spread information throughout the League in three days.

Around a typical settlement a ditch was excavated, and wooden palisades, up to three rows deep, were imbedded at an angle into the earth from the ditch. A village enclosure might encompass from five to ten acres with fields of as much as several hundred acres spread beyond the fortified community. The dwellings within a settlement were of the well-known longhouse type. A longhouse was between fifty and one hundred and thirty feet long and about sixteen feet wide. Such a dwelling was built of seasoned posts, poles, and bark. The bark was stripped from trees which had been girdled previously. The sheets were piled on top of each other to retain a flatness after they had dried. Four stout posts with forked tops, one at each corner, formed the outline of the structure. Smaller forked poles were spaced between the main posts, and in the crotches of the forks were strung poles and then cross-poles as rafters. The roof was arched with bent poles; it and the sidewalls were covered with horizontal, overlapping sections of bark. The bark slabs were lashed into place and held firm by retaining poles.

The inside of a house was partitioned into two elevated sections, each about twelve feet in length; between the sections were separate compartments for the storage of maize and other provisions. Along the center of a longhouse were fireplaces with the families occupying opposite apartments using a single fire. The smoke from the fires drifted through an oblong opening in the roof which served also to admit light into the structure. In windy or rainy weather slabs of bark were placed over this opening. Each of the occupying families had an apartment with two platforms; there might be as many as twenty apartments. An upper platform some five feet above the ground and six feet from front to back was covered with bark, then with mats of reeds, and finally with skins. The lower platform of similar dimensions and covering was about a foot above the ground. It was on these platforms that family members lounged or napped during the day and slept at night. At each end of the structure were doorways leading into storage rooms which in turn opened to the outside. The outer doors were of bark and hinged at the top; in the winter a second door of skins was added.

For a small family or as a temporary residence, a less permanent dwelling might be constructed. It was triangular in outline, with poles at each corner converging at the top; additional poles in between served as further framing. Over the frame were placed overlapping bark slabs; an opening was left in one side for the entrance and one at the top of the structure for the smoke from the interior fireplace to pass out. In addition to the maize in the house storage compartments and storage rooms, some was placed in underground caches. Excavated pits were lined with bark, the maize deposited inside, and waterproof bark roofing was added, to be topped with soil. Similar underground storage containers were lined with deerskins to receive dried meats.

The right to use farmland belonged to the persons who cleared and cultivated the plots, and any uncleared land might be prepared for crops. Beyond the farmlands of an Iroquois settlement were hunting, fishing, and collecting areas belonging to the community. Residents of a settlement joined one another in war and hunting parties, in games, and in mutual assistance in times of stress. The landholding unit was conceived in family, village, and national, as well as League, terms. The boundaries between League nations were established, but sometimes they were modified.

The round of yearly subsistence pursuits included two distinct periods when people were well beyond the village boundaries. From the time of the crop harvest until midwinter families scattered to hunt, and again in the spring the settlements were abandoned when the occupants collected maple sap, hunted pigeons, and fished.

The most effective means for taking individual deer was with the use of a spring pole snare set in the animal's trail. When a snare peg was tripped, the spring pole righted itself, and the deer was caught by its hind legs and lifted into the air. Bears might be snared along their paths; as a bear tripped the snare, a heavy pole fell on its back and pinned it down. Bears likewise were hunted by pursuing them for long distances until they tired; then they could be approached and killed with arrows. A hunting technique employed against herds of deer was for hunters to drive the quarry into converging lines of brush, at the end of which were concealed bowmen who shot their arrows from ambush. In the winter when an animal was killed only a short distance from the hunter's settlement, it was placed on an improvised bark toboggan and taken to the village to be dressed. At other times the animal was butchered, and the venison was prepared for transport by removing the bones, drying the meat before a fire, and then packing it into bark containers for backpacking.

In the spring the men fished and took birds, while the women planted their crops. A common fishing method was to make an essentially cone-shaped basket some three feet in length from converging splints of black ash which were bound together with vegetable fiber cords. The fisherman placed the basket beneath the water facing a rapid or ripples over stones. With a stick he guided the fish downstream into the trap. After one had been taken, it was removed from the trap and the technique repeated. Birds were snared with elm bark nooses, and another technique for taking birds, particularly quail and pigeons, was with nets made from shredded bark. Most of the summer was passed by the men not in subsistence activities but participating in war parties, religious ceremonies, and council meetings.

All farming among the Iroquois was the obligation of women. They not only seem to have cleared the land, they sowed the seeds, cut the weeds, and harvested the crops. The most important domestic plant was maize, of which at least fifteen varieties are recognized. They cultivated some sixty varieties of beans and eight forms of squash. The most important farming tools were the digging stick and a hoe made from a scapula blade. The women also collected plant foods, including thirty-four different wild fruits and about fifty plant products varying from roots to leaves. The collected products were largely to vary the maize-bean-squash diet, or they were important foods when crops failed.

Summer travelers used overland trails, waterways, or a combination of the two. The canoe for travel over water was not made from birchbark since the birch trees were small, but from the bark of red elm or bitternut hickory trees. The bark was pried from a tree in a single section if possible, and the canoes ranged in length from twelve to forty feet. The rounded ribs and the gunwales were made of ash, and both ends of a canoe were alike with a slight upturn. They were propelled with single-bladed paddles. For winter travel snowshoes were constructed of hickory frames laced with babiche. Each snowshoe was about three feet long and sixteen inches at its broadest cross section. They were relatively short and broad and well adapted to travel in timber. It is reported by Morgan that a person could travel as far as fifty miles a day on snowshoes.

One rather notable aspect of the Iroquois was that they did not work stone so extensively as might be expected. They knew of stoneworking from their Algonkian neighbors, and stone was locally available; their failure to develop a larger inventory of stone artifacts seems to reflect a culture bias. The chipped stone manufactures included triangular and tanged arrowpoints and, more rarely, leaf-shaped knives or spearpoints. Ax blades of chipped stone did not occur among them, and drills were rare. Artifacts which were ground and polished were found more often than the chipped variety. Stone mortars were present, and adz blades were common. They employed a chisel that possibly was of ground stone. Ground stone knives and arrowpoints, long slender points with diamond-shaped cross sections, semilunar knives and gouges known among the Algonkian did not occur normally.

In order to fell a tree they built a fire at the base, chipped away the charred wood with a chisel, and then repeated the process as often as was necessary. Fire was kindled with the use of a pump drill, which consisted of a shaft weighted with a wooden spindle near the lower end. The string of a bow drill was wrapped partway around the shaft. The bottom of the shaft rested on a drill board on which was placed punk. The shaft was rotated in a pumping motion by drawing the drill bow back and forth, and fire soon was created from sparks produced on the punk. One artifact made with a fire-hollowing technique was the mortar for pulverizing maize. It was made from a section of a tree trunk about three feet high and two feet across. It was charred and chiseled to form a longitudinal cavity to receive the maize. The maize was ground by using a wooden pestle some four feet long and cylindrical in shape with a narrowed midsection for a hand grip.

The relatively permanent nature of Iroquois settlements made it possible for them to accumulate a variety of material objects for household use. One major category was bark vessels; these included barrel-shaped storage containers, trays for mixing cornmeal, deep folded trough-like receptacles for maple sap, and bark ladles. Other ladles of wood were deep-bowled, and soup or hominy was eaten with them. A special paddle-shaped wooden implement was used to stir hominy as it cooked. The grit-tempered pottery vessels were globular with necks that constricted to collared rims. The most common ornamental surface treatment consisted of lines in triangular patterns on the collar and rim projections. The vessels held from two to six quarts and were used for either cooking or storage. The varieties of basketry were limited and included one twined form which was somewhat globular with a narrow neck at the top; this form held salt. Containers from animal skins were used for storage of household items, and a skin bag which hung about the waist of a warrior or hunter contained most of the items he would require on a short or extended trip.

Among the diverse manufactures were elbow pipes of fired clay with bowls showing a variety of surface treatment forms. It was common to make encircling lines about the bowl and sometimes to decorate a bowl with an animal or human figure. The tobacco used was cultivated but required little attention between sowing and harvesting. After a crop was planted once, it seeded itself from year to year and required only thinning. The leaves were picked in the fall after a frost, were dried, and were then ready for use. Tobacco was smoked, never chewed, and often was kept in a weasel skin pouch which was attached to the man's belt.

In carrying a load a tumpline was passed over the forehead and could be attached to a basket, cradleboard, or pack frame. The frame was fitted to the back and made from sections of hickory wood. A loaded pack frame might be carried with a chest strap alone, with a tumpline, or with a combination of the two. A cradleboard was about two feet long and fifteen inches wide, with the bottom and the lower end made from boards. The outside of the foot of the cradleboard was carved, and at the head was an upright bow-shaped hoop. An infant was swaddled in a blanket and bound to the board with a belt, while a hood was attached to the hoop. When a cradleboard was carried by a woman, she attached a separate tumpline to it.

For ordinary meals at home the men ate first, followed by women

matrilineal
matrilocal

and children; the only scheduled meal was in the morning. At other times of day people ate whenever they were hungry, and a woman always offered food to her husband when he returned home during the day and to all visitors. Foods prepared from maize dominated the diet and occurred in a wide variety. Hominy, cornmeal "bread," succotash, roasted corn, and boiled corn probably were eaten most often. Of these the most important was a hominy gruel called saga-mite, which is an Algonkian term. The Seneca, according to Morgan, recognized three varieties of maize: red, white, and white flint, each with a different use. The red variety was roasted and dried for the future; white was preferred for cornmeal bread; and the white flint ripened earliest and was preferred for making hominy. In making bread the kernels were taken from the ear, boiled in water with wood ashes to remove the hulls, ground in a tree trunk mortar with a wooden pestle, passed through a sieve and then made into loaves which were boiled in water. For roasting, the maize was picked, and the ears were placed in a line next to a fire. After roasting, the ears were shelled and the grains dried further in the sun and stored. Maize to be stored on the cob had the husks stripped back; the husks then were braided into bundles of twenty ears each. To the maize diet might be added meats and soups of various types as well as wild vegetable products.

The typical occupants of an Iroquois longhouse were the females of a matrilineage, their children, and the in-marrying husbands. There was thus not only matrilineality but also matrilocal residence. The matrilineages were consolidated into fifteen matrisibs with names such as Bear, Wolf, Turtle, Deer, Beaver, and Hawk. Among the Cayuga, Onondaga, Seneca, and Tuscarora the matrisibs were divided into moieties. The Mohawk and Oneida recognized no moiety division, only the Bear, Turtle, and Wolf sibs; these were in one moiety among the other nations. The matrisibs cut across national identifications so that members of the Wolf sib, for example, were found in each nation, in different villages within a nation, and in one or more house-holds within a village. Where the moiety division existed, it once was said to have formed the exogamous unit; any combination between sibs of opposite moieties was permitted in marriage. By Morgan's time, however, there was sib exogamy and continuing matrilineal descent. Thus, the inheritance of rights would pass from a man to his brothers, to his sister's children, or to some other person in his matrisib. The importance of the sib cannot be underestimated in Iroquois society; not only was it the exogamous and property-holding unit, but it was empowered to invest, and remove if necessary, sachems as well as chiefs. Members cooperated with one another in economic and political activities and judged disputes with other sibs. Furthermore, each sib had a common burial ground, could adopt foreigners, and held certain religious ceremonies.

In the kinship terminology a person referred to his father and father's brother by the same word, and mother was termed the same as mother's sister. There were separate and different words for father's sister and mother's brother. The bifurcate merging avuncular terminology was accompanied by terms for parallel cousins (i.e., father's brother's or mother's sister's children) which were the same as for biological brothers and sisters. Cross-cousins (i.e., father's sister's or mother's brother's children) were "cousins." This then is an Iroquois type of cousin terminology. Furthermore, all individuals of one's matrisib, irrespective of their tribal affiliations, were drawn into the system as blood relatives.

The kinship basis of Iroquois political life was an extension of household and community ties at the national and League levels. Furthermore, when incorporating non-League tribes in the seventeenth century the kinship basis of the League was retained. In the original League the Cayuga, Onondaga, and Seneca each had a moiety system, with sachems for each moiety represented at League meetings. The Mohawk and Oneida did not have a moiety division among their sibs according to Morgan. However, for ceremonial occasions at the League level the Mohawk, Onondaga, and Seneca were regarded as in one moiety, whereas the Cayuga and Oneida were in another. In one early report of the Mohawk dating from 1644, it was noted that the Turtle sib settlement was the largest and most important and was separate from the Bear sib community as well as from the third community, that of the Wolves. The Wolves were said to be offspring of the Turtle and Bear. Later in time the Turtle and Wolf sibs formed a moiety, with the Bear sib members their opposites. If this is correct, then the Mohawk did have a moiety system comparable to three of the other League nations, but it had died out by Morgan's day. At Caughnawaga by 1735 the Turtle sib had become so large that it divided into Great Turtle and Little Turtle. It would be expected that with the passage of generations their close ties would be lost and intermarriage eventually would become possible between them.

The League of Hodenosaunee or Iroquois was in its general structure the same when described during the historical period as it was when conceived originally. At least this was so according to tradition, with one important exception. The original League included fifty permanent offices which were filled with individuals from each of the five member nations or tribes. The Onondaga contributed fourteen;

Cayuga, ten; Mohawk and Oneida, nine each; and the Seneca, eight. The holder of such an office has been termed a sachem in the literature. This title is derived from a word used by the speakers of diverse Algonkian languages in the eastern United States and refers to the holder of a hereditary office. Among the Iroquois a sachem was called a "Counsellor of the People." The sachems were drawn from the sibs of the nations, and among the Mohawk the three sachems were from each of the three matrisibs which existed among them: the Bear, Turtle, and Wolf. As examples of the names sachems assumed when they took office, we find that in the Bear sib of the Mohawk there were Going with Two Horns, Great Wood Drift, and Puts on the Rattles. The sachems of each nation collectively formed the Council of the League which had legislative, executive, and judicial authority over the entire League. Historically, the first annual League meetings were held at Onondaga in order to invest new sachems, but as League political power increased more time was devoted to dealing with other tribes and European nations. In theory and seemingly in fact, each of the member tribes of the League was equal in power and authority. The unequal distribution of the sachemships among the nations was not a key to power because any decision made in the name of the League was unanimous.

At some unknown time in prehistory the Tuscarora split from what was later to become the League and settled along the Roanoke and nearby rivers in the present states of North Carolina and Virginia. Hostilities with white settlers erupted in the Tuscarora wars of 1711 and 1712–1713. The second war ended with some Tuscarora moving north to join the League members. They were adopted formally by the Oneida in 1722 as members of the League. The last remnant of the Tuscarora population did not move northward, however, until 1802. When the initial group was accepted into the League, it was not accorded rights equal to the other member nations since no sachemships were created for it.

The stated purpose of the League was to avoid the constant wars which occurred before its foundation. League meetings were called to deal with internal and external affairs, to invest new sachems as well as to mourn the ones replaced, or to carry out religious obligations. The influence of any particular sachem depended on his abilities as a speaker, and his primary obligation was to maintain civil order. Occasionally there was conflict between different members of the same sib in different nations. An individual's allegiance was strongest toward his own household, less important toward the sib in general, and least important beyond the nation to the League. Warfare, or more properly feuds, sometimes erupted between sibs of diverse League nations, but no doubt such conflicts were quickly brought before the League council for settlement.

The sachems did not seek glory as individuals, and except for deeds committed by the founders of the League, Daganoweda and Hiawatha (Hayowentha); the great shaman and conqueror of the Cayuga and Seneca, Tododaho; and Logan, their achievements have gone largely unrecorded. Logan was a Cayuga sachem who achieved fame for torturing and murdering white settlers in revenge for the murder of relatives by whites. The sachems acted collectively so that the achievements of an individual could be reflected only in group decisions. By contrast the outstanding Iroquois leaders known to whites usually were chiefs, a category of leaders who will be discussed shortly.

Only when the Council of the League sat did the League function, and even in these meetings the sachems were not free to decide any issue according to their personal feelings. They were obligated to reflect the opinions held by the people they represented. Since there was considerable intercourse among the member tribes and the kinship bonds were regarded as close, there existed a feeling of League unity even when the organization was not meeting. The member tribes frequently joined one another in parties to hunt or fight and participated in mutual religious ceremonies. If a group of individuals, such as a band of warriors, chiefs, or women, thought a particular matter was important, they met to discuss the issue and then appointed an orator among them to convey their views to a sachem. If the subject was considered important enough to be considered by the League, it would be introduced at a meeting of the body by a sachem. In an example provided by Morgan of a League meeting, it was cited that an alien tribe might desire to submit a question to the League. The foreign ambassador first went to the Seneca since this nation decided whether a question of foreign origin was important enough for a League meeting. If so, they sent runners to the Cayuga with a wampum belt into which had been "read" the time, place, and purpose of the meeting. Each member nation in turn notified those to the east. When the topic for consideration was of widespread interest, people from all over the League territory gravitated to the meeting place. A meeting opened with prayers, and then the matter at hand was put forth by the envoy, who then withdrew from the meeting. There were discussions, and orators spoke about the issue. When the time to reach a decision arrived, different groups of sachems consulted among themselves until they agreed. The next step was for one from each group to act as a spokesman in consultations with other sachems who were similarly selected. Finally, the varying conclusions were offered. If unanimity could not be reached, the matter was set aside. When a unanimous decision was reached, an orator summarized the proceedings and gave the decision to the envoy. Only once, it appears, was the principle of unanimity set aside; this was when the Oneida sachems refused to agree with the others to side against the colonists during the American Revolution. The conclusion then was to permit each member nation to decide its own position.

In the original League there were fifty permanent sachems. Among the original sachems were Daganoweda and Hiawatha, whose offices were not filled upon their deaths. Although in theory each sachem had the same power and authority as any other, there still were certain sachemships which were more honored than others. The most notable example was the Onondaga sachem titled Tododaho who had two sachems as his assistants. The Seneca sachem Donehogaweh was the Keeper of the Door in the council house, and the Onondaga sachem Honowenato was the Keeper of the Wampum for the League.

Certain obligations were attached permanently to a particular nation of the League. The Onondaga, since they were centrally located in the League, were in charge of the council brand and wampum. In ordinary session the Council of the League met each fall among the Onondaga. Special sessions, however, might be convened among any member nation. The Seneca were the Keepers of the Door because they faced the hostile tribes to the west. Logically too, the two hereditary war chiefs were Seneca, but these individuals were not sachems. When a war was declared by the League in council, it was these two men who were the overall coordinators. The Mohawk, the easternmost of the League tribes, were given the right to receive tribute, suggesting that the non-Iroquois to the east were subject peoples.

It was the accepted custom to validate any important League decision through the medium of wampum. In treaties with whites as well as with other Indians wampum belts were exchanged to bind a contract. The decision of agreement was "talked into" the beads and the Keeper of the Wampum taught the associated texts to his successor. The wampum beads were spiral-shaped, freshwater shells strung together or made into belts. The word wampum is derived from the Algonkian term which is a condensation of a morpheme meaning "a string of white beads." In general, among the Iroquois white beads were used in a religious context and purple ones as a mnemonic device to recall the details of political decisions.

On the death, or removal from office, of a sachem, his successor was "raised-up" in a council of the League. His former name, the one acquired as an infant, was dropped, and his new name was taken from the one of the office he was to hold. A new sachem was invested at a League meeting held at the council headquarters or capital of the nation involved in the replacement.

During the rituals in which the tribe of the deceased sachem served as the hosts to the League there were prayers, a mourning rite for the sachem to be replaced, and recitations of ancient traditions by reading the wampums, and finally the investiture of the new sachem. The religious ceremonies were punctuated with feasting, games, and social dances which relieved the solemnity of the occasion. A sachemship was passed along a particular matrilineage of a specific sib in one particular tribe. A former sachem's office normally would pass to a brother or to a sister's son. What appears to have been most important was the ability of possible successors; the person considered most fitted for the office was invested with it. If no such individual existed, which was rare, then the selection was made by the localized segment of the sib. In this case the office passed from one matrilineage to another. The most influential person in selecting a sachem was the oldest woman in the particular matrilineage down which the sib title passed. In the event that it was necessary to displace a sachem before his death, this action could be taken by the sib council of the nation to which the sachem belonged.

The League in council dealt primarily with problems relative to the common good of all member nations, and the sachems of each nation handled their own domestic problems. Thus the nine Mohawk sachems were the final authorities on Mohawk internal affairs, and they functioned in the same manner as did the League council as a whole. Furthermore, if a sachem from one tribe visited another in the League, he was accorded the same status that he enjoyed at home.

After the League had been functioning for an unknown length of time, a new office, that of chief or Pine Tree Chief, was created. Among the Iroquois such a person was called An Elevated Name or Brace in the Long House, for which the term chief often has been substituted. Chiefs were nonhereditary office holders elected by the sibs of a nation for the lifetime of the individual. There was no set number of chiefs, and they were selected on the basis of such qualifications as oratorical skills or deeds in warfare. The chiefs first served as local leaders and as advisers to the sachems. Later they sat in League councils with the sachems and rivaled the sachems in authority; at the same time they were invested by the sachems. According to tradition the creation of the office of chief was the only innovation in League structure. In general the League was bound to follow as closely as possible the organization and purposes established at its founding.

Considering the unique nature of the League of the Iroquois in American Indian political life, it is desirable to discuss the League's creation. A summary of the founding, recorded by John N. Hewitt in 1888 from an Onondaga, provides the general background, although a number of different versions of the creation exist. An Onondaga shaman named Tododaho used his supernatural powers to further his own ambitions. Repeatedly he prevented the other Onondaga leaders from meeting in council to decide what could be done about his tyranny. At one proposed council meeting the leader Hiawatha had arrived. Tododaho found out about this meeting, and when he reached the group of people who had gathered, he caused them to knock to the ground Hiawatha's heavily pregnant daughter, who died as the result. Since this was the third of Hiawatha's children to be destroyed by Tododaho, Hiawatha left the tribe because of Tododaho's evil power. He came to the house of a man and was taken in, but he was not admitted to the councils of the leaders. He traveled on to the home of Daganoweda, a Mohawk. Two spies who changed themselves into crows went from Daganoweda's settlement and found the sorcerer's home. They entered in human form and saw that Tododaho had assumed a weird appearance. His head was covered with snakes, his hands were like the claws of turtles, and his feet were like those of a bear. The spies left quickly, turned again into crows, and returned home to report what they had seen. Daganoweda was determined to go to the shaman to make him human again. He took Hiawatha and some of his people to Tododaho's village, and they sat in council with the leaders of the settlement. They sang the Six Songs, which Daganoweda had earlier composed; on hearing these, Tododaho started slowly to turn into a rational being. They also brought with them thirteen strings of wampum which had been prepared earlier and into which had been spoken matters of importance. The Six Songs again were sung and other songs as well, and Tododaho was transformed into fully human form. The next effort was (Hewitt, 1892, 140) "to work, first, to secure to the nations peace and tranquillity." To realize peace among the Iroquois was proposed, and the message was carried to the tribes. The names of the sachems were recited, the allotment of sachems to the different nations, and other specific regulations governing League functioning were set forth. Finally, the consent of all the nations was obtained, and the Tree of the Great Peace, with roots in each direction, was planted among the Onondaga to symbolize the unity of the new League. The question of when the League was founded is open to dispute. Some authorities would place it as early as around A.D. 1400 and others as late as about 1600; the latter date possibly is nearer the time of the founding.

The original and guiding purpose of the League was to bring peace to the warring Iroquois tribes, and yet much of the League's concern was with war. Since the League structure was designed to handle civil affairs only, any military operations were organized outside of the League. If a sachem wanted to participate in warfare it first was necessary for him to resign his office temporarily. The chiefs were the customary leaders of raiding parties. Each party was organized by an individual as a small contingent; these might join forces with one or more other parties. There was no overall command in a combined expedition, but each party leader was responsible for his own force. In warfare the individual was free to act according to his own feelings, and proper behavior could not be dictated. After returning from a raid or war, the temporary war leaders ceased to have authority. Since warfare was a primary focal point in the lives of men, the organizer of a war party could recruit a following readily, for most men sought glory and the accompanying prestige. The Iroquois considered themselves at war with all other Indian tribes with whom they had no alliance; there were always potential victims to be found. When war was declared against an enemy tribe by the League as a whole, the warriors were under the coordination of the Seneca war chiefs, although these men did not necessarily play a part in the direct conflict.

The principal weapon of war was a self-bow which was up to four feet in length and had a slight outward curve at the ends. The bow could be strung only with practice and skill since the wood was inflexible. The arrows were vaned with two twisted feathers and tipped with arrowpoints of flinty material or antler. About fifteen arrows were carried in an animal skin quiver which was hung on the back, with the feathered ends of the arrows situated just above the left shoulder. For close combat a club was employed. One form was some two feet long and was made from ironwood, with a large knot at the end. Another war club had a slightly curved wooden handle, and set into the convex surface was a sharp, curved antler point which likewise was highly effective in close combat. When not in use, a war club was hung from the owner's belt. The famous tomahawk was apparently not an aboriginal weapon of the Iroquois but was known among the eastern Algonkians from whom the word is derived. The blade was hafted in the manner of a modern hatchet, and tomahawks soon came to be manufactured by Europeans from metal, sometimes with a pipe bowl at the head. In use they either were thrown or held in the hand.

Hostilities were initiated by the League in council or by a member nation acting alone. A chief who sought to organize a fighting party went about the village making war whoops and then went to the war post, one of which was erected near the center of each settlement. Into it he stuck a red tomahawk adorned with red feathers and then performed a War Dance around it. Any man desiring to join the party participated in the dance. After a band of warriors had been enlisted, further preparations were made. The most important of these was for the women to prepare food for the trip. The standard fare for war parties was maize which had been parched twice to dry it thoroughly, ground into flour, mixed with maple sugar, and placed in a bearskin bag. The war parties from various communities might join forces, but each was under the supervision of its originator. While traveling to seek out the enemy, the men moved in a single-file formation. At their nightly camps they marked trees with symbols of where they were going and their number. Likewise, at their home settlement just before they departed, they peeled the bark from a large tree and with red paint depicted, for example, the number of canoes departing and the number of paddlers. An animal symbol representative of the group of people they were setting out to conquer was painted on the bows of the canoes. When the party returned, they painted on this tree or one nearby a pictorial account of the venture. The canoe paddlers faced the settlement, scalps were represented in black paint, and the number of prisoners was indicated by bindings employed to fetter individual captives.

When a returning war party with prisoners passed through a League village the captives were forced to run the gauntlet naked, and according to Cadwallader Colden (1755, v. 1, 9), "The Women are much more cruel than the Men." As the party approached their home village, they sounded a war whoop as they neared and danced as they led their captives. At the war post they were welcomed and praised by an elder. A reply was made by the warriors, who narrated their exploits; then they performed the War Dance. For a captive repatriation did not occur except in most extenuating circumstances. Either a man was adopted into the tribe or he was tortured to death. The one exception was to free an extremely brave but captured enemy warrior. If the warriors had lost one of their number to an enemy, the Iroquois wife suffering the loss could adopt any male

426   *This Land Was Theirs*

prisoner to take the place of her husband. First, however, he was obliged to run a gauntlet to his new home. The women and children lined up with whips, and the potential adoptee ran between the lines. If he stumbled and fell, he was considered an unworthy person and was killed; if he ran the lines successfully, he was then considered a member of the tribe. The balance of the male captives were tortured to death. It thus would appear that widows had first choice concerning the fate of captives. This fact, coupled with the rights of sib matrons to select the sachems, has been cited as evidence for the importance of women in decision-making. In addition to these observations there are records of women inducing men to go on war parties or restraining them if they thought it fitting. All of these factors have led to the generalization that the Iroquois were a matripotestal society, one in which the power and authority of women were great, the nearest known approach to the ideal of a matriarchy. This interpretive stance has recently been challenged by Cara B. Richards. A review of the earliest historical accounts about the fate of prisoners by Richards points to the pattern that the fate of captives was in the hands of the captor and the council. When a woman disagreed with their decision, she could not take an effective counteraction, for it was only after a prisoner had been released by the captor and council that the women had any voice in his fate. Later, women obtained jurisdiction over prisoners after the mere formality of their release by the council, a development which clearly is indicative of increased female authority. One factor leading to the increased importance of women in decisions of this sort may have been the instability of community life as a result of the warriors fighting more often after the introduction of firearms, and with deadlier effects.

It was the general League pattern to assimilate defeated tribes who were related distantly to them. Thus, when they destroyed the Erie, Huron, Neutral, and other peoples, they were brought into the League, but not with a voice equal to that of the original Five Nations.

The League nations are famous not only for their complex political structure and its successful implementation, but for their treatment of prisoners. The tortures conceived were diverse and diabolical. A summary of their methods prepared by Nathaniel Knowles (1940, 188) gives a good idea of the variations. Among the techniques "were: applying brands, embers, and hot metal to various parts of body; putting hot sand and embers on scalped head; hanging hot hatchets about neck; tearing out hair and beard; firing cords bound around body; mutilating ears, nose, lips, eyes, tongue, and various parts of the body;

searing mutilated parts of the body, biting or tearing out nails; twisting fingers off; driving skewers in finger stumps; pulling sinews out of arms; etc." The usual practice, except for a person slated for possible adoption, was to begin abusing a captive soon after he was taken. Only the Onondaga tortured young and old, male and female; the other nations reserved their tortures for men. The general pattern was to begin the systematic torture of a victim when he arrived in the settlement of the captor. The prisoner was forced to run around inside a longhouse as young men burned him, primarily on the legs, until he fainted. While he was being tortured slowly, he was expected to sing about his lack of fear. After a captive fainted, he was revived and the tortures repeated. Care was taken so that he did not die from the tortures in order to have him mount a platform at dawn. Here he was bound so that he could move about and was tortured more before the entire community (see Note 3). When the captive was very near the point of dying, he was stabbed to death or his head was smashed. Normally the body of a tortured person was cooked and eaten.

For the Iroquois the world was occupied by a host of invisible spirits. The greatest deity was Hawenneyu, translated as the Ruler, or termed Great Spirit. It was he who created men, other animals, plants, and additional forces for good in nature. Great Spirit guided indirectly the lives of Indians, but he could not be reached through direct appeal by men. Great Spirit was capable of counteracting Evil Spirit if he applied his energies, and men passed through life standing between these two forces. These fraternal deities were aided by lesser spirits. Among the lesser supernaturals doing good was Heno, the Thunderer, who was capable of bringing rain or exacting vengeance, particularly against witches. Associations of Heno with fertility are found in the prayers offered to him when planting crops and the thanks expressed after a harvest. Gaoh, the Spirit of the Winds, commanded the winds which could help or harm man. The Three Sisters, the spirits of Maize, Beans, and Squash, were conceived of as lovely women always termed collectively as Our Life. Everything that in one manner or another aided man had its spiritual associations; there were even helpful spirits of particular plants, fire, and water. Some assumed human form and were assigned specific obligations, and all were called by the general name, the Invisible Aids. It was possible to communicate with the lesser spirits for good by burning tobacco, for it was thought that through this medium prayers and special needs were made known to the gods. Men acknowledged their gratitude to the spirits with thanksgiving statements. Evil Spirit controlled a host of lesser spiritual beings who brought pestilence to men and crops, but these forces were not systematized in detail as were those for good. One organized group of evil supernaturals were the False Faces who existed only as contorted and evil-appearing faces with hair. They existed in out-of-the-way places, and if they chanced to be seen, their viewer was paralyzed. They were able because of their great powers to send death and destruction to the people.

The religious specialists known as Keepers of the Faith were chosen by elders, both male and female, of the matrisibs. These individuals, with males and females represented in approximately equal numbers, were expected to serve when called on. Each was given a new name, which was announced at the next general meeting of the nation; this constituted investiture. Such persons were accorded respect by the population, but the members realized no special honors in either dress or in social recognition. A person could at his choosing relinquish his obligations as a Keeper of the Faith by again assuming his old name. The primary duty of these specialists was to arrange and conduct the major religious ceremonies. There was no set number of such persons, and all held the same rank. The sachems and chiefs were ex officio Keepers of the Faith. A second function performed by the Keepers of the Faith was to censure the antisocial behavior of persons. In the case of a serious transgression they reported the individual to the tribal council; this was a serious form of censure.

During a year, according to Morgan, there were six major religious ceremonies, with the first five quite similar in character and the final one somewhat distinct. In sequence of occurrence they were the Maple, Planting, Strawberry, Green Maize, Harvest, and New Year's (Midwinter) ceremonies, with the first three ceremonies held on a single day. The first five ceremonies shared the common feature of individual public confessions prior to the group religious observances. When offering a confession, each person held a string of white wampum as a symbol of sincerity. The assembled throng did not pass judgment on any transgression, but future behavior was to reflect renewed purpose and intent. During the days of ceremonies it was the pattern for the sacred rituals to be held before noon. The religious aspects of the ceremonies included speeches by the Keepers of the Faith on the precedent and purpose of the ceremony; offerings of burnt tobacco; prayers; and speeches of thanksgiving. The social festivities included dances and feasting in the afternoon and evening. One of the most popular dances was the Feather Dance, which consisted not only of a dance but accompanying songs of thanksgiving. A specifically designated Thanksgiving Dance was performed at the Green Maize and Harvest ceremonies. When the sap began to flow in the maple trees during the spring, the Keepers of the Faith announced when and where the Maple Ceremony would be held. It was a localized celebration with observances held in diverse settlements. The Planting Ceremony followed the patterning of the Maple, and the purpose of the former was to make the seeds which were planted productive (see Note 4). In the event that rain did not fall, a special ceremony was performed later and addressed to the Thunderer for rain. The Strawberry Ceremony was celebrated with the harvest of these berries and a feast in which strawberries mixed with maple sugar were consumed. The Green Maize celebration lasted four days and was held when the first maize of the year was harvested. Inasmuch as maize was the most important staple, it is not surprising that this was an important ceremonial event. One departure from the usual pattern was that on the third day individuals offered personal speeches of thanks for individual blessings. The final day was devoted to gambling, which was secular, and feasting. The Harvest Ceremony, like the one preceding, was celebrated over four days and was a general thanksgiving for the harvest of all crops.

In a War Dance there were about twenty principal performers, although as many as three hundred persons might participate. The dance costume for the principal performers, who were male, consisted of a deerskin kilt plus ornaments. Limb adornments consisted of bands about the arms and knees; from these might be hung deer hoof rattles. The headdress consisted of a semicircular wooden frame over which probably was fitted a piece of deerskin. Attached to the frame near the top and slanting backward was a long eagle feather; behind it was a small cluster of feathers. The Feather Dance was performed as a religious obligation; reportedly, it first was introduced by Tododaho. Accompanying the dancers were two singers who shook turtleshell rattles to keep time. The songs praised the Ruler or were thanksgiving offerings. The male dancers attempted to out-endure each other in the performances. Women might dance too, but they wore ordinary clothing. The War Dance was the one which appealed most to the Iroquois. It was performed on many different occasions such as before setting out on a war party, when returning from a war party, investing a sachem, adopting a captive, or entertaining visitors. The dance was said to have been borrowed from the Sioux, and before a performance a Keeper of the Faith stated its purpose. The dance was violent in nature and was accompanied by drums as well as war whoops from the performers and audience.

The New Year's Ceremony usually was held early in February and lasted for seven days. Before the ceremony began, individuals who had dreamed went from house to house asking the residents to guess the nature of their dreams. Dreams were regarded as important supernatural signs and were treated seriously. When someone suggested a text and interpretation for a dream that seemed reasonable to the dreamer, he ceased his quest for an interpretation. If the accepted text and its meaning included statements about the future behavior of the dreamer, he was obligated to behave as directed. This account of dream interpretation taken from Morgan is idealistic. An account by Jesuit missionaries who witnessed the dream procedure in 1656 shows that it was a violent affair, with the threatened and actual destruction of a great deal of household property by the dreamer until he was satisfied with an interpretation. The New Year's events were initiated by two Keepers of the Faith disguised in skin robes with cornhusks hanging from their heads, over their bodies, and attached to the arms and ankles. Their skins were painted, and they carried pestles for pounding maize as they visited every household. In each dwelling during the morning they made a formal statement concerning the ceremony (see Note 5) and sang a song of thanksgiving. In the afternoon they returned to recite a second speech and sing another song. The day's activities included strangling one or two white dogs which symbolized purity. The sacrificed dog was spotted with red paint and adorned with feathers; white wampum was hung from its neck, and the body was suspended from a branch of a pole erected for this purpose. The following day in the morning, around noon, and in the evening the Keepers of the Faith returned to the houses dressed as warriors. They stirred the ashes in the fireplace with a shovel, sprinkled ashes over the hearth, and offered a prayer, followed by a thanksgiving song. The people dressed in their best clothing and visited each house twice during the day. The next two days, the third and fourth, were allotted to dancing and additional visits. This was the time too when groups of boys, accompanied by an old woman carrying a large basket, visited each house. The boys danced for the family, and if they were given presents they went to the next dwelling. If they received nothing, they attempted to steal whatever they could before they moved on; if caught in the theft, they gave the item back without hesitation. After they had visited the houses, they feasted on their take. On the fifth day the white dog or dogs were taken from the poles and placed on a platform in the council house. A speech was made by a Keeper of the Faith concerning the precedent for the sacrifice and expressing thanks to Great Spirit. A song was sung and the dog's body carried out to be burned in a fire built by Keepers of the Faith. This ritual was to purge any evil and transfer it to the sacrificed animal, who car-

ried the message of contrition to Great Spirit. The offering additionally was to reflect the thanks of the people for the rewards of the year.
As the dog burned, a Keeper of the Faith recited an invocation three
times to gain the attention of Great Spirit (see note 6). Another series
of songs were sung and a lengthy speech delivered to the Ruler. While
the dog continued to burn, the people gathered at the council house
to witness a Feather Dance and other dances. The most important
event of the sixth day was the Thanksgiving Dance, and the final day,
which was devoted to gambling, ended the ceremony. There is some
evidence that although the sacrifice of a white dog occurred among
the Iroquois in aboriginal times, it was not associated with the New
Year's Ceremony.

The information about the ceremonial round from Morgan's ethnography may be supplemented by Fenton's compilation from historical and ethnographic sources of the Tonawanda Seneca ceremonial
round. The most important omission by Morgan appears to be the
Green Bean Ceremony, held when the beans ripened in late July or
early August. The festivities lasted a single day and were thanksgiving
in their purpose.

The most dreaded antisocial behavior emanated from witches who
were in league with Evil Spirit. It was possible for anyone to ally himself thus and to assume the form of an animal, bird, or reptile in his
evil doings. Witches were difficult to detect since they could at will
transform themselves into inanimate objects. There was thought to be
a society of witches with regular initiations. The most important test
for the initiate was for him to kill his closest friend by supernatural
means. Anyone who saw a witch practicing black arts was free to kill
him, and the normal punishment for unconfessed witches was death.
It was possible for a council meeting to establish whether someone
were a witch; if the accused confessed before the accuser, he was freed
if he promised to reform.

One group organized in order to counteract Evil Spirit and
his emissaries was the famous False Face Society. Members were persons who had dreamed that they were participants, and one left the
association by dreaming that he no longer was a member. All members
were male except for a woman who was the Keeper of the False Faces.
She not only kept the ceremonial paraphernalia, but was supposed to
be the only person who knew who the members were. A False Face
Society probably was present in each community, and the duties of
members included curing illness as well as keeping evil spirits at bay.
If a person was taken ill with a disease often treated by the society
and if he dreamed of the false faces, this was considered to be a sign

that he could be cured by False Face Society activities. The False Face Society was most noted for its ability to cure nosebleeds, toothaches, swellings, and eye inflammations. The Keeper of the False Faces was notified when someone desired to be cured, and she assembled the members, each of whom was covered with a face mask and a blanket and carried a rattle made from a turtle shell. There was a ritual sprinkling of the patient with hot ashes, and the members performed a dance, after which they withdrew. Fenton records another function of the False Face Society members, which was to clear disease from a village at regular times during the early spring, late fall, and midwinter. Also according to Fenton, there were the one-night performances in June and October by the Little Water Medicine Society to renew their sacred medicine bundles.

The false face masks were inspired by mythological beings and creatures seen during dreams. A mask was carved from a living basswood tree and would be one of about a dozen facial types. Some had crooked mouths, others a smile, some a protruding tongue, and so on, as their most distinguishing feature. In color they might be painted black, brown, red, or white. Another type of mask was made from braided and sewn corn husks. These were representative of deities important in farming and hunting. Corn husk masks too may be divided into types according to the facial features.

Systematic information about the life cycle of a typical Iroquois is unavailable. Morgan's material on the subject seems to apply best to the 1841–1850 period when he did most of his fieldwork and was corresponding with Ely S. Parker concerning the Iroquois. From Morgan's published descriptions it is clear that by the mid-nineteenth century women dominated family life. The earlier sources discussed and summarized by Cara B. Richards concerning various aspects of mating and marriage support an earlier historic patterning which differs from Morgan's presentation. An account from 1624 states that a person could not marry a cousin on either side of the family, but in 1724 matrisib endogamy was possible when no genealogical ties were traceable; at the time about which Morgan wrote, the matrisibs were exogamous. The choice of a spouse in 1624 ultimately was in the hands of the couple, but by 1724 the mother of a son sought his wife. The young man approved the selection, and further arrangements were made by the parents, with the couple usually following their parents'

wishes. By 1850 the couple might be unaware that marriage arrangements for them were being negotiated by the maternal lines. In the
ceremony the bride was taken to the home of the groom by her mother
and the latter's female friends. The bride gave her mother-in-law corn
bread as a symbol of her domestic accomplishments. The mother of
the groom in turn offered meat which had been killed on a hunt, and
this exchange concluded the formal ceremony. The couple assumed
residence with the wife's family and ideally remained in this household.

It would appear too that before Morgan's field study there existed
plural marriages of a polygynous nature; however, by his time monogamy was observed strictly. In instances of divorce Morgan makes
it clear that the children of a couple were under the general control
of their mother and members of her sib. In the event of a divorce the
mother had unquestioned control of all children from the marriage.
From 1624 and 1724 records it appears that during these times a father had considerable voice in the disposition of children after a divorce. It was most common for him to take the older males and
for the small males and all females to stay with their mother. The
reader should remember that this information on mating and marriage is drawn from scattered accounts for diverse tribes. It must be
considered as tentative but highly suggestive of rather dramatic
changes taking place in Iroquois society between about 1624 and 1850.

Morgan presents a strong case for the matripotestal nature of Iroquois society, and even stronger evidence might be introduced for a
somewhat earlier period, just before 1800. From a description of Mohawk women living along the Grand River in Ontario we obtain the
following view. All the products of a hunt and a man's labor became
the property of women, and a wife allotted money to her husband for
his needs (Johnston, 1964, 31); "indeed every possession of the man
Except his horse & his rifle belong to the Woman, after Marriage."

The Iroquois made clear dividing lines between the activities of
men and women. There were no close bonds with members of the opposite sex. Men sought the company of men, and women preferred to
associate with other women. The primary duties of women were to
care for the children; to plant, cultivate, and harvest crops; to collect
wild food products, and to prepare foods for consumption. Men by
contrast never farmed; they devoted their intellectual and physical
energies to hunting, warfare, and politics. The ideals of behavior were
set forth in the oral traditions of the people. Recitations of a sacred

nature played an important part in most religious activities and at social events as well. At such times the audience heard from the elders the proper norms of behavior.

Each individual was identified with the totemic group of his mother but additionally possessed a personal totem, or perhaps more aptly a guardian spirit or *oki* comparable to the Algonkian manitou. The *oki* was acquired in a dream or vision quest and aided the possessor. The object, animate or inanimate, was represented in his personal medicine bundle.

The analysis of historical references to Tuscarora personality characteristics by Anthony F. C. Wallace furnishes what possibly are general guidelines for the aboriginal Iroquois. The most striking trait noted by Wallace was what he termed their "demandingness," which was a mask for their extreme dependency. This is best exhibited in their expectations from others; they never ceased, it seems, to expect goods and services. The same attitude is reflected in their desire for intoxicants; this desire apparently knew no limits in early historic times. They blamed the difficulties resulting from intoxication on the white traders or on the rum itself but not on the person drinking it. Another striking characteristic of the Tuscarora and apparently of other Iroquois was the absence of fear of heights. It was observed that they walked over creeks on small poles without hesitancy and could walk on the peak of a gabled house roof casually and without any fear.

Wallace also has analyzed early historic records of the form and meaning of dreams among the Iroquois. He found that the meanings they attached to dreams in some respects were similar to ideas developed by Sigmund Freud. The Iroquois in general believed that dreams expressed the desires of the most inner realm of the soul and that the fulfillment of a dream was absolutely essential. Dreams stemmed from inner and symbolic unconscious desires which if frustrated could cause psychosomatic illness. An individual could not always interpret his dream properly, in which case he consulted a shaman versed in such matters. The dreamers most often mentioned in the literature were adolescent boys who embarked on vision quests, warriors who feared torture, and the ill who feared death. Boys seeking spiritual guardians were among those who had dreams of the visitation form according to the twofold Iroquois dream classification of Wallace. In these dreams the supernaturals communicated with the dreamer, bestowing diverse powers such as good fortune in hunting or war, or some other inordinate ability. One of the most important gifts from the most powerful supernaturals was a capacity to predict the future. Symptomatic dreams differed from visitation dreams in being an expression of the desires of one's soul. Wallace (1958, 244) writes, "that the only way of forestalling realization of an evil-fated wish was to fulfill it symbolically. Others were curative of existing disorders, and prophylactic only in the sense of preventing ultimate death if the wish were too long frustrated. The acting out patterns can also be classified according to whether the action required is mundane or sacred and ceremonial." It was under the compulsion of fulfilling a symptomatic dream that men were tortured by their friends, some material object sought even if it meant great hardships, traditional but special ceremonies held, or a new ritual introduced. In summary Wallace's (1958, 247) concluding paragraph is best quoted. "The culture of dreams may be regarded as a useful escape-valve in Iroquois life. In their daily affairs, Iroquois men were brave, active, self-reliant, and autonomous; they cringed to no one and begged for nothing. But no man can balance forever on such a pinnacle of masculinity, where asking and being given are unknown. Iroquois men dreamt; and, without shame, they received the fruits of their dreams and their souls were satisfied."

Diversion in the form of games of chance and skill played an important part in Iroquois religious and social life. The contests were between individuals or teams organized within a community or beyond it, even including different tribes. The teams seem to have been divided along sib lines. These Indians were avid gamblers, and betting on the outcome of a game was intensive. A man might even gamble away all of his property on a game. The favorite game was played with a ball and often is known as lacrosse. It was played by two teams with from six to eight men; each player carried a crook with netting strung from the curved end to about halfway up the racket. The object was to drive a deerskin ball from midfield through the opposing team's goal, which consisted of two poles set in the ground near each other and about four hundred and fifty yards from the opposite goal. The rules allowed a variation from five to seven in the number of goals necessary to win a game. Substitutions were possible, and the ball could be driven or thrown only with the racket. Another game was to throw a javelin at a rolling hoop or to distance-throw a javelin. The snow snake game was played mainly by children. The snow snake was a thin, smoothed hickory shaft some six feet in length, with the forward end increased in diameter and slightly upturned. There were up to six players, with three to a side, and each hurled his snow snake across a snow surface. The game was scored according to the distance achieved until the specified number of points had been reached by one side. The snow boat game was based on the snow snake principle. A snow boat was constructed from a solid piece of beech wood and looked like a round-bottomed vessel with an upturned bow. The boat had small feathers at the top of the stern and an oblong central opening in which was placed an arched piece of wood from which rattles hung. On a hillside each player trampled a runway in the snow and iced the depression. Up to about a dozen parallel courses, one for each player, might be prepared; the players formed teams for the game. Each player iced his two or three boats and propelled them along the chute and as far as possible across the snow below. A point was made by each boat that outdistanced all of the opposite team's boats. Two different dice games were played, one with dice made from disk-shaped gaming pieces ground down from pieces of antler, and the second with similarly shaped dice of wild plum seeds. One side of each die was burned to blacken it. The games were played with six dice, using bean counters to score the varying combinations of natural and burned surfaces which turned up when the dice were shaken and thrown. The games were played by two individuals against each other or by partners who took turns. The game furthermore had religious associations which are only sketchily recorded.

According to Morgan, in early historic times the dead were buried in a sitting position facing the east. At the grave after the burial a captured bird was released in order to carry away the spirit. Grave goods left with a man's body included his bow and arrows, his pipe, and food for the trip to the world of the dead. From the dwelling of each man to the home of Great Spirit was a path, and it was along this route that the soul traveled. Prior to this form of burial, bodies were placed on scaffolds where they were exposed to decay. The bones later were collected to be deposited in the household of the deceased or in a separate nearby structure. Just before a house and settlement were abandoned or after an unstated number of years the accumulated bones were buried in a mound. The aboriginal mourning period was probably of a year's duration. For a single season the soul lingered near the place of burial, and it required a year before reaching its final resting place. At the end of the mourning period the relatives assembled and held a feast to signify the soul's arrival among the dead. After this time the name of the deceased never again was mentioned.

When a woman died, her farmland, along with her material property of a domestic nature, was most likely inherited by her children, but it also was possible for her to will them to other individuals. A man's property normally was passed to his matrilineage, to be disposed of as they desired. The matrilineage members disposed of his separate dwelling or apartment in a longhouse as well as his other property. The members might also keep items by which to remember the deceased. A man could will his property to his wife or children if he made his desires known before a witness.

The afterlife of an individual was spent in the upperworld home of Great Spirit. Here there was a peaceful existence where sexual desires were unknown and where families again lived together. In heaven it was always summer, and the occupants passed their time in games and feasts. Here were found only the spirits of Indians, for whites were not created by the Indian gods. However, there was a partial exception to this rule. The spirit of George Washington existed in a compound just outside the land of Great Spirit. Washington's heavenly home was built like a fort, and he reportedly walked silently back and forth. The special consideration given this one white man resulted from the great humanitarian efforts of Washington for the Iroquois after the American Revolution.

It is necessary to reemphasize that the preceding descriptions of the Iroquois have been drawn largely from Morgan's ethnography, which presents an idealistic view of their lifeway. Then too the information gathered by Morgan was primarily from one group of Seneca long after they had their first contacts with Europeans. Thus what has come to be regarded as typically aboriginal Iroquois is really a view of acculturated Seneca. At the same time material has been introduced from studies other than the one by Morgan in order to correct errors and to add greater substantive detail. No attempt will be made to follow systematically the patterning of later historic changes among the Iroquois. Instead summary remarks will be made about particular historical events and trends following the American Revolution. Then the scene will be shifted to the modern Iroquois, and the Mohawk in particular, again with awareness that the generalizations may only be applied to Iroquois as a whole with caution.

Frank G. Speck made a number of comments about the nature of Iroquois material culture which are worth repeating. He observed that Morgan reported eighty-three classes of artifacts for 1841–1850; when Speck was writing in the early 1940's, most of the artifacts still were employed. The proportions unquestionably differed at the two time periods, but there was at least a one hundred-year stability in material forms. The change from aboriginal materials to those largely from traders took place around 1800, and the adaptations became crystalized by about 1820. The major changes were from deerskin to cloth as clothing material and from porcupine quills to trade beads for decorative patterns on clothing.

As was mentioned earlier the League disintegrated at the time of the American Revolution because the member nations could not agree on a unanimous course of political action. In 1777, the critical year of the League split, the Seneca were torn in two directions. The eastern segment was pro-British, whereas some of the western group favored neutrality and others the British cause. Among the western Seneca leaders was Cornplanter, who received a British commission as a "captain." In order effectively to neutralize the Iroquois the Americans laid waste to their villages and farmlands in 1779, and about 1780 Cornplanter and his followers moved to the upper Allegheny River drainage. When the American Revolution was over, the western Seneca in general occupied the unenviable position of having supported the losers. The Americans at this time were searching for an Indian leader to counteract the influence of Joseph Brant with his pro-British Mohawk, and they selected Cornplanter. He accepted the responsibility and actively sought supporters for the Americans. In the course of his official travels he went to Philadelphia on different occasions and became acquainted with the Quakers. In 1795 the Commonwealth of Pennsylvania granted Cornplanter a fee patent title to three separate plots of land very near the New York State line on the Allegheny River; one of the three tracts, each about a mile square, was Burnt House. Soon after this time Cornplanter had gathered about him some four hundred persons in thirty dwellings. One of the individuals living in the home of Cornplanter was his half-brother, Handsome Lake or Ganiodayo.

In 1798 five Quaker missionaries went to Burnt House, and one man, Henry Simmons, who had previous experience with the Oneida as a missionary, was selected to live at the settlement and teach the children. In the analysis by Merle H. Deardorff of what occurred at Burnt House during this general time period we have an ethnographic gem in the presentation and interpretation of the Simmons and other Quaker diaries. We learn that Simmons was asked by Cornplanter about his beliefs, and answers were supplied cautiously. As Deardorff (1951, 90) writes:

> Questions about theology and morals had been referred to Simmons, and answered in the Quaker way: Look inside. You have a Light in there that will show you what is good and what is bad. When you know

you have done wrong, repent and resolve to do better. Outward forms and books and guides are good; but they are made by men. The Great Spirit himself puts the Inner Light in every man. Look to it. Learn to read and write so that you may discover for yourself whether or not the white man's Book is true. Learn to distinguish good from evil so that you may avoid the pricks of conscience in this world and prosper; and that you may avoid punishment in the next.

The missionary, however, did not see many forms of behavior which were compatible with his beliefs. He particularly was annoyed at the preparations for a "Dancing Frolick," and the council decided to stop them, in part as a result of Simmons' objections. Furthermore, the men returned from Pittsburgh where they had traded many of their furs for intoxicants, and this led to a community binge of several weeks' duration. This brought reproval from the Quaker, and the contrite Indians resolved that two chiefs would be appointed to curb drinking. The killing of a witch and dances held for the dead were other distressing events which Simmons witnessed.

At the house of Cornplanter in June, 1799, his half-brother Handsome Lake appeared to be near death. On the fifteenth of the month Handsome Lake had a vision, the details of which were recorded by Simmons. In summary, Handsome Lake saw three men carrying different types of berry bushes upon which there were berries. The men asked him to eat some berries off the bushes, and by doing so he would live to see the berries of summer ripen. The men told him that Great Spirit was unhappy about the drunkenness of the people, and that if Handsome Lake recovered he was not again to drink intoxicants. The three men said further that a fourth man would visit him later. When he regained consciousness, he asked Cornplanter to call together the council, to repeat what had happened to Handsome Lake and to have each person eat a dried berry; these instructions were followed. Handsome Lake still was very ill, and within a short time he had a vision in which the fourth man, assumed to be Great Spirit, came to take him because he pitied him for having to suffer. When Handsome Lake awoke, he sent for Cornplanter and after talking with him fell into a trance for seven hours. Simmons (Deardorff, 1951, 91) wrote, "his legs and arms were cold, his body warm but breathless." Handsome Lake revealed later that he was led by a man with a bow and a single arrow who was clothed in a "clear sky colour." Soon he met his dead son and Cornplanter's daughter who recently had died. The girl told of her unhappiness because her father and her brother argued, while the son of Handsome Lake revealed that he was sorry that he did not care for his father better. The guide in turn stated that sons should treat their fathers well. The guide went on to say that Handsome Lake must not drink intoxicants and must give up all dances save the Green Maize Ceremony. The man with the bow and arrow pointed toward a river where there were canoes loaded with barrels of whiskey. There was an evil man in charge of the cargo who was (Deardorff, 1951, 91), "going about very busy doing and making all the noise and mischief he could amongst the people." Furthermore, Handsome Lake was told that if all the people agreed, it would be proper to accept whites as teachers. Finally, the guide said that Handsome Lake was to return among the living and he would see no more of these things until he died; in death he would return to this setting if he behaved properly while alive. When Cornplanter heard the second series of revelations, he again called a council meeting to which Henry Simmons was invited. When asked what he thought of the revelations, Simmons cautioned that Handsome Lake may not have reported precisely what he had seen and (Deardorff, 1951, 92), "I told them there had been instances of the same kind amongst white people even of the Quakers, falling into a trance, and saw both the good place, and bad place, and saw many wonderful sights which I did believe."

A White Dog Ceremony was held, in accord with another of the guide's instructions, to prevent illness, and following the Green Maize Ceremony the missionary Simmons left Burnt House. He was replaced by Halliday Jackson, who continued the record of what was happening at Cornplanter's village. Handsome Lake preached his doctrine, which came to include the rejection of schools and a return to a subsistence-based economy. In 1802 his cause received American support when Handsome Lake went to Washington, D. C., with other Iroquois and President Thomas Jefferson condoned his teachings. Partly because of this official sanction Handsome Lake became an acknowledged prophet. Cornplanter, however, thought schools for children should be accepted, and he did not agree with Handsome Lake's witch hunting. From the time of his recovery until his death Handsome Lake visited Seneca communities to influence the behavior of others. By 1807 his fame as a prophet had spread widely among the Iroquois and to other eastern tribes as well. When the War of 1812 began, the Iroquois had learned their lesson, and most of them did not participate. Handsome Lake in particular preached neutrality because of his continuing close ties with the Quakers. In 1815 the prophet moved to Onondaga, and it was here that he died the same year.

As Deardorff has noted, the Handsome Lake revelations or Gaiwiio (Good Message) came to include not only the revelations but biographical material, prophecy, law, parable, and anecdote. Its members call the entire system the New Religion. It should be noted that the Good Message does not under analysis stand as highly unique in the content of the revelations. Some of the more important aspects of the revelation already were initiated before Handsome Lake went into his series of trances. If only the text of the revelations had survived, it might have been assumed that Handsome Lake was a great innovator, but from the diaries of the Quaker missionaries it is obvious that the revelations were in step with what were recognized and pressing problems at Burnt House. Like all prophets, Handsome Lake is remembered because he was the right man at the right moment in history. Most important, and unlike many other Indian prophets, he was willing to adapt his basic ideas to accommodate Quaker beliefs and even certain material aspects of white culture such as agricultural methods. This flexibility contributed in a meaningful manner to the realities of Iroquois life in his times and unquestionably aided in the long-range survival of the Good Message. Soon after Handsome Lake's death, various Christian missionaries began to proselytize among the Seneca, and the Indians labored in council to establish a uniform approach to religion. The time-honored pattern of unanimity, however, could not be reached, and by 1820 the New Religion was of necessity separate from all others but the Quakers. It was not until 1845 that the Good Message was recorded systematically, but no single text has become standard. In 1949 there were ten ceremonial structures, each termed a longhouse, on the Six Nations meeting circuit of the New Religion. For most of the preachers four days were required to relate the Good Message, but the range was between three and five days' recitation time. The Tonawanda Longhouse was the Central Fire, and here were kept the most sacred strings of wampum which had belonged to Handsome Lake.

The New Religion includes the following tenets: the prohibition of intoxicants; obedience of children toward their parents, for children to care for aged parents, and faithfulness of married couples to each other; individuals should not gossip maliciously or boast; witches should be killed; there is a hell which will receive sinners and heaven awaits persons who have lived good lives or repent having lived evil lives; and the ways of whites may be accepted save for schools. As was written recently by Wilson (1960, 87) about the New Religion, it "has a scope and a coherence which have made it endure as has the teaching of no other Indian prophet, and it is accepted at the present time by at least half the Iroquois world as a source of moral guidance and religious inspiration."

A surviving stronghold of Iroquois culture today is among the ancestors of Six Nations members who followed Joseph Brant to Canada. The Six Nations Reserve population in 1956 consisted of about sixty-five hundred Iroquois, on seventy-two square miles of land. The reserve is far from homogeneous in its members' approach to life; in fact, great diversity in any facet of the sociocultural system is the norm. Also, since there has been so much intermarriage among the Iroquois tribes, a confusion in descent systems, and other related problems, it is not realistically possible to determine clear tribal identity with any accuracy. The study of the Six Nations Reserve by Annemarie A. Shimony ranks with the *League of the Iroquois* by Morgan and is the second great Iroquois ethnography. To attempt a summary of Shimony's analysis does violence to the wealth of detail in her compilation. Nonetheless, the major aspects of Six Nations Reserve life will be presented briefly with some stress on the New Religion. The study by Shimony concentrates on the conservative or native-oriented segment of the population. These are persons who accept some white material items but reject the road to rapid assimilation, following the New Religion, supporting the hereditary matrilineal chiefs, and stressing sib as well as moiety ties. These people are most likely to live on the reserve; they may be rich or poor, although the New Religion de-emphasizes material wealth.

The Six Nations Reserve population resides on homesteads scattered about the reserve. The land still belongs to the band as a group, but individual holdings are inherited by members. The stress placed on patrilineal inheritance by the Canadian authorities confuses the traditional matrilineal system of the Indians. If a man owns land, it passes to his wife and children if he made no will to the contrary, and when there are no heirs the land reverts to the band. Individual rights to band membership, like inheritance rights, are calculated in a patrilineal line according to the Canadian authorities but matrilineally by the Iroquois. This leads to complications when a Six Nations woman marries someone from outside the band. Although the Canadian government does not normally interfere with the decisions of the elected council in determining band membership and is in sympathy with the old system, there always is the possibility that the government may interfere in the future. Understandably, girls are encouraged to marry band members. The nuclear family as an important social unit is comparatively new to the Indians, and the Canadian emphasis on it robs the sibs of important functions.

There are no sib landholdings, and the original settlement pattern of localized areas for particular tribes has broken down except that the Cayuga and Mohawk have tended to retain geographical sections. A newly married couple establishing residence on the reserve will live with either the husband's or wife's relatives initially, depending on which side of the family can best accommodate them. Such residence is temporary, and the couple will establish a neolocal household as soon as they are in an economic position to do so. The combined matrilineal and matrilocal family no longer exists; for different women the family may mean the nuclear family or the matrilineage. The matrilineages are important in selecting sachems and chiefs of the sib, and disputes arise over which are the leading lineages with the vested rights. Members of the leading lineages of a sib are most likely to be familiar with their own sib ties and so are able to establish their political and religious authority. A real difficulty, however, stems from the fact that even some conservative families may be unsure or not know their sib affiliations. As would be anticipated, many earlier functions of the sibs have been dropped. At the time of Shimony's studies, 1953–1960, the sibs invested the sachems and chiefs; the sibs also could remove them from office. The sibs still bestowed names on members as they did in the past, but this function was of rapidly declining significance. The exogamous nature of the matrisibs continues to be observed by some persons, but others feel it is satisfactory to marry anyone to whom genealogical ties cannot be established on either side of the families involved.

The New Religion, based mainly on the Good Message of Handsome Lake, has four local congregations, each symbolized by a "fire" and centered at a different longhouse. The "head fire" is at the Tonawanda Longhouse in New York State; here each preacher on the longhouse circuit is invested. Each longhouse has its wampum, which validates the legitimacy of the local organization in the circuit, but the head fire has no jurisdiction over the "home" fires. The rituals of the four longhouses of the Six Nations Reserve vary in details in their yearly cycle but are essentially the same. The particular longhouse to which a person belongs is guided by matrilineage ties, not tribal affiliations, and by its proximity, although all four are within eight miles of each other. For active members it is most desirable to live near one's longhouse in order not to miss out on any events because of not being informed of their occurrence.

The physical structure of a longhouse is in the form of a rectangular wooden building, usually with doors at each end; wood-burning stoves are near the ends, with each stove serving as the fire for a moiety. Benches are along the walls, and the central area of the room is dominated by neither moiety. In fulfilling social and ceremonial

obligations as well as maintaining the structure the moieties reciprocate in their activities. Reciprocity is a basic characteristic of the longhouse organization. The moiety alignments are not the same as those
reported for earlier historic times, and although three of the four longhouses are named for tribes (Cayuga, Seneca, and Onondaga) plus
Sour Springs, there is no clear indication that the longhouses are affiliated with these respective tribes. Considering the present confusion,
it is not unexpected that the sibs associated with the Mohawk are not
in the same moiety.

The leaders in a longhouse are the Keepers of the Faith, or deacons, as they more commonly are called by the Six Nations people.
Each moiety has two leading Keepers of the Faith who are male and
female respectively, selected from among the Keepers of the Faith of
the longhouses on the basis of their merit. The Keepers of the Faith
oversee all longhouse functions, their advice on secular and ceremonial matters is sought, and they tend to represent the longhouse at
political functions. With a breakdown of the sib structure the Keepers of the Faith have an increased voice in general community affairs.
Some Keeper of the Faith offices are inherited in matrilineal families;
others, with no fixed number, are selected by the existing deacons
because of their abilities or ties with a sachem. One personality trait
expected of all these individuals is that they be nonaggressive in dealing with each other and the congregation. The most capable longhouse leaders successfully and without obvious pressures induce the
members to participate in the longhouse as fully as possible. A second
longhouse functionary is the Keeper of the Fire, who is the guardian
of the longhouse wampum. His moiety and sib affinities are unimportant, but it is regarded as important that he be a staunch believer in
the New Religion. The wampum is highly symbolic of the longhouse
traditions, and the people believe that Canadian officials would like
to destroy the wampum in order in turn to destroy the longhouses.
A third and final category of longhouse leaders is the Speaker, who
presents to the congregation traditional and extemporaneous speeches.
Such persons are not invested in any formal office, nor are they usually
preachers on the longhouse circuit. All that is required of a speaker is
an established talent for public speaking and a knowledge of traditional speeches.

A longhouse clearly serves many diverse functions in the members'
efforts to resist becoming like other Canadians. The organization has
come to fulfill social, medical, economic, and political functions. Social gatherings include softball or lacrosse games, raffles, and dances.
Organized social activities outside of the longhouse usually are closed

to longhouse members by their own dogma. The longhouse ceremonial round is rich in detail and, since the Handsome Lake revelations, has come to include these teachings and supplementary beliefs plus the round of aboriginal planting and harvest ceremonies and old and new means for curing. An important aspect of almost any longhouse function is the recitation of a formal address of thanks to Great Spirit for the continued life of the persons attending and thanks to the participants for attending. The text of an address follows the general patterning of thanks to the diverse levels of supernatural forces. In all longhouse activities the ritual and social language is Iroquois; speaking English is disapproved in any context. The dialects most often spoken are Cayuga, Onondaga, and Seneca, with Mohawk distinctly associated with Christian Iroquois. To the members, participation in longhouse events gives real purpose to life and at the same time offers a systematic philosophy for living. People are encouraged to remember the teachings of Handsome Lake and to live good lives. At other times the younger members are told not to imitate such fashion extremes of whites as high-heeled shoes and low-cut dresses for girls. Neither should one listen to the radio, watch television, or drink intoxicants, for such behavior is not in keeping with the New Religion. Behind it all is the real fear that the longhouse members will come to imitate their white Canadian neighbors. The conflict created seems often to lead to trauma at the time of death for those individuals who at one time or another in their lives followed forbidden white ways.

For members of the New Religion and other Iroquois as well there is a sociocultural focus on death which unquestionably is deeply rooted in being Iroquois. The death ceremonies were not detailed for the reconstructed past, but the present Six Nations attitudes and practices seem steeped in tradition. A person's death may be caused by failure to take a time-honored view about the spirit world, by showing a lack of respect for plants or animals, or by failing to hold rituals as directed. Furthermore, the dead possess great power over the living, and to neglect them, especially right after someone has died, is an invitation to disease and death. Today there are many diverse attitudes toward the nature of a soul. In general, they feel that souls reside in a pleasant upperworld or else they suffer punishments. Souls bent on evil may take animal forms but in ordinary instances may be nonmaterial second and invisible bodies, or a light, vapor, and so on. All of this concern with death and the dead necessitates the proper performance of obligations to the dead. To avert death and illness for the community or the individual the Ceremony for the Dead was and is held. Currently the Ceremony for the Dead is supervised and arranged by a woman from each moiety in a particular longhouse. She receives the office and a name through her matrilineal line. Other functionaries include a man selected from each moiety; persons who joined because they wanted to, because of dreams, or because they were told to join by fortunetellers; and those members who regard membership as hereditary in their families. Ideally, two Ceremonies for the Dead are held each year, in the spring before planting and in the fall after the harvest. After one or more planning meetings the members assemble to clean the longhouse cemetery, lunch at the longhouse and later hold a social dance. The formal ceremonies are held at night, with all members participating. There is first a speech of thanksgiving which explains the purpose of the ceremony, then tobacco offerings, followed by Ceremony for the Dead songs and dances. Later, there is feasting, the distribution of gifts, and perhaps more dances before daybreak. The singing and dancing not only make the dead content but benefit the living as well.

The destiny of the hereditary chiefs or sachems is in many respects tied to the New Religion. The sachems represented traditional authority and functioned as the recognized political body until 1924. Sachems were either Christian or adherents of the New Religion. This religious division was very serious since the longhouse sachems considered that their Christian counterparts could not legitimately hold office unless invested at a longhouse ceremony, which was comparable to raising up a sachem in the old League. Thus, installation to the longhouse members required sacred sanction for secular power. The sachems divided also over whether they were tradition-oriented or favored closer rapport with Canadian officials. In 1924 a group of World War I veterans and other more acculturated persons, collectively termed "warriors," sought governmental recognition of an elected council. In a subsequent investigation of Six Nations Reserve affairs the sachems would not present their case to the governmental representatives; thus the government heard only the faction supporting elected chiefs. The Canadian government favored elected leaders since it received little cooperation from the sachems. An elected council was installed during 1924. The sachems were locked out of the council house, and Royal Canadian Mounted Police officers enforced the government's decision. The sachems were bitter against the Canadians as well as against their factional opposites. Continuing opposition on the part of the sachems and their supporters is shown in their refusing at least some forms of Canadian aid such as Family Allowance payments and Old Age Assistance payments. The elected council clearly does not have widespread support. This is reflected in the election returns; although there are burning political issues, from a total population of seven thousand only about six hundred ballots are cast in typical elections. It is not disinterest that keeps the conservatives from voting but the idea that to vote constitutes recognition of the elected council and the Canadian government's right to validate the elected council's position.

The ability of the aboriginal Iroquois to work with ease at heights exists still. Among the modern Tuscarora of New York State many of the men who entered the armed services during World War II chose to become paratroopers or to find duty with the air forces. Likewise, there are men over sixty years of age who are capable pruners of high trees, painters of roofs, and carpenters working on scaffolds. Jobs of this nature attract them in spite of the dangers involved. Futhermore, the people prefer to live in two- or three-story houses.

From the studies of modern Mohawk by Morris Freilich, Joseph Mitchell, and Fred Voget, we learn a great deal about how the Caughnawaga have come to find a secure place in the economic development of modern Canada and the United States. It will be recalled that Mohawk began to be attracted to Canada by Jesuit missionaries in the late seventeenth century. They were known as the Praying Indians and came to occupy their present reservation after three short moves before 1719. The land they occupied until 1830 was a mission holding, but in that year it became a reservation. Land was allotted to families, and other ground was held for future generations. The holdings may be leased to anyone but sold or given only to another member of the reservation. The Caughnawaga Reservation extends about eight miles along the St. Lawrence River and is up to four miles in width. The community of Caughnawaga, in the 1940's, consisted of about fifty homes in addition to an Indian Affairs Branch office, Roman Catholic and United Church of Canada churches, Protestant and Catholic schools, a Catholic hospital, post office, grocery stores and gasoline stations. The highway from Montreal to Malone, New York, passed through the reservation, and to attract tourists to his souvenirs one man had a striking advertising display. Before his house he placed a bark-covered tepee, two totem poles, and a sign which read (Mitchell, 1960, 5), "Stop! & Pow Wow With Me. Chief White Eagle. Indian Medicine Man. *Herbages Indiens.*" It might be added that the advertising efforts of this enterpriser were not approved by the other reservation residents. The dwellings at Caughna-waga were frame structures, a combination of framing and stone masonry, or log cabins. A yard was likely to contain a garage, stable, chicken coop, and privy, as well as fruit trees and an assortment of miscellaneous items. The stable was for a horse which was needed to carry water from the river and to haul firewood.

The homes appear to have been occupied by extended families, and the total reservation had nearly three thousand. Some twenty-seven hundred were Roman Catholics and two hundred fifty were Protestants. Fewer than one hundred belonged to the New Religion. The Roman Catholics have been losing ground since the 1920's. Some persons have become Protestants, and since World War I others in small numbers have been attracted to the doctrines of Handsome Lake. A longhouse in which the New Religion members met was constructed on a hillside at the cemetery.

After the move to Caughnawaga in the early 1700's, the economy of the migrants underwent a series of diverse adjustments. When they arrived at their new home, the Jesuit priests attempted to teach the men to farm. This activity of course was regarded as work for women, and the men continued to be hunters, unquestionably fight-ing their enemies at every opportunity. Before long more and more men were attracted to the fur trade and served as canoemen or voy-ageurs for French trading parties, sometimes fighting as they moved through hostile country. After the British became the political con-trollers of the area, the Mohawk continued working in the fur trade until its decline which began about 1800. Next, some of the men found employment in the logging industry by rafting timber through rapids and along fast water; this work was as dangerous as being a canoeman or warrior. At about the same time some men finally turned to farm-ing, while others were among the first medicine show Indians, travel-ing about New England by horse and buggy selling Indian medical preparations. Others seem to have performed with circuses during the summer months and then returned to the reservation for the winter. Another part of the population was obsessed by the desire for alcohol; they found temporary employment in Montreal but drank excessively.

In 1886 the Dominion Bridge Company began construction of a cantilever bridge across the St. Lawrence River, using reservation land for a bridge abutment. In obtaining permission to use the land the company agreed to hire reservation Indians, but only for unskilled labor jobs. The Mohawk were unhappy with this arrangement, and they could not be kept off the bridge structure as the span was being built. Soon it became quite apparent that they not only were unafraid of heights but seemed to enjoy the new experience. Neither did the din of the riveting faze them in the least. After pestering the crew foremen, a few men finally were hired, and they turned out to be excellent workers. It appears that three crews were trained on this bridge. In the erection of a bridge of this sort precut and drilled beams and girders were hoisted into place with a crane or derrick, temporarily bolted and plumbed, then riveted. The Iroquois were to become members of riveting crews, the most daring as well as the most lucrative type of job. A four-man riveting crew consisted of a heater, bucker-up, sticker-in, and riveter. The heater heated the rivets at a portable forge on a wooden platform. With tongs he tossed a red-hot rivet to the sticker-in who caught it in a metal container. The bucker-up removed the temporary bolt, and the sticker-in pushed the mushroom-shaped rivet in place. The next step was for the bucker-up to brace the rivet head. The riveter attached his pneumatic hammer to the cylindrical end of the rivet and pressed back the hot rivet until it was secure. The job of riveter was the most difficult, and the men of a crew rotated in handling the air hammer.

After this introduction the Caughnawaga Mohawk worked on other bridges and systematically trained more and more riveting crews. By 1907 there were over seventy skilled workers, about half of whom were employed on the Quebec Bridge which spans the St. Lawrence River near Quebec City. On August 29, 1907, "the disaster" occurred; the span fell and ninety-six men, including thirty-five Caughnawaga, were killed. Bridgework now took on a new meaning, for obviously it was dangerous. It became a more attractive form of employment than either timber rafting or performing in circuses. For the reservation women the disaster was a great tragedy, and one of their first moves was to force the gangs to work on many different projects so that a similar disaster could not affect so many families. Since there were relatively few bridge jobs in Canada, the men found employment on diverse high steel projects. The women also demonstrated that their Christian faith had not been shaken by purchasing a large crucifix of St. Francis Xavier for the church.

About 1926 three or four reservation high steel gangs went to New York City to work, and three more gangs arrived in 1928. With the construction of Rockefeller Center in the 1930's, seven more gangs arrived in the city. They became members of the Brooklyn local of the International Association of Bridge, Structural, and Ornamental Iron Workers and roomed nearby in the North Gowanus area. By the late 1940's the North Gowanus locality was occupied by about one hundred twenty-five steel workers and their families. The families live in Brooklyn, but the men span the country working first on one job and then another. The reason offered for moving about is the overtime wage at distant jobs, but this simply is a rationalization of their desire to wander. They hear of a new and distant job, and before long they have left for it with little or no warning.

The area of Brooklyn called North Gowanus consists mainly of tenements and some factories. The Mohawk live in the best houses and are within ten blocks of each other. The household occupants consists of a series of related females and their families in one or adjacent apartment buildings. The residences are furnished in the manner typical for local whites with the addition of Mohawk artifacts on a wall or mantel. In these homes where the men frequently are away many women spend their free time making what have come to be regarded as typically Indian craft items. The raw materials are most likely to be obtained from the Plume Trading and Sales Company of New York City, which specializes in the Boy Scout and Indian markets. Beaded belts, handbags, and dolls are made. These are sold at fairs in the New York State area by the most Indian-looking men of the group. Other members of a household are likely to include single girls from the reservation who are employed in nearby factories. Not infrequently they marry non-Indians and become lost to the Iroquois community. The boys raised in these households are in general intelligent and adjust well to school life, but they drop out of school after fulfilling the minimum state requirements to become workers in high steel. Inasmuch as very little training is necessary, it is not long before a boy can work as an adult in a work gang and earn about $150 a week (ca. 1955).

Social life of the Brooklyn Mohawk centers at one particular bar in the North Gowanus neighborhood. The high steel men drop by there at the end of the work day; on weekends and in the evening they bring their wives. On the walls of the bar are a reproduction of "Custer's Last Stand," drawings of Iroquois warriors, and steel workers' helmets. According to Freilich (1958, 479), "Periodically, the Indians tear the place apart; they feel it their right, since it is their home. If outsiders give any sign of attempting to make it their clubroom too, blood flows fast and furious." The combative nature of the individual Mohawk exists still, and examples of bloody fights are not uncommon. Furthermore, there is not only the element of daring in their jobs and in dealings with other individuals, but a continued use of intoxicants which leads to other forms of recklessness. Again to quote from Freilich (1958, 478), "Some examples from my field work include driving 90 miles per hour on a winding road at night in the mountains of New York State in an old car while inebriated; accepting a dare to go faster than the speedometer could register and two men having sexual intercourse with a girl while her fiancé was asleep beside her."

Ties with Caughnawaga are still maintained by the Brooklyn residents. The reservation members are required only to have an identification card issued by the Indian Affairs Branch of Canada to cross the international border. In addition to the girls who come to find work in Brooklyn, the relatives of established members of the Mohawk colony visit, especially in any time of crisis. A man might take his family to the reservation for the summer, but he would not be likely to remain there for very long. When a steel worker retires, he is likely to return to the reservation, but his adjustment to the uneventful and sedentary life is difficult. One response seems to be to return to Indians ways to the point of not speaking English and to become deeply involved in reservation politics and social life.

In a search for the reasons for the striking success of the Mohawk in high steel work Freilich has made some noteworthy observations. First, he thinks that they are behaving in the pattern of warriors, exhibiting no fear of heights as a warrior would in theory not fear the enemy or death. He thinks, from listening to a conversation about heights among moderately intoxicated Mohawk, that they do in fact fear heights. They subordinate their fear because of what they think of themselves and to maintain the white view that they are unafraid. Surprisingly, work in high steel is highly compatible with many essential features of the old Mohawk way of life. The men leave home to work for extended periods as they left to hunt and fight in aboriginal times. There is danger and possible death in what they do as there was danger of old. When a man returns, he can boast of the tall building on which he has worked, just as he once boasted of his combative skills. Today, the steel worker is subject to little authority, and if he is displeased he can quit his job just as he could drop out of a war party formerly if he so desired. These and other parallels support the traditional status of the male in an unpredictable setting.

With the long tradition of being Roman Catholics, many of the Brooklyn Mohawk attend a local Catholic church. Others have been attracted to the Cuyler Presbyterian Church. The minister, David M. Cory, noted that a few Mohawk began attending his church in 1938,

and he decided to learn Mohawk, which he did. He now holds one
evening service each month entirely in Mohawk, and he is by far the
most trusted white in Brooklyn.

In a study of only the most conservative or Indian-oriented
Caughnawaga Reservation people, Fred Voget supplies anthropological
insight into the way of life in the 1940's. What is most apparent is the
extreme importance of the New Religion in focusing their world view.
The position of these people, or the native-modified population as
they have been called by Voget, is that they were forced by the French
to become Roman Catholics, and since that time they have lost physical strength and stature, as well as their lands. Such has been their
punishment for abandoning their old religion, which is conceived in
terms of the Good Message of Handsome Lake and his followers. In
order to regain their physical strength and political powers of old it
is essential to return to a religion that is Indian. They consider themselves chosen people and advocate retention of their racial identity
as a means for consolidating and achieving their purposes. As Edmund
Wilson has popularized, Fred Voget (1951, 223) also has stressed, "the
important historic role of the Iroquois has awakened a national consciousness based on their original autonomy and structured according
to the traditional organization of the League of the Five (or Six)
Nations." The efforts of these Caughnawaga have led to a modern
nativistic movement striving for the freedoms of old. Some persons
look to the councils at the Grand River Reserve in Ontario and the
Onondaga Reservation in New York State as centers of their movement.

The personality characteristics of the modern Tuscarora, as presented by Wallace, may be extended cautiously to the Iroquois in
general. The people have retained their strong desire for alcohol, but
its consumption now is more channelized than in early historic times.
When the study of the New York State Tuscarora was made in 1948–
1949, the Indians still were prohibited from legally consuming intoxicants, but this restriction had not been successful in the past nor was
it at the time of the study. The Indians frequented bars which were
known to sell intoxicants to Indians. By drinking mainly in bars they
were subject to the authority of the bartender concerning how much
they consumed, and there was always the possibility of police intervention if there were disturbances. Furthermore, since the drinking
was away from home, at least one man in a group by necessity re-

mained sober to drive the others home. Thus there were regularized controls over the behavior of drunken persons. A counterforce also had developed in the Indians' attitudes toward intoxicants. Some persons rejected alcohol because of traumatic childhood experiences with drunks, and some were reformed middle-aged drinkers. A nearby Baptist Church to which most of the Tuscarora belonged rejected drinking, and there was also a local Temperance Society. Thus there were possible ways out of drinking problems for individuals, and gossip was an important means for attempting to curb drinking.

Iroquois and white American attitudes are in so many ways fundamentally different that it is little wonder the people fail to understand one another. Certain examples will serve to illustrate their differences. Whites are in general thrifty, coveting wealth to accumulate more wealth; the Iroquois are generous and wasteful with money and material things. Whites are orderly in keeping house, and their dwellings are built by contractors and follow standard plans. Indian houses are untidy, jerrybuilt, and often left unfinished. The whites are time-oriented, considering promptness as a great virtue, but there is "Indian time," which means being late or not appearing at all. The old Tuscarora demandingness runs wild in their dealings with the state of New York. The state supplies schools, school busses, welfare, road maintenance and other services. The Indians not only accept these but expect more and more. Their dependency, to their thinking, is based on obligations of the Federal and state authorities stemming from old injustices which are both real and imagined.

The attempts in recent years by the Iroquois to assert their nationalism have led to diverse protests; for example, most of the United States Iroquois population refuses to vote, although they have had the right to do so since the passage of the Citizenship Act of 1924. They feel that by not voting they are not recognizing United States political domination over them and in the process are reinforcing their own identity. During World War I they separately declared war on Germany. In World War II when subject to selective service as a result of the Citizenship Act, some went to jail, and some in other way evaded the draft. The Iroquois in New York State have resisted strongly all attempts by state officials to intervene in their affairs. Justification for the Indian position is based upon their treaties with the Federal government and the implication of equality in national standing between the Six Nations and the United States. Predictably, the Iroquois have resisted both state and Federal income taxes and have fought efforts to use reserved lands for the St. Lawrence Seaway,

the Power Authority of New York State, and the relocation of highways. All of these disputes usually are complicated by the fact that
the elected chiefs are willing to cooperate with the whites, but the
hereditary chiefs backed by the members of the New Religion resist
any and all efforts toward increased outside control. The conflict
between the Tuscarora and the Power Authority of New York State
is a sad example of a recent effort by the state to obtain about a fifth
of the Tuscarora Reservation for a reservoir. The Power Authority
was at that time headed and controlled by Robert Moses, who later
became chairman of the Triborough Bridge and Tunnel Authority.
There was a great attraction in taking Indian lands through the
process of eminent domain, for unlike other possible land, that of the
Iroquois contained so few improvements that its value was comparatively little. Furthermore, reservation lands are not taxable, and by
using them there would be no reduction in the local tax base. The
callous immorality of the Power Authority campaign need not be
detailed. The outcome was, however, as might be expected. The case
was carried to the United States Supreme Court and the Power
Authority won.

The stance of the Iroquois in the United States is similar to that
of the Six Nations Reserve residents near Brantford, Ontario. Protests
of the conservative and traditionally oriented Six Nations population
in Canada stem in part from a 1924 decision by the Canadian government to dispose of the hereditary chiefs because of their slow response
to change. The leaders were replaced by an "elected" council which
was appointed by the Indian Affairs Branch. This led to various protests carried by delegates, who issued their own passports "good anywhere in the world," to the League of Nations and to the King of
England, but without success. Later appeals to the United Nations
were equally futile. Revolution broke out on the Six Nations Reserve
in 1959 when the government-backed council and chief met in closed
session. Some thirteen hundred supporters of the hereditary chiefs
removed the front door of the council house. In a subsequent meeting, attended by about five thousand, a proclamation was read doing
away with the government-supported political structure, reinstating
the hereditary leaders, and creating an Iroquois Police to replace the
Royal Canadian Mounted Police officers who had local jurisdiction.
Further plans were made to make the reserve self-sufficient economically. Before long a schoolteacher was tried for treason for writing
to a newspaper that the movement did not have widespread support.
The offender was freed when he swore on wampum that he would
support the new authorities, under the threat of expulsion from the

reserve if he failed in his vow. The Canadian government reasserted itself when R.C.M.P. officers attempted to dislodge the Iroquois Police from the council house. The men were passive until some Iroquois women attacked the Mounties; a general fight followed. The defenders finally withdrew, and warrants issued by the police were forgotten when the lawyer representing the hereditary chiefs assured the Canadian authorities that such violent action would not take place in the future.

In 1958 the very dynamic nationalistic Iroquois leader Mad Bear accepted an invitation to Cuba, where he visited Fidel Castro. Mad Bear and his followers hope that they may be admitted to the United Nations under Cuban sponsorship. The Iroquois, along with the balance of the world, are witnessing the current emergence of highly nationalistic governments. The day of political domination by white colonial powers over aboriginal peoples seems to be passing quickly. This gives the Iroquois hope, it strengthens their position, and contributes to the consolidation of their own nationalism; perhaps the day will come when the League of the Iroquois or Hodenosaunee again will guide the destiny of its people.

Note 1. At the end of Cresap's War the Iroquois sachem Logan delivered an oration praised by Thomas Jefferson (Stone, 1838, v. 1, 46).

I appeal to any white man to say if he ever entered Logan's cabin hungry, and he gave him not meat; if ever he came cold and naked, and he clothed him not . . . Such was my love for the whites, that my countrymen pointed, as they passed, and said, "Logan is the friend of the white men." I had even thought to have lived with you, but for the injuries of one man. Colonel Cresap, the last Spring, in cold blood and unprovoked, murdered all the relations of Logan, not even sparing my women and children. There runs not a drop of my blood in the veins of any living creature. This called on me for revenge. I have sought it; I have killed many; I have fully glutted my vengeance. For my country, I rejoice at the beams of peace; but do not harbour a thought that mine is the joy of fear. Logan never felt fear. He will not turn on his heel to save his life. Who is there to mourn for Logan? Not one.

Note 2. This letter written by Joseph Brant to Lord Sidney, the Secretary of State for the English Colonies, illustrates the skillful use of English by Brant (Stone, 1838, v. 2, 252–253).

My Lord,

The claims of the Mohawks for their losses having been delivered by Sir John Johnson, His Majesty's Superintendent General for Indian affairs, to General Haldimand, and by him laid before your Lordship, who cannot but be well informed that their sufferings, losses, and being drove from that coun-

try which their forefathers long enjoyed, and left them the peaceable possession of, is in consequence of their faithful attachment to the King, and the zeal
they manifested in supporting the cause of His country against the rebellious
subjects in America.

From the promises made by the Governor and Commander-in-chief of
Canada, that their losses should be made good, and that soon, when I left
them, I was desired to put His Majesty's ministers in mind of their long and
sincere friendship for the English nation, in whose cause their ancestors and
they have so often fought and so freely bled,—of their late happy settlements,
before the rebellion, and their present situation,—and to request their claims
might be attended to, and that orders may be given for what they are to
receive to be paid as soon as possible, in order to enable them to go on with
the settlement they are now making; in some measure stock their farms, and
get such articles and materials as all settlements in new countries require, and
which it is out of their power to do before they are paid for their losses.

On my mentioning these matters, since my arrival in England, I am informed orders are given that this shall be done; which will give great relief
and satisfaction to those faithful Indians, who will have spirit to go on, and
their hearts be filled with gratitude for the King, their father's, great kindness,
which I pray leave, in their behalf, to acknowledge, and to thank your Lordship for your friendship.

JOSEPH BRANT, Captain, or
Thayendanegea.

London, 4th January, 1786.

Note 3. In *The Jesuit Relations and Allied Documents* for 1637 is
described the torture of a prisoner by the Iroquoian-speaking Huron. At the
point the quote begins, the captive has already been tortured for hours
(Thwaites, 1898, v. 13, 65–79).

But the Captains prevented them from going any farther, and ordered
them to cease tormenting him, saying it was important that he should see the
daylight. They had him lifted upon a mat, most of the fires were extinguished,
and many of the people went away. Now there was a little respite for our
sufferer, and some consolation for us . . . While he was in this condition, their
only thought was to make him return to his senses, giving him many drinks
composed of pure water only. At the end of an hour he began to revive a little,
and to open his eyes; he was forthwith commanded to sing. He did this at first
in a broken and, as it were, dying voice; but finally he sang so loud that he
could be heard outside the cabin. The youth assemble again; they talk to him,
they make him sit up—in a word, they begin to act worse than before. For me
to describe in detail all he endured during the rest of the night, would be
almost impossible; we suffered enough in forcing ourselves to see a part of it.
Of the rest we judged from their talk; and the smoke issuing from his roasted
flesh revealed to us something of which we could not have borne the sight.
One thing, in my opinion, greatly increased his consciousness of suffering—
that anger and rage did not appear upon the faces of those who were tormenting him, but rather gentleness and humanity, their words expressing only

raillery or tokens of friendship and goodwill. There was no strife as to who should burn him,—each one took his turn; thus they gave themselves leisure to meditate some new device to make him feel the fire more keenly. They hardly burned him anywhere except in the legs, but these, to be sure, they reduced to a wretched state, the flesh being all in shreds. Some applied burning brands to them and did not withdraw them until he uttered loud cries; and, as soon as he ceased shrieking, they again began to burn him, repeating it seven or eight times,—often reviving the fire, which they held close against the flesh, by blowing upon it. Others bound cords around him and then set them on fire, thus burning him slowly and causing him the keenest agony. There were some who made him put his feet on red-hot hatchets, and then pressed down on them. You could have heard the flesh hiss, and seen the smoke which issued therefrom rise even to the roof of the cabin. They struck him with clubs upon the head, and passed small sticks through his ears; they broke the rest of his fingers; they stirred up the fire all around his feet. No one spared himself, and each one strove to surpass his companion in cruelty. But, as I have said, what was most calculated in all this to plunge him into despair, was their raillery, and the compliments they paid him when they approached to burn him. This one said to him, "Here, uncle, I must burn thee"; and afterwards this uncle found himself changed into a canoe. "Come," said he, "let me calk and pitch my canoe, it is a beautiful new canoe which I lately traded for; I must stop all the water holes well," and meanwhile he was passing the brand all along his legs. Another one asked him, "Come, uncle, where do you prefer that I should burn you?" and this poor sufferer had to indicate some particular place. At this, another one came along and said, "For my part, I do not know anything about burning; it is a trade that I never practiced," and meantime his actions were more cruel than those of the others. In the midst of this heat, there were some who tried to make him believe that he was cold. "Ah, it is not right," said one, "that my uncle should be cold; I must warm thee." Another one added, "Now as my uncle has kindly deigned to come and die among the Hurons, I must make him a present, I must give him a hatchet," and with that he jeeringly applied to his feet a red-hot hatchet. Another one likewise made him a pair of stockings from old rags, which he afterwards set on fire; and often, after having made him utter loud cries, he asked him, "And now, uncle, hast thou had enough?" And when he replied, "onna chouatan, onna," "Yes, nephew, it is enough, it is enough," these barbarians replied, "No, it is not enough," and continued to burn him at intervals, demanding of him every time if it was enough. They did not fail from time to time to give him something to eat, and to pour water into his mouth, to make him endure until morning; and you might have seen, at the same time, green ears of corn roasting at the fire and near them red-hot hatchets; and sometimes, almost at the same moment that they were giving him the ears to eat, they were putting the hatchets upon his feet. If he refused to eat, "Indeed," said they, "dost thou think thou art master here?" and some added, "For my part, I believe thou wert the only Captain in thy country. But let us see, wert thou not very cruel to prisoners; now just tell us, didst thou not enjoy burning them? Thou didst not think thou wert to be treated in the same way, but perhaps thou didst think thou hadst killed all the Hurons?"

Behold in part how passed the night, . . . One thing that consoled us was to see the patience with which he bore all this pain. In the midst of their taunts and jeers, not one abusive or impatient word escaped his lips . . . He himself also entertained the company for a while, on the state of affairs in his country, and the death of some Hurons who had been taken in war. He did this as easily, and with a countenance as composed, as any one there present would have showed. This availed him at least as so much diminution of his sufferings; therefore, he said, they were doing him a great favor by asking him many questions, and that this in some measure diverted him from his troubles. As soon as day began to dawn, they lighted fires outside the village, to display there the excess of their cruelty to the sight of the Sun. The victim was led thither . . . Meanwhile, two of them took hold of him and made him mount a scaffold 6 or 7 feet high; 3 or 4 of these barbarians followed him. They tied him to a tree which passed across it, but in such a way that he was free to turn around. There they began to burn him more cruelly than ever, leaving no part of his body to which the fire was not applied at intervals. When one of these butchers began to burn him and to crowd him closely, in trying to escape him, he fell into the hands of another who gave him no better a reception. From time to time they were supplied with new brands, which they thrust, all aflame, down his throat, even forcing them into his fundament. They burned his eyes; they applied red-hot hatchets to his shoulders; they hung some around his neck, which they turned now upon his back, now upon his breast, according to the position he took in order to avoid the weight of this burden. If he attempted to sit or crouch down, someone thrust a brand from under the scaffolding which soon caused him to arise . . . They so harassed him upon all sides that they finally put him out of breath; they poured water into his mouth to strengthen his heart, and the Captains called out to him that he should take a little breath. But he remained still, his mouth open, and almost motionless. Therefore, fearing that he would die otherwise than by the knife, one cut off a foot, another a hand, and almost at the same time a third severed the head from the shoulders, throwing it into the crowd, where someone caught it to carry it to the Captain Ondessone, for whom it had been reserved, in order to make a feast therewith.

Note 4. The Planting Ceremony speech of the Seneca is typical of ceremonial prayers (Morgan, 1954, v. 1, 188).

Great Spirit, who dwellest alone, listen now to the words of thy people here assembled. The smoke of our offering arises. Give kind attention to our words, as they arise to thee in the smoke. We thank thee for this return of the planting season. Give to us a good season, that our crops may be plentiful.

Continue to listen, for the smoke yet arises. (Throwing on tobacco.) Preserve us from all pestilential diseases. Give strength to us all that we may not fall. Preserve our old men among us, and protect the young. Help us to celebrate with feeling the ceremonies of this season. Guide the minds of thy people, that they may remember thee in all their actions.

Note 5. A Keeper of the Faith among the Seneca delivered the following speech at each dwelling the morning of the first day of the New Year's Ceremony (Morgan, 1954, v. 1, 200–201).

Listen, Listen, Listen:—The ceremonies which the Great Spirit has commanded us to perform, are about to commence. Prepare your houses. Clear away the rubbish. Drive out all evil animals. We wish nothing to hinder or obstruct the coming observances. We enjoin upon every one to obey our requirements. Should any of your friends be taken sick and die, we command you not to mourn for them, nor allow any of your friends to mourn. But lay the body aside, and enjoy the coming ceremonies with us. When they are over, we will mourn with you.

Note 6. When a white dog was sacrificed among the Seneca as a part of the New Year's Ceremony, the following speech was given three times (Morgan, 1954, v. 1, 209).

Hail, hail, hail. Thou who hast created all things, who rulest all things, and who givest laws and commands to thy creatures, listen to our words. We now obey thy commands. That which thou hast made is returning unto thee. It is rising to thee, by which it will appear that our words are true.

References

Beauchamp, William M. "The Principal Founders of the Iroquois League and its Probable Date," *Proceedings of the New York State Historical Association*, v. 24, 27–36. 1926.

Colden, Cadwallader. *The History of the Five Indian Nations of Canada.* 2 v. London. 1755.

Cory, David M. *Within Two Worlds.* New York. 1956.

Deardorff, Merle H. "The Religion of Handsome Lake: Its Origin and Development," *SI, BAE,†* *Bulletin* 149, 79–107. 1951.

*Fenton, William N. "Problems Arising from the Historic Northeastern Position of the Iroquois," *Essays in Historical Anthropology of North America.* Smithsonian Miscellaneous Collections, v. 100, 159–251. 1940. An excellent study of the Iroquoian tribes from the time of early historic contact until the modern period.

*———. "Tonawanda Longhouse Ceremonies: Ninety Years after Lewis Henry Morgan," *SI, BAE, Bulletin* 128, 140–166. 1941. Included is a detailed summary outline of the Tonawanda Seneca ceremonial calendar which provides comparable detail for each event.

———. "Locality as a Basic Factor in the Development of Iroquois Social Structure," *SI, BAE, Bulletin* 149, 35–54. 1951.

———. "The Concept of Locality and the Program of Iroquois Research," *SI, BAE, Bulletin* 149, 1–12. 1951.

† Smithsonian Institution, Bureau of American Ethnology

————. "Iroquois Studies at the Mid-Century," *Proceedings of the American Philosophical Society*, v. 95, 296–310. 1951.

————. "Long-Term Trends of Change among the Iroquois," *Cultural Stability and Cultural Change*, 30–35. American Ethnological Society. 1957.

Freilich, Morris. "Cultural Persistence among the Modern Iroquois," *Anthropos*. v. 53, 473–483. 1958.

Gridley, Marion E., ed. *Indians of Today*. 3rd ed. Chicago. 1960.

Griffin, James B. "The Iroquois in American Prehistory," *Papers of the Michigan Academy of Science Arts and Letters*, v. 29, 357–374. 1944.

————. "The Northeast Woodlands Area," in *Prehistoric Man in the New World*, Jesse D. Jennings and Edward Norbeck, eds., 223–258. Chicago. 1964.

Hewitt, John N. "Legend of the Founding of the Iroquois League," *American Anthropologist*, v. 5, 131–148. 1892.

Indians of Quebec and the Maritime Provinces. Department of Citizenship and Immigration, Indian Affairs Branch. Ottawa. No date.

Johnston, Charles M. *The Valley of the Six Nations*. Toronto. 1964.

Knowles, Nathaniel. "The Torture of Captives by the Indians of Eastern North America," *Proceedings of the American Philosophical Society*, v. 82, 151–225. 1940.

Lounsbury, Floyd G. "Iroquois-Cherokee Linguistic Relations," *SI, BAE, Bulletin* 180, 9–17. 1961.

Lydekker, John W. *The Faithful Mohawks*. Cambridge. 1938.

Martin, Paul S., et al. *Indians Before Columbus*. Chicago. 1947.

*Morgan, Lewis H. *League of the Ho-De-No-Sau-Nee or Iroquois*. 2 v. 1851. (The 1901 edition was edited and footnoted by Herbert M. Lloyd and was reproduced in 1954 by the Human Relations Area Files.) The standard Iroquois ethnography and a key Iroquois source; more precisely, a detailed description of one group of Seneca living between 1841 and 1850 and capable of recalling the past.

Mitchell, Joseph. (*see* Wilson, Edmund.)

Parkman, Francis. *A Half-Century of Conflict*. 2 v. Boston. 1892.

————. *The Conspiracy of Pontiac and The Indian War after the Conquest of Canada*. 2 v. Boston. v. 1, 1901; v. 2, 1902.

Richards, Cara B. "Matriarchy or Mistake: The Role of Iroquois Women through Time," *Cultural Stability and Cultural Change*, 36–45. American Ethnological Society. 1957.

Schoolcraft, Henry R. *Notes on the Iroquois*. New York. 1846.

*Shimony, Annemarie A. *Conservatism among the Iroquois at the Six Nations Reserve*. Yale University Publications in Anthropology, no. 65. 1961. The best comprehensive study of the Iroquois since Morgan's ethnography, the second key Iroquois source, and one of the finest studies of North American Indians.

Speck, Frank G. *The Iroquois*. Cranbrook Institute of Science, Bulletin no. 23. 1955.

Stone, William L. *Life of Joseph Brant-Thayendanegea*. 2 v. New York. 1838.

Thwaites, Reuben G. *Travels and Explorations of the Jesuit Missionaries in New France.* v. 13. 1898.

Voget, Fred. "Acculturation at Caughnawaga: A Note on the Native-Modified Group," *American Anthropologist,* v. 53, 220–231. 1951.

Wallace, Anthony F. C. "Some Psychological Determinants of Culture Change in an Iroquoian Community," *SI, BAE, Bulletin* 149, 55–76. 1951.

———. "Dreams and the Wishes of the Soul: A Type of Psychoanalytic Theory among the Seventeenth Century Iroquois," *American Anthropologist,* v. 60, 234–248. 1958.

*Wilson, Edmund. *Apologies to the Iroquois.* (Includes a reprinting of "The Mohawks in High Steel," by Joseph Mitchell.) New York. 1960. The study by Mitchell is the most complete discussion of the history of Iroquois work in high steel and should be consulted in conjunction with the study of the same subject by Morris Freilich. The balance of Wilson's book is a sensitive analysis of the modern scene in New York State and in Ontario, Canada.

Wintemberg, William J. "Distinguishing Characteristics of Algonkian and Iroquoian Cultures," *Annual Report, 1929, National Museum of Canada,* 65–125. 1931.

10

The Natchez:

Sophisticated Farmers of the Deep South

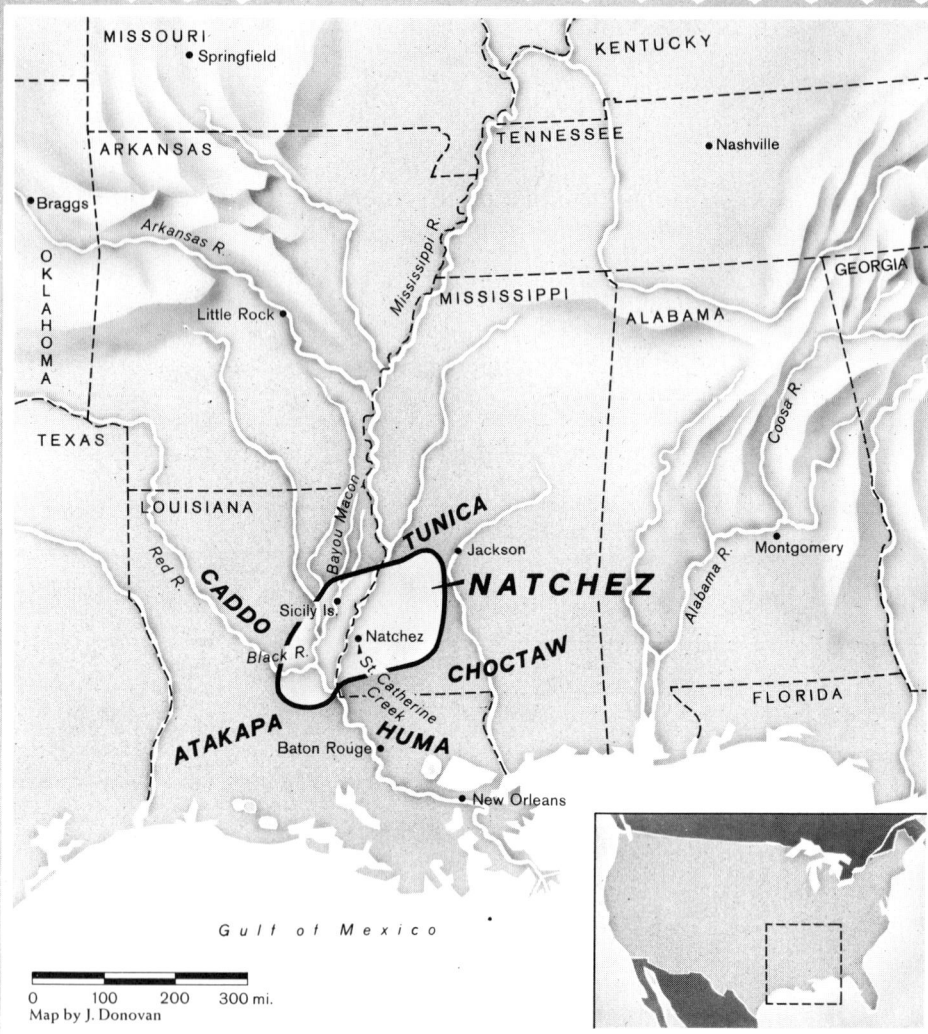

Gulf of Mexico

0   100   200   300 mi.
Map by J. Donovan

A long the eastern bank of the lower Mississippi River emerged the most elaborate American Indian culture to be found north of Mexico. Nowhere else were there similar heights of complexity in social, political, and religious life. The people who best represented this climax of achievements were the Natchez. The word Natchez apparently is derived from a French interpretation of the name for one settlement occupied by these people, a community called Naches. However, the people of this and the associated communities termed themselves the Theloel. The Natchez or Theloel maintained a highly developed system of social class which stressed rank and birth, they possessed material luxuries of rare elaboration, and there was an overriding formalized religious system which gave focus and direction to the sociocultural system. In all likelihood some of their neighbors, such as the Taensa, were as complex, but only the Natchez were described in reasonable detail by early observers. The prime reason for discussing the Natchez is that they were complex and also well described for the period of their early contact with Europeans. In addition, they passed through rather well-defined stages of relationships with the French which in many respects are similar to developments between Europeans and other Indian groups in North America. Then too, Natchez social structure was unique in its form, and it has attracted considerable attention from anthropologists interested in its interpretation. Finally, these people were systematically destroyed by the French, which in some ways typifies a not unusual approach to dealing with Indians by Europeans.

The Natchez occupied an area of land on the eastern bank of the Mississippi River along St. Catherine Creek about three miles southeast of the present city of Natchez, Mississippi. This was their main area of settlement, but they may have controlled the sector of land along the opposite bank of the Mississippi River. The general area of occupancy is within the Austroriparian biotic province. Characteristically, the region is one of pine and hardwood forests, with swamps and marshes numerous in the lowlands. During the French period the Natchez locale along the eastern riverbank was a rolling plain of black soil covered with grasses, hickory forests, and cane thickets in the draws. The settlements were inland from the steep riverbank. Perhaps nine communities existed in the earliest historic period; generally five are listed by later sources. The total population numbered about thirty-five hundred at the end of the seventeenth century. In 1720 it was estimated that the Natchez, the refugees absorbed into the community of Grigas, and the Tiou, a dependent people among them, still could assemble about twelve hundred warriors. By

1731 there were only three hundred warriors, and in 1735 among the
Chickasaw were some one hundred eighty in addition to an unknown
number elsewhere. By then the Natchez were a remnant people; however, a few Natchez survived into the present century. Actually by 1731
the old way of life was destroyed, but the account of this destruction
is a topic for later consideration.

The language of the Natchez is classed as of the Hokan-Siouan
phylum, the Siouan-Muskogean stock, the Natchez-Muskogean family,
and the Natchez language. It is interesting to note that while the
women spoke the same language as the men, women were said
(Le Page du Pratz, 1774, 312) to "soften and smooth their words,
whereas the speech of the men is more grave and serious." Since the
French acquired their knowledge of the language from women, their
pronunciation was that of the women and was ridiculed by Natchez
men and women alike.

The rapid historic decline of Natchez culture was preceded by
two or more millenniums of prehistory coursing toward a complex
way of life. At the present time the beginnings of man's occupancy of
the lower Mississippi River are mysterious even among those who
have studied the problem with greatest care and intensity. It would
appear that the present alluvial valley surface is not an extremely old
configuration, but dates from about 3000 B.C. It is reasoned that if
man had lived in the area at that time or previously, the remains
would now be deeply buried beneath the ground or else have washed
away. One of the oldest excavated sites along the lower Mississippi
River drainage is Poverty Point in northeastern Louisiana. The remains from this settlement do not reflect a simple way of life for the
inhabitants. The site was occupied around 700 B.C. and includes an
artificial mound which is almost seventy feet in height. The mound
is aligned closely to the cardinal directions, and the base measures
some six hundred forty by seven hundred ten feet. To the east a series
of six slightly-rounded ridges in concentric order form half an octagon measuring some three quarters of a mile across at the outer ridge.
About five feet high, the ridges are regularly spaced at one hundred
fifty-foot intervals and are broken by a series of gaps. It may be
that the octagon originally was more nearly complete, but the
Bayou Macon has cut into the ridges, leaving only about half of a
geometric figure. About a mile and a half from the octagon is another
mound which is essentially the same shape as the one at Poverty Point,
and it has been suggested that both of these mounds originally were
intended to represent birds. Beneath the ridges at Poverty Point was
a thin layer of cultural debris, indicating that the area had been occu-

pied for at least a brief period before the construction of the ridges. No evidence of structural remains was found on the ridges, but because of surface erosion none would be expected. Still it is probable that the ridge tops were for house structures. Found on the site were hundreds of tons of small, irregularly shaped lumps of fired clay. To say that these clay objects were probably heated in fires and then dropped into vessels in order to cook food is a reasonable assumption; heating stones are common over parts of North America, but stone in any form is rare in this area. A few crude clay figurines were found; they seem to have represented individuals who were seated and were most probably females, although the features were not clearly represented. Fiber-tempered pottery was present, but very few sherds were recovered. Considering the large number of steatite container fragments recovered, it is likely that the pottery was not of local manufacture. At the same time, steatite vessels, or at least the raw material, were imported from the southern Appalachian region. Some vessels were shaped like deep bowls, and a few were decorated at the rim with lines. There existed a significant use of nonlocal raw materials, such as a particular type of banded green slate from southern Ohio, of which there was one artifact; red sandstone from northern Mississippi; galena and gray-white chert from the Ozark Mountains; and even an artifact of copper from the Lake Superior area. All of this implies established routes of trade, but the reuse of flaked stone, the repair of steatite vessels and other patchings suggest that raw materials or artifacts from afar were not abundant. The people made a wide variety of projectile points. Knife blades were of chipped stone, and they had small flint tools made of microblades struck from polyhedral cores. They possessed also the technological skills necessary to grind and polish stone, which led to the manufacture of celts, plummet stones, and gorgets. The general cultural complex had affinities with the developmental level termed Archaic, with the addition of farming which very likely was the basis for their economic system. In summary, the excavators of the site, James A. Ford and Clarence H. Webb, consider that the occupants represented two different classes of people, a lower class stemming from an Archaic background and an upper, ruling class of Ohio River drainage people called Hopewell.

Joseph R. Caldwell has proposed that we recognize what he would term the Gulf Tradition along the northern part of the Gulf of Mexico, with the Natchez of Mississippi and the Timucua of Florida as the best examples reported for early historic times. The tradition was derived from an Archaic base, but received strong or weak Mississippian influence from the north depending on the locality. The Gulf

Tradition features would include class-stratified societies with retainer sacrifice, elaborate burials, temple mounds and plazas, effigy vessels of pottery, and painted clay vessels. It is proposed by Caldwell that these characteristics had their origins in Mesoamerica and spread northward in a west-to-east direction. The rise of the later Mississippian Tradition is viewed as an integration of the Gulf Tradition with local cultures in the heart of the Southeast. The Mississippian Tradition was based on intensive maize cultivation in the rich bottomlands and gave rise to towns, temple mounds, extended burials, and elaborate ceramic forms. About A.D. 1300 the Southern Cult or Southern Death Cult climaxed from a local Southeastern base, but with influence from Mesoamerica. Included were elaborate grave goods such as engraved shell gorgets with representations of the sun, death, and winged serpents. The elaborate late prehistoric cultural manifestations in the Southeast were apparently on the decline by the time the French arrived, but their essence was preserved among the Natchez. What we see in the lower Mississippi River area are long-established prehistoric traditions of cultural complexity based on rather intensive farming. The Natchez and closely related peoples with similar cultural foci controlled both sides of the Mississippi River between the junctions of the Arkansas and the Red rivers.

History dawned in the lower Mississippi with the arrival of a Spanish expedition under the original command of Hernando de Soto. The party descended the Mississippi River in 1543, and the Natchez attacked and pursued the explorers along the lower course of the river. The next contacts known to be with the Natchez took place in 1682 with the visit of the French explorer Sieur de La Salle. It was he who first recorded the name Natchez. In an important study of the course of French and Natchez relationships, Andrew C. Albrecht labeled this as a first phase, one of visiting explorers. The Natchez were gracious hosts to the La Salle party. They provided the French with food and smoked the peace calumet with them, but the Indians were not overawed by the Europeans. La Salle was respectful toward the Indians, for he was well aware that they were the most powerful tribe in the region. Friendly relations temporarily were disrupted when two Frenchmen were killed in 1690, but in 1698 four missionaries sent from French Canada to the lower Mississippi stayed briefly among the Natchez. In 1700 one returned and baptized one hundred eighty-five children. In the same year Pierre de Iberville established friendly relations between the Natchez and the French who were penetrating from the lower Mississippi River. De Iberville attempted to wrest political control from the French in Canada in order to establish an independent colony. With the arrival of missionaries and traders from Canada a new phase of contact began, but neither the *coureurs de bois* nor the Roman Catholic missionaries were very successful. As will be understood later, the religious system of the Natchez was so highly integrated with the social and political life that the task of making Christians of these people was virtually impossible. Additionally, the great distance between the lower Mississippi River and eastern Canada made these trading and mission ties tenuous. The French administration independent of Canada, which was established by de Iberville, became the most influential force in the lives of the Natchez. During the early 1700's English traders operating from the Carolinas were successful in winning the support of a leading Natchez called Bearded Chief, who apparently controlled the communities of White Apple, Hickory, and Grigras. The settlements of Grand Village, the home of the Great Sun who was the reigning ruler, and Flour were loyal to the French.

The next phase of Natchez relations developed in 1713 with the establishment of a French trading post in their midst. Antoine Crozat was granted a monopoly on all the trade in Louisiana, with the stipulation that he was to bring slaves from Africa and settlers from France. The Natchez post of Crozat possibly was built at Grand Village, but it did not succeed. Intrigue by English traders and Bearded Chief apparently led to its being plundered in 1715. The French now found themselves in a tenuous position; the obvious solution was to subjugate the Natchez and establish military control over the area. In 1716 with a force of no more than fifty men Jean de Bienville tricked the Indians so that he was able to seize and kill those individuals who had plundered the trading post and had killed some Frenchmen. The Natchez agreed to maintain peace with the French and aided in the construction of the stockaded Fort Rosalie, which was built to the west of their villages and overlooked the Mississippi River. For the moment relations temporarily became stabilized, with the Natchez controlling their settlements and the small French garrison representing the outposts of an empire. In 1717 Crozat terminated his monopoly, and soon after this the Western Company of John Law assumed the responsibility for trading and colonizing. It had the right to grant lands to private individuals and proceeded to do so. The company attempted to settle the country with a French landed nobility who would bring with them tenants, skilled craftsmen, and slaves. In 1718 the concession holders began to settle the area, and two years later the immigrants were well established. One even owned large tracts of land near Grand Village; the land evidently had been sold to him by the Indians. The French farmers prepared the land for raising tobacco, and Indian-French relationships were quite congenial. In 1718 the particular Frenchman to whom we owe most of our knowledge of the Natchez settled in the area. Antoine S. Le Page du Pratz, a Dutchman by birth, remained in Louisiana until 1734. The French were provided land and food by the Indians, who in turn were offered guns, powder, lead, intoxicants, and cloth; this was highly satisfactory to both parties. Then in 1723 at Fort Rosalie an old Natchez warrior was needlessly killed by a soldier, and his murderer went unpunished by the French commander of the fort. In retaliation the Natchez killed some French settlers. Peace was reestablished within a few days, but a course toward hostilities had been set. After the peace the French attacked White Apple, demanding and receiving the head of a leader who had been hostile to them. The Natchez could not understand the deception of the French and subsequently avoided contacts with them.

At this crucial period in Natchez-French relations two deaths occurred among the Natchez which quite possibly led to temporary Indian disorganization. In 1725 the younger brother of the Great Sun, Tattooed Serpent, died, and three years later the Great Sun himself died. Thus in 1728 a young and inexperienced Great Sun was in power. In the next year, 1729, a new commander of the Fort Rosalie garrison decided quite arbitrarily that he required the land of White Apple to settle. When he told the Natchez noble who was the leader of the settlement of his decision, the noble refused, and the commander became furious. The Natchez parleyed to decide what course of action should be taken. It was decided that because the French were becoming more numerous, were corrupting the Natchez youth, and were breaking their promises, the French should be destroyed. The Great Sun agreed on this general course of action, and the Natchez sought the aid of neighboring tribes. In spite of an attempt by the leaders to keep their decision from the women, one noblewoman, Tattooed Arm, the mother of the Great Sun, prodded her son into revealing the general plan. She managed to warn the French, but the commander would not take this and other warnings seriously. Finally the Natchez fell upon the French and killed over two hundred persons who were at or near the fort. As an aside it is perhaps noteworthy

that the Natchez warriors had such great contempt for the French
commander that he was not killed until late in the massacre and then
was beaten to death by a commoner who used a wooden war club.
The Yazoos, allies and neighbors of the Natchez to the north, killed
the small number of French among them but not until after the massacre by the Natchez. Tattooed Arm, the woman who had warned
the French, apparently altered the time of the attack by removing
secretly one or two of the rod counters from the bundle in the temple.
This bundle was similar to others that had been taken to adjacent
allied tribes. One rod was to be destroyed each day, and when all
were gone it was time to attack. Because of Tattooed Arm's change
in the bundle, the Natchez uprising was premature, which angered
their allies. The Choctaw were to have aided the Natchez in the
attack but did not do so because of its premature nature. They were
angry, too, because the Natchez did not share the spoils with them,
and so the Choctaw turned to aid the French against the Natchez.
In late January 1730 a French and Choctaw force, estimated between
seven hundred and sixteen hundred attacked the Natchez at two
forts they had constructed. A larger French force arrived in mid-
February and bombarded the Natchez with cannon fire. Before long,
however, the French began to run low on ammunition, and their
Choctaw allies talked of withdrawing. By mutual agreement the
Natchez released the captives they still held, and the French with-
drew to the Mississippi River. Then the Natchez with their loot
slipped across the Mississippi River and made good their escape.
They ascended the Red River to the Black River and built a fort at
Sicily Island. In 1731 another French and Indian force was sent
against the Natchez, and about four hundred, including the Great
Sun, were forced to surrender, although others escaped. John R.
Swanton, whose study of Natchez sources is monumental, stressed
that these people were not destroyed by the two French campaigns
against them; in fact, the French efforts were quite clumsy. What did
destroy the Natchez were the numerous skirmishes with other Indians
and physical exposure which led to illness and death in the swamps
where they took refuge. Those who escaped or were not at the fort,
some one hundred and eighty warriors, eventually joined the Chickasaw, against whom the French turned for having received the refugees.
The Chickasaw were allied with the English but were forced to surrender and hand over a few Natchez to the French. Some of the
Natchez did not remain with or join the Chickasaw after their defeat,
but lived with the Creek. This group probably included the largest

number of survivors. They came to occupy a town near the Coosa River in Alabama, and in 1764 they had about one hundred and fifty warriors. In 1832 the Natchez together with the Creek went to Indian territory in what is now Oklahoma. This move was made as a result of the removal policy of the Federal government which was designed to have all the Indians living east of the Mississippi River seek new homes to the west of it. To complicate the matter further some of the Natchez joined the Catawba after their wars with the French, but later left the Catawba and lived with the Cherokee. In 1907 Swanton located some Natchez near Braggs, Oklahoma, in the southwestern part of the Cherokee nation, and he found five individuals who still knew some of the language. In 1934 when Mary R. Haas worked among the Natchez living near Braggs, she found that only two Natchez speakers had survived.

The mythological origins of the Natchez provide particular insight into the type of sociopolitical structure which developed among them. According to tradition two individuals entered their already established community which was to the southwest of historic Natchez country. The newcomers, a man and his wife, were so bright in appearance that they were considered figuratively to have come from the sun. The man said he noted that the people did not have any effective means for governing themselves and that he had come down from the sky to instruct them. He told the people about the Great Spirit and what they must do to please it. Among the rules of behavior were a series of prohibitions: do not kill except in one's own defense; do not have sexual intercourse with a woman not one's own; do not steal, nor lie, nor become intoxicated. Finally, he said that the people should give freely of what they had to those in need. After hearing these rules of conduct, the people agreed to their wisdom and asked the man to be their leader. He said he would but only under certain conditions. Among these were that the people must obey him but no other and that they must move to another country to which he would lead them; finally, he set forth the rules for selecting his successor. He said too that they should build a temple in which the leaders could communicate with the Great Spirit. In the temple would be an eternal fire which he would bring from the sun. The people agreed to all of these and other conditions, and the sacred fire was brought from the sun. This man then became the first Great Sun.

It is difficult to state with certainty the precise configuration of structures in a typical Natchez settlement. While a composite reconstruction may not have had reality for any particular community, the characteristics which follow would have been found in at least one of the five major areas of settlement in the historical period. The principal settlement, Grand Village, which may have been termed Natchez, was the residence of the Great Sun, and the other villages were nearby. These included Grigras, a community of refugees among the Natchez; Hickory, sometimes termed Walnut; Flour; and White Apple, which has also apparently been called White Earth. It is by no means certain that there were five distinct villages; the designations simply may have been references to neighborhoods about Grand Village. Furthermore, only the physical location of Grand Village has been identified with reasonable certainty. It has been excavated in part and the finds reported on by archaeologists.

In Grand Village there was an open plaza which measured two hundred and fifty by three hundred paces in width and length. At one end was a flat-topped temple mound, and at the opposite end of the square was another similar mound upon which was built the home of the Great Sun. The temple mound at Great Village was elevated some eight feet and was relatively steep on three sides but gradually sloping along the fourth side. The gentle slope which was the ramp to the top faced the east and the open plaza. The temple probably measured about thirty feet in length and was somewhat less than thirty feet in width. It was constructed of thick cypress logs extending some ten feet above the top of the mound. Over the logs of the outer walls a layer of mud was plastered, and the structure was topped with a ridged roof with three large wooden figures of birds along the peak. The temple was entered through a rectangular doorway, and the inside was divided into two separate rooms. In the larger outer room was a perpetual fire, and nearby on a platform was a cane coffin which contained the bones of the most recently deceased Great Sun. The contents of the inner room to the south included two boards to which were attached various unidentified items. It was probably in this room that a wooden box was to be found which contained the stone statue of the first Great Sun who reportedly turned himself into this form for fear that if he were buried in the ground his remains would become tainted.

The dwelling of the Great Sun was on an earth mound some eight feet in height, and the house was twenty-five feet wide and forty-five feet long. All other dwellings were at ground level. Eight were noted to be near the home of the Great Sun, and all the other houses were considerably smaller. Upon the death of the Great Sun his house was burned, and probably the same mound was increased in size and used as a foundation for the home of his successor. The houses in general appear to have been square, rectangular, or less often round. The walls of the former forms were not less than fifteen feet in length along one side. At the four corners the trunks of individual hickory trees were embedded in the ground, bent over at their tops, and tied to form a dome-shaped framework. Along the sidewalls similar poles were embedded in the earth, bent, and tied at the top to the four main poles. Along each inner wall a pole was laid, and to this all the other poles were fastened with split cane. On the inner and outer walls was spread a clay and moss plaster, with split cane mats covering the plastered walls. To the roof was added a mixture of sod and grass, and over the entire structure were cane mats held in place with vines. A rectangular doorway was left, but windows were not included. In the winter a fire was built for warmth, and the smoke filtered out the entrance. It appears that houses were not necessarily near each other but may have been scattered widely. Somewhere near a village were raised platforms on which the bodies of deceased persons were placed. Covering a body was a woven mat smeared with mud; the head of the individual was left uncovered so that food offerings might be placed there. After the flesh had decayed, the bones were moved to the temple.

To the French who first lived among them the Natchez were striking in their physical appearance. They had the proud air and noble bearing which have come to be the ideal expected of American Indians. Du Pratz described them as usually five and a half feet or more in height, lean, sinewy, with regular features, coarse black hair, and black eyes. To him these people were "naturals," but to the other French observers they were savages. As infants their foreheads had been flattened by the thongs which held them in a cradleboard. A woman's dark hair hung over her forehead in short bangs, whereas in back her hair was long and bound with a mulberry thread net with tassels at the ends of the net. Her ears were pierced, and from each large hole hung an elongated ornament of shell. Around her neck she might wear strings of small stones or perforated shell disks. Around a man's head was a band of short hair; a few hairs were allowed to grow long at the crown. Often the young Natchez dandies painted themselves with red paint and wore bracelets of deer ribs which had been bent into circles by steaming and then polished to a high luster. They wore the best of white feathers in their scalp locks and might even have carried fans of turkey tail feathers. Furthermore, they wore stone-beaded necklaces like those of the women. The people plucked their axillary hair, and the men plucked out the hair from their beards. The tattoos of these people were impressive in their diversity and complexity. In their youth males and females were tattooed with a line over the bridge of the nose, and some females had vertical lines on their chins. Persons of the nobility and warriors were elaborately tattooed on the body, head, and limbs. The patterns were of serpents, suns, and other undescribed forms. Warriors who had slain an enemy were permitted to tattoo themselves to give evidence of their kills, and for a brave deed a man had the right to tattoo a war club on his shoulder, with a sign beneath it to symbolize the people involved in his conquest. Warriors pierced their earlobes and made a hole about an inch in diameter into which they inserted decorative plugs. The process of tattooing involved pricking the skin until blood flowed freely and then rubbing charcoal or red or blue pigment into the openings.

The clothing of the people was made of either skins or plant fibers. The boys, however, went without clothing until they were about twelve years old, and the girls were nude until about nine years of age. An older girl's clothing consisted of a short, fringed skirt made from the inner bark threads of the mulberry. Adult women wore a dressed deerskin which fitted about the waist and reached the knees. Ordinary men wore a length of white deerskin as a breechclout; this was held in place with a belt about the waist. The breechclouts of chiefs were usually the only ones dyed black. Some upper-class women wore cloaks with a mulberry inner bark netting made on a two-pole frame loom. The netting was covered with overlapping rows of bird feathers. In cold weather a woman wore a cape, probably of skins, which passed under her right armpit and fastened over the left shoulder. As protection against the cold a man wore a poncho-like shirt of two dressed deerskins which reached beneath the knees and was sleeved at the shoulders. The leggings of men reached from their thighs to the tops of their footwear. The deerskin moccasins that reached above the ankle were worn only when traveling. When the weather was severe, a bison-skin robe with the hair intact and facing inward was worn. Deerskin garments, which were the most numerous form, were sewn together with sinew with the aid of an awl for piercing the skins. Certain distinctions in dress and adornment apart from those mentioned have been recorded. The elaborate tattoos of the nobility, the feather-covered mantles of the noblewomen, and black breechclouts of the chiefs are all examples. Likewise, the infants who were of the nobility wore two or three pearls, taken from the temple, about their necks. When they were about ten years old, the pearls were returned to the temple.

A number of household artifacts were recorded specifically among the Natchez, and others excavated from a historic Natchez site may with assurance be attributed to them. Within the cane-walled dwellings, inhabitable for about twenty years, were household goods usually not found among American Indians, although they might be expected in permanent dwellings such as these. The most prominent furnishings were the beds around the sidewalls. Forked posts reaching about a foot above the ground supported two poles, across which were laid three more poles. Then lengths of cane were fitted next to each other, or else a woven cane mat was put down. Over this framework bearskins were laid, and a bison skin was used as a cover. A log served as a pillow. When relaxing during the day, people either sat on the beds or else on short-legged stools made from a solid piece of wood and standing about seven inches high. Pottery vessels were commonly used as containers around the houses. The various forms included shallow bowls with rounded or flat bottoms and necks that were constricted or flared. The vessels were decorated by making incised scrolls or meanders with a sharp implement. Some of the larger containers were described as receptacles for bear oil and held up to forty pints. The forms were manufactured by the coiling process, and the clay was tempered with grit, organic material, or shell fragments in order to prevent its cracking during firing and in later use. The people used wooden mortars and pestles, and they had spoons as well as ladles carved from the horns of bison. A wide variety of cane basketry included sieves of various grades for sifting maize, containers for small items of adornment, and hampers of cane for maize.

In order to dress a deerskin for clothing, the fresh skin was soaked in water for a few days, lashed on a wooden frame through holes cut into the skin, and then scraped with a hafted, flint-bladed scraper. In order to bleach and further process a skin, it was rubbed with a mixture of cooked deer brains and could be made more pliable by smoking it over a fire. Various colored designs were sometimes painted on skins, and embroidery of dyed, split porcupine quills added a decorative touch. The Natchez similary processed bison skins but left the hair or wool intact when the intended use was for bedding and robes.

Among the tools and weapons utilized by men were knives made from split sections of hard cane. For heavier cutting axes they perhaps had blades of fine-grained gray stone which was ground to a beveled edge, with a hole drilled through the head for hafting the ax to a wooden handle. To fell a large tree or to remove a section of wood to make a mortar the wood was charred and then chipped away. The hunting weapons included bows made from locust wood and strung with plant fiber or twisted sinew. Arrow shafts of wood or cane had feathered vanes attached to the nock end with a glue made from fish, and the same manner of attachment was applied to the points. The arrowpoints varied in form from splinters of bone, garfish scales, and fire-hardened shaft tips to stone points shaped like elongated triangles with notches knapped at the base for hafting. At the end of a cane spear, some six feet in length, was attached a flint blade; spears were employed for hunting large game such as bison, bear, and deer.

For water transportation vessels of two different types, rafts and canoes, have been reported. The rafts were made from bundles of cane which were lashed together; over these were attached additional cane poles. Rafts were used to carry relatively light loads. For transporting ten- to twelve-ton loads large canoes were made from hollowed-out cypress or poplar logs. The interior of the log was removed by controlled burning, followed by chipping away the charred wood. These dugout canoes were propelled with paddles and measured some forty feet in length with three-foot beams.

In Natchez subsistence activities farming was of greatest importance, followed by hunting and fishing which clearly were secondary. The principal crop was maize, and from the two different types some forty-two named dishes were prepared in the Natchez area. In order to prepare the soil for cultivation, it was first cleared of cane, and the ground was broken up with an L-shaped mattock of hickory wood. The Natchez probably also used a hoe consisting of a bison scapula hafted at right angles to a wooden handle. After the cane had been cut, it was allowed to dry and then set afire. Maize was planted by making holes in the ground by hand and depositing a few grains of corn in each hole. Additional crops included pumpkins and probably beans, plus two forms of wild grasses which were cultivated along riverbanks.

Hunting was most important in the fall of the year, and the large animals of greatest importance were the deer, bison, and bear. Deer were hunted by individuals wearing a deer disguise. If a deer grew cautious as it was approached, an imitation of a deer's call was made to attract it closer. Deer sometimes were hunted cooperatively as a sport by about one hundred men at a time. Once a deer was located, it was trapped in a surround of men who kept the animal running back and forth until it was exhausted. It was then taken alive to the Great Sun, or his representative, who killed it and divided the meat among the leaders of the hunt. This particular hunting method was a game, not an ordinary means for obtaining meat. Bison were hunted in winter on the grasslands away from the river and were approached by wearing a disguise or else by stalking them against the wind. When a kill was made near a settlement, the hunter returned with the choice parts and sent his wife to retrieve the remainder of the animal. The meat was either smoke-dried for future use or else soon cooked. Bear meat was eaten only if lean, but bears were killed when they were fat in order to obtain the oil. These animals were smoked out of their holes in trees, and if a cub was found it was sometimes taken alive to a village and tamed. The only domestic animal of the Natchez was the dog, used to tree turkeys so that the birds could be easily killed with arrows. Taking fish was a means of obtaining food which was less important than either farming or hunting. Among the fishing devices were gill nets made from organic fibers and fish arrows made with pointed bone tips, to which wooden floats were attached by a cord. Hooks likewise were used, and the species most often taken were carp and catfish.

Maize was prepared in many different ways—mixed with beans, smoke-dried, and ground into meal, prepared as hominy, or parched. Ground meal was made into cakes that were roasted in ashes, baked, or boiled in water. Salt for seasoning was obtained in trade with the Caddoan-speaking people to the north and west. The people made bread from walnuts and consumed chestnuts as well as acorns, but these were not important dietary items. There were no set mealtimes except for feasts. When an ordinary meal was served, the males, including those who were very young, ate before the females.

The cultivation of tobacco was one of the primary reasons for the plantations of the French in the Natchez region. This crop was cultivated by the Indians in aboriginal times, for the people were described as avid smokers. They smoked pipes of an unknown form and inhaled the smoke. To make the smoke mild, dried leaves from the sumac tree were mixed with the tobacco. Smoking was not merely a pleasant activity; pipes and smoking played an important part in events surrounding war and peace.

Natchez social life was structured primarily around each individual's relationship to the Great Sun. This leader held absolute control over his subjects and was served by the tribe as a whole but particularly by personal retainers and slaves. He was spoken to at a distance of four steps; he was thanked and bowed to no matter what he said, and when leaving his presence a person walked backward. He was saluted on all occasions when seen by ordinary persons, and he could have an individual killed by saying to a retainer, "Go and rid me of that dog," all of which is clear evidence of his exalted position. The administrative offices delegated by the Great Sun included two war chiefs, two leading priests at the temple, two men who dealt with the external affairs of war and peace, one in charge of public works, and four who arranged public feasts. The decisions of the Great Sun were tempered by the amount of influence brought to bear upon him by his near relatives, particularly his brother and mother. He consulted also a council of elders, the leaders of the various villages, and outstanding old warriors.

The reigning Great Sun was from the Sun matrilineage; consequently, his sister's son was his successor. According to Swanton's analysis of the system, it contained two distinct groups of persons: an upper class with three levels of descending rank, the Suns, Nobles, and Honored People, and a lower class consisting of Stinkards, who may be termed more euphemistically, Commoners. The upper-class individuals were required to marry into the Common class, and many Commoners also married Commoners. Furthermore, the offspring of any man of the upper class would assume a rank one step lower than that of the father. The essence of the system is as follows:

woman	= man	—— children
Sun	Common	Sun
Noble	Common	Noble
Honored	Common	Honored
Common	Common	Common
Common	Sun	Noble
Common	Noble	Honored
Common	Honored	Common

The persons numbered among the Suns were very few; estimates at two different times ranged from eleven to seventeen. In this marriage and class system, as Charles W. H. Hart has pointed out, the upper-class males would take women who otherwise would have become wives of Common men. Since polygyny commonly was practiced by the upper class, this would require still more Common women. The plural upper-class marriages would deplete the stock of Common women and would theoretically, in most marriages, produce even more upper-class children to intensify the problem. The Commoners would have a resulting loss of "mother-power" as Hart aptly has phrased it. He calculated that over a few generations there would not be enough marriageable Common women to sustain the system. How then could the Commoners maintain their numbers over the generations? Hart suggests as a possible explanation that the female children of Sun, Noble, or Honored fathers became Commoners, and there is a suggestion in a statement by du Pratz that this may have been the case. The next effort to solve the riddle of Natchez social structure was made by George I. Quimby. He accepts the validity of Hart's theory that the system could not have had stable structural form and goes on to demonstrate that it was through the assimilation of other peoples that the Commoner ranks received new members. To support his thesis he cites the village of Grigras, which was composed of Tunican speakers adopted by the Natchez as Commoners. Still other Tunican speakers identified as of the Tiou tribe were similarly assimilated. Quimby acknowledges fully that his explanation is not reconcilable to any balanced system, and indeed balance did not exist. The structure would have broken down but only when the large-scale assimilation of other Indians ceased. Quimby suggests also that the Natchez emerged only around A.D. 1600 as a dominant cultural form in the southeastern area, and rapidly were approaching, or had reached, a sociocultural climax when first visited by the French.

Another analysis of the system has been offered, this time by John L. Fischer. One of his statistical calculations, a projection based on the few population figures for the Natchez, concerns how many generations would have been required for the stable system to become nonoperative because of a scarcity of Commoners. The calculation is that it would require nine generations. He advances the idea that as a shortage of Commoners developed it would be the Noble and the Honored women who would have a more difficult time acquiring spouses, rather than the Suns who were required by society to produce heirs. If so, those two classes might have a lower rate of reproduction. It is known that in general both sexes married late, when about twenty-five years old, and Common men were reluctant to become the husbands of upper-class women since these women had absolute control over them. These factors, together with the practices of infanticide and birth control for nonlegitimate offspring, and the reluctance of some individuals to marry at all, would decrease the potential population. Perhaps, too, the imbalance of female Noble and Honored productivity was compensated for by overproduction of male Suns and Nobles who mated with Commoners. There are additional factors which may have operated simultaneously or else were more important than have been calculated. If there had been a more flexible class structure than is suggested in the literature, the system might have been able to function without recourse to the alternative postulates of Hart and Quimby. For example, upper-class individuals may have lost rank as they became increasingly distant from the leading matrilineages. Then too, it is known that a person could be raised in rank from a Commoner to an Honored or from an Honored to a Noble because of individual accomplishments, particularly in warfare. This would result in an increase in the upper-class numbers. At the same time a compensation may have been that casualties among the upper-class warriors were heavier than among the Commoner warriors, resulting in a continual depletion of the higher category of males. Thus the discussion by Fischer offers new and different dimensions to what he calls the "Natchez paradox."

In the ethnographic reconstructions of Swanton and Haas are embodied all of the information on Natchez social structure that is ever likely to be obtained. One fact that emerges clearly from the linguistic and ethnographic analyses by Haas is that the Natchez did not have a matrilineal sib system in aboriginal times when they maintained a class system. It is nonetheless quite clear that in recent years the Natchez have had matrilineal sibs; Haas demonstrates with authority that these must have been derived from the Abihka, a group of Creek who lived on the Coosa River in Alabama. The kinship terms of the Natchez for the first ascending generation above Ego included separate terms for each individual, that is, father, father's brother, mother's brother, mother, mother's sister, and father's sister, which is of the bifurcate collateral type. On Ego's generational level there was a generalized cousin term of the Eskimo type, in addition to a supplementary term of "little brother and sister" for parallel cousins. Older and younger sibling terms were included in the system as well.

From the nature of early French attitudes toward the Natchez as a military power, it is apparent that the Indians were successful warriors under able leadership. Although the Great Sun headed the entire nation, the Great War Chief at one period was Tattooed Serpent, the brother of the Great Sun and a very powerful individual in his own right. There were lesser war chiefs, probably leaders of different villages, and there were warriors who were organized into three grades: apprentice, ordinary, and true warriors. Most, if not all, men belonged to one of these three categories or were numbered among the old warriors. When hostilities were contemplated, a pole was erected in the ground at the entrance to the house where a decisive meeting was to be held. Attached to the pole was the war calumet, a pipe adorned with red feathers, tufted and tasseled in black, with the black skin from the neck of a buzzard surrounding the pipe itself. The meeting was attended by old warriors, the Great War Chief, lesser war chiefs, and the Great Sun. The grievance against the potential enemy was presented vividly by the Great War Chief. The rationale for aggressive action was real or fabricated; it might be that another people had hunted on Natchez lands. The offense was discussed, but the opinions of the old warriors were decisive. A delegation of warriors led by an old warrior went to the offenders carrying a peace calumet. It was decorated with valuable white eagle feathers with red tufts attached and the skin from a wood duck's neck along the stem. The party carried no gifts so that they could not be considered appeasers. Coming under these circumstances, they generally were received well and were sent home with gifts as an admission of the wrong done to them. Open conflict seldom erupted with this treatment of an offense.

When the Natchez anticipated an attack, they decided, usually in council, to defend themselves rather than to attempt appeasement of the aggressors. They first warned the outlying families to join the main group and then posted scouts to watch the approaches to their settlements so that they might have warning of any aggression. Another defensive move was to build palisaded fortifications. Forts were rather complex structures built around a tall tree which served as a watchtower. The trunks of trees were stripped of branches and buried in the ground so that they extended about ten feet above the surface. The palisades were arranged in a roughly circular form with an overlap at the ends. Inside were structures to protect the women and children from falling arrows. The entrance was protected by towers, and in the passage to the outside were placed brambles and thorns. When aggression was imminent, emissaries carrying a peace calumet were sent to enlist the aid of friendly peoples. In the meantime the Great War Chief among the Natchez cited in their council the reasons for defending themselves. He attempted to rally the full support of the war chiefs and warriors. He offered honor and vengeance to the older warriors and the hopes of glory to the youthful braves.

When it had been decided to make war on another people, the warriors hunted and returned with their kills to the dwelling of the Great War Chief. For the three-day ceremony that followed, the bodies of the warriors were painted in different colors. The warrior's only clothing was a breechclout held in place with a belt, to which was fastened rattles; stuck into this belt was a war club. In his left hand the warrior carried a round shield of bison skin about eighteen inches in diameter, and in his right hand a bow. His arrows were contained in a skin quiver. The warriors gathered at a clearing, in the center of which was erected a pole some seven feet in height. To this was attached the war calumet. Around the pole, about eight feet away, were arranged three foods in wooden dishes. At the base of the pole was a large dog which had been roasted for the occasion. The foods in the dishes included coarse cornmeal cooked in fat; the coarseness of the meal was a reminder that warriors did not require dainty foods. They ate deer meat, both roasted and boiled, in order to be swift as a deer. Before the meal the oldest warrior, a man who was no longer able to take part in raids, orated to the assembly. He recounted his deeds of bravery and instructed the party how to go into battle and to fight. Then the old man lit the war calumet and presented it to the Great War Chief to smoke first. All the others smoked in order of rank; the old orator drew on the pipe last and returned it to the pole. The Great War Chief took a piece of the dog meat to eat, and the others followed in succession. By partaking of the roasted dog a warrior demonstrated his willingness to participate in the pending hostilities. As they ate, one young warrior went a short distance away and screamed the death cry. The warriors rushed in a group to him, and after he screamed again, they returned the cry. This episode was repeated twice more during the meal. Later the war drink was brought forth; it was a powerful emetic which caused the drinker to vomit violently. The retching could be heard at a great distance according to one observer. In the next ritual act each man ran in front of the pole of the calumet. This post, carved to look like a man and painted red, represented the enemy, and each warrior uttered a death cry as he struck it. He then told the post of his past deeds of valor. After each of the seasoned warriors had done this, each apprentice warrior told of what he hoped to accomplish. A war dance was performed, and the ceremonials continued over a span of three days. During this time dances were held before the temple, along with recitations of personal accomplishments and the singing of death songs. Meanwhile, the women prepared food for the men to take on their expedition, and old men refurbished war clubs and incised graphic symbols on a bark tablet. On it a symbol of the sun representing the Natchez was set above a figure of a naked man with a war club. An arrow was shown as though about to strike a fleeing woman, near whom was the sign of the enemy nation. Another set of symbols recorded the forthcoming month, a moon, and the day when an attack in force would take place if this was included in the planning.

A raiding party could include about twenty or as many as three hundred warriors. As they approached the community they planned to attack, they traveled only at night and sent scouts to reconnoiter. The party carried fetishes attached to a long pole which was leaned

toward the enemy when they stopped to camp. If any sign were interpreted as an ill omen for the adventure, the warriors returned to
their villages in spite of their elaborate preparations. The same
course was followed when two hostile parties encountered each other;
they never fought pitched battles. An attack was made at daybreak
when it was unsuspected, and the persons to be killed were dispatched as quickly as possible. Women and children were taken
alive, as was at least one man if at all possible. The raiders
then departed as quietly as they had arrived, taking their prisoners
and leaving behind the inscribed bark, two red-painted arrows crossed
and stuck in the ground, and the scalped dead. If the raid was anticipated and the enemy prepared for the attack in a palisaded for-
tification, the Natchez were forced to search for hunting parties to kill.
When the raiders had one of their own number killed, they attempted
to scalp this slain comrade if at all possible to prevent the enemy
from gaining a Natchez scalp. Furthermore, upon the party's return
the Great War Chief compensated the dead man's family for its loss.
The party returned home in honor if they had captured a living enemy man. They planted two poles in the ground and lashed a crosspiece near the ground and another somewhat higher than a man's
head. The enemy man was stunned with a blow at the base of the skull
with a war club by the individual who had captured him. The victim
then was scalped by the same person, and afterwards tied naked in
spread-eagle fashion on the pole frame. The young persons in the assembled throng gathered canes which were lighted, and the first flaming cane was applied to the captive by his captor. The torturer was
free to apply the cane anywhere he chose, and it was most likely to
be on the arm with which the victim had best defended himself. The
victim was then burned by others as he sang his song of death. Some
sacrificial victims were reported to have sung for seventy-two hours
without pause before dying. However, not all captive males were
dealt with in this manner, for if a young woman whose husband had
been killed claimed the captive, he was given to her as a husband
without hesitation. Captive women and children had their hair cut
short and became the servants of their captors.

Warriors who had distinguished themselves were given new names
by the Great War Chief. These names were titles which denoted particular levels of achievement in warfare. For example, the name or
title Great Man Slayer could be claimed by a warrior after he had
taken twenty scalps or ten prisoners. Likewise, a warrior might tattoo
his body to commemorate an achievement, and he could be elevated
in class.

Natchez religion was a highly formalized supernatural system and included specialists who devoted all of their time to supernatural matters. Thus these individuals were priests in a generic sense. They were guardians at the major temple, and it was one of these priests who explained their religion to du Pratz. They believed in a Great Spirit who was all-powerful. He created all good things, and to do his bidding he was surrounded by lesser spirits. There existed, too, spirits of evil led by a particularly malignant spirit. However, the Great Spirit had tied him up forever, and as a result the lesser spirits of evil could do no great harm. The Great Spirit molded the first man from clay, and the figure grew to the proportions of a normal man. Woman probably was created in the same manner, but since man was created first, he was the stronger and more courageous. It was apparently the Great Spirit who sent the first Great Sun among the people, and this man established the line of Suns. His oldest son was to select a wife from the Common people, and his eldest daughter was likewise to marry a Commoner. Of this daughter's children, the eldest son was to become the next ruling Great Sun, while her eldest daughter became the mother of the next Great Sun. Thus the spiritual leadership was passed through a matrilineage to the oldest son.

The reigning Great Sun, the highest supernatural authority on earth, combined the qualities of a god and a king. His power and authority over things religious were paramount, and his decisions were very important in secular matters. In this theocratic state, religious, social, and political control was, in theory, in the hands of one individual. The Great Sun was surrounded by warriors and retainers who followed him wherever he went. When he traveled about, he was carried on a litter by eight warriors; in his dwelling he sat on a small wooden throne. The Great Sun was distinguished in his dress from others; for example, his normal headdress was a net covered with black feathers, around which was a red border some two inches wide and from which hung white seed beads; on the top were white feathers some eight inches long in front and four inches in length behind. The lesser Suns appear to have worn similar headpieces.

The core of the religious life focused on the preservation of the sacred temple fire by eight elders, two of whom cared for the fire continually and would be killed if they permitted the fire to die out. When an ordinary person walked in front of a temple, he put down any load that he might be carrying and extended his arms toward the temple as he wailed loudly. The same type of behavior was manifest when he passed before the Great Sun. The Great Sun visited the temple daily to make certain that the fire still burned, and each morning at sunrise he faced the east, bowed to the ground, and wailed three times. A special calumet was brought to him, and he blew smoke first toward the rising sun and then in each of the three other cardinal directions. Thus, the Great Sun venerated the sun and was in turn venerated by all other persons in the tribe. What we see is a direct line of continuity into the past functionally linked to the Great Spirit, the sun, the Great Suns, and an eternal fire.

The first products of any harvest were brought to the temple by the heads of families. These foods were received by the temple guardians and conveyed to the Great Sun, who was free to distribute them as he chose. Furthermore, the seeds to be sown were blessed at the temple before planting. Each of the thirteen months of the calendar was named for the most important food of the prior month, and the beginning of each month was celebrated by a feast in which either the Great Sun or a lesser Sun played a major role. The feast of the first month, corresponding roughly to the month of March, was called Deer, and this marked the beginning of the year. A commemorative celebration was held each year during the month of Deer in honor of a particular event said to have been historically true. The people reenacted the capture of the Great Sun by an enemy party, his liberation by Natchez warriors, and his return home in triumph. Afterwards there were other ritual acts, and gifts were presented to the Great Sun as he sat on his throne.

The month of the Great Corn was ushered in by the most important of all yearly ceremonies, which was for the first fruits of the harvest. This was in the seventh month of the year, and the maize for the feast was sown on virgin soil by the warriors. The warriors cared for the crop and notified the Great Sun when it had been harvested and stored in a granary of cane. The entire village assembled at the cache of corn to receive the Great Sun arriving on his litter, which was covered with a flower-decked canopy. A new fire was kindled by rubbing sticks together, and the first of the harvest was presented to the female Suns and then to all the women. The maize was cooked, and a feast followed additional ritual. After the people had eaten, the warriors recounted their brave deeds, and ambitious youths told of what they hoped to accomplish. When it grew dark in the evening, some two hundred poles of dry cane were lighted around the area, and the men and women danced until morning. The dance beat was provided by one man drumming on a pot covered with a deerskin. Around the drummer were a circle of women and then an outer circle of men who shook gourd rattles. The women moved in one direction and the men in the opposite direction, and as an individual tired he or she was replaced by someone from the audience. The following day a ball game was held in which the warriors divided into two teams. One was led by the Great Sun and the other by the Great War Chief. In the hair of the Great Sun's men were white feathers, and the opposite team wore red feathers. The object of the game was to force a ball to one or the other end of the plaza. The winning team was presented with gifts by the losing team captain, and the winners were permitted to wear their feather headdresses until the game again was played. After the ball game, a war dance was performed by the warriors. The celebration was not over until the harvested maize had been consumed completely. The two celebrations just described took place at the Natchez settlement, the capital of the tribe. Similar ceremonies, however, took place at the other settlements, and these were led by the different resident Suns.

Religion embraced more than the temple cult alone, for there existed a host of spirits that probably were lesser agents of the Great Spirit. There was power in the honey locust tree, and under one such tree near the temple was the wood for the sacred fire. A tree struck by lightning was burned completely by the Indians, and snakes were regarded with terror. The Great Sun and people of all classes fasted to bring rain. Commoners, when they fasted on certain days, smeared black paint on their faces and did not eat until the sun had set. The precise association between the shamans, who were curers, and the religious system centered on the sun is obscure, but the shamans seem to have been outside the general structure of the organized theocracy. Shamanistic power was sought by fasting for nine days, during which time only water was consumed. In this period of isolation a spirit presented itself to the aspirant, and from it he learned certain skills such as how to change the weather or to cure illnesses. The spirit aids were kept in a small basket and included such tangible items as plant roots, owl heads, animal teeth, pebbles or small stones, and hair from a deer. A shaman had very real obligations to his patient. Were an individual treated by him to die, the shaman might be killed, but success brought material gain. Among the techniques for curing and weather changes were fasting, smoking, singing, and dancing. A shaman could, after rubbing himself with a particular form of root, handle poisonous snakes without fear. One described cure included making an incision at the locus of an illness and sucking blood from the wound. When the shaman spit the blood into a container, not only blood was seen but also a foreign object such as a piece of wood, a straw, or bit of leather. It was to one of these items that the illness was attributed.

After bearing a neonate the first activity of the mother was to bathe it and herself. Afterwards the offspring was placed in a cradleboard made from cane. In this small bed was laid a mattress of Spanish moss, and a pillow of skin stuffed with moss was placed at the head. After the baby was bound into the cradleboard, strips of deerskin were bound over the forehead to flatten it artificially. The cradle rested in bed with the mother, where the infant was nursed intermittently. Infants were smeared with bear oil to keep flies from biting them and to make them supple. Strands of bison wool were bound under a month-old baby's knees and above its ankles, and these were worn until the child was about five years of age. When nearly a year old, the small child was encouraged to walk. It continued to nurse until it weaned itself or until the mother again became pregnant. As children grew they came under the influence of the elder male of the family, who as an extended family head was termed "father" but might be a great-grandfather or even a great-great-grandfather. Children were considered to belong to their biological father, and so long as he lived they were responsible to him as well as to the elder male in the extended family, who counselled all families responsible to him. Children who might have fought with each other feared to do so because of the threat that they would be sent away from the Natchez to live. Boys were encouraged to exercise and gradually acquire adult skills from about the age of twelve. The sexual division of labor was instilled in the youths. Hunting, fishing, fighting, some farming and manufacturing most of the artifacts were male activities. Carrying home game or fish, most of the farming, preparing food, manufacturing clothing, baskets, and pottery were female responsibilities, along with the raising of children.

After puberty the young males and females were free to have sexual intercourse. The girls apparently did not bestow sexual favors without material gain, and a potential husband was proud of the amount of property his future mate had accumulated in this way. A man was required to be about twenty-five years old before he married, and a girl appears to have been somewhat younger. Once the prospective couple had decided that they hoped to marry, the man went before the heads of their respective families to be questioned. If no close blood ties existed and if the pair loved each other, the elders would sanction the marriage. On the day of the wedding the girl was led by the elder of her family, and followed by the remainder of her family, to the home of the man. Here they were greeted, and they then entered the house where after a pause the elders of both families asked the couple whether they loved each other and were willing to be man and wife. The ideals of domestic harmony were set forth, there was an exchange of vows by the couple, and a gift was made to the bride's father. From her mother the bride was handed a laurel branch which she held in one hand and an ear of corn to hold in the other hand. She gave the corn to her husband, and he said, "I am your husband," to which she answered, "I am your wife." Finally the husband told his wife, "There is our bed, keep it tight," which was an injunction against committing adultery. After a special meal the couple and their guests danced from early evening through the night. In this description of a marriage by du Pratz it is not specified whether these customs were observed by everyone or just by one particular class. The need for such clarification is evident since other descriptions of Natchez marriages vary from this form. One record states that the couple went off into the forest, and while the man hunted the girl made a house of boughs. They ate together, returned to the home of the girl to give her relatives the game the man had killed, and then went to live permanently with the husband's family. This sojourn in the woods sounds as though it might be a trial marriage. Another marriage description was rather like that given by du Pratz but included a bride-price and stated that the couple ate from the same container; the groom then smoked a calumet with the bride's father and with his own father. In this description, too, the wedding night was spent at the girl's home, and then the couple lived with the family of the husband until they could build their own house nearby.

Plural marriages were known, and sororal polygyny was the most common form, although nonsororal polygyny also was practiced. Plural marriages were more common among the nobility than among commoners. A Noble with many wives retained only one or two in his house; the others lived at their natal home where they were visited by him. In the polygynous households the wife who bore the first offspring supervised the other wives. Divorce was extremely rare for most persons, but when an upper-class woman married a Common man, as she must, she was free to take other husbands. Furthermore, such a woman could have her husband put to death if he committed adultery. This appears to be a most unusual form of the double moral standard. Berdaches (transvestites) were reported, but their position in the society is not clear.

From the writings of du Pratz and a few other observers, it is possible to obtain a generalized perspective of the ideals which guided adult life. Complete tribal unity did not exist during the brief historical era, and it may be inferred that a struggle for power existed between the leading upper-class persons, which would have had an effect on intervillage affairs. In any event, some of the Natchez communities were friendly to the French while others were hostile, which is the historical evidence for a lack of unity. Under the power and control of the Great Sun and his relatives there was a conceptually rigid and well-defined hierarchy of sociopolitical control. The distinct impression is that the upper class did not abuse its power and village harmony was the norm. The people in general were strictly honorable in dealing with each other and with the French. In the story of the acceptance of the first Great Sun it will be recalled that certain specific rules of behavior were stated. These were supported by the guardians of tradition, the temple priests, and the upper class in general.

One of the most vivid descriptions left by du Pratz is of the death of the Great War Chief, Tattooed Serpent. He was the brother of the Great Sun and almost as powerful. When he died the tribe was confused completely, for each brother had vowed to kill himself at the death of the other. The temple guardians went to du Pratz, who was very influential among the Natchez and a friend of the Great Sun, to avert the leader's potential suicide. Du Pratz and other leading Frenchmen of the area went to the home of the Great Sun and talked with him. The Great Sun was grieved deeply over the death and had to be restrained from committing suicide. At the house of Tattooed Serpent his corpse lay on the bed he had occupied during his life. His face was painted red, and he was clothed in his finest garments, including a feather headdress. Attached to the bed were his weapons, displayed with the peace calumets he had received during his life. From a pole stuck into the ground were forty-six linked pieces of red-painted cane sections representing the number of enemies he had killed. Gathered around the body were his "chancellor," physician, chief domestic, pipe bearer, two wives, some old women, and a volunteer from among the Noblewomen, all of whom were to be killed as a part of the funeral ceremony. The next day included a "Dance of Death" and two rehearsals of the deaths of those persons who were to be killed. At about this time the Commoner parents of a child strangled their offspring out of respect for the death of Tattooed Serpent; by doing so they were raised to Noble standing and would not be killed when the Great Sun died. Some warriors also had apprehended a Common man who had been married to a Sun woman but had fled at her death to avoid being killed. His capture once again slated him for death, but three old women related to him offered themselves to be killed in his place. The man in turn was elevated to the upper class by the women's sacrifice. The activities on the day of the funeral were directed by a "master of ceremonies." The upper part of his body was painted red, and about his waist was a tight-fitting garment fringed to the knees with red and white feathers. On his head he wore a crown of red feathers. The red staff that he carried had a crosspiece near the top, and from the upper part of the staff hung black feathers. When this impressively arrayed individual approached the house of the deceased, he was greeted with "hoo" and then by a wailing to indicate death. The procession formed behind the master of ceremonies, who was followed by the oldest warrior carrying the staff from which hung the red cane rings and a war pipe that reflected the honor of the dead man. These men were in turn followed by six temple guardians who carried the body on a litter; then came those who were to be killed, each accompanied by eight relatives who served as executioners. Each of these relatives was subsequently freed from the probability of being killed at the death of the Great Sun and seemingly was raised to the class of Nobles. The procession circled the house of the deceased three times, and then the litter bearers walked in intersecting circles to the temple. The dead child was thrown in the path of the bearers and retrieved from it by its parents. When the body of Tattooed Serpent was placed in the temple, the sacrificial victims, their hair covered with red paint, were drugged with tobacco and then strangled. Within the temple the two wives of Tattooed Serpent and two men were buried in the same grave as the Great War Chief. The other victims were buried elsewhere, and the funeral ended by burning the home in which Tattooed Serpent had lived.

With a great man's death unrolled pomp, pageantry, and human sacrifice; the death of a Sun was a tragic highlight to life. The number of persons killed at the funeral of Tattooéd Serpent unquestionably was fewer than would have been considered fitting prior to the time of French influence. For others to die was of lesser moment; nevertheless, any death was surrounded with further deaths. When an outstanding female Sun died, her Common husband was strangled by their eldest son. Then the eldest surviving daughter ordered twelve small children killed and placed around the bodies of the deceased couple. In the plaza were erected fourteen platforms, and on each was a man who was to die during the funeral. These men danced before the house of the deceased every fifteen minutes and then returned to their public stations. It was said that after four days the "March of the Bodies" ritual took place. The dead children previously had been placed outside the dead woman's home, and with them were the live victims. The woman was carried out on a litter, and the small bodies were dropped repeatedly before the procession so that by the time the litter reached the temple the corpses of the children were in pieces. After the woman's body was inside the temple, the fourteen victims were strangled, but not before they had received water and wads of tobacco which drugged them into unconsciousness. The living mourned for an important deceased person by weeping for four days. In general, mourners cut their hair but did not paint their faces, and they avoided public gatherings. The temporary grave of a person was on a raised platform covered with a shelter of branches which formed a vault over the body. There was an opening at one end where food was placed near the head. The mourners grieved at the grave each day at dawn and at sunset for a month. Then after the flesh had decayed, the bones were placed in a basket in a temple.

The custom of executing persons at the death of the Suns and other upper-class individuals may seem barbaric and senseless, but it had very real advantages to the individuals involved. In their belief system one's spirit under such circumstances would accompany the deceased upper-class person to the world of the dead and serve him or her there in perennial happiness. The same fate awaited all other persons who observed the rules of the society during their lifetime. It was thought, too, that a person who had broken the rules of the people would go to a place which was covered with water; naked, he would be bitten by mosquitoes and have only undesirable foods to eat.

It was only a few short years after the dramatic death and burial ceremonies for Tattooed Serpent that the Natchez became extinct as a people. It seems fitting to record a speech which Tattooed Serpent delivered to Le Page du Pratz (1774, 40–41) after a war with the French and shortly before the Natchez were destroyed.

> I did not approve, as you know, the war our people made upon the French to avenge the death of their relation, seeing I made them carry the *pipe of peace* to the French. This you well know, as you first smoked in the pipe yourself. Have the French two hearts, a good one to-day, and to-morrow a bad one? As for my brother and me, we have but one heart and one word. Tell me then, if thou art, as thou sayest, my true friend, what thou thinkest of all this, and shut thy mouth to every thing else. We know not what to think of the French, who, after having begun the war, granted a peace, and offered it of themselves; and then at the time we were quiet, believing ourselves to be at peace, people come to kill us, without saying a word.
>
> Why . . . did the French come into our country? We did not go to seek them: they asked for land of us, because their country was too little for all the men that were in it. We told them they might take land

where they pleased, there was enough for them and for us; that it was good the same sun should enlighten us both, and that we would walk as friends in the same path; and that we would give them of our provisions, assist them to build, and to labour in their fields. We have done so; is not this true? What occasion then had we for Frenchmen? Before they came, did we not live better than we do, seeing we deprive ourselves of a part of our corn, our game, and fish, to give a part to them? In what respect, then, had we occasion for them? Was it for their guns? The bows and arrows which we used, were sufficient to make us live well. Was it for their white, blue, and red blankets? We can do well enough with buffalo skins, which are warmer; our women wrought feather-blankets for the winter, and mulberry-mantles for the summer; which indeed were not so beautiful; but our women were more laborious and less vain than they are now. In fine, before the arrival of the French, we lived like men who can be satisfied with what they have; whereas at this day we are like slaves, who are not suffered to do as they please.

References

Albrecht, Andrew C. "The Location of the Historic Natchez Villages," *Journal of Mississippi History*, v. 6, 67–88. 1944.

———. "Indian-French Relations at Natchez," *American Anthropologist*, v. 48, 321–354. 1946.

———. "Ethical Precepts among the Natchez Indians," *Louisiana Historical Quarterly*, v. 31, 569–597. 1948.

Caldwell, Joseph R. *Trend and Tradition in the Prehistory of the Eastern United States*. American Anthropological Association, Memoir 88. 1958.

Fischer, John L. "Solutions for the Natchez Paradox," *Ethnology*, v. 3, 53–65. 1964.

Ford, James A., and Clarence H. Webb. *Poverty Point, A Late Archaic Site in Louisiana*. Anthropological Papers of the American Museum of Natural History, v. 46, pt. 1. 1956.

Griffin, James B., ed. *Archaeology of Eastern United States*. Chicago. 1952.

Haag, William G. "The Archaic of the Lower Mississippi Valley," *American Antiquity*, v. 26, 317–323. 1961.

Haas, Mary R. "Natchez and Chitimacha Clans and Kinship Terminology," *American Anthropologist*, v. 41, 597–610. 1939.

Hart, Charles W. M. "A Reconsideration of the Natchez Social Structure," *American Anthropologist*, v. 45, 374–386. 1943.

*Le Page du Pratz, Antoine S. *The History of Louisiana*. London. 1774 (reprinted at New Orleans in 1947). Between the years 1718 and 1734 the author lived most of the time near the Natchez, where he owned a plantation. The observations by du Pratz concerning these Indians are the most systematic of all the firsthand accounts. The book is very enjoyable to read and is at the same time highly informative.

Quimby, George I., Jr. "The Natchezan Culture Type," *American Antiquity,* v. 7, 255–275. 1942.

——. "Natchez Social Structure as an Instrument of Assimilation," *American Anthropologist,* v. 48, 134–137. 1946.

Swanton, John R. *Indian Tribes of the Lower Mississippi Valley and Adjacent Coast of the Gulf of Mexico.* Bureau of American Ethnology, Bulletin 43. 1911.

——. *Social Organization and Social Usages of the Indians of the Creek Confederacy.* Bureau of American Ethnology, Annual Report 42. 1928.

*——. *The Indians of the Southeastern United States.* Bureau of American Ethnology, Bulletin 137. 1946. Virtually all that is known about Natchez ethnography is in this volume. It is a monumental regional culture history and a key secondary source on the Natchez.

——. *The Indian Tribes of North America.* Bureau of American Ethnology, Bulletin 145. 1953.

11

Various Perspectives

The foregoing descriptions of aboriginal Americans have been presented in terms of histories and ethnographies for particular segments of the population. There has been no attempt to discuss subjects of general interest; this objective has been reserved for the present chapter. Some of the topics discussed here have already been mentioned; others have been ignored. Each, however, is important to an overall understanding of the position of the modern Indian in the United States and Canada. It admittedly is presumptive to deal with diverse aspects of Indian life by devoting only a brief space to each topic, but my purpose is to present an overview of select subjects concerning Indians. The interested reader will find a wealth of detail on most subheadings by consulting the bibliographic items.

What Is an Indian? When persons of European background first came to North America, there was no difficulty in establishing who was an Indian. The gulf between Indians and Europeans was obvious to all. The Indian was racially of the Mongolian stock, and to distinguish between a red man and a white man was an easy matter. In terms of language the Indians clearly were not speakers of Indo-European tongues, and attempts to discover linguistic relationships between Indians and Europeans have not succeeded. The cultural dissimilarities between Indians and whites were obvious. Although there were striking differences in the achievements of diverse Indian tribes, in general a European could with a clear conscience label Indians as savages. The problem of defining an Indian became more complex after traders, trappers, settlers, and missionaries began to live among them. It would appear that three sets of ensuing conditions were important: first, white men mated with Indian women and produced individuals of mixed blood; second, Indians captured whites and sometimes made "Indians" of the captives; and third, some Indians lost their clear identity by becoming at least partly assimilated into white society. To identify an Indian with clarity after the period of early historic contact we are forced to deal with two primary sets of factors—racial and sociocultural. It can be imagined that whites who were assimilated into an Indian tribe would become "Indians," in spite of their racial identity, and this has occurred. Likewise there were Indians who disassociated themselves from other Indians and came to be judged as "whites." These two types of situation are rather straightforward, but with individuals of mixed Indian and white ancestry the categories are not so clear. Such persons may be Indian in one context and white in another, Indian or white exclusively throughout their lives, or Indian at one time in life and white at another. The identification of an Indian has become a matter of definition and is best considered in a legal sense.

In the history of United States Indian law there has never been a precise and uniform definition of an Indian. In general, however, legal precedent has been established that if a person is regarded as an Indian by other individuals in his community, he is an Indian. The degree of Indian blood in an individual may be important, but under most circumstances this is secondary to his sociocultural standing in the community in which he lives. Perhaps some examples will illustrate why there is so much confusion. For instance, if an individual is on the roll of a Federally recognized Indian group, then he is an Indian; his degree of Indian blood is of no real consequence, although he generally has at least some Indian blood. In the definitive study, *Federal Indian Law,* it is stated that a person may, on some reservations, be considered an Indian even if over four generations fifteen of sixteen immediate ancestors were not Indian. In each case the purpose of defining an Indian is with reference to a piece of legislation at some particular time. A person who is on the roll of a tribe and lives on a reservation clearly is an Indian; if he moves from the reservation but remains on the roll, he continues to be an Indian. If he receives a clear title to allotted reservation land, he may or may not remain an Indian, depending on the circumstances. It would appear that in order to lose one's status as an Indian, it is necessary to disassociate oneself voluntarily from other Indians and become identified with some other social segment of American society.

The Canadian Indians, as a result of the Indian Act of 1951, became generally subject to the same laws that apply to other Canadians. For instance, they may vote in national elections, and in most instances they may vote in local elections. The primary difference between a full Canadian citizen and an Indian is that the latter could not, until after 1951, consume intoxicants legally. Neither could an Indian become a full citizen unless "enfranchised," which means a voluntary and formal renunciation of his status as an Indian.

Citizenship. In the United States it was not until 1924 that all Indians became American citizens. The Citizenship Act passed in that year made citizens of about one hundred twenty-five thousand. At that time approximately two hundred fifty thousand other Indians previously had acquired citizenship. As early as 1817 individuals might be granted citizenship under treaty arrangements if they met certain provisions, such as the acceptance of title to individual lands in contrast to living on tribal lands. It was for many years the prevailing opinion of the Federal government that when Indians were bound to their tribal ways and were not under control of the state or territory in which they lived they could not be citizens;

tribal identity was considered separate and different from citizenship, which meant following a "civilized way of life." Becoming a citizen was made simpler with the passage of the Dawes Act of 1887. It was designed to break up reservation lands into individually allotted holdings for individuals and families. After an individual received a clear title to his land he became a citizen, or if he adopted civilized ways and lived apart from any tribe he also became a citizen. He might still retain a special status because he was an Indian and receive treaty or other benefits. Thus he was a citizen, but one with special privileges not granted to other citizens. In 1888 a law was passed making Indian women citizens if they married citizens, the assumption being that these women were following the path of civilization. Indians were not inducted into the armed services during World War I since they were not citizens. However, those that volunteered were made citizens by Congressional action. It is noteworthy that by 1938 some seven states still refused to allow Indians to vote, and only in 1948 were voting rights granted to Indians in Arizona and New Mexico. Opposition to Indian suffrage was based on the fact that they still retained a special relationship to the Federal government.

One of the provisions of the Canadian Indian Act of 1876 was that any Indian who had a university education or its equivalent became a citizen under a mandatory stipulation of the act. In other instances, the individual or the band by majority vote initiated enfranchisement proceedings which required a probationary period before becoming effective. When a man with a wife and minor unmarried children became enfranchised, his family assumed the same legal status as the husband. These provisions did not in general apply to the Indians of British Columbia, Manitoba, the Northwest Territories, or Keewatin District. In 1880 the mandatory enfranchisement was made voluntary. Prior to 1895 an enfranchised Indian received a land allotment by the band; after this time he received land as well as his share of funds belonging to the band. In 1920 it became possible for officers of the Superintendent General to enfranchise an Indian, male or female, without a prior request from the Indian for full citizenship. Such a person still received land and his share of tribal funds. In 1922 the involuntary process leading to citizenship was repealed, and it again was necessary for an individual or a band, by vote of its majority, to apply for enfranchisement. Again in 1933 involuntary enfranchisement was possible by a new amendment to the Act. Consideration was given in 1917 and 1948 to granting full citizenship to Canadian Indians in general, but no legislation to this effect was passed. With the Indian Act of 1951 an Indian woman who married a white man had only to prove the legal validity of the marriage, and enfranchisement became a formality. At present an adult Indian may become a full Canadian citizen by presenting character references and evidence that he has lived away from a reserve for a considerable period of time and has steady employment. The comments of the band to which the person belongs are solicited, and formal application is made through the local superintendent. Upon enfranchisement he receives his share of band assets in cash and henceforth has none of the Indian's legal rights. In general the Indians of Canada have resisted enfranchisement, and very few make application for it. In British Columbia during the 1950's it is estimated that from five to ten Indians a year became citizens because they sought to assimilate into Canadian society. The most important advantage of full citizenship is not voting rights, which a reserve Indian has for any local elections, but the right to buy intoxicants in a liquor store. This he could not do as a reserve Indian until very recently. In 1959–1960 for all of Canada there were eleven hundred twenty-three enfranchisements approved.

Treaties. In the sector of North America that later was to become the United States, the earliest explorers and colonists everywhere found aboriginal Americans on the lands they desired. The Spanish, who initiated the earliest contacts, debated theological and legal issues surrounding the status of Indians. With their prior experience in enslaving African peoples, the question was raised whether or not the Indians in the Americas should likewise be made slaves and their property rights ignored. The problem of whether Indians were fully human and in possession of immortal souls was resolved to the affirmative by a Papal Bull in 1537. Likewise, in theory, Spanish representatives were to recognize the Indian rights of prior possession for their lands. The Dutch and English in the 1700's held that the Indian tribes were sovereign powers and the legitimate claimants to the lands they occupied. Any land acquired from Indians was obtained on a national, not an individual, basis. The pre-Revolutionary War treaties of the British dealt primarily with the question of boundaries and the acquisition of lands from Indians; their overall approach to Indian problems was quite paternalistic. As early as 1670, during the reign of Charles II, England was concerned that those tribes desiring her protection should receive it. There are treaties and agreements with New England tribes dating from 1664, and by 1755 a bureau was founded to deal with Indian matters. Formal recognition given to Indian land titles was later to guide policy in both Canada and the United States. In contrast with English policy the French in general viewed the Indians with a kindly paternalism but did not normally recognize Indian land rights.

Between the years 1778 and 1871 the United States government negotiated formal treaties with Indian tribes in the same manner as it dealt with foreign powers. Indian tribes were viewed by Federal authorities as "dependent nations," and treaties were considered in the same light as other statutes of the United States Congress. In some instances early treaties prohibited U. S. citizens from venturing onto Indian lands without passports. The subordinate position of Indian tribes to the United States is clear by the provisions in most treaties. The tribes were politically weak and economically dependent on the United States. It may come as a surprise that in spite of the hostilities between the Federal government and various tribes, the United States never drew up a formal declaration of war against hostile Indians.

In spite of the fact that no new treaties have been made with Indians for nearly a century, there are still treaty obligations being fulfilled by the Federal government, and Indian treaties have an important place in the development of Federal Indian laws. It is clear that the Federal government reserved the right to regulate affairs with Indians, and only rarely was this right relinquished to a particular state. Once a treaty was negotiated and ratified, it could not be regarded as invalid owing to fraud, duress, or improper Indian representation. Treaties might be renegotiated by the mutual consent of the Indians and the Federal government, and a treaty could be superseded by other Congressional action. Hostilities with a tribe could invalidate a treaty, and a treaty could be modified or nullified under other circumstances. It has, however, been a general policy of the government to interpret ambiguities in treaties in favor of the Indians involved and to consider the circumstances under which a treaty was negotiated. At the same time the courts could not interpret a treaty in a manner not intended in the original wording.

Treaties with Indians were negotiated by the President of the United States and were binding when approved by the Indians and two thirds of the U. S. Senate. It is important to note that a treaty could not provide funds for Indians; monetary commitments required separate Congressional action. The subjects dealt with in Indian treaties varied widely and, in all of the nearly four hundred separate treaties, were negotiated. The greatest number, nearly two hundred sixty, were negotiated between 1815 and 1860, during the great westward expansion of white settlers following the War of 1812. Two hundred and thirty, the majority of all treaties made between 1790 and 1871, involved Indian lands. These concerned the exchange and cession of lands or the establishment of boundaries for Indian lands. A block of seventy-six treaties called for Indian removal from their lands and resettlement on other lands. As early as 1818 there was a treaty setting aside or reserving lands for specific Indian tribes; however, the majority of the reservations were established much later. Nearly a hundred treaties dealt primarily with boundaries between Indian and white lands and affirmed the existence of friendly relations between a tribe and the United States. This was the general nature of most early treaties. Two tribes, the Potawatomi and Chippewa each negotiated forty-two separate treaties, which is a record number.

Most of the early treaties dealt with the relationship of a tribe, or tribes, to the United States government, and no attempt was made to regulate or control the internal affairs of a tribe. As Federal power over Indians increased, this policy was changed, and treaties came to stipulate certain rules for the behavior of tribal members in their own communities. This change took place in 1849 in a treaty with the Navajo which included the provision that the Federal government could (*Federal Indian Law*, 1958, 163) "pass and execute in their territory such laws as may be deemed conducive to the prosperity and happiness of said Indians." By the 1860's the Federal government made treaties which could be amended unilaterally by Congress. This was an anticipation of the end of treaty-making. By the mid-nineteenth century it was becoming increasingly apparent that treaties with Indian tribes were unrealistic because of the increased Indian dependence on the Federal government. It was not until 1871, however, that the last treaty was negotiated and ratified by the U. S. Congress. The end of treaty-making came as a result of a dispute between the U. S. Senate and the House of Representatives. The Senate approved treaties, but the House was obliged to appropriate money relative to the treaties. This finally brought an end to the treaty period (see Note 1).

An interesting sidelight in Federal dealings with Indians was the attempt to have Indian representation at the national level. In the first treaty of the United States with Indians, the Delaware in 1778, there was the provision that at a future date this tribe might consolidate with others and form a state, with the Delaware as the leaders. The state was to have Congressional representation, but nothing ever developed from the possibility. In a treaty of 1785 and another of 1830 it was proposed that Indians send a representative to Congress, but again this possibility was never realized.

The cornerstone of Canadian Indian rights originated with the

Proclamation of 1763, which prohibited the displacement of Indians from their lands except with their consent and Crown approval. This was the guiding principle to direct Indian affairs in Canada, and it has been justly administered. The first Canadian treaties were with the Ojibwa Indians and date from 1850; between that time and Confederation there was one additional treaty negotiated. After Confederation, between 1871 and 1923, thirteen other treaties were approved, but there have been none since 1923. The key provisions in any treaty were usually the following: to set aside lands reserved for exclusive use by Indians; perpetual trusteeship by the Crown; the payment of annuities; the provision of schools; control of liquor traffic; control of hunting and fishing; and the end of Indian title to the land.

Administration. The Continental Congress of the United States in 1775 created three agencies to deal with Indian affairs. These were in the three geographical areas, the northern, middle, and southern. The commissioners in charge of the respective areas were instructed to make treaties and to establish friendly relations with Indians to prevent them from aiding the British. The general structure of Indian administration was the same as had existed under British control. It is worth noting that the individuals in charge of the middle department included Benjamin Franklin and Patrick Henry. Their leadership is indicative of the importance attached to Indian affairs. In 1786 the administration of Indians was placed under the Secretary of War with two departments, the north and south, whose administrators were empowered to grant licenses to trade and live among Indians. With the adoption of the Constitution of the United States, the War Department maintained jurisdiction over Indians. The first Congress of 1789 appropriated funds for negotiating treaties and placed the governor of a particular territory in charge of Indian affairs in his area. The following year Congress began licensing traders among Indians; this was an important step toward Federal control. The year 1824 saw the creation of the Bureau of Indian Affairs, which supervised the problems of Indian administration. This agency remained under the War Department, and its basic organization was established by a Congressional act in 1834. The only major alteration in structure occurred in 1849 when the overall control of the Bureau passed from military control into the hands of the newly created Home Department of the Interior. Owing to the flagrant corruption and mismanagement of the Bureau, a Board of Indian Commissioners was created in 1869, composed of ten outstanding citizens who were appointed without compensation by the President and who reported to him. The Commissioners were overseers of the expenditure of funds for Indians and served to advise the Bureau of Indian Affairs; the Board was abolished in 1933.

In Canada the direction of Indian affairs was delegated to the Commander of the Forces in the British North American Provinces in 1816. In 1830 the management of Indian affairs of Upper Canada passed into civilian control, but that in Lower Canada remained under military jurisdiction. By the Act of Union in 1841 the two Indian Affairs departments were joined into a single Department of Indian Affairs, and in 1860 the Crown Lands Department assumed the responsibility for Indian management. With the Confederation of Canada in 1867 the administration of Indians passed into the hands of the Dominion of Canada. At this time the Department of the Secretary of State directed Indian affairs, but in 1873 with the creation of the Department of the Interior the Indian branch was made a part of this agency. A few years later in 1880 a separate Department of Indian Affairs was founded with a minister who was the Superintendent General of Indian Affairs. The portfolio of this minister always was held by an individual with another ministerial post, usually the Minister of the Interior. In 1936 the Department of Indian Affairs was changed into a branch and placed under the new Department of Mines and Resources. Finally in 1950 the Department of Citizenship and Immigration assumed control of the Indian Affairs Branch.

The Dominion Parliament alone is responsible for legislating for Indians. The general structure for rights and services was framed in the Indian Act of 1876. The administration controls the management of Indian lands—both the reserves and other lands set aside for use only by Indians—as well as the Indian Trust Fund, which is an accumulation of money derived mainly from the sale of natural resources on Indian lands. The Indian Act of 1876 recognized also that the Dominion government was responsible for relief, education, health services, and Indian-based agriculture and industry. Finally the Parliament was made responsible for the enfranchisement of Indians to full Canadian citizenship.

The next major revision of Indian policy in Canada, the Indian Act of 1951 with its subsequent revisions, is the legal basis for current policy. The Act sets forth in exact terms the authority and power of the Governor in Council, the Minister and the Minister's field representatives, the superintendents. Robert W. Dunning, in discussing the effects of the Act on the Indians, stresses the power of the superintendent on a reserve and his flexibility in formulating and administering local policy. Among the duties of a reserve superintendent are to consider what nonlegitimates may become members of a band and to screen enfranchisement applicants, in addition to administering welfare, relief, and education on a reserve. He furthermore may accept or veto the nomination of an Indian to a band council.

Treaties and laws referring to both Canadian and United States Indians often made reference to the consumption of intoxicants. In Canada an Indian, unless he was enfranchised, could not buy liquor legally for ordinary consumption until 1951. The Indian Act of 1951 permitted the provinces or territories, with the approval of the Governor in Council, to allow Indians to consume intoxicants in public places. This condition existed over most of Canada until 1958. Between 1958 and 1963 the restriction was lessened in most provinces and territories to permit Indians to buy alcoholic beverages in the same manner as Canadian citizens in general, that is, either in a public place or from a package store. At the same time a band still may elect to prohibit intoxicants on reserve lands. In the United States the first Federal regulation of intoxicants among Indians originated in 1802. The law was periodically modified to ease enforcement and to cover loopholes. It was not until 1953 that the Federal government repealed this law. Prohibition on any reservation still was possible under local option. Before Indians could consume intoxicants in some states, the state laws against the sale of liquor to Indians had to be changed.

Major Legislation in the United States. The first Congress of the United States in 1789 enacted four statutes which were to be of lasting significance in the development of Indian policies. During this Congressional session the administration of Indian affairs was placed under the jurisdiction of the Department of War. Furthermore, after creating the Northwest Territory, Congress used its "plenary" authority to legislate over all the inhabitants. This was to be the pattern in the future for the development of territories. Funds were appropriated for Indian treaties and for salaried officials among Indians. In 1790 an act was passed by Congress regulating trade with Indians by licensing traders and setting forth guides for the sale of Indian lands under treaty arrangements only. At this time, too, legislation was enacted concerning the punishment of whites for crimes against Indians. These statutes were interim arrangements which were later, in 1802 and again in 1834, crystallized into a lasting Indian Trade and Intercourse Act. Between 1796 and 1822 the Federal government operated trading houses for Indians under Presidential control. Even after the abandonment of these establishments, the Federal government was to retain control over Indian trade by licensing traders. Indian country was legislatively defined in 1796, and in 1817 a system of criminal law for Indians and non-Indians was established within Indian country. Indians remained free to punish other Indians according to their own norms of behavior, however. An important act passed in 1819 was designed to help Indians along the frontier to adopt civilized ways (see Note 2); funds to implement this goal were appropriated in the act.

An act of 1830 was of major significance since it set forth the policy to be followed during any removal of Indians from the eastern United States. The Indians affected were those living east of the Mississippi River; they were to be given lands west of the Mississippi in exchange for those that they forfeited. This act stated that removal was to be voluntary and that payment was to be made by the Federal government for improvements on lands the Indians relinquished. Removal was not a concept new to Indian affairs. It had been advanced in the treaty with the Delaware and was first advocated as a policy by President Monroe. The major groups who successfully resisted removal were the Cherokee and Seminole.

The position of Commissioner of Indian Affairs was created in 1832, but the administration was still under the Secretary of War. The general administrative structure of a new agency to deal with Indians was created in 1834, and part of the same act was the general prohibition against selling intoxicants to Indians. The Indian Trade and Intercourse Act became the structural framework upon which subsequent policies were built. Federal administrative and regulatory jurisdiction was broadened in 1847 on the previously established base, and finally in 1849 the administration of Indian affairs passed from the War Department to the new Department of the Interior.

During the 1850's treaty-making took precedence over legislation, whereas in the decade to follow the reverse was true. In the 1860's laws were enacted to protect private land holdings of Indians and to abrogate treaties with hostile tribes. Likewise an investigation was made into the administration of Indian affairs in 1865. The bureau was consolidated in 1868, and treaty-making was ended by Congressional action in 1871. Direct Federal control increased after this decision.

The most important legislation of the 1880's was the General Allotment or Dawes Act. In 1887 the President was authorized to allot the lands of most reservations to individual Indians. The Indians were to select their acreage, and the Federal government was to hold a trust title for twenty-five years or longer, during which time the land could not be encumbered. Surplus reservation lands then were to be sold to the government, and the funds derived were held in trust for the tribe, subject to use for education and civilizing the tribe when

Congress approved this use. Over the next ten years the General Allotment Act was modified in some of its aspects in order to permit the leasing of allotted lands and to validate claims of descendants from those marriages that were in keeping with tribal customs. Indian education came to be stressed with particular enactments from 1892 to 1897. These provided for schools and virtually forced the attendance of Indian children, while Federal support of church schools was withdrawn. An important supplement was made to the Dawes Act in 1906; it permitted the President to extend the trust period for allotted lands. Again in 1910 the General Allotment Act was revised to resolve problems arising from inheriting allotments, leasing timber lands, and replacing trust patents for reservoir lands with others of comparable value. The tribal funds held by the U. S. Treasury were to be dispersed to members of such tribes as a result of legislation in 1919, but this provision was repealed in 1938.

The Johnson-O'Malley Act of 1934 was a systematic effort to improve the economic and educational facilities available for Indians. It provided that (*Federal Indian Law,* 1958, 128) "the education, medical attention, agricultural assistance, and social welfare" among Indians be the responsibility of qualified state agencies, supported by Federal money, rather than remain under the Bureau of Indian Affairs. In the history of legislation centering on Indian affairs there were three major pieces of legislation: the Indian Trade and Intercourse Act, the General Allotment Act, and finally the Wheeler-Howard Act or Indian Reorganization Act of 1934 (see Note 3). The major provision of the Wheeler-Howard Act was designed to end the alienation of Indian lands through the allotment process. In fifty years under the allotment system the Indians had lost nearly ninety million of their one hundred thirty-eight million acres of land, with about half the remaining lands being nearly useless desert. The major device for fostering the retention of the remaining land base was through extending the period of trust holding. Furthermore, additional land was acquired for Indians, declared exempt from taxes, and placed under Federal control. Indian tribes were encouraged to form chartered corporations, and a revolving credit fund was established to bring viability into the tribal economies of those choosing to incorporate. It also was now possible for the Indians to obtain loans for furthering their education, and preferential hiring was given to Indians in the Bureau of Indian Affairs. One very important section of the law was that it would apply only to those tribes in which a majority voted to come under its provisions. Initially, one hundred and eighty-one tribes accepted, and seventy-seven rejected the Indian

Reorganization Act. Fourteen groups came under it because they did not vote, and the Act was extended in 1936 to include Alaskan and Oklahoman peoples without their vote of approval. Since Indians in general had come to distrust deeply the Federal government, the Indian response to this enlightened legislation was not so great as had been hoped for by its creators. Some tribes favored allotments and were able to obtain clear title to their land in spite of the Indian Reorganization Act.

House Concurrent Resolution 108 of the First Session of the Eighty-third Congress in 1953 brought an acceleration of Federal withdrawal from Indian affairs (see Note 4). This resolution set forth the attitude that the Federal government should divest itself of its Indian interests and hand over to the Indians and the various states the supervision of Indian matters. This decision had been anticipated, particularly in the 1940's, when the Federal government began to divest itself of certain obligations which heretofore had been Federal responsibilities. Certain Indian schools were abandoned, and the children were sent to public schools. In other instances Indians on reserved lands became subject to the legal jurisdiction of the state in which they lived. To settle old injustices by the United States against Indians the Indian Claims Commission Act was passed in 1946; this also was a move toward Federal withdrawal. In 1954 the U. S. Congress initiated steps for terminating Federal responsibilities to the Menominee of Wisconsin and the Klamath of Oregon, as well as for a few smaller reservations. The only positive change in Indian policy in this general time period took place in 1955 when the U. S. Public Health Service assumed the responsibility for Indian health services from the Bureau of Indian Affairs.

House Concurrent Resolution 108 ushered in the policy of "termination" which by some Indians was welcomed as an opportunity to receive their share of tribal wealth held in trust. For others, probably a great majority, it was viewed as a new effort of whites to take their lands and strip them of their Indian identity. The language of the resolution implied that the Indian was henceforth to be regarded as a fully participating citizen. Indians already had these rights and privileges; the differential treatment they received was based on treaty or statutory obligations and included services as well as keeping trust lands off tax rolls. The results of the termination policy were soon likely to lead to the general withdrawal of Federal economic support to reservations as well as a turning over of Federally held trust lands to individual Indians and tribes. These lands would then, with normal expectations, be added to the local tax base. Vocal hostility against termination by most Indians and interested whites caused Congress to pause, particularly after it was realized how costly the ill-conceived and rapid effort to terminate the Klamath Reservation in Oregon had become (see Note 5).

Land. It is only truistic to write that the Indians came to America first; however, this point is extremely important in that it establishes their rights of aboriginal occupancy. No significant portion of North America which was to be of value to whites did not have its earlier Indian settlers. It still was necessary, however, for some legal action recognized by whites to be brought forth to validate the claims. In the United States, Indians have land rights based on aboriginal possession, treaty, a Congressional act, Executive order, purchase, or by the action of some colony, state, or foreign nation.

Indian reservations were created by treaty arrangements before 1871, by acts of Congress after that time, and by Executive orders of the President. In each instance the Federal government usually retained the title to reservation lands. Treaty reservations were created in some instances in recognition of aboriginal title and in others in exchange for different lands or for the privilege of joining another Indian group on its reservation. Occasionally during the treaty-making era and often thereafter, reservations were established by Congressional action. Such statutory reservations consisted usually of an area of public domain or land purchased by the Federal government for use by a designated segment of the Indian population. The legality of reservations established by Executive orders was uncertain, but their validity was established in the General Allotment Act. Reservations were created by Executive order between about 1855 and 1919. The practice, however, met continuing resistance from Congress and was brought to an end, except that some Alaskan reservations have been a partial exception. It has happened also that from time to time Indians have purchased lands with their own funds for their group as a whole; such land has been administratively supervised by the Federal government. Since virtually all of the territory which is now the United States was held earlier by a European-based power, the rights of Indians under British, Dutch, French, Mexican, Russian, and Spanish rule have been taken into consideration when there was a transfer of sovereignty. In each instance at least some implicit recognition was given to aboriginal rights of occupancy by the Indians.

In Canada the earliest significant grant of lands to Indians was made in 1680 by Louis XIV to a band of Iroquois in Quebec, and the land still is occupied by the Iroquois. The next major grant of land was to the Six Nations, who were Iroquois, in 1784. They received nearly 700,000 acres for their loyalty to the British during the American Revolution. By 1821 the Six Nations had alienated nearly half of the original grant by selling lands to whites before this practice was prohibited. In the early 1940's there were some 5,500,000 acres of land held in trust by the Dominion government for Indians. Under the Canadian Act of 1870 reserved lands may be held by a particular Indian under an allotment system. This means that the allottee has exclusive rights of use and occupancy. He may pass the land on to heirs or sell it to another Indian of his group, but he does not receive clear title to the holding. Indians with more land than is necessary for their welfare may surrender land and use the money derived from the sale for the benefit of the group. Under certain rare conditions an individual Indian may obtain a clear title to his land; for example, it is possible if he requests Canadian citizenship or enfranchisement and it is granted. Title to his land is obtained by receiving the consent of his group and the Dominion government, but he must pay the band for the land.

Population. It is estimated that the aboriginal population of the United States at the time of historic contact was nearly 850,000, in addition to 73,000 others in Alaska and 221,000 in Canada. The accepted estimate for the area north of Mexico, for the earliest period of historic contact in each area, is about one million. The population declined to some 406,000 by about 1910. The major cause of the decline probably was disease, with the most horrible example of what could happen being recorded among the Mandan. In 1837 a smallpox epidemic reduced them from 1600 to 31 individuals. In certain areas, such as Texas and California, more Indians probably were murdered by whites than died from disease. Further factors of unquestioned importance, particularly in the United States proper, were the debilitating effects of intoxicants and removal, which led to substandard living conditions and innumerable accompanying deaths. Around 1900 the Indian population began to increase at a much higher rate than that for whites so that by 1960 there were 550,000 Indians in the United States and Alaska, of whom 28,000 were Aleuts or Eskimos, and another 200,000 in Canada. It is estimated that in Alaska and the United States some direct services are provided to approximately 370,000 persons of aboriginal descent. The racial composition of the current Indian population is of course not what it was at the time of historic contact. There are probably relatively few tribes, possibly some of the pueblo peoples, the Navajo, and isolated communities of Northern Athapaskans, and Eskimos, who have retained their racial homogeneity. Then, too, many Indians have lost their identity as Indians. In the United States it is estimated that between 1930 and 1960 some 30,000 Indians became assimilated in the general population.

A 1962 estimate of the Indian population by state indicates the following numbers, which have been rounded off, for states with 20,000 or more Indians: Arizona, 82,000; Oklahoma, 62,000; New Mexico, 52,000; Alaska (including Eskimos), 38,000; South Dakota, 28,000; and Montana, 21,000. In 1963 the total amount of land held by tribes was nearly 39,000,000 acres; allotted land consisted of nearly 12,000,000 acres, and government-owned land associated with Indian administration amounted to nearly 5,000,000 acres.

The Indian population of Canada for the early 1960's was as follows: Alberta, 19,000; British Columbia, 37,000; Manitoba, 24,000; New Brunswick, 3500; Nova Scotia, 4000; Ontario, 47,000; Prince Edward Island, 350; Quebec, 21,000; Saskatchewan, 23,000; Northwest Territories, 5000; and Yukon Territory, 2000. The total Eskimo population for all of Canada, including Labrador, is approximately 13,000.

Urban Population. The movement of Indians into cities is an old and established pattern of off-reservation adjustment, but it seldom has been studied by social scientists, and rarely have the results of such studies been published. One of the recommendations of the Meriam Survey of 1928 was that broader employment opportunities should be made available to Indians; there was very little potential for such a program during the depression of the 1930's. During World War II it was not difficult for Indians leaving their reservations to find employment, but the scene changed after the war when Indians employed in war industries and those in the armed services returned to the reservations. The problem of overcrowding on the reservations became critical in the face of the multiple problem of wartime stagnation of economic development programs, the inadequate land-base, and the rapid increase in Indian population growth. The problem was most acute on the Navajo Reservation. In 1948 a program was initiated to find seasonal employment for single Navajo men in Denver, Los Angeles, and Salt Lake City, where Indian placement offices were established. In late 1951 a general Indian relocation program was begun, and a relocation office was opened in Chicago. The previously established placement offices were also incorporated into this program. In 1954 a relocation office was started in Oakland and the one in Salt Lake City closed. Eight additional relocation offices were opened in the Midwest, Southwest and far west in 1956–1957. By 1956 around $1 million was alloted to relocation, and in 1957 the money spent for it was in the neighborhood of $3.5 million. In 1957 nearly 7000 Indians were relocated and received financial aid from the Federal government to establish themselves. The relocated individuals and families received funds for transportation, establishment of a new household, temporary medical insurance, plus other services of this nature if required. Finally the Bureau found work for individuals and family heads. The Bureau of Indian Affairs reported that during the mid-1950's approximately 75 percent of the relocated Indians did not return to their reservations.

As might be expected one step toward urban living for an Indian is to move to a town or city near his reservation home. This pattern of urbanization has been studied for the Sioux moving to Yankton in southeastern South Dakota. The study was made by Wesley R. Hurt, Jr., between 1955 and 1959. Yankton had a population of about 9300 in 1960; it had several small industries and was also a trading center. In 1940 there were only twenty-nine Indians in Yankton, but by late 1959 the number was estimated at two hundred and sixty. During the span of the study a number of particularly noteworthy characteristics of the Indian population were recorded. First, over half of the Indians in Yankton in 1955 had moved away by 1959. Second, the bulk of the Indians were from nearby reservations. By and large they were young, with a median age of 11.5 years in 1958; in 1950 the median age in the United States was 30.2 years. Finally, women were more numerous in town than men. The Indians in Yankton lived in poorer sections of the community but not in segregated housing.

If there was any dominant reason for most Indians' moving to Yankton, it probably was to improve their economic condition. One group, about fifty individuals, left the reservation each summer for seasonal employment in town and then returned to the reservation. Another category, estimated at 20 percent of the total, resided in Yankton more or less permanently because they did not have reservation-based resources to support themselves. These people, however, longed to return to the reservation and disliked urban life. About 40 percent liked living on the reservation less than living in Yankton, and thus the city had an attraction as a lesser of evils. Another segment of the population was attempting to integrate itself into white society either through stable city residence or as migrant workers. Finally, there were Indians who seemingly rejected both white and Indian values and spent most of their time in jail. A common difficulty of all the Indians was that they rarely had the job skills which made steady employment likely; generally, also, they did not have the attitudes toward work which would make them reliable workers. It seems that these Indians as a whole did not desire to be like whites, but they were unable to maintain themselves at home except at a very low economic level.

One recent analysis of city Indians under the relocation program has been published by Harry W. Martin. It deals with an unidentified metropolitan center in the southwestern United States between 1957–1961 and compiled and analyzed three hundred eleven case histories of Choctaw, Navajo, and Sioux who went to the urban area as individuals or as heads of families. Martin's study relates adjustment to various population factors. The conclusions reached were that the Navajo were the best adapted to their new environment. The percentage of well-adjusted individuals was greater for Navajo women than for men, and young Navajo males were better adjusted than older ones. Next to the Navajo men in adjustment were the Choctaw and then the Sioux. In an attempt to determine whether a correlation existed between the degree of Indian blood and urban adjustment the Choctaw and Sioux were compared. The Navajo were not considered since virtually all were full-blooded Indians. For the Choctaw there was no relationship between Indian blood and adjustment. The situation among the Sioux was different, for nearly 70 percent with less than half Indian racial identity were high on the adjustment scale. Sioux with one half or more Indian blood rated only slightly better than 30 percent for high adjustment. In view of the military experience of all the Indian men, it was found that nearly 60 percent with no military experience rated high on adjustment, whereas about 40 percent of those with military experience rated high in adjustment. Thus it would seem that for an Indian to become a member of the armed services decreased the probability of his adjusting to urban life under relocation. This study as a whole demonstrates that urban adjustment of Indians is a complex subject, and to offer generalizations about Indian adjustments in cities is likely to be dangerous.

In 1961–1962 a study was made by Joan Ablon of relocated Indians in the San Francisco Bay area communities of San Francisco, Oakland, and San Jose. Among Ablon's concluding ideas are the following statements (1964, 303).

> The adjustments most Indians make in learning the cues for living successfully in the white world seem to be superficial to their established basic personality structures. Such basic qualities of Indianness—as Indian identity and continuing belief in early teachings and values—are strongly resistant to change, despite efforts of the Bureau of Indian Affairs and the dominant white society to effect fundamental changes during the process of adjustment.

In order to understand the meaning behind the resistance of urban Indians to assimilation it is essential to realize the basic reason for their move to a city. Most relocated Indians left their reservations because they could not find regular employment at home. It was not bright lights that lured them, but what to them seemed to be economic necessity. Most of the relocated persons would return to their home reservations if they could find employment there. Thus they are striving not for assimilation but for a better standard of living.

The San Francisco Bay area reportedly has some ten thousand Indians from more than a hundred different tribes, two thirds of whom have participated in the relocation program. When the program began in 1954, some 75 percent of the initial participants returned to their reservations, a contradiction of Bureau of Indian Affairs statistics, but now the return rate is about 35 percent. Most of the relocatees are unskilled or semiskilled workmen, and like whites in their educational category they are so susceptible to layoffs that any job security is minimal. In general they do not meet with discrimination in the San Francisco Bay area, but they rarely make close friendships with whites. Whites may be willing to cultivate Indian friends, but the Indians do not respond in such a manner that friendships can develop. The Indians distrust whites and fear white rejection. At the same time they recognize that potentially they are dependent on whites. We find that Indians seek the company of other Indians, particularly those who are relatives. At the beginning of their stay in a city they orient themselves by participating in one of the sixteen voluntary social groups created for Indians. Thus they live in a social setting that centers about being Indian, carrying with them their earlier feelings about whites which they developed while living on a reservation.

Current Federal Policies. In the United States the Federal government appears to be guided along two general policy lines. One is to encourage and facilitate Indian adjustments off the reservations, and the second is to support programs of economic development for Indians on or near reservations. The off-reservation program is built around "Operation Relocation." Initially, the relocation program was concerned entirely with finding jobs in cities for Indians who were willing to relocate. However, by 1958 the emphasis of the program had begun to change at least in part. The 1958 budget called for about $3.5 million for relocation and $1.5 million for adult vocational training. An emphasis toward adult education began in 1956 with pilot programs on a number of reservations. The initial project was expanded so that by 1959 some fifteen hundred Indians were direct participants in adult education projects. It would appear that these moves are in line with the general policy of termination, and yet between 1954 and 1958 there was little effort made for Federal withdrawal from Indian supervision. In 1959 a renewed attempt was made in Senate Concurrent Resolution 12 to reestablish termination as a Federal policy; as in 1953, termination was to be without any necessary approval by the affected tribes. The attempt failed but suggests that the possibility of unilateral termination exists still.

The United States Bureau of Indian Affairs budget appropriation in fiscal 1964 amounted to $206 million. In terms of millions of dollar units the budgetary breakdown was as follows: 66, education of children; 58, construction of buildings, utilities, and irrigation systems; 38, resources management; 15, road construction; 11, welfare; 9, employment assistance and occupational training; 4, administration; and 2, revolving loan fund. To these funds should be added the 64 million spent by the U. S. Public Health Service on Indian health through the Division of Indian Health.

In 1961 a Task Force appointed by the Secretary of the Interior studied Indian affairs and issued a report on Federal goals, both for the present and for the future. The previous Bureau of Indian Affairs policy, according to the Task Force, attempted the following programs: improving social, economic, and political achievements to a level comparable for whites; fostering increased Indian self-sufficiency; and terminating Federal responsibilities. The Task Force reported that increased stress should be placed on development programs and less on termination. Another aspect of the findings pointed out the ambivalent position of the Indians and of the organizations interested in them, who seek Federal aid to improve Indian life and yet at the same time censure the Federal attempts to destroy the old Indian ways.

In early 1964 the President met with the leaders of diverse tribes and made a statement about poverty among Indians. President Lyndon B. Johnson acknowledged that Indians are the most impoverished segment of the American population. He stated that 90 percent of their housing is substandard; unemployment is about 50 percent; the high school dropout rate is 60 percent; the income for reservation Indians is one third of the national average; and finally the average life expectancy of reservation Indians is forty-two years, in contrast with a national average of sixty-two. Furthermore, the President pledged to offer new opportunities for Indians. A statement later the same year by the Commissioner of Indian Affairs, Philleo Nash, seemed to stress vocational training as the most reasonable means for solving Indian economic problems away from the reservation. It was stressed, too, that the training alone was not enough; counseling and job placement services were needed along with other aids, in order for the training to be most effective.

Pan-Indianism. As various tribes of American Indians have declined in numbers and been relocated voluntarily or forcefully, they have come into contact with other Indians of diverse backgrounds. One product of this association has been an increasing emphasis by Indians on being Indian irrespective of tribal affiliations. Pan-Indianism is a synthesis of those things Indian. The Ghost Dance of 1890 was the first great example of this type of movement, and the peyote cult is another. Both of these are religious in nature, but another aspect of Pan-Indianism is secular. Accompanying this realignment of the Indian population has been the influence of that which whites consider to be typically Indian; thus Indians have partially come to see themselves through the eyes of whites. As a result certain aspects of aboriginal life now regarded as Indian per se are accepted by diverse tribes. For example, the plains Indian headdress of eagle feathers is now symbolic of Indians irrespective of the area.

In Oklahoma, where there is the greatest concentration of tribes of diverse origins, we might expect and do find a center for the pan-Indian movement. Here we have what James H. Howard (1955, 215) justly calls "supertribal culture." Apparently pan-Indianism has a different meaning among the participating tribes. For most of the larger tribes the elements are added to their existing ideas of what is Indian, but for some of the smaller tribes pan-Indianism alone represents Indian culture. A war dance reportedly of Pawnee origin is what Howard (1955, 216) terms the "prime secular focus of pan-Indianism." The appeal of this dance is that it usually is considered secular and requires no preparation for peformance. Another advantage of the war dance is that it may be performed by a single individual or by many persons at the same time. The costume includes a feather roach patterned after the plains and Eastern Woodland hair roaches. On the dancer's back at hip and shoulder level are circular attachments of feathers called bustles. Their origin is from the plains, but the arm bustles worn have no obvious earlier form. Again, the neckband and moccasins are of plains derivation. A stomp dance originating in the eastern United States is recognized as pan-Indian; although it formerly was sacred, it now is secular. Another aspect of the movement in Oklahoma is the "Indian store," which stocks items with appeal to Indians. We find that English is the language spoken when members of different tribes participate jointly in a powwow. The mobility provided by the automobile is important in the spread of pan-Indian ideas. Indian solidarity is furthered by a general attitude of whites that Indians are lower-class individuals. Interestingly enough, when Indians move to a city and are not inclined to assimilate, pan-

Indian identification may become the most important way to retain recognition as an Indian (see Note 6).

"White" Indians. There exists a fascinating and highly romantic aura surrounding those instances of white Americans becoming Indians socially and culturally. How many such transformations took place along the frontier will never be known, but there likely were thousands of cases. In general, anthropologists and historians have noted such instances but have not studied the phenomenon systematically. At least such was the condition until Alfred I. Hallowell turned his perceptive attention to the problem. Hallowell divided the instances of Indianization, a word dating from the late seventeenth century, into two categories: the individual white being taken by Indians as a captive, or the attachment to Indian society being voluntary. At the time of the expanding American frontier, when most of these instances took place, it was considered remarkable by most colonists that anyone would refuse to be identified with Europeans. And yet in numerous instances this is precisely what happened. The refusal of a voluntary Indian to rejoin the dominant society was not so startling as the decision of a liberated white captive to remain Indian. It may be asked how it was that Indians so readily assimilated white Americans, and the answer seems to rest primarily with the form of institutional adoption common among many if not most tribes. In times before historic contact it was a frequent custom to adopt captives in warfare and in this way assimilate fully alien Indians. Thus there was ample precedent for the adoption of individuals with diverse backgrounds. When such tribes came into contact with whites, the practice of adoption was extended to include them. A white could become a fully participating individual in Indian society and even rise to a position of power and authority; white chiefs of Indian groups were not unknown. At the same time comparable adoption patterns did not exist among whites, and it was impossible for an Indian to become fully assimilated into colonial American society. Hallowell has termed Indianization as transculturalization and defines it as that process which occurs under conditions where an individual of one culture accepts an alien culture to a greater or lesser degree. He has noted also that such transculturalization of whites is not unique among American Indians but has occurred elsewhere in the world.

Material Borrowings of White Americans. One perspective in which to view Americans north of Mexico is to cite those items from Indian culture that have been adopted into contemporary American life. To consider material examples the most important contributions would be moccasins, parkas, birchbark canoes, kayaks, snowshoes, and toboggans, and possibly one plant, the sunflower. This list is perhaps surprisingly short, and yet it does reflect rather accurately the narrow range of borrowings. The list also reflects the vast differences between Americans today and aboriginal Americans. Modern American materialism is of such complexity that North American Indians could not be expected to have contributed a great deal to it. We have freed ourselves from the intimate environmental associations which characterized virtually all North American Indian cultures.

One enormously important borrowing by white Americans occurred in eastern North America during colonial times. The early colonists who were precariously settled along the eastern seaboard borrowed the entire maize complex from local Indians. They did not absorb the social or religious associations but were taught by Indians how to cultivate the plant, how to process the harvest, and how to prepare maize as a food. The event may not seem of great importance today, but in the context of the time at which it took place it was immensely significant.

If we were to include Indian discoveries or inventions for all of the Americas, the list of contributions would be greater, because American Indian cultures climaxed in Central and South America rather than in North America. To the list would be added potatoes, beans, tomatoes, tobacco, and various drugs, as well as a few material items such as pipes, hammocks, and the rubber syringe. Again, this list is not long, but some of the plants are economically very important around the world today. It still may be asked if American Indians in general were not woefully unimaginative in devising items with utility in the modern world, and the answer would be an obvious yes. To the question of why, the answer seems to stem not from any lack of intelligence on the part of the Indians but rather from their total environmental setting and its potential for the development of civilization. The New World was devoid of such animals as the horse, cow, and pig which had great potential as domesticates, and neither were there grains such as wheat and barley. More important, in the New World the animals and plants which had potential as domesticates were not concentrated in one restricted geographical area. A contrary situation existed in the Old World, for in the Near East, about 7000 B.C., there emerged the basis for all Old World civilizations. New World developments, however, are not to be cast aside as failures if one considers the complex societies that emerged in aboriginal Mexico and Peru. It is simply that these peoples could not go as far toward civilization, in western terms, because of their general setting. To explain why the New World Indians did not develop civilizations comparable to those of the Old World and at the same rate as in the Old World requires an awareness of the limitations of localized New World environments.

American Indians and American "Culture." By employing the word "culture" in a nonanthropological sense and again drawing on the scholarly endeavors of Alfred I. Hallowell, we will be able to see the American Indian in yet another dimension. In American literature, for example, there is no subject of greater appeal than the Indian, but the literary image of the Indian has been by no means uniform through time. The first entry of Indians into the literature of America was directly from Indian speeches composed during treaty-making. The oratorical skills of Indians were appreciated and orations printed for general circulation in the eighteenth century. When Indians were nearby in the eastern United States and the whites sought their lands, Indians were more likely to be viewed as foes. With the first half of the nineteenth century the frontier drifted westward, and the image of the Indian in the eastern sector was cast in a new and different light. He was no longer a threat, but became a romantic figure. Drawing on Indian ethnographic accounts, James F. Cooper wrote his great novels and produced the character of Leatherstocking, a white Indian with no literary equal. Then, too, Henry W. Longfellow's *Hiawatha* is a literary monument of this era.

In the frontier region to the west, the Indian once again assumed a different cast for those white Americans who quested for Indian lands. The Indian was now a sort of vermin to be exterminated since he impeded progress. When the Indian wars and skirmishes in the West had been won and the remnant Indian population confined to reservations, these people again could be viewed romantically, but even before the West was seized, the Indian was a standard figure in nearly half the three hundred twenty-one dime novels that originated in the 1860's. The Indian theme never died but was recast in different mediums with the introduction of motion pictures and radio. Needless to say, American television owes a great debt to the Indian, nor is he forgotten in contemporary novels.

Words and phrases in American English derived from a background of Indian contacts continue to be a part of our daily vocabulary. Examples such as Indian summer, happy hunting ground, wild Indian, Indian giver, and "to bury the hatchet" are known widely. When place names on the land are considered, the number with an Indian origin is staggering, not only for lakes and rivers but for states and cities. Indian trails, also, were later to become roads and highways for white Americans.

Indians played a major role in shaping the belief system of one of the few large and lasting religions originating in the United States, the Church of Jesus Christ of Latter-day Saints or Mormons. The Book of Mormon relates that Indians originated from a segment of the Jewish population which came to the New World before Christian times. For the members of this faith the Book of Mormon supplements the Bible and records the history of these migrants in the New World. According to the Mormon belief system, Jesus Christ returned to earth and was seen in Mexico as a White God. In Mormon theology the Indians descended from the Lamanites, a degenerate people, but still the Mormons have been inordinately kind in their dealings with Indians. The inclusion of population theory in a religious dogma "could hardly have occurred anywhere but in early 19th-century America," as noted by Hallowell (1958, 461). It might be added further that the nondoctrinal part of the Book of Mormon most likely originated from a novel written but not published by Solomon Spaulding.

In other diverse aspects of American culture the Indian has not only been recognized but immortalized. One of the most popular nineteenth-century American plays was "Metamora," and playwrights have continued to build plots around Indians. In the first American opera in 1794, "Tammany," there was a Cherokee melody, and the Indian exists in American folk songs. In more recent times we have Charles Cadman's "From the Land of Sky Blue Waters," and Thurland Chattaway and Kerry Mills' "Red Wing" as two examples of Indian themes in modern American music. Other Indian contributions which are now a part of American history include the Wild West show, the Indian medicine show, the cigar store Indian, and the romantic appeal of the Indian as a subject for painters.

Note 1. The end of treaty-making among Indians of the United States (*Federal Indian Law*, 1950, 211).

When the appropriation bill for the fiscal year 1871 came up in the second session of the Forty-first Congress the fight of the previous year was renewed, the Senate insisting on appropriations for carrying out the new treaties and the House refusing to grant any funds for that purpose. As the end of the session approached it appeared as if the bill would fail entirely, but after the President had called the attention of Congress to the necessity of making appropriations, the two houses finally reconciled their differences.

The strong fight made by the House and expressions of many members of the Senate made it evident that the treaty system had reached its end, and the Indian appropriation act for the fiscal year 1872, approved on March 3, 1871 (*16 Stat. L.*, 566), contained the following clause, tacked on to a sentence making an appropriation for the Yankton Indians: "*Provided,* That hereafter no Indian nation or tribe within the territory of the United States shall be acknowledged or recognized as an independent nation, tribe, or power with whom the United States may contract by treaty: *Provided further,* That nothing herein contained shall be construed to invalidate or impair the obligation of any treaty heretofore lawfully made and ratified with any such Indian nation or tribe."

Note 2. Section one of "An act making provision for the civilization of the Indian tribes adjoining the frontier settlements," adopted in 1819 (*Federal Indian Law,* 1958, 101).

That for the purpose of providing against the further decline and final extinction of the Indian tribes, adjoining the frontier settlements of the United States, and for introducing among them the habits and arts of civilization, the President of the United States shall be, and he is hereby authorized, in every case where he shall judge improvement in the habits and condition of such Indians practicable, and that the means of instruction can be introduced with their own consent, to employ capable persons of good moral character, to instruct them in the mode of agriculture suited to their situation; and for teaching their children in reading, writing, and arithmetic, and performing such other duties as may be enjoined, according to such instructions and rules as the President may give and prescribe for the regulation of their conduct, in the discharge of their duties.

Note 3. The purposes of the Wheeler-Howard Act as summarized by Senator Burton K. Wheeler, one of the sponsors of the legislation (*Federal Indian Law,* 1958, 129).

1. To stop the alienation, through action by the Government or the Indian, of such lands, belonging to ward Indians, as are needed for the present and future support of these Indians.

2. To provide for the acquisition, through purchase, of land for Indians, now landless, who are anxious and fitted to make a living on such land.

3. To stabilize the tribal organization of Indian tribes by vesting such tribal organizations with real, though limited, authority, and by prescribing conditions which must be met by such tribal organizations.

4. To permit Indian tribes to equip themselves with the devices of modern business organization, through forming themselves into business corporations.

5. To establish a system of financial credit for Indians.

6. To supply Indians with means for collegiate and technical training in the best schools.

7. To open the way for qualified Indians to hold positions in the Federal Indian Service.

Note 4. U. S. Congress, House of Representatives Concurrent Resolution 108, of the 83rd Congress, First Session, August 1, 1953.

Whereas it is the policy of Congress, as rapidly as possible, to make the Indians within the territorial limits of the United States subject to the same laws and entitled to the same privileges and responsibilities as are applicable to other citizens of the United States, to end their status as wards of the United States, and to grant them all of the rights and prerogatives pertaining to American citizenship; and

Whereas the Indians within the territorial limits of the United States should assume their full responsibilities as American citizens: Now, therefore, be it *Resolved by the House of Representatives (the Senate concurring)*, That it is declared to be the sense of Congress that, at the earliest possible time, all of the Indian tribes and the individual members thereof located within the States of California, Florida, New York, and Texas, and all of the following named Indian tribes and individual members thereof, should be freed from Federal supervision and control and from all disabilities and limitations specially applicable to Indians: The Flathead Tribe of Montana, the Klamath Tribe of Oregon, the Menominee Tribe of Wisconsin, the Potowatamie Tribe of Kansas and Nebraska, and those members of the Chippewa Tribe who are on the Turtle Mountain Reservation, North Dakota. It is further declared to be the sense of Congress that, upon the release of such tribes and individual members thereof from such disabilities and limitations, all offices of the Bureau of Indian Affairs in the States of California, Florida, New York, and Texas and all other offices of the Bureau of Indian Affairs whose primary purpose was to serve any Indian tribe or individual Indian freed from Federal supervision should be abolished. It is further declared to be the sense of Congress that the Secretary of the Interior should examine all existing legislation dealing with such Indians, and treaties between the Government of the United States and each such tribe, and report to Congress at the earliest practicable date, but not later than January 1, 1954, his recommendations for such legislation as, in his judgment, may be necessary to accomplish the purpose of this resolution.

Note 5. Statement in *A Program for Indian Citizens* (1961,   10–11) concerning Klamath Reservation termination.

The consequences of the Klamath Termination Act (P. L. 587, 83d Congress) had obviously not been adequately weighed either by the Department of the Interior or by Congress; hence four successive changes in the basic measure proved necessary.

The law and its amendments, taken together, furnish an example (not the only one in Indian history) of ill considered and unsuccessful attempts to deal (in an all-inclusive measure) with Indians irrespective of their special way of life, their location, and property holdings. It also demonstrates that no termination of tribes, especially those with large properties, should ever be deemed merely an Indian problem. It is inevitably a national problem, one upon the solution of which depends the welfare of people both near and far.

In still another sense termination offers no pat answer to "the Indian problem," for the Indians themselves remain. They remain mostly where they were and as they were. For the government to act out of a sense of frustration and of haste to rid itself of the vexing questions involved in administering Indian affairs is bound to ensure failure. American policy, if it is to succeed, must aim at helping Indians to prepare themselves in advance of termination for self-reliant living in whatever is their prevailing social and economic framework. As this is accomplished tribe by tribe, termination will follow and follow from the Indians' own desire. Termination so conceived will be an act of statesmanship in the best American tradition.

Note 6. Joan Ablon (1964, 303) writes about pan-Indianism among the San Francisco Bay area Indians.

In the city the alternative of passing into white society is often an easy one, but still it appears that not many take that course. To the contrary, many become more positive of their Indianness after they arrive. Perhaps the self-image of Indianness stands out more sharply in the white world for people who come from reservations where the old ways are dying out and no meaningful new identity-action patterns have developed for the individual. In the city a person may dramatically realize that he is an *Indian,* because for the first time his identity stands in high relief in the midst of his all-white neighbors and workmates. As a result he begins to seek out Indian groups, to "dance Indian" for the first time or to take pride in his children's dancing. Perhaps he will take an active interest in Indian political problems. Thus a neo-Indian type on a new level of self- and group identity with a pan-Indian as well as tribal orientation may be born from the necessity of mingling with members of other tribes.

References

Ablon, Joan. "Relocated American Indians in the San Francisco Bay Area," *Human Organization,* v. 23, 296–304. 1964.

Bureau of Indian Affairs. U. S. Department of the Interior. Washington, D. C. (mimeographed releases).

The Canadian Indian. Department of Citizenship and Immigration, Indian Affairs Branch. Ottawa. 1963.

Dunning, Robert W. "Some Aspects of Governmental Indian Policy and Administration," *Anthropologica,* n.s., v. 4, 209–231. 1962.

*Federal Indian Law. U. S. Department of the Interior. 1958. The definitive work on the relationship between Indians and the government of the United States. A truly great compilation of the legal aspects of American Indian affairs.

Federal Indian Legislation and Policies. Department of Anthropology, University of Chicago. 1956.

*Hagan, William T. *American Indians.* Chicago. 1961. This small volume traces the history of Indian and white relationships from the colonial period through the 1950's. It is a masterfully written synthesis which could only have been produced by a historian of Hagan's stature.

Hallowell, Alfred I. "The Impact of the American Indian on American Culture," *American Anthropologist*, v. 59, 201–217. 1957.

———. "The Backwash of the Frontier: The Impact of the Indian on American Culture," *Annual Report of the Smithsonian Institution, 1957-58*, 447–472. 1958.

———. "American Indians, White and Black: The Phenomenon of Transculturalization," *Current Anthropology*, v. 4, 519–531. 1963.

*Hawthorn, Harry B., Cyril S. Belshaw, and Stuart M. Jamieson. *The Indians of British Columbia*. Berkeley. 1958. This is the best modern study of any regional segment of the American Indian population. The development of historical policies is weak, but this dimension purposefully was not covered.

Howard, James H. "Pan-Indian Culture of Oklahoma," *Scientific Monthly*, v. 81, 215–220. 1955.

Hurt, Wesley R., Jr. "The Urbanization of the Yankton Indian," *Human Organization*, v. 20, 226–231. 1961-1962.

Indian Affairs. New York. The newsletter, "Indian Affairs," issued by the American Indian Fund and the Association on American Indian Affairs, Incorporated, is an invaluable source on current happenings among Indians in the United States. This organization is often somewhat militant in its views but is at the same time one of the most effective private organizations interested in Indians.

Indian Affairs Branch. Department of Citizenship and Immigration. Ottawa (offset printed releases).

Lindquist, Gustavas E. "Indian Treaty Making," *Chronicles of Oklahoma*, v. 26, 416–448. 1948-1949.

Loram, Charles T., and Thomas F. McIlwraith, eds. *The North American Indian Today*. Toronto. 1943.

Martin, Harry W. "Adjustment Among American Indians in an Urban Environment," *Human Organization*, v. 24, 290–295. 1964.

*Meriam, Lewis, director. *The Problem of Indian Administration*. Baltimore. 1928. The Institute for Government Research was commissioned by the Secretary of the Interior in 1926 to compile a comprehensive report on Federal Indian policy and administration. The report is the most far-reaching study of its type and is still regarded as the most informative and enlightened analysis of the Bureau of Indian Affairs. The report's recommendations still serve as a guide to many changes in administrative policies.

Mooney, James. "The Aboriginal Population of America North of Mexico," *Smithsonian Miscellaneous Collections*, v. 80, no. 7. 1928.

National Fellowship of Indian Workers, (newsletters). New York.

A Program for Indian Citizens. The Fund for the Republic. 1961.

Ritzenthaler, Robert, and Mary Sellers. "Indians in an Urban Situation," *Wisconsin Archeologist*, v. 36, 147–161. 1955.

*Simpson, George E., and John M. Yinger, eds. "American Indians and American Life," *The Annals of the American Academy of Political and Social*

Science, v. 311, May, 1957. Diverse authors contributed articles on specific topics dealing with Indians in the United States to make this publication one of the best, if not the best, recent discussions of the emergence of modern Indian life.

Voget, Fred, ed. "American Indians and their Economic Development," *Human Organization,* v. 20, no. 4. 1961–1962.

Bibliography*

Brebner, John B. *The Explorers of North America.* London. 1933 (reprinted, New York. 1955).

Dice, Lee R. *Biotic Provinces of North America.* Ann Arbor. 1943.

Driver, Harold E. *Indians of North America.* Chicago. 1961.

———— and William C. Massey. "Comparative Studies of North American Indians," *Transactions of the American Philosophical Society,* v. 47, pt. 2. 1957.

Hodge, Frederick W., ed. *Handbook of American Indians North of Mexico.* Smithsonian Institution, Bureau of American Ethnology, Bulletin 30, pts. 1, 2. 1907.

Kroeber, Alfred L. *Cultural and Natural Areas of Native North America.* University of California Publications in American Archaeology and Ethnology, v. 38. 1939.

Mooney, James. "The Aboriginal Population of America North of Mexico," *Smithsonian Miscellaneous Collections,* v. 80, no. 7. 1928.

Swanton, John R. *The Indian Tribes of North America.* Smithsonian Institution, Bureau of American Ethnology, Bulletin 145. 1953.

Tax, Sol. *The North American Indians, 1950 Distribution of Descendants of the Aboriginal Population of Alaska, Canada, and the United States* (map). 1960.

Trager, George L., and Felicia E. Harben. "North American Indian Languages: Classification and Maps," *Studies in Linguistics, Occasional Papers,* no. 5. 1958.

U. S. Indian Population (1962) and Land (1963). United States Department of the Interior. Bureau of Indian Affairs. 1963.

* Items consulted for more than one chapter.

Index

Duncan, Father, 341
Dunning, Robert W., 504
Dutch, language, 406
  missionaries, 405
  nationals, 403, 404, 405, 470, 500, 509

Eagle, 156, 158–159, 167, 296, 318, 320,
    347, 359, 366, 371
  crest, 333
  Killing Ceremony, 158–159, 173
Earthworks, 189, 243, 402, 466–467
Easter, 53
  Russian, 131
Eclipse, 103, 281
Education, by elders, 56–57, 59, 98–100,
    126–127, 132–133, 164, 165, 218, 276–
    277, 320, 321, 359, 365, 382–383, 393,
    488
  Federal Bureau of, 335
  formal, *see* School
Eek, 85
Eekchuk, 86, 116
Eggan, Fred, 35
Elections, 447
Elephant, 189, 242
Elk, 189, 257, 401
Elopement, 219
Enfranchisement, 498, 499, 500, 505, 510
England, 69, 405, 409, 410
English, language, 56, 57, 129, 130, 249,
    334, 389, 445, 451, 519–520
  nationals, *see* British nationals
Eototo katcina, 369, 374
Epidemic, 137, 247, 389; *see also* under
    the name of the epidemic
Epiphany (Russian), 131
Equalization Bill, *see* Public Law 86–339
Erie Indians, 426
Ermine, 47, 296, 331
Eskimo, Alaskan, 34, 67, 68, 69, 83, 84,
    104, 296, 297, 300, 307, 336, 510, 511
  language, *see* Language, family, Inuit,
    or Yuit
  meaning of name, 83
  see also specific tribe
"Eskimo Point," 22
Espejo, Antonio de, 351
Estudillo, Jose Maria, 169
Ethnobotany, 145, 216, 361
*Ethnographic Bibliography of North
    America,* 347
Eulachon, 296, 306

Europeans, 168, 169, 190, 293, 325, 497
Evening Star, 266, 274, 275, 279
  sacred bundle, 265, 272–273
Evil Spirit, 411, 427, 431
Exploits Island, 79
Exploits River, 68, 70, 71, 72, 77, 79
Explorers, among Beothuk, 68–70, 78
  Cahuilla, 168
  Chipewyan, 22–24
  Fox, 190–191
  Hopi, 351–353
  Iroquois, 403–404
  Kuskowagamiut, 83, 87–88
  Natchez, 468, 469
  Pawnee, 244–246
  Tlingit, 309, 310, 320, 321, 340
Eyak Indians, 20, 294

Fages, Pedro, 168
Fairbanks, 117
False Face Society, 428, 431–432
Family, Cahuilla, 155, 165, 175
  Chipewyan, 20, 27, 33, 50
  Fox, 208, 225, 231, 233–234
  Hopi, 382–384, 391, 393
  Iroquois, 417–418, 433, 442, 447, 450
  Kuskowagamiut, 106–108, 118, 120–121,
    131–135
  Natchez, 478–481, 488
  Pawnee, 252, 260–261
  Tlingit, 309, 310, 320, 321, 340
Family Allowance (Canadian), 49–50, 446
Family size, Chipewyan, 31, 35, 51
  Fox, 209, 224, 231
  Kuskowagamiut, 92
  Pawnee, 252
Famine, Chipewyan, 33, 40–41, 42, 60
  Hopi, 389
  Kuskowagamiut, 96, 103
Farming, Cahuilla, 169, 171, 172, 175
  Fox, 201, 209, 222, 224
  Hopi, 356, 360–362, 369, 370, 377, 379,
    382, 383, 388, 390–391
  Iroquois, 404, 413, 414–415
  Natchez, 477
  Pawnee, 249, 252, 256–257, 259, 268
  prehistoric, 348, 349
  Tlingit, 328
Feather Dance, 428, 429, 431
Federal agencies, *see* specific agencies
Federal Census of 1880, 116
Federal Indian Law, 498

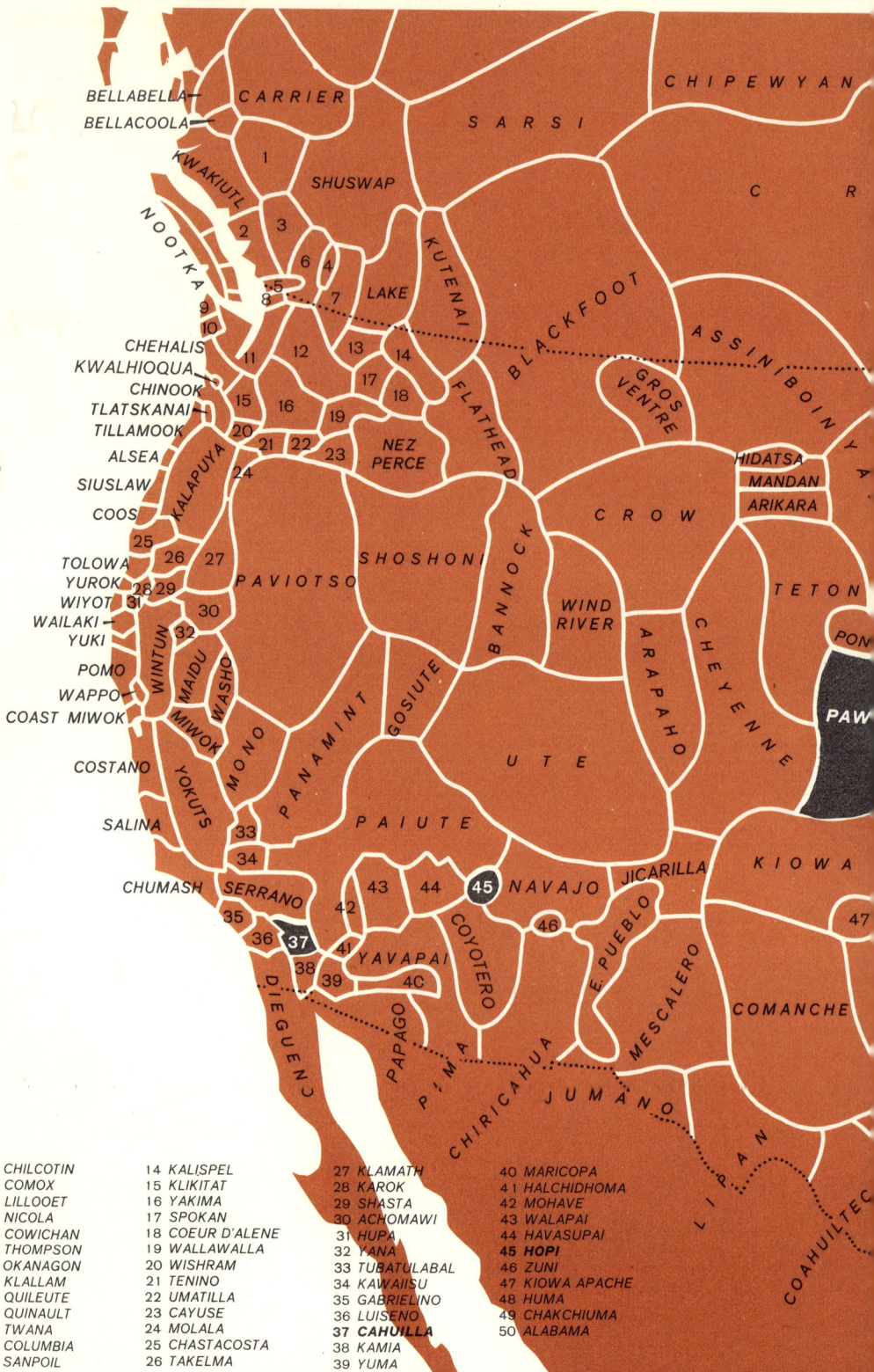

BELLABELLA—
BELLACOOLA—
CARRIER
CHIPEWYAN
SARSI
C R
KWAKIUTL
1
SHUSWAP
NOOTKA
2 3
6 4
5
8
9
7
LAKE
KUTENAI
BLACKFOOT
ASSINIBOIN
10
CHEHALIS
11
12
13
14
KWALHIOQUA
17
GROS VENTRE
CHINOOK
15
16
18
FLATHEAD
TLATSKANAI
19
HIDATSA
TILLAMOOK
20
MANDAN
ALSEA
21 22
23
NEZ PERCE
ARIKARA
24
KALAPUYA
SIUSLAW
CROW
COOS
25
SHOSHONI
TOLOWA
26 27
WIND RIVER
TETON
YUROK
28 29
PAVIOTSO
WIYOT
31
BANNOCK
WAILAKI
30
ARAPAHO
YUKI
32
CHEYENNE
PON
POMO
WINTUN
GOSIUTE
PAW
WAPPO
MAIDU
MONO
WASHO
COAST MIWOK
PANAMINT
MIWOK
UTE
COSTANO
YOKUTS
SALINA
33
PAIUTE
34
KIOWA
CHUMASH
SERRANO
43 44
45
NAVAJO
JICARILLA
35
42
46
47
36
37
41
YAVAPAI
E. PUEBLO
38
39
4C
COYOTERO
MESCALERO
COMANCHE
DIEGUENO
PAPAGO
PIMA
CHIRICAHUA
JUMANO
LIPAN
COAHUILTEC

1 CHILCOTIN	14 KALISPEL	27 KLAMATH	40 MARICOPA
2 COMOX	15 KLIKITAT	28 KAROK	41 HALCHIDHOMA
3 LILLOOET	16 YAKIMA	29 SHASTA	42 MOHAVE
4 NICOLA	17 SPOKAN	30 ACHOMAWI	43 WALAPAI
5 COWICHAN	18 COEUR D'ALENE	31 HUPA	44 HAVASUPAI
6 THOMPSON	19 WALLAWALLA	32 YANA	45 HOPI
7 OKANAGON	20 WISHRAM	33 TUBATULABAL	46 ZUNI
8 KLALLAM	21 TENINO	34 KAWAIISU	47 KIOWA APACHE
9 QUILEUTE	22 UMATILLA	35 GABRIELINO	48 HUMA
10 QUINAULT	23 CAYUSE	36 LUISENO	49 CHAKCHIUMA
11 TWANA	24 MOLALA	37 CAHUILLA	50 ALABAMA
12 COLUMBIA	25 CHASTACOSTA	38 KAMIA	
13 SANPOIL	26 TAKELMA	39 YUMA	

(after George P. Murdock, Ethnographic Bibliography of North America, New Haven, 1960)   Map by J. Donovan